Eli Heckscher,
International Trade, and
Economic History

Eli Heckscher, International Trade, and Economic History

edited by Ronald Findlay,
Rolf G. H. Henriksson, Håkan
Lindgren, and Mats Lundahl

The MIT Press
Cambridge, Massachusetts
London, England

MIT Press books may be purchased at special quantity discounts for business or sales promotional use. For information, please email special_sales@mitpress.mit.edu or write to Special Sales Department, The MIT Press, 55 Hayward Street, Cambridge, MA 02142.

This book was set in Palatino on 3B2 by Asco Typesetters, Hong Kong.
Printed and bound in the United States of America.

Library of Congress Cataloging-in-Publication Data

Eli Heckscher, international trade, and economic history / Ronald Findlay ... [et al.], editors.
   p.   cm.
Includes bibliographical references.
ISBN 0-262-06251-8 (hc : alk. paper)
1. International trade. 2. Economic history. 3. Mercantile system. 4. Heckscher-Ohlin principle. 5. Heckscher, Eli F. (Eli Filip), 1879–1952. I. Findlay, Ronald.

HF1379.E4   2006
382.01—dc22   2005056285

10   9   8   7   6   5   4   3   2   1

Contents

Preface

When the faculty of the Stockholm School of Economics met on November 8, 1928, Eli F. Heckscher, professor of economics and statistics, offered a proposal calling for the establishment of an institute for research in economic history. The faculty, followed one week later by the School's Board of Trustees, gave its assent, and on June 18, 1929, Heckscher was awarded a personal professorship in economic history and appointed director of the new institute.

The research tradition to which Eli F. Heckscher gave his imprimatur still characterizes much of the work performed within the Institute for Research in Economic History (EHF) at the Stockholm School of Economics. This is especially true of the cross-disciplinary nature of the research, but it also applies to the emphasis on business history and historical economics. With the approach of the fiftieth anniversary of Heckscher's December 23, 1952 death, it seemed only fitting that the EHF Institute should participate in marking the occasion. Thus, a symposium celebrating Heckscher's many scholarly contributions was organized under the auspices of the Institute. An organizing committee consisting of Ronald Findlay, Rolf G. H. Henriksson, Håkan Lindgren, and Mats Lundahl was given responsibility for the planning and scholarly content of the symposium.

The planning was based on our conviction that Eli F. Heckscher, together with Knut Wicksell, Bertil Ohlin, and Gunnar Myrdal, belongs to a group of Swedish economists who have received wide-spread international recognition for their work. At least in Heckscher's case, his major contributions go beyond economics as such to include the discipline of economic history. Among economists, he is primarily known for his path-breaking work on international trade, while among economic historians his fame rests on his now classic works on *Mercantilism*, *The Continental System*, and *Swedish Economic History*, all of which have appeared in English translation. In Sweden, Heckscher founded, and indeed molded, economic history as a scholarly discipline. Thanks to his grounding in economic theory and his extensive list of publications, Heckscher remains relevant to this very day. Inevitably, his research results have been modified in numerous regards. Nevertheless, for many modern scholars his body of work remains both a starting point and a challenge. The goal of the symposium, therefore, was to create a forum where economists and economic historians could meet to develop a picture of how relevant Heckscher's research program and results are perceived to be by current practitioners of the two disciplines.

The results of the conference "Eli F. Heckscher, 1879–1952: A Celebratory Symposium," are presented in this volume. Many individuals have made valuable contributions to the creation of this book. First and foremost there are the authors, who have patiently awaited the results of their labor, as well as the numerous commentators, who are as follows: Lena Andersson-Skog, Bob Coats, Richard Friberg, Ylva Hasselberg, Maths Isacson, Jan Jörnmark, Olle Krantz, Jonas Ljungberg, Anders Ögren Jan Ottosson, Tom Petersson, Ronny Pettersson, Lars Pålsson-Syll, Örjan Sjöberg, Hans Sjögren, Bo Södersten, Richard Sylla, Kersti Ullenhag, Daniel Waldenström, and Kurt Wickman. The insights provided by these commentators have without question facilitated the work of preparing the contributed papers for publication.

The conference would not have been possible without the support of the SSE and its president Leif Lindmark. Administratively, success, before, during, and after the conference can largely be credited to the self-sacrificing and unselfish work performed by the staff of the EHF Institute, especially Britt-Marie Eisler and Krim Talia. Moreover, without contributions from a number of leading Swedish research funding sources, the conference could not have been held. Thus the organizing committee wishes to extend its heartfelt appreciation for the financial support provided by the Central Bank of Sweden, Jan Wallander's and Tom Hedelius's Foundation, Prince Bertil's Foundation, the Bank of Sweden Tercentenary Foundation, Marianne and Marcus Wallenberg's Foundation, the Swedish Research Council, and Timbro AB.

Last, but certainly not least, a special thank you is due the grandchildren of Eli F. Heckscher: Eva, Einar, Sten, and Ivar. They participated in the project with great enthusiasm, providing family photographs and Eli's school essay. Their personal recollections of their grandfather, which are included in this volume, shed important light on Heckscher as a private person. Our picture of this great scholar would be incomplete without their contributions. Tragically, Eva Heckscher died before she could see her loving account of her grandfather in print. We wish to honor Eva by dedicating this book to her memory, and to thank Dag Klackenberg for the brief sketch of her life that he has provided.

New York and Stockholm, 7 June 2005

Ronald Findlay
Rolf G. H. Henriksson
Håkan Lindgren
Mats Lundahl

1

Introduction

Ronald Findlay, Rolf G. H.
Henriksson, Håkan Lindgren,
and Mats Lundahl

The name of Eli Heckscher will forever be associated with two great ideas in economics: the factor proportions theory of comparative advantage and international trade, which bears his name along with that of his distinguished pupil Bertil Ohlin, and mercantilism, that complex and controversial body of thought that he illuminated, as no one has before or since, in his great two-volume treatise of the 1930s. What is perhaps even more remarkable is that most of Heckscher's relentlessly active scholarly life was spent on neither of these topics but on his unfinished multivolume masterpiece on the economic history of Sweden. Almost incidentally, he also found the time to write another perennial classic, his study of the Continental Blockade, along with numerous other major works in an amazing bibliography of well over a thousand items. It is certain that we will never see a scholar like Heckscher again; among his great contemporaries perhaps only Jacob Viner was comparable in combining theoretical insights with a depth and breadth of knowledge of both economic history and the history of economic thought.

In the present volume we attempt to delineate and assess the contributions that this truly extraordinary man made to economic history and economic theory, to the nature of the relationships between these two very different varieties of economic inquiry, and to the controversies over economic policy that he actively engaged in over the course of a scholarly life that spanned two world wars and the Great Depression. Heckscher was both a patriotic Swede and an uncompromisingly cosmopolitan nineteenth-century liberal citizen of the world. To honor his memory, we are fortunate to have been able to assemble a team of Swedish and international scholars whose own research programs have all been inspired by his ideas and example.

A Biographical Sketch

Eli Filip Heckscher was born in 1879.[1] His father came from Denmark
to Sweden to work with his brother in a banking firm. The two represented the eighth generation of a family of wealthy Jewish bankers
who had begun their activities in Hamburg as far back as the sixteenth
century.

After graduating from high school in 1896, Eli Heckscher began his
academic studies in Uppsala the following year, specializing in history.
He gravitated to the circle of historians headed by Harald Hjärne, a
well-known and charismatic figure in Swedish academic life. Hjärne
was also a major participant in public policy debates, taking a social-
conservative stance and strongly advocating social reform. It was in
history that Heckscher wrote his *licentiat*[2] thesis in 1903, on the Swedish Navigation Act (Produktplakatet) of 1724 (Heckscher 1908). His
studies towards this degree also included economics, taught by David
Davidson, and political science. Not surprisingly, Heckscher opted for
economic history when it came to selecting a topic for his Ph.D.

Before writing his doctoral dissertation, however, Heckscher wrote
the first in a long series of papers on methodology, a topic that would
concern him for the rest of his life (Henriksson and Lundahl 2003a), especially the relationship between economic history and economic
theory. Heckscher argued that the task of economic history is exploring
the development of economic life and that in order to do so the economic historian necessarily has to make use of economic theory
(Heckscher 1904). During his entire career Heckscher displayed something of a Janus face, being both an economic historian and an economist, and he was forced to come to grips with the similarities and
differences between the two subjects, constantly reevaluating and
deepening his views.[3]

Heckscher wrote his doctoral dissertation (Heckscher 1907) in a
mere two years. The topic was the economic effects of the development
of the Swedish railway system, and the explicit consideration of a
counterfactual in some parts of the book makes the work an early precursor of the New Economic History movement (Henriksson 1991:
145). Incidentally, one of the leaders of this intellectual movement,
Robert Fogel, also wrote on the railroad's economic impact in the United States. Heckscher's thesis earned him the position as docent (the
equivalent of an associate professorship) in political economy at Stockholm College in 1907. After two years he was appointed to the chair in

economics and statistics at the new Stockholm School of Economics, which was founded that same year.

Holding this position brought Heckscher increasingly into economics and away from economic history, but his activities during the first decade as a professor were also partly a response to the World War I. This focus led to a monograph on the wartime economy (Heckscher 1915), and he also got involved in the Swedish War Commission, first as secretary and then as its executive head. Heckscher's activities for the commission provided a foundation for his extensive work on this topic in the 1920s for the Carnegie Foundation (Bergendal et al. 1930), and also proved fruitful in other ways. The World War I experience had an obvious historical parallel in the Napoleonic Wars, and this similarity led Heckscher to begin his study of the Continental Blockade System in 1916. It was completed in 1918, and four years later an English edition appeared (Heckscher 1922).

In 1919, Heckscher published the work for which he is renowned, not only by economic historians but also by economists, the seminal paper on foreign trade and the distribution of income that provided the foundation for the Heckscher-Ohlin (or factor proportions) theory of foreign trade. This paper was one of only four that by and large comprise Heckscher's entire theoretical output, all of which were published within a narrow time span between 1916 and 1924.[4] Thereafter, Heckscher left his theoretical work behind and set out to fulfill what he considered to be his "real" task in life: writing an economic history of Sweden. The work was delayed, however, because before embarking on this major undertaking he had to complete a few "minor" research tasks.

One of these tasks, by no means a minor one, was his theoretical history of mercantilism. The monumental study was published in 1931 and translated into English four years later (Heckscher 1935a). It immediately became a standard work and was hailed as a classic. In 1931 Heckscher also published his survey of the Industrial Revolution (Heckscher 1931), a work that became a long-lived textbook in Swedish universities, appearing in several editions, but that has unfortunately never been translated into English. A second task that Heckscher could not refuse was active participation in the formation of Swedish economic policy. After World War I he became a member of the Commission on Tariffs and Treaties, whose final work very much bore the imprint of Heckscher's free trade views, and in 1926 he was a member of an unemployment committee. Throughout his life Heckscher considered it more or less a duty to contribute to government policy making and to the public debate of economic issues in general. The (incomplete) bibliography of his published output (*Eli Heckschers bibliografi* 1950) lists no less than 1,148 works, most of which are newspaper articles and similar projects. Altogether the 1910s and (to a lesser extent) the 1920s were the decades of Eli Heckscher the policy-making economist, as distinct from the economic historian.

Heckscher held the economics and statistics chair at the Stockholm School of Economics until 1929, and he was quite influential when it came to the organization of teaching there, striking a balance between the curriculum's scientific foundations and his endeavor to provide the young men who would later make careers mainly in private business with a grounding in economics that allowed them to deal efficiently with practical problems. He attempted to uphold high standards, and was widely feared as an examiner. Only a handful of the approximately one thousand students that he examined obtained the highest grade, one of them Bertil Ohlin. A lively description of Eli Heckscher the teacher during this period was provided in the mid-1960s by Ruben Rausing, the founder of the Swedish corporation Tetra Pak. Rausing had entered the Stockholm School of Economics in 1916 and, like Ohlin, had become part of the select group of Heckscher's best students:

He greatly influenced my life. It is also of him that I have my richest and warmest mental image of those years. When heading for the lectures he never walked. Instead he ran and jumped nimbly up. In formal instruction, he was an extraordinary lecturer, lively, clear and fully engaged with his students. This contact was even further intensified during seminars. There could be sharp exchanges between professor and student. He combined this ability to relate to the students with a remarkable and unpretentious dignity. He himself was always punctual to the minute. If a student arrived late, he would pause meaningfully. The person in question would learn that punctuality is a requirement of all organized work and of all civilization.[5]

Heckscher's involvement with the Stockholm School of Economics changed in 1929, after an incident that ended on a sour note. When the president of the school, Carl Hallendorff, unexpectedly died that year, Heckscher regarded himself as the natural successor, but his colleagues did not, especially those who saw him as condescending, sarcastic, and arrogant. The result was that Heckscher found himself without support and considered leaving the school. The problem was, however, happily solved by the creation of a special chair in economic history under the auspices of the new Economic History Institute. This position freed Heckscher from teaching duties and allowed him to concentrate entirely on research.

With this new appointment, Heckscher the economist took the opportunity to finally become Heckscher the economic historian. He chose to leave theoretical work and contemporary economic issues aside, except for when exceptional circumstances called for his presence in ongoing policy debates, and to concentrate on what he considered his real mission in life. Without the newly established chair, which Heckscher occupied until reaching retirement in 1944 and then by special extension to 1949, it would probably not have been possible for him to write his projected four-volume magnum opus, *Sveriges ekonomiska historia från Gustav Vasa* (*The Economic History of Sweden since Gustav Vasa*). Heckscher had begun this work in the early 1920s, but it was not until he could concentrate more or less exclusively on research that he could fully master the material necessary for his monumental survey.

The first installment, on the sixteenth century, was ready in 1935 (Heckscher 1935b), and the volume on the seventeenth century followed duly in 1936 (Heckscher 1936), but the third part on the eighteenth century did not appear until 1949 (Heckscher 1949a, 1949b). The reason was simple. The amount of work involved had increased as Heckscher's study advanced chronologically in time. The material grew richer and the statistical series longer. Heckscher, whose research increasingly was based on the painstaking accumulation and analysis of statistics, ended up overtaxing his health, and by the time the two-part eighteenth-century volume was completed the notorious workaholic (who had had two collapses in 1942 and 1943) was a physically broken man who only had a few years left to live. The last volume, on the nineteenth century, remained unwritten. The approach that Heckscher used, basing his analysis on the close examination of voluminous statistical series, would simply have been too onerous to allow him to complete the work.[6]

Eli Heckscher died in December of 1952. Among economists he is known mainly for his seminal contribution to international trade theory. Had he been alive in 1977 he would no doubt have shared the Nobel Prize in economics with Bertil Ohlin and James Meade. Among economic historians Heckscher's reputation rests mainly on his monumental works exploring mercantilism, the Continental Blockade, and Sweden's economic history. As we have already pointed out, he presented to the scholarly world something of an intellectual Janus face. Yet during his entire scientific life Heckscher struggled with the question of how to bridge the divide between economics and economic history. The purpose of the present work, which emanates from the fiftieth anniversary of his death, is to provide readers with a complete portrait of Heckscher's scientific contributions, both in economics and in economic history, and furthermore to link his distinctive approach to later developments in both areas. The book also gives a portrait of Heckscher the private person.

Theory, Methodology, and History

Håkan Lindgren starts off his discussion of methodological issues in chapter 2 with the research program for the new field of economic history that Eli F. Heckscher, at the tender age of twenty-four, published in 1904. In this programmatic paper, the German historical school is criticized for either getting lost in a sea of details or else trying to squeeze history into some ill-fitting stage theory of economic development. On the other methodological flank, Heckscher argued that deductive economics suffers from a tendency to view economic laws as universal laws of nature, not as historical categories. It was his contention that a new field, economic history, could be based on a melding of the best features of both these parent disciplines.

During recent decades, the methodologies employed in economics and history have moved even further apart. History has become receptive to micro history and to social constructivism, while economics has become ever more deductive and mathematical. Given these divergent methodological trends, Lindgren poses the question of whether the young Heckscher's hope of merging history and theoretical and empirical economic inquiry still has relevance, or if his proposal was stillborn.

A review of the Swedish experience leads to the conclusion that Heckscher's 1904 program still remains relevant today. Both the historian's evaluation of sources and the economist's models are needed to resolve problems in economic history. Social constructivism, in the sense that there are "cultural codes" that must be deciphered, is an essential element in all historical research, while economic models have great explanatory power when applied to appropriate economic historical questions. As Heckscher argued, however, economic history is not historical economics and should not evolve into a branch of economics.

Economic history is an empirical, inductive discipline, but by no means is it nontheoretical. Knowledge of modern "pure theory," as well as of previously accepted theories, can be very helpful in explaining how economies have been organized and how these systems functioned during different historical eras and in different cultural settings. Lindgren therefore argues that the emphasis placed on economic theory and econometric methods in the current economic history curriculum should be increased, furthering the agenda Heckscher articulated 100 years ago.

In chapter 3 Rolf Henriksson elaborates on the methodological discussion initiated in the previous chapter. Heckscher's position, occupying the middle ground between history and economics, as presented in his 1904 manifesto, is traced back to the formative years of his academic career. When the eighteen-year old Heckscher matriculated at Uppsala University in 1897, history became his major field, and he was admitted to Professor Harald Hjärne's inner circle of top students. Hjärne was an avid supporter of Leopold von Ranke's program for historical methodology and its focus on historical understanding, striving for objectivity and the critical evaluation of sources.

In the course of his economics studies, Heckscher came into contact with Professor David Davidson, who held the economics and fiscal law chair on the law faculty. Davidson had been influenced by the historical school and by socialist economic thinking. Although he was a great admirer of David Ricardo, he was not receptive to the ongoing neoclassical revolution in economics. At that time, the great majority of economics students were candidates for a law degree. Thus, when Heckscher chose economics as the second field in his *licentiat* degree program, he became one of a select few students who seriously pursued graduate studies in this discipline. Moreover, during the last few years of his university studies, Heckscher worked very closely with Davidson as an unofficial assistant.

On the basis of Heckscher's program of university studies, as well as on his early writings (including his *licentiat* thesis in history), Henriksson identifies and traces three different lines of influence that would become the pillars of the 1904 manifesto. Having been trained in the Hjärne tradition, reliance upon and critical evaluation of primary sources were basic principles of Heckscher's scholarly program. Indeed, its importance to him only increased over time. His plea for deductive economic analysis and his conceptualizing approach to the social sciences can be traced back to Davidson's influence. As for

Heckscher's advocacy of the use of statistics, this can be related to his study of political science, even though, like Hjärne, he remained skeptical of the official variety. The originality in Heckscher's 1904 manifesto lay in his having selected some, and rejected other, aspects of these three traditions and then forging his choices into a whole new program.

Heckscher-Ohlin Trade Theory

The second section of the present volume focuses on Eli Heckscher the trade theorist. Heckscher's 1919 paper on international trade was not translated into English until thirty years later, and then only partially. (It was not until the appearance of the 1991 volume edited by Harry Flam and June Flanders [Heckscher and Ohlin 1991] that a full translation of the original article became available.) Before this, scholars without a reading knowledge of Swedish were unable to evaluate the extent and originality of Heckscher's own contribution to the model that bore his name jointly with that of Bertil Ohlin.

In chapter 4, however, Ronald Jones deconstructs the 1919 paper, pointing out exactly what Heckscher did and did not do in that celebrated piece. He notes that Heckscher clearly stated the possibility that free trade between economies endowed with different factor proportions would lead to a *complete* equalization of factor prices and would therefore be a *perfect substitute* for international factor mobility. Jones also observes that Heckscher, along with Ohlin, did not state some of the crucial assumptions necessary for the factor-price equalization theorem to hold: that the number of factors could not exceed the number of goods that are traded, and that the possibility of factor-intensity reversals has to be excluded. Yet in 1919 nobody had the technique necessary to appreciate these aspects of the complex mathematical structure underlying the theorem's proof, which only became known after the work of Paul Samuelson in the late 1940s and early 1950s. Indeed, a completely rigorous proof did not exist until after the work of the mathematicians David Gale and Hukukane Nikaido (1965) on the global univalence theorem. That Heckscher, an economic historian by temperament and training, was single-handedly able to first envision and grasp the underlying economic logic of this deep and beautiful theoretical result is nothing short of astonishing.

In chapter 5 we turn from the logical abstractions of the factor-price equalization theorem and related theoretical issues of the Heckscher-Ohlin model to some very basic empirical tests of the predictions that the model makes about individual attitudes across countries toward globalization, or more specifically toward national policies on trade and immigration. Kevin O'Rourke begins with the simplest version of the model, with skilled and unskilled labor as the two factors. Since trade favors the abundant factor and harms the scarce one, skilled workers should be against protection in richer, more skill-abundant countries and in favor of it in poorer, less skill-abundant countries. Similarly, skilled workers in richer countries should favor the immigration of unskilled workers, who are complementary to them, but skilled workers in poorer countries should be against immigration of skilled workers, who are competitive with them. Unskilled workers in each type of country should of course have the opposite preferences to those of their skilled compatriots.

O'Rourke tests these predictions rigorously on cross-country data from a sample of twenty-four countries and generally finds them to hold remarkably well, with the results also supported by independent studies undertaken by Matthew Slaughter, Dani Rodrik, and others. As O'Rourke points out, these results refute the plausible hypothesis that more educated skilled workers everywhere support globalization because they are more "enlightened" than their less educated unskilled fellows, who are everywhere against it. It is thus not a question of what type of worker one is, regardless of location, but whether one is the abundant or the scarce factor in a given location, that seems to matter for attitudes toward globalization. This conclusion is just as the model predicts.

Historical Applications of Heckscher-Ohlin Theory

The third section deals with the application of Heckscher-Ohlin trade theory to historical material. Strangely enough, Heckscher himself never attempted to apply his seminal 1919 paper to the analysis of historical material (Findlay and Lundahl 2002). His use of trade theory was limited to the discussion of current economic problems (Henriksson and Lundahl 2003a). Nevertheless, as the three chapters by Peter Temin, Ronald Findlay and Mats Lundahl and Jeffrey Williamson demonstrate, the factor proportions approach provides a powerful tool in a wide variety of historical settings and episodes, across a time period of over two millennia.

In chapter 6 Peter Temin deals with trade in the Mediterranean during biblical times. Temin bases his discussion of the existence of trade and the reasons for it on archaeological evidence: two sunken ships from the latter half of the eighth century B.C., found north of the Egyptian coast, transporting amphorae containing wine from Phoenicia to Egypt, obviously to be traded there. Archaeological evidence for early trade in the Mediterranean also comes from a thirteenth-century B.C. wreck off the coast of Turkey and from a painting in a Theban tomb of Syrian ships arriving in Egypt. Thus, interregional trade existed in the Mediterranean during the Bronze Age. This trade, however, appears to have been broken off during the transition to the Iron Age in the twelfth century B.C. but to have been revived in the eighth, and there is further evidence of trade in the fifth century B.C.

Temin deals with trade in bulky commodities—like grain, oil, and wine—commodities that required a lot of coordination between different agents in the commercialization chain. He argues that this coordination was achieved through the market mechanism, with unminted silver being used as the medium of exchange. Temin also attempts an explanation of the trade pattern along Heckscher-Ohlin lines. Egypt exported wheat and Phoenicia exported wine. According to Temin, fertile land was a scarce factor in Egypt, its extension being determined by the flooding of the Nile, so wheat ought to have been the labor-intensive commodity, while wine was land-intensive, unless trade was determined by climatic factors alone.

Finally, Temin deals with the risks of trade, the high transaction costs these entailed, and the attempts to bring the costs down. The three main risks were natural disaster on the voyage, piracy, and nonpayment or faulty payment. The first could be managed by not venturing too far on to the high seas. Piracy required arms and/or escorts, and payment, in the absence of international treaties, had to be ensured by a reputation equilibrium signaling fair deals. Temin argues that piracy must have been responsible for much of the break-off of trade in the twelfth century B.C., and that as trade revived in the eighth century B.C. deliberate efforts were made to reduce trade risks.

Chapter 7, by Ronald Findlay and Mats Lundahl, moves the time perspective to the eight centuries that elapsed between the Plague of Justinian and the Black Death, that is, from the sixth to the fourteenth centuries A.D. The issue is how the advent of the earlier plague affected three civilizations or economic regions and the extent to which each of these was able to recover from or perhaps even transcend its effects: the Byzantine Empire, where the plague struck directly and where the economy barely recovered centuries later; the Islamic world, which fared much better and even experienced a green revolution based on crops introduced from the east; and Western Europe, which initially was the most economically backward region but eventually expanded most rapidly of all on the basis of land clearance and the use of the heavy plow and other agricultural innovations.

Findlay and Lundahl develop a factor proportions–based model that produces some key predictions regarding the impact of demographic change and can be used to shed some light on the difference in performance between the three geographical regions. The model rests on a Malthusian specification of birth and death rates in combination with an endogenous land frontier, the extension of which is subject to increasing marginal costs. It produces a steady state determining population and labor force size, per capita consumption, total output, and the land area under cultivation, as well as the rewards to land and labor. The model can be subjected to different kinds of exogenous shocks, notably a reduction of the population but also, for instance, technological change in production. Findlay and Lundahl show that when the population shrinks, wages increase and land rents decline. The amount of new land cleared is reduced and so is the area under cultivation. Per capita output and consumption rise and trigger new population growth. Eventually the price of land rises and the real wage declines. New land is added and the economy returns to the steady state. It is also demonstrated that technological change will increase both the population and the area under cultivation.

The model can be used to shed some light on the difference in performance between the three geographical regions. In the Byzantine Empire the plague caused the economy to contract and the agricultural frontier to retreat, but higher per capita income and wages made the population grow back, altering the labor market balance in favor of landowners. Ultimately, the absence of technological progress and the deterioration of political and military conditions made the empire lose territory and collapse. The Islamic world, on the other hand, filled the vacuum created by the plague in the eastern Mediterranean. At the outset of the period it enjoyed territorial expansion, but by conquest rather than land clearance. This expansion was accompanied by technological progress in agriculture and population growth. However, the latter was constrained by the region's harsh geographical conditions and by the Mongol conquests toward the end of the period. Western Europe, finally, was the area that fared best. There the ravages of the plague were not as harsh as in regions further east, and the recovery was accompanied by technological progress on the one hand,

and eastward territorial expansion by conquest on the other. Altogether these developments made for, comparatively speaking, spectacular population growth, to the point of overpopulation shortly before the Black Death arrived in Western Europe.

With chapter 8 we move four to five hundred years further ahead in time. Jeffrey Williamson's essay deals with the determinants of tariff policy in thirty-five countries from 1870 to 1938. During this period two great surges in tariff levels took place, the first from 1865 to about 1900, and the second in the 1920s and 1930s, with great geographical variations both between and within regions. Latin America, the European overseas offshoots and the European periphery led the pre-1914 backlash, while in the second surge tariff levels rose everywhere.

Williamson's chapter concentrates on a discussion of the mechanisms that may have caused the tariff increases. Four possible explanations are introduced: Stolper-Samuelson tariffs driven by the scarce factors in each region (the factors that stood to gain from tariffs), infant industry tariffs (intended to foster industrialization), revenue tariffs, and, finally, strategic trade policy tariffs (tariff increases triggered by high tariffs among the trading partners). The infant industry argument is ruled out because high tariffs were correlated with slow, not rapid, growth, and hence would not have caused these increases.

Williamson proceeds to test the remaining three explanations econometrically, controlling for the effect of inflation on ad valorem tariff rates (during a period when the actual duties were specific) and other factors affecting these rates. The results of the time series regressions indicate that all three explanations played a part. The most important determinant of tariff increases for the entire 1870–1938 period turns out to be increases in the tariff levels of the trading partners. However, as demonstrated by other recent contributions, before 1900 the picture was more divided. Fears of deindustrialization in the periphery and cheap grain imports in the core both played a major role. Political economy effects resulting from increased urbanization and increased skill levels also had an impact. Partner tariffs were more significant in the European periphery, compensation for transport cost reductions influenced events in the industrialized European core, in Asia, and in the non-Latin American overseas offshoots of Europe. The reduction of tariff levels from the 1890s to the outbreak of World War I was caused by rising income levels in Europe and its overseas offshoots, including Latin America, as a result of mass migration and capital movements.

Finally, the rising tariff levels during the interwar period were driven almost exclusively by strategic motives.

The cross-section regression results differ from the time series data by not conceding any importance to partner tariffs. Tariff *levels* (as opposed to *changes*) were not determined by partner levels but by other considerations. For example, the low initial tariff levels in Asian countries were the result of their colonial status vis-à-vis trading partners with high tariff levels; that is, these were forced on the colonies by their European rulers.

Mercantilism

Heckscher's *Mercantilism* is the first modern work on the topic. As such it has been the natural starting point for subsequent research in the field. The study was begun during his years in Uppsala but was not published until 1931. The focus is on economic policy rather than on actual historical events, and Heckscher paints a panoramic picture extending from the Middle Ages until the age of liberalism in the nineteenth century. The work benefited from employing hitherto unused sources, but it was also informed by theoretical knowledge. To a very large extent *Mercantilism* is a work of synthesis, (Montgomery 1953: 168), a consideration that constantly occupied Heckscher (Olsson 1992).

In different ways all the four chapters in the fourth section relate modern research on mercantilism to the foundation provided by Heckscher. In chapter 9 Lars Magnusson traces the evaluation of *Mercantilism* over time by using an explicitly historical strategy: exploring how the interpretation of mercantilism has changed over time, and how these changes have been influenced by the context of each period. He rejects attempts to reconcile mercantilist ideas with modern theory because this approach anachronistically uses the wrong yardstick by failing to do justice to the early theories.

When *Mercantilism* was published it was criticized on the basis that the relationship between economic ideas and political action was tenuous, and that Heckscher's attempt to come up with a synthesis melding the two did not hold water. Magnusson reconstructs Heckscher's general argument that the mercantilists had a set of ideas. The goal of the mercantile system was to maximize state power, not wealth: the core of the system was the means employed to reach the goal, and the state was the propelling agent of the system. This view was criticized by Jacob Viner, who argued in favor of the approach that modern theory takes as its point of departure: the mercantilists confused money and wealth, they were bullionists to the core, and they were the representatives of a policy built on special interests.

British economists during the 1950s, 1960s, and 1970s regarded Heckscher's conception of mercantilism as too broad, as it simply gave too much unity to what were in reality disparate events. The notion of a mercantile state was rejected as a straw man. The basis of mercantilist ideas was sought in (sometimes very specific) contemporary events of the seventeenth and eighteenth centuries. The obsession with bullion was seen as the outcome of bilateral trade (Heckscher denied that bilateral trade was common).

Magnusson concludes by providing a current perspective on *Mercantilism*, asserting that many of these criticisms remain valid. Economic ideas and policy practice are not as closely related as Heckscher argued, and it is hardly possible to draw any clear demarcation line between "mercantilist" and "liberal" ideas. Still, Magnusson argues, *Mercantilism* is worth reading. There was definitely a "mercantilist" economic worldview, and mercantilism displays at least some of the system-like characteristics emphasized by Heckscher. His impressive knowledge of ideas and policies still has a lot to offer. Finally, even though he might overstate his case, Heckscher's insistence on the nexus between ideas and policies cannot be neglected. Although the ability of the early modern states to carry out coherent economic policies left a lot to be desired, policymakers were to a certain extent influenced by ideas.

Chapter 10, by Douglas Irwin, takes as its point of departure the discussion between Heckscher and Jacob Viner of whether mercantilism was mainly about power (Heckscher) or plenty (Viner). With the aid of the modern theory of strategic trade behavior, Irwin analyzes the competition between the English and Dutch East India companies during the first decades of the seventeenth century and demonstrates that there need not be any conflict at all between the two goals. Power and wealth may be complementary rather than competing ends.

Irwin begins with a brief exposition of strategic trade policy in a Cournot duopoly model and shows how once a Nash equilibrium has been established between the two firms, government export subsidies may shift this equilibrium in favor of the domestic firm. This finding provides the theoretical foundation for the rest of the chapter. Next, Irwin recapitulates some mercantilist economic ideas: the desire to export is linked to government export promotion, establishing the relevance of strategic trade policy. The following section is devoted to a reconciliation of the empirical facts of the East India trade with the strategic trade policy model, and to a comparison of Dutch and British policy. Irwin argues that the English East India Company was simply maximizing profits, while its Dutch competitor maximized a linear combination of profits and revenue. The difference arose from the fact that the English company was a purely private firm seeking profits while the Dutch company's policy was determined by the so-called *bewindhebbers*, who received both dividends and a provision based on turnover. The creation of the state-supported Dutch East India Company made it possible for the Dutch to increase both sales volume and profits and made the Dutch company a Stackelberg leader.

Chapter 11, by Joel Mokyr, deals with the "end" of mercantilism as ushered in by the Enlightenment and the Industrial Revolution. Heckscher identified intellectual changes as one of the roots of the latter, and one of the main strands of the Enlightenment was the stress on economic progress. The Enlightenment also brought institutional changes of rules, norms, and beliefs, to a large extent because this period's leading actors were favorably disposed to innovations. Mokyr concentrates on these institutional changes.

Rent seeking was an important part of mercantilism. The European economies were caught in a high rent seeking equilibrium with low returns to productive efforts. L'ancien régime to a large extent was a machine that redistributed wealth and income. The French Revolution put an end to this, and in the wake of revolution a number of deregulations and eliminations of entry barriers followed. These went hand in hand with a change in the dominant ideology guiding rulers and civil servants. The attitude toward protectionism changed. Whether this was the result of Enlightenment ideas is, however, debatable, especially since contemporary writers were not in agreement on the subject, and in Prussia the concept of *Nationalökonomie* eventually superseded free trade. The Enlightenment also encouraged inventions, notably through the patent system, although some thinkers cautioned against the potentially destructive forces inherent in technological change.

Mokyr concludes by stressing the role of institutional progress in the Industrial Revolution. If institutions had not changed, the fruits of technological change might easily have ended up in the hands of rent seekers, tax collectors, and the like, and this would have slowed the pace of growth. It was the combination of ideological and institutional change on one hand and the growth of knowledge on the other that produced and fed the Industrial Revolution. What produced the Enlightenment is a more difficult question to answer, but clearly scepticism and rejection of old ideas had a great deal to do with it, and the new ideas went hand in hand with the emergence of free markets and international trade.

Deepak Lal, in chapter 12, applies one of the findings of Heckscher's *Mercantilism* to today's international economy. The phenomenon that he investigates is the cycle of economic repression and liberal reform. Lal's starting point is the creation of dirigiste states, eagerly desired by rulers intent on nation building, in most third world countries during the 1960s and 1970s, followed by liberal reforms from the 1980s onward in the face of combined fiscal and balance-of-payments crises. As Eli Heckscher argued in *Mercantilism*, dirigisme was a pattern that characterized the rise of the European states during the Renaissance but that fostered corruption, tax evasion, rent seeking, and illegal economic activities. These problems led to an erosion of the tax base during the eighteenth century, before reforms set in during the nineteenth century. The "crisis theory of economic liberalization" is thus applicable to both historical episodes. It is not until the state begins to wither away and society threatens to break down in a crisis situation that wholehearted reform is triggered.

Lal also applies the crisis theory to the question why dirigiste policies made a comeback during the twentieth century. To this end he adopts the distinction between the state as a civil association that does not impose any preferred pattern of goals and the state as an enterprise association that uses the law for its own purposes. Classic liberalism embraces the former viewpoint and socialism the latter one. The dissolution of the "morality of communal ties" inherited from the Middle Ages produced individuality, but it also bred an "anti-individual" who, placing a high premium on security, preferred not to make his or her own choices but left these to the government. This collectivist morality tipped the balance in favor of the enterprise view of the state and produced a new wave of dirigisme.

Finally, Lal attempts to answer the question of whether the present age of reform is likely to be more long-lived than its nineteenth-century counterpart. The worldwide growth in tax resistance and the virtually complete integration of financial markets plus the recent moves of China and India from planned to market economies all tend to work in favor of reform. However, the social democratic political agenda, the realization of the European Union, the fear in the West of economic competition from the East, the increasing substitution of high-skill jobs for low-skill ones in Western countries, and the financial crises in Asia all point in the direction of less globalization, more protectionism, and more dirigisme. Possibly, a third Heckscherian cycle will emerge.

The Continental Blockade

Heckscher's study *The Continental System* grew out of his research on the economic aspects of the 1914–18 World War, when Sweden and most of continental Europe were cut off from overseas trade as a result of the hostilities. From the outset he characterized the Contintental System as Napolean's gigantic exercise in mercantilist economic policy, aimed at defeating the "nation of shopkeepers" by denying them their export markets and not, as might seem more rational, by depriving them of imports of food and other necessities. Needless to say, the liberal cosmopolitan Anglophile Heckscher did not look kindly on the economic policies of the interventionist emperor in whose mind "France was first and foremost." Heckscher claims that the blockade failed to cripple Britain economically, but also that this failure was inevitable. Furthermore, the stimulation to French industry was artificial and short-lived despite successes in some sectors such as cotton textiles, sugar beets, and chemicals. Heckscher concluded that the "selfish" way in which Napoleon enforced the blockade on his allies in Europe was severely detrimental to their interests.

In chapter 13 Francois Crouzet provides a warm and generous, but not uncritical, appraisal of a work that he calls a "masterpiece." He agrees with Heckscher that the attempt to strangle Britain by depriving her of export markets was in the end a failure, but he vigorously denies that this outcome was necessary or inevitable and not contingent on circumstances. He points to the severity of the economic crisis in Britain from 1810 to 1812, when exports fell to two-thirds of their 1809 level. Who knows what would have happened if Napoleon's Russian campaign had not ended in disaster before Moscow in 1812? Crouzet approvingly quotes his "old master," Georges Lefebvre, to the effect that "it was not the laws of economics but the Russian winter" that caused the blockade to fail. Crouzet finds Heckscher guilty of anachronism in several of his judgments on Napoleon's actions and perhaps overly critical in his assessment of the blockade's effects on France.

The appraisal of the Continental System continues in chapter 14, written by Lance Davis and Stanley Engerman, who embed their narrative and appraisal of this episode's main events within a broader survey of the history of naval blockades and economic warfare. They extend the discussion beyond Europe to consider relevant events in the New World, such as the slave revolt in Haiti, the War of 1812, and British trade with Latin America, which was stimulated by the restriction of exports to Europe. After an extensive examination of the more recent literature, they conclude that Heckscher seems to have anticipated most of its main results and that his work survives essentially unscathed. They also observe, ironically, that it is Heckscher's much more controversial work on mercantilism that has continued to keep his name before the scholarly public outside Sweden rather than *The Continental System*, his less ambitious but more definitive study.

Any reader convinced by Davis and Engerman that Heckscher's analysis of the Continental Blockade is no longer controversial will be startled to read chapter 15 by Patrick O'Brien. Casting his paper as a "conversation" with Heckscher, O'Brien challenges the master head-on. Whereas Heckscher frames his account of the blockade as a defeat of Napoleon's irrational and misguided mercantilist ideology by the pure light of liberal Smithian reason that guided Britain, O'Brien places it in a much broader context: the sustained geopolitical rivalry between France and Britain for power and profit from 1688 to 1815 in which high and rising levels of investment in the Royal Navy gave Britain mastery of the seas and global trade despite France's continued military strength on the European mainland. Britain was able to do this because the superiority of her fiscal and financial system sustained a balance of overall military power in her favor, with subsidies to allies on the mainland complementing her own command of the sea.

In O'Brien's opinion the blockade was a desperate and doomed attempt to strike at Britain and cause her to accede to French domination of Europe. The plan was to force Britain to lose specie through a negative trade balance by shutting off her access of European export markets, thus undermining the linchpin of her monetary and fiscal system. Even though the policy failed, it should not be condemned as irrational since it was the only option available to France in a protracted geopolitical struggle. O'Brien criticizes Heckscher for two failures of historical objectivity: his Anglocentrism and what O'Brien regards as an excessive attachment to the tenets of classical economics that prevented him from appreciating the practical difficulties and wartime exigencies that economic policy makers on both sides had to contend with. It was only after her great continental rival had been decisively defeated by 1815 and her own global hegemony safely assured that Britain could turn to the implementation of the liberal world economic order based on free trade and the gold standard. This stability would be sustained until 1914 and the emergence of another continental challenger.

Eli Heckscher and Swedish Economic History

In the sixth section of the book some of Heckscher's basic concepts and interpretations concerning the Swedish economy and its history are reevaluated in light of recent research in the field. Lennart Schön's contribution in chapter 16 discusses the explanatory value of the Heckscher-Ohlin theorem in relation to the process of Swedish industrialization from 1890 to 1930. Schön makes a distinction between two different types of forces that drove this process: an external, or exogenous, force based on international integration and specialization and an internal, or endogenous, force based on the ability of the domestic economy to interact with new market opportunities and technological innovations. He makes this distinction operational by classifying Swedish industries as consisting either of Heckscher-Ohlin firms, exploiting abundant factors of production, or Schumpeterian firms, exploiting new knowledge and innovations.

For Heckscher and Ohlin, international trade was the principal force behind the integration of and factor-price equalization among different national economies. Trade and other open-economy forces worked to increase the price of relatively abundant factors and to reduce the price of those that were relatively scarce. Schön finds that the importance of the two types of industries changed over time. Until the 1890s, Swedish exports were based mainly on abundant raw materials and cheap labor ("Heckscher-Ohlin" industries). When changing relative factor prices eroded the advantage originally held by these industries, the Swedish industrial structure responded. During the so-called Second Industrial Revolution, electricity-utilizing and knowledge-intensive industries ("Schumpeterian" industries) took the lead. The convergence of factor prices that had characterized the earlier period, both internationally and within Sweden, slowed down and ceased. Indeed, starting in the 1890s and accelerating during World War I, it was replaced by factor price divergence.

In chapter 17 Johan Söderberg places Heckscher within the research tradition that has dealt with the overarching question of the long run evolution of economy and society. Here can be found almost all of the great classical economists of the eighteenth and nineteenth centuries; Adam Smith, David Ricardo, John Stuart Mill, and Karl Marx, as well as original thinkers of the early twentieth century such as Thorstein Veblen and Joseph Schumpeter. Eli Heckscher also devoted considerable thought to more "existential" questions, such as the eventual consequences of economic growth and the general forces, both economic and noneconomic, underlying growth.

Despite the fact that Heckscher never endowed his model with a formal theoretical structure, Söderberg concludes that he maintained a vision of the process of long-term economic and societal growth. Economic activity—in Heckscher's terminology, all human behavior intended to deal with the problem of scarcity—had a single purpose: to make life as rich and worthwhile as possible (that is, to produce economic welfare in the broadest sense). According to Heckscher's universal interpretation of long-run social development, preferences are endogenous. As wealth increases, the propensity to consume decreases and consumer preferences shift in the direction of nonessential goods and services, thus destabilizing core demand. The role of economic factors in long-run change was limited, especially before the nineteenth century. Noneconomic factors, such as perceptions and attitudes, were the principal sources of economic growth.

As to the ultimate outcome of long-term economic development, Heckscher's expectations for the twentieth century were distinctly gloomy. In this regard, he might be perceived as a prophet of the dismal science along the lines of Ricardo and Malthus. His gloom, however, was his own. Heckscher believed that progress was possible, but by no means was it an inevitable feature of the economic system. The liberal spirit that characterized the nineteenth century had made it an epoch of not only monumental economic growth, but also one of extraordinary cultural progress. The experience of the interwar period, however, did not bode well for the rest of the twentieth century. Changing consumer preferences made the economy less stable, and the market economy, the true source of wealth and prosperity, proved unable to resist the inroads of the state. Individual freedom was being restricted, and the individual was doomed to become the serf of an ever more oppressive state. Clearly, Heckscher's forebodings were not unlike those of Schumpeter and Hayek.

A number of Heckscher's conclusions concerning Swedish economic history have been questioned and revised by subsequent scholarship. Prominent among these is his series of estimated food consumption in Sweden for the extraordinarily long period 1550 to 1815, which Heckscher also argued could be used as a proxy for the overall standard of living. Immediately following its publication as part of the first volume of *Sveriges ekonomiska historia*, Heckscher's analysis of Swedish food consumption in the sixteenth century spurred an intense debate among Swedish scholars concerning his choice of methods and sources. That, however, did not discourage Heckscher from extending his study of the Swedish standard of living up to the end of the Napoleonic wars. His entire series is contained in *An Economic History of Sweden* (Heckscher 1954), posthumously published in English in a translation by the late Göran Ohlin, nephew of Bertil and a fine economist and economic historian in his own right.

Mats Morell has carefully examined Heckscher's work concerning Swedish food consumption, and in chapter 18 he presents a critical evaluation of the methods Heckscher used. Heckscher opted for a physiological approach, weighting various foodstuffs by their calorie content, over the more economics-based real-income approach that relies on incomes and prices. According to Morell, his preference resulted from his extensive research on food and calorie requirements during the blockade-induced food shortage Sweden suffered during World War I. Subsequent research has concluded that Heckscher's handling of his sources, especially his transformation of old measures, was far from accurate. The net effect was that he greatly exaggerated the consumption of calories during the sixteenth century, and thus that the "barbaric prosperity" he claimed to have found never existed. Despite these shortcomings, however, a number of Heckscher's results are still valid. These include his discovery of the "vegetabilization" of the Swedish diet during the eighteenth century, as well as the observation that diets in preindustrial times consisted largely of vegetable foodstuffs, particularly grains.

The Man

Eli Heckscher left an indelible imprint on the Swedish academic world, both as a giant in his field and as an academic entrepreneur. He belonged to a pioneering generation of economists, and as the founder of economic history as an academic discipline in Sweden, he remains a prominent figure. Heckscher's extensive scholarly output, as impressive in its breadth as in its depth, makes his research the starting point for later generations of Swedish economic historians even to this day. Numerous stories about the rather eccentric professor have circulated for several generations, and frequent testimony to his teaching skills is found in memoirs and biographies. Heckscher himself, however, wrote no memoir and a comprehensive biography still remains to be written.

The reminiscences that comprise the last section of the book are intended to present the human side of Eli Heckscher. In descending order of age, the grandchildren Eva, Einar, Sten, and Ivar relate their personal childhood memories of their grandfather in chapter 19. They confirm that he was a true workaholic, a continuously working scholar with set routines and a distinctly ascetic personality. Other than at family meals, when visiting their grandparents in Baldersgatan, they always met their grandfather in his study where Eli presided at his desk and the children were invited to sit briefly on his lap. Ivar relates that even those visits were dominated by ritual: first a survey of the items on the desk and then the offer of a piece of candy—the one at the top. No digging through the box in search of a favorite was permitted.

On these occasions Eli could be rather distracted and have difficulty totally abandoning his work. A serious accident was narrowly averted when young Einar, on a visit to his grandfather's study during World War II, was allowed to play with a loaded revolver so that Eli could continue his labors undisturbed. Of course, a shot went off. Eli's comment, "Well Einar, I think you had better go and play with grandma for a while," displays a degree of self-control that says a good deal about his character. Indeed, so does the fact that he kept a loaded revolver on his desk, a remarkably un-Swedish practice.

The older grandchildren, Eva and Einar, were teenagers, sixteen and fourteen years old, when Eli died in 1952. Thus they have a somewhat more mature perspective on their grandfather than that of a child. Their images are different, but it is possible to merge them into a single portrait. Einar did not live up to Eli's strict requirements for hard work and success in school. As a result, their relationship became cold and impersonal. Eva, on the other hand, became very close to her grandfather, even though they seldom talked about personal matters. Rather, their frequent conversations concerned issues. In these discussions, regardless of his true convictions, Eli frequently took positions at odds with Eva's view simply in order to encourage her to think. He remained a demanding teacher and an intellectual guide his entire life, even towards his grandchildren.

Interestingly enough, the adult Heckscher's reluctance to speak of himself and his preferences also can be detected in the school essay his grandchild Ivar discovered stashed away. The topic assigned by his teacher encouraged the pupils to reflect personally on their future choice of profession. Sixteen-year-old Eli, however, responded with a totally impersonal discussion of the general factors that influence a person's choice of profession, with no hint whatsoever as to where his own ambitions lay.

His skill as a storyteller is attested to by Sten, the second youngest of the grandchildren: "We small children sat at his feet and listened to fascinating stories based on his scholarly research." The grandfather he knew, of course, was elderly. Sten Heckscher's description of his grandfather as a singular mixture of warmth and intimacy, on the one hand, and distance and analytical restraint, on the other, reveals personality traits that also had been noted by contemporaries earlier in Eli's life.

Together with David Davidson, Knut Wicksell, and Gustav Cassel, Eli F. Heckscher has come to be regarded as a member of the first generation of modern Swedish academic economists by virtue of the Heckscher-Ohlin theory. At the time, however, Heckscher was best known as a participant in economic policy debates. In a seemingly endless series of newspaper articles, most of them published in the leading liberal morning paper *Dagens Nyheter*, he analyzed and commented on current problems. Moreover, he was heard repeatedly on the radio, the revolutionary new medium of the period, as a lecturer and debater.

Nonetheless, it is principally as an economic historian that Heckscher became known to posterity. This is clearly demonstrated in chapter 20 where Bo Sandelin examines how frequently Eli Heckscher still is cited in scholarly journals. Between 1986 and 2002, Heckscher's principal publications in economic history, *Mercantilism, Sveriges ekonomiska historia*, and *An Economic History of Sweden*, accounted for more than two-thirds of all his citations, while less than one-fifth referred to his publications in economics. Of the latter, almost all were citations of his the seminal 1919 article.

As Sandelin stresses, Eli Heckscher's citation frequency as measured by the ISI databases, the Social Science Citation Index, and the Arts and Humanities Citation Index, seriously understates his continuing scholarly importance. These sources are biased against Heckscher for a number of reasons, chiefly because they are based largely on English language journals and thus fail to provide a worldwide result. In addition, the foreign trade article presents special problems. From the database available it is impossible to tell if these citations refer to the Heckscher article or Bertil Ohlin's thesis, both of which are included in *Heckscher-Ohlin Trade Theory* (Heckscher and Ohlin 1991), or to Harry Flam and June Flanders's introductory chapter in the same volume.

Even allowing for these shortcomings, however, the results are not without interest. Heckscher's most cited work is *Mercantilism*, which during the 1930s was published in Swedish, English, German, Spanish, and Italian. Two subsequent English editions appeared in 1935 and 1994. Compared to other contemporaneous Swedish economists of the first or second generation, such as Knut Wicksell, Gustav Cassel, Bertil Ohlin, Gunnar Myrdal, and Erik Lindahl, Heckscher places third, ahead of Ohlin, Cassel, and Lindahl, but behind Myrdal and Wicksell.

In chapter 21, Benny Carlson deals with Eli Heckscher's political conversion, which occurred during the 1910s. Heckscher's image is that of one of the most liberal Swedish economists who never deviated an inch from his free trade position. As a young man before World War I, however, he had appeared on the national scene as a conservative. Indeed, he verged on being a state socialist, advocating government intervention in the economy. At the time he was strongly influenced by his teacher and mentor Harald Hjärne, who was a leading conservative thinker.

Carlson bases his analysis of Hecksher's conversion from social conservatism to economic liberalism on a number of sources. These include the testimony of colleagues and other associates, Heckscher's own published writings, and even his personal correspondence with his mother. Heckscher himself believed that his study of economics, together with the unsatisfactory experience with wartime socialism, was decisive for his altered political views. This is also the conclusion that scholars and other observers have tended to reach. After reviewing Heckscher's writings on the state, however, Carlson argues that Heckscher actually changed his position sometime during 1910 or 1911, a timing that may well be associated with the franchise reform of 1909 and the shift from a right wing to a leftist government in 1911.

Heckscher's views on Jewish assimilation and Zionism are examined by Harry Flam in chapter 22. His well-known credo that he considered himself "first and foremost as a citizen of Western society...only second as a Swede, and third as a Jew" did not prevent him from writing about and discussing the so-called Jewish Question. He was a second-generation Swede, an assimilated Jew, raised in an economically comfortable and socially well-established family, and married to a Swedish gentile. Like most of his generation of Swedish Jews, Eli Heckscher was totally integrated into Swedish society and did not consciously identify with any Jewish culture or nationality.

Heckscher believed that the promotion of Western civilization and its scholarly expression in an unfettered search for truth was the highest of all callings. Jews, just like everyone else, should contribute to that quest rather than to the nationalism that was rampant throughout Europe after World War I. Thus, he argued, the establishment of a Jewish state in Palestine would be disastrous. It would increase anti-Semitism in the nations of the diaspora and create a bloodbath in Palestine. Instead of creating a Zionist state, Jews, in his opinion, should support Western civilization by continuing the process of assimilation. Heckscher was a rational intellectual and moralist, a man of principle, whose worldview was consistently antinationalistic, internationalist, and multicultural.

Eli F. Heckscher is one of the greatest Swedish names in the social sciences. For his entire academic career, spanning over fifty years, Heckscher straddled two disciplines, economics and economic history, and during these five decades he was constantly striving to find a way to produce a successful crossbreeding between the two. He did not always succeed, and sometimes he voluntarily abstained from making the attempt. Nevertheless, the plea for incorporating economic theory in economic history, and its mirror image, the plea to make use of history in economic theorizing, were always present in his thinking. The chapters in this book are intended to reflect this preoccupation. By bringing economists and economic historians together we have endeavored to work in the spirit of Eli Heckscher, echoing and resounding his pleas to join economic history in economic analysis, and vice versa.

Notes

1. This section draws on Montgomery (1953), Henriksson (1979, 1990, and 1991), and Henriksson and Lundahl (2003a).

2. A *licentiat* degree was a preliminary step on the road to the Ph.D. Usually, obtaining it would take three or four years after the *fil. kand.* (B.A.). It involved the writing of a thesis which had to be defended at an internal departmental seminar. Only a handful of carbon-copied, or even handwritten, versions of the works were made, and basically the degree was an affair between the professor and the student. Hardly any coursework was involved, but the main activity other than the thesis took place in the so-called higher seminar (research seminar).

3. Heckscher's most important methodological papers are collected in Henriksson and Lundahl 2003b.

4. The other three dealt with exchange rate determination under a paper standard (Heckscher 1916), with a criticism of Gustav Cassel's purchasing power parity doctrine (continued in Heckscher 1930), Wicksell's cumulative process (Heckscher 1921) and fixed capital and free goods (Heckscher 1924). Heckscher's (1918) book on Swedish production problems also contain interesting chapters on overcapitalization and cooperative firms, and in the chapter on tariffs and trusts (originally Heckscher 1913), he anticipates Wilfred Salter's (1960) vintage approach to capital formation and technological change.

5. Ruben Rausing, unpublished and undated manuscript (ca. 1966), archives of the Stockholm School of Economics.

6. Heckscher (1954) gives an idea about how Heckscher conceived what the final product would have looked like.

References

Bergendal, K., et al., eds. 1930. *Sweden, Norway, Denmark and Iceland in the World War, Part III.* New Haven and London: Carnegie Endowment for International Peace.

Eli F. Heckschers bibliografi 1897–1949. Stockholm: Ekonomisk-historiska institutet.

Findlay, R., and M. Lundahl. 2002. "Toward a Factor Proportions Approach to Economic History: Population , Precious Metals, and Prices from the Black Death to the Price Revolution." In R. Findlay, L. Jonung, and M. Lundahl, eds., *Bertil Ohlin: A Centennial Celebration (1899–1999)*, 495–528. Cambridge, MA: MIT Press.

Gale, D., and H. Nikaido. 1965. "The Jacobian Matrix and the Global Univalence of Mappings." *Matematische Annalen*, 159:81–93.

Heckscher, E. F. 1904. "Ekonomisk historia: några antydningar." *Historisk Tidskrift* 24:167–198.

———. 1907. *Till belysning af järnvägarnas betydelse för Sveriges ekonomiska utveckling.* Stockholm: Centraltryckeriet.

———. 1908. "Produktplakatet och dess förutsättningar. Bidrag till merkantilismens historia i Sverige." In *Historiska studier: tillägnade Harald Hjärne på hans sextioårsdag den 2 maj 1908*, 693–784. Uppsala: Almqvist & Wiksell.

———. 1913. "Tullpolitik och trustväsen. Med anledning af förslaget om sockertullens sänkande." *Ekonomisk Tidskrift* 15:1–29.

———. 1915. *Världskrigets ekonomi.* Stockholm: P. A. Norstedt.

————. 1916. "Växelkursens grundval vid pappermyntfot." *Ekonomisk Tidskrift* 18:309–312.

————. 1918. *Svenska produktionsproblem.* Stockholm: Albert Bonniers.

————. 1919. "Utrikeshandelns verkan på inkomstfördelningen. Några teoretiska grundlinjer." *Ekonomisk Tidskrift* 21, part II: 1–32.

————. 1921. "Verkan av för låg räntefot." *Ekonomisk Tidskrift* 23:49–56.

————. 1922. *The Continental System: An Economic Interpretation.* Oxford: Clarendon Press.

————. 1924. "Intermittent fria nyttigheter." *Ekonomisk Tidskrift* 26:41–54.

————. 1931. *Industrialismen. Den ekonomiska utvecklingen 1750–1914.* Stockholm: P. A. Norstedt.

————. 1930. "Monetary History from 1914–1924 in Its Relations to Foreign Trade and Shipping." In K. Bergendal et al., eds., *Sweden, Norway, Denmark and Iceland in the World War, Part III,* 127–268. New Haven and London: Carnegie Endowment for International Peace.

————. 1935a. *Mercantilism.* London: George Allen & Unwin.

————. 1935b. *Sveriges ekonomiska historia från Gustav Vasa. Första delen. Före Frihetstiden. Medeltidshushållningens organisering 1520–1600.* Stockholm: Albert Bonniers.

————. 1936. *Sveriges ekonomiska historia från Gustav Vasa. Första delen. Före Frihetstiden. Andra boken. Hushållningen under internationell påverkan 1600–1720.* Stockholm: Albert Bonniers.

————. 1949a. *Sveriges ekonomiska historia från Gutav Vasa. Andra delen. Det moderna Sveriges grundläggning. Första halvbandet.* Stockholm: Albert Bonniers.

————. 1949b. *Sveriges ekonomiska historia från Gustav Vasa. Andra delen. Det moderna Sveriges grundläggning. Andra halvbandet.* Stockholm: Albert Bonniers.

————. 1954. *An Economic History of Sweden.* Cambridge, MA: Harvard University Press.

————. 1991. "The Effect of Foreign Trade on the Distribution of Income." In E. F. Heckscher and B. Ohlin, *Heckscher-Ohlin Trade Theory,* 39–69. Cambridge, MA: MIT Press.

Heckscher, E. F., and B. Ohlin. 1991. *Heckscher-Ohlin Trade Theory.* Cambridge, MA: MIT Press.

Henriksson, R. G. H. 1979. "Eli Heckscher och svensk nationalekonomi." *Ekonomisk Debatt* 7:510–520.

————. 1990. "Eli Heckscher." In C. Jonung and A.-C. Ståhlberg, *Ekonomporträtt: svenska ekonomer under 300 år,* 165–186. Stockholm: SNS Förlag.

————. 1991. "Eli F. Heckscher: The Economic Historian as Economist." In B. Sandelin, ed., *The History of Swedish Economic Thought,* 141–167. London: Routledge.

Henriksson, R. G. H., and M. Lundahl. 2003a. "Eli Heckscher, ekonomisk teori och ekonomisk historia." In R. G. H. Henriksson and M. Lundahl, eds., *Janusansiktet Eli Heckscher: nationalekonom och ekonomisk historiker,* 17–49. Stockholm: Timbro.

————, eds., 2003b. *Janusansiktet Eli Heckscher: Nationalekonom och ekonomisk historiker.* Stockholm: Timbro.

Montgomery, A. 1953. "Eli Heckscher som vetenskapsman." *Ekonomisk Tidskrift* 55:149– 185.

Olsson, C.-A. 1992. "Eli Heckscher and the Problem of Synthesis. A Methodological Note." *Scandinavian Economic History Review* 40:29–52.

Salter, W. E. G. 1960. *Productivity and Technical Change.* Cambridge: Cambridge University Press.

Part I

Theory, Methodology, and History

2

On the Continuing Need for Both the Critical Evaluation of Sources and the Utilization of Economic Theory: Recent Methodological Developments in Economic History

Håkan Lindgren

Nearly one hundred years have come and gone since the then twenty-four-year-old Eli F. Heckscher published a paper in the Swedish journal *Historisk Tidskrift* that introduced and justified a new social science discipline—economic history. Even today, Heckscher's manifesto seems remarkably fresh, and it has definitely retained its relevance. He positions himself midway between history and economics while skillfully managing to distance himself from the extremes of both fields. The German historical school is criticized both for "its extreme historical" treatment of economic events and developments, and for its "nomothetic" historical writing. The former all too often loses itself in a sea of detail while the latter, within the context of various stage theories of development, results in history being squeezed "into all too easily manipulated formulas."[1]

According Heckscher, deductive economics suffers from an "absolute blindness towards the concept of development" and a total lack of "historical perspective." Economic regularities and theories are not universal natural laws, but rather historical categories. They are determined, and will change with, the development of society and the "living conditions of classes of people." When previous theories and earlier economic policies are treated, it is usually to illustrate the mistakes of the past. Economists "elevate ... the principles of free competition to ethical doctrines and take every opportunity to express their purely moral indignation at the crimes that have been committed since the beginning of time against the orthodox teachings."[2]

Given these methodological shortcomings of history and of economics, Heckscher drew the logical conclusion that the new field should combine the best features of both its parent disciplines. The task of economic history, according to Heckscher, was to examine three aspects of the evolution of economic life: *conditions*, *policy*, and *perspective*. Conditions referred to the development of the economy and the living conditions of the population, and were the heart of the new discipline. The history of economic thought, "perspectives," also was an essential part of the field. It conveyed knowledge concerning how people, at various points in time, understood the interaction among economic variables. Heckscher used the expression "how the construction of economic activity evolved." That, in turn, determined what economic policies were pursued. Thus, the young Heckscher was well aware that people's experiences, values, and ideas concerning the true nature of reality form the basis for how the economy was organized during various historical eras and under different cultural systems.[3]

This essay poses the question of whether Heckscher's 1904 manifesto is relevant to the economic historian of today and tomorrow. Methodological developments in the fields of history, economics, and economic history during recent decades are contrasted with Heckscher's vision. This then forms the background to some reflections on the current relationship between economic history and the two disciplines from which it emerged. The concrete examples and the reality, I assume, are largely Scandinavian. The problems I treat, however, have a global and, to some degree, a timeless character.

Micro History and Social Constructivism

Within the discipline of history, recent decades have witnessed a distinct shift in the focus of research, a development that also has affected the set of methods used to solve problems. This methodological reorientation is also apparent in a number of other humanistic fields such as archaeology, anthropology, and ethnology. It can be summarized as a declining interest in artifacts as such, accompanied by greater attention to the values and the mental framework that can be inferred from the historical remains. Thus, for example, during the 1960s and 1970s, research in social history had a solid positivistic foundation. It was to a great extent dedicated to the quantification of the characteristics of large social aggregates. Class status was by far the most frequently used such category. The reaction against this quantification and aggregation paradigm that occurred during the 1980s and 1990s received its sustenance from French historical psychology and the Annales school. Historians such as Lucien Febvre, Fernand Braudel, and Emmanuel Le Roy Ladurie led the charge.

In Sweden, these new trends were noted during the early 1990s in several newspaper articles contributed by two of the leading professors in the field, Rolf Torstendahl of Uppsala University and Eva Österberg of Lund University. Rolf Torstendahl emphasized that anthropologically oriented, historical mentality research was in the process of displacing the previously totally dominant quantitative social history.[4] Eva Österberg, for her part, noted that hermeneutics, anthropological culture analysis, and the gender theories of women's studies had gradually shifted the interpretive framework of historical research. Nonetheless, she predicted that both materialism and social theory were about to experience a renaissance.[5]

Currently, little remains of the old quantitative social history. It has been almost entirely replaced by research on mentalities and perspectives, on attitudes towards time and space, suicide, death and religion, as well as toward other persons. Court records have become a diligently exploited source of material. Correspondence, diaries, and other narrative sources are also utilized, often for textual analysis. These materials yield new knowledge concerning people's life experiences, such as carnivals, café socializing, and folklore.

Paradoxically enough, the growing interest in cultural analysis and mentality research has resulted in a major restriction in the scope and geographic extent of historical research. The Annales school's initial demand for a "*histoire totale*," in practice, has brought on a renaissance for detailed descriptions, local history, and the so-called *micro history*. Striving to gain insight into the actions and experiences of individual actors has replaced the goal of producing total history. Ironically enough, the fact that the new sources are analytically demanding and very labor intensive to use, has actually reinforced the micro trend.[6] As a result, now, ten years after Torstendahl and Österberg brought up the issue, micro history directed at charting people's perspectives and individual fates is the height of fashion in Swedish history departments. When such analysis has been broadened to include groups and experiences at an "intermediate level," it has even been endowed with a new name intended to differentiate it from macro and micro history: *mezzo history*.[7]

During 1999, Arne Jarrick, professor of history at Stockholm University, initiated a new public debate concerning historical scholarship with an article in one of Sweden's largest morning newspapers, *Svenska Dagbladet*.[8] Basically, the ensuing discussion concerned what constitutes scholarly research and writing in history. Is the search for truth, with a capital T, the essential mission? Indeed, is there a truth to be found, or are our interpretations of various events only cultural constructions that are determined, or in any case influenced, by our own perspectives and values? The answers offered to these questions depended greatly on the writer's epistemological and theoretical address.

To the outsider, the role of the search for truth in legitimizing history as a scholarly discipline might seem trivial. On further reflection, however, it is a highly relevant, and perpetual, problem for all scholarship that seeks to investigate so-called reality. At one extreme, there are scholars who emphasize the primacy of the search for truth and the critical evaluation of sources in order to separate fact from fiction. Even though most modern historians distance themselves from the "primitive positivism" of Comte, Carnap, and Neurath, it is not totally incorrect to refer to this group of scholars as being inspired by positivism. The opposite extreme is represented by modern idealism. In technical jargon, it has been labeled "social constructivism," "postmodern relativism," or even "postmodern constructivism."

The extreme relativists maintain that every statement concerning reality is a social construct and that, therefore, there are as many truths as there are speakers. As Håkan Arvidsson argued in the above-mentioned debate, history "ultimately is a construction and a narrative that bears the imprint of the values, insights and biases of its time." In his contribution, Arvidsson does back away from the extremes by drawing a methodological distinction between the determination of the "particularities of the past," on one hand, and the merging and interpretation of actual events into a unity, or narrative, on the other hand. In the former case, the critical evaluation of sources is needed, even though in practice it seldom yields simple answers as to what is true or false. In the latter case, however, history is caught up in a spider's web of relativism. Interpretations of our past will always be followed by reinterpretations, simply because "history is a communication between the past and the present, between then and now."[9]

Economics: A Social Science Apart

The new methodological currents with the cultural disciplines, to various degrees and in various ways, have also influenced the social sciences. This indicates that these changes are an expression of a broad scholarly renewal. They constitute a profound reaction against the materialistic and generalistic direction of research that totally dominated the 1960s and 1970s and that one critic aptly called "the tyranny of aggregations."[10]

Within the area of economic research, the leadership in this process of renewal undoubtedly has come from business economics. This new discipline expanded rapidly at the existing Swedish universities during the 1980s, and, at the same, was represented at most of the new regional campuses that were established during this time. Measured by the number of students and faculty, business economics quickly grew to become the incomparably largest subject among the social sciences. Its multidisciplinary character gave rise to new questions and new methods for illuminating various aspects of business activity. That part of economic history that deals with business history has especially been inspired by the rapidly expanding research concerning company organization and leadership. Research in business economics is, by definition, inductive and theory-testing, often utilizing case studies of individual enterprises. Its predisposition toward such case studies has helped increase the scholarly legitimacy of studies of "micro structures," even in other areas and in other disciplines.

Nor did research in economics remain unaffected by the shift from macro to micro. During the last few decades, the firewall that previously divided macro from micro theory has been breached. In particular, the tools of micro theory have made major inroads into macro territory. This flowering of microeconomics is clearly related to the shift in paradigms that occurred in the 1970s, when it became apparent that reality no longer agreed with the Keynesian road map. There was no room in Keynesian business cycle theory for the combination of accelerating inflation and increasing unemployment. Instead, this unhappy duo had to be given a new name—stagflation.

At the same time, faith in Keynesian growth theory was being undermined by the absence of economic growth in the low income countries, despite the massive capital transfers from the industrial countries that had been ongoing since the 1950s. Simply put, the use of broad aggregates to explain the mechanisms underlying the business cycle and economic growth had failed. Thus, an intensive search for the microeconomic basis of macroeconomic variables was undertaken. Monetarism got wind in its sails, while new approaches such as "supply side economics" and the "economics of entrepreneurship" emerged, as did "post-Keynesian economics," with ambitions to open up for a more nonorthodox economic theory and "abductivist" views of explanation. At the same time, older, so-called heterodox theories, such as Austrian economics, Schumpeterianism, and institutional economics, reappeared and were adapted to mainstream economics.[11]

Still, economics has remained relatively impervious to the various schools of postmodern thought. The reason for this resistance is that the discipline, or at least its mainstream, rests on a unifying analytical base, a product of its roots in neoclassical theory. No other social science can rely on such a compact core of axioms and premises as does microeconomics. In combination with a strictly logical, deductive methodology, which is particularly well suited to mathematical and statistical expression, economics has with great success applied its hard core of marginal utility maximization and rational behavior based on self interest to many new and, reformulated old, areas of research.

This constant theoretical core has both strengths and weaknesses. The deductive analysis and the strong emphasis on mathematical and statistical models have successfully been applied to new problems, but it has also contributed to isolating economics from the other social sciences. During recent decades, economic analysis has made major incursions into other areas of research, including the economics of education, of the environment, of energy, and of health care. Not surprisingly, other social scientists have not hesitated to criticize what they see as inappropriate intellectual imperialism by economists.[12]

Ever since deductive methods and mathematical models had their breakthrough in economic analysis during the late 1800s, a debate has raged as to whether these methods actually have screened economics from the very social problem it was intended to solve. Stanley Jevons and Léon Walras laid the groundwork for the two principal approaches that won wide acceptance and for a long time dominated "mainstream economics." From Jevons, and later Alfred Marshall, emerged the idea that the principal task of economics is to utilize statistical methods to test theoretically based conclusions with empirical data. For some time, this was referred to as applied economics. Walras, with his strictly deductive and mathematical model of general equilibrium, originated the paradigm that eventually came to dominate research and graduate education: that the function of economic science is to develop its internal theoretical apparatus, "positive economics," with the help of increasingly refined abstract models and ever more advanced mathematical methods.[13]

More recently, the ever increasing specialization and "technification" of the subject according to Walrasian principles has led to a new debate among economists as to whether or not the discipline puts excessive emphasis on the solution of technical problems at the expense of social relevance. Assar Lindbeck, professor emeritus at Stockholm University, has forcefully warned against economics abandoning the social sciences to become a pure natural science. Lindbeck's successor in the Stockholm chair in international economics, Lars Calmfors, emphasized several years ago in a discussion paper that technification has increased the distance from empirical reality. In order to give economic scholars perspective and a more relativistic view of their mathematical and statistical models, the history of economic thought and economic history should be required subjects for graduate students, he argued.[14]

Economics and History

At the end of World War II, research and instruction in economic history in Sweden was constrained to one single academic setting: the Institute for Economic History Research that had been founded by Eli Heckscher. Its institutional home was at the Stockholm School of Economics and what was then called Stockholm University College. As part of postwar university reform, however, and thanks to Heckscher's influence at the ministerial level, the field was given more independence from the departments of history than had been proposed by the prelegislative committee proposals. New readerships in economic history were filled in Lund by Oscar Bjurling (1948), in Gothenburg by Artur Attman (1949), and in Uppsala by Karl-Gustaf Hildebrand (1951). All had been active in the history departments of their respective universities. Heckscher's own pupil Ernst Söderlund was appointed to the professorship in Stockholm (1949), and a separate economic history department was created. Of these scholars, only Bjurling was an economist. All the rest had their roots in the field of history.

The institutional liberation of the field was completed, first when the readerships were converted into professorships during the 1950s, and second when the humanistic faculties were divided up during the mid-1960s. Since then, training and research in economic history have been located in separate departments of economic history. Over time, they have developed a consensus as to what constitutes good research in the field. In 1966, these departments of economic history were transferred to the faculties of social science, thus, at least in the long run, strengthening their contacts with the other economic disciplines.

Courses in time series analysis, growth theory, and the history of economic thought were introduced, but methodologically the field was, and remains, firmly anchored in the inductive empirical tradition.[15]

A clear indication that the roots of Swedish economic history lay in the cultural field of history is that the discipline remained relatively unaffected by the "new economic history" and the cliometric movement that emerged in the United States during the 1960s and 1970s. The historical economics that flourished among American economic historians at that time was intended to widen the boundaries of neoclassical economics through a conscious application of the logical deductive approach to historical problems. Critics, however, argued that deductive models based on simple assumptions are incompatible with historical research which is intended to explain complicated (multicausal) empirical relationships. The ensuing methodological struggle petered out during the 1980s, with neither side being able to claim victory. The methodological chasm between economic and historical thinking was just too deep.[16]

As in the other Scandinavian countries, Swedish economic history has been characterized by a *relativistic perspective*. This has found expression in a marked openness toward new trends, both with regard to theory and to choice of topics. Marxist-inspired research on the transition from one mode of production to another had its day. It was succeeded by work-life research during the 1980s and by women's history, now called historical gender research, during the 1990s. On a more basic level, however, the methodological unanimity has been great: formal theory, at various levels of abstraction, regardless of origin, is to be tested against a concrete, multifaceted reality. To the law-seeking "nomotetists" this was justified by the argument that a theory continually has to be confronted with reality to prevent if from becoming a shackling dogma. To the empiricists it was argued that detailed descriptions of "the living past" must be imbedded in more general explanations and theories in order to have scientific interest.

The epistemological basis of this consensus has been materialistic in the sense that is founded on a belief that a reality, about which it is possible to gain knowledge, exists independent of the individual's perceptions.[17] In recent years, this consensus has been challenged by micro history and postmodernism, the latest fashions in history and the other cultural disciplines. Especially at Stockholm University, where research in social history has had a long tradition, people's experiences and perceptions has become an area of research within

economic history. A number of monographs and theses with a sociological and anthropological bent have recently been written there.
Their principal inspiration has been the French cultural sociologist
Pierre Bourdieu. One interesting example is the research project entitled "A History of Human Conceptions." From a social and mentality
perspective, it examines questions such as how gender relations, crimi-
nals, suicides, and children were perceived in the past.[18]

These trends within the academic discipline of economic history naturally raise the question of whether or not it has a hard core. What
should be considered its central area of concern and what should be
viewed as peripheral? Even if we opt for inclusion rather than exclusion, it must still be asked if postmodernism and social constructivism
is relevant to the internal development of the discipline. What does a
far reaching social constructivist perspective add and what are its dangers? That question is not so easy to answer.

As long as I can remember, in our methodology courses we have
taught our students that scholarly research in history requires a critical
examination of myths and socially useful metaphors. Otherwise our
defenses against all sorts of propaganda and biased information are
likely to be inadequate. This scholarly attitude is operationalized in
various ways: the explicit formulation and analysis of problems, critical and independent thinking, and an understanding of the context.

Not least, the requirement of insight and understanding calls for
consideration and respect for other points of view and the values of
other people. This applies not only to colleagues in one's own discipline, but also to those who work in adjoining fields, and who pose
somewhat different questions. In the historical disciplines, however, it
is especially respect for the values and perspectives of previous generations that is essential. Any serious current researcher must, to the best
of his or her ability, strive to unravel the cultural code that permeates
human relations in all societies.

In a recently published book, Sören Barlebo Wenneberg, a scholar
at the Copenhagen Business School, has analyzed the problems and
possibilities of social constructivism in an understandable and easily
grasped presentation. He works with four different methodological
standpoints, all of which fit within, or are associated with, the concept
of social constructivism. The first two of these are in a sense related.
The first is simply a critical perspective based on the conviction that social phenomena are the product of human actions, not natural laws.
The second consists of various theories of how this social reality is

structured and holds together. A third viewpoint concerns epistemology and the nature of knowledge. In its most radical version, it
maintains that knowledge and scientific concepts exclusively are determined by social factors (such as "power" and "interests") and subjective factors. The fourth and final position can be regarded as the
ultimate consequence of the other three. It rejects realism and supports
the idealistic point of view that "reality" (especially social reality) is
created by our perception and knowledge of it.[19]

No historian is likely to have trouble accepting the first two of these
methodological positions. Indeed, they are the basis of our belief in
path dependence, usually expressed in terms such as saying that some
phenomena are "historically determined" and that special theories,
such as Hegel's theory of history, are needed to explain the relationship between continuity and discontinuity in the process of change. In
my opinion, however, today's intellectual fashion of including epistemological and ontological analysis creates a two-pronged danger for
historical scholarship. First, if two assertions that contradict each other
constitute *competing* descriptions of reality and can be equally true,
depending on the authors' different perspectives, then logic indicates
that all conclusions have scholarly validity. Even those that actually
are nothing more than a confirmation of the scholar's own values
could not be excluded.[20]

Second, there is apparent peril in a one-sided reliance on "today's
narratives" to determine what is of historical importance. Namely, the
risk that the norms of our time, or our society, become the basis for
value judgments concerning phenomena and events of the past. Writing history backwards also makes it possible to enlist history in the service of political propaganda, something frequently practiced in the
past.

Without an open mind and an honest intent, the cultural codes of
the past will never be deciphered, and without that it will never be
possible to understand why people acted as they did in various historical situations. For example, understanding changes over time in the
concept of "childhood," that is, to understand its character as a social
construct, is essential for studies of the treatment of children in the
past. With such a content, the social constructivist approach has important strengths. That, of course, was the reason that Eli F. Heckscher in
his 1904 manifesto so strongly emphasized the key role of the history
of thought in economic history. Economic theories are historical categories, and the history of economic thought reveals how, at various

points in time, people understood the functioning of the economy. That, in turn, determined their economic behavior.

It is, of course, rewarding to study historical actors with hindsight. As Göran B. Nilsson put it, however, it also leads "to a trivialization and simplification of events." All history, including economic history, should be written forward. It should be based on a holistic perspective, carefully examine its sources, and strive to understand historical actors and their behavior. Knowing in retrospect what actually came to pass, the historian is tempted to ignore the expectations for the future held by his subjects. That, however, would be a mistake. As Nilsson argues, "the historian should take the anticipations of his subjects seriously, even though he knows better than them."[21] This prescription constitutes a well-thought-out and articulated alternative to the moralizing history writing that unquestionably has grown in popularity. In fact, of course, the latter is a return to the older history writing that flourished before the breakthrough of "Rankeism" during the nineteenth century.

The fundamental rules for scholarly historical research that first were preached in the middle of the nineteenth century by Leopold von Ranke, an influential professor at the University of Berlin for almost half a century (1824–72), are still valid today. They require a critical evaluation of sources and a striving for objectivity, as well as *historical understanding*. That is to say, the scholar should endeavor to set aside the values of his or her time and attempt to understand and interpret historical events in light of the then existing conditions. This demand to free oneself of one's own values requires that the scholar not only have a profound knowledge of the historical period being studied—how did people think then?—but also that the subject be approached with considerable humility and respect for the actions of the historical actors.

In 1824, Ranke's manifesto was summarized in an appendix to his first major work, *Geschichte der romanischen und germanischen Völker*: no longer was historical research intended to judge the past, but, to the greatest extent possible, to determine what had actually happened, "wie es eigentlich gewesen."[22]

Economic History as Economic Science

Economic history is an inductive, empirical discipline. Even though the purpose of economic historical analysis is to describe reality, to discover repetitive phenomena and to reveal similarities and patterns in economic development, it is not atheoretic. Perhaps its most important task is to test various economic theories, and thereby to contribute to the development of new theoretical constructs concerning the nature of reality. Thus, the field has clear connections to "applied economics" in the spirit of Jevons and Marshall, even though the economic historical method has fundamental differences from that of economics. The latter works with a theoretical-deductive approach to analysis. Thus, economics treats as *constants* factors that in economic history are considered short-run *parameters* and long-term *variables*. As Heckscher emphasized in a 1947 article, the practice in economics of abstracting away portions of economic reality inevitably means that it can not provide the inclusive analysis of events that economic history strives to deliver.[23]

The extent, if any, to which the abstract deductive approach of economic theory is compatible with pronouncements concerning empirical reality was the subject of a lively debate among nineteenth-century classical economists. After all, modern economics emerged from seventeenth-century mercantilism, where the point was to determine how economic policy should be formulated so as to increase a nation's political power. Normative economics, which provides advice and counsel on economic policy, thus has a long tradition. This background is also reflected in the name given to the new discipline; until the end of the nineteenth century it was called *political economy*.

During the nineteenth century, economics slowly freed itself from simply being a provider of policy prescriptions, and became established as a *positive* discipline, an "economic science" distinct from the "art of policy." The basic distinction between positive and normative economics is usually credited to Nassau William Senior and his 1836 work *An Outline of the Science of Political Economy*. In a famous pronouncement, Senior maintained that the conclusions drawn from an economist's scientific work "do not authorize him in adding a single syllable of advice." The overriding idea was that reality is so complicated that the conclusions reached through use of deductive economic theory cannot serve as the sole basis for recommendations concerning which actions should be taken in a given situation.[24]

The idea of divorcing theoretical (that is, scientific) economics from the empirical variant was perhaps argued most forcefully by the Cambridge economist Henry Sidgwick, at the time highly respected but now largely forgotten. In the Introduction to his *Principle of Political*

Economy (1883), he declaimed that "it is very rarely, if ever, that practical economic questions which are presented to the statesman can be unhesitatingly decided by abstract reasoning from elementary principles. For the right solution of them full and exact knowledge of the facts of the particular case is commonly required; and the difficulty of ascertaining these facts is often such as to prevent the attainment of positive conclusions by any strictly scientific procedure."[25]

During the twentieth century, economics has evolved in the direction of "pure" theory, with an ever-increasing emphasis on deductive models, relying on sophisticated mathematical and statistical methods. This development has increased the methodological chasm separating theoretically oriented economists, not just from economic historians, but also from policy oriented economists. Within one school of thought, the "Austrian," the discussion concerning whether it is possible to draw empirical conclusions on the basis of deductive theoretical models has been kept alive. A common conviction of all those economists who describe themselves as "Austrian," or today even "neo-Austrian," is that no discipline that ultimately deals with relations among people can yield exact predictions, such as those generated by physics and other natural sciences. Thus, the apparent exactness of orthodox economic's mathematical models is misleading. As the basis for economic policy decisions, it can sometimes be catastrophic.[26]

These difficulties have been clarified by, among others, Friedrich von Hayek. His installation lecture, given in conjunction with his assumption of the chair in economics at the University of Freiburg in 1962, was devoted to an extremely illuminating discussion of the principles underlying the relationship between scientific professionalism and participation in practical decision making. Hayek's most important justification for drawing a clear boundary between economics and politics was methodological. Abstraction and theorizing are essential for the development of economic science, as "knowledge of facts as such is not science." By themselves, however, theoretical relationships do not make it possible to predict the results of one or another economic policy action in a given historical situation. The analysis of economic relationships requires not only insight into theoretically deduced relationships, but also knowledge of the actual conditions that in a concrete situation will affect the outcome. This problem affects all science that deals with complex process involving human beings. According to Hayek, however, economists appear to be more prone than other researchers to forget that advanced theoretical insights are insufficient when it comes to predicting the consequences of a particular action in a given situation.[27]

In my judgment, the methodological tendencies of "mainstream economics" during recent decades have made Hayek's argument more relevant than ever. As the problem areas subjected to economic analysis have been broadened and given a time dimension, the economist's tool chest has been further supplemented with mathematical models a la mode. It also seems as if economists actually have become less aware of the limited empirical validity of theoretical reasoning applied to a concrete economic situation. Apparently this has resulted from the increasing study-time-related displacement of graduate courses intended to convey a broad perspective and a realization that real-world phenomena are indeed complex, by ever more technical courses. Much has no doubt been gained by this development, but something has also been lost.

None of the above said implies that economic history should dump its economic ballast. On the contrary, as long as the practitioners of both economics and economic history are aware of the basic methodological differences between the fields, and of the limits and the strengths of the deductive and inductive approaches, major synergetic effects may arise. Ultimately, the nature of the research problem addressed is crucial; naturally, not all questions in economic history can be resolved by economic theory. Nonetheless, as long as examining "how the problem of satisfying needs, broadly defined, has been solved through time" remains the central task of economic history, all theorizing concerning the efficient allocation of scarce resources will be of interest. The principal of scarcity, as well as its antithesis, the principal that individuals with given preferences rationally strive to maximize their payoffs, thanks to their simplicity and general applicability, have impressive explanatory power.[28]

Let me make the benefits of economic theory for research in economic history tangible by giving two examples, one hypothetical and one from a doctoral thesis recently presented here at the Stockholm School of Economics. The price system is crucial for the allocation of resources in a society. Should, let us say, the price of grain greatly increase in a single year, the economic historian with training in economics immediately will know where to look. He or she will analyze the phenomena in light of the general principles of supply and demand, consider the functioning of the market, and give thought to the substitutability among various grains and of grains with other foodstuffs, both in production and in consumption. Thus, abstract economic theory, although not the entire explanation, becomes the gateway to an explanation. For a complete and exhaustive explanation, it is at least as important to know if the price rise resulted from an increase in demand for grain as a result of a domestic potato crop failure or from a general crop failure in North America.

In his thesis, entitled "Empirical Studies in Money, Credit and Banking," Anders Ögren studies the nineteenth century Swedish financial system, which was based on private note issuing banks. One of the questions he poses is how the rapid expansion of the country's money supply could have been compatible with the fixed change rate that the Swedish central bank maintained between 1834 and 1913. In answering this question, the thesis exemplifies not only how good empirical research requires a firm grasp of both economic theory and of econometric methods, but also the importance of historical knowledge concerning how things actually functioned. Ögren's gateway to an analysis of the functioning of the specie standard in an international perspective is various economic theories of monetary and exchange rate systems. He then utilizes econometric techniques to explain how central bank reserves, the money supply, and prices interacted. The results of his causality tests indicate that reserves affected the money supply, which in turn affected the price level, all in accord with the classical specie flow mechanism.

At the same time, both Swedish prices and central bank reserves moved in general accord with those of the country's principal trading partners. Supplementing the analysis with empirical information leads to the conclusion that the specie standard system was more flexible than predicted by theory. This result was a consequence of the Swedish central bank's policy of accumulating foreign assets, which could be drawn upon when domestic reserves shrunk. The international connection was of decisive importance for the exchange rate regime. Prices followed the monetary expansion, but so did economic growth, and they were all international phenomena during the gold standard era.[29]

To Be a Historian While Remaining an Economist

In this essay, I have shown how the methodological developments of the two fields that have traditionally constituted economic history's closest neighbors, history and economics, have developed in diametrically opposite directions. The growing interest among historians in mentality and cultural analysis has given social constructivism and micro history wind in their sails. By contrast, economists have stuck with their hard core and have further developed the strictly logical deductive approach with the help of increasingly advanced mathematical and statistical techniques. The instinctive conclusion ought to be that economic history has arrived "at the end of the road" and now has to choose its scholarly partner. Is it now even possible to maintain, along with Eli F. Heckscher, that an economic historian both must "be familiar with the abstract method and habit of reasoning on the basis of simplified assumptions of theoretical economics" and also "have the historians ability to synthesize and his sensibility to the multifaceted nature of reality"?[30]

I would argue that it is perfectly possible. Social constructivism, in the sense that there are "cultural codes" that must be deciphered, is perfectly familiar to historically trained scholars. Thus, for example, in economic history the basic justification for studying the history of economic thought is that people's conceptions of how reality is constructed determines the framework for interpretation and action during various epochs. It is only when social constructivism is interpreted in terms of epistemology and ontology that it becomes a danger to historical scholarship (and other disciplines). The problem, above all, is that it opens the door to absolute methodological individualism and subjectivity, as well as a one-sided reliance on "today's narratives" to determine what is historically meaningful. Materialism and realism must remain the epistemological base of economic history, nor should we revert to the pre–Leopold von Ranke, moralizing style of writing history.

Of course the need for insight into abstract economic theory and deductive model building depends on how the field of economic history is defined. As long as the label is "economic" history, however, economic questions must be *the heart of the discipline*. Other aspects of human activity, no matter how closely related to economics, are *secondary*. If the broad definition that recurs, in various formulations, throughout Eli F. Heckscher's writings, that the field concerns "how human needs have been met throughout time," is maintained, then the principle of scarcity is raised to a general phenomena that all people in all societies at all times have been obliged to face. It is therefore easy to agree with Heckscher when he continues: "Methodologically speaking, this is the explanation why economic theory is indispensable."[31]

A conscious utilization of economic theory in empirical research, however, does not excuse the economic historian from the customary critical evaluation of sources. It is thus essential to be fully aware of the assumptions underlying economic theory and of the limits on the conclusions drawn from deductive reasoning when they are confronted with a complicated and multicausal reality. Such an empirical confrontation, however, can also serve to enrich theory. Thus, economic history can make important contributions to economic theory and, indeed, can be developed in a theory-generating direction.

It is important to emphasize that my pleading in favor of a deliberate rapprochement with economic theory does *not* mean that I in any sense find it desirable for economic history to evolve into a branch of economics. Economic history is by no means historical economics. The boundary is crystal clear. Economic history is an empirical, inductive discipline, deeply rooted in historical method and the critical evaluation of sources. What I do hope, however, is that the trend toward estrangement from economic theory and growing distaste for econometric modeling, which recently can be observed within the field in Sweden, will be broken.

Making the application of economic theory explicit and more energetic, however, requires a considerable increase in the qualifications of our economic historians. The next generation of Swedish economic historians must acquire a considerably better knowledge of modern economic theory and of the history of economic thought than is possessed by the current generation. Graduate training in economic history is still dominated by the humanistic educational tradition, with long reading lists and insignificant training in economic theory and methodology. It is the duty of the currently active generation to see to it that graduate education in the field be at least partly reorganized. Multidisciplinary methodology and theory courses, as well as training in quantitative methods, should be given a substantially larger role. If this can be accomplished within the framework of national graduate course cooperation, it simultaneously would satisfy both myself and the evaluation section of the Swedish National Agency for Higher Education.

Notes

The title of this essay is an echo of that used by Göran B. Nilsson thirty years ago in *Historisk Tidskrift* (1973: 173–211). That paper opened my eyes to one of the central problems in historical research, and I am pleased to be able to associate my essay with his work.

1. Hecksher (1904: 188, 197).

2. Hecksher (1904: 169, 173, 185). In current usage, one would say that economic theories are "social constructs" or "socially and historically embedded."

3. Hecksher (1904: 185–186).

4. Torstendahl (1991: 1).

5. Österberg (1992: 24).

6. Högskoleverket (2003: 12); Tosh (2000: 110–118, 240–242).

7. Odén (1998: 11).

8. Jarrick (1999: 16–17); Nordqvist and Wiklund (1999: 12); Magnusson (1999: 18); Arvidsson (1999: 14).

9. Arvidsson (1999: 14).

10. Dahmén (1979: 256).

11. Dahmén (1979: 258–262); Lindgren (2003: 14); Sellstedt (2002: 131–133).

12. Högskoleverket (2002: 17–29); Bergström (1996: 77–78).

13. Landreth and Colander (1994: 231, 236, 266–281).

14. Calmfors (1996: 239–240); Lindbeck (2001: 31).

15. Högskoleverket (2003: 30–32); Hettne (1980: 151–155).

16. Högskoleverket (2003: 30–32); Hettne (1980: 146).

17. Eva Österberg is presumably using the term "materialism" in this sense.

18. Hedenborg (1997: 22–23). For theses inspired by Bourdieu, see Gustavsson (2002, especially pages 10–27), and Eriksson (2004: 9–27, 245–249).

19. Wenneberg (2001: 62, 69–70, 80–81, 92–93).

20. This, of course, does not constitute a denial of the well-known fact that our view of reality affects the construction of scholarly concepts and theories. The complexity and multifaceted nature of reality makes it highly likely that two scholars, working independently, will produce two different descriptions of a given aspect of reality, both of which are "reasonably true." What is more, these descriptions are more likely to be complementary than competitive in nature. Thus, the constant rewriting of history is not a result of arbitrary or relativistic scholarship. Rather, it is the infinitely multifaceted and multidimensional state of reality that enables the scholarly community to constantly produce new insights into the past as society evolves and the focus of interest shifts.

21. Nilsson (1989: 3); Nilsson (1990: 67).

22. Torstendahl and Nybom (1988: 25–36).

23. Heckscher (1947: 3–4).

24. Schumpeter (1954: 536–541). It should be noted that the classic distinction between normative and positive economics has nothing whatsoever to do with the role of values in scholarly work. For historians and historically trained economists, the importance of

the attitudes and the concept of reality prevalent during various epochs is so apparent that it would never occur to them that positive economics is value-free.

25. Reproduced in Schumpeter (1954: 805 n. 11).

26. Hakelius (1995: 31–37, 62–76).

27. Hayek (1967: 259–265).

28. The quotation is from Hecksher (1922: 15).

29. Ögren (2003: 177–212).

30. Hecksher (1922: 36).

31. Hecksher (1936: 17).

References

Arvidsson, H. 1999. "Historiker måste konfrontera da med nu." *Svenska Dagbladet*, August 19.

Bergström, V. 1996. "Ar ekonomerna samhällsvetare?" In L. Jonung, ed., *Ekonomerna i debatten—gör de någon nytta?* Stockholm: IVA and Ekerlids.

Calmfors, L. 1996. "Nationalekonomernas roll under det senaste decenniet—vilka ar lärdomarna?" In L. Jonung, ed., *Ekonomerna i debatten—gor de nagon nytta?* Stockholm: IVA and Ekerlids.

Dahmén, E. 1979. "Kan den företagshistoriska forskningen bidra till den ekonomiska teoriens utveckling?" *Historisk Tidskrift* 99, no. 3: 255.

Eriksson, P. 2004. *Stadshypoteks plats och bona inom det svenska kreditväsendet 1909–1970—en socialhistorisk studie*. Stockholm: Almqvist & Wiksell.

Gustavsson, M. 2002. "Makt och konstsmak. Sociala och politiska motsättningar på den svenska konstmarknaden 1920–1960." Ph.D. diss., University of Stockholm.

Hayek, F. A. 1967. "The Economy, Science, and Politics." In *Studies in Philosophy, Politics and Economics*. London: Routledge & Kegan Paul.

Heckscher, E. F. 1904. "Ekonomisk historia. Några antydningar." *Historisk Tidskrift* 23, no. 4: 13–198.

———. 1922. "Ekonomi och historia." In *Ekonomi och Historia*, 11–50. Stockholm: Albert Bonniers.

———. 1936. "Den ekonomiska historiens aspekter." In *Ekonomisk-historiska Studier*, 9–69. Stockholm: Albert Bonniers.

———. 1947. "Ekonomisk historia och dess gränsvetenskaper." *Historisk Tidskrift* 67, no. 1: 1–17.

Hedenborg, S. 1997. *Det gåtfulla folket. Barns villkor och uppfattningar av barnet i 1700-talets*. Stockholm: Almqvist and Wiksell.

Hettne, B. 1980. "Ekonomisk historia i Sverige under femtio år. Institutionell utveckling och forskningsinriktning." *Historisk Tidskrift* 100, no. 1–2: 140–175.

Högskoleverket (National Agency for Higher Education). 2002. *Utvärdering av utbildning i nationalekonomi vid svenska universitet och högskolor.* Högskoleverkets rapportserie 2002:9 R.

————. 2003a. *Utvärdering av ämnet ekonomisk historia vid svenska universitet.* Högskoleverkets rapportserie 2003:11 R.

————. 2003b. *Utvärdering av grundutbildning och forskarutbildning i historia vid svenska universitet och högskolor.* Högskoleverkets rapportserie 2003:12 R.

Jarrick, A. 1999. "Vetenskapen hotar förfalla till kollektiv monolog." *Svenska Dagbladet,* June 20.

Jonung, L. 1996. "Inledning." In L. Jonung, ed., *Ekonomerna i debatten—gör de någon nytta?* Stockholm: IVA and Ekerlids.

Landreth, H., and D. C. Colander. 1994. *History of Economic Thought.* Boston: Houghton Mifflin.

Lindbeck, A. 2001. "Economics in Europe." *CESifo Forum* (Spring 2001): 31–32.

Lindgren, H. 2003. "Scandinavian Business History at the End of the 1990s: Its Prior Development, Present Situation, and Future." In F. Amatori and G. Jones, eds., *Business History Around the World,* 146–169. Oxford: Oxford University Press.

Magnusson, L. 1999. "Allsköns vidskepelse framkallar rysningar." *Svenska Dagbladet,* August 11.

Nilsson, G. B. 1989. "Historia som humaniora." *Historisk Tidskrift* 109, no 1: 1–15.

————. 1990. *Den lycklige humanisten. Tio offensiva essäer.* Stockholm: Carissons.

Nordqvist, S., and M. Wiklund. 1999. "Historikerna måste bidra till nuets berättelser." *Svenska Dagbladet,* July 16.

Oden, B. 1998. *Leda vid livet: Fyra mikrohistoriska essäer om självmordets historia.* Lund: Historiska Media.

Ögren, A. 2003. "Empirical Studies in Money, Credit and Banking. The Swedish Credit Market in Transition under the Silver and Gold Standards, 1834–1913." Ph.D. diss., Stockholm School of Economics.

Osterberg, E. 1992. "Historieforskare, lyft näsan en smula!" *Svenska Dagbladet,* November 11.

Schumpeter, J. A. 1954. *History of Economic Analysis.* London: Allen & Unwin.

Sellstedt, B. 2002. "Metodologi för företagsekonomer. Ett försök till positionsbestämning." Stockholm: SSE/EFI Working Paper Series in Business Administration. Available online: http://swoba.hhs.se/hastba/abs/hastba2002_007.htm.

Torstendahl, R. 1991. "Historieforskning: Kultur och makt." *Svenska Dagbladet,* September 2.

Torstendahl, R., and T. Nybom. 1988. *Historievetenskap som teori, praktik, ideologi.* Stockholm: Författarförlaget.

Tosh, J. 2000. *Historisk teori och metod.* 3rd ed. Lund: Studentlitteratur.

3

The Making of the Economic Historian: Eli F. Heckscher, 1897–1904*

Rolf G. H. Henriksson

Eli Heckscher's fame as both an economic historian and an economic theorist also entails recognition of him for his methodological position. He was already noted internationally for his writings on the methodological theme in the inter warperiod when he, somewhat in opposition to an early mainstream in the field, made a plea for theory in economic history and followed it up arguing for a more quantitative statistical approach.[1] Then in the skirmishes caused by the emergence of the so-called new economic history in the 1960s, he met renewed attention as somewhat of a precursor to that movement (Fogel 1965).

The basic motive for the attention in this essay to Heckscher's methodological views is that comprehending them is central to the task of reassessing also his substantive contributions.[2] In 1904, at the outset of his career as an economic historian, Eli Heckscher made a much noted methodological declaration (Heckscher 1904b). Methodological issues concerning the interface of economics and history then remained a central concern for him throughout his life.[3] But in a life of research and thinking spanning more than five decades of scholarly pursuits, Heckscher's methodological views were considerably reformulated. However, in my view the early declaration of 1904 stands as a manifesto, whose core tenets Heckscher never abandoned.[4] The present essay seeks to lay bare Heckscher's conception of the task, scope, and method of the field as stated in the manifesto of 1904. This is done by presenting the manifesto generically as the result of exposures to the fields of history, political science, and economics, which were Heckscher's three main subjects during his study years at Uppsala University (1897–1904). By especially scrutinizing more closely the background of the manifesto it is possible to interpret its content and message more deeply than has so far been done.

The content and argument of the essay is as follows: a first lengthy section, reviewing Heckscher's various lines of study, seeks to clarify his starting position before the 1904 declaration as mainly that of a general historian. However, it points out that already in this phase Heckscher had received at least elementary research experiences in social science that prepared for his later breakaway from the established track of historians. He had familiarized himself with the statistical approach in political science and the conceptual approach in economics.

The next section offers an appraisal of Heckscher's work with the licentiate thesis (Heckscher 1903; 1908a). Here Heckscher, in his first major research project as a historian, is seen to have arrived at an intermediary position in his transition from history to economic history. As the thesis is but a first synoptic anticipation of his later work on mercantilism and merely an embryo of his *Economic History of Sweden*, he had not yet fully conceived of how to employ either the statistical or the conceptual approaches that his exposure to the two social sciences might have suggested.

The subsequent section deals directly with the manifesto of 1904. Here Heckscher took the decisive step in assuming an identity as an economic historian. The account expounds on and offers an interpretation of the content of the manifesto as regards the roles of economics and other social sciences in defining the task, scope, and method of economic history. A brief conclusion sums up the survey and the argument.

Apprentice in Uppsala

When Heckscher, at age eighteen, entered Uppsala University, in early 1897 he first spent some time shopping around and orienting himself in academic life before settling for his chosen line of study. After a while, he reported to his parents that he had never dreamed that he would earn his first income as an actor in a play. This public activity of Heckscher illuminates a passionate side of his personality that may easily be forgotten in an intellectual portrayal that will in the main underscore the rational and systematic way in which this very focused man, dedicated to high moral principles, sought to go about his duties and solve the problems he encountered.

Heckscher had graduated from the so-called Latin line at Nya Elementar, the high school in Stockholm where he had prepared himself for the university. This line aimed quite exclusively for humanistic and law subjects rather than "sciences." Facing his academic options thus confined, Heckscher seems at first to have considered mainly linguistic subjects in his study program.[5] However, Heckscher's basic inclinations were early bent towards historical studies. He appears to have made a predisposing acquaintance with that field already during his next to last year at Nya Elementar. In the summer of 1895 he attended courses at Uppsala University, where he gained his first impressions of a number of leading university professors, including the historian Harald Hjärne, which as a sanguine father figure was later to become his main mentor.[6]

Although, Heckscher appears to have spent considerable time before finally committing himself to a study program he had already in his first year at Uppsala enrolled in historical studies and did seminar work assigned by Hjärne. However, these studies under Hjärne were broken off in the spring of 1898 by a sojourn at Gothenburg University.[7] Here he had the opportunity to pursue studies under the Ludvig Stavenov, who in 1895 had been appointed to the chair of history and politics set up at that new university.[8] Stavenow had less of the flashing brilliance that was the prime mark of Hjärne's excellence, but was nevertheless a historian of wide perspectives and intuition who no doubt influenced Heckscher's later thesis work for the *fil. lic.* degree.

Thus history became Heckscher's primary choice and hence to be the subject where he wrote a thesis. On returning to Uppsala in the fall of 1898 he was more tightly drawn into the circle of historians gathering around Hjärne. This socializing with the Hjärne group appears to have been the decisive influence not only for his studies in history but for his other studies as well.[9] Of special importance was the friendship Heckscher made with a more advanced history student, who like himself was a graduate of Nya Elementar, the charismatic Gunnar Hazelius.[10] Hazelius was a leading personality in Uppsala student life in the 1890s and exerted an intellectually as well as morally kindling influence on student minds in a wide network. Hazelius seems to have played an important role in guiding Heckscher on his initial study program. Apparently Hazelius was the major influence in making Heckscher the first in the circle of history students to formally sign up for economics in a *fil. lic.* degree as an option available after a university reform act of 1891. On recommendation from Hazelius, who had no doubt read Wicksell's favorable review, Gide's *Nationalekonomins Grunddrag* (1899) seems to have been the primer for Heckscher's studies in economics.[11] That study was a newly conducted translation into Swedish of a French classic that offered, as far as a text book goes, a solid up-to-date overview of the state of economic science, covering also the recent advent of neoclassical theory. Such a textbook introduction was no doubt important to Heckscher, inasmuch as economics was at Swedish universities only taught as an examination subject in the Faculty of Law, which made it somewhat inaccessible to history students.

The chair in economics, including fiscal law, at Uppsala University was held by David Davidson.[12] He had in 1899, in response to the increasing interest in economics outside the law faculty, set out as initiator and editor of *Ekonomisk Tidskrift*, Sweden's only professional journal in economics. The reason economics had become so attractive outside the faculty of law, especially among history students, was generally that this subject seemed highly relevant to many of the social issues that agitated politically concerned academicians at the turn of the century. Interest in the subject was at the time enhanced by the presence in Uppsala of Knut Wicksell,[13] who was "a celebrity of ill repute" in respectable circles after his many "scandalous" lectures and writings. Wicksell, now in his late forties, had in the 1890s made his fundamental theoretical contributions to economics and was then studying for the law degree, which university regulations required before he could be accepted to the position of docent.

However, despite the general interest in economics, very few students outside the faculty of law enrolled for that subject. No doubt picking economics was considered a bit adventurous for a history student who would meet with a different tradition in terms of teaching and examinations than he was used to. Studies in history were centered on participation in a seminar with presentation of assigned works as more important than the examinations of course literature and checks on knowledge from attendance at lectures. In law studies the reading of course literature constituted the main workload for students who generally had little contact with the professors in the field.

But a further reason for hesitation in committing study time to economics was apparently Davidson himself, whose personality made him notorious as a teacher in failing to stimulate students and who was furthermore considered somewhat of an examination risk factor. In the fall of 1899, Heckscher deplored that he did not have the opportunity to listen to Wicksell, who as a newly appointed docent now taught a well received lecture course. Heckscher added that, alas, he had therefore to fall back on Davidson, who was "almost as boring as his examinations were impossible." However, Heckscher was not a man to take counsel of his fears and, with Hazelius as an informant, he proceeded with economics under Davidson.[14]

Heckscher's Political Interest and Work in Political Science

In deciding on his study program, Heckscher, while no doubt yielding to his quest for a challenge, was also economizing on his time and effort. As he set out for a goal both boldly direct and rationally circumspect, he had taken advantage of the examination reform of 1891. This made it possible to aim directly for the higher degree of *fil. lic.* Thus, in opting to skip the lower level degree, *fil. kand.*, he had to study three fields instead of five. The field Heckscher picked, in addition to history and economics, was political science.[15]

Much of Heckscher's continued work through 1900 and 1901, in addition to his historical studies, was his seminar work in political science. That subject had no prominent front figure in Uppsala to fascinate Heckscher in the same way as Hjärne in history or representing as much pristine authority as Davidson in economics. This may have been one reason Heckscher, as previously noted, spent a semester at Gothenburg University.

What seem to have generally attracted Heckscher to political science, as well as to economics and history, were apparently his now growing political concerns as may be inferred from his participation in organized student union and coterie life. Heckscher had in the fall semester of 1898 joined the conservative student society, Heimdal, to which also most of the above-mentioned Hjärne group of history students belonged.[16] Heimdal became very much Heckscher's habitat in integrating his many diverse intellectual activities related to the studies for which he had signed up as well as a number of extramural pursuits.[17] He was, as the representative of Heimdal, central in the organizing committee for the Nordic meeting of student unions in 1901. As an officer to the meeting he reported thoroughly on its proceedings (Heckscher 1901a;b).

It was on political issues that Heckscher, already in his "freshman" year, wrote the first printed items listed in his bibliography (Heckscher 1897). Political issues were also the subject area for his next published writings (Heckscher 1898a;b). These publications dealt with the issue of international arbitration as a way of promoting a more peaceful world. In the fall of 1897 Heckscher had in the main Uppsala daily reviewed a study written by the Hjärne disciple Karl Hildebrand (1897), who argued that only a certain type of international conflicts, called conflicts of "rights," could be resolved through institutions of international arbitration, while so-called conflicts of "interests" could not be resolved through such procedures.[18] As regards the latter point, Heckscher argued to the contrary. The next year in the same daily, Heckscher followed up with a discussion of the possibility of abolishing international warfare. He now advanced an argument for the establishment of a progressive global "legal state" (*rättsstat*).

In his political studies Heckscher interacted with other members of the Hjärne group in a deepened focus on the eighteenth century parliamentary proceedings, which were in some degree parallels to the contemporary constitutional issues in Sweden at the tine. Heckscher himself contributed a paper on "Tillfälliga utskott" (occasional committees) dealing with the eighteenth-century organization of work in the Swedish parliament. This paper was subsequently printed (Heckscher 1902) and should be noted as his first published research contribution.

The political science paper is of great interest as evidence of Heckscher's early orientation towards social science as an aberration from the main methodological tenets to which he as member of the Hjärne group so far had subscribed. The paper was a product of a rather prolonged seminar participation in the spring of 1901. Heckscher had here been forced to try his hands at some statistical fact gathering and elementary processing in dealing with an historical issue. Generally the stern Rankean principles of source criticism, to which all professional Uppsala historians in those days subscribed, had led most of them to shun "historical statistics," a term referring to the numerical information generated by the past about itself. In consequence of the source-critical view, most Swedish historians in those days, were apparently negative toward statistical research methods. Getting one's hands dirty in any type of statistical fact-gathering was not the virtue it is today, but was rather, especially in the high Hjärne quarters, frowned upon. Thus, Heckscher had already in his political science work taken a first step on his course of methodological separation away from being purely a political historian.

However, the most immediate importance of Heckscher's work in political science was that it seems to have settled his mind for the choice of licentiate thesis topic in history. Heckscher's earlier attention to arbitration topics, as well as other aspects of political conflict, alerted him to economic policy issues focused in his work on the mercantile system and later central also in his work on the economic history of Sweden. Thus, since eighteenth-century parliamentary life was the theme on which Heckscher had done his most intense research before setting out on his licentiate thesis work, one may rather safely conclude that political science was the main breeding bed for Heckscher's conception of his thesis topic. Most notably, Heckscher's research for this paper was a quite integral part of his historical studies at the time when he was already working on his thesis topic. But the question that still needs an answer is to what extent political science contributed to shaping the approach of the licentiate thesis.

Studies in Economics Under Davidson

Heckscher's studies in economics are of course a central chapter both in the making of the economic historian and in the shaping of his methodology. Here the Davidson's impact was a rather complex and intriguing one. Heckscher's own testimony of the role of Davidson as a teacher of economics was negative. According to Heckscher, Davidson seems not to have been very anxious to increase the enrollment in his subject. He actually appears to have dissuaded Heckscher from attending his lectures. This somewhat shirking attitude to his teaching obligations made him, as noted earlier, problematic to an enthusiast for economics like Heckscher. Also, Davidson was generally too negative and little appreciative in his views on the state of the art in his field. Very few of the received works in economics passed muster under his critical eyes. Furthermore, during the years when Heckscher studied under him, Davidson seems to have become more influenced by the historical school than formerly and did not offer much of the synthesis brought to the fore internationally in neoclassical economics at that time.

However, Davidson's well-known strong inclination toward Ricardo was now beginning to dominate, possibly reinforced by the constructive influence of Wicksell. Heckscher was despite his antipathy to Davidson's instruction methods impressed by that feature of Davidson's teaching where Davidson displayed his analytical edge and ability to hold on to long chains of deductive reasoning, a trait Heckscher might have considered an asset also in his own intellectual equipment (Heckscher 1952).

But not much is known about Heckscher's studies under Davidson. Some clue may be obtained from the fact that Heckscher had in a meeting with Davidson in 1901 asked for a reading course that fitted his thesis plans. This indicates that he seems to have had his thesis topic somewhat defined when he set out on his studies in economics. Whether this meant that he had a set of specific questions that economics should help him answer is far from clear, however.

Having made economics one of the three fields in his licentiate degree, Heckscher from 1901 on worked closely under Davidson in the later phase of his studies in Uppsala. Highly motivated, Heckscher devoured the learning that Davidson, despite his noninviting lectures, offered in economics. Because the great majority in the audience obtaining Davidson's instruction were law students who seldom aspired for more than a "pass" in the subject, Heckscher stood out as one of a select few, who seriously pursued higher studies under Davidson at that time. After the departure of Hazelius he may have been the only one and assumed the position as somewhat of an unofficial assistant to Davidson. In that capacity, Heckscher played quite a major role. He carried out what should be considered amanuensis chores for Davidson by setting up the guidelines for studies in economics, first for students in the faculty of law and then also for students in the faculty of philosophy (Heckscher 1904a). Furthermore, toward the end of his degree work he assisted students with examination difficulties, apparently with Davidson's blessing, by offering private tutoring.

A most important event in Heckscher's studies under Davidson occurred already in 1902. He was after only one year of concentrated work in economics, appointed by Davidson to assist as an official discussant of a doctoral dissertation in the faculty of law.[19] The occasion was the assessment of how a an independent-minded law student, Nils Stjernberg, also at the time chairman of the Uppsala Student Union, had handled his subject matter (Stjernberg 1902). Stjernberg, after straying away from the beaten track in his field, had produced a tract with the title "Till frågan om de s k rent ekonomiska kategorierna" (On the so-called purely economic categories).[20] Assessing a dissertation on that topic required the expertise knowledge not only in jurisprudence but also in economics. As Heckscher, with the exception for Davidson, was the only one around who was sufficiently versed in economics, he was called upon to serve as the second discussant.

Stjernberg's dissertation was exceptional in many ways. First of all, a doctoral degree was seldom awarded in the Faculty of Law. Secondly, dealing with the conceptual issues on the interface between law and economics was a daring enterprise in Uppsala in those days. Heckscher reports, quite stirred, that Stjernberg's study was met with ridicule in the camp of jurisprudence and with condescension by the economists, meaning Davidson.

Unfortunately, what Heckscher said in his capacity as opponent is not known. He had prepared fifteen points, but his discussion was cut short as he ran out of time. This opposition may have been much more important to Heckscher than the passing event Heckscher's later reporting held it to be. At least some of Heckscher's points must have dealt with the clash between the conceptualization approach of jurisprudence and the anticonceptualization approach of the historians. The latter had become an issue among Hjärne's disciples following some noted works by Edén (1896, 1900) and the previously mentioned Hildebrand (1897). Heckscher's views on this score had undoubtedly a bearing of central importance for his later plea for theory in economic history.

But in contending with the perplex that nomothetical theory posed for the historians, Heckscher had little support from the social sciences he had included in his degree in addition to history. While political science opened up toward statistics, it was still conceptually too under-developed to open up for nomothetical theory. Therefore political scientists were almost as negative to covering law tendencies as were the historians. Thus historians, who disregarded that positivistic social science approach, could still feel quite at home in political science.

Things were a bit different in economics. That field was more advanced as a nomothetical science, but that feature was not sufficiently pursued and underlined in Davidsons's presentation. Davidson had once written a dissertation querying about the laws of capital formation and had followed it up with a study of the theory of rent (Davidson 1878, 1880), but he had as much a legal as an economic mind. While the training in jurisprudence sharpened his conceptual powers, the analytic taxonomy of that field was more normative than behavioural. This made his method of reasoning casuistic and little bent on driving points home in a generalising fashion. Furthermore, Davidson had in his young days been much exposed to the teaching of Knies at Heidelberg, who through his abstract, excruciating approach had impugned Davidson's attitude toward economic theory.[21]

In his above-mentioned doctoral dissertation of 1878, Davidson had actually been influenced by the Austrian approach, but only more narrowly by Menger. In working out a theory of capital formation he had absorbed the idea of the hierarchy of wants, but without accepting Menger's related implicit notion of marginalism. Thus, since Davidson had missed out on the emergence of the neoclassical revolution, he was not the one to push Heckscher into the neoclassical camp. Heckscher had his first encounter with neoclassicism, basically as mentioned earlier, through his reading first of Gide (1899) but then especially also Marshall (1890) and Wicksell (1901). Davidson had all these writers on his reading list, but one should note that it was Heckscher who had compiled that reading list.

Thus, although Heckscher's studies in economics at Uppsala may have entailed only a select absorption of economic theory compared to his vast reading of history, they were by no means minor and far from shallow. Heckscher no doubt became rather well groomed in classical economics during his Uppsala years. But he also accepted the criticism expressed by the historical school against "the whigism" of the classical authors. This criticism made clear that classical theory was mainly a specific model, which had an "institutional fit" only to the particular time and place of England in the early Industrial Revolution. More generally, like the historical economists, Heckscher noted the blindness of the classical economists to the fact of institutional evolution in response to technological change. The institutional specificity deprived their theoretical conceptions of any universal applicability. The only general validity of classical theory that Heckscher retained as his "keep" was what might be called "the economic logic in the small," the type of partial deductive reasoning demonstrated by Ricardo. This was the residue of classical theory that had been transferred into the now emerging neoclassical theory, where it was expanded into a stringent general theory of markets and the market system.

Thus, Heckscher never went as far as some of the most extreme members of the historical school, who totally rejected classical theory. Like most members of that school Heckscher only criticized the institutionally specific model set forth by the classical economists. What Heckscher had retained via Davidson was their more rigorous general economic market logic, which made it possible for him to absorb and digest also the neoclassical involution. On that basis Heckscher arrived, through reading and efforts of his own, at what we might today identify as the textbook neoclassical reconstitution of a Millian stationary state, the neoclassical macro system model. This conception served as Heckscher's point of departure for his later application of economic theory in clarifying historical economic policy issues. That Millian basis would, at the side of Heckscher's later reading of Marshall and Wicksell, account also for the quite Ricardian qualities of his later contribution to international trade theory. That contribution of his appeared properly enough in a festschrift to Davidson (Heckscher 1949b).[22]

It should also be pointed out that Heckscher, because he had obtained a fundamental grasp of Ricardian deductivism from Davidson, also learned a lot about deductive socialistic thinking from him. Here Heckscher especially absorbed the theory of Davidson's favorite, Rodbertus. Understanding Rodbertus also made for a fundamental understanding of Marx, whose deductive approach Davidson had penetrated in his above mentioned dissertation. All this made Heckscher well equipped to take on the socialists in his later heated controversy with them (Heckscher 1908b).

It may be argued that since Davidson did not give Heckscher a fully satisfactory overview of economics, Heckscher had himself to put together the synthetic whole. However, for this he equipped Heckscher well, by making Heckscher's grounding in the field conceptually solid. Thus Heckscher's logical mind could probably perform that task well enough to rescue him from surrendering to the overall antitheoretical teachings of the historical school.

But it is important to note, as a major deficiency in the teaching that Heckscher received from Davidson during the Uppsala period that he was inadequately informed about the increasingly predominant neoclassical economic theory. Heckscher's exposure to Wicksell and to available literature, which must soon have included also Marshall, was probably not enough to make up for these lacunae in his overview of economics. Heckscher probably did not begin to make up for this deficiency until he sat down to write the manifesto.

We may, as a summing up of Heckscher's studies under Davidson note that he became much more knowledgeable in economics than has generally been recognized. We may then conclude that the study of economics as a conceptual approach served as a second source of aberration from the tenets taught by Hjärne. But, as with the statistical approach to which he was exposed in political science, the impact of the conceptual approach in economics may not, as we shall note, have had an effect rapid enough to influence his work on the licentiate thesis. The influence of these aberrations from the Ranke school guidelines did not show up until in the manifesto. To see the historical "musts

and must nots," there is a need to take a closer look also at the holds
that Hjärne's teaching had on Heckscher.

The Grounding of the Historian and the Importance of Hjärne

While Davidson, despite his cooling influence, may be seen as important for Heckscher's intellectual development by ushering him into the
world of academic economics, he obviously never served as the mentor
to Heckscher in the same way as Hjärne. The latter seems to have
exerted a strong not only professional but also ideological, influence
on Heckscher as well as on his other disciples. However, while it seems
clear that what we have called the making of the economic historian
was a process during which Heckscher gradually emancipated himself
from the methodological tenets of Hjärne, this did not mean a weakening of the ideological bondage to his mentor. This bondage is of importance in understanding "the making of the economic historian" insofar
as it had an at least indirect bearing on Heckscher's conception of the
task of economic history. But the character of this bondage seems too
complex for a ready assessment here.

More pertinent and less remote to the overall theme of the present
essay was the influence that Hjärne exerted on the professional level.
Abiding by Hjärne's strictures regarding the pursuit of historical craftsmanship on the level of the work floor was for his students almost a
matter of obedience to second-nature lifestyle imperatives. The inculcation of the principles of historical source criticism was the mark of
a professional historian. Thus the teaching of the techniques and
methods of historical research, in the spirit of Ranke, was basic to the
training of the historians in the Hjärne seminar. As an example of
what Heckscher's work under Hjärne on that score involved, may be
mentioned the first historical writing that Heckscher got published
(Heckscher 1898c). In that paper, titled "Vår äldsta kungaätt" (Our
oldest royal ancestry line), Heckscher offered an account of the most
recent controversy and fate concerning the *Yngliga Saga*, a tale by the
medieval Icelander Snorre Sturlasson. Heckscher could report that as a
result of a sharp Rankean scrutiny in the hands of scientific historians,
that story about the birth of Sweden as taught to all Swedish schoolchildren in those days, had now to be relinquished as completely a
myth.

Heckscher praised this result highly, not only because it demonstrated the power of the Rankean source critical approach, but also be-

cause it fitted his vision of history mediated by Hjärne, implying that the emergence of Sweden as a state and nation had to be placed in the wider European context as the rise of the West out of the age of antiquity rather than as a purely Germanic or Nordic genesis.[23] This wider perspective on Swedish history, was an essentially "medievalist" vision in the sense that it required an overview extending both forward to the present and backward in time to antiquity. Heckscher's "medievalist" outlook made him especially receptive to the Hjärne message that the historian's "ulterior motive" always was a concern for the time in which he lived. What Heckscher seems especially to have absorbed in Hjärne's teaching was a type of Whig interpretation of history that can be called "methodological presentism." Hjärne projected a perspective on the past that was implicitly comparative in search for universal features in the historical process implying also a central understanding of the present day and age. Generally, historians, in turning to the past, often quite intuitively choose those periods or problems that seemed to be parallels to the present, but this should be done more consciously in order that the methodological problems of this approach should be clarified. In searching for basic parallels to the present the historian should, because history never fully replicated itself, also be alerted to the contrasts with the present which in that way would be even further illuminated.

In his methodological presentism Heckscher, in the writing of the *Economic History of Sweden*, eventually went even farther than Hjärne. This Heckscher's advance meant that the historian in his searchlight on the past was looking for factors that pointed forward in the historical process and thus ultimately also to the contemporary world to which the historian did his reporting. It meant asking in what way a past was part of the root system for what followed. This deeper Whig interpretation of history involved an effort at perceiving those particularities in the onward frontier that linked up to the present.

Aside from informing about the important content of Hjärne's teaching that Heckscher absorbed and extended, the above informs also about the methodological approach that Hjärne by example implanted in his students. It makes clear that Hjärne turned them into more than Ranke proselytes. He also taught them much about the essentials of synthesis in historical reconstruction. Reconstruction must necessarily be based on interpretation, but interpretation presumes the existence of an object to be interpreted. Thus interpretation is both a matter of analysis of causal links in the nodal core of a historical web and of putting together the larger picture of historical change and context. Heckscher, who in general was Hjärne's foremost follower in emphasizing the need for synthesis, was also on that score holding a view beyond Hjärne in pushing for the need to make syntheses as much as possible empirically objective. The reason he did that, or could do that, is to be found in his deviation from Hjärne's anticonceptualist stance. Heckscher tried to escape from Hjärne's reluctance to offer too daring historical interpretations premised on abstract concepts. Hjärne's main ambition, following Ranke, was confining history to the task of establishing "wie es eigentlich gewesen" through resort only to the source-critical approach, where all problems of synthesis were to be solved through a purely creative act of overall assessment that could not be anything but subjective. Heckscher held that historical syntheses may, like castles in the sand, be obliterated when there are no supportive conceptual pillars. Heckscher's explicit advocacy for the necessity of abstract premises—and, we should add, statistically reinforced—for historical syntheses was his basic deviation from Hjärne. In Heckscher's view Hjärne's position precluded the study of social and economic progress as a subdiscipline within the field of history. Actually, Hjärne's embracing the uniqueness of historical events implied a global vision that ruled out a comparative approach as regards the total process. Hjärne's position meant to Heckscher a radical taboo against all attempts to deal with history in theoretical terms.[24]

However, although Heckscher did not accept Hjärne's anticonceptualism, he agreed in his formative years to Hjärne's opposition to positivism and also to his opposition to nomothetic explanations of historical change. In the early phase of his productive life as an economic historian Heckscher only accepted nomothetical theory insofar as his query about the past was confined to the workings of the system as opposed to its evolution (Heckscher 1922a, 1929, 1930b, 1933, 1936b). But as he in the later phase adopted a statistical outlook and applied a statistical approach, nomothetical theory eventually had to be resorted to even in accounting for economic-historical change (Heckscher 1951a; Henriksson and Lundahl 2003). Thus Hjärne long had a confining influence on Heckscher's methodological position and may be said to have shaped his stance not only as regards the conception of the task for economic history, but also as regards its scope and method. Not until Hjärne's hold on Heckscher's conception of its task began to ease did Hjärne's confining influence on Heckscher's views regarding the scope and method of economic history soften.

But with this we are back facing the issue of Hjärne's ideological importance and we shall therefore on that score only make one point previously touched upon in a footnote. The ideological lead of Hjärne implied for Heckscher a moral adherence to a universalizing western European culture perspective, to which Swedish nationalistic concerns were subordinated. This wide perspective was not only the basic framing for Heckscher's work on mercantilism but also what inspired him in the writing of the *Economic History of Sweden*. Here Heckscher, influenced by Hjärne's conception of history, actually transcended the narrow economic perspective and opened to the spiritual dimension even of economic life. This strongly permeated Heckscher's pursuit of economic history from the start. Heckscher's Hjärne-inspired conception of historical craftsmanship as a calling for economic historians in the service of a cultural mission should be kept in mind for understanding "the making of the economic historian" as that process unfolded in Heckscher's licentiate thesis and subsequently in the methodological manifesto.

The Licentiate Thesis: A Specimen for the Historian's Craft

After having spent the first Uppsala years in apprenticeship for the craft of historian, Heckscher finally turned to the task of doing the specimen work required for the *fil. lic.* degree, which was considered the lower entry level to the profession before the doctorate. In 1903 he submitted a licentiate thesis to Hjärne with the title "Studier till Produktplakatets förhistoria och historia" (Studies in the prehistory and history of the Navigation Act) (Heckscher 1903). This study dealt with the Swedish Navigation Act of 1724, which was a decree favoring Swedish vessels in the import and export of goods to and from the country.[25] Not revealed by the overall title, the thesis also entailed, as a framing background, an overview of the evolution of the system of economic policy prevalent in the Western world before the age of economic liberalism called the mercantile system.

With this thesis Heckscher initiated what in his vernacular may be referred to as the two "Faustian" ventures in his scholarly life.[26] Through the inclusion of the lengthy background survey of the mercantile system, the thesis was first of all the very beginning of his great work on mercantilism, the major study of the history of economic policy that evolved as the central theme in his historical research during the early half of his scholarly life (Heckscher 1935a). Secondly, from the main part of the thesis unfolded his massive work on Swedish economic history, his so-called real task, which became his predominant preoccupation in the later half of his life (Heckscher 1935b; 1936a; 1949a; 1954).

The thesis was presented to Hjärne as a handwritten manuscript in November 1903. Apparently most of the writing had been done during 1903. Judging from purchasing dates of books preserved in the Heckscher book collection and from library loan records, one may conclude that his research on the framing part dealing with the mercantile system took place mainly in 1902. But preparation for this part, as well as for the rest of the thesis, may have been initiated much earlier. As noted above the idea for the thesis topic in general may have arisen already in 1898 during Heckscher's study period under Stavenov in Gothenburg. However, the most likely starting year for the substantial work on the project, dealing with the specifics of the Swedish navigation act, is 1901. As was noted above, in that year Heckscher asked Davidson about a reading list that fitted his thesis plans.

As only the embryo of his monumental study, Heckscher's general introductory discourse on the mercantile system of course lacked many features of his later work, but some are already strikingly present in this early presentation. The account had all Heckscher's general characteristics of writing style and eloquence and, of course, his meticulousness.[27] The main difference to his later work was that his presentation was not based on primary sources. It was only a synopsis derived from his reading of the secondary literature. The central authors were Schmoller and Cunningham, but there were of course references also to all other leading commentators on the mercantile system such as Ashley and Hewins. Heckscher even referred to Marshal, but not as approvingly as he did later. In general, he was in many ways critical of the main authorities he built on. In particular, Schmoller was singled out for not drawing sufficiently on primary sources.

As regards detailed facts, Heckscher's general discussion of the mercantile system was in no way original, and even his overall conceptions hinged much on the literature he referred to. But on that level he often made startling remarks and arrived at questions that called for the explorations he was later to undertake. Of course some queries posed in the thesis had later to be discarded, but other observations proved to stand subsequent validation research well. But any applications of the economic theory he had learnt from Davidson are strikingly absent.

Actually, Heckscher's early vision of the mercantile system, albeit with major deficiencies, was stated in this first tract with a vigor and clarity that Heckscher was not always to repeat in the later treatise. When his main points were put forth within a more explicit conceptual scheme and in greater detail, their immediate intuitive appeal, that is part of the persuasive qualities of a good interpretation, were somewhat lost. The account in his later presentations often seems stale in comparison with his youthful impressionistic text in the thesis.

The second and major part of the thesis, dealing specifically with the Swedish Navigation Act of 1724, was in contrast to the introductory part, a report on archival research covering the background of the act and its antecedents. Here Heckscher's approach was not very different from what might have been expected from any political historian. Yet, his focus back in time on the antecedents of the act was notably deep even for a historian. Before providing a thorough account of the processing of the act in parliament and of the politics of its implementation, it offered a penetrating overview of earlier Swedish foreign trade and shipping policies since the seventeenth century. The methodologically interesting part of the inquiry, anticipating a central feature of his own later study on the economic history of Sweden, concerned his emergent attention already at this time to the views and understanding of the policy makers and the debaters. Heckscher, in commenting on the deficiency and lack of data at the time on the Swedish commercial fleet, showed how fatally inaccurate their perceptions of the real world could be. It is notable that he constructed a statistical table of information based on primary materials in an attempt to assess the impact of the act, but in this he only succeeded in capturing a short-term partial effect. But Heckscher's statistical efforts are of course very interesting as evidence of his ambitions, which meant illuminating the wider and long term implications of the act.

It would here take us too far to account in more detail for the content of the thesis as we are only looking for evidence that illuminate Heckscher's progress toward becoming an economic historian and his advance of a proper methodology for that field. On that score, the licentiate thesis showed how Heckscher, schooled as a historian and equipped with the historical method of source criticism, at an early phase of his work tried to explain the development of economic policy with surprising little use of economic theory. We may especially note that he had little to say on the effects of economic policy. He was more interested in its causes. But in his attention more to motives than to contexts, Heckscher in fact pointed to the factor that made the policy efforts ineffective. This opened for his later more systematic observations on the policy makers' perception of the world. Heckscher already in the thesis extended his coverage of this perception to include economic thinking.

It is clear that Heckscher, despite having made advances in resorting both to statistics and to some conceptualizing, was still far from being an economic historian. In his attention to economic policy and thinking, his approach was essentially that of a general political historian. Further, he did not cover the state of the economy in any modern sense, that is, of economic life as the object of economic policy. Although he had studied economic theory this did not show up neither explicitly nor in the structuring of his approach. Thus he had little to say on questions of method in exploring past economic life and its evolution. Heckscher's main deviation from Hjärne so far was his choice of topic. But from what we know, Hjärne had raised no objection to Heckscher's thesis topic and was pleased with the work.

A Manifesto for Economic History

The licentiate degree Heckscher earned in 1904 was an intermediate-level degree, which had taken seven years of university studies. Naturally the question whether he should go on for a doctorate or try some alternative career had now to be faced. Applying for a position with the Kommerskollegium (Board of Trade) had loomed as an option at the time of setting out on the thesis work, but now his ambitions were higher. While Heckscher had been far from pleased with his performance on the examinations for the *fil. lic.* degree, Hjärne had thought highly of his thesis of which also Heckscher felt proud. Thus, although Hjärne appears not to have much encouraged Heckscher to go on for an academic career, Heckscher was himself mentally set to follow up on the licentiate degree with a doctoral degree.

The main factor in the scales was apparently that the financing of further academic studies seemed somewhat uncertain. Heckscher's parents were probably enough well off to support him through for a further prerequisite period of dissertation research, but quite understandably Heckscher, now twenty-five, wanted to become economically independent. However, the uncertainty about the financing of further studies was soon resolved. Heckscher had, some time in the early spring of 1904, been approached by the board of the Swedish state railroads for a coming anniversary study about the economic significance of the development of Sweden's state railroad system. This was to become the subject for his later doctoral dissertation (Heckscher 1907). Soon after the railroad proposal in early 1904, Gustav Cassel, who had just been appointed to the chair in Economics at Stockholm University, inquired if Heckscher would be willing to do some teaching in that year's summer courses. This contact with Cassel then led to Heckscher being in the fall of 1904 appointed amanuensis without pay in the Institute of Social Science that Cassel had just initiated at Stockholm University. During the five year sojourn under Cassel (1904–1909) that followed, Heckscher was completing his dissertation, was appointed associate professor in 1907, and in 1909 was called to a chair in Economics and Statistics at the Stockholm School of Economics. This may seem to have been the beginning of a career quite far from the field of economic history that Heckscher conceived of in 1904. But with the manifesto of 1904, the making of the economic historian had become inevitable as was made evident by his later career.

The Presentation of the Field of Economic History

It was probably with the noted academic opening at Stockholm University secured, that Heckscher, in anticipation of the methodological issues in his coming dissertation work, in the fall of 1904 submitted the renowned paper to *Historisk Tidskrift* where, in the manner of a manifesto, he presented economic history as a distinct special field of academic study (Heckscher 1904b). Here, after surveying earlier work in the field, he outlined what he, in somewhat of a personal declaration of intent, considered to be its task, scope, and method.

Heckscher's paper is divided into two main parts. Drawing on his thorough acquaintance with the literature built up during the work on the licentiate thesis, Heckscher offered in part one a comprehensive account of how the field of economic history originated. Although he took pains to note that it had important antecedents also among pure historians dealing with the Middle Ages, his central contention was that it originated mainly in economics. He presented its rise as a criticism of classical economists for "their total blindness to the historical and evolutionary aspects of economic life." Heckscher described the phases of the development of this criticism in various countries and commented incisively on various schools of thought. In so doing he offered a very interesting account of the early socialist writings pertinent to the theme with attention not only to Marx but also and especially to Rodbertus.

However, his main attention was devoted to the historical school. He noted the leading German names of its older generation, where in addition to the previously mentioned Knies he also of course included Roscher and Hildebrand. Yet his focus in the review of the historical school concerned the younger fraction, which Heckscher saw as the real breakthrough for economic history. Here the Germans Schmoller and Wagner received due attention, but Heckscher's most interesting presentation concerned the English branch. Ashley, Toynbee, and Cunningham were presented with apparent enthusiasm as the central figures. With the mercantilist system on his mind, Heckscher could give a quite enlightened presentation. He of course gave key attention to Cunningham for clarifying broadly the nature of state power and the emphasis on defence in the evolution of mercantilist policies, while Schmoller was noted for his attention to the territorial dimension and the importance of transport and communication costs as a central conditioning factor in that process.

It is impossible here to offer a full and fair review of Heckscher's impressive survey. Although it was polemically peppered it was still authoritative. It was richly sprinkled with incisive comments on details but offered also many startling vistas. One may note as a gem in the account of the writings of the professional historians, Heckscher's comments on Macaulay. These reveal his appreciation of Macaulay's colorful descriptions of the state of the English economy at various moments in the past. They would please even schoolchildren for which such pages in a history book were usually pure horror, Heckscher noted. Another interesting part in Heckscher's broad overview was his commentary on the evolution of the writings in the *History of Economic Thought*.

The Task and Scope of Economic History

In the second part of the paper Heckscher set forth his much noted methodological statement of what economic history purported to be. In this were also included didactic declarations about what it did not purport to be. In drawing that latter line he made two important demarcations. In response to what he saw as a central message in the somewhat hegemonic Marxist dogma on the socialist side, he pointed out that economic history was not the same as the economic interpretation of all history that he conceived to be the Marxist point of view. He strongly distanced himself from such a one-sided perspective on the totality of history. Further, in an important addition in the final proofs before printing, he criticized the view on economic history stated by Wicksell in his recent inaugural lecture at Lund University (Wicksell 1903). Wicksell, in clarifying his disagreements with the historical school, had argued that economic history was an important empirical base for the development of economic theory insofar as the inductive generalizing from that type of field experiences rested on the interpretation of historical events as "laboratory" outcomes of "as if" staged experimental situation for deductive retrodictive testing of general causal hypotheses. Heckscher offered no compliments to Wicksell for that view on the making of theory. While thanking Wicksell for his supportive attention to economic history, Heckscher instead faulted him for not understanding its scientific task, which according to Heckscher was not at all to develop theory, but rather to explore the development of economic life (Heckscher 1904b; Henriksson 1991).

In his reply to Wicksell Heckscher had thus also stated in a more direct way what he considered economic history to be by pointing to its task. The task of studying and explaining economic development was to him entirely different from the task of economics which was to explore the laws regulating the workings of economic life. Heckscher's made some seemingly rather ambiguous comments on his adherence to the so-called historical school, but his position becomes crystal clear once we recognize that sharp division of labor he imposed on the two fields. In following up on his criticism on Wicksell that the task of economic history was not at all to offer an alternative way to reach a better economic theory, he pointed out that that, unlike the historical school at the time, economic history had no aspirations to replace theoretical economics with historical economics. In his general elaboration in the paper he clarified that the ambition of economic history was not to offer a substitute to economic theory. As an economist Heckscher was the opposite of a proponent of the historical school although he may have remained sceptical of the Wicksellian view. But as an economic historian he saw no inconsistency in accepting the central critical stance of the historical school against economic theory in so far as the task of economic history, as Heckscher pointed out to Wicksell, was to study and explain economic development. However, Heckscher's position did not rule out the application of economic theory in historical research, but this was confined to clarifying only the workings of past economic life and, to repeat, not to be resorted to in explaining economic evolution. Economics and economic history had entirely different objectives.

In stating the above views on the task of economic history, Heckscher made quite a breach with the position that was implicit in his licentiate thesis. The breach was quite thoroughgoing as it entailed a new view of the object or scope for the analysis. In writing the thesis Heckscher had methodologically still been a political historian dealing with a specific instance of economic policy and the related economic thinking. The basic change that had occurred, as recorded in his position of 1904 in comparison with the position in the licentiate thesis, was a shift in scholarly focus that meant the elevation of economic life more narrowly conceived, to center stage of the historical study. Instead of being merely a background in a political account of government economic measures, economic life should in an economic-historical account be its very core part. Of course, in general the scope of economic history would, in addition to its core object, still include both economic polices and economic thinking. But only the core, that is, economic life in a more narrow sense, should, in Heckscher's view, be the constitutive part of the general object of that discipline.

In his more detailed presentation of the conception of economic history to which he had now arrived, Heckscher elaborated on this broad scope of the discipline. He first reverted to the coverage of the notion of "economic life" for a further fine but crucial point. He advanced what in the following might be called a dualistic view on the economy as the object of inquiry. According to this dualistic view, economics and economic history both had the economy, defined as an economic system, as their object of study, thereby sealing a logical tie between these two disciplines. Heckscher strongly underlined this formal identity of the scope of economics and the scope of economic history. To cite from Heckscher 1904b: "As long as economic life is a closed system, i.e. as long as economics is an independent science—also economic history is a closed entity, but no further."[28]

However, by stating this identity of the formal object of inquiry in the two fields, Heckscher was able to make a very clear demarcation between them as regards their research and study assignments. Despite their common focus, the two fields had entirely different analytic and synthetic tasks. While economics had to clarify the workings of economic life; that is, its mechanism of short-term performance, economic history was, as stated in Heckscher's comment on Wicksell, concerned with the long term evolution of economic life.[29]

Having set forth the above noted segmented view of the scope of economic history as a field covering not only the history of economic life in the narrow sense referred to as the core, but also the historical realms of economic policy and economic thinking, Heckscher had, as a major issue for analysis, raised the question about the interrelationship between the components in the triad.

His views on the interdependencies between the core and the two other components of economic life may be summed up in a number of quotes. A first point concerned their relationship in general. Heckscher wrote: "These three parts of total economic life were of course in many ways interrelated, but each of them was at the same time influenced by its own specific factors and forces that were separate from the influences affecting the other parts" (p. 186).

He then attended separately to each of the components. The first point now concerned the above noted focus on the core object of economic history. He clarified what the coverage of the core entailed; that is, what the study of past economic life and its evolution implied. In his words it "concerned the different branches of productive life, such as the history of agriculture from the times of Germanic extensive husbandry to modern intensive forms of land cultivation, the history of industrial life from domestic production to handicraft and from cottage industry to manufacturing, the transition from natural economy to a money economy, the history of credit and capital etc" (p. 185).

To that he added the following important rider: "On the basis of such accounts the economic historian then has to construe a picture of the living conditions of the different classes of people" (p. 185).

Turning to economic policies and economic thinking, as subsidiary elements of economic life, Heckscher argued, what he had already noted in the licentiate thesis, that they evolved only tenuously related to the hard facts of economic life i e to the core. Economic policies had according to him for ages been determined "more by dynastic and military interests than by economic considerations" (p. 186), and as regards economic thinking his view was that it had been "similarly dominated by the old hegemonic moral and philosophical systems of a period" (p. 186).

These points on the relationship between the core of economic history and its overlay of economic policy and thinking, Heckscher no doubt had derived from his studies of medieval economic life. But while his formulations leave open the possibility, that economic policies and thinking during the following period of the mercantile system were more conditioned by economic needs and constraints than Heckscher believed, he appears generally to have held that this medieval character of economic policy and thought prevailed strongly even in that later period.

But as regards economic policies in the modern age, Heckscher seems to have argued that a central task for the economic historian was to find out how and to what extent economic conditions and considerations influenced economic policy decisions. This followed from the duty of an economic historian, who as the general rule "had to show how the representatives of society from the village commune to the state conceived of their task in relation to economic life; what they fought against, what they promoted and what they left untouched" (p. 185).

Heckscher also made the point that, as a general rule, the task of the economic historian with respect to economic thinking; that is, the history of economic ideology and of economic science, was to show "how the conception of economic life has evolved; what in different ages was conceived as its functions and forms" (p. 186).

While it is clear that Heckscher's segmented view of economic life was present already in his thesis, it was in the manifesto underscored as fundamental in marking out what was to be analysed as the core of the object. As the most central point relating to the mercantile system, Heckscher now held that there had been no close connection between the development of the state of the economy in the narrow core sense and economic policy and economic thinking. As regards the influence of economic policy and economic thinking on early "capitalism," a term for that narrow core conception of the economy that he had not yet discarded, Heckscher argued that the authorities lacked the administrative muscles to achieve anything whatsoever, that any measures were just "thrusts in the air." But he also noted the role of information failures making the policy efforts have unexpected outcomes and side effects that were generally negative. He also recognized that, as much as the information failure was due to deficient statistical and other factual information, it was also due to inadequate theoretical understanding of the economy.

As regards the reverse influence of the economic core on economic policy working, through the understanding that would be generated among the politicians through the confrontations with facts, Heckscher of course admitted the possibility that the advance of economic thinking might evolve out of repeated experiences. But here he held a very pessimistic view, as experiences may not have been fully perceived due to the unreliability of or the lack of statistical information, which of course also slowed the advance of theoretical understanding.

Interestingly enough, Heckscher did not much elaborate on the possibility of a divergence between developments in economic thinking and developments of economic policy. But such a divergence seems to be implied in the vision set forth already in the licentiate thesis about economic liberalism being the executioner of what mercantilism wanted to achieve. However, he did not offer a major historical interpretation on the premise of a segmentation between economic policies and economic thinking. Such a divergence could perhaps not arise until the emergence of economic science as distinct from the general popular understanding and lay discourse on economic policy issues. It would only emerge as a point in Heckscher's later writings dealing with the modern phase of economic history.

The Methods of Economic History

Recognizing Heckscher's segmentation of the object of economic history is fundamental for understanding his views on methods. As long as the object of study was past economic policies and economic thinking, Heckscher had little reason to reconsider the established approach of general history. Accordingly he said little on the problems of method they raised.[30] In contrast, he had much to say on the methods of studying the evolution of the core of economic life in the narrow sense. This requires a number of comments.

Heckscher of course recognized that the study of the evolution of economic life in the narrow core sense of the term required methods that are quite different from the methods used in the study of past economic policies and thinking. However, it is important to note, as a first framing point, that Heckscher in fact betrayed a disregard also for methodology. In this he showed the usual impatience and disdain of the creative mind for pedagogic didactics. Heckscher always underscored the need to see issues from a practical point of view, although he usually added that the most practical thing is a good theory. With

Heckscher's adverse view to formal methodological discourse went a similar lack of appreciation of the kind of assistance he might have obtained from the professional philosophers at the time. He actually betrayed a clear dislike of philosophy.

The negative attitude to methodology and philosophy was probably an inculcation from Hjärne.[31] Heckscher appears as yet not to have been especially well read in philosophy, and there is not much evidence from which to infer about where he stood as regards the different philosophies that might be invoked when stating a methodological position in economic history. Therefore it seems somewhat meaningless to query into which philosophical camp he belonged. Quite clearly he was not a utilitarian like Wicksell, nor can he be called a positivist. As an adherent to the Ranke-Hjärne view his philosophy of history, if any, was more in the neo-Kantian idealistic tradition.

Of particular interest as regards Heckscher's historical approach as an empirical method is his view on so-called historical statistics. Here Heckscher still advanced the position noted earlier, which was in the main the one common to all historians at the time. He devoted much space in the paper to a commentary on the use of statistics in economic history. Here he could draw on his own earlier experiences from statistical work in political science. These views seem to have been little changed by his experience of writing the licentiate thesis. It is of course not surprising that he made no substantial advance in statistics even in his thesis work, considering that economics was taught in the law faculty.

As an historian Heckscher had previously not expressed much thought on questions of principle regarding the handling of primary statistical material for historical reconstruction of economic life narrowly conceived, because he had little need for it. He had been trained to disregard this issue. As long as his main purpose was confined to reconstruct and explain the history of economic policy, as in the licentiate thesis, he had not seen any need for such research. When he wrote his 1904 paper he still had not done any such research. But, with the dissertation project soon engaging him, he had at least responded to the necessity to think about what it meant concretely.

Concluding Summary

The story told above about the making of the economic historian and the shaping of his methodology underscores that this was a process of gradual transformation from a starting position that might be called that of a pure political historian over an intermediate transient phase before finally arriving at the position of 1904. The account has sought to pinpoint the factors that made for the slowness of this process and the notable resilience of his first views. The inculcation into the mores of a general political historian meant a crucial conditioning of the subsequent shaping of his methodology as an economic historian.

The creed of the general and political historian in the Hjärne tradition meant one "must" and two "do nots." The "must" meant adopting the source-critical method of fact gathering as the main method in writing history. The first "do not" prevented the use of generic "historical statistics" and the second prevented the use of "abstract concepts."

The two "do nots" were hurdles for Heckscher to overcome before he arrived at his research program. Although Heckscher's position meant a breakaway from Hjärne's hold on him, insofar as he violated the two "do nots" he still accepted the Hjärne "must." In that way Heckscher as an economic historian never cut off from history completely. In reaching his research program for economic history, Heckscher still accepted the "must" in the historical research program, but refuted the two "do nots." Instead, he now pleaded for both a statistical and conceptual approach. However, the Heckscher program of 1904 had no use for nomothetical theory in pursuing the main task of explaining economic development. Only the exploration of the workings of the old economic system at a given point in time would call for nomothetical economic theory. Only in that latter case can the Heckscher program be seen as precursor to the cliometric program. That program does not include the source-critical "must" of the history program, and while not refuting the two "do nots," it is one level higher up by pleading for the use of fully specified models, which presumes a resort also to nomothetical theory and empirical procedures grounded in statistical theory.

Heckscher's research program for economic history comprising tenets about the task, scope, and method of the field may be summed up as follows. Heckscher strongly underscored that the scope of economic history has to be exactly the same as the scope of economics, "no more, no less." What fundamentally separates the two fields, he declared, are their tasks. While the prime task of economic history is to study and explain the evolution of economic life, the prime task of economics is to explore and explain its workings. The economic historian was by Heckscher here assigned the task of studying economic development apparently as a long term process, while the allotment to the economist was by Heckscher conceived as the study of the short-term behavior of the economic system, its "mechanism" as he called it.

Turning then to the point concerning the method of economic history, Heckscher made a declaration that in part followed rather neatly from his declarations about its scope and task. Insofar as economic history was only concerned with the task of studying and explaining economic development as a unique historical process there was no use of economic theory, or for that matter, of any other type of nomothetical social theory. The method called for was simply the method of historians as worked out especially by the Ranke school, namely the principles of source criticism in the assessment of factual events and their causal origins. According to the pure Ranke school, to which Heckscher's major mentor Hjärne belonged, there was no further need for either the conceptual or the statistical approach.

But on this point, Heckscher differed from Hjärne. Heckscher recognized the need for labels such as mercantilism and the Industrial Revolution in the same manner as the general historians had names for broad phenomena such as the Renaissance and the Reformation. But the strictures of the historical method accepted by Heckscher did not allow abstract labeling of phenomena on the historical time/space coordinates in the manner of the positivists, who urged the study of history for finding the laws of historical development and hoped that the study of the past would yield normative lessons.

However, the 1904 statement was formally too narrowly confined in the conception of the task. There was one notable lapse in the 1904 declaration seen as the formal tenets of a research program. In the manifesto Heckscher visualised that the tasks of economics and economic history were neatly complementary. But as soon as he set out on "doing" economic history, he recognized that his declaration had missed the area of overlap comprising the workings of the economic system in the past. This too, of course, was a study that in practice had to be assigned to the economic historian. Regardless of whether such a study was conducted as part of a project with the ulterior purpose of explaining economic development or not, the study of the workings of economic life in the past called for economic theory as much as the study of the workings of economic life in the present. It was for that endeavor that Heckscher later made his well-known plea for theory in economic history.

This did not mean, however, that he retracted from the core position of the manifesto. To repeat: Heckscher's famous plea for theory in economic history only concerned the explanation of a repetitive state in the past. The manifesto, as well as all later restatements of the method of economic history, gave economic theory little role as a tool in the explanation of economic development.

Acknowledgments

The essay builds on research in progress on an intellectual biography of Heckscher. That project was initiated in the 1970s with benign encouragement from his son, the late Gunnar Heckscher. For the present essay I am grateful to Ivar Heckscher and the other Heckscher grandchildren, Eva, Einar, and Sten Heckscher, for having entrusted me with some of the literary remains of Eli Heckscher. Earlier reports of this project are Henriksson (1979, 1987a, 1987b, 1989, 1990, 1991a, 1991b, 2001, 2002a, 2002b, 2003). See also Henriksson and Lundahl (2001, 2003). This essay draws largely on Heckscher's correspondence, which is available in the Heckscher collection at the Royal Library in Stockholm. The research has been financed by the Jacob Wallenberg Fund.

Notes

1. Very few of Heckscher's methodological writings are available in English, and these cover only his position for a brief ten-year period of the interwar decades (Heckscher 1929, 1930a, 1933, 1939). The first two of these are reprinted in Lane and Riesmera (1953).

2. That task should claim priority in the much neglected field "the history of economic history." Here an intellectual biography of Eli Heckscher is still missing, especially in view of the attention that in recent years has been devoted mainly to Heckscher's participation in the public economic policy discourse. For the important work in this latter area, see Carlson (1994). Some work on Heckscher as an economic historian was, however, done by Utterström (1982) and later also by Magnusson (1991).

3. In addition to his writings in English, mentioned in note 1, the list of Heckscher's most important writings in Swedish include Heckscher (1904b, 1908c, 1920, 1922a, 1930b, 1936b, 1941a, 1947, 1948) and Heckscher 1951a and 1951b. The last two items are not listed in the Heckscher bibliography (Ekonomisk-historiska institutet 1950) that was published two years before he died in 1952, A selection of Heckscher's methodological writings in Swedish together with a commentary has recently been reprinted in Henriksson and Lundahl (2003).

4. My view, as previously expressed in Henriksson (1979, 1990, 1991), that Heckscher's 1904 statement is to be considered a manifesto, has been criticized by C-A Ohlsson (1992). As the issues he raised require an extensive discussion beyond the purview of the

present essay, his points will not be specifically commented on in this presentation. However, the approach in the present essay may be seen as an indirect response to his position.

5. This seems to have been a response mainly to pressures from his somewhat dominant mother, Rosa Heckscher (1856–1944). Heckscher's father, Isidor Heckscher (1848–1923) was probably of a different view concerning his son's studies.

6. H. Hjärne (1848–1922) was professor in history at Uppsala University through 1885–1913. The summer course in Uppsala in 1895 dealt with constitutional issues in Sweden during the seventeenth century. Thus it is clear that Heckscher, even before he entered Uppsala University, was quite set on studying history. In high school, Heckscher, as his examination paper in Swedish, had written about Robespierre. Only a few formal spelling and grammatical errors seem to have prevented the grading teacher from giving him the highest mark. The teacher informed Heckscher that the paper was stylistically a very impressive achievement.

7. The basic explanation for that transfer was undoubtedly the appointment of Heckscher's father as Denmark's consul to Sweden with office in Gothenburg. It led to the family's moving there from Stockholm. Concern for Heckscher's study expenses may here have been the primary reason, but Gothenburg University, as a newly opened university in 1891, with examination rights from 1893, may also have offered some purely academic attractions to Heckscher.

8. Ludvig Stavenov (1864–1950) was professor in history at Gothenburg University (1895–1913) and at Uppsala University (1914–1929). Because Stavenow had earned his doctorate in history in Uppsala in 1890, he, too, was at least formally a disciple of Hjärne.

9. It provided the nucleus for Heckscher's build up of his wider social network that evolved from the "eating team," the so-called *matlag*, he was invited to join. The social organizing of student daily food consumption into rather fixed table groups at local restaurants had become an institution of student living in Uppsala. Becoming a member in such a group, and in the right kind of group, was in many ways a crucial part of an Uppsala study period for a student. In such a group Heckscher made the closer acquaintances that were to channel his studies.

10. Gunnar Hazelius (1874–1905) was called on the death of his father in 1901 from further academic work to take over the management of the Nordic Museum and Skansen in Stockholm, the great cultural and natural history bequest of his father. However, Hazelius appears to have remained a summoning name for Heckscher and the student circle in Uppsala even after his departure. After the premature death of Hazelius in 1905, this absentee role seems to have elevated Hazelius into somewhat of a symbolic cult figure or icon for an inner circle of his network, which in that phase emerged as a social compact of close friends somewhat later called the Junta. Heckscher was a key member of the Junta and instrumental in seeing the doctoral dissertation of Hazelius through to a posthumous publication (Hazelius 1906).

11. This translation was a main addition to a rather meagre economic literature available in Swedish. There was before Gide no modern Swedish text. Gide's text did not especially advance the outlook of the historical school, nor was it partisan with the Austrian view or any other specific school of neoclassicism. It is of some note that Heckscher's first textbook was not *Marshall's Principles*, which he later referred to as his early beacon of economic light (Heckscher 1935). This is not denying the importance of Marshall, but the impact of Marshall on Heckscher appears to have been of a somewhat later date. In addi-

tion to Gide one may also note the work by Nicholson (1893, 1897, 1901) as an early text of some importance for Heckscher.

12. Davidson (1854–1942) held the chair from 1880 to 1919. His dissertation dealt with the economic laws of capital formation (Davidson 1878). A second publication dealing with the history of rent theory was written after a sojourn in Heidelberg under Knies (Davidson 1880). For an understanding of Davidson's influence on Heckscher, one must also recognize the role of Wicksell as important for Davidson's thinking from the 1890s and on. For Heckscher's account of his dependence on Davidson, see Heckscher (1952).

13. Wicksell (1851–1926) was professor in Lund (1901–16). Wicksell had after his doctoral dissertation in 1895 been denied a docentship in the faculty of philosophy, but had been advised by Davidson that he would qualify for a docentship in the faculty of law if he first passed the basic law degree, the *jur. kand.* (Gårdlund 1958).

14. In retrospect, Heckscher's apprehensions must have seemed to him quite justified. After Heckscher had begun work under Davidson in 1901, Heckscher's father intervened on behalf of his son by pointing out to Davidson that the course composed for Heckscher was a bit too substantial. However, the only result was that Davidson refrained from adding any works to the list.

15. Heckscher made a similar decision later in life, when at age forty he finally assessed the possibility of carrying out his long planned "real task" of writing the *Economic History of Sweden*. After considering the difficulties, he first concluded that the project was impossible, but then valiantly went ahead with it. Although Heckscher always had everything carefully planned it might appear that he also knew how to make intellectual life a perpetual adventure. But what most spurred him from not spending his life in "vegetating" security was not as much a quest for challenge as the moral obligation under the pledge in his Latin ex libris: *Non propter vitam vivendi perdere causas* (modified from Juvenal's *Satires* (8.33)), which in free translation, admonishes a person against indulgent living that may cause him to lose touch with life's deeper meaning.

16. As a follow-up to his entry to Heimdal, Heckscher became in 1899 a founding member of Nordiska Föreningen (the Nordic Society) that signaled the return of Scandinavianism, the movement that had died in the 1860s when Denmark was let down in the conflict with Prussia on the Schleswig issue. The new Scandinavianism at the turn of the century was, however, a more cultural than political movement. What could be called common Nordic issues were always to remain matters of close concern for Heckscher. More than any other of the Swedish historians and economists, his network extended into the other Nordic countries, Denmark, Norway, and Finland.

17. His general position in Heimdal was that of a librarian combined with a position in charge of some university extension teaching and lecturing services for non-academicians and working people. Generally Heckscher, here appears to have been engaged in Hjärne's political program, "defense and reforms." Following Hjärne, Heckscher supported the suffrage movement as a rational conservative stance for gaining the support of labor on the issue of general conscription, which had been proposed as an enhanced measure of national defence. But it was probably also as a Heimdal representative that Heckscher on February 3, 1902, lectured in Gävle on labor protection laws. This appears to have been his first extramural public lecture on a central issue of the day.

18. Karl Hildebrand (1870–1952) was one of the earliest to influence Heckscher through his writings (Hildebrand 1897a). Among Hjärne's disciples, he was also among the earliest to review writings in the field of economic history (Hildebrand 1897b). He was also

a member of the aforementioned junta and remained long politically influential, especially as editor of the conservative daily, *Stockholms Dagblad*, which up to the 1920s was a major outlet for Heckscher's contributions to the daily press. He was finally appointed chief of Sweden's public debt office.

19. As evidence of Heckscher's early special position under Davidson, one may note that Davidson on that occasion dropped titles with Heckscher. This was a formal act signifying collegiality.

20. Stjernberg (1873–1943) was, in the build-up of Stockholm University, called to the first chair in its Faculty of Law when it was established in 1907. It is of some interest to note that Stjernberg in turn served as a discussant when Heckscher in 1907 presented his doctoral dissertation in history.

21. The position of Knies as a member of the historical school is intriguing. According to Heckscher (1952), Knies cannot really be called an historical economist. In "bony abstractions" he was little different from the classical or neoclassical theorists. This may go far in explaining also Davidson's somewhat unclear attitude to received theory. In pointing to Davidson's dependence on Knies and what he may have imparted to Heckscher there is reason to ponder as a memento the fact that Knies had also influenced both Schmoller and J. B. Clark.

22. In his final testimony about Davidson, Heckscher (1952) ranked him as the sharpest in his generation of Swedish economists. What Heckscher referred to in that assessment was the performance stemming from Davidson's mastery of classical economic theory and especially his ability to apply Ricardian thinking not only to problems in the present but to issues in economic history as well. Admittedly, Davidson did not do much historical writing, but he made major contributions to the history of Sweden's central bank, most notably his publication in the anniversary series (Davidson 1931).

23. Before he completed his magnum opus, *The Economic History of Sweden*, Heckscher wrote his interim synoptic overview *Svenskt arbete och liv* (Swedish Labor and Life) in 1941, which was later translated into English as *An Economic History of Sweden* (Heckscher 1941b and 1954). It was a work of patriotism at the time when Sweden was virtually besieged by the German avalanche in northern Europe. But Heckscher held his Swedish identity only in the second place. He declared himself to be first of all a citizen of the world and notably allotted his Jewish descent only the third place in such a ranking (Henriksson 1991). For an overview of Heckscher's position on Zionism and the related issues of what Jewish culture and genes meant to him, see Henriksson (1979).

24. Hjärne was of course opposed to the positivism that toward the end of the nineteenth century turned many historians into following Lamprecht's search for the sociological laws of history in an evolutionary (Darwinian?) direction. That approach had been discussed by Edén (1896, 1900). In these writings Edén may be seen to have expressed the majority view of the Hjärne disciples at the time when Heckscher joined the group. In 1903 Edén (1871–1945) was appointed the second professor in history in Uppsala and was thus, together with Stavenow, who succeeded Hjärne himself in 1911, the caretaker of the hold of the Hjärne school in Uppsala.

25. The second part of the thesis, omitting the background part dealing with international mercantilism, was published (with little revision) in the Hjärne festschrift in 1908 (Heckscher 1908a). The first part of the thesis dealing with the mercantile system was never published. However, a very good summary was made available as an encyclope-

dia article in 1913 (Heckscher 1913). That summary goes to show that Heckscher had as late as 1913 done little further work on the theme of the mercantile system.

26. Heckscher named his licentiate thesis "Urfaust," referring, no doubt, to the fact that Goethe's *Faust* was a life project in which the second part appeared many years after the first part.

27. One may note his painstaking attention to the bibliographical part, which was a very impressive list of readings and references to sources. He was himself aware of the some-what notable length of the list and made a remark about that in the preface.

28. The Swedish original text runs, "Så långt som det ekonomiska livet är något i sig självt slutet—alltså lika långt som nationalekonomin är en självständig vetenskap—är även den ekonomiska historian ett avslutat helt, men ej längre" (Heckscher 1904b, p. 186).

29. One may here note, as a somewhat startling and seemingly paradoxical consequence of Heckscher's demarcation line, that the workings of economic systems in the past must logically be seen as the domain of the applied economist rather than the economic histo-rian. In responding to possible objections he could of course retort that what this meant was simply that the practicing economic historian had also to acquire competence as an economist. However, Heckscher did not make that obvious point until the 1920s, when he advanced his much-noted "plea for theory" in economic history (Heckscher 1929).

At the time of writing, Heckscher seems to have been so focused on this dynamic task of economic history, and perhaps so blinded by his logic, that he did not realize how seri-ously he disregarded the intellectual property rights of economic historians. He forgot the rather trivial "must" for economic historians, that they must of course—and perhaps above all—be concerned also with the past economic life as an equilibrating entity in it-self; that is, as conceived by economists.

The explanation of Heckscher's lapse is of course partly that, so far, he had not done any empirical historical research beyond the explorations of the economic policies and thinking of the mercantile system. These explorations had not required that he delve into the actual state and development of economic life conceived in the more detailed narrow sense of the activities of consumption, production, and trading. Heckscher was not to be confronted with the need to repair for the lapse until after World War I, when he finally resolved to start work on this real task, the writing to the *Economic History of Sweden*.

30. One reason Heckscher has so little to say on the history of economic policy is that most of the economic history research he reviewed in the paper had dealt with the Mid-dle Ages. In that era economic policy was mainly undertaken by such powers in eco-nomic life as the church and the city-states, while territorial dynastic authorities were administratively weak as public policy organ insofar as they were feudally decentralized.

31. In the introduction to his paper Heckscher presents his own account as only an "un-philosophical little" preview of the field while awaiting an apparently more authoritative account to come from a senior colleague of his. Needless to say, Heckscher's account pre-empted the need for such a further contribution.

References

Ashley, W. J. 1889–93. *An Introduction to English Economic History and Theory*. London: Longmans & Co.

———. 1900. *Surveys Historic and Economic*. London: Longmans & Co.

Carlson, B. 1994. *The State as a Monster: Gustav Cassel and Eli Heckscher on the Role and Growth of the State*. Lanham, MD: University Press of America.

Carr, R. 1950. Review of Heckscher, E. F. (1949). *The Economic History Review*, n.s., 3:246–249.

Coats, A. W. 1957. "In Defence of Heckscher and the Idea of Mercantilism." *Scandinavian Economic History Review* 5:173–187.

Coleman, D. C. 1957. "Eli Heckscher and the Idea of Mercantilism." *Scandinavian Economic History Review* 5:1–25.

Cunningham, W. 1892. *Growth of English Industry and Commerce in Modern Times*. 2nd ed. Cambridge: Cambridge University Press.

———. 1896. *Growth of English Industry and Commerce During the Early and Middle Ages*. 3rd ed. Cambridge: Cambridge University Press.

———. 1898–1900. *Western Civilization in its Economic Aspects, Ancient Times; Medieval and Modern Times*. Cambridge: Cambridge University Press.

Davidson, D. 1878. *Bidrag till läran om de ekonomiska lagarna för kapitalbildningen*. Uppsala: Lundequistska bokhandeln.

———. 1880. *Bidrag till jordränteteorins historia*. Uppsala: Esaias Edquists.

———. 1931. *Sveriges Riksbank 1834–1860*. Stockholm: P. A. Norstedt.

Edén, N. 1896. "Ett nytt program för den historiska vetenskapen." *Historisk Tidskrift* 16:321–331.

———. 1900. "Frågan om en ny historisk metod." *Historisk Tidskrift* 20:205–248.

Ekonomisk-historiska institutet. 1950. *Eli F Heckschers bibliografi 1897–1949*. Stockholm: Albert Bonniers.

Elvander, N. 1961. *Harald Hjärne och konservatismen*. Stockholm: Almqvist & Wiksell.

Fogel, R. W. 1965. "The Reunification of Economic History with Economic Theory." *American Economic Review* 40:93–98.

Gårdlund, T. 1958. *The Life of Knut Wicksell*. Stockholm: Almqvist & Wiksell.

Gerschenkron, A. 1954. "Acknowledgments" and "Preface." In E. F. Heckscher *An Economic History of Sweden*, v–vii, xiii–xlii. Cambridge, MA: Harvard University Press.

Gide, C. 1899. *Nationalekonomins Grunddrag*. Helsingfors: G. V. Edlund.

Hazelius, G. 1906. *Om hantverksämbetena under medeltiden*. Stockholm: Nordiska Museet.

Heckscher, E. F. 1987. "Skiljedom och allmän fred." *Uppsala Nya Tidning* 8:12.

———. 1898a. "Fredsfrågan och historian." *Uppsala Nya Tidning* 16:5.

———. 1898b. "Försvaret och kriget." *Uppsala Nya Tidning* 18:5.

———. 1898c. "Vår äldsta kungaätt". *Föreningen Heimdals uppsatser* 4.

———. 1901a. "Studenternas folkbildningsmöte i Upsala." *Nordisk Universitetstidskrift*. pp. 157–161.

————. 1901b. "Studenternas nordiska folkbildningsmöte i Upsala. Några intryck och anmärkningar." *Nordisk Universitetstidskrift*. pp. 238–249.

————. 1902. "Tillfälliga utskott." *Statsvetenskaplig Tidskrift* 4:32–59.

————. 1903a. "Grunddragen av merkantilsystemet i 16 och 17 århundradena, särskilt med hänsyn till den yttre handelspolitiken." Unpublished MS.

————. 1904a. "Nationalekonomi." *Studiehandbok för examina vid Uppsala universitet*. Uppsala: Föreningen Verdandi.

————. 1904b. "Ekonomisk historia: några antydningar." *Historisk Tidskrift* 24:167–198.

————. 1905. "Statistik och ekonomisk historia." *Historisk Tidskrift* 25:104–110.

————. 1907. *Till belysning af järnvägarnas betydelse för Sveriges ekonomiska utveckling*. Stockholm: Centraltryckeriet.

————. 1908a. "Produktplakatet och dess förutsättningar. Bidrag till merkantilsystemets historia i Sverige." In *Historiska studier tillägnade professor Harald Hjärne på hans sextioårsdag den 2 maj 1908*. Uppsala and Stockholm: Almqvist and Wiksell.

————. 1908b. *Socialismens grundvalar*. Stockholm: Foreningen studenter och arbetare.

————. 1908c. "Prishistoriska metodfrågor." *Statsvetenskaplig Tidskrift* 10:161–171.

————. 1913. "Merkantilsystemet." *i Nordisk Familjebok* 18:174–177.

————. 1920. "Historia och nationalekonomi." *Historisk Tidskrift* 40:1–22.

————. 1921. *Gammal och Ny Ekonomisk Liberalism*. Stockholm: Norstedts.

————. 1922a. "Ekonomi och historia." In *Ekonomi och historia*. Stockholm: Albert Bonniers Förlag.

————. 1922b. *The Continental System: An Economic Interpretation*. Oxford: Clarendon Press.

————. 1929. "A Plea for Theory in Economic History." *Economic Journal* 39, *Historical Supplement* 4:523–554.

————. 1930a. "Monetary History from 1914–1925 in its Relations to Foreign Trade and Shipping." In K. Bergendal et al., eds., *Sweden, Norway, Denmark and Iceland in the World War, Part III*, 127–268. New Haven, CT: Carnegie Endowment for International Peace.

————. 1930b. "Den ekonomiska historiens aspekter." *Historisk Tidskrift* 50:1–85.

————. 1930c. "Natural and Money Economy as Illustrated from Swedish History in the Sixteenth Century." *Journal of Economic and Business History* 3:1–29.

————. 1933. "The Aspects of Economic History." In *Economic Essays in Honour of Gustav Cassel*, 705–720. London: George Allen & Unwin.

————. 1935a. *Mercantilism*, vols. 1–2. Trans. Mendel Shapiro. London: Allen & Unwin.

————. 1935b. *Sveriges ekonomiska historia från Gustav Vasa. Medeltidshushållningens organisering Första boken 1520–1600*. Stockholm: Albert Bonniers Förlag.

————. 1936a. *Sveriges ekonomiska historia från Gustav Vasa. Hushållningen under internationell påverkan Andra boken 1600–1720*. Stockholm: Albert Bonniers Förlag.

————. 1936b. "Den ekonomiska historiens aspekter." In *Ekonomisk-historiska studier.* Stockholm: Albert Bonniers Förlag.

————. 1937. "Materialistisk och annan historieuppfattning." *Svensk Tidskrift* 27:109–120.

————. 1939. "Quantitative Measurement in Economic History." *Quarterly Journal of Economics* 53:167–193.

————. 1940. "Harald Hjärne och den moderna historievetenskapen i Norden." *Historisk Tidskrift* 60:133–152.

————. 1941a. "Historieforskningens objektivitet." *Svensk Tidskrift* 118–131.

————. 1941b. *Svenskt arbete och liv: från medeltiden till nutiden.* Stockholm: Albert Bonniers Förlag. (This first Swedish edition was in 1957 followed by a second Swedish edition that took into account the revisions offered in the English edition of Heckscher 1954.)

————. 1947. "Ekonomisk historia och dess gränsvetenskaper." *Historisk Tidskrift* 67:1–17.

————. 1948. "Objektivititet och subjektivitet i historieforskningen." In *Historia och religion* G. Landberg and K. G. Hildebrand, eds., *Historia och religion.* Stockholm: Förlag.

————. 1949a. *Sveriges ekonomiska historia från Gustav Vasa. Det moderna Sveriges grundläggning Tredje boken 1720–1815, Vol. 1–2.* Stockholm: Albert Bonniers Förlag.

————. 1949b. "The Effect of Foreign Trade and the Distribution of Income." In H. S. Ellis and L. A. Metzler, eds., *Readings in the Theory of International Trade,* 272–300. Philadelphia: Blakiston Company.

————. 1951a. *Studium och undervisning i ekonomisk historia.* Lund: C.W.K. Gleerups Förlag.

————. 1951b. "Om historiska misstag och deras behandling." *Historisk Tidskrift* 71:1–13.

————. 1952. "David Davidson." *International Economic Papers* 2:111–135.

————. 1953. "A Survey of Economic Thought in Sweden 1875–1950." *Scandinavian Economic History Review* 1:105–125.

————. 1954. *An Economic History of Sweden.* Trans. Göran Ohlin. Cambridge, MA: Harvard University Press.

Henriksson, R. 1979. "Eli F. Heckscher och svensk nationalekonomi." *Ekonomisk Debatt* 7:510–520.

————. 1987a. Montgomery, Gustaf Arthur." *Svenskt Biografiskt Lexikon.* Stockholm: Norstedts.

————. 1987b. "Konjunkturbevakning före Konjunkturinstitutet." Mimeo. Konjunkturinstitutet.

————. 1989. "The Institutional Base of the Stockholm School: The Political Economy Club 1917–1951." *History of Economics Society Bulletin* 11:59–97.

————. 1990. "Eli Heckscher." In C. Jonung and A.-C. Ståhlberg, eds., *Ekonomporträtt: Svenska ekonomer under 300 år,* 165–186. Stockholm: SNS.

————. 1991a. "Eli F Heckscher: The Economic Historian as Economist." In B. Sandelin, ed., *The History of Swedish Economic Thought,* 141–167. London: Routledge.

————. 1991b. "The Facts on Wicksell on the Facts: Wicksell and Economic History." In J. Mokyr, ed., *The Vital One: Essays in Honor of Jonathan R.T. Hughes*, 33–50. Greenwich, CT: JAI Press.

————. 2001. "Nationalekonomiska Föreningen." *Royal Economic Society Newslettter* 113:11–15.

————. 2002a. "Nationalekonomiska Föreningen 1877–2002." *Ekonomisk Debatt* 30:569–599.

————. 2002b. "Eureka Unter den Linden: A Reinterpretation of Ohlin's Early Contributions to the Heckscher-Ohlin Theme." In R. Findlay, L. Jonung, and M. Lundahl, eds., *Bertil Ohlin: A Centennial Celebration, 1899–1999*, 125–137. Cambridge, MA: MIT Press.

————. 2003. "Eli F Heckscher." *Oxford University Press Encyclopedia of Economic History*. New York: Oxford University Press.

Henriksson, R. G. H., and M. Lundahl. 2001. "Eli Heckscher, Economic History and Economic Theory." Paper presented to the conference Trade, Development and History. Columbia University, New York, April 20–21.

————, eds. 2003. *Janusansiktet Eli Heckscher: Nationalekonom och ekonomisk historiker*. Kristianstad: Timbro.

Hettne, B. 1980. "Ekonomisk historia i Sverige under femtio år." *Historisk Tidskrift* 100:140–175.

Hildebrand, K. 1897a. "Skiljedom och allmän fred." *Meddelanden från Uppsala Försvarsförbund* 11.

————. 1897b. "Nationalekonomisk historieskrivning." *Historisk Tidskrift* 17:171–208.

Hildebrand, K.-G. 1954. "Planhushållning." *Svenska Dagbladet*, February 15, 1954.

————. 1980. "Emil Hildebrand och Historisk Tidskrift." *Historisk Tidskrift* 100:62–91.

Lane, F. C., and J. C. Riemersma, eds. 1953. *Enterprise and Secular Change: Readings in Economic History*. Homewood, IL: Irwin.

Lundberg, E. 1952. Obituary of E. H. Heckscher. *Dagens Nyheter*, December 30, 1952.

Magnusson, L. 1994. "Eli Heckscher and Mercantilism: An Introduction." *Uppsala Papers in Economic History Research Report* 35.

Marshall, A. 1890. *Principles of Economics*. London: Macmillan.

Montgomery, A. 1956. "Eli F. Heckscher." In J. F. Lambie, ed., *Architects and Craftsmen in History: Festschrift für Abbot Payson Usher*, 119–156. Tübingen: Mohr (Siebeck).

Nicholson, J. S. 1893–1901. *Principles of Political Economy*. 3 vols. London: Adam and Charles Black.

Odén, B. 1975. *Lauritz Weibull och forskarsamhället*. Lund: Gleerup.

Olsson, C.-A. 1992. "Eli Heckscher and the Problem of Synthesis: A Methodological Note." *Scandinavian Economic History Review* 40, no. 3: 29–52.

Schmoller, G. 1919. *Grundriss der allgemeinen Volkswirtshaftslehre*. 2 vols. Munich: Duncker & Humblot.

Söderlund, E. 1946. "Heckscher Eli Filip." *Svenska Män och Kvinnor* 3:336–338.

————. 1953. "Eli F. Heckscher." *Scandinavian Economic History Review* 1:137–140.

Stjernberg, N. 1902. *Till frågan om de s k rent ekonomiska kategorierna.* Uppsala: Akademiska Boktryckeriet.

Uhr, C. 1979. "Eli F. Heckscher 1879–1952 and His Treatise on Mercantilism Revisited." *Economy and History* 23:3–39.

Utterström, G. 1982. "Eli Heckscher, Bertil Boethius och Sveriges Ekonomiska Historia från Gustav Vasa." Meddelanden från institutionen för ekonomisk historia 2, Umeå Universitet.

Wicksell, K. 1899. Review of Gide 1899. *Ekonomisk Tidskrift* 1:534–537.

————. 1901. *Föreläsningar i nationalekonomi Häfte 1.* Lund: Gleerup.

————. 1903. "Mål och medel i nationalekonomin." *Ekonomisk Tidskrift* 4:457–474.

————. 1907. Review of Heckscher, E. F. (1907). *Statsvetenskaplig Tidskrift* 10:337–341.

Part II

Heckscher-Ohlin Trade Theory

4

Eli Heckscher and the Holy Trinity

Ronald W. Jones

Eli Heckscher died in 1952, just one year earlier than Wassily Leontief's famous article appeared proclaiming what has become known as the Leontief paradox concerning the trade pattern in the United States. Received doctrine from the Swedish pair of Eli Heckscher and Bertil Ohlin had prepared us to expect that American exports would be capital-intensive in their production techniques compared with its import-competing sector. Not so, argued Leontief, and this bombshell spurred a raft of theoretical dissertations among young students on both sides of the Atlantic as well as a plethora of empirical work that continues to this day. Fortunately for English speakers, a few years before Heckscher's death, Svend Laursen and his wife prepared a translation from the Swedish of Heckscher's 1919 article for the 1949 *Readings in the Theory of International Trade* (edited by Howard Ellis and Lloyd Metzler). This article received a revised translation in a gem of a book, *Heckscher-Ohlin Trade Theory* (1991), prepared and edited by Harry Flam and M. June Flanders. Although the primary objective of this latter work was to provide a translation, for the first time, of Bertil Ohlin's 1924 dissertation, *The Theory of Trade*, it also served to confirm the importance of Heckscher's pioneering article, written five years previously. It is perhaps ironic that, almost the entire academic career of Eli Heckscher was concerned with issues of economic history, whereas this single article on international trade theory was sufficient to award him the lead position in a "hyphen trophy" of the label, "Heckscher-Ohlin Trade Theory."

In the prefatory remarks to the 1949 translation of his article, Heckscher, in referring to the work of his former student, Ohlin, remarks: "My previous treatment...does not, in the eyes of its author, contain much of value over and above Ohlin's books" (Flam and Flanders 1991:43). An innocent reader of such a remark might conclude that Ohlin's work appeared first, and that Heckscher was admitting that he did not have much more of substance to add. Such modesty is seen clearly to have been misplaced on rereading the Heckscher article, as well as the foreword (by Paul Samuelson) and the introduction (by Flam and Flanders) in the 1991 book. Some years ago Wilfred Ethier (1974) arranged the main substantive contributions of Heckscher-Ohlin theory into four subcategories. Two of these, the Heckscher-Ohlin theorem about the nature of trade, arguing that with technologies assumed the same everywhere trade patterns reflected differences in relative factor endowments, and the factor-price equalization theorem, positing that free trade in commodities could bring about an absolute equalization of wage rates and other factor returns even without any international mobility of the factors of production, were spelled out rather clearly in Heckscher's original treatment. Furthermore, his discussion of the effect of tariff protection on the distribution of income foreshadows the later classical account provided by Stolper and Samuelson (1941), while his remarks on the international mobility of factors stimulated by a protective tariff can be said to anticipate some of Mundell (1957).

Whereas Ohlin would later prove reluctant to accept that trade could bring about full factor-price equalization, Heckscher was perhaps too eager to push this possibility since in talking about quality variations in factors he states that "the number of factors of production is thus practically unlimited" (Flam and Flanders 1991:48). The problem with this is the "numbers game"; if the number of factors exceeds the number of produced commodities, commodity prices by themselves do not determine factor returns. Factor endowments have a role to play so that trade in commodities cannot be expected to equalize the returns to factors among the trading nations. (More on this below.)

Putting quality differences aside, both Heckscher and Ohlin make frequent reference to what I refer to as a classical *holy trinity* of factors, namely *land*, *capital*, and *labor*. As Samuelson remarks about Ohlin in his foreword to the Flam and Flanders volume: "Already in 1924 Ohlin has melded Heckscher and Walras. But neither then, nor in 1933 and 1967, did Ohlin descend from full generality to strong and manageable cases—such as two factors of production and two-or-more goods. What a pity. Not only did Ohlin leave to my generation these easy pickings, but in addition he would for the first time have really understood his own system had he played with graphable versions" (Flam and Flanders 1991:ix).

The same is not quite true of Heckscher, in that he briefly discusses a 2 × 2 example in which wheat and textiles are produced by labor and land. But his example is rather constrained. He assumes that with trade the price of textiles is cut in half relative to the price of wheat, and that this causes the wage rate also to be cut in half. No basis for this relationship is given. It implies that textiles only use labor (and wheat only land) and in this sense is a quite special 2 × 2 example.[1]

In the rest of these remarks I concentrate on what can be said about Heckscher-Ohlin trade theory if the classical trinity of land, capital, and labor is maintained. In short, if Heckscher had taken the route of laying out the propositions that would be valid in this three-factor case, what remarks would be justified? And how did he connect the three-factor case to the factor-price equalization possibility?

The Holy Trinity with One Commodity in Each Country

Most simple models of trade in the Heckscher-Ohlin tradition assume that each country can produce a (same) pair of commodities. But this is not necessary. In a two-commodity world, trade could take place with each country specialized to a different commodity. In such a case, whether there are two factors of production or three makes little difference to the conclusion that free trade will generally *not* result in factor price equalization. And an explanation of the trade pattern is trivial— each country exporting the sole commodity produced there, regardless of any comparison of autarky factor prices. So what extra is added by having a third factor?

The existence of a third factor of production introduces the possibility that two of these factors have a complementarity relationship with each other, whereby an increase in one factor's return would, at given output, cause the other factor to be used less intensively. (Of course, the third factor must be used more intensively in order to maintain output since less must be utilized of the factor that has gone up in price.) Even without complementarity, a factor may have a different degree of substitutability with each of the other two. As will be seen, this can matter for the issue of the effect of trade on the distribution of income, an issue of primary concern to Heckscher.

The Specific Factors Model

The specific-factors model, with an early treatment by Gottfried Haberler (1936) and formally developed by Jones (1971) and Samuelson

(1971), is perhaps the most simple way of sticking with the trinity of land, labor, and capital, but avoiding the complications that enter when any productive activity uses all three factors. That is, simplicity of the type familiar from 2 × 2 Heckscher-Ohlin models is maintained by positing that each sector uses a productive factor not used in the other while both make use of a factor that is freely mobile between sectors. Many of the subsequent uses of the model consider the pair of specific factors to be of the same general type (e.g., capital), so that over time one kind of specific factor can be transformed into the other. This interpretation suggests the specific-factors model is a short-run version of the 2 × 2 Heckscher-Ohlin model (e.g., as proposed by Neary 1978). Alternatively, this model might consider the three factors as distinct, as in the holy trinity. Thus suppose labor is completely mobile between sectors, capital is used only to produce manufactures, and land is used only in the production of agricultural goods.

With this interpretation the model can yield strong results on the two issues of primary concern to Heckscher, namely, the effect of countries having different factor endowments on the pattern of trade and the consequences of such trade on the distribution of income. Certainly a country that is relatively land-abundant is apt to be an exporter of agricultural products, and one that is relatively capital-abundant will tend to export manufactures.

As an aside, it is useful to recall that in the development of trade theory, two distinct meanings of relative factor endowments have been highlighted. On one hand is the comparison of relative physical volumes in endowments. On the other is a comparison of how relative factor returns would compare before international trade takes place. Heckscher's interpretation of relative factor endowments clearly belongs to this latter category, and developments in Heckscher-Ohlin theory have pointed out not only that the two interpretations are different, but also that the price definition of relative factor intensity is the stronger of the two: asymmetric demand conditions in two countries could account for a physically relatively capital abundant country finding capital relatively dear in autarky if tastes there are biased heavily toward the capital-intensive good. In such a case, the pattern of trade predicted by the Heckscher-Ohlin theorem would be violated if a comparison of physical proportions was the criterion of relative factor abundance, but nonetheless would be upheld with the price version that was used by Heckscher (Jones 1956).

Although dissimilarities either in land rents or returns to capital in autarky would have strong effects on relative commodity prices (and hence trade patterns), what is the significance of one country having relatively cheap labor before trade? As the theory points out, such a difference in the (price version of) endowment patterns has less of an effect on commodity prices because labor is used in both industries. However, by itself a lower wage rate in one country would tend to make relatively inexpensive the commodity in which labor's distributive factor share is higher. Factor endowments all count in influencing the trade pattern, just as they do in the simple 2×2 Heckscher-Ohlin model.

As suggested earlier, factor-price equalization with trade is not to be expected in this setting since the number of factors (3) exceeds the number of produced commodities (2). What can be said that is similar to results of the Stolper-Samuelson type for the 2×2 model is that returns to the specific factors are *magnified* reflections of any change in relative commodity prices. An increase in the relative price of manufactures, say, unambiguously improves the real return to capital and reduces that to land. The fate of laborers is subject to what has been called "the neoclassical ambiguity," the nominal wage rising in terms of agriculture and falling in terms of manufactures. The magnification effects for the specific factors are reflections of the asymmetry in production technology whereby in each sector it takes both factors to produce, separately, each commodity (the assumption of no joint production).

The General 3 × 2 Model

Letting all three factors in the holy trinity be involved in both commodities produced is a natural extension of the specific-factors model, and was examined in detail by Raveendra Batra and Francisco Casas (1976), Katsuhiko Suzuki (1983), and Ronald Jones and Stephen Easton (1983). Just as in the earlier case of a single commodity produced, different degrees of substitutability among factors and the possibility of complementarity can no longer be avoided. Changes in the terms of trade affect the returns to each of the three factors, but the possibilities are wider than in the specific-factors model. The difference in the ranking of factor intensities by industry is, of course, less extreme than in the specific factors model. Suppose, nonetheless, that in such a ranking land is the most intensively used input in agriculture, capital in manufacturing, and once again labor is the "middle" factor. The effect of commodity price changes on income distribution could be similar to that in the easier-to-analyze specific-factors case. But it need not be, since asymmetry in substitutability among factors counts. As an extreme example, suppose that land and capital are better substitutes for each other than is either with labor. This means that it would be fairly difficult for a commodity price change to alter the ratio of land's return to that of capital by very much. But if the relative price of manufactures, say, goes up, in a competitive market place in which commodity prices are matched by unit costs, the relative cost of manufactures must rise. If labor's distributive share in manufactures is larger than it is in agriculture, one way of having relative costs in manufactures go up to match the price increase is to have a large relative increase in the nominal wage rate, with land's return rising very little, or perhaps falling, so as not to vary much from the return to capital.

Heckscher's Example of Factor-Price Equalization

If two economies share the same technological knowledge, with each input possessing the same skills from country to country, but with different relative endowments, trade in two commodities would generally *not* serve to equalize factor returns because the number of commodities is smaller than the number of factors. Heckscher (Flam and Flanders 1991:54–55) discusses an example in which he seems to disagree. His discussion of this example is, in my view, rather opaque, but he seems to be saying that with common fixed coefficients in the two countries, with two commodities (meat is commodity 1, machinery is commodity 2), and with one unit of each factor required per unit of commodity 1 as the fixed input-output coefficients and, for the second commodity, one unit of land, 3 units of capital and 4 units of labor required as inputs per unit output,[2] he concludes: "Exchange will thus continue until equalization is complete."

There are two pitfalls I see in this example. First, with rigid input/output coefficients and only two commodities produced, there is only a restricted set of possible factor supplies that could result in full employment and thus positive factor returns. The restrictions that are required can be revealed, first, by considering the full-employment conditions for capital and labor:

$$X_1 + 3X_2 = K$$

$$X_1 + 4X_2 = L$$

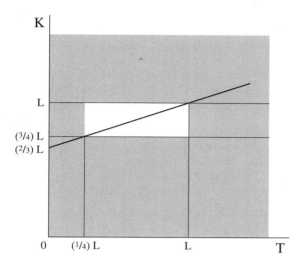

$$T = 3K - 2L \; ; \; 1/4\, L < T < L \; ; \; 3/4\, L < K < L$$

Figure 4.1
Allowable endowments

where the X_i denote the two outputs and fixed factor endowments of capital and labor are denoted by K and L. The solutions obtained are that X_1 equals $(4K - 3L)$ and that X_2 equals $(L - K)$. In order that these market-clearing relationships can be obtained with positive outputs of the two commodities, K must exceed $\frac{3}{4}L$ but fall short of L. In addition, the market for land (T) clears if $X_1 + X_2 = T$, requiring that

$$K = (1/3)T + (2/3)L,$$

and this, with the previous restriction, implies that T lies between $\frac{1}{4}L$ and L. Figure 4.1 illustrates for given arbitrary labor endowment the only possible (linear) combinations of capital and land that allow full employment and positive outputs for the prescribed rigid technological coefficients. Note that it is not a unique endowment bundle; the two economies under consideration could have different endowments but identical techniques, full employment, and positive levels of output.

The second problem emerges from a consideration of the competitive profit conditions of equilibrium in which costs are equal to commodity prices. Suppose the return to land, r_T, is arbitrarily chosen. Then for positive equilibrium production of the two commodities:

$$r_K + w = (p_1 - r_T)$$

$$3r_K + 4w = (p_2 - r_T)$$

where the return to capital and the wage rate are denoted by r_K and w, respectively. As for the commodity prices, p_i, not only must they both exceed r_T (to allow non-negative returns to the other two factors), but as well,

$$4(p_1 - r_T) > (p_2 - r_T) > 3(p_1 - r_T) > 0.$$

The dependence of the return to capital and the wage rate on given commodity prices and the return to land satisfying the above set of inequalities is shown by the solutions:

$$r_K = 4(p_1 - r_T) - (p_2 - r_T); \quad w = (p_2 - r_T) - 3(p_1 - r_T).$$

Figure 4.2 illustrates, by the intersection point of the two lines, D, a possible joint solution for the return to capital and the wage rate given commodity prices and the return to land with both commodities produced. The heavy broken line is the *factor-price frontier* for wages and the return to capital.

If the required inequalities are satisfied, can two economies that share this inflexible technology and face the same set of commodity prices have different factor endowments but end up with exactly the

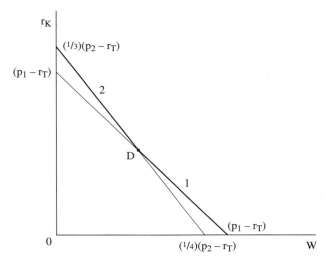

Figure 4.2
Factor-price frontier

same factor returns without any international factor mobility being allowed? Yes. But *must* trade serve to equalize factor prices? No. For example, in one country there might be a slightly lower return to land than in the other country, shifting upwards the pair of linear loci in figure 4.2. Factor returns would thus be different in the two countries, with factor markets clearing in both and price equal to cost in both industries in each country.

Heckscher compounds his difficulties by suggesting that in each country outputs adjust in the movement from autarky to free trade. This is not possible for a given set of factor endowments and rigid coefficients of production. Allowing smooth factor substitutability in both commodities would help in that factor prices could then change, and with them outputs of both commodities as techniques of production adjust. But the problem remains that the three-factor, two-commodity setting is not conducive to Heckscher's conclusion that factor price equalization will be complete. In fairness to Heckscher, however, he does leave himself some wiggle room. He later mentions a third commodity (with unit input-output requirements for land, capital and labor of 1, $\frac{1}{2}$, and 15, respectively) (see Flam and Flanders 1991:55–56), and earlier in his two-commodity illustration he does *not* state explicitly that these are the *only* two commodities produced. It was left to Samuelson and followers to point out more explicitly the balance between the number of factors and commodities required to get factor price equalization. As well, he does link factor-price equalization to the situation in which "techniques of production are the same in all countries" (54). If techniques were flexible, it would be the case that factor prices are uniquely linked to the techniques chosen, so that factor returns would be lined up between countries if, with trade, these techniques were the same. However, in his example the techniques were inflexible and *assumed* to be the same between countries, and this inflexibility disrupts the link between techniques and factor prices.

Another problem with the numbers chosen by Heckscher in his illustration is revealed by a closer analysis of figure 4.2. In his discussion of how the United States and Europe differ in factor returns (58–59), he stresses that land rents are low in the United States and thus wages are high—fostering immigration from Europe if international trade in commodities does not suffice to equalize factor prices. Would a country with the technology assumed by Heckscher experience an increase in labor's wage rate if the return on land were to be reduced? Both loci in figure 4.2 would be shifted upward, but in such a way that the

return to capital rises and *the wage rate falls.* To use more modern terminology, the reduction in land rents lowers the relative effective price in
the second sector—that is, $(p_2 - r_T)/(p_1 - r_T)$—and the second sector
is relatively labor intensive.

The 3 × 3 Case

The objections raised above to the argument presented by Heckscher to
establish the proposition that international trade suffices to bring
equality of factor prices among countries even without any international factor mobility (as long as they share a common technology)
cease to have relevance if the number of productive inputs is matched
by the number of produced commodities, as in the 3 × 3 case. Even
if production coefficients are rigid, alterations in the composition of
commodity outputs *often* suffice to clear factor markets when factor
endowments are altered, even without any change in factor prices. The
qualification refers to the necessity (in order to clear markets) that the
vectors of techniques for the three commodities contain the factor endowment vector. (In the 2 × 2 case, this is stated as requiring the
endowment vector to lie within the *cone of diversification*).[3] If so, two
countries with different endowments would find their factor returns
brought to equality with free trade. And Heckscher's argument would
be even stronger if the common technologies were flexible in allowing
techniques actually adopted to be sensitive to factor prices.

Even if technologies are flexible, there is no guarantee that in this
3 × 3 case a country will actually produce all three commodities in a
free-trade equilibrium, although it could do so in the absence of international trade. Perhaps the most basic feature of trade is that it allows
a country to consume many more commodities than it produces. In the
present scenario a country might produce all three commodities, or
perhaps just two, or, indeed, may be specialized completely to the
commodity in which it has the greatest comparative advantage. Two
countries that share the same technology but have different factor
endowments may thus very well produce different commodities, or
perhaps have an overlap of a commodity produced in common with a
commodity that is not. Heckscher was well aware of this possibility,
and he stressed that in such a case factor returns would *not* be equalized by trade, any commodity produced in common would not have
the same technique utilized in each country, and that international migration would result if allowed. He discussed this possibility in the
context of trade between the United States and Europe.

There is a reservation about trade and factor-price equalization that was not brought out explicitly by Heckscher, but was the focus of much of the literature some decades later. That reservation has to do with the possibility of *factor-intensity reversals*. This phenomenon is typically discussed in the 2 × 2 setting. Although a country's factor prices are usually assumed uniquely to determine productive techniques (i.e., no "flats" on the isoquants) and thus the cost of production (equal to price in a competitive equilibrium in which the commodity is produced), uniqueness may not work in the other direction. That is, commodity prices may not uniquely determine factor prices. (An early discussion of this is found in Samuelson's factor-price equalization articles [1948, 1949]). A pair of countries might each produce the full complement of commodities (that is, the same number as the number of factors), but their endowment vectors could lie in different cones of diversification. Although much of the mathematical literature concerned with the conditions for the univalence of the commodity price-factor price relationship pays no attention to factor endowments, trade theorists from Samuelson's 1948 article have always stressed that a necessary condition for factor-price equalization is that countries' endowments be fairly similar.

The questions most intensely debated in the literature concerning the 3 × 3 scenario have to do with the pair of "Heckscher-Ohlin propositions" not stressed by Heckscher, nor by Ohlin, namely, the Stolper-Samuelson theorem (1941) and the Rybczynski theorem (1955). Are there strong general results that can be stated for the effect of a commodity price change on the distribution of factor income or for the effect of endowment changes on the composition of output for a country facing given commodity prices? In a sense the answer is in the negative, in that more structural detail is required, having to do with factor intensity comparisons. For example, John Chipman (1969) showed that an increase in any commodity price would unambiguously raise the real return to the factor most intensively used in that sector if that factor's distributive share in that sector exceeded its share in the other two industries.[4] Heckscher did not explicitly concern himself with either of these propositions. The Stolper-Samuelson kind of result rests heavily upon the assumption that productive activities are not joint. That is, in each a combination of inputs yields a unique individual output. The factor-price equalization result, I would argue, does not (Jones 1992b).[5] Of course the Heckscher-Ohlin theorem, discussing the relationship between factor endowments and trade patterns, is related to the Rybczynski type of theorem. In the 3 × 3 case, Ed Leamer (1987 and 1994) has extensively explored possible relationships among physical factor endowments and trade patterns as well as trade and factor returns.[6] In this context it is useful to recall that Heckscher adhered to the price version of relative factor endowments.

The Holy Trinity and Many Commodities

I have often maintained that Heckscher-Ohlin theory can best be seen (and is more easily understood) in the context in which many commodities can technically be produced. The reason for this is that with trade a country can be highly specialized, even to the extent of producing only a single commodity. Thus the interesting question can be raised: With trade, *what* commodities does a country produce? This is Ricardian in its tone. If world prices are not necessarily reflected in a country's own technology, the country need not produce more commodities than it has productive factors, and may produce an even smaller number. Thus, if there are more commodities than three, there is much room for production patterns to differ among countries and for their factor returns to be different even with commodity trade. The stage is set for a discussion of international mobility of productive factors, and Heckscher was very much involved with discussions of Swedish emigration. This is a setting in which Heckscher's unique and great role in trade theory can well blend in with his voluminous published work on economic history.

Concluding Remarks

There is no doubt that Heckscher's 1919 article is a classic. Since its translation into English (thirty years after its publication) it became clear that Eli Heckscher's contribution to the modern theory of international trade (as it was then called) had to be put on a par with that of his brilliant student, Bertil Ohlin. Ohlin added more technical material, borrowing from Cassel (and, indirectly, from Walras), and, especially in his 1933 Harvard University Press volume, delved deeply into historical episodes as well as into the importance of economies of scale. (This was later picked up in so-called new trade theory. See, for example, Paul Krugman's remarks [1999]). In his earlier and shorter presentation, Heckscher also brought up the possibility that scale in production was important, and could lead to lower costs and better technology.

In retrospect, perhaps the major difference in the contributions of these two Swedish economists concerned the effect of international trade on a nation's distribution of income. Although I have argued above that Heckscher's illustration of why factor prices might be fully equalized with trade is subject to reservations, he was absolutely clear that such a result was possible. In particular, he was explicit on the fact that having factor prices brought to equality with trade would not signal the end of trade. Instead, trade would merely have reached its equilibrium level and would not expand further (unless conditions changed). In this he was bolder than Ohlin, who, perhaps with a keen eye on actual trading conditions, was reluctant to accept that international trade by itself could bring about full equalization of factor returns. Heckscher remarked on the possible mobility of factors between countries in case countries were sufficiently dissimilar that trade would not equate factor returns. As well, he considered the case in which changes in factor returns would alter their domestic supply. In this he was correct in asserting that variable factor supplies would result in greater differences in factor endowments between countries as a consequence of trade (which would serve to lessen the possibility of factor price equalization).

I was first introduced to the English translation of Heckscher's article when Heckscher was still alive. It was tough reading then, and it remains so for me to this day. As Samuelson has remarked, both Heckscher and Ohlin missed the opportunity to spell out their model in simple terms, such as in the two-commodity, two-factor case that proved of such worth in countless succeeding articles and books. (But I am thankful for the great employment opportunities this provided to subsequent generations.) I think this reflects the nature of the times. After all, which of the holy trinity of labor, capital, and land could be denied, especially in a time and place in which each of these factors was deemed to be so important in production, especially by an economic historian? With the holy trinity maintained, Heckscher still did a remarkable job in laying out the foundations of what has since become known as Heckscher-Ohlin theory.

Notes

1. The assumption that wheat uses only land and no labor is necessary for Heckscher's remark that the wage rate is cut in half *relative to the rental on land*. If wheat uses labor as well as land in this 2×2 example, and the price of wheat is constant, the rental on land

would be driven up, and thus the wage rate would be cut by more than half relative to land's rental.

2. Curiously enough, the input coefficients of capital and labor in machinery (industry 2) cited by Flam and Flanders are 4 and 5 (instead of 3 and 4). The latter pair of numbers corresponds to the 1949 translation and, according to Mats Lundahl, to the original Swedish 1919 article as well.

3. See Chipman (1966).

4. In the same issue of the journal in which Chipman's contribution appeared, Murray Kemp and Leon Wegge (1969) provided even more strict conditions on factor shares that would suffice, in the 3×3 case, to establish that an increase in any commodity price would raise the real return to the factor used intensively there and lower the returns to the other two factors. In both of these articles the criteria used to establish results in the 3×3 case were shown *not* to be sufficient in the 4×4 case. Sufficient conditions for each of these cases in higher dimensions were provided later in Jones, Marjit, and Mitra (1993) and Mitra and Jones (1999).

5. For a divergent view, see Samuelson (1992).

6. For agreements and disagreements with Leamer, see Jones (1992a).

References

Batra, R., and F. Casas. 1976. "A Synthesis of the Heckscher-Ohlin and the Neoclassical Models of International Trade." *Journal of International Economics* 6:21–38.

Chipman, J. S. 1966. "A Survey of the Theory of International Trade, Part 2." *Econometrica* 33:685–760.

———. 1969. "Factor Price Equalization and the Stolper-Samuelson Theorem." *International Economic Review* 10:399–406.

Ellis, H., and L. Metzler, eds. 1949. *Readings in the Theory of International Trade*. London: George Allen and Unwin.

Ethier, W. 1974. "Some of the Theorems of International Trade with Many Goods and Factors." *Journal of International Economics* 4:199–206.

Flam, H., and M. J. Flanders, eds. 1991. *Heckscher-Ohlin Trade Theory*. Cambridge, MA: MIT Press.

Haberler, G. 1936. *The Theory of International Trade*. London: William Hodge.

Heckscher, E. 1919. "The Effect of Foreign Trade on the Distribution of Income." *Ekonomisk Tidskrift* 21:497–512.

Jones, R. W. 1956. "Factor Proportions and the Heckscher-Ohlin Theorem." *Review of Economic Studies* 24:1–10.

———. 1971. "A Three-Factor Model in Theory, Trade and History." In J. Bhagwati et al., eds., *Trade, Balance of Payments and Growth*, 3–21. Amsterdam: North-Holland.

———. 1992a. "Factor Scarcity, Factor Abundance and Attitudes Towards Protection: The 3×3 Model." *Journal of International Economic Integration* 7:1–19.

————. 1992b. "Jointness in Production and Factor-Price Equalization." *Review of International Economics* 1:10–18.

Jones, R. W., and S. Easton. 1983. "Factor Intensities and Factor Substitution in General Equilibrium." *Journal of International Economics* 15:65–99.

Jones, R. W., S. Marjit, and T. Mitra. 1993. "The Stolper-Samuelson Theorem: Links to Dominant Diagonals." In Robert Becker et al., eds., *General Equilibrium, Growth and Trade II*, 429–441. San Diego: Academic Press.

Kemp, M. C., and L. Wegge. 1969. "On the Relation Between Commodity Prices and Factor Rewards." *International Economic Review* 10:407–413.

Krugman, P. 1999. "Was It All in Ohlin?" In Ronald Findlay et al., eds., *Bertil Ohlin: A Centennial Celebration*, 389–405. Cambridge, MA: MIT Press.

Leamer, E. 1987. "Paths of Development in the Three-Factor n-Good General Equilibrium Model." *Journal of Political Economy* 95:961–999.

————. 1994. "Commemorating the Fiftieth Birthday of the Stolper-Samuelson Theorem." In Alan Deardorff and Robert Stern, eds., *The Stolper-Samuelson Theorem: A Golden Jubilee*, 289–308. Ann Arbor: University of Michigan Press.

Leontief, W. 1953. "Domestic Production and Foreign Trade: The American Capital Position Re-examined." *Proceedings of the American Philosophical Society* 97:332–349.

Mitra, T., and R. W. Jones. 1999. "Factor Shares and the Chipman Condition." In James Melvin et al., eds., *Trade, Welfare and Econometrics*, 135–143. New York: Routledge.

Mundell, R. A. 1957. "International Trade and Factor Mobility." *American Economic Review* 47:321–335.

Neary, J. P. 1978. "Short-run Capital Specificity and the Pure Theory of International Trade." *Economic Journal* 88:488–510.

Ohlin, B. 1924. *The Theory of Trade* (Handelns Teory), in Flam and Flanders 1991:75–214.

————. 1933. *Interregional and International Trade*. Cambridge, MA: Harvard University Press.

Rybczynski, T. 1955. "Factor Endowments and Relative Commodity Prices." *Economica* 22:336–341.

Samuelson, P. A. 1948. "International Trade and the Equalisation of Factor Prices." *Economic Journal* 58:163–184.

————. 1949. "International Factor-Price Equalisation Once Again." *Economic Journal* 59:181–197.

————. 1971. "Ohlin was Right." *Swedish Journal of Economics* 73:365–384.

————. 1992. "Factor-Price Equalization by Trade in Joint and Non-joint Production." *Review of International Economics* 1:1–9.

Stolper, W., and P. A. Samuelson. 1941. "Protection and Real Wages." *Review of Economic Studies* 9:58–73.

Suzuki, K. 1983. "A Synthesis of the Heckscher-Ohlin and the Neoclassical Models of International Trade: A Comment." *Journal of International Economics* 14:141–144.

5 Heckscher-Ohlin Theory and Individual Attitudes Toward Globalization

Kevin H. O'Rourke

The factor proportions theory of trade developed by Eli Heckscher and Bertil Ohlin is so intuitively appealing that it remains the bedrock of modern trade courses. Despite its popularity, however, doubts have persistently been raised about its empirical applicability, from the Leontief paradox (Leontief 1953) to the stylized facts (high levels of intra-industry trade; high levels of trade between similar countries) that motivated the development of new trade theory in the 1980s. In an influential paper that was particularly damaging to the theory's credibility, Bowen, Leamer, and Sveikauskas (1987) showed that the Heckscher-Ohlin-Vanek model was of no help when trying to predict the net factor content of a country's trade.

However, recent work by Don Davis, David Weinstein, and others has suggested that Heckscher-Ohlin theory does indeed help to explain trade patterns, so long as the researcher bears in mind the fact that countries are not distinguished by differences in factor endowments alone; for example, Davis and Weinstein (2001) show that Heckscher-Ohlin-Vanek theory is consistent with the data, as long as it is modified to take account of the (self-evidently true) facts that technology differs across countries, that factor price equalization does not hold, that some goods are nontraded, and that international trade is not costless.

In this essay, I take an entirely different approach in assessing the empirical usefulness of Heckscher-Ohlin theory. I do not ask whether it explains trade patterns, which is what the theory is supposed to do; rather, I ask whether individuals' attitudes toward globalization (and more specifically, their attitudes toward trade and immigration) are consistent with factor proportions theory. In particular, I start from the premise that trade and migration patterns are today driven largely by differences in the relative endowments of skilled and unskilled labor in different countries; it follows from Heckscher-Ohlin theory that skilled and unskilled workers should differ in their attitudes towards globalization, in a predictable manner. Do these predictions hold true when confronted with the data?

In a series of papers, Kenneth Scheve and Matthew Slaughter have addressed these issues and found evidence for the Heckscher-Ohlin worldview. Scheve and Slaughter (2001a) examined individual-level survey data for the United States in 1992 and found that low-skilled workers were more likely to support "new limits on imports" than high-skilled workers; they also found that factor type (i.e., skill level) was more important than the sector in which individuals were employed in explaining preferences. This finding was consistent with Heckscher-Ohlin models in which factors of production are mobile between sectors, but inconsistent with specific factors models in which agents are intersectorally immobile. Scheve and Slaughter (2001b) use U.S. survey data for 1992, 1994, and 1996 to examine attitudes toward immigration. They find that high-skill workers are less likely to support restrictionist immigration policies than their low-skill counterparts.

While such findings may be consistent with a Heckscher-Ohlin worldview, single country studies cannot convincingly demonstrate that factor proportions models are relevant in explaining individual preferences regarding globalization. The reason is straightforward: Heckscher-Ohlin theory predicts that the impact of skill on attitudes should vary in a systematic way across countries. In skill-abundant countries, high-skill workers should favor trade; in low-skill-abundant countries, it is the unskilled who should favor trade. The Scheve and Slaughter findings, on their own, do not preclude the possibility that the high-skilled are in favor of globalization everywhere—for example, because better educated people understand the intellectual arguments in favor of international integration. Such a world would be at dramatic variance with the predictions of Heckscher-Ohlin theory.

In order to test the theory, therefore, we need data giving attitudes toward globalization in a number of different countries. The crucial issue then becomes whether the relationship between skills and attitudes varies across countries in a manner consistent with theory. This paper will survey recent attempts to do precisely this, looking separately at attitudes toward trade and attitudes towards immigration, and drawing on my work with Richard Sinnott (O'Rourke and Sinnott 2001, 2006).[1] The next sections will discuss what theory has to say about how individuals in different countries should feel about trade and immigration; the data used; the determinants of individual attitudes toward trade; the determinants of individual attitudes toward immigration; and the determinants of attitudes toward both trade and immigration.

Theoretical Expectations

Trade

Standard Heckscher-Ohlin trade theory is quite clear in its predictions regarding who should benefit and who should lose from free trade in commodities. Imagine a two-factor world in which countries are distinguished only by their relative endowments of skilled and unskilled workers. The relative wages of skilled workers will be lower, other things being equal, in skill abundant countries (which we will denote by R and refer to as rich countries) than in unskilled labor abundant countries (denoted by P and referred to as poor countries): we have $(w_S/w_{US})^R < (w_S/w_{US})^P$, where w_S and w_{US} denote skilled and unskilled wages respectively. It is this inequality that drives comparative advantage: the rich countries will export skill-intensive goods, while the poor countries will export unskilled labor-intensive goods. The result is then relative factor price convergence (or, in the limit, factor price equalization): when countries move toward freer trade, the relative price of skilled labor rises in rich countries and falls in poor countries. Moreover, the abundant factor gains in real terms in all countries, while the scarce factor loses. Thus the skilled should favor free trade in rich countries, while they should favor protection in poor countries; the unskilled in rich countries should favor protection, while the unskilled in poor countries should support free trade.

Note that Heckscher-Ohlin theory argues that individuals' interests are related to countries' factor endowments; in order to test the theory, we ought in principle to see whether the relationship between skills and protectionist sentiment varies across countries in a manner related to their skill endowments (for example, their average educational levels). For reasons outlined later, however, the available educational data are not satisfactory, and in testing the theory we assume that GDP per capita is strongly and positively correlated with human capital endowments. We therefore have Prediction 1: that the impact of skills on protectionist sentiment should be related to a country's GDP per capita. In the richest countries, being high-skilled should have a negative impact on protectionist sentiment. In the poorest countries, being high-skilled should have a positive impact on protectionist sentiment. More generally, an interaction term between skills and GDP per capita should enter with a negative sign in a regression explaining protectionist sentiment.

Immigration

In a pure Heckscher-Ohlin world in which technology is identical across countries, and in which countries are only distinguished by their relative endowments of skilled and unskilled labor, it is again possible to make unambiguous predictions about who should favor immigration and who should not. This is the case, even though international migration is not driven by comparative advantage and relative factor prices, but by absolute advantage, and by absolute factor price differentials. In a pure Heckscher-Ohlin world, the real wages of skilled workers will be higher in poor countries (where skilled workers are scarce) than in rich countries (where they are abundant), while unskilled wages will be higher in rich countries than in poor countries: we have (in real terms) $w_S^P > w_S^R$, but $w_{US}^R > w_{US}^P$. Thus, we should observe skilled workers migrating from rich to poor countries, and unskilled workers migrating from poor to rich countries. Immigration will hurt skilled workers in poor countries, but benefit the unskilled there; therefore in poor countries the unskilled should favor immigration, while skilled workers should oppose it. The situation is the reverse in rich countries: immigration will hurt the unskilled, but benefit skilled workers. Thus skilled workers should be pro-immigration, while the unskilled should oppose it.

We thus have Prediction 2: the impact of skills on anti-immigrant sentiment should be related to a country's GDP per capita. In the richest countries, being high-skilled should have a negative impact on anti-immigrant sentiment. In the poorest countries, being high-skilled should have a positive impact on anti-immigrant sentiment. More generally, an interaction term between skills and GDP per capita should enter with a negative sign in a regression explaining anti-immigrant sentiment.

Note that in such a pure two-country, two-factor Heckscher-Ohlin world, in which countries are distinguished solely by their relative factor endowments, agents are consistent in their attitudes toward globalization. That is, in rich countries skilled workers favor both trade and immigration, while unskilled workers are protectionist and anti-immigration. In poor countries, it is the unskilled who are liberal in their attitudes toward both trade and immigration, while the skilled favor both protection and immigration restrictions. This symmetry reflects the fact that in a pure two-factor Heckscher-Ohlin world in which technology is identical across countries, trade and factor flows are substitutes: they have identical effects on factor prices (i.e., they both lead to relative and absolute factor price convergence), and thus, the more you have of one dimension of globalization, the less incentive there will be for the other dimension to take place. In such a world, scarce factors lose as a result of either trade or immigration, while abundant factors gain from either. One immediate political consequence of the fact that trade and migration are substitutes for each other is that agents who are protectionist should also be anti-immigration: both trade and immigration have to be simultaneously restricted, since either phenomenon will hurt the scarce factor. Protection without immigration restrictions will not work, since protection without immigration restrictions will simply lead to more immigration; immigration barriers without protection will not work, since immigration barriers on their own will simply lead to more trade (Mundell 1957).

We thus have Prediction 3: all other things being equal, being protectionist should increase the likelihood that an individual is anti-immigrant; while being anti-immigrant should increase the likelihood that an individual is protectionist.

Things get a lot more complicated if technology differs across countries, or if there are more than two factors of production. Any test of Heckscher-Ohlin theory will in all likelihood do better by admitting such possibilities (recall that it is precisely by admitting the existence of such complications that the empirical trade literature has to some extent rehabilitated the theory in recent years). If technology is superior in the rich country, or if the rich country is better endowed with some third factor of production than the poor country, then it no longer follows from an inequality such as $(w_S/w_{US})^R < (w_S/w_{US})^P$ that skilled workers will migrate from rich to poor countries: it is quite possible that $(w_S/w_{US})^R < (w_S/w_{US})^P$, but that (in real terms) $w_S^R > w_S^P$. In this case, skilled workers will move from poor (unskilled labor abundant) countries to rich (skill abundant) countries: unskilled workers will move in the same direction as skilled workers. This is, of course, what happens in the real world, suggesting that richer countries do indeed enjoy superior technology to poor countries, and that endowments alone cannot explain differences in income, or for that matter trade patterns and factor flows. The issue of whether skilled or unskilled workers should be more anti-immigration in rich countries thus becomes unclear. Presumably it depends upon whether immigration predominantly involves skilled or unskilled workers; but which is true is not immediately obvious.[2]

In fact, there is a large theoretical literature which asks whether migrants are more likely to be skilled or unskilled, but this literature tends not to be located within standard Heckscher-Ohlin trade models. For example, Katz and Stark (1984) argue that asymmetric information can lead to migration flows disproportionately involving unskilled workers, since employers in rich countries may not be able to correctly discern the skill levels of potential migrants, although the equilibrium outcome can change if various devices reinstating informational symmetry are employed (Katz and Stark 1987). While appealing, it is not clear to me how this theory could be empirically tested with the data at my disposal.

An alternative theory is provided by Borjas (1987), who adapts Roy's (1951) model of occupational self-selection to the issue of migration. The conclusion of the analysis is that there will be positive self-selection of migrants if (a) the correlation between the earnings which they receive in the home and destination countries is sufficiently high; and (b) if income is more dispersed in the destination country than in the home country. On the other hand, there will be negative self-selection if (a) the correlation between the earnings which they receive in the home and destination countries is sufficiently high; and (b) if income is less dispersed in the destination country than in the home country. The theory thus predicts that immigrants into more unequal countries should be higher-skilled than immigrants into more equal countries: it follows that the high-skilled should be less favorably disposed toward immigrants in more unequal countries than in more equal countries. We have Prediction 4: the impact of skills on anti-immigrant sentiment should be related to a country's level of inequality. In the most unequal countries, being high-skilled should have a positive impact on anti-immigrant sentiment. In the most equal countries, being high-skilled should have a negative impact on anti-immigrant sentiment. More generally, an interaction term between skills and inequality should enter with a positive sign in a regression explaining anti-immigrant sentiment.[3]

The Data

The 1995 International Social Survey Programme (ISSP) module on national identity provides the kind of cross-country survey data[4] that are needed to test the hypotheses outlined above. The ISSP national identity survey was conducted in twenty-four countries in 1995–96. The countries concerned were: Australia, West Germany and East Germany (divided again for purposes of the survey), Great Britain, the United States, Austria, Hungary, Italy, Ireland, the Netherlands, Norway, Sweden, the Czech Republic, Slovenia, Poland, Bulgaria, Russia, New Zealand, Canada, the Philippines, Japan, Spain, Latvia, and Slovakia.

The survey provides two questions that are relevant in assessing attitudes toward globalization. The first asks respondents how much they agree or disagree with the statement that their country "should limit the import of foreign products in order to protect its national economy." The second asks respondents if the number of immigrants to their economy should be increased a lot (1), be increased a little (2), remain the same (3), be reduced a little (4), or be reduced a lot (5). Table 5.1 reports the mean response to these questions in each country: a score greater than 3 indicates that on average respondents were leaning towards greater restriction, rather than freer trade or immigration. In every country in the sample, respondents on average favored lowering the number of immigrants; in every country in the sample bar two (the Netherlands and Japan) respondents on average favored limiting imports.

Answers to these two questions constitute the dependent variables that are to be explained in the analysis which follows. The data set also provides individual-level measures of a range of demographic, socioeconomic, and political variables that are of relevance in understanding attitudes toward globalization. Among the socioeconomic variables, the most valuable from the point of view of testing the implications of the theories surveyed earlier is the respondent's skill level. This is arrived at by coding the answers to questions on respondents' occupation using the International Labor Organization's ISCO88 (International Standard Classification of Occupations) coding scheme. While a complex coding scheme of this sort allows for very fine distinctions between different occupations, it makes most sense to focus on the four main skill categories provided by ISCO88. In brief, these are: (1) "elementary occupations" (i.e., "manual labor and simple and

Table 5.1
Summary statistics, selected variables

Country	Protect		Anti-immigrant	
	Mean	Std. Dev.	Mean	Std. Dev.
Australia	3.997	0.988	3.768	1.042
W. Germany	3.083	1.232	4.226	0.910
E. Germany	3.563	1.189	4.338	0.871
Britain	3.723	1.004	4.052	0.962
USA	3.707	1.016	3.873	1.044
Austria	3.873	1.163	3.804	0.933
Hungary	4.047	1.075	4.402	0.817
Italy	3.571	1.216	4.151	0.900
Ireland	3.65	1.128	3.071	0.829
Netherlands	2.912	0.992	3.826	0.924
Norway	3.144	1.038	3.847	0.982
Sweden	3.228	1.081	3.961	1.017
Czech Rep.	3.415	1.294	4.158	0.880
Slovenia	3.465	1.174	3.939	0.868
Poland	3.787	1.083	3.888	1.060
Bulgaria	4.190	1.09	4.219	0.990
Russia	3.670	1.282	3.717	0.971
New Zealand	3.406	1.147	3.742	1.053
Canada	3.264	1.135	3.317	1.135
Philippines	3.624	0.918	3.796	1.102
Japan	2.919	1.282	3.391	1.008
Spain	3.813	0.906	3.401	0.813
Latvia	4.042	1.18	4.182	0.884
Slovakia	3.488	1.273	4.004	0.911

Source: Data from ISSP National Identity Survey (1995).

routine tasks, involving ... with few exceptions, only limited personal initiative" [ILO 1990:7]); (2) "plant and machine operators and assemblers; craft and related trades workers; skilled agricultural and fishery workers; service workers and shop and market sales workers; clerks"; (3) "technicians and associate professionals"; and (4) "professionals." A fifth group, "legislators, senior officials, and managers," do not have a skill coding under this four-step skill classification and were included as a separate, fifth, skill category. Finally, members of the armed forces were excluded, since it was unclear what their skill levels were. Skill data were available for twenty-one of the twenty-four countries; the other three (Italy, Sweden, and Japan) were omitted when estimating models involving skill.

The analysis also uses a subjective economic variable, namely the stated willingness of people to move from one location to another in order to improve their standard of living or their work environment. Respondents were asked: "If you could improve your work or living conditions, how willing or unwilling would you be to move to another neighbourhood or village; another town or city within this county or region; another county or region; outside [named country]; outside [named continent]?" Based on the responses to these questions, two binary variables were derived, indicating whether or not individuals were nationally mobile, and internationally mobile.[5] Arguably, those willing to relocate within the country should be less affected by any dislocation implied by immigration or free trade than those who are immobile. This will be particularly true if national labor markets are not perfectly integrated; and if immigrants tend to concentrate in particular regions or cities, or if import-competing industries are similarly concentrated. The rationale behind including the international mobility variable is to test Rodrik's (1997) argument that globalization is currently favoring internationally mobile factors of production (i.e., physical and human capital) over immobile factors such as unskilled labor; alternatively (in the context of migration), being willing to live overseas may signal an openness to other cultures, and hence a greater tolerance for immigrants. The survey also indicates whether the respondent had ever lived abroad; previous experience of living abroad may provide a signal regarding willingness to move again (or, again in the context of immigration, it may indicate familiarity with foreigners). In addition, the survey provides information on respondents' age; their gender; their religion; on whether they and their parents are native-born or not; on their marital and employment status; and on a variety of other personal characteristics and attitudes.

The ISSP national identity data set includes a wide range of indicators of nationalist attitudes. The analysis here focuses on the following seven questions (versions implemented in Ireland, other country/ nationality labels substituted as appropriate):

• "Generally speaking, Ireland is a better country than most other countries"

• "The world would be a better place if people from other countries were more like the Irish"

• "I would rather be a citizen of Ireland than of any other country in the world"

• "It is impossible for people who do not share Irish customs and traditions to become fully Irish"

• "People should support their country even if the country is in the wrong"

• "Ireland should follow its own interests, even if this leads to conflicts with other nations"

• "How important do you think each of the following is for being truly Irish?" . . . "to have been born in Ireland"

In each case, respondents were asked to rank their responses along a scale, in the case of the first six items, from 1 (strongly disagree) to 5 (strongly agree) and, in the case of the seventh item, from 1 (very important) to 4 (not at all important). The seventh item was reordered to make it consistent with the other six. Principal components analysis of these responses yielded two factors or underlying dimensions of nationalist attitudes. As can be seen from the rotated factor loadings in table 5.2, the first factor is a straightforward preference for and sense of the superiority of one's own country (here labeled patriotism). The second factor identifies a narrow or exclusive sense of nationality com-

Table 5.2
Factor analysis of nationalist items in ISSP National Identity Survey (1995)

	Factor 1	Factor 2
[COUNTRY] better country than most other countries	0.86	0.02
World better place if people from other countries more like the [NATIONALITY]	0.78	0.2
Rather be citizen of [COUNTRY] than of any other country in world	0.61	0.29
Impossible for people who do not share [NATNL.] traditions to be fully [NATNL.]	−0.01	0.71
People should support their country even if country is wrong	0.20	0.63
Importance of having been born in [COUNTRY] to be fully [NATIONALITY]	0.16	0.63
[COUNTRY] should follow own interests, even if conflicts with other nations	0.23	0.55
Percent variance	**26.34**	**24.50**

Extraction Method: Principal Component Analysis. Rotation Method: Varimax with Kaiser Normalization.
Source: O'Rourke and Sinnott (2001). Data from ISSP National Identity Survey (1995).

bined with a degree of chauvinism of the "my country right or wrong" variety (here labeled chauvinism). On the basis of this analysis, patriotism and chauvinism scores have been calculated by averaging responses across the relevant subsets of items identified in the factor analysis.

Finally, in order to test the various hypotheses outlined in the previous section, data on GDP per capita in 1995 were collected from the World Bank's *World Development Indicators* (these are PPP-adjusted figures, in 1995 international dollars); the same source yielded information on inequality (namely, Gini coefficients).[6] Data on educational attainments are also available; the standard source is the Barro and Lee (2000) dataset on average years of schooling in each country. However, the transition countries account for nine of the twenty-four countries in the ISSP dataset, and the Barro-Lee figures for schooling in several transition countries are very high: for example, average schooling is higher in Slovakia, Bulgaria, Latvia, and Poland than in the Netherlands, Ireland, and Austria. It seems doubtful that these figures provide a genuine reflection of the economically relevant human capital endowments of these countries; it is for this reason that GDP per capita data are used when testing Heckscher-Ohlin theory.

Understanding Protectionist Preferences

Table 5.3 presents results of a series of ordered probit regressions in which the dependent variable is "protect," an ordered variable running from 1 (least protectionist) to 5 (most protectionist). The results differ from those presented in O'Rourke and Sinnott (2001) in that the specification of the equations is altered to make them more comparable with the results for anti-immigrant sentiment.[7]

Equation (1) shows that nationalist sentiment is an extremely strong determinant of attitudes toward trade, with patriotism, and especially chauvinism, having a large positive effect on protectionist sentiment. This result is robust across all specifications, and confirms the importance of ideology in determining attitudes towards globalization.

Is there also a role for interests in shaping voter preferences? The other equations suggest that there is. Equation (2) provides a test of Prediction 1. It adds a skill variable, Skill345, to the specification, as well as an interaction term between Skill345 and GDP per capita. Skill345 is a variable indicating whether the respondent is high-skilled or not; it is equal to one if the respondent belongs to one of the three

Table 5.3
Determinants of protectionist preferences (ordered probit)
(dependent variable: protect)

	(1)	(2)	(3)	(4)
Patriotism	0.2009***	0.1954***	0.1767***	0.1605***
	[0.0182]	[0.0197]	[0.0173]	[0.0159]
Chauvinism	0.3559***	0.3483***	0.3385***	0.3044***
	[0.0203]	[0.0213]	[0.0219]	[0.0198]
Skill345		−0.0378	−0.0287	−0.0518
		[0.0802]	[0.0777]	[0.0858]
Skill345*GDPCAP		−0.0088**	−0.0089**	−0.0069
		[0.0042]	[0.0039]	[0.0044]
National mobility			−0.0066	−0.0164
			[0.0234]	[0.0240]
International mobility			−0.0809***	−0.0728***
			[0.0227]	[0.0270]
Never lived abroad			0.0863***	0.0855***
			[0.0201]	[0.0200]
Native			0.0027	−0.0276
			[0.0561]	[0.0640]
Native parents			0.0269	0.0055
			[0.0600]	[0.0584]
Age			0.0122***	0.0105***
			[0.0037]	[0.0039]
Age squared			−0.0001***	−0.0001**
			[0.0000]	[0.0000]
Female			0.1854***	0.1906***
			[0.0296]	[0.0283]
Married			0.0178	0.0046
			[0.0157]	[0.0196]
Catholic			0.0587***	0.0636***
			[0.0177]	[0.0170]
Unemployed			0.0676**	0.0834***
			[0.0291]	[0.0278]
Anti-immigrant				0.1325***
				[0.0136]
Cut1	−0.1478*	−0.2508***	0.1814	0.3936**
	[0.0798]	[0.0951]	[0.1584]	[0.1621]
Cut2	0.7823***	0.7348***	1.1821***	1.4377***
	[0.0646]	[0.0570]	[0.1161]	[0.1258]
Cut3	1.4824***	1.4147***	1.8688***	2.0943***
	[0.0659]	[0.0573]	[0.1107]	[0.1150]
Cut4	2.4691***	2.4185***	2.8782***	3.1462***
	[0.0887]	[0.0801]	[0.1169]	[0.1367]
No. of observations	30082	26501	24147	21191
Log likelihood	−41427.54	−36037.20	−32712.35	−28318.23
Pseudo-R-squared	0.08	0.08	0.08	0.09

Robust standard errors in brackets assume clustering at country level. * significant at 10%; ** significant at 5%; *** significant at 1%. Country dummy variables included; coefficients not reported.

high-skill categories mentioned earlier (categories 3, 4, and 5) and zero otherwise. The results are a triumphant confirmation of Heckscher-Ohlin theory, in that the interaction term between Skill345 is negative and statistically significant. It is in fact the case that the high-skilled are more likely to support free trade in rich countries than in poor countries, just as the theory predicts. This result is also robust across specifications (although the coefficient is only at the margins of statistical significance in equation (4), with a p-value of 0.116).

Equation (3) adds a variety of control variables to the regression, but the basic Heckscher-Ohlin result remains. A stated willingness to move within the country has no impact on attitudes, but international mobility is associated with free trade preferences, consistent with Rodrik (1997). Women, Roman Catholics, and older people tend toward more protectionist viewpoints, as do the unemployed.

How important quantitatively is this Heckscher-Ohlin effect? Taking the specification in equation (3), and setting all right-hand side variables equal to their median values, the expected probability that a respondent will give the most protectionist response possible (protect = 5) is 31.3 percent. In a country with a per capita GDP of $5000, being high-skilled reduced this probability by just 2.6 percent; but being high-skilled reduces the probability by 5.5 percent in a country with a per capita GDP of $15,000, and by 8.2 percent in a country with a per capita GDP of $25,000. It appears that income matters a lot in determining the impact of being high-skilled on preferences.[8]

Finally, equation (4) tests Prediction 3 by adding a measure of anti-immigrant sentiment. Prediction 3 is vindicated, in that those who are more anti-immigrant also tend to be more protectionist: trade and immigration policy are viewed as complements rather than as substitutes, just as Heckscher-Ohlin theory predicts.

An alternative way of testing Heckscher-Ohlin theory is to run a series of regressions for individual countries, and see how the relationship between skills and protectionist sentiment which comes out of these regressions varies across countries. The table that makes up appendix 1 gives the result of a series of country-specific regressions, which include most of the variables in equation (3) of table 5.3.[9] Figure 5.1 plots the coefficients on Skill345 for each of these countries, against that country's GDP per capita. Again, Prediction 1 is confirmed, in that there is clearly a negative relationship between the impact of skill on protectionist attitudes, and GDP per capita. Indeed, in four of the poorest countries in the sample (Poland, Bulgaria, the Philippines, and

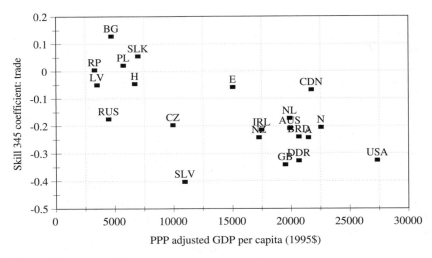

Figure 5.1
Impact of skill and GDP

Slovakia) being high-skilled is actually associated with being more protectionist, rather than less protectionist, although the effects are small and statistically insignificant. Ideally, of course, one would like to have information on even poorer countries, and see if skills are strongly and positively related to protectionist preferences, but this is not possible with the ISSP dataset.

The robustness of these results is confirmed by Mayda and Rodrik (2005), who independently arrived at the same conclusions using slightly different methods and specifications. In particular, they

• ran ordered logit rather than ordered probit regressions

• used years of education rather than occupational skill-level to measure human capital

• use other control variables, such as individuals' relative incomes, and their sector of employment (which they infer from the data on occupations).

Despite these differences, their basic findings are strikingly similar to the ones presented here. Moreover, the Heckscher-Ohlin results carry over when Mayda and Rodrik employ data for a larger sample of countries (taken from the World Values Survey). It appears that people's preferences regarding trade policy are fully consistent with the predictions of factor proportions theory.

Understanding Anti-immigrant Preferences

Table 5.4 presents the results of a series of regressions explaining "anti-immigrant," which is an ordered variable running from 1 (least anti-immigrant) to 5 (most anti-immigrant). The same variables are used as in the previous analysis, and as before patriotism, and especially chauvinism, are important determinants of anti-immigrant sentiment. Equation (2) tests the unconditional version of Prediction 2, and this time the results are not favorable to Heckscher-Ohlin theory: the coefficient on the interaction term between Skill345 and GDP per capita is negative, as expected, but the effect is statistically insignificant. Similarly, equation (3) tests the unconditional version of Prediction 4, and again the results are disappointing for the Borjas self-selection theory. The coefficient on an interaction term between Skill345 and the Gini coefficient is positive, as expected, but again insignificant.

Equation (4) tests a conditional version of Prediction 2, and this time the results are favorable. Controlling for international differences in income distribution the interaction term between Skill345 and GDP per capita is negative and statistically significant, just as theory predicts. This result remains robust when other control variables are used (in equations 5 and 6), although the coefficient on the interaction term between Skill345 and GDP per capita becomes statistically insignificant at conventional levels in equation 6 (with a p-value of 0.113). Moreover, controlling for international income differentials, the interaction term between Skill345 and the Gini coefficient is positive in equation (4), and on the margins of statistical significance (with a p-value of 0.136). When further control variables are added to the specification in equations (5) and (6), this positive coefficient on the interaction term between Skill345 and the Gini coefficient becomes statistically significant at conventional levels, confirming a conditional version of Prediction 4.

How strong are these effects? Again, taking the specification in equation (5), and setting all the explanatory variables equal to their median values, yields an expected probability of the most anti-immigrant response of 48.6 percent. Assuming that the Gini coefficient is held at its median value, 31.6, being high-skilled reduces the expected probability of the most anti-immigrant response by 3.4 percent at a per capita income of $5,000, but by 6.1 percent at per capita incomes of $15,000, and by 8.7 percent at per capita incomes of $25,000. Assuming that per capita income is held constant, at its median value

Table 5.4
Determinants of anti-immigrant preferences (ordered probit)
(dependent variable: anti-immigrant)

	(1)	(2)	(3)	(4)	(5)	(6)
Patriotism	0.1090***	0.1001***	0.0988***	0.0997***	0.0787***	0.0606***
	[0.0193]	[0.0209]	[0.0209]	[0.0208]	[0.0148]	[0.0140]
Chauvinism	0.3606***	0.3415***	0.3432***	0.3418***	0.3204***	0.2833***
	[0.0461]	[0.0483]	[0.0483]	[0.0484]	[0.0516]	[0.0497]
Skill345		−0.0569	−0.3366*	−0.2662	−0.2784*	−0.3045**
		[0.0705]	[0.1721]	[0.1765]	[0.1625]	[0.1544]
Skill345* GDPCAP		−0.0061		−0.0072*	−0.0068*	−0.0060
		[0.0047]		[0.0041]	[0.0039]	[0.0038]
Skill345* Inequality			0.0056	0.0070	0.0072*	0.0083**
			[0.0052]	[0.0047]	[0.0043]	[0.0041]
National mobility					−0.0133	−0.0119
					[0.0197]	[0.0195]
International mobility					−0.0806**	−0.0700**
					[0.0326]	[0.0338]
Never lived abroad					0.1228***	0.1106***
					[0.0276]	[0.0274]
Native					0.1842***	0.1860***
					[0.0569]	[0.0581]
Native parents					0.2002**	0.1996***
					[0.0779]	[0.0730]
Age					0.0075***	0.0064***
					[0.0025]	[0.0024]
Age squared					−0.0001**	−0.0000*
					[0.0000]	[0.0000]
Female					0.0327	0.0096
					[0.0261]	[0.0251]
Married					0.0018	0.0006
					[0.0233]	[0.0231]
Catholic					−0.0230	−0.0281
					[0.0418]	[0.0418]
Unemployed					0.0370	0.0284
					[0.0535]	[0.0533]
Protectionism						0.1228***
						[0.0134]
Cut1	−1.0700***	−1.1802***	−1.2106***	−1.2007***	−0.7171***	−0.5098***
	[0.1347]	[0.1409]	[0.1342]	[0.1354]	[0.1577]	[0.1621]
Cut2	−0.3720***	−0.4830***	−0.5134***	−0.5032***	−0.0075	0.2024
	[0.1356]	[0.1463]	[0.1387]	[0.1409]	[0.1468]	[0.1547]
Cut3	0.8796***	0.7786***	0.7478***	0.7585***	1.2907***	1.5100***
	[0.1293]	[0.1420]	[0.1342]	[0.1366]	[0.1589]	[0.1643]
Cut4	1.6979***	1.5894***	1.5586***	1.5695***	2.1098***	2.3363***
	[0.1426]	[0.1561]	[0.1485]	[0.1511]	[0.1659]	[0.1720]

Table 5.4
(continued)

	(1)	(2)	(3)	(4)	(5)	(6)
No. of observations	26484	23246	23246	23246	21220	21191
Log likelihood	−32707.20	−28675.13	−28676.30	−28671.76	−25883.56	−25709.22
Pseudo-R-squared	0.07	0.07	0.07	0.07	0.08	0.08

Robust standard errors in brackets assume clustering at country level. * significant at 10%; ** significant at 5%; *** significant at 1%. Country dummy variables included; coefficients not reported.

for this sample of countries of $19,270, being high-skilled reduces the expected probability of the most anti-immigrant response by 9.0 percent when the Gini coefficient is 25, by 6.3 percent when the Gini coefficient is 35, and by only 3.5 percent when the Gini coefficient is 45. The net impact of being high-skilled is positive for Gini coefficients of 58 and over.

As before, national mobility is unrelated to attitudes to globalization, but a stated willingness to move internationally, or a history of such mobility, reduces the probability that a respondent will express anti-immigrant opinions. Both natives and the children of natives are more anti-immigrant, as are older people. In contrast with the results for trade, being a woman or a Roman Catholic does not have a statistically significant impact on preferences (and the coefficient for Roman Catholics is actually negative). Neither does being unemployed have any such effect, which is surprising.

Finally, equation (6) tests Prediction 3, by including "protect" as an additional explanatory variable; protectionism is positively and statistically significantly correlated with anti-immigrant sentiment, just as Heckscher-Ohlin theory would predict (although, as noted above, when "protect" is included in the specification the interaction term between Skill345 and GDP per capita becomes statistically insignificant).

Again, another approach to testing the Heckscher-Ohlin and self-selection theories is to run a series of regressions explaining attitudes towards immigration in individual countries, and compare the coefficients on Skill345 across countries. The table that makes up appendix 2 gives the results of doing this using the specification in equation (5) (without country dummies or the two interaction terms). Figure 5.2

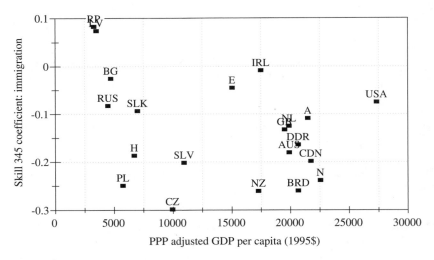

Figure 5.2
Impact of skill and GDP

plots the resultant coefficients on Skill345 for each country, against that country's level of GDP per capita. As can be seen, support for the HO predictions is in this case unclear. There is indeed a negative relationship between the coefficient on Skill345 and per capita GDP for the poorer countries in the sample (i.e., the Philippines and the transition economies of Central and Eastern Europe); and in two of the poorest countries, Latvia and the Philippines, the impact of skills on anti-immigrant attitudes is actually positive. However, for the richer countries in the sample the relationship is unclear. This methodology provides much stronger evidence for the Borjas theory: figure 5.3 shows a positive relationship between the Skill345 coefficient and the Gini coefficient (with a correlation coefficient of 0.401).

Of course, figure 5.2 just plots the bivariate relationship between the Skill345 coefficient and GDP per capita; while the regressions in table 5.4 control for a simultaneous relationship between the Skill345 coefficient and inequality. It appears that the evidence for the predictions of Heckscher-Ohlin theory is weak when the unconditional version of that theory is tested; however, conditional on other factors the predictions of the theory hold up well. The Borjas theory does better than factor proportions theory when tested unconditionally, but does even better yet when tested conditional on other factors.

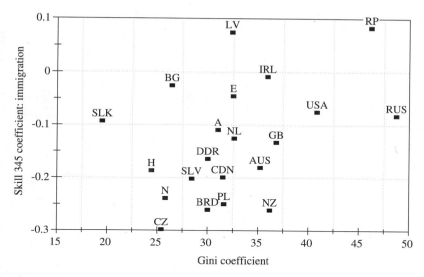

Figure 5.3
Impact of skill and inequality

The above exercises are fairly simple in their methodology. However, Mayda (2006) has recently and independently arrived at similar conclusions to these, using the same data set, as well as the World Values Survey, but going into much greater detail and employing many additional individual- and country-level variables to test the basic Heckscher-Ohlin predictions. She uses both education and skills as measures of human capital, and runs probit regressions explaining a dichotomous "immigrant opinion" variable. Her results are even more favorable for factor proportions theory than mine, even though she does not correct for differences in inequality across countries. The findings in this section thus appear to be robust.

Explaining Attitudes Toward Trade and Immigration Simultaneously

The previous sections have documented relationships between attitudes toward globalization that conform well with factor proportions theory. One objection to the results, however, is that they do not take adequate account of the fact that attitudes toward trade and immigration are correlated with each other, and (crucially) that unobserved

Table 5.5
Determinants of anti-globalization preferences
(seemingly unrelated bivariate probit)

Dependent variable	(1) Highly protectionist	(2) Highly anti-immigrant
Patriotism	0.1967***	0.0803***
	[0.0214]	[0.0225]
Chauvinism	0.3677***	0.3754***
	[0.0285]	[0.0479]
Skill345	0.0387	−0.2137
	[0.0717]	[0.1703]
Skill345*GDPCAP	−0.0137***	−0.0093**
	[0.0040]	[0.0038]
Skill345*Inequality		0.0057
		[0.0040]
National mobility	−0.0301	0.0063
	[0.0189]	[0.0176]
International mobility	0.0029	0.0233
	[0.0324]	[0.0292]
Never lived abroad	0.0330	0.0537
	[0.0310]	[0.0363]
Native	0.0873	0.2182**
	[0.0827]	[0.0873]
Native parents	−0.0466	0.2515***
	[0.0690]	[0.0785]
Age	0.0164***	0.0204***
	[0.0049]	[0.0031]
Age squared	−0.0001***	−0.0002***
	[0.0000]	[0.0000]
Female	0.0985***	−0.0301
	[0.0262]	[0.0224]
Married	0.0086	−0.0239
	[0.0194]	[0.0231]
Catholic	0.0588***	−0.0082
	[0.0226]	[0.0293]
Unemployed	0.0917**	0.0986*
	[0.0362]	[0.0580]
Constant	−2.8535***	−2.7675***
	[0.1675]	[0.1754]
No. of observations	24180	
Rho [standard error of rho]	0.221349 [0.013959]	
Wald test of rho = 0	Chi-squared(1) = 235.13, p-value = 0.0000	

Robust standard errors in brackets assume clustering at country level. * significant at 10%; ** significant at 5%; *** significant at 1%. Country dummy variables included; coefficients not reported.

determinants of globalization could have similar effects on both variables. Table 5.5 therefore presents the results of seemingly unrelated bivariate probit regressions explaining attitudes toward both trade and immigration. It estimates two regressions with the same explanatory variables as before, but allows the disturbance terms in both regressions to be correlated with each other.[10] The dependent variables in both cases are binary variables, indicating whether the respondent gave the most anti-globalization response possible: "Highly protectionist" is 1 if "protect" = 5, while "Highly anti-immigrant" is 1 if "anti-immigrant" = 5; otherwise both variables are zero. The "rho" coefficient reported at the bottom is the correlation between the disturbances in the two equations, or "(roughly) the correlation between the outcomes after the influence of the included factors is accounted for" (Greene 2000:854). The results confirm Prediction 3 in that "rho" is strongly positive. Predictions 1 and 2 are also confirmed, in that the interaction terms between Skill345 and GDP per capita are negative. There is less strong support for Prediction 4: while the interaction term between Skill345 and the Gini coefficient in equation (2) is positive, it is statistically insignificant at conventional levels (with a p-value of 0.151). The other big difference between the results here and those obtained earlier is that unemployment now has a positive effect on anti-immigrant sentiment, as well as on protectionism, while the international mobility variables are no longer statistically significant.

Conclusion

Presumably, the debate about to what extent factor proportions theory explains trade flows will continue in the decades ahead. However, it appears that people's attitudes toward globalization are strikingly similar to those that would be predicted if Heckscher-Ohlin trade theory accurately described the world. The high-skilled are proglobalization in rich countries, confirming the results of Scheve and Slaughter. Even more tellingly, in some of the very poorest countries in the ISSP sample, being high-skilled has a negative (if statistically insignificant) impact on pro-globalization sentiment. More generally, an interaction term between skills and GDP per capita has a negative impact in regressions explaining antiglobalization sentiment. Furthermore, individuals view protectionism and anti-immigrant policies as complements rather than as substitutes, which is what simple Heckscher-Ohlin theory predicts.

Appendix 1. Country-specific regressions: Protectionism

	(1)	(2)	(3)	(4)	(5)	(6)
	Australia	West Germany	East Germany	Great Britain	USA	Austria
Patriotism	0.2555*** [0.0446]	0.1199** [0.0508]	0.3298*** [0.0782]	0.1764*** [0.0590]	0.2807*** [0.0572]	0.0536 [0.0559]
Chauvinism	0.3432*** [0.0368]	0.4638*** [0.0466]	0.3975*** [0.0682]	0.4947*** [0.0558]	0.4284*** [0.0464]	0.4504*** [0.0520]
Skill345	−0.2087*** [0.0531]	−0.2394*** [0.0792]	−0.3260** [0.1269]	−0.3403*** [0.0822]	−0.3248*** [0.0646]	−0.2427*** [0.0940]
National mobility	0.0235 [0.0555]	−0.2382*** [0.0726]	−0.3146*** [0.1079]	0.0942 [0.0839]	0.0487 [0.0762]	−0.1706** [0.0841]
International mobility	−0.1063 [0.0707]	−0.2263*** [0.0870]	−0.0530 [0.1604]	−0.1316 [0.0946]	0.0031 [0.0925]	−0.1257 [0.1088]
Never lived abroad	0.1358** [0.0618]	0.1356 [0.0956]	0.3172 [0.2088]	0.0415 [0.0930]	0.0682 [0.0835]	0.1329 [0.1085]
Native	0.0804 [0.1517]	0.1661 [0.2457]	1.5934* [0.8838]	0.0019 [0.2363]	0.1027 [0.2778]	−0.5752** [0.2689]
Native parents	−0.1709 [0.1401]	−0.2020 [0.2223]	−1.1386 [0.7053]	0.1710 [0.2337]	0.0563 [0.2653]	0.6279** [0.2465]
Age	−0.0159 [0.0119]	0.0147 [0.0131]	−0.0106 [0.0205]	0.0254** [0.0128]	0.0286** [0.0113]	0.0099 [0.0116]
Age squared	0.0002 [0.0001]	−0.0002 [0.0001]	0.0001 [0.0002]	−0.0002* [0.0001]	−0.0003** [0.0001]	−0.0001 [0.0001]
Female	0.3258*** [0.0522]	0.3708*** [0.0668]	0.6695*** [0.1010]	0.2217*** [0.0755]	0.1663*** [0.0634]	0.3016*** [0.0720]
Married	−0.0235 [0.0634]	−0.1244 [0.0789]	0.0247 [0.1160]	−0.0310 [0.0777]	0.0839 [0.0639]	0.1429* [0.0796]
Catholic	0.0695 [0.0608]	0.0535 [0.0670]	0.0606 [0.2462]	0.1018 [0.1176]	−0.0142 [0.0720]	−0.1011 [0.0910]
Un-employed	−0.0572 [0.1382]	0.0887 [0.1957]	0.2491 [0.1553]	0.2157 [0.1599]	0.1846 [0.1864]	−0.2144 [0.1736]
Cut1	−0.7244** [0.3403]	0.3004 [0.3233]	0.6345 [0.6688]	0.5813 [0.3619]	1.1999*** [0.3562]	0.0154 [0.3222]
Cut2	0.4602 [0.3263]	1.4560*** [0.3247]	1.7858*** [0.6661]	1.8647*** [0.3469]	2.1036*** [0.3574]	0.9426*** [0.3209]
Cut3	0.9978*** [0.3274]	2.1714*** [0.3276]	2.5158*** [0.6701]	2.6709*** [0.3517]	2.8997*** [0.3616]	1.4623*** [0.3235]
Cut4	2.2817*** [0.3301]	3.1295*** [0.3332]	3.5303*** [0.6753]	3.9466*** [0.3615]	4.2290*** [0.3708]	2.4259*** [0.3289]
No. of observations	1877	1067	512	923	1225	985
Log likelihood	−2212.59	−1480.28	−664.43	−1139.25	−1530.54	−1251.86
Pseudo-R-squared	0.07	0.10	0.14	0.10	0.09	0.09

	(7)	(8)	(9)	(10)	(11)	(12)
	Hungary	Italy	Ireland	Nether-lands	Norway	Sweden
Patriotism	0.0551 [0.0542]	0.1766*** [0.0493]	0.2146*** [0.0575]	0.0781* [0.0400]	0.2171*** [0.0522]	0.3390*** [0.0520]
Chauvinism	0.2131*** [0.0476]	0.2984*** [0.0541]	0.3735*** [0.0579]	0.4806*** [0.0395]	0.2797*** [0.0437]	0.3575*** [0.0469]
Skill345	−0.0455 [0.0832]		−0.2143** [0.0857]	−0.1716*** [0.0540]	−0.2049*** [0.0614]	
National mobility	−0.0302 [0.0842]	0.0660 [0.0727]	−0.0353 [0.0832]	−0.0325 [0.0551]	−0.0931 [0.0639]	−0.1104 [0.0710]
International mobility	−0.1429 [0.1267]	−0.0231 [0.0893]	−0.1055 [0.1072]	−0.0973 [0.0675]	−0.2835*** [0.0833]	−0.2649*** [0.0847]
Never lived abroad	0.0184 [0.1599]	0.2647** [0.1078]	0.1836** [0.0811]	0.1485** [0.0736]	0.1604** [0.0742]	0.1952** [0.0852]
Native	−0.8959** [0.3914]	0.1237 [0.5965]	−0.4066 [0.2558]	0.1089 [0.2538]	0.2799 [0.2240]	0.4316 [0.3256]
Native parents	0.3273 [0.2724]	−0.0242 [0.2703]	−0.3261* [0.1917]	−0.1300 [0.2327]	−0.2287 [0.1932]	−0.6031* [0.3105]
Age	0.0062 [0.0122]	0.0143 [0.0148]	0.0111 [0.0138]	0.0103 [0.0093]	−0.0081 [0.0105]	0.0118 [0.0130]
Age squared	−0.0000 [0.0001]	−0.0002 [0.0002]	−0.0001 [0.0001]	−0.0001 [0.0001]	0.0001 [0.0001]	−0.0001 [0.0001]
Female	0.0656 [0.0735]	0.2150*** [0.0659]	0.3492*** [0.0730]	0.3406*** [0.0506]	0.2370*** [0.0577]	0.5068*** [0.0638]
Married	−0.0063 [0.0757]	0.1162 [0.0815]	−0.0776 [0.0829]	0.0852 [0.0605]	0.0588 [0.0695]	−0.0739 [0.0731]
Catholic	−0.0219 [0.0776]	−0.1304 [0.1710]	0.0698 [0.1343]	0.0584 [0.0624]	−0.9099** [0.4175]	−0.3315 [0.2897]
Un-employed	0.1306 [0.1418]	0.0745 [0.1792]	0.2189* [0.1273]	−0.0491 [0.1251]	0.1349 [0.1483]	0.2740** [0.1245]
Cut1	−1.4153*** [0.4183]	0.5839 [0.6489]	−0.3938 [0.4560]	0.3055 [0.2599]	−0.2325 [0.3207]	0.8668** [0.3583]
Cut2	−0.7563* [0.4138]	1.4071** [0.6476]	0.9237** [0.4419]	1.7456*** [0.2603]	0.9902*** [0.3185]	1.8561*** [0.3574]
Cut3	0.0136 [0.4110]	1.9248*** [0.6479]	1.3130*** [0.4431]	2.6989*** [0.2623]	1.9691*** [0.3204]	2.9802*** [0.3637]
Cut4	0.7238* [0.4111]	2.8932*** [0.6488]	2.5078*** [0.4463]	3.9858*** [0.2709]	3.1494*** [0.3264]	4.0949*** [0.3734]
No. of ob-servations	983	1084	942	1853	1391	1186
Log likelihood	−1251.18	−1553.23	−1221.08	−2363.53	−1844.13	−1540.38
Pseudo-R-squared	0.02	0.04	0.06	0.07	0.07	0.11

	(13)	(14)	(15)	(16)	(17)	(18)
	Czech Rep.	Slovenia	Poland	Bulgaria	Russia	New Zealand
Patriotism	0.1547*** [0.0534]	0.2286*** [0.0544]	0.2071*** [0.0600]	0.1000* [0.0517]	0.2281*** [0.0402]	0.1223* [0.0631]
Chauvinism	0.3188*** [0.0496]	0.3749*** [0.0538]	0.2448*** [0.0597]	0.3817*** [0.0551]	0.2932*** [0.0388]	0.4073*** [0.0521]
Skill345	−0.1966*** [0.0729]	−0.4022*** [0.0838]	0.0222 [0.0794]	0.1294 [0.0894]	−0.1738** [0.0728]	−0.2421*** [0.0827]
National mobility	−0.0649 [0.0740]	−0.0985 [0.0780]	−0.0263 [0.0715]	0.0296 [0.0856]	0.1257* [0.0709]	−0.0346 [0.0808]
International mobility	−0.1304 [0.1167]	−0.0340 [0.1209]	−0.0222 [0.0885]	−0.2124** [0.1004]	−0.0401 [0.0995]	0.0059 [0.0920]
Never lived abroad	0.0703 [0.1133]	0.1370 [0.0851]	0.1406 [0.1188]	0.1380 [0.1066]	−0.1945 [0.1458]	0.1621* [0.0839]
Native	−0.6694* [0.3824]	−0.3807** [0.1882]	0.6276* [0.3690]	−0.0129 [0.4177]	0.5217 [0.3919]	−0.2263 [0.2239]
Native parents	0.1537 [0.2525]	0.1932 [0.1671]	−0.6299** [0.2523]	0.7981*** [0.2394]	−0.1941 [0.3528]	0.1369 [0.2065]
Age	−0.0031 [0.0134]	−0.0186 [0.0138]	0.0113 [0.0126]	0.0276** [0.0133]	0.0284*** [0.0101]	0.0027 [0.0141]
Age squared	0.0001 [0.0001]	0.0002 [0.0001]	−0.0002 [0.0001]	−0.0002* [0.0001]	−0.0002 [0.0001]	0.0000 [0.0001]
Female	0.2132*** [0.0692]	0.1194* [0.0710]	0.0244 [0.0697]	0.0169 [0.0739]	0.0790 [0.0567]	0.2428*** [0.0725]
Married	0.0694 [0.0803]	−0.0053 [0.0812]	−0.0713 [0.0826]	0.0705 [0.0878]	0.1401** [0.0613]	−0.1726** [0.0843]
Catholic	0.0933 [0.0734]	0.0747 [0.0855]	0.0614 [0.1025]	−0.6094*** [0.1692]	0.0478 [1.0353]	−0.0675 [0.1089]
Un-employed	−0.0565 [0.2562]	−0.0549 [0.1308]	0.0915 [0.1404]	0.1030 [0.1172]	0.0663 [0.1117]	−0.0226 [0.1867]
Cut1	−0.1467 [0.4185]	−0.4850 [0.3470]	−0.1140 [0.4521]	1.6706*** [0.5222]	1.2945*** [0.3445]	0.0797 [0.4284]
Cut2	0.6079 [0.4191]	0.7362** [0.3388]	0.7941* [0.4528]	1.9691*** [0.5197]	2.0614*** [0.3423]	1.1461*** [0.4187]
Cut3	1.2235*** [0.4211]	1.4911*** [0.3422]	1.5049*** [0.4545]	2.6696*** [0.5225]	2.6419*** [0.3448]	1.7926*** [0.4196]
Cut4	2.0054*** [0.4233]	2.3164*** [0.3460]	2.4589*** [0.4574]	3.4136*** [0.5250]	3.3397*** [0.3481]	2.8628*** [0.4217]
No. of observations	994	993	1043	1050	1566	893
Log likelihood	−1458.69	−1370.44	−1446.36	−1184.65	−2195.17	−1251.33
Pseudo-R-squared	0.06	0.07	0.03	0.06	0.06	0.06

	(19)	(20)	(21)	(22)	(23)	(24)
	Canada	Philip-pines	Japan	Spain	Latvia	Slovakia
Patriotism	0.0908** [0.0447]	0.1929*** [0.0572]	0.1441*** [0.0500]	0.1269** [0.0550]	0.1048** [0.0477]	0.2921*** [0.0449]
Chauvinism	0.3879*** [0.0457]	0.1903*** [0.0626]	0.3015*** [0.0400]	0.2956*** [0.0619]	0.2569*** [0.0497]	0.1678*** [0.0404]
Skill345	−0.0678 [0.0695]	0.0055 [0.1654]		−0.0578 [0.1019]	−0.0494 [0.1027]	0.0559 [0.0743]
National mobility	0.1580** [0.0767]	0.1235* [0.0719]	0.0061 [0.0694]	0.1569** [0.0726]	0.0121 [0.0894]	0.0271 [0.0643]
International mobility	−0.0961 [0.0804]	0.1248 [0.0765]	−0.1388 [0.1269]	0.0937 [0.0965]	−0.0213 [0.1166]	−0.1289* [0.0765]
Never lived abroad	0.0458 [0.0787]	0.0118 [0.1171]	0.1447 [0.1487]	−0.1946* [0.1074]	−0.0255 [0.1042]	0.1228 [0.1011]
Native	0.2452 [0.1626]	−0.5194 [0.3208]		0.3537*** [0.0976]	0.0017 [0.1354]	−0.4517 [0.3207]
Native parents	−0.1970 [0.1428]	−0.4163* [0.2182]	0.3030 [0.2244]	0.3334 [0.2699]	0.2176* [0.1247]	0.2845 [0.2072]
Age	−0.0086 [0.0123]	0.0005 [0.0116]	−0.0541*** [0.0113]	0.0116 [0.0108]	0.0244 [0.0154]	0.0152 [0.0118]
Age squared	0.0001 [0.0001]	−0.0000 [0.0001]	0.0005*** [0.0001]	−0.0002 [0.0001]	−0.0002 [0.0002]	−0.0001 [0.0001]
Female	0.2290*** [0.0633]	−0.0045 [0.0637]	0.4068*** [0.0628]	0.1372** [0.0658]	−0.0664 [0.0786]	0.1365** [0.0594]
Married	0.0760 [0.0714]	0.0617 [0.0755]	0.1528* [0.0860]	0.0892 [0.0809]	−0.0918 [0.0808]	−0.0006 [0.0683]
Catholic	0.0195 [0.0652]	−0.0529 [0.0920]	0.4129 [0.5195]	0.4218*** [0.1240]	0.1623 [0.1013]	0.0851 [0.0611]
Un-employed	0.4242** [0.1828]	0.2199 [0.1582]	−0.1006 [0.3267]	0.1069 [0.1091]	0.0133 [0.1253]	−0.1245 [0.1239]
Cut1	−0.1839 [0.3475]	−1.9101*** [0.4886]	0.0324 [0.3559]	0.1656 [0.4003]	0.0510 [0.3569]	0.2988 [0.3721]
Cut2	0.8776** [0.3463]	−0.4834 [0.4759]	0.5485 [0.3576]	1.3108*** [0.4099]	0.6901* [0.3542]	1.0663*** [0.3739]
Cut3	1.6362*** [0.3490]	0.0950 [0.4757]	1.5325*** [0.3596]	2.0450*** [0.4106]	1.2806*** [0.3593]	1.6687*** [0.3762]
Cut4	2.6894*** [0.3530]	1.7006*** [0.4790]	2.1536*** [0.3624]	3.4891*** [0.4165]	1.8672*** [0.3615]	2.4750*** [0.3789]
No. of observations	1149	1197	1228	1184	974	1346
Log likelihood	−1631.23	−1444.71	−1806.41	−1420.20	−1230.11	−1967.98
Pseudo-R-squared	0.04	0.02	0.05	0.04	0.04	0.05

Note: Robust standard errors in brackets. * significant at 10%; ** significant at 5%; *** significant at 1%.

Appendix 2. Country-specific regressions: Anti-immigration

	(1)	(2)	(3)	(4)	(5)	(6)
	Australia	West Germany	East Germany	Great Britain	USA	Austria
Patriotism	0.1691***	0.1265**	0.1589*	0.0990	0.1471**	0.0634
	[0.0432]	[0.0548]	[0.0833]	[0.0674]	[0.0579]	[0.0544]
Chauvinism	0.4498***	0.5690***	0.4891***	0.5841***	0.2095***	0.4231***
	[0.0358]	[0.0588]	[0.0764]	[0.0616]	[0.0499]	[0.0514]
Skill345	−0.1802***	−0.2595***	−0.1637	−0.1326	−0.0748	−0.1088
	[0.0521]	[0.0931]	[0.1359]	[0.0857]	[0.0676]	[0.0992]
National mobility	0.0224	0.0363	0.0700	−0.0544	0.0067	−0.2066**
	[0.0555]	[0.0871]	[0.1231]	[0.0887]	[0.0849]	[0.0855]
International mobility	−0.0030	−0.2028**	0.1327	−0.1020	−0.3167***	−0.2189
	[0.0692]	[0.0957]	[0.1935]	[0.1084]	[0.1008]	[0.1362]
Never lived abroad	0.2430***	−0.0019	0.3382	0.0314	0.1171	0.0214
	[0.0609]	[0.1107]	[0.2487]	[0.0976]	[0.0948]	[0.1147]
Native	0.0029	0.1572	−0.3647	0.0397	−0.2970	−0.1517
	[0.1328]	[0.2965]	[0.7416]	[0.2545]	[0.2391]	[0.2823]
Native parents	0.0076	0.4100	0.0633	0.1442	0.6886***	0.2090
	[0.1227]	[0.2581]	[0.6680]	[0.2566]	[0.2241]	[0.2570]
Age	−0.0158	0.0198	−0.0120	0.0229*	0.0177	0.0171
	[0.0112]	[0.0145]	[0.0236]	[0.0132]	[0.0122]	[0.0134]
Age squared	0.0001	−0.0002	0.0001	−0.0002*	−0.0002	−0.0002
	[0.0001]	[0.0001]	[0.0003]	[0.0001]	[0.0001]	[0.0001]
Female	0.2092***	0.0680	−0.0099	−0.1179	0.1091	−0.0283
	[0.0519]	[0.0783]	[0.1118]	[0.0802]	[0.0686]	[0.0742]
Married	0.0659	0.1019	0.1030	0.1176	0.0198	−0.0454
	[0.0632]	[0.0935]	[0.1361]	[0.0835]	[0.0691]	[0.0879]
Catholic	−0.2299***	0.0076	0.1096	−0.1125	−0.1233	−0.1587
	[0.0639]	[0.0774]	[0.2781]	[0.1231]	[0.0754]	[0.0990]
Un-employed	0.0093	0.4226	0.1199	−0.0102	−0.2691	−0.3207
	[0.2047]	[0.2809]	[0.1963]	[0.1775]	[0.2093]	[0.1979]
Cut1	−0.6585**	−0.2309	−1.1444*	0.2445	0.0459	−0.8801**
	[0.3214]	[0.4137]	[0.6673]	[0.3795]	[0.3831]	[0.3892]
Cut2	0.2559	0.6449*	−0.6495	0.8527**	0.5854	−0.1508
	[0.3163]	[0.3734]	[0.6349]	[0.3865]	[0.3856]	[0.3699]
Cut3	1.3103***	2.0472***	0.7616	2.3958***	1.6754***	1.6863***
	[0.3186]	[0.3683]	[0.6215]	[0.3963]	[0.3945]	[0.3726]
Cut4	2.2328***	2.8951***	1.5257**	3.1593***	2.5030***	2.4364***
	[0.3212]	[0.3737]	[0.6265]	[0.4011]	[0.3998]	[0.3760]
No. of observations	1831	963	478	870	1074	927
Log likelihood	−2322.91	−970.49	−462.17	−959.05	−1381.60	−1061.30
Pseudo-R-squared	0.08	0.13	0.09	0.10	0.05	0.07

	(7)	(8)	(9)	(10)	(11)	(12)
	Hungary	Italy	Ireland	Nether-lands	Norway	Sweden
Patriotism	0.0786	0.0861*	−0.0342	0.0331	0.1340**	0.0822
	[0.0588]	[0.0490]	[0.0604]	[0.0423]	[0.0533]	[0.0536]
Chauvinism	0.0909*	0.3801***	0.2621***	0.6969***	0.6451***	0.7179***
	[0.0513]	[0.0545]	[0.0595]	[0.0438]	[0.0465]	[0.0495]
Skill345	−0.1860**		−0.0084	−0.1249**	−0.2383***	
	[0.0881]		[0.0832]	[0.0580]	[0.0659]	
National mobility	0.0275	−0.0722	−0.2395***	−0.0418	−0.0327	0.0017
	[0.0890]	[0.0795]	[0.0868]	[0.0598]	[0.0672]	[0.0755]
International mobility	0.0242	−0.0076	−0.0514	−0.1015	−0.2068**	−0.1199
	[0.1422]	[0.0899]	[0.1164]	[0.0688]	[0.0926]	[0.0860]
Never lived abroad	0.1301	0.0751	0.1356	0.0093	−0.0838	0.0153
	[0.1721]	[0.1189]	[0.0833]	[0.0801]	[0.0829]	[0.0952]
Native	0.4473	−0.1864	−0.2027	0.0823	0.3568*	−0.6224**
	[0.4180]	[0.4917]	[0.3183]	[0.2817]	[0.2144]	[0.2758]
Native parents	−0.0329	−0.6629	0.0064	0.5540**	0.2391	0.6648***
	[0.3814]	[0.4079]	[0.2273]	[0.2314]	[0.1512]	[0.2473]
Age	0.0015	−0.0101	−0.0242	0.0052	0.0072	0.0088
	[0.0124]	[0.0158]	[0.0149]	[0.0103]	[0.0113]	[0.0140]
Age squared	0.0000	0.0001	0.0003*	−0.0000	−0.0001	−0.0002
	[0.0001]	[0.0002]	[0.0001]	[0.0001]	[0.0001]	[0.0001]
Female	0.1316*	0.0808	0.0160	0.0123	−0.0850	0.0205
	[0.0787]	[0.0713]	[0.0750]	[0.0534]	[0.0616]	[0.0676]
Married	0.0267	0.0776	0.0646	0.1711***	−0.1830**	0.0413
	[0.0802]	[0.0881]	[0.0872]	[0.0652]	[0.0752]	[0.0762]
Catholic	−0.0222	0.0705	0.4111**	0.1286*	0.1722	0.7988*
	[0.0797]	[0.1558]	[0.1744]	[0.0661]	[0.8406]	[0.4165]
Un-employed	0.1279	0.0711	0.0742	−0.1916	0.1571	−0.0086
	[0.1434]	[0.2171]	[0.1375]	[0.1485]	[0.1823]	[0.1165]
Cut1	−1.2354***	−1.8930***	−1.5440***	0.1337	0.1577	0.2074
	[0.4452]	[0.4957]	[0.5401]	[0.3170]	[0.3268]	[0.3848]
Cut2	−0.9748**	−1.2968***	−0.4081	1.0221***	1.1489***	0.7844**
	[0.4370]	[0.4949]	[0.5339]	[0.2985]	[0.3170]	[0.3851]
Cut3	0.2251	−0.1063	1.3235**	2.6047***	2.5250***	1.9677***
	[0.4422]	[0.4947]	[0.5381]	[0.3013]	[0.3212]	[0.3864]
Cut4	1.0080**	0.8108	2.0470***	3.6460***	3.5019***	2.9487***
	[0.4466]	[0.4958]	[0.5440]	[0.3061]	[0.3247]	[0.3916]
No. of observations	937	1033	885	1744	1311	1105
Log likelihood	−939.29	−1169.78	−1004.79	−1962.22	−1515.48	−1275.69
Pseudo-R-squared	0.01	0.05	0.03	0.12	0.13	0.12

	(13)	(14)	(15)	(16)	(17)	(18)
	Czech Rep.	Slovenia	Poland	Bulgaria	Russia	New Zealand
Patriotism	0.1340** [0.0532]	0.1365** [0.0590]	0.1544** [0.0671]	0.0786 [0.0554]	0.0562 [0.0464]	0.1622*** [0.0627]
Chauvinism	0.1895*** [0.0536]	0.3389*** [0.0584]	0.1338** [0.0682]	0.0030 [0.0666]	0.1177** [0.0484]	0.3535*** [0.0531]
Skill345	−0.2979*** [0.0805]	−0.2013** [0.0859]	−0.2489** [0.0975]	−0.0252 [0.1012]	−0.0819 [0.0853]	−0.2602*** [0.0883]
National mobility	0.1201 [0.0809]	0.1017 [0.0846]	−0.0107 [0.0908]	−0.3727*** [0.1060]	0.0729 [0.0881]	−0.0163 [0.0855]
International mobility	−0.1818 [0.1399]	0.0830 [0.1225]	0.1208 [0.1144]	0.2454** [0.1187]	0.0381 [0.1067]	−0.2254** [0.0928]
Never lived abroad	−0.1228 [0.1266]	0.0812 [0.0976]	0.2199 [0.1387]	−0.0297 [0.1355]	−0.0582 [0.1751]	0.1516* [0.0864]
Native	−0.0004 [0.3340]	0.2128 [0.2691]	−0.0964 [0.3124]	0.4477 [0.3495]	0.2104 [0.2758]	0.0660 [0.1790]
Native parents	0.0567 [0.2680]	0.4725* [0.2545]	0.1278 [0.2438]	0.6822** [0.2762]	0.0877 [0.2276]	0.2620* [0.1578]
Age	0.0120 [0.0150]	−0.0088 [0.0161]	0.0074 [0.0148]	0.0154 [0.0179]	−0.0050 [0.0126]	−0.0012 [0.0144]
Age squared	−0.0001 [0.0002]	0.0001 [0.0002]	0.0000 [0.0002]	−0.0001 [0.0002]	0.0001 [0.0001]	−0.0001 [0.0001]
Female	0.0534 [0.0769]	−0.1809** [0.0736]	0.2130** [0.0840]	0.2781*** [0.0917]	0.1357** [0.0677]	−0.0276 [0.0744]
Married	−0.1638* [0.0917]	−0.0041 [0.0973]	0.0352 [0.0991]	0.0434 [0.1128]	0.0112 [0.0728]	−0.0024 [0.0922]
Catholic	−0.0630 [0.0809]	0.1290 [0.0916]	0.0175 [0.1219]	−1.7180*** [0.6228]	0.2830 [0.2286]	−0.3312*** [0.1084]
Un-employed	−0.1091 [0.3196]	−0.3149** [0.1358]	−0.0932 [0.1559]	0.4441*** [0.1616]	0.2550** [0.1215]	0.3429* [0.1931]
Cut1	−1.6894*** [0.4608]	−0.9011** [0.4053]	−0.2647 [0.4545]	−0.0772 [0.5203]	−1.1187*** [0.4171]	−0.5046 [0.4168]
Cut2	−0.9684** [0.4264]	−0.3209 [0.3966]	0.3146 [0.4513]	0.3136 [0.5037]	−0.4916 [0.4123]	0.3382 [0.4084]
Cut3	0.4433 [0.4312]	1.5952*** [0.4029]	1.4038*** [0.4560]	1.1781** [0.5015]	0.7046* [0.4134]	1.3349*** [0.4081]
Cut4	1.2302*** [0.4342]	2.5002*** [0.4067]	2.1029*** [0.4589]	1.9981*** [0.5033]	1.6143*** [0.4153]	2.2716*** [0.4098]
No. of observations	886	932	718	672	1031	848
Log likelihood	−992.49	−1028.82	−931.24	−753.32	−1360.55	−1095.52
Pseudo-R-squared	0.03	0.06	0.04	0.04	0.01	0.08

	(19)	(20)	(21)	(22)	(23)	(24)
	Canada	Philip-pines	Japan	Spain	Latvia	Slovakia
Patriotism	−0.0562	0.0889*	0.2460***	0.0649	−0.0313	0.0284
	[0.0489]	[0.0513]	[0.0582]	[0.0539]	[0.0570]	[0.0506]
Chauvinism	0.4963***	−0.1309**	0.1261***	0.1415**	0.2737***	0.1093**
	[0.0502]	[0.0572]	[0.0450]	[0.0588]	[0.0581]	[0.0426]
Skill345	−0.1985***	0.0834		−0.0449	0.0744	−0.0930
	[0.0751]	[0.1556]		[0.1099]	[0.1091]	[0.0802]
National mobility	0.0289	0.0543	−0.1525**	−0.0344	0.0483	0.1247*
	[0.0820]	[0.0701]	[0.0763]	[0.0817]	[0.1011]	[0.0719]
International mobility	0.0106	−0.2241***	−0.0058	0.0264	0.1233	−0.0101
	[0.0840]	[0.0790]	[0.1367]	[0.0939]	[0.1339]	[0.0893]
Never lived abroad	0.2446***	0.2315*	0.5870***	−0.1017	0.1460	0.1228
	[0.0792]	[0.1187]	[0.1416]	[0.1084]	[0.1117]	[0.1167]
Native	0.3823**	0.1799		−0.0818	0.5318***	0.7441***
	[0.1645]	[0.2733]		[0.1426]	[0.1630]	[0.2658]
Native parents	−0.2197	−0.2215	0.2651*	0.3677**	0.5376***	−0.0520
	[0.1463]	[0.2722]	[0.1445] .	[0.1804]	[0.1372]	[0.1569]
Age	0.0110	0.0126	0.0023	0.0182	0.0221	0.0222*
	[0.0126]	[0.0129]	[0.0132]	[0.0125]	[0.0183]	[0.0133]
Age squared	−0.0001	−0.0001	0.0001	−0.0001	−0.0001	−0.0002
	[0.0001]	[0.0001]	[0.0001]	[0.0001]	[0.0002]	[0.0001]
Female	0.0876	−0.0773	0.3401***	−0.0379	−0.1101	0.0038
	[0.0687]	[0.0642]	[0.0678]	[0.0692]	[0.0913]	[0.0667]
Married	0.0100	−0.0137	0.0660	−0.0845	−0.1132	−0.0474
	[0.0745]	[0.0802]	[0.0971]	[0.0859]	[0.0968]	[0.0787]
Catholic	−0.2589***	0.1281	−0.9550	0.2370*	0.0848	0.1233*
	[0.0724]	[0.0909]	[0.5857]	[0.1351]	[0.1110]	[0.0689]
Un-employed	0.1409	0.1958	−0.1018	0.0173	−0.1497	0.1495
	[0.2236]	[0.1881]	[0.2741]	[0.1147]	[0.1408]	[0.1564]
Cut1	−0.1012	−1.4339***	0.6026*	−0.7925**	−0.6815	−0.5833
	[0.3762]	[0.4578]	[0.3466]	[0.3760]	[0.4748]	[0.3766]
Cut2	0.6242*	−0.8690*	1.4900***	0.0852	1.7902***	−0.0320
	[0.3711]	[0.4544]	[0.3525]	[0.3657]	[0.4396]	[0.3708]
Cut3	1.8080***	0.0535	2.8113***	1.7354***	2.4255***	1.4411***
	[0.3743]	[0.4555]	[0.3596]	[0.3744]	[0.4437]	[0.3703]
Cut4	2.5966***	0.7908*	3.6732***	2.8048***		2.2202***
	[0.3794]	[0.4567]	[0.3650]	[0.3791]		[0.3716]
No. of observations	1009	1144	1024	1045	813	1102
Log likelihood	−1380.09	−1586.02	−1335.87	−1211.95	−758.86	−1318.47
Pseudo-R-squared	0.06	0.01	0.06	0.01	0.12	0.02

Note: Robust standard errors in brackets. * significant at 10%; ** significant at 5%; *** significant at 1%.

Acknowledgments

This essay was in part written while the author was an IRCHSS Government of Ireland Senior Fellow. I thank the Irish Research Council for the Humanities and Social Sciences for its generous support. I am extremely grateful to Richard Sinnott for allowing me to draw on our joint work, and I also wish to thank Kevin Denny, Chris Minns, and participants at the Eli Heckscher Celebratory Symposium for helpful suggestions. The usual disclaimer applies.

Notes

1. Since beginning this project, Sinnott and I became aware of the independent work that was being done on the same issues by Anna Maria Mayda and Dani Rodrik (Mayda and Rodrik 2005; Mayda 2006). While their findings confirm our own, they use different methods and measures of skill, and the essay will allude to these differences when our own empirical findings are discussed.

2. Furthermore, it is no longer the case that trade and factor flows are necessarily substitutes: they could instead be complements. For example, Markusen (1983) shows that technological differences between countries can lead to trade and factor mobility being complements; while in the context of a three-factor model such as the specific-factors model, trade, and factor mobility can be either substitutes or complements (O'Rourke and Williamson 1999).

3. In principle, self-selection should depend not only on income distribution within host countries, but also on the relationship between host-country and source-country income distribution. A complete test of the Borjas theory would thus involve calculating source country distributions for each host country. In this essay I make the simplifying assumption that source-country distributions are sufficiently similar for all host countries that self-selection varies across host countries based on differences in host-country distributions alone.

4. The next section draws on O'Rourke and Sinnott (2001).

5. Details available on request.

6. The data are available online at http://devdata.worldbank.org/dataonline/.

7. Note that in the context of an ordered probit model, a significant positive coefficient indicates that increasing the relevant independent variable increases the probability that "protect" takes on the value 5, and reduces the probability that "protect" takes on the value 1. The impact on the probabilities that "protect" takes on the values 2–4 is, however, a priori unclear. Nonetheless, in what follows I will speak loosely of variables being either positively or negatively related to antiglobalization sentiment. See Greene (2000:875–879) for further details.

8. These results, and similar ones quoted in the next section, were calculated using the CLARIFY programme described in Tomz, Wittenberg, and King (1999) and King, Tomz, and Wittenberg (2000).

9. Country dummy variables are obviously omitted from these regressions, as is the interaction term between Skill345 and GDP.

10. See Greene (2000:849–856).

References

Barro, R. J., and J.-W. Lee. 2000. "International Data on Educational Attainment: Updates and Implications." *Harvard Center for International Development Working Paper* No. 42. Available at http://www.cid.harvard.edu/ciddata/ciddata.html.

Borjas, G. J. 1987. "Self-Selection and the Earnings of Immigrants." *American Economic Review* 77:531–553.

Bowen, H. P., E. E. Leamer, and L. Sveikauskas. 1987. "Multicountry, Multifactor Tests of the Factor Abundance Theory." *American Economic Review* 77:791–809.

Davis, D. R., and D. E. Weinstein. 2001. "An Account of Global Factor Trade." *American Economic Review* 91:1423–1453.

Greene, W. H. 2000. *Econometric Analysis*. London: Prentice-Hall.

ILO. 1990. *International Standard Classification of Occupations: ISCO-88*. Geneva: International Labour Organization.

Katz, E., and O. Stark. 1984. "Migration and Asymmetric Information: Comment." *American Economic Review* 74:533–534.

———. 1987. "International Migration Under Asymmetric Information." *Economic Journal* 97:718–726.

King, G., M. Tomz, and J. Wittenberg. 2000. "Making the Most of Statistical Analyses: Improving Interpretation and Presentation." *American Journal of Political Science* 44:341–355.

Leontief, W. 1953. "Domestic Production and Foreign Trade: The American Capital Position Re-Examined." *Proceedings of the American Philosophical Society* 97:332–349.

Markusen, J. R. 1983. "Factor Movements and Commodity Trade as Complements." *Journal of International Economics* 13:341–356.

Mayda, A. M. 2006. "Who Is Against Immigration? A Cross-Country Investigation of Individual Attitudes Towards Immigrants." *Review of Economics and Statistics*, forthcoming.

Mayda, A. M., and D. Rodrik. 2005. "Why Are Some People (and Countries) More Protectionist than Others?" *European Economic Review* 49: 1393–1691.

Mundell, R. A. 1957. "International Trade and Factor Mobility." *American Economic Review* 47:321–335.

O'Rourke, K. H., and R. Sinnott. 2001. "What Determines Attitudes Towards Protection? Some Cross-country Evidence." In S. M. Collins and D. Rodrik, eds., *Brookings Trade Forum 2001*, 157–206. Washington, DC: Brookings Institute Press.

———. 2006. "The Determinants of Individual Attitudes Towards Immigration." *European Journal of Political Economy*, forthcoming.

O'Rourke, K. H., and J. G. Williamson. 1999. *Globalization and History: The Evolution of a Nineteenth-Century Atlantic Economy.* Cambridge, MA: MIT Press.

Rodrik, D. 1997. *Has Globalization Gone Too Far?* Washington, DC: Institute for International Economics.

Roy, A. D. 1951. "Some Thoughts on the Distribution of Earnings." *Oxford Economic Papers* 3:135–146.

Scheve, K. F., and M. J. Slaughter. 2001a. "Labour Market Competition and Individual Preferences Over Immigration Policy." *Review of Economics and Statistics* 83:133–145.

———. 2001b. "What Determines Individual Trade-Policy Preferences?" *Journal of International Economics* 54:267–292.

Tomz, M., J. Wittenberg, and G. King. 1999. CLARIFY: Software for interpreting and presenting statistical results. Version 1.1.1. Available at http://gking.harvard.edu.

Part III

Historical Applications of Heckscher-Ohlin Theory

6   Mediterranean Trade in Biblical Times

Peter Temin

.This essay analyzes trade in the Mediterranean Sea in biblical times, revealing that the forces Heckscher identified as stimulating trade were effective even before coinage was invented. The first part of the essay describes how we have come to be aware of this trade and what this trade appears to have been like. The second part inquires into the economics of this trade, inferring economic actions and organizations from the physical evidence.

Heckscher said in his classic 1919 paper, "The prerequisites for initiating international trade may thus be summarized as different relative scarcity, that is, different relative prices of the factors of production in the exchanging countries, as well as different propor-tions between the factors of production in different commodities" (Heckscher and Ohlin 1991:48). In the modern world, we reason as Heckscher did from relative scarcities and prices to the existence of in-ternational trade. When we study the ancient world, we are at the mercy of our sources, that is, to the accidents of history by which some evidence is preserved and much is lost. We therefore have to reason in the reverse direction, from the existence of trade to relative scarcities and prices. Some of these backward inferences can be verified from the archaeological record, but typically not prices.

Archaeology

Underwater archaeology until recently was confined to the exploration of shallow waters. There is no lack of ancient shipwrecks in the coastal waters of the Mediterranean, and some of them have been found and described. It seemed reasonable to archaeologists that these ships were representative of ancient shipping, as opposed to representing what they could find. They therefore inferred that ancient shipping followed the coastline.

This view has changed in the past generation as our ability to explore the seabed has improved. The biggest single innovation was in sonar, where "Doc" Edgerton developed side-scan sonar. This new technology allowed modern investigators to find shipwrecks in deep water, even if they were imbedded in the mud bottom. Sonar has been used to find modern wrecks, from the *Bismarck* in the Atlantic Ocean to Israeli warships in the Mediterranean. It also was used to find ancient shipwrecks in deep water.

Deep-water wrecks are very different from those in shallow water. Wrecks in shallow water landed on the bottom at all angles. They also typically have been buffeted by tides and currents, disturbed by fishermen, or looted by earlier explorers. Ships that foundered in deep water sank far through the water to the sea bottom, turning upright as the shape of their hulls offered the least resistance to the water. The ships then sat on the bottom or sank into the mud bottom upright, as if at sea. The wood used in ship construction rotted or was eaten, leaving the cargo in place or laying it down in a kind of projection of the ship onto the sea floor.

Two such sunken ships date from the latter half of the eighth century BCE, and they provide the central evidence for this paper. This evidence will be supplemented by customs records a little later and from older coastal wrecks. I need at this point to acknowledge my debt to the marine archaeologists who have found and described these relics of the past, and to Lawrence Stager of Harvard University, who has guided me through the archaeological literature.

The two eighth century ships were found far from the shore on a line from the northern Sinai coast and the Nile Delta. Ancient ships had their galleys in the rear, which indicates that the ships probably were going west toward Egypt. (This is only a probable determination since the ships may have been fleeing a storm when they foundered.) The ships might have been destined for the new Phoenician colony at Carthage, but their location and cargo suggest they were bound for Egypt. The ships can be identified as Phoenician and dated to the eighth century by the pottery that was on board.

The two ships were 14–14.5 meters long and ·5.5–6 meters wide. Their wide berth, one-third of their length, marks them as cargo ships rather than the sleeker and faster warships of the time (Casson

1991:75–80). They are roughly the same size as a thirteenth century BCE shallow-water wreck. Each of the ships was full of amphoras, approximately four hundred to a ship. Amphoras were the common container of the ancient world, like the plastic gallon jugs of the modern era. Amphoras were made in three parts, a cylinder about as long as a potter's forearm, a pointed bottom, and a top with a small opening. The shape seems odd to us, living in a world of flat surfaces. But amphoras were made to be packed into ships with sloping sides, in overlapping rows held in place by ropes through their small handles. They were stored on land in structures with dirt or sand floors into which the amphora bottoms could be sunk. They were not used much for overland transport.

The amphoras, surprisingly, are of roughly the same size. Eleven of them have been raised, and they average eighteen liters capacity, ranging only from sixteen to twenty liters. Their external dimensions were even more uniform. The presence of four hundred virtually identical amphoras on each of these ships suggests strongly that some form of trade was under way when these ships foundered. A computer-generated image of the shipwreck as it was found, showing the amphoras still in some sort of order on the sea floor, is shown in figure 6.1. This picture was the first evidence I saw of this trade, and it stimulated me to write this essay.

These amphoras were made in Phoenicia, an identification that can be made definitively from the presence in the pottery of an algae found only in coastal deposits of what is now Lebanon. They were made in a shape found in sites around that area, a shape that was recognizable elsewhere as being from Phoenicia and quite possibly as a guarantee of the standardized volume of the amphoras. A few amphora "factories" consisting of several kilns have been found from this period, and it is likely that the amphoras in our ships came from one or two of them. Amphoras made in Phoenician style have been found in many Egyptian sites of slightly later dates, suggesting that these ships—or other ships if not these particular ones—could have been destined for Egypt (Maeir 2002).

The amphoras originally contained wine, though they were full of mud, not wine, when found. The unbaked stoppers on the amphoras had dissolved, and mud had scoured out the amphora interiors. The mud did not clean the amphoras completely, and we can see that they had been lined with pine pitch from a common conifer found at

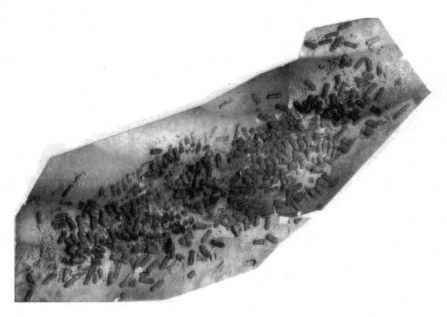

Figure 6.1
An eighth-century shipwreck as it "appears" today
Source: Ballard et al. (2002:156). Courtesy of H. Singh and J. Howland

the time in the Mediterranean area. This resin lining had trapped tartaric acid, found in grapes and grape products, from the amphoras' contents.

The Phoenician hinterland produced wine, some of which was regarded highly in ancient sources. The wine would have been grown away from the coast and shipped overland to the Phoenician coast. It appears to have been carried in *dannu* vessels that contained ten times as much as amphoras. Ezekial spoke of *danê yayin me'uzal*, which can be translated as "(large) containers of wine from Izalla," an ancient town in modern Turkey (Ballard et al. 2002).

Far earlier in time, the discovery of a thirteenth century BCE shipwreck off the coast of Turkey, the Uluburun wreck, "is yet another indicator of an eastern Mediterranean sea route for the east-west transport of copper, tin, and other raw materials during the Late Bronze Age" (Pulak 1998:191). This ship contained about 500 copper ingots, 150 jars containing glass beads, olives, and—mostly—what appears to be resin. The ship may have been transporting wine like the later ships, but this ship may have been simply transporting the resin as there is no tartaric acid in these amphoras. There also was a variety of glass beads, jewelry, and ceramics. And there were some weapons: four short swords and several daggers, arrowheads, and spearheads.

The shipwreck contained remains of three balances and almost 150 weights. Half the weights had been carefully finished in a variety of zoomorphic shapes. The weights are not marked to indicate their weight, but we presume that ancient merchants did not have to choose among the full set. They each probably had a few sets, whose weights were easily distinguished. Archaeologists, being without the cloth or leather pouches that originally contained the weights, have had to search for order among them. They hypothesized a base weight and looked to see if many weights were simple multiples or fractions of this weight. Assuming a standard unit of 9.3 grams, they found weights that appeared to range from simple fractions of this value up to fifty units. Not all weights fit into this scheme, and statistical analysis suggested that there were at least three different weight standards represented on this ship. The main standard, based on 9.3 grams, "undoubtedly represents a *shekel* of the 'Syrian' standard, a standard that was based on the Egyptian *qedet*" (Pulak 2000:259). The second most frequently found group of weights was slightly lighter, about 8.3 grams, and corresponded to a Mesopotamian standard. A third group was even lighter, and there was a hint from a few weights of even a fourth group.

We have also from about this time a Theban tomb painting that shows the scene of Syrian ships arriving in Egypt. The scene records several ships, some in the process of discharging their cargo, ranging from amphoras to live bullocks. Near the ships are three stalls where Egyptian men and women are engaged in what appear to be sales. They have textile samples hanging with other possible goods below, and two men in separate booths are holding balance scales. The disposition of most of the cargo is unclear, as the surviving picture shows them being carried to a missing destination. Archaeologists therefore have interpreted the stalls as private enterprise set up to deal along the margins of trade. This painting clearly shows the presence of market transactions in interregional trade, but it leaves open the extent to which the trade was bought and sold, as opposed to being accepted as tribute or other obligation (Davies and Faulkner 1947).

The Uluburun wreck and Egyptian painting reveal the existence of trade in the Bronze Age. There was an interruption in trade, or at least in our evidence for it, in the transition between the Bronze and Iron

Ages in the twelfth century BCE. Once stability returned, trade appears to have revived in old patterns, as shown by the two eighth-century shipwrecks. The evidence from the wrecks can be augmented by an Aramaic palimpsest on papyrus (that is, papyrus written on more than once with the underwriting still visible) containing records of the inspection, registration and taxation of ships arriving in Egypt for ten months of the fifth-century year, 475 BCE. The largest of the ships contained almost 1,500 amphoras of wine, four times as much as the two eighth-century ships. (It was about the same size as Columbus's *Niña*.) Other ships also contained amphoras of wine, typically in larger numbers than in the earlier ships, as well as copper, tin and iron ingots. Phoenican ships as a whole brought over 6,000 amphoras of wine to Egypt in the fall of 475 BCE, indicating a large demand for northern wines in Egypt. This large volume of Egyptian wine imports in the fifth century strengthens the case for an Egyptian destination for the eighth-century ships.

Economics

The first point to make is that there is abundant evidence of trade in bulk commodities even before the invention of coinage, much less of more sophisticated arrangements. This is powerful support for Heckscher's argument that regional differences made for trade. Water transportation was far cheaper than land transportation, as it would stay until the invention of the railroad after the Industrial Revolution. The Mediterranean Sea provided a route for long-distance transportation that was cheap enough to use for grain, oil, and wine. Local advantages therefore made for interregional trade.

This trade required a lot of coordination. It cannot have been a solitary activity to engage in trade, for the simple matter that there needed to be suppliers and recipients. In addition, not all products were found or grown at seaside; they had to be brought to a port and transshipped to a boat. When they arrived, the goods probably had to be transported again to the location of consumption. As we have seen, containers were needed for liquid cargoes—and probably for solid ones as well. These containers had to be manufactured and allocated to trade. The extent of this coordination can be surmised from the presence of hundreds of virtually identical amphoras in each ship. There must have been many groups involved in this trade: growers, land transporters, transshippers, amphora makers, ship operators, receivers, and consumers. There may have been middlemen in addition at several points. Coordination of all these far-flung and quite disparate people was a formidable task.

How was this coordination achieved? There are only a few models in the literature of ways to organize such complex interactions. Pryor (1977) provided a useful taxonomy. He distinguished between what he called exchanges and transfers. Exchanges are balanced transactions where goods or services are exchanged for other goods or services of equal value. This of course is the kind of behavior most often observed in markets. Transfers are one-way transactions where goods and services are given without a direct return. Grants, tributes, and taxes are all transfers. Pryor excluded "invisibles" from this accounting, so that taxes are considered to be transfers rather than an exchange of goods or money in order to purchase social order or military success.[1]

Pryor subdivided exchanges into those in which the ratio of goods or services exchanged can vary and those in which it cannot. The former may or may not involve money; the latter do not. He termed the former "market exchange," the latter "reciprocal exchange." The use of money is a good index of this distinction, as are changes in the exchange ratio over time. In the presence of money, of course, changes in exchange ratios are expressed as changes in prices. Pryor divided transfers into centric and noncentric ones. Centric transfers are between individuals in a society and "an institution or an individual carrying out a societal-wide role" (Pryor 1977:34).

Heckscher, of course, analyzed market exchanges, and we need to ask if the ships we have found were engaged in this kind of reciprocal activity. The evidence from the eighth century is ambiguous; the ships may have been going to Phoenician colonies or to Egypt. If the former, we have no way of knowing if they were transfers or exchanges. The presence of balances aboard the Uluburun wreck and in the Egyptian painting, however, indicates the prevalence of market activity. The key as always is how these artifacts were used. What were the ancient traders doing with their balances?

The archaeological evidence indicates that they were comparing the weights of materials to some standard. In other words, they were dividing whatever was being weighed into units of a standard, identified by Pulak as a *shekel*. We normally speak of a standard of value as money, although we ask that any putative money have more than this single attribute. The other functions of money are as a means of transaction and a store of value. There is no indication that the weights found in the Uluburun shipwreck were traded, and we must look elsewhere for money performing these other functions.

Related evidence suggests that silver was used for transactions and as a store of value, divided into *shekel* units. There were no coins as yet, and it was the weight of silver that determined the value of a transaction. Numerous written examples point to the use of silver for transactions. We do not find loose silver, perhaps because it dissipates in the water, but we do find what is called *Hacksilber*: cut-up silver jewelry, ingots, or figurines that appear to have been stored in fabric pouches. These jewelry fragments could not have functioned as coinage, but they easily could have functioned as silver in larger units than loose silver. If so, they probably were both means of exchange and stores of value. While we cannot infer that all trades across the Mediterranean in biblical times were exchanges, we can confidently assert that some of it—perhaps most of it—was market exchange.

Heckscher phrased his proposition in terms of relative prices. We do not observe prices until the end of this period, but there was knowledge of relative scarcities even if people did not convert them into prices. And when we do have records that appear to be prices at the end of this period, they have the characteristics of modern prices. For example, Slotsky (1997) recorded what appeared to be a series of monthly market prices for six agricultural commodities for four hundred years in ancient Babylon, starting in the fifth century BCE. They appeared to provide much more evidence of ancient market activity than had been available earlier, and Slotsky argued that her observations were market prices. I conducted an econometric analysis of these prices and confirmed that they indeed were market prices; they moved with a great deal of randomness, and they varied over time. More precisely, the Babylonian agricultural prices moved like the random walk of modern prices, and they varied together in response to exogenous events that affected all crops. These changes are clearly understood within a market framework; they are impossible to understand within an administrative one. I concluded therefore that the scribes recorded prices set in functioning markets, that is, they were examples of what Pryor called market exchanges (Temin 2002).

I infer from this mixture of evidence from different times and places that much of the Mediterranean trade of the biblical era was exchange, coordinated by market activities; it was market exchange. If so, then the trade was in response to the forces analyzed by Heckscher, a response to differing comparative advantage around the Mediterranean basin. Given the technology of the time, wine could not be produced in North Africa. It was imported from more northern localities. Egypt exported wheat as shown by the description of the traders of Sidon in Phoenicia in Isaiah (23:2–3); they imported grain from Shihor (Lower Egypt), which was "the harvest of the Nile." It had been the reliable result of the annual flooding of the Nile since the times of Joseph and his brothers and would remain so into Roman times. Egypt also exported natron, a form of sodium carbonate used to make glass, bleach textiles, and treat sick people, that was found in the Nile delta, but not on the northern shores of the Mediterranean. Even if these products were not all the object of market exchanges, they all were articles of reciprocal trade.

Heckscher talked of relative factor scarcities as well as relative scarcity of goods. It is even harder to find evidence of returns to factors than of product prices in this era, but we can at least pose the question. It is likely that land was the scarce factor in Egypt, since the agricultural area was limited to the flooding of the Nile. If trade was the result of differing factor proportions rather than different climates, if must have been the case that wheat was a labor-intensive commodity, while wine was a land-intensive one. In Phoenicia, trade raised the relative price of wine and therefore, if the assumption of relative factor proportions is correct, the return to land. The opposite effect in Egypt may well not have been relevant since Egypt was specialized in wheat production. Phoenician landowners may have been the primary gainers from trade as well as its apparent instigators.

These gains, however, were offset in part by increased risks. Three kinds of risks can be identified. There was the risk of natural disaster along the way, of the ship sinking or getting lost. There also was a risk of trouble in the form of attack by pirates along the way or hostile people when the ship landed. And there was the risk of not being paid, or not paid what was due, by the recipients of the cargo. I discuss them in turn.

While it certainly was bad for ancient sailors and traders that sailing was hazardous in the ancient world, we are the beneficiaries. If we did not find ships at the bottom of the sea, we would have only a few clues to the existence of ancient trade. We cannot know if the risk changed over time. Archaeologists and ancient historians have tended to assume that the risk of shipwreck stayed constant; they have used the frequency of wrecks as an index of the volume of trade (Hopkins 1980).

Ancient mariners were conscious of these risks, and they took actions to minimize them. They did not sail, or not often, in the winter. The port records in Egypt showed that ships vanished only in January and February, a short winter even for the Mediterranean. Roman shipping at a later date stopped for a longer period in the winter (Duncan-Jones 1990, chapter 1). It was thought earlier that sailors also reduced the risk of loss by staying close to shore. We now know that some ship captains were willing to brave the open seas. Given the primitive tools for navigation available at the time, they probably were not willing to make voyages for very long out of the sight of land. Hence the importance of trade along the hypotenuse of a triangle at the corner of the Mediterranean or across the strait opposite Carthage. These probably were the deep-water shipping lanes of the biblical era (Ballard et al. 2000).

The risk of capture was quite different, but even harder to recover at this late date. A time when governments had limited jurisdiction and no single empire ruled the Mediterranean must have been a time when pirates abounded. Yet the ships that we have found in deep water do not appear to have been fortified. There are three possibilities: either the arms were so small as to be invisible in the wreckage, or they simply have been lost, or there were no pirates to fear. There were some weapons aboard the Uluburun wreck, but they do not seem enough to repel pirates. There also is evidence of warships, leaner and faster than the merchant ships I have described, that would provide another defense against pirates. Two ships containing eight hundred amphoras of wine between them must have been very tempting to a potential pirate.

Or was it? Casson (1991:178) asserted that ancient pirates sought people rather than goods. It may have been hard for a pirate to sell eight hundred amphoras of Phoenician wine without the guarantee of both quantity and quality that came from Phoenician merchants. However poor people could be sold as slaves; rich people, held for ransom. The incentives can be illustrated by a story from the years just before the Romans cleared the Mediterranean of pirates. Pirates captured the young Julius Caesar on a voyage in the eastern Mediterranean. They sought and received a large ransom, made larger by Caesar's boast that he was worth more than their original request. However Caesar, once free, hired ships and soldiers and returned to capture the pirates. He recovered his ransom and crucified the pirates, as he had threatened while still their captive (Plutarch, *Caesar*, 1–2).

This story suggests a small theory of ancient piracy. Pirates wanted to find rich and powerful people at risk, because they could earn more from ransom than from the sale of captives as slaves. Human capital was worth more to the relatives and colleagues of captives than to strangers who might purchase slaves. This relation was not monotonic, however. Capturing someone who was exceedingly rich or powerful was potentially dangerous as well as profitable, as the story about Caesar illustrates. There must have been an optimum wealth for ancient pirates to aim for, quite possibly one that shifted over time.

The existence of pirates in earlier times can be inferred from the political record. The break between trade in the Bronze and Iron ages noted earlier was due to the invasion of the "Sea Peoples." This invasion appears in the literature as a political operation, but it had an important economic dimension as well. Much later, Norsemen invaded England and France in the ninth century CE, starting with piracy and marauding and progressing to settlement (Bloch 1961). The earlier invasion, about which we know far less, undoubtedly exhibited the same progression. The heightened risk of piracy provides a good explanation for the dearth of Mediterranean trade in the twelfth century BCE (Sherratt and Sherratt 1993:366).

Assuming the ship arrived safely to its intended port, there also was the risk of confiscation or commercial double-dealing. There were no international treaties or World Trade Organization to monitor these transactions. There must have been less formal arrangements that shippers could count on enough to launch two ships containing four hundred amphoras of wine each into the Mediterranean. The most obvious of these arrangements is a reputation equilibrium, that is, an arrangement where people receiving shipments deal fairly with importers and are known to do so. They maintain this behavior in order to encourage trade, forgoing the obvious short-term gain from confiscating a new cargo.

This organization was used in Bronze Age Assyrian overland trade, where family firms prospered by sending out sons and other relatives to make the actual sales (Larsen 1976:92–105). Almost three millennia later, the Maghrebi traders of Alexandria had a highly developed form of reputation equilibrium. They sent associates, typically family members and almost exclusively fellow Jews, around the Mediterranean to conduct repeated transactions. They expected their agents to deal honestly with them, but they did not rely solely on this expectation to do business. If an agent cheated, the injured trader shared this information widely with his colleagues. The resulting loss of reputation was reflected immediately in a loss of employment. An agent who cheated then had the prospect of losing not only his present employment, which he would have lost when he cheated in any case, but also any future employment as a trading agent with the Maghrebi traders. The agent would not cheat under any reasonable circumstance, since the anticipated cost of doing so would be far larger than the gain he could get from pocketing the results of a single voyage (Greif 1994).[2]

These motives were in force also in the early Iron Age, but they were not totally compelling. The Israelite prophets noted the use of false balances and dishonest scales among the other evils of their contemporaries (Amos 8:6; Hosea 12:8). In modern parlance, the transaction costs of international trade in the biblical era were very high. We presume that the gains from trade were even higher, which is why traders found it worthwhile to ship even bulk commodities like wine and wheat across the sea in normal times.

After trade revived in the Iron Age, in the eighth century, traders and Israelite kings appear to have made efforts to reduce transaction costs in trade. They appear to have done this in a variety of ways. Traders began to label their weights with the units in *shekelim* that the weights represented. This enabled their transactions to be monitored more easily. The Israelite kings introduced jars labeled *lemelek*, meaning "of the king," which probably functioned as guarantors of the standardized volume of the jars. Of course, if the king owned the contents of the jars as well as the jars themselves, then the thousands of *lemelek* inscriptions indicate centric transfers rather than market exchanges. The reforms of Hezekiah (eighth century) and Josiah (seventh century), which have been celebrated for their religious aspect, appear also to have contained attempts, which evidently had to be repeated, to standardize weights and measures (King and Stager 2002:312–314). All of these actions must have reduced transaction costs by increasing standardization and verifiability. They encouraged international trade and market exchanges—if they did not indicate the growth of a centralized state with centric transfers.

Prevailing archaeological thought supports the existence of markets rather than a centralized state. Larsen (1987:54) described "a highly interactive world in which it is possible to follow commodities flowing from one end to the other" in the Middle Bronze Age. The Bronze Age trade was organized as a mixture of controlled flows directed by central authorities and commercial transactions, but it was primarily limited to overland trade east of the Mediterranean. Liverani (1987) described the shift from the Bronze Age to the Iron Age as a shift from centralized empires to trading city-states, from a pattern of gift exchanges to profit-oriented commercial activity. (In Pryor's terminology, the shift was from reciprocal to market exchange.) Sherratt and Sherratt (1993:362) agreed, stating that, "merchant enterprise, rather than state-controlled exchange, became the dominant mode of trading activity" of Mediterranean trade in biblical times. Archaeologists, however, have focused primarily on trade in luxury goods, perhaps because they find evidence of them in archaeological sites. The point I want to make here is that transport and transaction costs fell enough by the Iron Age to create incentives for extensive international trade in bulk commodities.

A vivid window into transaction costs is given by the account of Wen-Amon's trip from Egypt to Phoenicia around 1050 BCE. This was about fifty years after the troubled time when the "Sea Peoples" destroyed the established networks of trade; the "Sea Peoples" in the Levant had changed from raiders to traders. Wen-Amon tells the story in the first person, and we presume that he was able to complete his journey, even though the surviving narrative is incomplete. We do not know if he wrote this account because it was typical or atypical; in the absence of other accounts, we take it as the former.

Wen-Amon went to Phoenicia to buy cedars of Lebanon for use in the Temple of Amon at Karnak. We know Wen-Amon went to buy the cedars because he brought silver with him to pay for them. And when he said to his host that his host should do as his father and grandfather had done in supplying cedars, his host responded that he would do so—as long as Wen-Amon gave him something in return. This was a market exchange, not a centric transfer. The story's context suggests strongly that the seller expected silver. The historical context was the breakdown of the Egyptian state.

But the sale was not completed quickly. Wen-Amon took with him about a kilogram of silver and some gold. However, all this money was stolen as soon as he reached Dor, a port on the eastern shore of the Mediterranean occupied by one of the "Sea Peoples" called the Sikkel, located between the Phoenicians to the north and the Philistines to the south. The Sikkel had been pirates before they were traders, illustrating the transition described earlier (Stager 1995:337). It therefore should not be surprising that Wen-Amon's appeal for restitution was denied. Archeologists recently have unearthed a jar containing seventeen linen bags of silver, each weighing half a kilogram, in Dor from about the time of Wen-Amon's voyage (Stern 1998). Could this jar have been the eventual destination of his silver?

Finding himself in a tough place, Wen-Amon stole a comparable amount of silver from another ship and, apparently, used it in place of his own. Negotiations for the cedars dragged on for a long time with lots of histrionic speeches. It took months if not years to make the purchase and arrange for the cedars to be shipped to Egypt. When Wen-Amon started back to Egypt, he was shipwrecked in a storm in hostile territory. He persuaded his captors not to kill him, and the narrative breaks off (Pritchard 1955:25–29).

Three lessons emerge from this colorful tale of commerce in difficult times. The first is how hard it was to conduct international trade when the world was composed of many small political entities. The second is that international trade in quite heavy commodities took place despite these large transaction costs. And the third is that the reforms of the eighth and seventh centuries are easily understood as attempts to reduce these enormous transaction costs.

Conclusion

This essay bridges two disciplines. I hope that it indicates how economics can inform archaeology, framing questions and focusing the search for evidence. More relevant for this conference, it shows that the forces leading to international trade are very old. We know that trade in luxury goods and special items existed since time immemorial; the added information here is that trade in bulk commodities was present in the early Iron Age if not even earlier. I have argued here that this trade conforms to the patterns analyzed by Heckscher that have become staple items in the analysis of more recent trade. One does not need to have modern ships or communication technology or even coinage to engage in extensive international trade. It is unlikely that there was anything like factor price equalization in the Iron Age, but I have argued that there were tendencies in that direction.

Acknowledgments

I thank Lawrence E. Stager for his extensive advice, encouragement, and help and M. June Flanders and Elhanan Helpman for their helpful comments and suggestions. All errors, of course, are mine alone.

Notes

1. This exclusion is necessary because one can always hypothesize an invisible gain that makes all transactions balanced. In that case, there is no way to discriminate between different forms of behavior.

2. Larsen referred to the medieval traders in explaining his views on Assyrian trade, albeit to authors who predated Greif.

References

Ballard, R. D., L. E. Stager, et al. 2002. "Iron Age Shipwrecks in Deep Water off Ashkelon, Israel." *American Journal of Archaeology* 106:151–168.

Ballard, R. D., A. M. McCann, et al. 2000. "The Discovery of Ancient History in the Deep Sea Using Advanced Deep Submergence Technology." *Deep-Sea Research* 47:1591–1620.

Bloch, M. 1961. *Feudal Society*. London: Routledge and Kegan Paul.

Casson, Lionel. 1991. *The Ancient Mariners*. Princeton, NJ: Princeton University Press.

Davies, N. de G., and R. O. Faulkner. 1947. "A Syrian Trading Venture to Egypt." *Journal of Egyptian Archaeology* 33:40–46.

Duncan-Jones, R. 1990. *Structure and Scale in the Roman Economy*. Cambridge: Cambridge University Press.

Greif, A. 1994. "Cultural Beliefs and the Organization of Society: A Historical and Theoretical Reflection on Collectivist and Individualist Societies." *Journal of Political Economy* 102:912–950.

Heckscher, E. F., and B. Ohlin. 1991. *Heckscher-Ohlin Trade Theory*. Cambridge, MA: MIT Press.

Hopkins, K. 1980. "Taxes and Trade in the Roman Empire (200 B.C.–A.D. 400)." *Journal of Roman Studies* 70:101–125.

King, P. J., and L. E. Stager. 2002. *Life in Biblical Israel*. Louisville, KY: Westminster and John Knox.

Larsen, M. T. 1976. *The Old Assyrian City-State and Its Colonies*. Copenhagen: Akademisk Forlag.

———. 1987. "Commercial Networks in the Ancient Near East." In M. Rowlands, M. Larsen, and K. Kristiansen, eds., *Centre and Periphery in the Ancient World*, 47–65. Cambridge: Cambridge University Press.

Liverani, M. 1987. "The Collapse of the Near Eastern Regional System at the End of the Bronze Age: The Case of Syria." In M. Rowlands, M. Larsen, and K. Kristiansen, eds., *Centre and Periphery in the Ancient World*, 66–73. Cambridge: Cambridge University Press.

Maeir, A. M. 2002. "The Relations Between Egypt and the Southern Levant During the Late Iron Age: The Material Evidence from Egypt." *Ägypten und Levante* 12:235–246.

Pritchard, J. B. 1955. *Ancient Near East Texts Relating to the Old Testament*. 2nd ed. Princeton, NJ: Princeton University Press.

Pulak, C. 1998. "The Uluburun Shipwreck: An Overview." *International Journal of Nautical Archaeology* 27:188–224.

————. 2000. "The Balance Weights from the Late Bronze Age Shipwreck at Uluburun." In C. F. E. Pare, ed., *Metals Make the World Go Round: The Supply and Circulation of Metals in Bronze Age Europe*, 247–266. Oxford: Oxbow.

Pryor, F. L. 1977. *The Origins of the Economy: A Comparative Study of Distribution in Primitive and Peasant Economies*. New York: Academic Press.

Sherratt, S., and A. Sherratt. 1993. "The Growth of the Mediterranean Economy in the Early First Millennium BC." *World Archaeology* 24:361–378.

Slotsky, A. L. 1997. *The Bourse of Babylon: Market Quotations in the Astronomical Diaries of Babylonia*. Bethesda, MD: CDL Press.

Stager, L. E. 1995. "The Impact of the Sea Peoples (1185–1050 BCE)." In T. E. Levy, ed., *The Archaeology of Society in the Holy Land*, chapter 20. London: Leicester University Press.

Stern, E. 1998. "Buried Treasure: The Silver Hoard from Dor." *Biblical Archaeology Review* 24:46–62.

Temin, P. 2002. "Price Behavior in Ancient Babylon." *Explorations in Economic History* 39:46–60.

7

Demographic Shocks and the Factor Proportions Model: From the Plague of Justinian to the Black Death

Ronald Findlay and Mats Lundahl

All of his professional life, Eli Heckscher was concerned with the methodology of economics and economic history. Straddling both disciplines, it was essential for him to come to grips with the problem of what one discipline could learn from the other and vice versa (Findlay 1998; Findlay and Lundahl 2002; Henriksson and Lundahl 2003). Gradually he also introduced the use of statistical time series in his works, notably his four-volume magnum opus about the economic history of Sweden from the time of Gustav Vasa (1523–1560) to "the present," which in practice meant the early nineteenth century. As he moved from the sixteenth to the eighteenth century the availability of quantitative material increased, and Heckscher made use of it. However, he steadfastly refused to be bound by the strict limits imposed by the "hard" facts when it came to the interpretation of a certain epoch. He certainly took great care to weed out hypotheses not grounded in facts, but he was no stranger to hypothetical reasoning either. Such reasoning was needed for arriving at a historical synthesis, and the refusal to go beyond just what the sources would reveal, after thorough critical scrutiny, was for him to stop short of attempting a synthesis.

The present essay should be seen as the effort of two economists to provide a building block for a historical synthesis. We would like to combine Heckscher's plea for economic theory in economic history with his insistence on historical synthesis into a plea for economic theory in historical synthesis. The roots of the essay are found in economic theory, which we employ very much in the fashion that Heckscher used it in his historical works: as a device for explaining the equilibrating processes in economic history during a determined period. We also share with Heckscher the conviction that it is difficult to use economic theory to explain transitions from one historical epoch or era to another. Here factors exogenous from the point of view of economics must be invoked, and we begin and end our story with two such events: the so-called Plague of Justinian in the mid-sixth century AD and the Black Death eight hundred years later.

What our analysis deals with is precisely the period between these two events, and the synthesis that concerns us is one based on a marriage between the historical facts, as provided by the professional historians, and an economic theory that may serve as reading glasses when it comes to the interpretation of the events. Our aim is to provide a reading of some of the fundamentals of eight centuries of the history of Western Europe, Eastern Europe, and Islam that is consistent with the interplay of the probable basic economic mechanisms at work; that is, we want to put history on a sound theoretical footing, to heed Heckscher's (1929) plea for the use of theory in economic history, and simultaneously to allow economic history to influence theorizing. Heckscher made it clear that theory was useful when it came to organizing the questions to be put to the historical material, and we agree, but any old theory won't do. In order to be efficient, our theory must spring out of the historical material itself. Its categories must be chosen in a way that properly reflects the characteristics of the period we have chosen to deal with. It is only through the interaction between the given historical material and the specific tools we need to construct to reveal its hidden secrets that we can arrive at a better understanding of the underlying processes that made economic history take a particular turn at given moment in time.

The Plague of Justinian and Its Aftermath

The waves of bubonic plague that swept the world of Late Antiquity and the Early Middle Ages have taken their name from the Emperor Justinian I, ruler of the eastern Roman Empire from 527 to 565. It was during his reign that the first outbreak occurred in Constantinople in 542, killing hundreds of thousands of people according to the historian Procopius, secretary to Justinian's general Belisarius. Procopius, who was an eyewitness, has provided us with the first incontestable description of bubonic plague in history (quoted by Bray 2000:22–23):

During these times there was a pestilence, by which the whole human race came near to being annihilated, . . . it did not come in a part of the world, nor upset certain men, nor did it confine itself to any season of the year . . . but it embraced the whole of the world, and blighted the lives of all men, though differing one from another in he most marked degree, respecting neither sex nor age . . .

With the majority it came about that they were seized by the disease without becoming aware of what was coming. They had a certain fever.... The body showed no change from its previous colour, nor was it hot...nor did any inflammation set in.... But on the same day, in some cases, in others on the following day, and in the rest not many days after, a bubonic swelling developed; and this took place not only in the particular part of the body which is called the "boubon," that is below the abdomen, but also inside the armpit, and in some cases also beside the ears and at different points on the thigh .... For there ensued with some a deep coma, with others a violent delirium...for neither physicians nor other persons were found to contract this malady through contact with the sick or with the dead, for many were constantly engaged in burying or attending those in no way connected with them.... With some the body broke out in black pustules about as large as a lentil and these did not survive even one day, but all succumbed immediately. With many also a vomiting of blood ensued without visible cause and straightaway brought death.... In some cases when the swelling rose to an unusual size and discharge of pus had set in, it came about that they escaped from the disease and survived.

The emperor himself was infected, but survived. The first wave of the 540s–550s was followed by several others of varying intensity, persisting intermittently until the middle of the eighth century (Biraben and LeGoff 1969). While there is wide disagreement as to the extent of the impact (cf., e.g., Harrison 1999:141–153, for a critical view), there is little doubt that it was a demographic catastrophe on a scale not exceeded till the Black Death of the fourteenth century. Russell (1968:180) estimates a 20–25 percent loss for the first epidemic of 541–544 and a total loss of 40–50 percent of the pre-plague population over the period 540–700.

The plague is believed to have entered the Mediterranean world at the Egyptian port of Pelusium through Ethiopia and the Red Sea, before spreading both east and west. The populations of Egypt, Syria, and Palestine, then all under the sway of the Byzantine Empire, were severely affected. What happened farther east is not clear (Bray 2000:27):

Its distribution to the east of Syria is something of a puzzle. It would seem that the Arabs did not bring the plague back to the Hejaz.... Equally it would seem that the Arabs did not bring he plague to Afghanistan, the Indus, Ferghana and Transcaucasia and thus into the Indian subcontinent and China, as all observers have the plague ceasing at about the present western border of Iran and at the Caucasus. Whether it penetrated Africa south of Egypt is anyone's guess.

The Middle East as well was hit by successive outbreaks of the plague. Dols (1974) lists six "major" epidemics between 627 and 717.

The westward spread to Italy, Gaul, and Spain was through the sea-
ports of Genoa, Marseilles, and Narbonne, proceeding inland along
the rivers and trade routes. The impact on the northern lands seems to
have been much less severe, though not necessarily negligible. The
arrival of the plague at Marseilles in 588 was vividly described as follows by the contemporary Gallo-Roman historian Gregory of Tours
(1974:510–511):

A ship from Spain put into port with the usual kind of cargo, unfortunately
also bringing with it the source of the infection. Quite a few of the townsfolk
purchased objects from the cargo and in less than no time a house in which
eight people lived was left completely deserted, all the inhabitants having
caught the disease. The infection did not spread through the residential quarter
immediately. Some time passed, and then, like a cornfield set alight, the entire
town was suddenly set ablaze with the pestilence... at the end of two months
the plague burned itself out. The population returned to Marseilles, thinking
themselves safe. Then the disease started again and all who had come back
died. On several occasions later on Marseilles suffered from an epidemic of
this sort.

Before the plague struck, the eastern Roman Empire under Justinian
was at the height of its power, with plentiful resources of manpower
and revenue. Not only was he able to secure the eastern frontier
against the Persians but also to stabilize and push back the frontiers
against the Avars, Lombards, Berbers, and others, while soundly
defeating the Vandals in North Africa in 534–535. The great scheme of
once again unifying the eastern and western halves of the empire was
not impossible, though of course extremely difficult. The devastating
effects of the plague on both manpower and revenue, however, rendered it impossible. Nevertheless, although his plans for expansion
failed he was still able to retain most of the eastern territories of the
empire.

As often noted, the nomads of the Arabian Peninsula escaped the
ravages that the plague wrought on the more settled Byzantine and
Sassanid empires. After the unification of the tribes under the Prophet
and his early successors, the "rightly guided" Caliphs, at the beginning
of the seventh century, the Arabs rapidly captured Syria, Palestine,
Egypt, North Africa, and western Mesopotamia from the Byzantines.
Sassanid Iran was conquered later by the Arabs under the Ummayad
Caliphate. The Byzantine emperor Heraclius (610–641) and his successors could not match the élan of the Arab onslaught with the depleted
resources at their command. They retreated to the Anatolian Plateau,

behind the security of the Taurus mountain range, and then suc-cessfully resisted successive Arab attacks on Constantinople from the sea.

The empire was to survive for eight hundred more years but it had lost the bulk of its territory, population and revenue to the Arabs. In the west, the empire's hold on Italy was rendered extremely tenuous, and the Lombard invasion of the peninsula, beginning in 568, could not be checked before most of it had been occupied. Gaul was left to the Merovingian Franks. Spain, under Visigothic rulers, was invaded in by the Muslims in 711, who established the powerful Emirate of Cordoba that occupied most of the Iberian Peninsula. The popes in Rome ceased to look to Constantinople and eventually allied them-selves with the rising dynasty of the Frankish warlord Charles Martel, who checked the Arab advance at Poitiers in 732 or 733.[1] Around the same time, say 718 or 722 (Collins 1995:182), after a Christian victory over Muslim forces at Covadonga in Asturias, the Spanish *Reconquista* began.

By the second half of the eighth century the territory of the Roman Empire at its height had come to be divided between three great powers, the Greek Orthodox Byzantine Empire under the vigorous new Isaurian Dynasty, with its capital at Constantinople, the Muslim Abbassid Empire, with its capital at Baghdad and the Latin Catholic Carolingian Empire with its capital at Aachen. Beyond the frontiers of these empires were Anglo-Saxon England in the west, the pagan Scan-dinavian and Saxon tribes in the north and in the east the Slavs and Bulgars in the Balkans.

Population figures for such early periods in history are notoriously unreliable and can only be taken as the best guesses made by scholars on the basis of extremely scanty evidence. Issawi (1981), citing Russell (1968), gives figures of 16.6 million in 350 for the eastern Roman Em-pire, falling to 10 million by 600, indicating the devastating effect of the early waves of the Plague of Justinian. Treadgold (1997:278) gives a figure of as much as 26 million for the empire under Justinian in 540, before the plague, falling to 17 million in 610 before the Arab invasions and collapsing to 7 million in 780 after that disaster, rising back to 12 million by 1025. Issawi cites 15 million at least for 1000, or about 25 percent more than Treadgold. The general qualitative picture, how-ever, is similar, with a heavy loss of population due to plague, more loss due to the Arab invasions, and then recovery within the restricted territory.

Issawi's main contribution is an estimate of the area and population of the Arab Empire at its height in 750. He puts the population at between 28 and 36.5 million over the vast arc stretching from Spain to India. The breakdown is 10–13 million in the former Byzantine territories of Egypt, Syria and North Africa; 5–6 million in Spain; 1.5–2 million in the Arabian peninsula; 5–6 million in Iraq; 3–4 million in Iran; and 3.5–5.5 million in Central Asia, Afghanistan, and India. The gross area he puts at 9.8 million square kilometers and the inhabited area at 2.1 million, only slightly more than one-fifth, indicated the highly arid inhospitable nature of much of the terrain.

For the tenth to eleventh centuries Issawi estimates only a very modest rise of the population to 35–40 million, or about 25 percent over three centuries. The Abbassid Empire was about twice as big in both population and inhabited area as the contemporary Byzantine Empire. The only comparable source of population history for the world as a whole is McEvedy and Jones (1980). We have checked Issawi's figures against the comparable estimates that they provide. While their figures are generally lower they are not too far below the bottom range of Issawi. The figures based on their estimates of individual countries are 21 million for 700, 26 million for 1000, and 22 million for 1300. Thus the trend of population for the Islamic world is a modest 25 percent over three centuries for both Issawi and McEvedy and Jones. The fall from 26 million in 1000 to 22 million in 1300 is attributable to the ravages of the Mongol invasion in Iran and Iraq in the east and the Bedouin raids in North Africa in the west.

For Europe excluding Russia, McEvedy and Jones report a peak of 33 million in 200, falling to a trough of 23 million in 600, rising back to 32 million by 1000, and then accelerating upward to the huge figure of 70 million in 1300 on the eve of the Black Death.[2] This gives annual growth rates of less than 0.1 percent per annum for the earlier period and 0.25–0.3 percent after the turn of the millennium. David Grigg (1980:53) reports some figures for individual countries: 0.43 percent per annum for England and Wales from 1086 to 1340, 0.49 percent for France from 1100 to 1328, less than 0.2 percent for Italy from 950 to 1300 and for Denmark from 1000 to 1300, 0.46 percent for the Moselle valley between 1000 and 1237, and an average rate of increase for Europe between 1000 and 1340 of 0.26 percent.

While these figures are notoriously uncertain, representing a tendency only, the beginnings of the higher demographic growth that was to last for three centuries can be dated. "It was 930–50 in Sabina and Lombardy, 940–90 in Catalonia, 980–1010 in Languedoc, Provence, Poitou and the Auvergne, 1010–30 in Flanders and Picardy, Bavaria and Franconia, Burgundy and Normandy, 1050–80 in England and the Rhineland, after 1100 in central Germany" (Fossier 1999:62). If we are to believe the McEvedy-Jones estimates, the increase from the trough in 600 to the peak in 1300 is a remarkable threefold or 200 percent over the seven centuries. For comparison, China increased from the 200 peak of 60 million back to 60 million in 1000, just like Europe, before rising further to a peak of 115 million in 1200, before falling to 85 million in 1300 as a result of the Mongol invasions at the other end of the European peninsula. This approximate doubling took place under the Sung Dynasty, generally regarded as the golden age of imperial China. Yet it does not come close to the European achievement.

Why did the Western Europe of the so-called Dark Ages perform so spectacularly well, relative to what were at that time the much more advanced Byzantine, Islamic, and Sung Chinese civilizations? Clearly, the foregoing leads us to suspect that the demographic change caused by the plague had something to do with it.[3] As it seems, the economic trend of late antiquity was a downward one in the Mediterranean area. In his monumental work on the "dark" centuries of the European economy, Michael McCormick (2001:41) concludes his chapter of the end of the ancient world thus:

Settlement patterns suggest that ill-understood processes of demographic stagnation and decline moved slowly across the old Roman space. They finally reached the east in the sixth or early seventh century. Around the same time, the history of disease marks a new configuration in the health experience of the population. The new pathocoenosis [the array of diseases characteristic of a society] could not by itself have been the leading cause of wide-reaching economic change, for change had started earlier in most of the Mediterranean world. But it surely must have reinforced some aspects of that change, if only by debilitating or destroying part of the work force. Both settlement patterns and disease encourage us to believe that the overall trend of the late Roman world was downward between c. 200 and 700.

The next section of this essay will develop a model of demographic-economic-ecological interaction that could perhaps provide some clues to the very fundamental problem of the unequal patterns of decline and, later, rebirth.

The Model

The model presented in this section draws on our previous work (Findlay 1993; Findlay and Lundahl 2002) combining the Malthusian demographic specification with the concept of an endogenous land frontier, while stripping away the other features of those models.

The Production Function

The economy is considered as producing a single input, denoted Y, with land, A, and labor, L, as inputs, according to the production function

$$Y = Y(A, L) \tag{1}$$

which is taken to have the usual neoclassical properties of constant returns to scale, positive first and negative second derivatives with respect to each input and complementarity between the inputs. Constancy of returns to scale enables us to write

$$y = y(a) \tag{2}$$

where y and a denote Y and A divided by L, respectively. We can also write the rent per acre and the real wage as

$$r = y'(a) \tag{3}$$

$$w = y(a) - y'(a)a \tag{4}$$

The Malthusian Mechanism

The fertility and mortality rates of the population are specified as positive and negative functions, respectively, of the per capita *consumption*, c, of the population

$$f = f(c), \quad f'(c) > 0 \tag{5}$$

$$m = m(c), \quad m'(c) < 0 \tag{6}$$

These relations are depicted in figure 7.1 below. The population is in equilibrium at the per capita consumption level of c^* that equates $f(c^*)$ and $m(c^*)$ at f^* and m^*.

Labor Productivity and Per Capita Consumption

Labor productivity, as defined above, is

$$y = Y/L \tag{7}$$

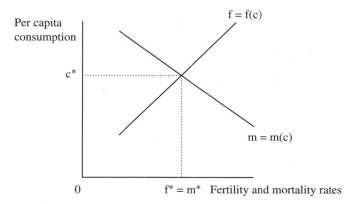

Figure 7.1
The Malthusian mechanism

Suppose that we are in a "stationary state" with zero net investment. Total consumption will then be equal to total output and the per capita consumption of the population as a whole will be

$$c = Y/P \tag{8}$$

where P denotes the entire population.

Suppose that the labor force is proportional to the population so that

$$L = \alpha P \tag{9}$$

where α is some fraction. In the preindustrial economic conditions that we are considering, the non-working population will consist of warriors, priests, and other "unproductive" occupations as well as those too old or too young to work. Taking a more "physiocratic" view, we could even include in the $(1 - \alpha)P$ artisans, traders, and so on who are "supported" by the surplus generated by agriculture, the only truly "productive" sector from this standpoint. From equations (7) to (9) it follows that

$$y^* = c^*/\alpha \tag{10}$$

so that y^* is the level of labor productivity that will maintain output, population and the labor force of the "stationary state" levels compatible with the Malthusian equilibrium level of per capita consumption, c^*.

From (2) we can obtain the value a^* of the land-labor ratio that defines y^* as

$$y^* = y(a^*) \tag{11}$$

We have therefore determined the long-run stationary values of the intensive magnitudes c^*, y^*, and a^*, but we yet have to determine the absolute levels of Y, C, A, and P.

Land and the Frontier

The marginal productivity of land and hence the rent per acre is determined in the stationary state as

$$r^* = y'(a^*) \tag{12}$$

We assume that an acre of land deteriorates in fertility at a rate of μ unless it is maintained. Suppose that the constant rate of time preference in the economy, and hence the rate of interest, is equal to δ.

Then by the usual asset pricing formula, the price of an acre of land would be

$$p^* = y'(a^*)/(\delta + \mu) \tag{13}$$

Figure 7.2 depicts the determination of p^* by the intersection of the demand and supply curves for the stock of land in the stationary state. The downward-sloping curve $p(a)$ in figure 7.2 shows the demand price for an acre of land as a function of the land-labor ratio. Since

$$y''(a) < 0$$

by the "diminishing returns" property of the production function (2), the value of $y'(a)$ capitalized by the reciprocal of $(\delta + \mu)$ is the nega-

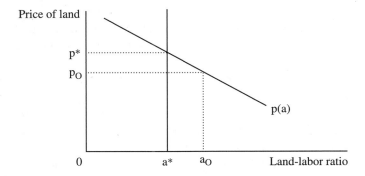

Figure 7.2
Stock equilibrium in the land market

tively shaped curve $p(a)$ in figure 7.2. The intersection with the vertical supply curve of land per unit of labor a^* in the stationary state yields p^* as in (13).

We now turn to the determination of the actual size of the land area A^* of the economy in the stationary state. Once this is determined, of course, the levels of L^*, Y^*, P^*, and C^* can all be obtained as well since we know the equilibrium intensive magnitudes a^*, y^*, and c^*.

The area of arable land A^* ultimately available in an economic system depends upon climatic or geographical factors, on the one hand, and the technology of land clearance and maintenance, on the other. Population, and hence the labor force, is endogenously determined within a Malthusian framework by the same factors and hence is not an independent variable in its own right.

In figure 7.3 below we consider the arable land available, A, as a function of the labor L_a, that is needed to "establish the frontier," that is, to ensure that A acres are available to the economy. To express it differently, L_a is the *cumulative* amount of labor that has gone into the clearance of the A acres of land currently available in the economy. We postulate that

$$L_a = L_a(A), \quad L_a'(A) > 0, \quad L_a'' > 0 \tag{14}$$

where $L_a'(A)$ is the marginal labor cost of clearing an additional acre, which increases with the amount of land already cleared, as indicated by the second derivative being positive as well. This formulation illustrates the Ricardian idea that extending the margin of cultivation is an

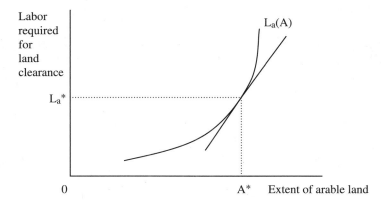

Figure 7.3
Determination of the land frontier

increasingly costly enterprise. The convex function (14) is plotted as the convex graph of $L_a(A)$ in figure 7.3.

In the long-run stationary equilibrium it will be true that

$$w^*L_a'(A) = p^* \tag{15}$$

that is, that the real marginal cost of clearing an additional acre, the left-hand side of (15), must be equal to the equilibrium price per acre p^*. Note that w^* and p^* in (15) have already been obtained by (4) and (13) alone. This enables us to solve (15) for the unique value A^* of A that satisfies this equation. This solution is depicted graphically in figure 7.3 where the slope of the convex function $L_a(A)$ at A^* is the value of $L_a'(A)$ that satisfies (15), given w^* and p^* as determined already. It is instructive to substitute for p^* from (13) into (15) to obtain the relation

$$w^* = y'(a)[1/L_a'(A)][1/(\delta + \mu)] \tag{16}$$

The right-hand side of (16) can be interpreted as the "indirect" marginal productivity of labor in clearing additional land, the marginal productivity $y'(a)$ of which is capitalized by the "gross" discount factor, the reciprocal of $(\delta + \mu)$. Since w^* is also equal to its direct marginal product by (4), we have the "efficiency condition" for labor allocation that it requires its direct and indirect marginal productivities to be equal.

Having now determined the absolute magnitude A^* of arable land and knowing already the equilibrium values a^*, y^*, and c^* of the intensive magnitudes, we can easily obtain the absolute values L^*, Y^*, P^*, and C^* of the labor force, total output, population, and consumption. We have thus fully determined the equilibrium values of all the variables in the model.

The relation between Y, A, and L is depicted in figure 7.4. Given A^* the concave function shows the relation between Y and L determined by the production function (1). The ray from the origin has a slope equal to y^*, so that the intersection with the concave function determines L^* and Y^*.

Employment in Land Clearance

We have established the cumulative labor effort needed to provide the economy with an arable land area of A^*. However, since land is assumed to depreciate at the rate μ, for example through reforestation

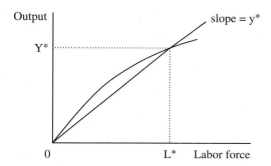

Figure 7.4
Determination of total output

or soil erosion, it must continuously be replenished by the clearance of
new land for the stationary state to be maintained. The amount of new
land cleared will be an increasing function of the price of land and
a decreasing function of the real wage, equal to p^* and w^*, respectively, in the stationary state. Letting N denote the amount of *new* land
cleared (as opposed to the cumulative total, A) and L_n the amount of
current labor required for this task, in the stationary state we must
have

$$N(L_n) = \mu A^* \tag{17}$$

and

$$L_n^* = L_a(A^*) - L_a[(1-\mu)A^*] \tag{18}$$

Assuming land clearance to be an explicit economic activity, "profits"
equal to $(p^*N - w^*L_n)$ must be maximized, which requires that

$$P^*(\partial N/\partial L_n) = w^* \tag{19}$$

which is precisely the condition (15) obtained earlier to determine
A^* by equating the price p^* to the marginal cost of land clearance
$w^*L_a'(A)$. (At the margin it does not matter whether we use A or N.)

Where does L_N^* come from? The number of production workers L is
equal to αP by assumption, so the L_N^* workers required for the land
clearance come out of the remaining pool of $(1-\alpha)P$. Thus the labor
force is the sum of the production workers and the members of the
"land-clearing brigade," and if we add the "unproductive" members
of society we get the total population.

What happens outside of the steady state? Corresponding to any point (A, L) in the input space the production function determines $r(a)$ and $w(a)$ by the marginal productivities of each input. Capitalizing $r(a)$ by the reciprocal of $(\delta + \mu)$ and ignoring expected capital gains and losses we can always obtain $p(a)$ for every $r(a)$. Taking $p(a)$ and $w(a)$ as given the land-clearing sector maximizes profits in determining the amount of land cleared $N(p, w)$ as an increasing function of p and a decreasing function of w as indicated by

$$N = N(p, w) \quad \partial N/\partial p > 0, \quad \partial N/\partial w < 0 \tag{20}$$

Since the point (A, L) is arbitrary it is clear that $N(p, w)$ may exceed, equal or fall short of μA, allowing A to rise or fall over time depending upon the direction of the inequality.

Dynamic Stability

From a dynamic perspective the model can be represented by the following two-dimensional system of differential equations

$$\dot{L} = \dot{L}(L, A) \tag{21}$$

$$\dot{A} = \dot{A}(L, A) \tag{22}$$

where the dots indicate the time derivatives dL/dt and dA/dt respectively.

The equilibrium state of this system is reached when the values of L and A are such that (21) and (22) are both equal to zero. These values are precisely the L^* and A^* that we have obtained above for the long-run stationary state. What is investigated here is whether the system will move towards the point (L^*, A^*) when $L(t)$ and $A(t)$, the state variables of the system are not equal to these equilibrium values.

The system will be dynamically stable, that is, $L(t)$ and $A(t)$ will approach (L^*, A^*), when the Jacobian matrix of the partial derivatives of (22) and (23)

$$J \equiv \begin{vmatrix} \partial \dot{L}/\partial L & \partial \dot{L}/\partial A \\ \partial \dot{A}/\partial L & \partial \dot{A}/\partial A \end{vmatrix}$$

evaluated at the equilibrium point (L^*, A^*) satisfies

$$\partial \dot{L}/\partial L + \partial \dot{A}/\partial A < 0 \tag{23}$$

$$(\partial \dot{L}/\partial L)(\partial \dot{A}/\partial A) - (\partial \dot{A}/\partial L)(\partial \dot{L}/\partial A) > 0 \tag{24}$$

The first of these is called the "trace," and the second the "determinant" condition. Together they ensure that the characteristic roots of the matrix are negative, and have negative real parts, as required for dynamic stability.

We may now evaluate each of the four partial derivatives to obtain their signs.

The rate of change of population, and hence the labor force, is given by the difference between fertility and mortality rates:

$$\dot{L} = [f(c) - m(c)]L \tag{25}$$

from equations (5) and (6) above. Noting that per capita consumption c is proportional to per capita output y as given by (10), we obtain the sign of the partial derivative

$$\partial \dot{L}/\partial L = [f'(c) - m'(c)]\alpha(\partial y/\partial L) < 0 \tag{26}$$

Since $f'(c)$ is positive and $m'(c)$ is negative, the expression within parenthesis is positive. But

$$\partial y/\partial L = y'(a)(-A/L^2) < 0 \tag{27}$$

since average productivity per worker falls when L is increased with A constant, ensuring (26).

Partially differentiating (25) with respect to A we obtain

$$\partial \dot{L}/\partial A = [f'(c) - m'(c)]\alpha y'(a) > 0 \tag{28}$$

From the previous section we have seen that

$$\dot{A} = N(p, w) - \mu A \tag{29}$$

Both p and w are functions of A and L, so we have

$$\partial \dot{A}/\partial A = (\partial N/\partial p)(\partial p/\partial A) + (\partial N/\partial w)(\partial w/\partial A) - \mu < 0 \tag{30}$$

since

$$\partial N/\partial p > 0, \quad \partial p/\partial A < 0, \quad \partial N/\partial w < 0, \quad \partial w/\partial A > 0$$

and

$$\partial \dot{A}/\partial L = (\partial N/\partial p)(\partial p/\partial L) + (\partial N/\partial w)(\partial w/\partial A) > 0 \tag{31}$$

since

$$\partial p/\partial L > 0, \quad \partial w/\partial L < 0$$

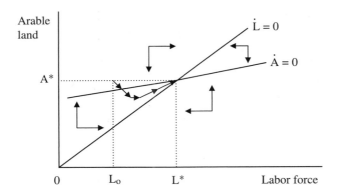

Figure 7.5
The dynamic stability of the model

The trace condition (23) is clearly satisfied, since both diagonal elements of the matrix J have been shown to be negative.

Figure 7.5 is the "phase diagram" of the dynamic system (21)–(22). It shows combinations of the state variables A and L that leave $dL/dt = 0$ and $dA/dt = 0$ along each of the respective functions, with the equilibrium point being (A^*, L^*) where these two functions intersect. It is easy to see that the determinant condition (24) is satisfied if the slope of the $dl/dt = 0$ function is steeper than the slope of the $dA/dt = 0$ function, that is,

$$(\partial \dot{L}/\partial L)/(\partial \dot{L}/\partial A) > (\partial \dot{A}/\partial L)/(\partial \dot{A}/\partial A)$$

The $dL/dt = 0$ function is a ray through the origin with a slope equal to a^*, the land-labor ratio that equates the fertility and mortality rates to maintain the Malthusian equilibrium. For any given value of A points to the left of the $dL/dt = 0$ ray have a greater than a^* and hence c greater than c^*, so population, and hence the labor force, must increase. By the same reasoning L must increase for a given A from any point to the right of the $dL/dt = 0$ ray. Similarly, for any given L and amount of A above the $dA/dt = 0$ line will result in A falling vertically to it or rising toward it from any value of A below that line. The $dA/dt = 0$ locus has a flatter slope than the $dL/dt = 0$, as required by the determinant condition for stability. The state variables will move according to the pattern of the arrows in each of the four regions of the input space.

Demographic Shock

An immediate exercise is the impact of a demographic shock such as the bubonic plague. If we start from the equilibrium point (A^*, L^*) in figure 7.5, the population and hence the labor force as well collapses instantly from L^* to L_O, while A^* is initially fixed. The real wage rises above w^* while the rent per acre falls below r^*. Hence, the land price also falls below p^*. In terms of figure 7.2 the land-labor ratio moves to the right, to a_O, so that p falls from p^* along the demand curve to the point corresponding to $p_O(a_O)$. The fall in p and rise in w make the amount of new land cleared fall below μA^*, and so the area of land cultivated contracts. The rise in per capita output and consumption stimulates the recovery of population and the labor force so the state variables move down and to the right along the path indicated in figure 7.5. Once the $dA/dt = 0$ line is crossed from above the rising price of land and the falling real wage result in the new land cleared exceeding the depreciation μA, and so the area cultivated rises along with the labor force back to the equilibrium point (L^*, A^*).

Comparative Steady States

Suppose that there is Hicks-neutral technological progress in the production function (1). At the original land-labor ratio this will raise productivity and hence consumption per capita, so as to increase population growth. To keep $dL/dt = 0$ it is clear that the land-labor ratio a^* has to fall. This implies a rotation to the right of the $dL/dt = 0$ ray as in figure 7.6. The $dA/dt = 0$ line remains unchanged and so the new equilibrium point (A^{**}, L^{**}) involves an increase in both the labor force and the area of cultivation, with a lower land-labor ratio. Initially A remains fixed at A^*, since both p^* and w^* rise in the same proportion. But the increase in labor lowers the real wage rate and raises the rent and the price of land, and thus induces an expansion in the area cultivated as well.

An improvement in the cost of land clearance, due either to better technology or to climatic conditions, will shift the $L_a(A)$ function in figure 7.3 downward for each value of A, and reduce the slope $L_a'(A)$ as well. Thus, for each value of L on the $dA/dt = 0$ line, the area cultivated, A, will have to rise until $p(a)$ has fallen and $w(a)$ has risen sufficiently to equate the price to the marginal cost of land clearance. As we

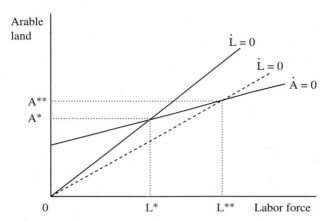

Figure 7.6
Technological progress

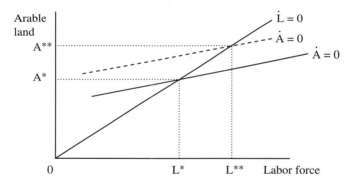

Figure 7.7
A reduction of the cost of land clearance

can see from figure 7.7 this will result in A^{**} and L^{**} both higher than the previous values A^* and L^*.

From (13) it also follows that a reduction in the rate of time preference δ or the depreciation rate μ of land will raise the value of the marginal acre and hence require an increase in A to leave dA/dt still equal to zero for each value of L, while leaving the $dL/dt = 0$ function unchanged. The result is therefore the same as in figure 7.7.

As a final exercise a leftward shift in the fertility function $f(c)$ will raise c^* and hence y^* and c^*. The result is to rotate the $dL/dt = 0$ locus

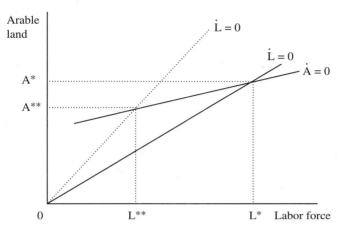

Figure 7.8
A fertility reduction

to the left, which results in a new equilibrium with A^{**} less than A^* and L^{**} less than L^*, as in figure 7.8.

Performance: The Byzantine Empire

In the next three sections we will briefly examine the economic performance of the three systems, mainly with respect to population, labor force, cultivated area, and output, but also looking at other factors such as urbanization and trade as indicators of these developments. The intention is to see whether we can relate these outcomes to the implications of the model and what we know of the exogenous shocks that occurred in each case.

As we have noted, the Byzantine Empire before the plague struck in 542 was at its peak in terms of territory and population, put at about 26 million by Treadgold (1997:278) on the basis of estimates by McEvedy and Jones (1980). It is easy to imagine, with Cyril Mango (1994:68–69), what must have happened to the economy:

All normal occupations were interrupted, prices of goods trebled and quadrupled, starvation set in, fields were deserted and the remaining farmers were burdened with additional taxes on the non-productive land of their deceased neighbours.

There can be little doubt that the plagues of the sixth century, combined with an unprecedented sequence of natural disasters were a factor, perhaps the determining factor in the collapse of urban life. For it is a fact (though some historians still refuse to recognize it) that all round the Mediterranean, the cities, as they had existed in Antiquity, contracted and then practically disappeared.

By 610, as a result of the plague, the Byzantine population had fallen to 17 million, and it continued to fall to a mere 7 million by 780 after the loss of Egypt, Syria, Palestine, and North Africa to the Arabs and further outbreaks of the plague. The population of Constantinople, which was at least 300,000 at the time of Justinian, fell to a mere 40,000 by the middle of the eighth century, after another disastrous outbreak of the plague in 747, "probably ... the lowest point in the medieval history of Constantinople" (Mango 1994:78). Antioch and Alexandria, the next largest cities after Constantinople, were lost to the Arabs in the seventh century. Thessalonica was the only other remaining city of any size. Several of the cities of Asia Minor declined to mere *kastra*, citadels surrounded by small civilian settlements (Mango 1994; Cameron 1993). That this development should not have been related to the appearance of the plague is difficult to believe. Even an author as cautious as Averil Cameron (1993:164) is quite emphatic:

The effects are certainly hard to quantify ... but it is hard not to think that plague must have been a factor in undermining the generally thriving state of cities in the Near East in the early part of the sixth century .... Historians vary sharply in the amount of weight that they are willing to attach to the sixth- and seventh-century plague. Yet the fact remains that this seems to have been the first appearance of bubonic plague in Europe; its impact must therefore have been far greater than that of the regular diseases which ravaged ancient cities as a matter of course.

The period 641–780 is described by Treadgold (2002) as the "Struggle for Survival" against the twin enemies of the Arabs and the plague. Byzantium may have escaped total collapse by a slim margin. State revenue fell drastically as people died (Treadgold 2001:67):

The evident explanation for this decline in state spending is the same as that for most of Justinian's failures: the effects of the plague after 541. These were so different from most historical events in magnitude and kind that they were inevitably underestimated by most Byzantine observers, as indeed they have been by most modern historians. Not even the return of the plague in the thirteenth century wreaked such havoc, because it recurred less often and reduced a denser population. If the first outbreak had killed Justinian, as it almost did, it might well have brought on the fiscal and military collapse of the empire that he barely adverted.

It was bad enough as it was.

While revenue and population shrank, the size of the army did not fall in the same proportion, so a greater share of resources was devoted to the military, and a reorganization of society along military lines, in so-called *themata* (military districts, each with its own army), took place. As our model predicts, however, per capita income appears to have been on the rise and income disparities were being reduced. Treadgold (2002:150) states that in "comparison with earlier Byzantine times the rich appear to have been poorer and the poor richer," which is consistent with the rise in the land-labor ratio lowering rents and raising wages, in terms of our model. He also observes that peasants benefited from the greater availability of land. Labor had become a scarce factor and the peasants benefited from this. It became difficult to tie them to the soil. Their freedom of movement increased and they had "complete and unlimited legal disposal over . . . [their] land. The Byzantine sources show quite clearly that peasant land was handed down from generation to generation by inheritance and that it could be freely alienated by the possessor just as he chose—by sale, by gift, or limited lease" (Ostrogorsky 1966:210). The Byzantine Empire had uncultivated land at its disposal, in its very heartland, Asia Minor, where the military holdings granted out in return for military service could not obtain labor without bringing in foreigners, mostly of Slavonic origin. The rise in per capita income that all this seems to indicate could also explain how a greater than proportionate military burden was borne, relative to the pre-plague years. In relation to our model the situation would be ripe for the rise in per capita consumption to induce a recovery of population and an associated increase in the area under cultivation.

While the empire had survived, its prospects around the year 800 did not look too good in the ongoing tripartite struggle for power against its two great rivals, the Carolingian Empire of the West and the Abbasid Empire of Haroun al-Rashid in Baghdad. Byzantium had to contend not only with the Arabs but with formidable barbarian peoples on its frontiers, such as the Bulgars and the Pechenegs. In the west the aggressive Normans intruded successfully into Byzantine possessions in southern Italy and the Balkans, after taking Sicily from the Arabs (Norwich 1991, 1997).

Population, and with it manpower and revenue, began to revive from 7 million in 780 to 12 million in 1025 on the death of the Macedonian Emperor Basil II, who crushed the Bulgars and stabilized the Balkan frontiers. Also significant, particularly for the future, was the conversion to Christianity of the Kievan Rus ruler Vladimir and his marriage to a Byzantine princess to cement a mutually beneficial alliance. Meanwhile the Carolingian Empire was fragmented in the succession struggles between Charlemagne's heirs and the power of the Sunni Abbasid caliphs was challenged by the Shia Fatimid caliphate in Cairo, while Byzantium preserved its political and religious unity.

As the population recovered, the man-land ratio increased, and the relative bargaining power shifted in favor of the larger landholders, who proceeded to buy up peasant property. Efforts on part of the rulers to protect the peasants proved to be of little avail (Ostrogorsky 1966:221–222):

After the death of Basil II [in 1025] the long series of these laws came to an end.... For, as even the government regulations of the tenth century, in spite of their extreme severity, had been unable to suppress the buying-up of peasant and military lands, now the passively benevolent attitude of the government meant that the great landowners' capacity for expansion could develop to the full. The destruction of the small freehold properties continued unrestricted; the great landowners absorbed the land of the peasants and soldiers and made the owners their serfs.

...Certainly there were free peasants in the late Byzantine period; but whereas in the middle Byzantine period, from the seventh to the beginning of the eleventh century, the free and moving peasantry is the chief factor in agrarian development and the backbone of Byzantine agriculture, from the eleventh century onward, just as in the early period, the great landlord dominates the scene. The agrarian history of the late Byzantine period is that of great landowners and their dependants.

Just when it seemed that the empire could continue its revival a fateful new challenge arose with the emergence of the Seljuk Turks. They took over much of the interior of the Anatolian Plateau after defeating the Byzantines at Manzikert in 1071. This shifted the center of gravity of the empire from the interior of Asia Minor to the coastal regions of the Balkans and the Black Sea. The rising commercial and naval power of Venice, Pisa, Genoa, and the other Italian cities was accommodated by the Byzantines with increasing diplomatic concessions, such as exemptions from customs duties and "extraterritorial" rights in Constantinople (Nicol 1988). The relative expansion of the West was strikingly displayed in the Crusades, which liberated Jerusalem and Antioch and established new kingdoms in the Holy Land (Runciman 1951; Riley-Smith 1987). These Christian allies did not accept the authority of Byzantium, and the Fourth Crusade of 1204 that sacked Constantinople and established the so-called Latin Empire that lasted until 1261 was a fatal wound from which the empire never recovered until its fall at the hands of the Ottoman Turks in 1453 (Queller and Madden 1997).

Despite the economic expansion from the tenth century onwards, part of which has been well documented by Harvey (1989), it is difficult to resist the impression that the economic history of the Byzantine Empire was one of protracted demographic collapse, due to plague and the Arab invasions, from about 550 to 780, followed by a long recovery during which power systematically shifted in favor of the large landowners, set back by the intrusions of the Fourth Crusade and the Turks. Something akin to a new demographic-economic equilibrium was being restored, within the restricted post-plague area imposed by the Muslim advances, as would be implied by our model. This restoration is symbolized by the fact that Constantinople seems to have had the same population, about 300,000, at the time of Justinian and the onset of the plague, as it had when it was sacked by the Crusaders in 1204, after having fallen to as low as 40,000 in the middle of the eighth century. This was also about as many inhabitants as it had on the fateful day of May 29, 1453.

There does not appear to have been any notable technological progress or other economic innovation in the entire history of the empire:

In general, Byzantine technology was extremely conservative. Byzantine agricultural implements remained virtually unchanged from Roman times. The peasant continued to use the light plow dragged by a pair of oxen. It was made of wood and had a removable iron plowshare; it did not have wheels, so the plow bit rather than cut the soil. The scythe was not in use in Byzantium, and the image of Death with its scythe in hand, so popular in the West, would have left the Byzantines unmoved. (Kazhdan and Epstein 1985:27)

The large estates remained partly uncultivated, very much due it seems to faulty techniques (Ostrogorsky 1966:211):

The difficulty of making proper use of the larger estates was partly due to the primitive conditions of economic technique; for in this respect the Byzantine Empire, so far ahead in culture, was in many ways far behind the West. Thus Byzantium to the end of its days continued to employ an extremely uneconomic and antiquated harness for draught animals, while by the tenth century the West had evolved a greatly improved method of harnessing.

Byzantium maintained and adopted the administrative, military, and economic institutions that it had inherited from antiquity, but did not make any significant new breakthrough, as far as one can gather, other than "Greek fire," the lighted naphtha that was used successfully in naval battles against the Arabs in an early form of chemical warfare, and the importation of the silkworm from China in the sixth century in an early example of commercial espionage. Characteristically, this led to a significant but "luxury" industry, which was also imitated and supplanted in due course by both of its great rivals, the Muslims and the Latins. The critical frontier, in the case of Byzantium, was always a political and military one, not one of settlement and cultivation. As Harvey (1989) points out, there was considerable land reclamation accompanying the population growth from 900 to 1200, but this is not likely to have constituted any net addition to the cultivated area in the same regions before the onset of the plague. None of this should be taken as denigrating the great resilience and adaptability that the empire displayed in dealing with an almost uninterrupted succession of military and political challenges and the crucial role in world history that it played in relation to the Russians and the other Slavic peoples of Eastern Europe.

The Islamic World

The extent and rapidity of the Arab conquests of the seventh and eighth centuries is one of the most remarkable features of world history. "The speed, magnitude, extent and permanence of these conquests excite our wonder and almost affront our reason, but the historian who seeks to explain them is impeded by the deficiency of the evidence at his disposal," writes J. J. Saunders (1965:39). The first conquests, however, can perhaps be partly explained with the aid of the Findlay (1996) model of the extension of empires, or simply by interpreting the extension of the land frontier in the present model as a military operation. Justinian's attempt to reconquer the territories lost by Rome to the barbarians had turned the Byzantine frontier into a triple war frontier: Italy, Africa, and the east. The eastern frontier was weakened by the necessity to maintain troops in the two other war theaters.

The eastern war led to nothing, and the plague outbursts in the sixth and seventh centuries in the eastern Mediterranean and the western part of the Sassanid Empire left the two contending empires militarily weakened, with little power of resistance, whereas the Arabs had escaped the deadly disease and could take advantage of the population vacuum. Damascus, Jerusalem, and Alexandria fell to Islam in rapid succession between 635 and 642, and farther east the Arabs simultaneously penetrated Sassanid territory.

Islam, and Arabic, the language in which the Qur'ān was written, imposed a cultural unity over a vast extent of diverse peoples and physical environments, stretching from the shores of the Atlantic to the oases of Central Asia and the mountains of Afghanistan. This vast territory was never a single politically and administratively unified empire but it did maintain a unique identity as the *Dar al-Islam*, or Abode of Islam, as opposed to the *Dar al-Harb*, or Abode of War, that is, the infidel. Thus most of the welter of dynastic changes and power shifts that form so much a part of medieval Islamic history can be ignored for purposes of this paper since they mostly took place within the same system. It was only on the frontiers of Spain and in the Mediterranean islands, before the Crusades, that land and people moved in or out of the Islamic world itself as a result of political conflict. In Central Asia much of the conversion of the nomadic Turkish and later Mongol tribes and states took place peacefully. The Crusader kingdoms in Syria and Palestine were exceptions, but only temporarily, since they were eventually returned to the Islamic fold by Saladin and the Mamluks.

In the case of Islam, the extension of the frontier of cultivation was a military operation rather than a peaceful land clearance affair (Hitti 1970:144):

Islam did provide a new battle-cry, a convenient rallying-point and a party watchword. It undoubtedly acted as a cohesive and cementing agency for the heterogeneous masses never before united and furnished a large part of the driving force. But it is hardly in itself enough to explain the conquests. Not fanaticism but economic necessity drove the Bedouin hordes, and most of the armies of conquest were recruited from the Bedouins, beyond the confines pf their arid abode to the fair lands of the north. The passion to go to heaven in the next life may have been operative with some, but the desire for the comforts and luxuries of the civilized regions of the Fertile Crescent was just as strong in the case of many.

Fertile soil was available in abundance in the conquered territories, in the valleys of the Guadalquivir, Nile, Euphrates, Tigris, Oxus, and Jaxartes rivers, with the Indo-Gangetic plain being added by the Delhi Sultanate early in the thirteenth century. The string of oases from North Africa to Central Asia also yielded high returns. On the whole, however, the Abode of Islam was situated in one of the most arid zones of the civilized world, and "the struggle between the desert and the sown" has been a persistent theme of its existence.

To quote the eminent French geographer Xavier de Planhol (1959:102), "the heart of Islam remains that desert zone which, slanting across the globe from the Atlantic Ocean to Central Asia, includes the whole of the ancient world between, on the one side, the humid zones of intertropical Africa and monsoon-moistened Asia and on the other side the wet and temperate climate of Europe." In this zone, according to de Planhol (1959:124), the towns, linked to each other along the trade routes, dominate their rural agrarian environs, which, despite their density, are often no more than "a farming or truck-gardening suburb." Reflecting its origins in Mecca and Medina, Islam in this view is essentially a religion of traders and city-dwellers. It has always had difficulty penetrating mountainous and forested areas. Pastoral nomadism is well adapted to the environmental conditions of the Islamic zone, and Bedouin Arab, Berber, and Turkish nomadic tribes have all interacted positively and negatively with the sedentary cultivators and townsfolk over the centuries, providing the fourteenth-century Tunisian sage Ibn Khaldun (1958) with the theme of his great work. Interestingly, Khaldun says (1958, 1:302), "Arabs can only conquer flat territories" and also that (1958, 1:308) "desert tribes and groups are always dominated by the urban population."

Jared Diamond (1997) has popularized the idea that agricultural innovations can be diffused more readily across the same latitudes, since climatic conditions are similar, rather than on a north-south axis. With its largely "horizontal" extent around the globe, within a relatively narrow band, the early Islamic world provides an excellent example of this thesis. As Andrew Watson (1983) has demonstrated convincingly in a seminal work, the first three or four centuries of Islam were marked by a remarkable agricultural revolution that saw a very wide variety of new crops diffused from its eastern margins in India all the way to Morocco and Spain. These included such major crops as cotton and sugarcane, as well as rice, hard wheat, sorghum, citrus fruits, coconuts, bananas, artichoke, spinach, and eggplant. The introduction of these crops required complementary efforts in irrigation, the construction of canals and the opening up of new lands. The agents of such change were not only farmers and landowners but also rulers and officials who provided the necessary institutional infrastructure.

The following quotation (Watson 1983:129) describes a process that corresponds exactly to the implications of our model:

The agricultural revolution was bound up with an ill-documented but none the less real demographic revolution which seems to have touched most parts of the Islamic world from roughly the beginning of the eighth to the tenth century. Rising population levels and increasing levels of output of foodstuffs must continuously have interacted: though both were affected by other factors, at times demographic growth must have been the result of agricultural progress, at times its efficient cause.

Watson cites many instances of this agricultural expansion from all over the Islamic world, and the reader is referred to his book and the many sources cited therein for the evidence. Unfortunately, there appear to be no numbers. Perhaps the strongest evidence for the agricultural revolution of the early Islamic world is the extent and scale of its urbanization. Eric Wolf (1966:13) has defined the peasantry "in terms of its subordinate relationships to a group of controlling outsiders," and, conversely, urban areas are dependent on the surrounding countryside for their growth.

Watson (1983:132) challenges many published estimates of city size as biased downward, by sheer "Orientalist" prejudice or "on the grounds that it is more responsible to underestimate than to overestimate." Baghdad and Samarra, the two capitals of the Abbasid dynasty, could have had populations of close to a million, although half a million would be more plausible and impressive enough, since Constantinople at the time would not have exceeded 300,000. Basra seems to have had at least 200,000. One colorful citation (Watson 1983:131) says that "along the Tigris settlement was continuous, so that before dawn crowing cocks answered one another from housetop to housetop all the way from Basra to Baghdad." On the eve of the Black Death, the twin city of Fustat-Cairo also had a population that was of the order of half a million, and Nishapur in the ninth century is put at between 100,000 and five times that number. In the west Fez and Qairawan had several hundred thousand each but Cordoba at its peak was comparable to Baghdad at its height, estimated to be between half and one million. Cordoba also surpassed the one million mark. According to a census taken towards the end of the tenth century, the city had 1,600 mosques, 213,077 houses occupied by the lower and middle classes, another 60,300 inhabited by the higher bureaucracy and the aristocracy, and 80,455 stores (Ocaña Jiménez 1975:47). The Islamic world also had very many cities of lesser rank, far outstripping Byzantium and Western Europe.

Agriculture clearly had to be very productive to support urban set-tlements on such a scale, (as well as the Arab cultural advance in general). The relationship was not confined simply to food supply. Major processing industries such as sugar refining and textile manufactures relied on the supply of raw materials from the agricultural sector. In addition to cotton, raw silk and hemp for linen were important inputs to urban textile industries. Many of these manufactures were exported to other parts of the Islamic world, and also to Europe. In addition to these high value-added manufactured exports, the Islamic world, through the Red Sea and to Persian Gulf, was also the entrepôt for the precious spices from India and Southeast Asia to be distributed to Europe.

Looking at the admittedly unsatisfactory data provided by McEvedy and Jones, we see that the population of the Islamic world seems to have grown from about 21 million to about 27 million from 700 to 1000, say about 30 percent over three centuries. Issawi (1981) gives 28–36 million for 750 and 35–40 million for 1000. Taking the 28 million low estimate for 750 and the 40 million high estimate for 1000 we get what would be a maximum increase of 43 percent for two and a half centuries, as compared with 30 percent for three. While noticeably better than the performance of Byzantium at about 25 percent over three centuries, even the 43 percent over 250 years can hardly be called a "demographic revolution." Thus, while fully agreeing with Watson's picture of complementary agricultural and demographic expansions in the early Islamic world, we should not exaggerate the magnitude of either.

There is little doubt that what held back the further progress of early Islamic agriculture was the unfavorable nature of the physical environment and climatic conditions under which it operated. Once the power of conquest was gone, the character of the frontier changed from one of war to one of land clearance. In the "struggle between the desert and the sown" the sown had three good centuries, from 700 to 1000, but then the desert seems to have begun its counterattack. Islam was thus hemmed in by its unfortunate geographical circumstances. As Watson says, there is the possibility that the earlier expansion may have become over-extended, with excessive reliance on irrigation leading to soil erosion. Settlement was not continuous in many areas, raising costs of communication.

Warfare and the breakdown of central authority, and the raids of the ever-present nomads, also shrank the margin of cultivation. The social institutions of the *waqf*, donation of land for religious or charitable purposes, and the *iqta*, a revocable military fief, also were not conducive to sustaining agricultural productivity. The McEvedy-Jones population estimates decline from about 27 million in 1000 to about 23 million in 1300, reflecting the loss of cultivable area and the cessation of innovation. The impact of the Mongol invasion (Findlay and Lundahl, in press), the sacking of Baghdad in 1258 by Hülegü and the annihilation of the Abbasid Caliphate, was also of course an additional major factor in this regard.

Western Europe

Western Europe at the outset of our period had a Latin Christian core, soon to be flanked by a Muslim Spain in the west, with a pagan fringe in the Scandinavian north and in the east, with the Frisians, Saxons, Balts, and Slavs inhabiting the shores of the North Sea and the Baltic and the fertile plains beyond the Elbe, the Oder, and the Vistula. By the end of the period the pagan fringe had long since been almost entirely converted and the Muslims in the Iberian Peninsula had been pushed back all the way south to the narrow confines of the kingdom of Granada, and driven out of Sicily, Crete, and other Mediterranean islands that they had temporarily occupied.

Which were the factors behind this extraordinary advance, which the Roman Empire at its height was not even able to attempt, much less achieve? Lynn White (1962, 1978) had a deceptively simple answer, that could be colloquially phrased as "it was the stirrup and the plow, stupid," which led to his being roundly condemned by Sawyer and Hilton (1963) for the intellectual crime of "technical determinism."

The plow in question was the heavy wheeled plow with an iron coulter and plowshare, drawn by a team of horses or oxen, that cut deep into heavy soil in long straight furrows, turning the soil over with a moldboard. Though apparently known in antiquity it was not employed, being unsuitable for Mediterranean conditions, where the much lighter so-called scratch plow prevailed. The plains of northern Europe, however, were ideally suited to the heavier instrument. Horses also proved to be more efficient draft animals than oxen, after the invention of the horse collar multiplied the load that they could pull by up to a factor of five. The wear of the heavy loads on the horse's hooves required the complementary invention of the nailed horseshoe.

Another innovation, the three-field rotation in place of the more traditional two-field rotation, raised productivity per worker by 50 percent, if additional land were available, clearly providing a stimulus to land reclamation on a vast scale. In the two-field system, half the acreage was sown with winter crops, while the other half was left fallow. This made sense in the Mediterranean area where rainfall was concentrated to the winter, but in northern Europe, where sowing in the spring could bring another crop, one-third of the area was sown in the fall (wheat or rye), another third in the spring (barley, oats, or legumes), and the last third was left fallow. The following year the second field was sown in the fall, and so forth, until the cycle recommenced. The three-field system both increased the area under cultivation and the range of crops grown. The new system was introduced in France during the eighth century, but took time to spread, and it was not until after 1250 that the speed of diffusion became rapid. Even so, the two systems coexisted during the thirteenth and fourteenth centuries (Grigg 1980:73).

This new technology required changes in the social organization of the peasant community to adopt a more cooperative basis, in order to take advantage of the economies of scale offered by the more expensive plow and draft animals. The plow is a labor-saving device. It was introduced by a society that had undergone a population decline, but below a certain "threshold farm size" the introduction of the plow is not profitable, and when the cost of feeding the draft animals is taken into account this size increases (Lundahl 1979:590–591).[4] The need for oats to feed the horses stimulated greater variety in the mix of crops. These complementarities led to a highly productive system of mixed farming with cereal cultivation and livestock raising becoming the predominant form of agriculture in much of Western Europe.

The stirrup, unknown in antiquity despite its apparent simplicity, led to a revolution in warfare with the armored knight on his powerful warhorse relying on the lance to pulverize opposition. The high cost of horse and armor, and the long period of training required for knightly proficiency, would have been impossible without the surplus for rents and taxes over the peasant's consumption that the heavy plow provided. At a time such as the ninth and tenth centuries, with incessant raids by the Muslims in the south and west, Vikings on the northern coasts, and marauding Magyars from the east, the peasant also needed the protection of the knight, so that "stirrup and plow" together were the effective cultural package powering the rise of Western Europe during these centuries (Bloch 1962). Both peasant and warrior needed the consolation and spiritual guidance of the priest, who in turn was supported and protected in his cloister by the peasant and the warrior, together constituting the "Three Orders" of medieval feudal society as depicted by Georges Duby (1980).

Though the concept of the frontier is usually associated with Frederick Jackson Turner (1986) and the westward expansion of the United States in the nineteenth century, it is if anything even more applicable to early medieval Europe, as many authors have realized and pointed out in the excellent study edited by Bartlett and Mackay (1989). There clearly was an internal economic frontier in already settled areas, between stretches of arable land and the immense forests surrounding them. When reflecting over the data provided by the Domesday Book,[5] M. M. Postan (1966:549) unequivocally concludes that the "Domesday facts clearly denote dense, and hence ancient settlement, the product of at least six centuries of internal colonization."

The colonization pattern was generalized in Western Europe (North and Thomas 1973). Colonization took on different shapes. Trees and bushes were cleared in the neighborhood of villages or in the waste further away, contributing to the scattering of fields. New settlements were established in the forests between villages. Coastal areas were reclaimed by the construction of embankments, and marshes were drained. Most important was the advance into forests. During the first centuries after the plague, "the forest seems to have held sway over the whole natural landscape" of Western Europe, as Duby (1974:5) writes. Lowland forest was being cleared in the eleventh and twelfth centuries both in England and France, and at the end of the twelfth century the process continued into upland areas as well, in Brittany, above the Moselle, in the Vosges, the Alps, and the Pyrenées (Grigg 1980:71–72).

There also was an external military frontier, which required armed force to push back Muslim warriors in Spain during the entire *Reconquista*, or Saxon and Slav pagan tribes east of the Elbe, particularly after 1150, settling and cultivating the lands thus won and either converting, expelling, or killing the previous occupants. With land abundant and labor scarce, particularly on the eastern frontier, once the Saxons or Slavs accepted German rule, Jesus Christ as the "Deus Teutonicus," and the German heavy plow in place of their less efficient wooden one, they were valued and protected subjects of the German princes and bishops. After a few generations the population became culturally "German" despite the abundant and perhaps even dominant presence of Slavic genes. On the other hand, Polish and other Christian Slavic rulers also welcomed the efficient German peasants as settlers on their own lands. Assimilation was more difficult in Spain, where *cristianos nuevos* were regarded with considerable suspicion, and even in Ireland where there was tension between the native Celts and the Anglo-Norman feudal lords who were granted estates soon after the conquest.

The complementarity between the stirrup and the plow and the three orders on both the eastern and western frontiers is revealed in the vital role played by the military orders in both cases, the Teutonic Knights in the east and the Orders of Calatrava and Santiago in Spain. The *Reconquista* in Spain, with Santiago Matamoros and El Cid as its foremost symbols, and the wars against the Balts and Slavs, merged into the crusading mentality that swept Christendom, and also saw the excursions against the Albigensian heretics in Provence and into Syria and Palestine against the Muslims under the banner of the cross. Not surprisingly, the movement had permanent effects within the contiguous frontiers on the mainland of Europe but proved ephemeral in the Holy Land.

The role of Christianity in the extension of the frontier was not confined by any means to the inspiration of crusaders. As the greatest landowner in Europe the church took an active part in promoting land clearance and improving agricultural productivity in other ways. It has also been pointed out, by both Lynn White and Georges Duby, that Christianity induced a more instrumental and exploitative view of nature as something purely for the service of man, rather than as being imbued with a spirit of its own that had to be respected and propitiated. The great forests of beech and oak that were cut down to clear land for pasture and tillage were the abode of spirits that the animistic pagans worshipped. This cultural shift was thus no less important than the heavy plow or the three-field rotation in making the agricultural revolution possible, so the charge of "technical determinism" by White's critics is not entirely fair. Indeed most of their objections are on matters of the speed and scope of the technical changes and not on their ultimate significance. Hilton (Sawyer and Hilton 1963) says that rather than the causal sequence from plow and three-field rotation to food supply to population it might be the other way around, from exogenous increase in population to the need for more food and hence to the changes in agricultural technique, anticipating a thesis advanced by Ester Boserup (1965).

One advantage of the modeling approach adopted in this paper is that it enables us to escape from being trapped in chicken-egg arguments of this type. In our model both food supply and population are endogenous variables, depending upon the state of technical knowledge, geographic and climatic conditions, and the biological and behavioral determinants of fertility and mortality rates. The heavy plow may have been known to antiquity, and for that matter to the Islamic world, but there was no incentive to adopt it under Mediterranean environmental and social conditions, as White himself clearly says.

The results in terms of population growth in any case were spectacular, as seen from the figures already cited. The McEvedy-Jones numbers further indicate that growth was particularly rapid in the areas of modern Germany and Poland, where it trebled over the period from 1000 to 1340 and also in the areas of modern France and Great Britain. Italy doubled from 5 to 10 million over the same period, but even this was below the average for Europe as a whole. These patterns of population growth in the old and new areas of Europe are consistent with the frontier thesis adopted in this paper.

Hand in hand with the increase in area cultivated and population went an increase in the growth of towns and trade. While in 1000 there were only a hundred places in Europe that could be called towns, and half of them were in Italy, three hundred years later the figure had increased to between 4,000 and 5,000 (Grigg 1980:77). Western European cities, however, were far smaller than their Islamic counterparts. In 1292, Paris had a population of no more than 59,000 people, and as of 1328 the figure had possibly increased to 80,000. Toulouse, an example of a large provincial town, around the same time presumably had no more than 24,000 inhabitants. In Italy, where the larges cities were found, Milan had 52,000 in the thirteenth century, Padua 41,000 in 1320, Naples 27,000 in 1278, Venice 78,000 in 1363, Bologna 32,000 in 1371, and Florence 55,000 in 1381. Before the middle of the fourteenth century only Milan, Venice, Naples, and Florence, and possibly also Palermo, exceeded 50,000 inhabitants. Some of these cities may have approached the 100,000 mark. In the Low Countries, Ghent had some 56,000–60,000 inhabitants in 1356, and Bruges 25,000–35,000 in 1340. Antwerp was a small town of 18,000 in 1374. In England, London dominated completely, with 35,000–45,000 in 1377 followed by the far smaller York and Bristol, with figures somewhere between 10,000 and

14,000. Barcelona, Cordoba, and Seville (plus Granada in the Moorish zone) were the only cities in Spain with more than 40,000 inhabitants. Only Cologne in Germany was close to the 40,000 mark, while Metz, Strasbourg, Nuremberg, Augsburg, Vienna, Prague, Lübeck, and Magdeburg had populations around 20,000 (Russell 1958, tables 63–65; van Werveke 1963:38–39). Even with a generous allowance for the influence of the Black Death on the later figures the European cities were thus extremely small, relative to Constantinople and the Islamic world.

Trade took place not only within Europe but with the Byzantine and Islamic worlds as well, leading to the well-known identification by Robert Lopez (1976) of a "commercial revolution" of the thirteenth century that was also augmented by the growing trade with Asia both by sea and overland due to the Pax Mongolica. As is well known, a Genoese ship from the Black Sea port of Kaffa engaged in this lucrative trade returned to the Mediterranean in 1347 and opened another act in the drama of "Rats, Lice and History" (Zinsser 1935).

Even before the onset of the Black Death, however, the preceding century was marked by what Archibald Lewis (1958) termed "the Closing of the Medieval Frontier 1250–1350." The internal frontier was reaching its natural limits within the prevailing technology and there is the possibility that climate may have started to become less favorable. Tillage competed with pasture to the detriment of the proper balance between the two. Population continued to grow while the supply of land was not keeping pace, lowering wages and peasant incomes while raising rents (North and Thomas 1973:48), leading to growing inequality and social conflicts in both the countryside and the towns. The external frontiers of Europe also ceased to expand, with the Muslims recovering the Holy Land and the Byzantines Constantinople in 1261.

The second decade of the fourteenth century saw the outbreak of what William Jordan (1996) has called the "Great Famine" of 1315–22. A population of Europe in excess of 70 million, under the prevailing technology, was getting to be unsustainable within its geographical confines. A Malthusian crisis of major proportions was clearly looming. Population densities in certain rural areas in 1300 had increased to the point where they were comparable with those of the early nineteenth century, when the farming technology was vastly superior (Grigg 1980). David Grigg (1980:82) summarizes:

For perhaps two centuries the expansion of the cultivated area and the adoption of new techniques was sufficient to keep production up with population growth. But by the middle of the thirteenth century the supply of agricultural land was running out; it was in this century that there are most signs of attempts to intensify production by growing legumes and reducing the fallow but they seem to have been insufficient. The primary blockage to improving yields was the lack of livestock manure, and in the densely populated arable areas of south-eastern England and northern France this reflected the lack of grazing, as population growth led to the ploughing of grazing land.

Western European agriculture was getting into a situation typical of a number of today's developing countries, where the pressure of population leads to increasingly intensive cultivation, with diminishing returns to labor and falling productivity per acre, tantamount to a reduction of the effective land area, in a sequence that easily feeds itself (Lundahl 1979). The Genoese ship from Kaffa that brought the plague into the West was in the nature of a historically necessary accident waiting to happen.

Conclusions

In the middle of the sixth century AD, the Mediterranean world was struck by the so-called Plague of Justinian, an epidemic that would recur in further successive waves until the mid-eighth century. No good estimates exist with respect to death tolls, but there is not the slightest doubt that in the areas where it hit, the consequences were extremely severe. The diffusion in space was limited, however. Northern and northwestern Europe apparently escaped, and so did the areas that a century later would constitute the core areas of the new world religion: Islam.

As a result of the plague, the population of the Eastern Roman Empire hit a trough some time around the late eighth century and then began to rise until the advent of the Black Death in the mid-fourteenth century. Simultaneously, the Islamic population rose until the Mongol invasions in the mid-thirteenth century. Europe, in turn, saw a population decline in the wake of the plague, followed by a rise that accelerated after 1000 until the early fourteenth century, when famine was followed by another outbreak of the plague. Thus, all three geographical territories display a common demographic pattern: a decline in the size of the population, followed by a rise, continuing on beyond the previous peak.

As our essay demonstrates, this pattern can be made subject to analytical representation in the form of a simple Malthusian model where birth and death rates are functions of per capita consumption, production is a function of labor and land, and the extent of the arable area determined by the existence of an agrarian or military frontier that can be extended at a rising cost in terms of labor.

This simple model can be used to investigate the impact of a demographic shock. The shock leads to an instantaneous rise in the land-labor ratio due to the collapse of population, higher wages and lower rents, and a gradual reduction of the area under cultivation. Per capita consumption, among the survivors, increases and stimulates population growth. Due to the Malthusian characteristics of the model, however, this increase cannot continue, so the land-labor ratio must fall. The price of land increases and induces land clearance at the frontier and an expansion of the area under cultivation until the original levels of both land and labor are restored.

The model can also be used to investigate the effects of a discrete technological change. This raises labor productivity and consumption per capita and so makes the population grow. Population growth, however, cannot go on indefinitely, and in order to make it cease the land-labor ratio must fall. The larger population raises rents and the price of land, inducing an increase of the area under cultivation but less than proportionately to the increase in population, thus bringing about the fall in the land-labor ratio required to restore the Malthusian equilibrium. The extent of the resulting increases in population and the supply of land depend upon the magnitude of the technical change and the elasticity of the endogenous land frontier with respect to the rise in the price of land that it induces.

A reduction of the cost of land clearance, as a result of technological progress or more favorable climatic conditions, reduces the amount of labor necessary to sustain a given land area as well as the labor needed to clear an acre of new land. The area under cultivation has to increase until the land price has fallen enough and the wage rate risen enough to equate the land price and the marginal cost of land clearance. This, in turn, also increases the population and the labor force, in the same proportion as the increase in the supply of land, to preserve the Malthusian equilibrium.

Analogously, decreases in the rate of time preference or the exogenous rate of land destruction increase the price of land at the margin and hence also the area under cultivation and the labor force in the same proportion.

Finally, an autonomous fertility reduction leads to higher per capita consumption and production in the Malthusian equilibrium. The labor force shrinks, and with it also the area under cultivation, but less than in the same proportion, permitting the economy to enjoy a permanently higher standard of living as a result of the greater relative land-abundance induced by the exogenous reduction in fertility.

The model thus makes some explicit predictions, notably with respect to the demographic shock and the effects of technological change. These predictions can be checked against the historical performance of our three geographical areas: Byzantium, the Islamic world, and Western Europe.

In Byzantium the plague (and the subsequent invasions by the Arabs) led to a contraction of the economy. The area under cultivation was reduced and as a result urban life underwent a decline as well. Per capita income, however, increased as the land-labor ratio rose, which made it possible to shoulder a higher military burden per capita. The increase in per capita income induced population growth from some time between the late eighth century and the early eleventh, a process that also received some aid from the more peaceful conditions prevailing on the political frontier. As predicted by our model, when the population began to grow back, bargaining power in the labor and land markets shifted in favor of the landowners, and this resulted in harsher contractual conditions for the peasantry. Land rents increased at the expense of wages. At the same time, political conditions deteriorated, with the military frontier being pushed in by the Seljuk Turks and the Fourth Crusade. This opened the door for the eventual collapse of the empire with the fall of Constantinople in 1453. Nowhere in this process does technological progress appear to have been present, so that the Byzantine story was simply one of population change and military operations within a shrinking territory and a concomitant loss of population to superior military force.

The core territory of what would later become the Abode of Islam escaped the ravages of the plague. The cycle began by territorial expansion. The military frontier between the Byzantine and Sassanid empires was weakened by the loss of population due to the plague, and into this population vacuum the Arabs could move relatively easily, pushing both north and west into Byzantine territory in northern Africa and east into Iran all the way to the region of Sind in the west of India. The area of arable land was extended not by clearance but by conquest. Territorial expansion was, however, accompanied by remarkable technological progress in agriculture. New crops stimulated the use of irrigation and land clearance, industrial processing of agricultural products, and also demographic growth and urban development. The population of the Islamic world would grow from some time between 700 and 750 to 1000 at a rate that was superior to that of Byzantium, but not one that could be called a "demographic revolution." Such a revolution was not possible under the unfavorable conditions of the physical environment. The largely desertlike conditions in much of the territory of Islam could not support a higher population. To this can be added the unfortunate impact of certain social institutions and the devastating blow dealt to Islam by the Mongols.

The last of our three cases, Western Europe, emerges by a wide margin as the winner in our imaginary population race. Of course, we can only speculate about the reasons for this, in the light of our model. One factor was technological change: the improvement of the plow, the substitution of the horse for the ox, the horse collar, the horseshoe, the three-field system of crop rotation, and the change in the crop mix, as well as the concomitant changes in the social system. More important, however, was what took place at the frontier of cultivation. In different ways the frontier was spectacularly extended. The dense forests had to yield to the sown. While in the case of the Islamic world the desert increasingly encroached on the sown, in Western Europe population growth induced by technical progress ensured the retreat of the wilderness. The Germans advanced towards the east across the Elbe in an early *Drang nach Osten*, and the Spaniards pushed back the Moors, in an effort that would carry over to overseas conquests beginning in 1492, the very year that the military frontier was closed in the Iberian Peninsula itself. The results of all these frontier movements were spectacular, far above the achievements by Byzantium and Islam. Cities grew, albeit not to the size of those of Byzantium and Islam, but grow they did, both in size and in numbers. Western Europe experienced the same cycle as the other two regions, first a downswing, then an upturn in population. The upturn was nothing short of spectacular in the Malthusian age that we are dealing with, to the point where at the end of the period symptoms of serious overpopulation began to appear. The advent of the Black Death drastically raised the land-labor ratio back to a much more favorable level. In a perverse sense it came as a deliverer, triggering a new demographic-economic cycle that would last all the way up to the Industrial Revolution (Findlay and Lundahl 2002).

Notes

1. The traditional date is October 732, but it could also be October 733 (Fouracre 2000:87).

2. Livi-Bacci (2001:27), quoting Biraben (1979:16), has similar figures: 200, 44 million; 600, 22 million; and 1340, 74 million.

3. The plague may not have been the only disease to gain a strong foothold in late antiquity. As McCormick (2001:38–41) has pointed out, both malaria and leprosy appear to have been on the rise in the Roman world at about the same time as when the plague of Justinian struck.

4. Let us assume that the introduction of the plow saves N man-days per hectare, and that the daily wage rate is w. The annual capital cost (the sum of depreciation and interest, which we assume to be given), of plowing S hectares is $c = SNw$, and $S = (c/w)(1/N)$ defines the lowest ("threshold") farm size that makes it profitable to introduce the plow.

5. The Domesday Book was put together some time between 1108 and 1109 or between 1111 and 1113 (Poole 1955:1 n.).

References

Bartlett, R., and A. Mackay. 1989. *Medieval Frontier Societies*. Oxford: Clarendon Press.

Biraben, J.-N. 1979. "Essai sur l'évolution du nombre des hommes." *Population* 34:13–25.

Biraben, J.-N., and J. LeGoff. 1969. "La peste dans le haut moyen âge." *Annales: Économie, Société, Civilisations* 24:1484–1510.

Bloch, M. 1962. *Feudal Society*. 2nd ed. London: Routledge and Kegan Paul.

Boserup, E. 1965. *The Conditions of Agricultural Growth: The Economics of Agrarian Change Under Population Pressure*. London: George Allen and Unwin.

Bray, R. S. 2000. *Armies of Pestilence: The Impact of Disease on History*. New York: Barnes and Noble.

Cameron, A. 1993. *The Mediterranean World in Late Antiquity*. London: Routledge.

Collins, R. 1995. *Early Medieval Spain: Unity in Diversity, 400–1000*. London: Macmillan.

Diamond, J. 1997. *Guns, Germs and Steel: The Fates of Human Societies*. New York: Norton.

Dols, M. W. 1974. "Plague in Early Islamic History." *Journal of the American Orientalist Society* 94:371–383.

Duby, G. 1974. *The Early Growth of the European Economy: Warriors and Peasants from the Seventh to the Twelfth Century*. London: Weidenfeld and Nicolson.

———. 1980. *The Three Orders*. Chicago: University of Chicago Press.

Findlay, R. 1993. "International Trade and Factor Mobility with an Endogenous Land Frontier: The General Equilibrium Consequences of Christopher Colombus." In W. J. Ethier et al., eds., *Theory, Policy and Dynamics in International Trade*, 38–54. Cambridge: Cambridge University Press.

———. 1996. "Towards a Model of Territorial Expansion and the Limits of Empire." In M. R. Garfinkel and S. Skaperdas, eds., *The Political Economy of Conflict and Cooperation*, 41–56. Cambridge: Cambridge University Press.

———. 1998. "A Plea for Trade Theory in Economic History." *Economic and Social Review* 29:313–321.

Findlay, R., and M. Lundahl. 2002. "Toward a Factor Proportions Approach to Economic History: Population, Precious Metals, and Prices from the Black Death to the Price Revolution." In R. Findlay, L. Jonung, and M. Lundahl, eds., *Bertil Ohlin: A Centennial Celebration (1899–1999)*, 495–528. Cambridge, MA: MIT Press.

———. In press. "The First Globalization Episode: The Creation of the Mongol Empire, or the Economics of Chinggis Khan." In G. Therborn and H. H. Khondkar, eds., *Asia and Europe in Globalization: Continents, Regions, and Nations*. Leiden: Brill.

Fossier, R. 1999. "Rural Economy and Country Life." In T. Reuter, ed., *The New Cambridge Medieval History*, vol. III *c. 900–c. 1024*. Cambridge: Cambridge University Press.

Fouracre, P. 2000. *The Age of Charles Martel*. Harlow: Longman.

Gregory of Tours. 1974. *The History of the Franks*. Trans. L. Thorpe. Harmondsworth: Penguin.

Grigg, D. B. 1980. *Population Growth and Agrarian Change: An Historical Perspective*. Cambridge: Cambridge University Press.

Harrison, D. 1999. *Krigarnas och helgonens tid: Västeuropas historia 400–800 e Kr*. Stockholm: Prisma.

Harvey, A. 1989. *Economic Expansion in the Byzantine Empire 900–1200*. Cambridge: Cambridge University Press.

Heckscher, E. F. 1929. "A Plea for Theory in Economic History." *Economic History* (supplement to *Economic Journal*) 1:525–534.

Henriksson, R. G. H., and M. Lundahl. 2003. "Eli Heckscher, ekonomisk teori och ekonomisk historia." In *Janusansiktet Eli Heckscher: Nationalekonom och ekonomisk historiker. Texter i urval av Rolf G. H. Henriksson och Mats Lundahl*. Stockholm: Timbro.

Hitti, P. K. 1970. *History of the Arabs: From the Earliest Times to the Present*. 10th ed. London: Macmillan.

Issawi, C. 1981. "The Area and Population of the Arab Empire: An Essay in Speculation." In A. L. Udovitch, ed., *The Islamic Middle East 700–1900*. Princeton, NJ: Darwin Press.

Jordan, W. C. 1996. *The Great Famine: Northern Europe in the Early Fourteenth Century*. Princeton, NJ: Princeton University Press.

Kazdahn, A. P., and A. W. Epstein. 1985. *Change in Byzantine Culture in the Eleventh and Twelfth Centuries*. Berkeley: University of California Press.

Khaldun, Ibn. 1958. *The Muqaddimah: An Introduction to History*. 3 vols. Trans. F. Rosenthal. New York: Pantheon Books.

Lewis, A. R. 1958. "The Closing of the Medieval Frontier 1250–1350." *Speculum* 33:475–483.

Livi-Bacci, M. 2001. *A Concise History of World Population*. 3rd ed. Malden, MA: Blackwell.

Lopez, R. S. 1976. *The Commercial Revolution of the Middle Ages, 950–1350*. Cambridge: Cambridge University Press.

Lundahl, M. 1979. *Peasants and Poverty: A Study of Haiti*. London: Croom Helm.

Mango, C. 1994. *Byzantium: The Empire of the New Rome*. London: Phoenix.

McCormick, M. 2001. *Origins of the European Economy: Communications and Commerce, A.D. 300–900*. Cambridge: Cambridge University Press.

McEvedy, C., and R. Jones. 1980. *Atlas of World Population History*. Harmondsworth: Penguin.

Nicol, D. M. 1988. *Byzantium and Venice: A Study in Diplomatic and Cultural Relations*. Cambridge: Cambridge University Press.

North, D. C., and R. P. Thomas. 1973. *The Rise of the Western World: A New Economic History*. Cambridge: Cambridge University Press.

Norwich, J. J. 1991. *The Normans in Sicily*. Harmondsworth: Penguin.

———. 1997. *Byzantium: The Decline and Fall*. New York: Knopf.

Ocaña Jiménez, M. 1975. "Córdoba musulmana." In Juan Bernier Luque et al., *Córdoba: colonia romana, corte de los califas, luz de occidente*, 25–48. Madrid: Editorial Everest.

Ostrogorsky, G. 1966. "Agrarian Conditions in the Byzantine Empire in the Middle Ages." In M. M. Postan, ed., *The Cambridge Economic History of Europe*, vol. I, *The Agrarian Life of the Middle Ages*, 205–234. 2nd ed. Cambridge: Cambridge University Press.

Planhol, X. de. 1959. *The World of Islam*. Ithaca, NY: Cornell University Press.

Poole, A. L. 1955. *From Domesday Book to Magna Carta 1087–1216*. Oxford: Clarendon Press.

Postan, M. M. 1966. "Medieval Agrarian Society in Its Prime: England." In M. M. Postan, ed., *The Cambridge Economic History of Europe*, vol. I, *The Agrarian Life of the Middle Ages*, 549–632. 2nd ed. Cambridge: Cambridge University Press.

Queller, D. E., and T. F. Madden. 1997. *The Fourth Crusade: The Conquest of Constantinople*. 2nd ed. Philadelphia: University of Pennsylvania Press.

Riley-Smith, J. 1987. *The Crusades: A Short History*. New Haven, CT: Yale University Press.

Runciman, S. 1951. *A History of the Crusades*. 3 vols. Cambridge: Cambridge University Press.

Russell, J. C. 1958. "Late Ancient and Medieval Population." *Transactions of the American Philosophical Society* 48:3–152.

———. 1968. "That Earlier Plague." *Demography* 5:174–184.

Saunders, J. J. 1965. *A History of Medieval Islam*. London: Routledge and Kegan Paul.

Sawyer, P. H., and R. Hilton. 1963. "Technical Determinism: The Stirrup and the Plough." *Past and Present* 24:90–100.

Treadgold, W. 1997. *A History of the Byzantine State and Society*. Stanford, CA: Stanford University Press.

————. 2001. *A Concise History of Byzantium*. Houndmills: Palgrave.

————. 2002. "The Struggle for Survival (641–780)." In C. Mango, ed., *The Oxford History of Byzantium*, 129–150. Oxford: Oxford University Press.

Turner, F. J. 1986. *The Frontier in American History*. Tucson: University of Arizona Press.

Van Werveke, H. 1963. "The Rise of Towns." In M. M. Postan, E. E. Rich, and E. Miller, eds., *The Cambridge Economic History of Europe*, vol. III, *Economic Organization and Policies in the Middle Ages*, 3–41. Cambridge: Cambridge University Press.

Watson, A. M. 1983. *Agricultural Innovation in the Early Islamic World*. Cambridge: Cambridge University Press.

White, L. 1962. *Medieval Technology and Social Change*. Oxford: Oxford University Press.

————. 1978. *Medieval Religion and Technology: Collected Essays*. Berkeley: University of California Press.

Wolf, E. 1966. *Peasants*. Englewood Cliffs, NJ: Prentice-Hall.

Zinsser, H. 1935. *Rats, Lice and History*. London: Routledge and Sons.

8 Explaining World Tariffs, 1870–1938: Stolper-Samuelson, Strategic Tariffs, and State Revenues

Jeffrey G. Williamson

What determines tariff policy? It can't be conventional economics, since every mainstream economist agrees that free trade is a good thing (Smith 1776; Mill 1909; Krugman 1996; Bhagwati 2000). Yet, the politics of free trade have been surrounded by controversy ever since Alexander Hamilton tried shoving his protectionist policies down the throats of a new United States federal congress after 1789, and since Robert Peel ruined his political career by shoving free trade down the throats of the British Parliament in 1846. Political leaders have never been solely, or even largely, interested in maximizing national income, let alone maximizing world income. Rather, their main goal has always been "to get a larger slice [of the pie] for their supporters" (McGillivray et al. 2001:2). Protection and free trade have always been for sale in the political market place (Grossman and Helpman 1994), but having said so doesn't make the question—What determines tariff policy?—much easier to answer. After all, nations will adopt different tariff policies to the extent that there are different economic interests lobbying for those policies, to the extent that the economic environment impacting on those interests is different, and to the extent that different political institutions dictate which economic interests have the most votes.

Thus, to explain tariff policy, we need to understand the underlying economic, political and institutional fundamentals at work. As a recent book collaboration by four political scientists has pointed out so effectively (McGillivray et al. 2001:3–16), there are three ways that endogenous tariff theory has confronted fact as it has sought to uncover the fundamentals: first, by comparing tariffs by industries within countries; second, by comparing countries at various points in time; and third, by exploring tariffs over time. It is fair to say that the vast majority of the empirical work on endogenous tariffs has elected the first route—within-country variance across industries, and most of it is on the post–World War II United States (e.g., Magee, Brock, and Young 1989; but for pre–World War II United States, see Pincus 1977 and Marvel and Ray 1983, 1987). The second route—variance across countries—has been exploited less intensively (e.g., Kindleberger 1951; Conybeare 1983; Magee, Brock, and Young 1989). The third route—variance over time—has been exploited the least (e.g., Magee, Brock, and Young 1989). A fourth route has been added recently—panel data (Coatsworth and Williamson 2004a; Blattman, Clemens, and Williamson 2002; Clemens and Williamson 2002). This essay will exploit the second, third, and fourth routes by first exploring quantitatively annual tariff rate data for thirty-five countries between 1870 and 1938 (accounting for 82.8 percent of the world's 1900 population).

The next sections will review the pre–World War II tariff evidence, identifying the tariff facts most needing explanation; explore the familiar Stolper-Samuelson corollary and its recent extensions, showing why it is so important to find out whether it has been the central force driving tariffs in the past; do the same for the infant industry argument; and lay out the contending determinants of tariff policy and explore their role empirically. Here, world tariffs are treated as country and time fixed effects in the seven decades before 1938, a period that contains both the first global century up to World War I and the interwar autarkic disaster that followed. It appears that tariff policy before World War II was driven primarily by Stolper-Samuelson forces, revenue needs and strategic tariff behavior, not by infant industry.

World Tariffs 1870–1938: The Facts

This essay uses the computed average tariff rate[1] to explore the policy experience of thirty-five countries the world around between the 1860s and World War II: the United States; three members of the European industrial core (France, Germany, United Kingdom); three non-Latin European offshoots (Australia, Canada, New Zealand); ten from the industrially lagging European periphery (Austria-Hungary, Denmark, Greece, Italy, Norway, Portugal, Russia, Serbia, Spain, Sweden); ten from Asia and the Mideast (Burma, Ceylon, China, Egypt, India, Indonesia, Japan, the Philippines, Siam, Turkey); and eight from Latin America (Argentina, Brazil, Chile, Colombia, Cuba, Mexico, Peru, Uruguay). Figure 8.1 plots average world tariffs from the 1860s to the 1990s, and figure 8.2 plots it up to 1938 for some regional clubs.[2] There are six regions plotted in figure 8.2—the United States, the European

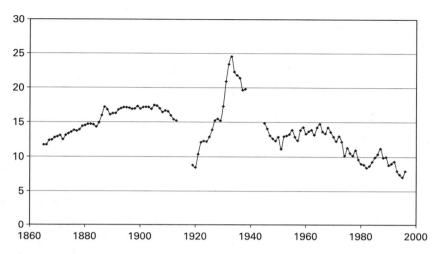

Figure 8.1
Unweighted world average own tariff, 35 countries
Source: Blattman, Clemens, and Williamson (2002, figure 1)

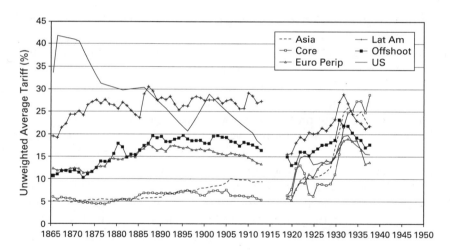

Figure 8.2
Unweighted world average of regional tariffs before World War II
Source: Coatsworth and Williamson (2002, figure 2)

industrial core, the European periphery, the European non-Latin off-shoots, Asia, and Latin America—the country members of which have just been identified.

Note first the powerful role played by inflations and deflations at key points in the past. Import duties were typically specific until modern times, quoted as pesos per bale, dollars per yard, or yen per ton. Under a regime of specific duties, abrupt changes in price levels can change import values in the denominator, but not the legislated duty in the numerator, thus producing big percentage point changes in equivalent ad valorem tariff rates. The impact of inflation during World War I was quite spectacular, and it had nothing to do with policy. Thus, tariff rates in all six regions fell sharply between 1914 and 1919,[3] and part of the rise in tariffs immediately after the war was also due to postwar deflation and the partial resumption of prewar price levels. The price deflation after 1929 was even more spectacular, and it too served to raise tariff rates at least on duties that were still specific (import values now declining). While the specific-duty effect certainly played a role worldwide at these critical points, it was not an important factor in accounting for differences between countries or for long run trends.

Second, the well-known surge to world protection in the 1920s and 1930s is certainly revealed in figure 8.1. What is less well known, however, is the pronounced protectionist drift worldwide between 1865 and about 1900. And what looks in figure 8.1 like a modest pre–World War I antiglobalization backlash—a retreat from the liberal proglobal trade positions in midcentury (Williamson 1998, 2002)—is *far* more dramatic when the world averages are disaggregated in figure 8.2. Indeed, there is a very pronounced rise in tariffs across Latin America, across the non-Latin European offshoots (the United States being the major exception) and across the European periphery. This steep rise up to the 1890s in the periphery's tariff rates *far* exceeds that of the European core, a notable fact given that almost nothing has been written on this antiglobal tariff trend in the periphery.

Third, note the enormous variance in levels of protection between the regional averages. The richer New World European offshoots had levels of protection almost three times that of the European core around the turn of the last century. When the United States is shifted to the rich European offshoot club, the ratio of European offshoot tariffs to that of the core is more than three to one. To take another example, in 1925 the European periphery had tariffs about two and a half times higher than those in the European part of the industrial core. To take yet another example, in 1885 the poor but independent parts of Latin America (Brazil, Colombia, Mexico, and Peru) had tariffs almost five times higher than those in the poor and dependent parts of Asia (Burma, Ceylon, China, Egypt, India, Indonesia, and the Philippines), while the poor but independent parts of Asia (Siam, Turkey, and Japan) had tariff rates about the same as the poor but dependent parts of Asia. Of course, colonial status, lack of autonomy, and "unequal treaties" all played an important role in Asia, and we will want to control for that fact in what follows.

Fourth, there was great variance *within* these regional clubs. In 1905, tariffs in Uruguay (the most protectionist land-abundant and labor-scarce country) were about two and a half times those in Canada (the least protectionist land-abundant and labor-scarce country). In the same year, tariffs in Brazil and Colombia (the most protectionist poor but autonomous countries in Latin America) were almost ten times those in China and India (the least protectionist poor and nonautonomous countries in Asia). The same high-low range appeared within the industrial core (the United States five times the United Kingdom) and the European periphery (Russia six times Austria-Hungary). Between 1919 and 1938, the tariff variance between countries was about the same as tariff variance over time, but between 1865 and 1914, the tariff variance between countries was more than twice that of the tariff variance over time. Thus, explaining differences in tariff policy between countries is at least as challenging as explaining changes in tariff policy over the eight decades after the 1860s, perhaps more so.

The empirical analysis later in this essay will treat countries as the unit of observation, but for a moment let us linger a little longer on the regional clubs. Prior to World War I, tariffs were much higher in the rich European offshoots than anywhere else. Furthermore, and as I have already mentioned, they would have been even higher had I allocated to this club one of the most protectionist, the United States (which is allocated instead to the core).[4] The European members of the industrial core (France, Germany, the United Kingdom) had the lowest tariffs, although the United States serves to raise the club average. Most members of the poor periphery in Asia were colonies or quasi-colonies of the industrial core (Burma, Ceylon, Egypt, India, Indonesia, the Philippines), or were forced to sign free trade agreements ("unequal treaties") with the core since the latter had naval guns trained on their potential trading partners (China, Japan), or viewed nearby gunboats as a sufficient threat to go open on their own (Siam). Thus, tariff rates in Asia were pretty much like those of the core early on, but they started drifting toward protection after the 1880s, long before the post–World War II independence movement.

It should also be stressed that colonial status did not necessarily imply lack of local influence on tariff policy. There are five colonies in our sample from Asia: Burma, Ceylon, India, Indonesia, and the Philippines, although foreign influence was strong enough (including occupation) to make Egypt behave like a colony. A previous paper (Clemens and Williamson 2002) has shown that while colonial tariff policy did indeed mimic that of their masters, local conditions mattered as well. Thus, I retain the full sample of thirty-five, although I will take care to control for colonial status and tariff autonomy.

In any case, while Asia had the lowest tariffs in 1865, they were approaching that of the protectionist rich European offshoots by 1914. The European periphery leaped to high levels of protection after the 1870s, with Russia leading the way. There is plenty of evidence of rising world protection before World War I (the unweighted average in the full sample rising from about 12 percent in 1865 to about 17.5 percent in 1900), but the much-studied European continental backlash plotted in figure 8.2 looks pretty modest compared with the rest of the world. Indeed, the pre-1914 global backlash took place mainly in Latin America, the European offshoots (excluding the United States, which retreated from its enormous Civil War tariffs), and the European periphery.

There are some surprises in these tariff data that have not been given much notice by previous scholars. For example, the traditional literature has made much of the tariff backlash on the continent to the "grain invasion" after the 1870s (Kindleberger 1951; Bairoch 1989; O'Rourke 1997): between the 1870s and the 1890s, average tariff rates rose by 5.7 percentage points in France (to 10.1 percent) and 5.3 percentage points in Germany (to 9.1 percent). However, this antiliberal move to higher tariffs by the leading economies on the continent is repeated in the European periphery (up 4.2 percentage points to 16.8 percent) and in our four poor Latin American countries (up 6.9 percentage points to 34 percent), regions where, one assumes, a "manufactures invasion" must have been the motivating event. The traditional literature also teaches that the Latin American reluctance to go open in the late twentieth century was the product of the Great Depression and the import substitution industrial (ISI) strategies that arose from it (Diaz-Alejandro 1984; Corbo 1992). Yet, Latin America already had by far the highest tariffs in the world by the mid- to late nineteenth century (Coatsworth and Williamson 2004a, 2004b). Thus, whatever explanation is offered for the Latin American commitment to high tariffs, it must search for origins well before the Great Depression. Finally, it is not true that Asia waited for post–World War II independence to switch to protectionist policies. I have already noted that there was an upward surge in tariff rates in Asia after the 1880s and early 1890s, illustrated best by Burma, India, the Philippines, Siam, and Turkey. With the exception of Egypt and Japan, all of the Asian countries underwent a surge to high tariffs in the 1930s, and most of these countries stuck with these higher tariffs into the 1940s and the modern era. How much of the surge in Asian tariffs from the 1880s to the 1930s was due to a weakening colonial grip and to the expiration of "unequal treaties" signed decades earlier, both of which would have given the region the increasing autonomy to set higher tariffs according to local political economy forces?

Tariffs took two big leaps upward in the interwar decades, and these took place world wide. The first leap was in the 1920s, which might be interpreted as a return to high prewar tariff rates. The second was in the 1930s, with the well-known and aggressive beggar-my-neighbor policies. The biggest interwar tariff hikes in the industrial core were initiated by Germany and the United Kingdom, but France and the United States were not far behind. Indeed, the rise in tariff rates was *so* pronounced in the core, that the big pre-1914 spread between the high-tariff autonomous periphery and the low-tariff industrial core evaporated. Still, tariffs rose in most of the European periphery and almost everywhere in Latin America, Asia and the Middle East. To give some sense of how large the rise in tariff barriers was around an Asian periphery dominated by allegedly passive and free-trading colonies, the tariff rate rose in India by 22 percentage points between 1920 and 1939, in Egypt it rose by 36.7 percentage points between 1920 and 1939, in Siam it rose by 26.9 percentage points between 1918 and 1936, and in Turkey it rose by 34.1 percentage points between 1923 and 1937.

So, what determined who protected and when in the century and a half before World War II?

Was It Stolper-Samuelson or Something Else, and Why Does It Matter?

Was the rise in tariffs and/or high tariffs before World War I driven by some antiglobal reaction, that is, by some backlash? Until the race towards autarky in the 1930s, the free traders were members of the industrial core, their colonies, or those who their gunboats had intimidated to open up. The rest had erected high tariff walls. Was the autonomous periphery exhibiting global backlash? In the three decades or so following 1865, the rise in tariff rates was ubiquitous worldwide. Was this upsurge a policy backlash response to the spectacular fall in transport costs which was serving to integrate world commodity markets and to blow the winds of international competition down the necks of import-competing industries which geography had protected before? It is essential to get answers to these questions if the modern debate about the future of globalization is to be properly informed by history. Simply to show high and/or rising tariffs is not enough. Did globalization backlash account for it?

The most elegant backlash explanation has its roots in Stockholm. Eli Heckscher and Bertil Ohlin told us how endowments could account for trade patterns, factor abundance dictating competitiveness in world markets and what would be exported by whom. In addition, Heckscher (1991) showed how foreign trade effects the distribution of income, but most economists had to wait for Wolfgang Stolper and Paul Samuelson (1941) to elaborate the corollary in English, namely that the scarce factor should favor protection and the abundant factor should favor free trade. A decade or so ago, (Heckscher-) Stolper-Samuelson thinking was used with great skill by Ronald Rogowski (1989) who applied it to country trade policy the world around from 1840 to the present. There are two limitations to the way Rogowski uses the Stolper-Samuelson corollary, however. The first limitation is that the corollary only tells us who votes for what, not who wins the voting. Since the landed elite dominated voting in land-scarce Europe,[5] the import-competing sectors got the protection from foreign grains that the landed elite wanted. Trade theorists have, in fact, offered an explicit rule (the "endowment effect") whereby the "equilibrium tariff increases with the square root of the ratio of the country's scarce factor to its abundant factor" (Magee, Brock, and Young 1989:25). Alternatively, as the scarce factor shrinks in relative size, its power at the polls shrinks too. However, what happens to such endowment rules when the scarce factor does not have the vote, as was true of labor through-out most of the world before the 1930s?[6] Did labor get the protection of import-competing manufacturing that it should have wanted in labor-scarce Latin America, in the labor-scarce English-speaking new world, and labor-scarce southeast Asia? The second limitation is that Rogowski uses the corollary to speak only to *levels* of protection rather than to *changes* in protection. We want to know whether a rise in protection can be attributed to globalization backlash and to compen-sation of the damaged scarce factor, so a dynamic version of Stolper-Samuelson is more relevant.

While the Ricardo-Viner-Cairnes specific-factor model yields results similar to the Stolper-Samuelson model—import-competing industries favor protection, (Heckscher-) Stolper-Samuelson thinking is probably more effective for long-run analysis like that contained in this essay. More generally, when the import-competing sector is damaged by an adverse price shock (an improvement in the country's terms of trade) induced by world market events or by declining seaborne transport costs that reduce import and raise export prices, is there always a "compensation effect" that drives up tariffs? The answer will depend largely on whether the factors in the slumping sector can escape to the booming sector. Stolper-Samuelson has a far better chance of explain-ing nineteenth-century tariff policy when, after all, most trade was in primary products and (immobile) specific factors played a big role. It has a far poorer chance of explaining modern tariff policy when trade is dominated by manufactures and most factors—labor, skills and capital—are mobile.[7]

There is no shortage of elegant backlash models. It's the evidence brought to bear that's scarce.

Was It Infant Industry or Something Else, and Why Does It Matter?

It has always been believed that a second powerful motivation for high tariffs on imported manufactures in the early-industrial periphery is development policy. Central authorities were persuaded for much of the twentieth century that industrialization was the only vehicle for development and that protection fostered that process. Indeed, they have often cited nineteenth-century experience to help support these claims. I will call this motivation the infant industry argument for short, with the understanding that it includes development and indus-trial policy.

Does protection help or hinder growth? It should be useful to answer this question first to see whether policy makers in the autonomous parts of the periphery could have used such evidence to support their protectionist policies in the century before the 1930s. Of course, policy makers of that time didn't have the models, methods, and evidence that we can exploit today, but they certainly would have had the intuition. Were we asking this question about the late twentieth century, then the evidence would strongly support the position that protection *hindered* growth. But what about the nineteenth century? Did protection foster[8] growth in the pre–World War I periphery where those tariff rates were so high?

Policy makers in those parts of the periphery which had tariff autonomy were certainly aware of the pro-protectionist infant-industry argument offered for the German *Zollverein* by Frederich List and for the United States customs union by Alexander Hamilton. This was certainly true of late-nineteenth-century Latin America (Bulmer-Thomas 1994:140). However, it is important to stress "late" in the previous sentence since the use of protection specifically and consciously to foster industry does not occur in Mexico until the early 1890s, Brazil and Chile a little later in the 1890s, and Colombia in the early 1900s (Coatsworth and Williamson 2004a, 2004b). So, the qualitative evidence suggests that domestic industry protection becomes a significant motivation for Latin American tariffs only near the turn of the previous century. It turns out that there is absolutely no pre–World War I quantitative evidence which would have supported infant industry arguments for Latin America either: high tariffs were correlated with slow growth, just like the late twentieth century (Coatsworth and Williamson 2004a). We must look elsewhere for plausible explanations for the exceptionally high (and often rising) tariffs in the autonomous periphery in the century before the Great Depression. One of the alternative explanations that I will explore in the next section involves the revenue needs of central governments. As a signal of things to come, I simply note here that the causation probably went the other way round in the autonomous periphery. That is, countries achieving rapid GDP per capita growth also had underwent faster growth in imports and in other parts of the tax base, thus reducing the need for high tariff *rates*. And countries suffering slow growth would have had to keep tariff *rates* high to ensure adequate revenues.

Why is it important to find no evidence supporting a protection-fosters-growth correlation in the periphery before the interwar decades? The answer, of course, is that such evidence would add more support to the view that those high and rising tariffs in the periphery represented a "globalization backlash" as it was "flooded with manufactures" from the industrial core.[9] The periphery *was* flooded with ever-cheaper manufactures, as the natural barriers of geography fell in response to the railroad and steamship, and as industrial Europe and North America underwent impressive productivity advance in manufacturing. If the periphery was in fact hoping to stimulate industrial development by protection, tariffs would have had to rise higher and higher to offset the continued fall in the landed price of imported manufactures.

The Political Economy of Tariffs: Some Preliminaries

Tariffs for Revenue

Were revenues a strong motive for high tariffs? If so, were those high pre–World War I tariffs in Latin America and the European periphery really all that the market could bear? As Douglas Irwin (1998a:8–12) has recently stressed for the United States, the revenue-maximizing tariff hinges crucially on the price elasticity of import demand. Tariff revenue can be expressed as $R = tpM$, where R is revenue, t is the average ad valorem tariff rate, p is the average import price, and M is import volume. Totally differentiating with respect to t, and assuming that the typical nineteenth century country in the periphery was a price taker for manufacturing imports, yields $dR/dt = pM + (tp)\,dM/dt$. The revenue-maximizing tariff rate, t^*, is found by setting $dR/dt = 0$—the peak of some Laffer curve—in which case $t^* = -1/(1 + \eta)$, where η is the price elasticity of demand for imports. Irwin (1998a:14) estimates the price elasticity to have been about -2.6 for the United States between 1869 and 1913. Since the import mix for countries around the periphery was similar to that of the United States, assuming the price elasticity for the former around -3 can't be too far off the mark. Under those assumptions, the revenue-maximizing tariff in the periphery would have been very high indeed, about 50 percent.

Suppose some government in the periphery—riding an export boom—had in mind some target revenue share in GDP ($R/Y = r$) and could not rely on foreign capital inflows to balance the current account (so $pM = X$), then $r = tpM/Y = tX/Y$. Clearly, if foreign exchange earnings from exports (and thus imports) were booming (an event which could be caused by a terms of trade boom, denoted here by a fall in the relative price of imports, p, or by a supply-side expansion which increased export quantities, X), then the target revenue share could have been achieved at lower tariff rates, t. The bigger the export boom, the higher the export share, the bigger the import share, and the lower the necessary tariff rate.

So, did independent governments in Latin America, the European periphery, and Asia act as if they were meeting revenue targets? *Ceteris paribus*, did they lower tariff rates during world primary product booms when export shares were high and rising, and did they raise them during world primary product slumps?

Of course, countries in the periphery that were successful in getting external finance from the European core would have had less reason to use high tariffs to augment revenues in the short run and medium term. Since world capital markets became increasingly well integrated up to 1913 (Obstfeld and Taylor 2003), high tariffs that were necessary in 1865 would no longer have been necessary in 1913 if "revenue smoothing" was a key motivation. However, there may have been plenty of motivation to raise them again when world capital markets fell apart in the interwar years. Furthermore, countries that developed internal (and less distortionary) tax sources would have had less need for high tariffs, an event that started in the late-nineteenth-century industrial core, accelerating during the interwar rise of the welfare state (Lindert 1994). Such developments lagged behind in the periphery, however.

The (Heckscher-) Stolper-Samuelson Theorem and Scarce Factor Compensation

The Stolper-Samuelson theorem tells us that protection benefits owners of factors in which that society is *poorly* endowed. According to this kind of thinking, Latin American capitalists should have been looking to form protectionist coalitions as soon as the *belle époque* began to threaten them with freer trade. In most cases, they did not have to look far, either because they managed to dominate oligarchic regimes that excluded other interests, or because they readily found coalition partners willing to help, or both (Rogowski 1989; Coatsworth and Williamson 2004a).

Why no scarce labor in the Latin American tale? Growth, peace, and political stability after 1870 did not necessarily produce democratic inclusion in Latin America. Most countries in the region limited the franchise to a small minority of adult men until well into the twentieth century. Literacy and wealth requirements excluded, as we have seen, most potential voters in virtually every country (Engerman, Haber, and Sokoloff 2000). Thus, the late nineteenth century tended to produce oligarchic governments in which urban capitalists—linked to external trade and finance—played a dominant role. In countries that specialized in exporting agricultural products, free-trading landowners formed the second dominant part of the governing oligarchy. Free-trading mineral export interests usually had less direct leverage in governmental decision making, despite the size and significance of their investments. Thus, unambiguous protectionist outcomes would hardly have been predicted for every Latin American country.

To the extent that Stolper-Samuelson thinking is useful in accounting for the variance in tariff rates the world around before World War II, we would expect plenty of regional differences, as Rogowski has argued. After all, very different endowments and political participation characterized various parts of the periphery. The land-abundant English-speaking New World countries were places where scarce labor had a powerful political voice to lobby for protection, joining scarce capital. The European periphery had scarce land and capital lobbying for protection, while the voices of free-trading labor were suppressed. Southeast Asia had scarce labor and capital, but with political participation limited to free-trading landed interests. The rest of Asia was pretty much land and capital scarce, but free-trading labor had little or no political voice. The important point here is that the Stolper-Samuelson theorem tells us who should vote for free trade and who should vote for protection, but it does not tell us who gets the most votes.

Productivity Advance Abroad, Deindustrialization Fears and Scarce Factor Compensation

Were high and rising tariffs in the periphery generated by deindustrialization fears and/or Stolper-Samuelson compensation of scarce factors at home in response to falling import prices?

Three things are essential to the survival of domestic industry (using scarce factors): low costs of inputs—like labor, power, and raw materials; high productivity in the use of those inputs; and high market prices of output. Policy makers in the periphery could not do much about the first two,[10] but they could do a great deal about the third by pushing up tariff barriers, excluding foreign imports and thus raising the domestic price of manufactures relative to other products produced for home or foreign markets. When industrial productivity advance in the core was fast, world market prices of manufactures would decline relative to other products, and foreign firms would be increasingly competitive in local periphery markets. Thus, policy makers in the periphery who favored industry, and/or the scarce factors used there, would have had reason to raise tariffs in response to any sharp decline in the relative price of manufactures, especially relative to prices of the primary products the periphery exported to Europe. In short, if the periphery had deindustrialization fears, or wanted to compensate the damaged scarce factors, it would have raised tariffs in response to falling prices of manufactures in world markets, that is in response to a rise in the world price of primary products, and thus to an improvement in the periphery's terms of trade.

Evaporating Geographic Barriers, Tariff-Transport Cost Trade-offs, and Scarce Factor Compensation

High transport costs on goods imported from one's trading partner are just as protective as high tariffs. When new transport technologies induce a dramatic fall in freight costs, the winds of competition thus created give powerful incentives to import competing industries (and scarce factors) to lobby for more protection. Since there certainly was a transport revolution across the nineteenth century (O'Rourke and Williamson 1999; Mohammed and Williamson 2004), there was plenty of incentive for manufacturing interests in the periphery and agricultural interests in the core to lobby for protection as the natural barriers afforded by transport costs melted away. This connection was confirmed long ago for the "invasion of grains" into Europe from the United States, the rest of the new world, and Russia. But what about the "invasion of manufactures" into the periphery from industrial Europe?

The transport revolution took many forms, but three mattered most: a decline in overseas tramp freight rates; the appearance of major canals such as the Suez and the Panama; and the penetration of railroads into interior markets. Tramp freight rates fell everywhere, but mainly on routes carrying high bulk intermediates and foodstuffs to Europe, much less on routes carrying low bulk manufactures to the periphery. Meanwhile, railroads penetrated everywhere, and this fact might have been especially relevant for tariff policy where markets were mainly located in the interior. If railroads exposed previously isolated interior local manufacturing to increased foreign competition, those interests should have lobbied for more protection, and railroad penetration of the interior was especially important in Latin America, Eastern Europe, and even India.

Strategic Trade Policy, the Terms of Trade, and Tariffs

A well-developed theoretical literature on strategic trade policy predicts that nations have an incentive to inflate their own terms of trade by raising tariffs, unless, of course, trading partners agree to mutual concessions (Dixit 1987; Bagwell and Staiger 2002). According to this kind of thinking, a country's own tariffs will depend at least in part upon the country's external tariff environment. Elsewhere, a principal-trading-partners'-tariff index has been calculated for our thirty-five countries (Blattman, Clemens, and Williamson 2002) and the index is revealing. In the two decades before World War I, every region except the industrial core and Latin America faced much lower tariff rates in their main export markets than they themselves erected against competitors in their own markets. The explanation, of course, is that the main export markets were located in the European core, where tariffs were much lower. Thus, most of the periphery faced much lower tariffs than did the core, although this was not true of Latin America for whom the protectionist United States was such an important market. During the interwar period there was convergence: every regional club faced very similar and high tariff rates in export markets, but those rates facing the periphery were rising very steeply as the core made that big policy switch from free trade to protection.

It might pay to repeat that Latin America, for example, faced far higher tariffs than anyone else since they traded with the heavily protected United States. So, did this "hostile" policy environment abroad trigger a like response at home? While the strategic trade thesis holds promise in helping account for higher tariffs in Latin America and in that part of the European periphery trading with more-protectionist France and Germany, it holds less promise for that part of the European periphery whose exports were sent to free-trading United Kingdom. Indeed, between 1900 and World War I a decline in partner tariffs took place everywhere in the periphery *except* in the European periphery, suggesting a leader-follower reaction that varied across the periphery depending on who the dominant trading partner was, for instance, an ultraprotectionist United States lowering tariffs, a moderately protectionist France and Germany raising tariffs, or a free-trade Britain standing pat (Blattman, Clemens, and Williamson 2002).

Controls: Price Instability and the Specific-Duty Effect

Inflations and deflations have had a powerful influence on average tariff rates. Recall that import duties were typically *specific* until modern times, quoted as pesos per bale, yen per yard, or dollars per bag. Under specific duty regimes, abrupt changes in price levels change import values in the denominator, but not the legislated duty in the numerator, thus producing big equivalent ad valorem or percentage rate changes. This specific-duty effect implies, of course, that debating the tariff structure is politically expensive, and thus is only infrequently changed by new legislation. The specific-duty effect has been explored most fully for the United States (Crucini 1994; Irwin 1998b:1017), but also for Mexico (Marquez 2002:307), and, more generally, for Latin America (Coatsworth and Williamson 2004a). The specific-duty effect has not, however, been explored at a global level. Nor does the literature tell us why specific duties seem to be much more common in young, nonindustrial, and poor countries. One answer might be this: Honest and literate customs inspectors are scarce in poor countries, but they are essential for implementing an ad valorem tariff where import valuation is so crucial. So, legislators impose specific duties to minimize the "theft" of state tariff revenues by dishonest and illiterate customs agents. Another answer might be this: Poor countries export primary products, concentrating on only a few, thus exposing themselves to price instability. Since export revenues and import expenditures are highly correlated, unstable export prices imply unstable export values and, finally, unstable tariff revenues. Specific duties tend to smooth out the impact of the export price instability on government finances.

Controls: Policy Packages and Real Exchange Rate Trade-offs

Few policies are decided in isolation. Indeed, there were other ways that governments could have improved the competitive position of import-competing industries, if such protection was their goal, and they explored many of these alternatives in the 1930s and in the ISI years that followed. Yet, they clearly understood these alternatives even before World War I. One powerful alternative involved manipulating the real exchange rate. If governments chose to go on the gold standard or to peg to a core currency, they got more stable real exchange rates in return (and an attractive advertisement for foreign capital). However, since protection via real exchange rate manipulation was forgone, tariff rates would have to go up to reclaim that protection lost. Did countries exploit this trade-off both during the years of gold standard commitment before World War I and during the interwar years when everybody went off gold?

The Political Economy of Tariff-Rate Setting: Empirical Analysis

The potential explanations for tariff policies discussed in previous sections can be allocated to three main motives: strategic trade policy, revenue needs, and scarce factor tariff compensation. I take the infant industry development goal to be a mid- to late-twentieth-century motivation. These four central motives need not have been competing. Still, even though each may have played a role before World War II, we would like to know which played the biggest roles, and in which periods and places. Elsewhere, an econometric attack has been launched on the problem two ways (Blattman, Clemens, and Williamson 2002; Clemens and Williamson 2002; Coatsworth and Williamson 2004a): first, by treating the experience as comparative world economic history and thus exploring time series only (TS); and second, by exploring the cross-section variance across these thirty-five countries using time fixed effects (CS). The cross-section results are transformed to remove serial correlation (using the AR(1) Cochrane-Orcutt correction), and the time series are estimated using random effects (RE) after likewise correcting for serial correlation (with a Baltagi-Wu estimator). What I report here summarizes the main findings.

Table 8.1 presents the time-series and cross-section results. Each of these contains five columns, necessitated by the fact that data coverage for inflation and the terms of trade is inferior to that of the other regressors. The right-hand side variables suggested by the previous section are the following (all but dummies in logs), allocated to the three central motives.

Revenue Motive

Lagged Export Share. This export/GDP ratio is a measure of export boom, where we expect booms in the previous year to diminish the

Table 8.1
Tariff Rate Determinants the World Around, 1870–1938
Dependent variable: ln Own Tariff
Includes AR(1) Baltagi-Wu (TS) or Cochrane-Orcutt (CS) serial correlation correction

Specification	TS, country RE					CS, year dummies				
Years	1870–1938	1870–1938	1870–1938	1870–1938	1870–1938	1870–1938	1870–1938	1870–1938	1870–1938	1870–1938
Countries	All	All	All	All	All	All	All	All	All	All
Revenue Motive										
ln Export Share	−0.0285 (−1.36)	−0.0832 (−3.02)	−0.0609 (−2.30)	−0.0463 (−2.07)	−0.0924 (−3.32)	−0.0397 (−1.37)	−0.0645 (−1.67)	−0.0601 (−1.60)	−0.0539 (−1.80)	−0.0753 (−2.02)
Strategic Tariff Motive										
ln Partner Tariffs	0.2490 (9.06)	0.2507 (6.64)	0.2992 (8.45)	0.2246 (7.54)	0.2526 (6.67)	−0.0440 (−1.22)	−0.0983 (−1.82)	−0.0338 (−0.60)	−0.0648 (−1.76)	−0.0953 (−1.73)
Stolper-Samuelson Scarce Factor Compensation Motive										
ln Terms of Trade Index				0.0798 (2.22)	0.1219 (2.68)				0.1037 (2.55)	0.1371 (2.66)
ln GDP per capita	−0.1412 (−2.40)	−0.2227 (−2.86)	−0.1745 (−2.28)	−0.1810 (−2.95)	−0.2260 (−2.90)	−0.1025 (−1.48)	−0.1445 (−1.44)	−0.1228 (−1.24)	−0.1439 (−2.00)	−0.1435 (−1.45)
ln Schooling	0.1640 (4.02)	−0.0560 (−0.82)	−0.0573 (−0.84)	0.1719 (4.30)	−0.0416 (−0.61)	0.0672 (1.49)	−0.3046 (−2.96)	−0.2993 (−3.01)	0.0548 (1.22)	−0.3053 (−2.99)
ln Effective Distance	−0.0735 (−4.86)	−0.1072 (−4.95)	−0.1267 (−5.97)	−0.0584 (−3.76)	−0.1086 (−5.02)	−0.0169 (−0.74)	−0.0644 (−1.53)	−0.0514 (−1.28)	−0.0309 (−1.29)	−0.0616 (−1.48)
ln Railway Mileage	0.0354 (3.38)	0.0639 (2.25)	0.0579 (1.98)	0.0347 (3.41)	0.0590 (2.08)	0.0055 (0.80)	0.0212 (0.93)	0.0190 (0.84)	0.0042 (0.56)	0.0219 (0.94)
ln Urbanization	0.0478 (2.13)	0.0198 (0.30)	0.0013 (0.02)	0.0462 (2.10)	0.0235 (0.36)	0.0242 (0.99)	−0.0890 (−1.58)	−0.0989 (−1.66)	0.0211 (0.79)	−0.0787 (−1.41)

Controls										
ln Population	−0.1084	−0.1716	−0.1441	−0.1172	−0.1721	−0.1224	−0.0433	−0.0545	−0.1302	−0.0504
	(−2.50)	(−3.35)	(−2.81)	(−2.58)	(−3.38)	(−2.85)	(−0.84)	(−1.12)	(−3.00)	(−1.00)
Federal						0.0100	0.0524	0.0585	0.0071	0.0509
						(0.35)	(1.45)	(1.55)	(0.25)	(1.35)
Colony						−0.0033	−0.1649	−0.2797	−0.0695	−0.1515
						(−0.05)	(−0.83)	(−1.58)	(−1.50)	(−0.79)
Inflation			−0.0004		−0.0005			−0.0004		−0.0003
			(−1.45)		(−1.46)			(−0.90)		(−0.69)
Inflation Squared			0.0000		0.0000			0.0000		0.0000
			(2.45)		(1.77)			(0.44)		(0.52)
Constant	2.7797	5.8022	5.4237	2.6333	5.1674					
	(4.75)	(7.80)	(7.45)	(4.28)	(6.68)					
N	2,138	1,169	1,300	1,951	1,169	2,067	1,116	1,238	1,889	1,116
Groups	35	30	35	35	30					
Avg. obs/group	61.1	39	37.1	55.7	39					
R-squared overall	0.224	0.271	0.25	0.251	0.266	0.144	0.203	0.195	0.149	0.211
DW original	0.222	0.242	0.251	0.227	0.245	0.083	0.107	0.115	0.083	0.111
DW transformed						1.972	1.979	1.948	1.982	1.987

t-statistics are in parentheses below each coefficient estimate. War years (1914–1918) omitted. Schooling is measured as the number of people per 10,000 below the age of 15 who are enrolled in primary school. The terms of trade = 100 in 1900.
Source: Blattman, Clemens, and Williamson (2002), Table 3 (revised).

need for high tariff rates this year—if government revenues are a key motivation—thus yielding negative coefficients in the regression.[11]

Strategic Tariffs Motive

Lagged Partner Tariffs. Strategic tariff policy suggests that countries should have imposed higher tariffs this year if they faced higher tariffs in their main markets abroad last year.

Stolper-Samuelson Scarce Factor Compensation Motive

Terms of Trade Index. In the periphery, this terms of trade variable measures the price of each jth country's primary product exports (Pxj) relative to the price of manufactures (Pm) in world markets. In the core, the opposite is the case. If deindustrialization fears in the periphery were dominant, a positive coefficient should appear: price shocks in world markets that were good for the periphery's export sectors were bad for import competing sectors inviting compensation for the injured parties. Thus, the sign on ln (Lagged Px/Pm) should tell us whether deindustrialization fears dominated in the periphery. In the European core and in land scarce Asia (like Japan), imports were dominated by foodstuffs and raw materials. Here, Px/Pm speaks to an "invasion of grain" fear, whether wheat or rice, inviting compensation for the injured parties in this case too;

GDP per capita and *Schooling*, the latter the primary school enrollment rate. These variables are taken as proxies for skill endowments, with the expectation that the more abundant the skills, the more competitive the industrial sector, and the less the need for protection, thus yielding a negative coefficient in the regression;

Effective Distance. The distance from each country to either the United States or the United Kingdom (depending on trade volume), adjusted by seaborne freight rates specific to that route. If protection was the goal, effective distance should have served as a substitute for tariffs, so the regression should yield a negative coefficient;

Railway Mileage added in kilometers. Poor overland transport connections to interior markets serve as a protective device. Railroads reduce that protection, requiring higher tariffs to offset the effect. Thus, the regression should yield a positive coefficient;

Urbanization, taken as share of population in cities and towns greater than 20,000. This urbanization statistic is taken to be a Stolper-Samuelson proxy for the lobbying power of urban capitalists and artisans in the periphery, thus yielding a positive coefficient in the periphery regressions.

Controls

Inflation and inflation-squared. To the extent that countries used specific duties, inflation should have lowered tariff rates, thus yielding a negative coefficient. However, very rapid inflation might well have triggered a speedier legislative reaction with increases in specific duties, thus yielding a positive and offsetting coefficient on the squared term in the regression;

Population. Large countries have bigger domestic markets in which it is easier for local firms to find a spatial niche. Alternatively, bigger populations imply higher density, which makes domestic tax collection easier and tariff revenues less necessary. In either case, the demand for protection should be lower in large countries, and the regression should produce a negative coefficient;

Federal, a dummy variable; if a federal system = 1, if centralized = 0. Federal governments had a stronger need for customs duties (joining members retained their tax authority), while centralized governments could better exploit internal revenue sources. Thus, the regression should report a positive coefficient;

Colony, a dummy variable; if a "colony" = 1, 0 otherwise.[12]

Comparative Tariff History Results

Turning first to the time series in table 8.1, we see that all coefficients have the expected sign with the exception of schooling (at least some of the time). Revenue motivation is revealed since export booms were associated with lower tariffs. Backlash and compensation forces are revealed too, and in many ways. Decreases in overseas transportation costs were associated with an offsetting rise in tariff barriers, and increases in the length of the domestic rail network were associated with a symmetric rise in tariffs. As geographic barriers evaporated, import-competing industries were compensated by higher tariffs. Also,

an improvement in a country's terms of trade in world markets gener--
ated a strong antiglobal reaction. For the periphery, this took the form
of a deindustrialization reaction since an improvement in the relative
price of their primary product export in world markets implied a fall
in the relative price of imported manufactures, inviting a tariff-raising
lobbying reaction by industrial interests at home. For the European
core, this took the form of a grain invasion reaction, as a rise in the relative price of their manufacturing exports implied a fall in the relative
price of their imported foodstuffs, inviting a tariff-raising lobbying
reaction by landed interests at home. There is strong support for strategic tariff motives, since partner tariffs has a positive and significant coefficient throughout. The results for both schooling and urbanization
depend on whether we control for inflation or not. Since including inflation reduces the sample size by almost half, however, we do not
know if the different results for schooling and urbanization are due to
the restricted sample or to the fact of controlling for inflation. In the
full sample, an increase in urbanization was associated with an increase in tariffs, just as the Stolper-Samuelson theorem would predict,
at least in the capital-scarce periphery. Tariff rates fell with increases in
GDP per capita, a result consistent with modern surveys of global attitudes (O'Rourke and Sinnott 2003), but which I also find consistent
with the Stolper-Samuelson theorem. Internal market size mattered in
the predicted way: large countries had lower tariff rates. Finally, note
that while inflation had the predicted effect throughout the period, it
was not statistically significant. Thus, while inflation had its predicted
effects during wartime (figure 8.1), it did not during peacetime. I believe this is due to the limited sample with inflation coverage underlying table 8.1.[13]

Judging by the estimated elasticities, increases in trading partner
tariffs were by far the most powerful determinant of increases in own
tariffs over the full seven decades, at least on the economic margin.
Changes in GDP per capita, population, and schooling had elasticities
next in size. The combined influence of geography—the sum of falling
effective sealane distance and rising railway mileage—also had high
elasticities, but they still were only half that of partner tariffs. The
same is true of the terms of trade index. Much to my surprise, the
lowest elasticity reported in table 8.1 is that attached to changes in the
export share, suggesting that a revenue motive was not the dominant
force *after* 1870. However, it was probably the dominant force *before*
that date.

Having analyzed both statistical significance and marginal economic importance, what about *historical* significance? To see the difference, consider this example: Suppose that own tariffs were highly responsive to partner tariffs in the European periphery. Suppose also we observe that own tariffs rose in the European periphery. Was this antiglobal tariff rise due to changes in partner tariffs or some other force? We cannot answer this question without knowing how much partner tariffs changed. To pursue this example further, if partner tariffs barely changed, then we would have to look elsewhere for explanations of the historical rise in own tariffs *despite* the fact that for a *given* change in partner tariffs we see a large change in own tariffs. This case illustrates the difference between big marginal economic impact and big historical significance.

Why were tariffs on the rise nearly everywhere in the decades before 1900? Elsewhere, it has been shown that growing GDP per capita and population size were serving to *lower* tariffs everywhere, but these were overwhelmed by tariff-raising forces (Blattman, Clemens, and Williamson 2002). The push for higher tariffs came mostly from two sources: first, domestic political economy forces associated with urbanization and schooling; and second, a protectionist reaction as a compensation to import-competing industries as openness was thrust upon them by advances in transportation technology (both on land and sea). Only in the European periphery do we observe partner tariffs making a major contribution to the antiglobal, tariff-raising dynamics during this period. Falling transportation costs certainly did contribute to rising tariff barriers in the European core, in the non-Latin European offshoots and in Asia. Yet, transport revolutions along the sealanes had little impact on tariffs in Latin America and the European periphery, simply because the fall in overseas freight rates were more modest there. In addition, there is strong evidence of deindustrialization fears in the periphery, joining deagricultural fears in the core. Overall, it appears to have been rising levels of railway penetration, schooling, urbanization (associated with changes in domestic politics) and improving terms of trade (at least up to the 1890s) that drove tariffs upward worldwide.

For the period from the 1890s to World War I, those antiglobal domestic political economy and (dissipating) transportation forces pushing tariffs upwards were finally overwhelmed by surging proglobal forces: falling tariffs are associated with rising per capita incomes in Europe, their non-Latin offshoots and Latin America, carried in large part by mass migrations and capital exports. Once again, the terms of trade effect was operative, but now in a proglobal way. As the long-run deterioration in the relative price of primary products (made famous by Raoul Prebisch) started after the 1890s, the relative rise in the price of imported foreign manufactures eased the competitive pressure on local industry in the periphery. During the interwar decades, the massive increases in tariffs were driven almost entirely by increases in partner tariffs, a force that seems to eclipse everything else.

Cross-section Results

Now consider the cross-section results in table 8.1. Here we control for two additional characteristics: colonial status—an indicator of autonomy over tariff policy, and federal status—an indicator of the decentralization of governance.

Three variables appear to have a different impact in time series relative to cross-section: partner tariffs, schooling, and urbanization. The partner tariffs variable is not significant in cross-section and appears to be negative. How can this be consistent with a world in which, as we have seen, *changes* in a country's own tariff is closely associated with *changes* in its trading partners' tariffs? This cross-sectional pattern suggests that initial conditions were such that, before reacting to *changes* in their partners' tariffs, countries began from a distribution in which high own tariffs just happened for other reasons to be associated with low partner tariffs and vice versa. This pattern would appear to fit Asia's initial conditions at the dawn of the twentieth century: their own tariffs were forced to be low, either as colonies or as victims of gunboat diplomacy, while high tariffs prevailed in their American and European trading partners. The European periphery would appear to fit this characterization too: their backlash before World War I left them with high tariffs at a time when their trading partners in the European core had recently moved toward freer trade. This shows up in time series as a positive coefficient on trading partner tariffs, but the initial distribution of tariffs shows up in cross section as a negative coefficient. A similar argument can explain the predominantly negative (but insignificant) cross-sectional coefficient on urbanization. I have no explanation for the nonrobust coefficients on the schooling variable.

What about historical significance? Why were tariffs so low before 1914 across Asia, the Middle East, and the European core? One reason was the large internal markets in these labor-rich and land-scarce economies. Another was the industrial competitiveness of the European core as captured by GDP per capita. Why were tariffs so high in both Latin and non-Latin European offshots? It appears that smaller domestic markets in the Latin and non-Latin European offshoots made it harder for firms to survive in a niche without walls to protect them, and, of course, they were less competitive. While the revenue motive is certainly present, and while the signs and magnitudes on the export share coefficient are the same in cross-section and time series, the influence is less powerful in the cross-section, a result I find surprising.

Where Do We Go from Here?

While surveying the political economy of trade policy, Dani Rodrik concluded that the "links between the empirical and theoretical work have never been too strong" (Rodrik 1995:1480). It appears that the boom in endogenous tariff theory over the past two decades has far outstripped the evidence brought to bear on it. My hope is that comparative tariff history like that offered in this essay will help redress the balance, and, in so doing, provoke new thinking on the political economy of tariffs.

This essay relies on a data base documenting average tariffs between 1865 and 1938 for thirty-five countries. While tariff policy for industrial Europe and the United States has been studied extensively, the rest of the world has not, and of our sample of thirty-five, the majority are from the periphery: ten are from the European periphery; another ten are from Asia and the Middle East; and the remaining eight are from Latin America. The advantage of this large panel database is obvious since it documents an enormous range of tariff policy experience, by period and by country.

What accounts for this immense variety in both cross section and time series? What were the underlying fundamentals driving tariff policy the world around? I think these questions should be at the top of the international economist's agenda. After all, even if we see high and rising tariffs out there in history, we need to know why they were high and rising if this history is to be used to understand the future of globalization in the present century. We have learned a fair amount in this essay: deindustrialization fears were a major determinant of tariff policy in the periphery before World War I, joining grain-invasion fears in the European core; revenue needs were an important determinant of tariff rates in the periphery, and especially for young republics;

geography mattered, so that where and when the natural protection of distance and topography was conquered by transport technology, tariffs rose to compensate the import competing industries; and, finally, there was strategic tariff policy behavior at work everywhere after World War I, and much earlier in most young republics forming customs unions.

There is much more to be done to uncover the fundamentals driving world tariff policy in the century before World War II. And while economic historians are doing it, one can only hope that economists will do the same for recent experience. Eli Heckscher would be pleased.

Acknowledgments

This project has received superb research assistance from David Clingingsmith, Martin Kanz, and István Zöllei. I have also benefitted by comments from Dick Baldwin, Gerry della Paolera, Graciela Marquez, Richard Cooper, Toni Estevadeordal, Ron Findlay, Jeff Frieden, Steve Haber, Elhanan Helpman, Doug Irwin, Jonas Ljungberg, Matts Lundahl, Ed Leamer, Peter Lindert, Stephen Meardon, José Manuel Ocampo, Kevin O'Rourke, Jonathan Pincus, Leandro Prados, Dani Rodrik, Dick Salvucci, Ken Sokoloff, Alan Taylor, Daniel Waldenström, and Nick Wills-Johnson; participants at the Conference on the Political Economy of Globalization (Dublin, August 29–31, 2002), the Economic History Association Meetings (St. Louis, October 11–13, 2002), the FTAA and Beyond Conference (Punta del Este, December 15–16, 2002), the RIN Conference (Punta del Este, December 17–19, 2002); and seminars at Adelaide, ANU, Australian Productivity Commission, Australian Treasury, Curtin, Harvard, UCLA, and UC-Davis. Most important, this essay draws extensively on a tariff project which has involved previous papers with four collaborators: Luis Bértola, Chris Blattman, John Coatsworth, and Michael Clemens. I am grateful to all of them, but errors remaining belong to me. I also acknowledge generous financial support from the National Science Foundation SES-0001362.

Notes

1. The average tariff rate is measured here as the share of customs revenues (import duties only) in total import values. It is part of the Williamson Tariff Project data base, used with collaborators in a series of papers (Bértola and Williamson forthcoming; Clemens and Williamson 2002, 2004; Coatsworth and Williamson 2004a; Blattman,

Clemens, and Williamson 2002). Toni Estevadeordal of the Inter-American Development Bank and I are now constructing a database documenting tariff structure in Latin America since the 1820s.

2. I have also calculated (but do not report here) weighted tariff averages for the regional clubs in figure 8.2, where weights are the country's total export share in regional exports or its GDP share. However, I prefer to treat countries as independent policy units regardless of size.

3. Of course, embargoes and soaring transport costs served to produce the same, or even bigger, protective effects.

4. The United States has always presented a problem to historians and economists alike. The canonical frontier economy with scarce labor and abundant resources, by 1900 it was also the world's industrial leader (Wright 1990) and a central market for the exports from the rest of the world, especially Latin America. So, while the United States was certainly a rich European offshoot, I allocate it to the industrial core.

5. In 1831, only 8.6 percent of the males in the United Kingdom had the right to vote, and even in 1866, after the First Reform Act in 1832, the figure was still only 17.8 percent. (See Lindert 1998: table 4.) These were, of course, the wealthy at the top of the distribution.

6. As late as 1940, the share of the population voting in Latin America was never higher than 19.7 percent (Uruguay), while the lowest figures were for Ecuador, Bolivia, Brazil, and Chile (3.3, 4.1, 5.7, and 6.5 percent, respectively). Engerman, Haber, and Sokoloff (2000:226, table 2).

7. Industrial manufactures have been a rapidly rising share of Third World output and exports. For example, for all "developing" countries, manufactures rose from only 17.4 percent of commodity exports in 1970 to 64.3 percent by 1994. Enough of the Third World is now labor-abundant and natural resource–scarce so that the growth of trade has helped it industrialize. The classic image of Third World specialization in primary products is obsolescing. See Lindert and Williamson (2003, note 22).

8. Caution suggests using the phrase "was associated with" rather than "fostered." I press on without caution, but subject to this understanding.

9. Any evidence favoring the Stolper-Samuelson hypothesis would, of course, also support the backlash view.

10. Except, of course, that they could keep the price of imported raw material intermediates low by giving such imports tariff concessions.

11. In a related paper on Latin America (Coatsworth and Williamson 2004a), capital inflows from Britain were added to the analysis for the years 1870–1913. This variable measured annual British capital exports to potential borrowing countries. Countries favored by British lending were shown to have had less need for tariff revenues and thus had lower tariffs. The variable does not appear here since our source does not report the period 1914–1938. Similarly, I do not report the gold standard effect here, although we now have the data to report the answer: being on the gold standard was associated with higher tariff rates, as predicted.

12. New analysis not reported here replaces the "colony" dummy with a "tariff autonomy" dummy—to include Asian countries with unequal treaties—and the results are even stronger than those reported in table 1.

13. Ongoing work is repairing this data limitation, and the specific-duty effect is confirmed in the larger sample. In addition, recall that the analysis in table 8.1 excludes World War I, and we know these years to have been ones during which the specific-duty effect was powerful.

References

Bagwell, K., and R. W. Staiger. 2002. *The Economics of the World Trading System*. Cambridge, MA: MIT Press.

Bairoch, P. 1989. "European Trade Policy, 1815–1914." In P. Mathias and S. Pollard, eds., *The Cambridge Economic History of Europe*, 3. Cambridge: Cambridge University Press.

Bértola, L., and J. G. Williamson. forthcoming. "Globalization in Latin America Before 1940." In V. Bulmer-Thomas, J. Coatsworth, and R. Cortés Conde, eds., *Cambridge Economic History of Latin America*. Cambridge: Cambridge University Press.

Bhagwati, J. N. 2000. *Free Trade Today*. Princeton, NJ: Princeton University Press.

Blattman, C., M. A. Clemens, and J. G. Williamson. 2002. Who Protected and Why? Tariffs the World Around 1870–1938. Paper presented to the Conference on the Political Economy of Globalization, Trinity College, Dublin, August 29–31.

Bulmer-Thomas, V. 1994. *The Economic History of Latin America Since Independence*. Cambridge: Cambridge University Press.

Clemens, M. A., and J. G. Williamson. 2002. "Closed Jaguar, Open Dragon: Comparing Tariffs in Latin America and Asia before World War II." *NBER Working Paper 9401*, National Bureau of Economic Research, Cambridge, MA.

———. 2004. "Why Did the Tariff-Growth Correlation Reverse After 1950?" *Journal of Economic Growth* 9: 5–46.

Coatsworth, J. H., and J. G. Williamson. 2004a. "The Roots of Latin American Protectionism: Looking Before the Great Depression." In A. Estevadeordal, D. Rodrik, A. Taylor, and A. Velasco, eds., *FTAA and Beyond: Prospects for Integration in the Americas* 37–73. Cambridge, MA: Harvard University Press.

———. 2004b. "Always Protectionist? Latin American Tariffs from Independence to Great Depression." *Journal of Latin American Studies* 36:205–232.

Conybeare, J. 1983. "Tariff Protection in Developed and Developing Countries: A Cross-Sectional and Longitudinal Analysis." *International Organization* 37, no. 3 (Summer): 441–467.

Corbo, V. 1992. "Development Strategies and Policies in Latin America: A Historical Perspective." *International Center for Economic Growth, Occasional Paper No. 22* (April): 16–48.

Crucini, M. J. 1994. "Sources of Variation in Real Tariff Rates: The United States 1900–1940." *American Economic Review* 84 (June): 732–743.

Diaz-Alejandro, C. 1984. "Latin America in the 1930s." In R. Thorp, ed., *Latin America in the 1930s*, 17–49. New York: Macmillan.

Dixit, A. 1987. "Strategic Aspects of Trade Policy." In T. F. Bewley, ed., *Advances in Economic Theory: Fifth World Congress*, 329–362. New York: Cambridge University Press.

Engerman, S., S. Haber, and K. Sokoloff. 2000. "Institutions, Factor Endowments, and Paths of Development in the New World." *Journal of Economic Perspectives* (Summer 2000): 217–232.

Grossman, G., and E. Helpman. 1994. "Protection for Sale." *American Economic Review* 84, no. 4 (September): 833–850.

Heckscher, E. F. 1991. "The Effect of Foreign Trade on the Distribution of Income." In H. Flam and M. J. Flanders, eds., *Heckscher-Ohlin Trade Theory*, 39–69. Cambridge, MA: MIT Press.

Irwin, D. A. 1998a. "Higher Tariffs, Lower Revenues? Analyzing the Fiscal Aspects of the Great Tariff Debate of 1888." *Journal of Economic History* 58 (March): 59–72.

———. 1998b. "Changes in U.S. Tariffs: The Role of Import Prices and Commercial Policies?" *American Economic Review* 88 (September): 1015–1026.

Kindleberger, C. P. 1951. "Group Behavior and International Trade." *Journal of Political Economy* 59 (February): 30–46.

Krugman, P. 1996. *Pop Internationalism*. Cambridge, MA: MIT Press.

Lindert, P. H. 1994. "The Rise in Social Spending, 1880–1930." *Explorations in Economic History* 31 (January): 1–36.

———. 1998. "Poor Relief Before the Welfare State: Britain Versus the Continent 1780–1880." *European Review of Economic History* 2 (1998): 101–140.

Lindert, P. H., and J. G. Williamson. 2003. "Does Globalization Make the World More Unequal?" In M. Bordo, A. M. Taylor, and J. G. Williamson, eds., *Globalization in Historical Perspective*, 227–271. Chicago: University of Chicago Press.

Magee, S. P., W. A. Brock, and L. Young. 1989. *Black Hole Tariffs and Endogenous Policy Theory*. Cambridge: Cambridge University Press.

Márquez, G. 2002. "The Political Economy of Mexican Protectionism, 1868–1911." Ph.D. thesis, Harvard University.

Marvel, H. P., and E. J. Ray. 1983. "The Kennedy Round: Evidence on the Regulation of International Trade in the USA." *American Economic Review* 73 (March): 190–197.

———. 1987. "Intraindustry Trade: Sources and Effects on Protection." *Journal of Political Economy* 95 (December): 1278–1291.

McGillivray, F., I. McLean, R. Pahre, and C. Schonhardt-Bailey. 2001. "Tariffs and Modern Political Institutions: An Introduction." In F. McGillivray et al., eds., *International Trade and Political Institutions: Instituting Trade in the Long Nineteenth Century*, 1–28. Cheltenham, UK: Edward Elgar.

Mill, J. S. 1909. *Principles of Political Economy*. London: Longmans.

Mohammed, S. S., and J. G. Williamson. 2004. "Freight Rates and Productivity Gains in British Tramp Shipping 1869–1950." *Explorations in Economic History* 41:172–203.

Obstfeld, M., and A. M. Taylor. 2003. "Globalization and Capital Markets." In M. Bordo, A. M. Taylor, and J. G. Williamson, eds., *Globalization in Historical Perspective*, 121–187. Chicago: University of Chicago Press.

O'Rourke, K. H. 1997. "The European Grain Invasion, 1870–1913." *Journal of Economic History* 57 (December): 775–801.

O'Rourke, K. H., and R. Sinnott. 2003. "Migration Flows: Political Economy of Migration and the Empirical Challenges." Unpublished paper (March).

O'Rourke, K. H., and J. G. Williamson. 1999. *Globalization and History*. Cambridge: Cambridge University Press.

Pincus, J. 1977. *Pressure Groups and Politics in Antebellum Tariffs*. New York: Columbia University Press.

Rodrik, D. 1995. "Political Economy of Trade Policy." In G. M. Grossman and K. Rogoff, eds., *Handbook of International Economics* 3:1457–1494. Amsterdam: Elsevier.

Rogowski, R. 1989. *Commerce and Coalitions: How Trade Effects Domestic Political Arrangements*. Princeton, NJ: Princeton University Press.

Smith, A. 1776 (1976). *An Inquiry into the Nature and Causes of the Wealth of Nations*. Oxford: Clarendon Press.

Stolper, W., and P. Samuelson. 1941. "Protection and Real Wages." *Review of Economic Studies* 9:58–73.

Williamson, J. G. 1998. "Globalization, Labor Markets and Policy Backlash in the Past." *Journal of Economic Perspectives* 12 (Fall): 51–72.

———. 2002. "Two Centuries of Globalization: Backlash and Bribes for the Losers." WIDER Annual Lecture, Copenhagen, September 5.

Wright, G. 1990. "The Origins of American Industrial Success, 1879–1940." *American Economic Review* 80 (September): 651–668.

Part IV

Mercantilism

9   Eli Heckscher and His Mercantilism Today

Lars Magnusson

There are two possible approaches to assessing mercantilism as a phenomenon, as well as to evaluate Eli Heckscher's contribution to our understanding of it. The first of these is that of mainstream economics: that is, to examine the doctrines and policies that constituted mercantilism, as well as the work of Heckscher and other interpreters of mercantilism, from the perspective of modern economic theory. This approach generates questions such as the following: Did the mercantilists, as Keynes argued, achieve economic insights that have been lost? What understanding can be gained by applying a public choice inspired (rent-seeking) analysis to seventeenth- and eighteenth-century mercantilist policies? Is it fruitful to utilize modern concepts, such as transaction cost and asymmetrical information, in our quest to understand the historical phenomenon of mercantilism? How, if at all, can Heckscher's, or Keynes's, reinterpretation of mercantilist ideas be reconciled with modern concepts and theories?

The second possible strategy is historical in nature. It emphasizes the necessity of placing the phenomenon, as well as its interpretation, in the proper historical context. The question of what constituted mercantilism and how it has been interpreted over time can be understood only in terms of its meaning during various historical epochs, including how it was interpreted by those who lived during the time when it was conceived and advocated. Thus, for example, the practices of state dirigisme are incomprehensible without a knowledge of the particular institutional setting of the time, including undeveloped markets and sticky factor prices. By the same token, any interpretations of ideas (or policies) also have their own history and can only be understood within that context.

Both approaches are clearly useful, although for different purposes, and they should not be treated as being totally contradictory. That, however, has not prevented modern (public choice) economists, such as Robert B. Ekelund and Robert D. Tollison, from scorning the use of the historical method—among whose practitioners they include Heckscher—as a "red-herring of historiography" (Coleman 1969:117), which "has yielded no cogent or consistent result if its aim has been a definition of mercantilism or an understanding of the period's events and institutional change" (Ekelund and Tollison 1997). According to them, historical interpretations invariably result in a "mess." Of course, it can be countered that the economist's method of reading history backward also has serious disadvantages. It frequently leads to anachronistic conclusions and judgments concerning historical pamphleteers and authors that miss the crucial point. That is, what it was that they actually were trying to say within their own historical context.

First of all, there is a tendency to headline thinkers and writers who were not well known as economists and who played no role in either the scholarly or the public debate of their time. This might not be a problem for understanding the development of pure analysis. It is a major difficulty, however, in trying to understand the broader history of economics. Second, there is a danger that the purely economic approach will lead to subjectivism. Thus an author's importance—no matter how historically obscure he may be—is measured by the extent he has contributed to, or been in tune with, the most recent version of economic theory (see, for example, Rothbard 1995).

Third, there is a danger that concepts, and even theories, might be reinterpreted in a fashion that obscures their original meaning. This makes it more difficult for us to understand what ideas the mercantilist writers wished to convey and why they presented them as they did. Thus, for example, twisting the arguments of earlier economists to make them seem to be precursors of modern concepts and theories is of doubtful value. The results of such an exercise are usually predetermined. We find what we wish to find. Moreover, doing so makes it harder to learn what there actually is to learn from these authors, namely that there are various ways of looking at economic problems and that economics as a subject is historically embedded. Surely the history of economic thought includes more than the logical perfection of what Arthur Lovejoy once called "unit ideas"? It also deals with how various individuals, be they rulers, merchants, or intellectuals, have tried to understand, and come to grips with, a complex and continually changing economic order, as well as with how these actors have distinguished what is good from what is bad in their world.

Eli Heckscher and Mercantilism

The first Swedish edition of Eli Heckscher's *Mercantilism* appeared in 1932 (Magnusson 1994b). It was translated into German the following year, and the first English edition was published in 1935. Virtually overnight, it made Heckscher well known to a wide international audience. However canonical this work seems now, when it was first published it received a mixed response from both economists and economic historians. The book's reviewers acknowledged the massive scholarly effort that had gone into writing it, as well as Hecksher's great learning and skill. Prominent economic and social historians, such as Marc Bloch (1934) and Herbert Heaton (1937), however, were highly critical of Heckscher's conceptualization of a "system of mercantilism." Bloch thought it had an unhistorical aura about it, and Heaton emphasized Heckcher's difficulty in establishing a synthesis among "the situation, the ideas and the actions" of mercantilism (Magnusson 1994a:32–36). Moreover, he found it hard to accept the argument that all the regulative policies practiced by governments starting in the Middle Ages had been based on a common and coherent set of intentions and goals. Finally, Heckscher's notion of a "fear of goods" as the principal explanation for the rise of mercantilism and as a reflection of the transition to monetized economies in Western Europe was judged to be both overly general and unrealistic.

It is certainly true that Heckscher interpreted mercantilism very broadly. In fact he treated it as a system of economic, regulatory, administrative, and political thinking with roots going back to the policies of the medieval cities. Thus, in essence, mercantilism was "a phase in the history of economic policy" (Heckscher 1994, 2:2). It was also, however, a systematic doctrine: a "system of protection and money." As such, he treated it as a species of timeless commonsensical, popular economic thinking. According to Heckscher, it was not limited to any specific historical period. But even this was not all. Mercantilism was also a particular conception of man and society: almost a (extremely materialistic) worldview. Moreover, it fitted neatly into a stages of history model of the type advocated by the historical school—an approach of which Heckscher himself was critical (Heckscher 1942). Heckscher's historicist tendencies are also displayed in his suggestive notion of a "fear of goods": that the hunger for money, taken to the level of a fetish, together with the corresponding "fear of goods," was a refection of the transition from a barter to a money economy.

One important reason for the cool reception given Heckscher's book was no doubt its complex structure. Thus, for example, it is often difficult to grasp how its various parts relate to each other. To a large extent, this problem is a product of Heckscher's own ambivalence concerning the nature of mercantilism. Indeed, this ambivalence is the principal explanation for his eclectic, unsynthesized treatment of the subject. He deals with various features of mercantilism, such as regulatory policies, economic doctrines, and general conceptions of society, separately and without clarifying how they relate to each other.

Heckscher's general argument, however, can be reconstructed as follows: He begins by emphasizing the systemlike character of mercantilism as a set of specific economic policies. He then asserts, as a matter of principle, that "everybody has certain ideas, whether he is conscious of them or not, as a basis for his actions, and mercantilists were plentifully provided with economic theories on how the economic system was created and how it could be influenced in the manner desired" (Heckscher 1994, 1:27). Furthermore, he suggests, mercantilism can only be understood by separating its ends from its means. The ultimate *goal* of mercantilist policies was to maximize the external power of the state. This explicitly contradicted Adam Smith and the liberal economists, who placed the wealth of the individual ahead of that of the nation state. This goal, however, was not mercantilism's most distinctive characteristic. Rather, Heckscher emphasized that the hallmark of the system was the set of means intended to achieve this general goal. These economic *means* designed to bolster the political strength of the state were inherent to mercantilism as a protectionist and monetary system. The ambiguity as to whether this "system" should be classified as economic policy or economic thinking—or both—is not initially resolved and haunts the reader throughout the two massive volumes.

Regardless of whether it was policy or doctrine, however, Heckscher stresses that mercantilism must not be seen as a rational reflection of how economic systems functioned during the early modern period. Thus, for example, he points out that "the description of the economic policy pursued in a particular period should never be regarded as a sufficient explanation of the economic circumstances of the time" (Heckscher 1994, 1:20). In a chapter added to the second edition, he is even more explicit. Now, however, he has reversed the argument to deal with the economic thinking of the period. His principal assertion is well known: "There are no grounds whatsoever for supposing that the mercantilist writers constructed their system—with its frequent and marked theoretical orientation—out of any knowledge of reality however derived" (Heckscher 1955, 2:347).

On the basis of this conceptualization, Heckscher informs the reader that he will deal with five different aspects of mercantilism. First, there is mercantilism as a policy of national unification and integration. Second, there is the desire for national power. The third and fourth aspects are protectionism and the monetary system. Here Heckscher takes his point of departure from Adam Smith. Finally, there is the concept of society inherent in mercantilism. As Heckscher observes, this last aspect has frequently been neglected. On the basis of this foundation, Heckscher's overall aim is to provide a synthesis of these five aspects and thus to provide a general interpretation of mercantilism as a systematic phenomenon.

The Economists' Critique of Heckscher

It is well known that the concept of a "mercantile system" was invented by the French physiocrats and subsequently made famous by Adam Smith. During the late nineteenth century, both in Germany and Britain, there was a reaction against the portrayal of mercantilism as being little more than a set of logical errors based on the false belief that money was identical with wealth. Instead, historical economists, such as Schmoller in Germany and Cunningham in Britain, argued that mercantilism had a rational basis. According to them, mercantilism could better be understood as a broad process of state, or nation, building. Thus, not only did they reinterpret mercantilism as a broad concept applicable to certain types of policy making and economic management of the state during the early modern period, they also brought into serious question Smith's assertion that mercantilism must be regarded as a doctrine pursued for the benefit of special, private interest groups. Instead, these revisionists argued that, at its core, mercantilism represented the interests of the national state. First and foremost, it reflected the "economic interests of whole states ... [which] found a rallying-point in certain generally accepted postulates" (Schmoller 1896:59). In "national policy" terms, the particular views and ideas of individual mercantilist thinkers and writers were of little interest. Thus, for example, "the whole idea and doctrine of the Balance of Trade ... was only the secondary consequence of economic processes" (Schmoller 1896:61). Instead, the true basis of mercantilism was the workings of particular institutions in given countries and the goals of statesmen and rulers.

Even though Heckscher was not always prepared to admit it, there is no doubt that his interpretation of mercantilism was greatly influenced by the historical economists. Thus, in accord with Schmoller and the historical school, he expanded the term "mercantilism" to be the kernel of a system of economic thought and a concept of society, not just a system of economic policy stretching back to the Middle Ages. Following in the footsteps of, among others, Schmoller and Cunningham, Heckscher made the state the principal agent of, and the chief propelling force behind, mercantilism. Although he conceded that opulence, as well as power, was indeed a goal of mercantilist policies, there is certainly some truth in Heaton's judgment that Heckscher "insists that mercantilism put power above opulence, in contrast with laissez-faire, which made the creation of wealth its lodestar, with small regard to the effect on power of the state" (Heaton 1937:379).

In a famous two-part essay published in 1930, Jacob Viner took the side of Adam Smith against the historical economists. Instead of trying to understand the mercantilists on their own terms, Viner maintained that one should start with "modern monetary and trade theory" and on this basis provide "an inventory of English ideas with respect to trade prevalent before Adam Smith, classified and examined in the light of modern...theory" (Viner 1930:250). He believed that such a critical evaluation of the evolution of doctrines would yield a greater understanding of them than would the historicists' approach, which was based on the belief that these ideas reflected the economic reality of the premodern world. Viner's argument, incidentally, is almost exactly echoed by Ekelund and Tollison in their current critique of the historical method (1997).

According to Viner, the mercantilists erred exactly as Adam Smith had claimed: they confused real wealth with money. There is no other way, he stressed, to explain the favorable balance of trade doctrine or their belief that foreign trade was the only possible path to national enrichment. Consequently, he maintains, the mercantilists "believed, momentarily at least, that all goods other than money were worthless" (Viner 1930:265). By relying on quotes taken out of their proper textual context, Viner is thus able, even more fervently than Adam Smith, to argue that at heart the mercantilists were out and out bullionists. At the same time, however, he was prepared to admit that the total identification of money with wealth was limited to some extreme mercantilists. The identification of gold and silver as the only "real" form of wealth by their more moderate compatriots must be understood from an institutional and historical perspective.

It is thus ironic that in his discussion regarding why money was considered so pivotal during the sixteenth and seventeenth centuries, Viner accepted an explanation which stressed the "material" (or institutional) basis of this fallacy. In this context, he maintained that "much more important in the writings of the abler mercantilist than the absolute identification of wealth with gold and silver was the attribution to the precious metals of functions of such supreme importance to the nation's welfare as to make it proper to attach to them a value superior to that of other commodities" (Viner 1930:270). In addition, Viner challenged another assumption made by the historical economists, namely that the mercantilist writers were disinterested and were arguing for the general good when they defended government policies and legislation. According to Viner, the opposite was true. They were first and foremost advocates of "special interests" (using modern terminology, they would be labeled rent seekers). Each interest group continually lobbied for legislative action in their own favor.

Viner's pair of articles appeared before Heckscher's work had been published and translated. Reading *Mercantilism*, however, only reinforced Viner's critical attitude toward historical economics. Thus, in his review of the book, as well as in an article published a decade later, he severely criticized the notion that power had been an end in itself for the mercantilists (Viner 1935, 1948). A more charitable reading of Heckscher, however, suggests that he saw power as only one of several mercantilist goals. After all, his intention was to present a general synthesis in which the struggle for power was just one aspect. Moreover, in principle Heckscher was always reluctant to advocate monocausal explanations. In his response to Viner, he was therefore prepared to grant that *both* power and opulence were central themes in mercantilist economic policy during its heyday. Furthermore, he suggested, underlying these two linked goals lurked a very peculiar social philosophy: the worldview of mercantilism.

The Response from the Economic Historians

The 1950s and 1960s were characterized by the rapid rise of economic history as an academic enterprise, especially in the Anglo-Saxon world. Undoubtedly, rapid industrial transformation, a high growth rate, and controversy over social issues lay behind this increase in its popularity. In Britain, however, one major theme of economic historical scholarship concerned mercantilism. This discussion focused on two issues in particular. The first of these was the usefulness of Heckscher's broad and encompassing definition of the concept. The consensus on this question was generally negative.

The second issue concerned the impact of new research on international trade relations on our understanding of the phenomenon of mercantilism. Here, a lively discussion intended to establish a sound economic and historical foundation for the superstructure of mercantilist thinking blossomed. It is only possible to speculate as to why mercantilism became such a popular topic during these decades. Very likely, the free trade versus protectionism controversy that had been ongoing in Britain since the nineteenth century was one factor. The "mercantilist fallacy," that a positive balance of trade was the road to national wealth, was perceived by many free traders—including Viner in America and Heckscher in Sweden—to be a useful weapon against protectionist theories. If mercantilism and protectionism could be shown to be built on a logical fallacy, it would be even easier to demonstrate the superiority of free trade (Magnusson 2004).

With regard to Heckscher's "totalitarian" ambitions, as early as 1939 A. V. Judges had vigorously rejected the notion of "a mercantile state." Formally, his campaign was directed against the *Historismus* of "German scholarship," including British fellow travellers such as William Cunningham and W. J. Ashley. Although he was only briefly mentioned, however, Judge's criticisms could just as well have been directed at Heckscher. Judges raised the question of whether or not it was appropriate to classify mercantilism as a coherent "system." Of course, he was certain of his own answer. Mercantilism "never had a creed; nor was there a priesthood dedicated to its service," he wrote. Moreover, he argued, it did not present a coherent doctrine, or "at least a handful of settled principles." Thus, mercantilism was a straw man constructed "in the eighteenth century by men who found security for their own faith in a system of natural law" (Judges [1939] 1969:35f).

Some two decades later, this standpoint was further elaborated by a leading British economic historian, D. C. Coleman, who directly confronted Heckscher's "synthesizing treatment" of mercantilism. In Heckscher's Hegelian-inspired hands, mercantilism had become a real entity, manifesting itself through the centuries in a variety of guises. Coleman's conclusion is widely accepted: "what was this mercantilism.

Did it exist? As a description of a trend of economic thought the term may well be useful. . . . As a label for economic policy, it is not simply misleading but actively confusing, a red-herring of historiography. It serves to give a false unity to disparate events, to conceal the close-up reality of particular times and particular circumstances, to blot out the vital intermixture of ideas and preconceptions, of interests and influences, political and economic, and of the personalities of men which is the historian's job to examine" (Coleman 1969:116; see also Earle 1950).

As already noted, in subsequent articles Coleman has extended this argument to include mercantilism as a trend in economic thought. In 1980 he conceded that the term mercantilism might have a certain heuristic value. Indeed, it was an example of such "non-existent entities that had to be invented in order to prevent the study of history of falling into the abyss of antiquarianism." As a description of a *real* specific stream of economic thought or economic policy, however, he maintained that the term was illegitimate and misleading.

A second important theme in the discussion of mercantilism since the 1950s has dealt with the relationship among economic ideas, events, and policies during the "age of mercantilism" (roughly the seventeenth and eighteenth centuries). Although Heckscher, as argued above, believed in a clear connection between thought and policy, he emphatically rejected the notion of a causative relationship between thought and events. In this regard, he was severely criticized by, among others, Coleman. Conversely, Coleman emphasized the materialistic foundation of economic ideas. Thus, the basis for "mercantilist" ideas must be sought in the historical reality of the seventeenth and eighteenth centuries (Coleman 1969:111).

Consequently, starting in the 1950s, Coleman's economic history colleagues set out to uncover the historical basis and origins of the theories regarding trade and growth that flourished before Adam Smith. The question they posed concerned the real historical foundation on which the writings of the mercantilists rested. Much historical research was devoted to this quest. Various scholars came up with alternative answers and interpretations. Generally speaking, these contributions have produced a much fuller understanding of the prevailing economic structures and conditions which are thought to have been the foundation of the mercantilist ideas and texts.

As an example, Charles Wilson has argued that a common weakness in attacks against the mercantilists, from Smith onward, has been their

denial of "the possibility that the obsession with bullion might have
rational historical roots" (Wilson 1969:64). Wilson, however, maintains that a central theme in early British mercantilist writings (Mun,
Misselden, and the like) was concern over particular trade balances,
especially in the Anglo-Baltic trade. As Wilson observes, much trade
during this period was bilateral in nature. The importation of grain,
timber, iron, and copper from the Baltic countries was crucial for Britain. It was an ongoing problem, however, that this trade required the
exportation of metallic money from Britain. An important reason for
this situation was the Dutch domination of exports to the Baltic area
(Wilson 1957). Consequently, this unavoidable outflow of specie had
to be offset by a positive "overplus" in the British trade with other
countries and regions. Wilson believed that it was this rather special
circumstance that explains the mercantilists' concern with maintaining
a positive balance of trade. As trade became ever more multilateral
during the seventeenth century, this doctrine became increasingly out-
dated and was ultimately discarded (Wilson 1949).

In his response to Wilson, Heckscher denied that bilateral trade was
common during the seventeenth century. According to Heckscher, the
existence of exchange bills argued strongly against Wilson's explanation (Heckscher 1950). In a rejoinder, Wilson reasserted his view that
"in a number of branches of international trade, precious metals played
a unique role which gives an element of rationality to mercantilist
thought" (Wilson 1951–52:242; see also Price 1961). Moreover, the
"hard currency" position was "rooted in the views of individual merchants about the requirements of their business." Therefore, he concluded, "Trading capital *in money* was regarded as an indispensable
link in the exchange of goods" (Wilson 1951–52:54).

During the early 1950's, another line of research, also openly intended to endow the mercantilist writers with historical rationality,
became the focus of intense debate. In two articles published in 1954
and 1955, J. D. Gould argued that the great British commercial and industrial depression of the 1620s played a major formative role in the
emergence of mercantilist doctrines. According to Gould, most contemporary observers agreed that the crisis primarily was caused by
"some shortcoming of the monetary system and the machinery of foreign exchange" (Gould 1954:82). From this it followed that: "To one
who studied the trade depression of the 1620s in detail...it is clear
that a very substantial part of *Englands's Treasure* [Mun's most famous
book] represents simply the fruits of reflection on the events and dis-

cussion of those years" (Gould 1955:123). In referring to the monetary situation, Gould unquestionably drew on De Roover's path-breaking study of Thomas Gresham and international exchange relations during the sixteenth century (De Roover 1949).

Gould's position on these issues was further elaborated by Barry Supple (1959). In his important contribution to this topic, Supple emphasized the existence of a "drain of silver" from England, especially during the 1620s. Its principal cause, in turn, was the monetary chaos and currency debasement on the Continent that followed in the wake of the Thirty Years War. The upshot was a severe drop in demand, especially for British cloth. This was the phenomenon, according to Supple, that underlay "so many contemporary complaints concerning a scarcity of money" (1957:251). The heated argument among Mun, Miselden, and Malynes thus hinged on how to explain this deflationary process and monetary shortage. Both Gould and Supple tended to favor Malynes's conclusion that the root of the problem lay in international currency manipulations. Since the pivotal issue was monetary problems, Malynes's position appeared to be more "realistic" than that of Mun and Misselden, who saw the shortage of British coin as a secondary result of a negative trade balance. The key point, however, Supple maintained was that "the reiterated claims of these years that England had an unfavourable balance of trade were founded on uncomfortable fact." From this, he immediately drew the conclusion that "much of the economic literature which historians have interpreted as 'typical' of mercantilism is, in fact, the product of a specific situation and a short-run crisis" (Supple 1957:251; see also Supple 1959:226f).

Against this backdrop, Supple shared Judges's, Coleman's, and Schumpeter's negative response to claims that mercantilism had systemlike characteristics. "In calling such writers 'mercantilist' there is the danger of implicitly attributing to them a continuity of doctrine, based on a set of supposedly logical principles, which was not theirs," he warns (Supple 1959:228). The fact that the mercantilist writings were "consistent and pragmatic responses to consistent fluctuations in an economic environment whose basic elements were slow to change" hardly justifies its "treatment as a full-blown system." Undoubtedly this argument might downgrade mercantilism's claim to be a coherent system or "school" of economic thought. A mere "pragmatic response" to economic "reality," however, does not preclude a process of interpretation or the use of concepts and even, crude as they might be, theories. Consequently, supposing that seventeenth-century authors of economic texts were nontheoretical or devoid of abstract thinking or ideological perspectives is unlikely to be a fruitful point of departure (Magnusson 1994a:1–20).

A Current Perspective on Heckscher's Mercantilism

Certainly some of the criticisms that were unleashed by the publication of Heckscher's work remain valid. The accumulation of subsequent economic-historical studies have provided a more realistic account both of economic policy making and of trade relations and monetary flows in Western Europe during the early modern period. In particular, few current scholars would accept the close relationship between economic ideas (however faulty) and the practice of economic policy that Heckscher argued existed during that historical epoch. Moreover, new theories concerning public policy formation, such as public choice based rent-seeking, have inspired new interpretations of mercantilism. Finally, increased knowledge of doctrinal history has forced a modification of Heckscher's analysis of the contemporary literature. Most especially, the supposed strict demarcation line between liberal and mercantilist ideas, as well as Smith's complete "otherness" vis-à-vis his older British "mercantilist" colleagues, has been undermined. Clearly, there was convergence as well as deviation between earlier writers, such as Child, Barbon, Davenant, and the "Smithians" (Magnusson 2004).

Against this backdrop, it is certainly debatable whether or not Heckscher's *Mercantilism* has anything to offer today. Is the book worth reading for other than antiquarian reasons? I believe it is, for three reasons that I will discuss in order.

First, I believe that it is still valid to speak of what might be called "mercantilist" economic "thinking" (for want of a better word). Surely, there are themes and systematic ideas in the economic literature between the early seventeenth century and Adam Smith that can legitimately be labeled "mercantilism." British authors from Mun, Misselden, and Roger Cooke in the seventeenth century to Theodore Janssen and James Stuart in the eighteenth century, certainly display some degree of coherence in terms of shared ideas, concepts, and formulations on the role of trade, the nature of economic growth, the crucial importance of supply and demand for prices, and the role of the dirigist state. This makes it useful to speak, at very least, of a mercantilist "quasi-system" (Schumpeter 1968:194) of economic discourse and thinking that flourished in seventeenth- and eighteenth-century Britain.

By the same token, however, it is extremely difficult to accept Schumpeter's assertion that the mercantilists (or "consultant administrators" as he preferred to call them in recognition of their practical role and attitude) did no theorizing whatsoever. Of course, they obviously did not use the theories developed by twentieth-century economists. It is also possible to agree with Schumpeter that they were poor theorists. But is that really all there is to the matter? It seems unlikely that even Schumpeter believed that the mercantilists did not think systematically, however faulty, at all (Schumpeter 1968:143–160). It seems more fruitful to posit that writers such as Mun, Misselden, Child, Barbon, Law, and Davenant struggled with a common set of questions: how can a nation become rich; what, in fact, constitutes national wealth; what is the importance of money; and what is the role of market forces in setting interest rates and prices? In so doing, they used a common conceptual vocabulary whose meaning they also discussed. They argued among themselves, both implicitly and explicitly. Together they ventured forth to discover answers to the new problems raised by the functioning of a market economy. Thus, Heckscher's conclusion that economic ideas in the seventeenth and eighteenth centuries shared at least some systemlike characteristics and cannot be regarded as just a type of ad hoc reasoning intended to solve particular practical problems, still seems valid.

Second, the principal contribution of Heckscher's treatment of the subject is not that he got everything right, but rather his impressive knowledge of the ideas and practices of the mercantilist era. Following Heckscher, perhaps in opposition to Viner as well as to Eklund and Tollison, I would argue that a skilled historical treatment of past economic ideas—including "mercantilism"—has a number of important advantages over any stylized version of history. All too often, the latter are principally intended to confirm some preconceived theoretical proposition. Only well executed historical research permits the drawing of useful conclusion—in this case, concerning mercantilism—that have implications for the modern interpretation and application of economics. The most important lesson to be learned, however, is how earlier writers, such as those of the seventeenth century, came to grips with the problems that still confront us: how markets work, how institutions influence economic behavior, and the importance of uncertainty in the real economic world. An appreciation of their efforts might provide modern economists with a suitable dose of humility, as well as a realization that the last word in these centuries-old debates has not been said.

Third, even though it has been severely criticized, Heckscher's discussion of the interrelationship between economic ideas and policies remains highly stimulating. Undoubtedly Heckscher overstated both the ambition and the ability of early modern states to pursue self-interested, coherent economic policies. They were usually too soft, too weak, and indeed too corrupt to succeed in such an endeavor. Nevertheless, Heckscher's insistence that economic policy making also must be placed in an intellectual context is certainly appropriate. Statesmen of the period, in addition to pursuing their private interests, also were motivated by ideas of how the economy operated and the world works and, perhaps, even by higher religious or moral ideals. As Coats has remarked, in principle it can not be illegitimate to generalize also about economic policy. Thus it is clear that "economic policies"—that myriad of decisions on various levels made by legislative or executive bodies of the state or subnational governments—must be guided by some visions and views concerning both how the "economy" operates and what are the ultimate ends of those policies. As Coats observed, "historians of economics recognise that without *some* conception of the way the economic system works, and the relationship between 'means' and 'ends', there can be no coherent policy making whatever." It is, of course, always possible to argue that such coherent policy making was entirely lacking during the eighteenth and early nineteenth centuries. Such a position, however, is hardly realistic. Surely it is more fruitful to posit that even at that time administrators and politicians were at least searching for a set of means that would satisfy the ends that they had set for themselves. That, of course, is not to say that they were successful in that quest.

At the same time, however, many of the interventions especially from the economic historians display, to a different degree, a reductionist tendency to immediately "explain" texts as the result of economical, political, and social circumstances. However, as we have argued, complex "circumstances" of the kind we deal with here are never immediately observable. They are always interpreted against the backdrop of a certain language, in concepts and words that are historically inherited and made intelligible to the actors. Once again we must stress that it is hardly enough to argue that Mun and Malynes were involved in a discussion that concerned merely pragmatic issues. Instead, it is totally clear that when they discussed "practical" economic matters such as the effect of monetary speculation on the trade balance, they did so with the help of a conceptual framework deeply rooted in earlier conceptions and views how the economy functioned and ought to be understood.

Acknowledgments

I want to thank especially Bob Coats for his valuable comments to an earlier draft of this essay.

References

Bloch, M. 1934. "Le mercantilisme, un état d'ésprit." *Annales* 6:160–163.

Coats, A. W. 1985. "Mercantilism, Yet Again!" In P. Roggi, ed., *Gli economisti e la politica economica*, 66–88. Naples: Edizione Scientifiche Italiane.

Cole, C. W. 1950. "The Heavy Hand of Hegel." *Nationalism and Internationalism*. New York: Richard R. Smith.

Coleman, D. C. 1969. "Eli Heckscher and the Idea of Mercantilism." In D. C. Coleman, ed., *Revisions in Mercantilism*, 92–117. London: Methuen & Co.

———. 1980. "Mercantilism Revisited." *Historical Journal* 23, no. 4: 773.

De Roover, R. 1949. *Gresham on Foreign Exchange*. Cambridge, MA: Harvard University Press.

Earle, E. M. ed. 1950. *Nationalism and Internationalism*. New York: Columbia University Press.

Ekelund, R. B., and R. D. Tollisson. 1997. *Politicized Economies*. College Station: Texas A&M University Press.

Gould, J. D. 1954. "The Trade Depression of the Early 1620s." *Economic History Review* 7:81–90.

———. 1955. "The Trade Crisis of the Early 1620s and English Economic Thought." *Journal of Economic History* 15:121–133.

Heaton, H. 1937. "Heckscher on Mercantilism." *Journal of Political Economy* 14, no. 3: 370–393.

Heckscher, E. F. 1942. "Den ekonomiska historiens aspekter." In *Ekonomisk-historiska studier*, 9–69. Stockholm: Bonniers.

———. 1950. "Multilateralism, Baltic Trade and the Mercantilists." *Economic History Review* 2:219–228.

———. 1955. *Mercantilism*. 2 vols. London: Allen & Unwin.

Judges, A. V. 1939. "The idea of a mercantile state." In D. C. Coleman, ed., *Revisions in Mercantilism*. London: Methuen (1969), 35–60.

Magnusson, L. 1994a. *Mercantilism: the Shaping of an Economic Language*. London: Routledge.

———. 1994b. "Introduction." In E. F. Heckscher, *Mercantilism*, xi–xxxv. London: Routledge.

———. 2004. *The Tradition of Free Trade*. London: Routledge.

Price, J. M. 1961. "Multilateralism and/or Bilateralism: the Settlement of British Trade Balances with the North, c 1700." *Economic History Review* 14:254–274.

Rothbard, M. 1995. *Economic Thought Before Adam Smith*. Aldershot: Edward Elgar.

Schmoller, G. 1896. *The Mercantile System and its Historical Significance*. New York: Macmillan.

Schumpeter, J. A. 1968. *History of Economic Analysis*. London: George Allen & Unwin.

Supple, B. 1957. "Currency and Commerce in the Early Seventeenth Century." *Economic History Review* 10:239–255.

———. 1959. *Commercial Crisis and Change in England 1600–1642*. Cambridge: Cambridge University Press.

Viner, J. 1930. "Early English Theories of Trade." *Journal of Political Economy* 38.

———. 1935. Review of Heckscher's *Mercantilism*. *Economic History Review* 6:99–101.

———. 1948. "Power versus Plenty as Objectives of Foreign Policy in the Seventeenth and Eighteenth Century." *World Politics* 1:1–29.

Wilson, C. 1949. "Treasure and Trade Balances: The Mercantilist Problem". *Economic History Review* 2:152–157.

———. 1951–52. "Treasure and Trade Balances: Further Evidence." *Economic History Review* 4:231–242.

———. 1957. *Profit and Power*. Cambridge: Cambridge University Press.

———. 1969. *Economic History and the Historians*. London: Weidenfeld and Nicolson.

10   Mercantilism: Power and Plenty Through the Lens of Strategic Trade Policy

Douglas A. Irwin

Ever since Adam Smith's vigorous attack on "the mercantile system," scholars have proposed and debated alternative ways of interpreting mercantilist economic thought and policy. Eli Heckscher's two-volume *Mercantilism* (1935) stands out as a landmark contribution to this endeavor and continues to influence the way scholars view the seventeenth and eighteenth centuries. But as is true with any work of enduring interest, Heckscher also stimulated an ongoing debate over his interpretations of the period.

Among the most important of the many reviews of *Mercantilism* in the leading economics journals was one by the formidable Jacob Viner. Viner (1935) clearly admired Heckscher's work, especially as it related to the history of economic policy, and called it "an absolutely indispensable guide." But he was less convinced that Heckscher had clearly stated or had accurately characterized English mercantilist thought on the relationship between national power and economic wealth. Far from subordinating factors such as wealth to considerations of power, as he understood Heckscher to say, Viner insisted that both power and wealth were desired goals and were viewed as complementary and not competing ends of mercantilist policy.[1]

Heckscher (1936) soon conceded that both "power" and "opulence" were always important goals of mercantilist economic policy. He reiterated, however, that greater significance was attached to power than to wealth, a ranking that was responsible for the "incessant commercial rivalries of the seventeenth and eighteenth centuries, which degenerated into military conflict." With the subsequent rise of laissez faire, Heckscher argued, power gave way to wealth as the chief goal of economic policy.

In a letter replying to Heckscher, Viner did "not deny that power was a more prominent objective of national policy in the 17th and 18th centuries than in the 19th .... All I dispute... is your argument that the mercantilists regarded power and prosperity as competing alternatives, as between which choice had to be made." With few exceptions, Viner insisted, "the English mercantilist literature treats power and prosperity as mutually supporting objectives... both were important objectives in their own right."[2] This exchange with Heckscher prompted Viner to write his famous 1948 essay "Power versus Plenty as Objectives of Foreign Policy in the Seventeenth and Eighteenth Centuries." In this article, Viner amassed an impressive array of textual evidence to support his contention that mercantilists believed that both wealth and power were ends to national policy and that each abetted the other.

Viner's exposition of mercantilist objectives proved convincing. The chapter entitled "Mercantilism as a System of Power" in the revised edition of Heckscher's book was changed considerably in light of Viner's article. In an addendum to the revised edition of *Mercantilism*, Heckscher (1955:359) conceded that Viner's "evidence impresses me as being sufficiently strong to make me abandon my original thesis on the issue .... I have come to the conclusion that the difference between the mercantilist position and that which succeeded it was a difference of degree and not a difference of kind," although Heckscher believed the difference to be a significant one.

This paper revisits the debate about the relationship between power and plenty during the mercantilist period by proposing that mercantilism be viewed through the lens of strategic trade policy. Strategic trade policy, it is argued, provides a structure in which we can better understand some of the long-distance trade policies pursued by the major countries in the seventeenth century. In addition, this economic framework shows how power and plenty were indeed compatible, as Viner contended.

The essential idea here is that, in many instances during the seventeenth century in particular, very few European firms competed over the same, potentially lucrative, long-distance trade routes. This competition among few players created conditions which were ripe for strategic behavior on the part of firms and governments. Under these circumstances, this trade competition was akin to a zero-sum game for the participants, and therefore state power could be exercised to the advantage of favored firms. Government promotion of a country's firms could have abetted both the power and the plenty of that country at the expense of its trading rivals.[3] The theory of strategic trade policy provides a framework in which we can better understand the relationship of government support for foreign trade monopolies.

The term "mercantilism" encompasses a wide range of doctrines and policies and refers to a period that exhibits much diversity in terms of history and ideas and policy. The multifaceted objectives of state policy in the seventeenth and eighteenth centuries cannot be reduced into a single idea. Therefore, the spirit in which this paper is offered is simply that this additional way of thinking about mercantilism may be useful—perhaps appropriate only for a narrow range of phenomena, in particular, state-chartered foreign trade monopolies—and can possibly supplement other interpretive approaches.[4]

This essay begins by describing the basic framework behind strategic trade policy, and then moves on to describe briefly how English mercantilist thought is similar in outlook to the perspective one gains from strategic trade policy. The essay considers at greater length the East India trade, as contested by the English and Dutch East India Companies in the first few decades of the seventeenth centuries. As K. N. Chaudhuri (1978:20) notes, "If there was a perfect example of what we today understand as the spirit of mercantilism, the East India Company embodied it in its policy of harnessing political power and privileges to commercial purpose." The economic characteristics of the East India trade, it turns out, map incredibly well into the assumptions underlying the canonical Brander and Spencer (1985) model of duopolistic trade competition. One of the strategic advantages of the Dutch over the English in this trade, it is suggested, is a subtle difference in the managerial compensation of the Dutch versus the English managers. A conclusion speculates on how far this analogy between strategic trade policy and mercantilism can work, and notes some of the qualifications to the analogy.

Strategic Trade Policy

Strategic trade policy arose as a part of the "new trade theory" in the 1980s which began exploring models of imperfect competition as applied to international trade.[5] A strategic situation is one in which a small number of firms make interdependent decisions. Strategic trade policy examines the implications for commercial policy when the actions of each firm or government affect the profits and revenues of all other competitors. In the standard approach of perfect competition, there is little scope for firms to engage in strategic behavior because prices are taken as given.

One of the leading, one might say canonical, models of strategic trade policy is the 1985 *Journal of International Economics* article by James Brander and Barbara Spencer entitled "Export Subsidies and International Market Share Rivalry." This paper examined trade policy in the context of a very simple Cournot duopoly model and yet succeeded in generating much controversy and a large follow-on literature. The basic idea can be described as follows. Suppose two firms from different countries produce a homogenous good that they sell by competing in a third market. In this duopoly situation, national welfare can be represented by the profits of the country's firm (there being no domestic consumption and hence no domestic consumer surplus to worry about). If the firms have identical costs and maximize profits by choosing the quantity of output to produce, then the Nash equilibrium is symmetric: each firm produces the same quantity and earns the same profit.

Under certain conditions in this framework, a government export subsidy enables one (say, the domestic) firm to commit itself to a higher level of output than without the subsidy, forcing the output of the other (foreign) firm to contract. This subsidy increases the profits of the domestic firm at expense of the foreign firm, thus shifting the international distribution of profits to the home country. In addition, Brander and Spencer actually show that the optimal subsidy can increase national welfare because the gain in profits to the domestic firm exceeds the cost of the government subsidy. Of course, if both governments undertake such subsidies, the resulting Nash equilibrium is inefficient in that the welfare of all countries could be higher in the absence of such subsidies.

Figure 10.1 illustrates firm behavior in this Cournot duopoly. The figure plots a schedule of the profit-maximizing level of output of each firm, taking as given various levels of output of the other firm. Notice that the higher is the level of foreign output, which drives down the market price, the lower is the profit-maximizing output of the domestic firm. The intersection of these "reaction functions" is the Nash equilibrium and determines the output levels of the two firms. In this setup, anything that the domestic firm can do to convince its foreign rival that it will produce more output will induce the foreign firm to reduce its output. The domestic firm will try to do this itself, but there are

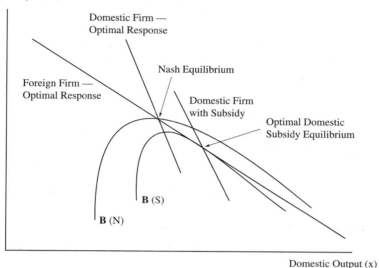

Figure 10.1
The Brander and Spencer (1985) model of strategic trade policy

limits to credible threats it can make. At this point, there is a role for government. As Grossman and Richardson (1985:11) point out, "in equilibrium, however, all such actions that are in the firm's interest have already been taken, and threats of further thrusts by one firm are dismissed by other firms as mere bluffs. The government, by contrast, may have the ability to threaten and credibly precommit even after the firms attain oligopolistic equilibrium, shifting the equilibrium to obtain a nationally desirable distribution of profits."

Thus, a credible government subsidy can shift the domestic firm's reaction function to the right, as illustrated in figure 10.1, and thus increase domestic output and lower foreign output. This "Stackelberg leader" equilibrium results in higher domestic profits and lower foreign profits. (Of course, the collusion equilibrium can increase the profits of both firms as they reduce output together.) Also shown on figure 10.1 are the associated "iso-profit" curves for the domestic firm—the combination of domestic and foreign output that leave domestic profits the same. The Stackelberg equilibrium, which involves higher domestic output and lower foreign output than the Nash equilibrium, is associated with higher profits for the domestic firm.

While this model provides just an example of a way in which a government export subsidy can be beneficial and is subject to many theoretical and practical qualifications, the entire literature on strategic trade policy focuses on precisely those situations in which strategic interdependence creates opportunities for welfare improving government interventions.

Mercantilist Economic Thought

There is a remarkable similarity between English mercantilist economic thought on trade and the thinking that underlies theories of strategic trade policy.[6] Both suggest that rents arising from imperfect competition are a prominent feature of international trade, both focus on capturing the gains from exporting for one's own country at the expense of others by displacing rivals from the market, and both imply that an activist government can assist domestic firms engaged in international competition to the benefit of national welfare.

A notable element of the mercantilist analysis was the perception that the gains from trade were derived from exporting domestic production or shipping goods between foreign markets. "Exportation is gain, but all Commodities Imported is loss," stated Carew Reynell (1695:12). William Petty (1680:23) maintained that "The National Gain, by Foreign Trade, consist[s] either in vending home Commodities to Foreigners, or in Trading from Port to Port." These gains from exports and the carrying trade, wholly unrelated to monetary concerns about the balance of trade, arose from the greater employment of labor, the larger mercantile profit, and the enhanced power and prestige of the nation which such commerce generated in increasing a country's domestic production and improving its maritime capability. Distant overseas trade received a disproportionate amount of attention from the mercantilists, as these trades were associated with extraordinary prestige and profit.

Yet mercantilists believed that increasing a country's trade to be a difficult task because they took the total volume of world commerce to be fixed. The idea that "there is but a certain proportion of Trade in the World" led easily to William Petty's conclusion (1690:82) that "the Wealth of every Nation consist[s] chiefly in the share which they have in the Foreign Trade with the whole Commercial World." A fixed volume of trade meant that the fixed gains from trade had to be distributed among the trading countries of the world. Consequently, international trade took on the characteristics of a zero-sum game. Trade was set along certain "channels" that could not accommodate more traffic, hence entry was only possible by displacing existing merchants.

This led to jealousy in trade and to the belief that one's own country could be made better off by making others worse off. As Josiah Child (1693:160) argued, trade should be managed to ensure "that other Nations who are in competition with us for the same, may not wrest it from us, but that ours may continue and increase, to the diminution of theirs." Child (1693:xxvi–xxvii) added that "no Trades deserve so much care to procure, and preserve, and encouragement to prosecute, as those that employ the most Shipping, although the Commodities transported be of small value in themselves; For, *first*, they are certainly the most profitable; for besides the gain accruing by the Goods, the Freight, which is in such Trades often more then the value of the Goods, is all profit to the Nation; besides, they bring with them a great access to Power."

The mercantilists concluded that activist trade policies in the form of export promotion schemes were essential to preserve and enhance national welfare. Widely advocated policies to increase exports included elimination of all government hindrances and disincentives to export, particularly export taxes; the enactment of direct financial support for exports, such as subsidies and drawbacks (tariff rebates on re-exported goods); and the implementation of indirect measures that would lower rates of interest and reduce wages. While mercantilists criticized importation of almost anything other than raw materials, the frequent association of the doctrine with high tariffs and import protection can be somewhat misleading because export promotion appears to have been the principal foreign trade goal of the mercantilists. Indeed, many writers recognized that import protection could adversely affect export volume. As Petyt (1680:61–62) explained, "for the opening of a sufficient Foreign Vent and Market for our Home Commodities ... it is not only necessary to remove all unequal cloggs on mere Exportations, but also those on Imported Goods; because ... the value of our English Exportation must be in a manner confined to the value of the Goods Imported."[7]

Yet competition over existing export markets was sure to be fierce if every government tried by export promotion to ensure that an ever larger share of world trade was captured by one's own country, even if demand in these markets was not perfectly inelastic. Indeed, seventeenth-century competition in international trade fostered commercial rivalries that extended beyond the marketplace, even spilling over into military conflict as the many commercial wars of the period attest. This was decidedly not the era of *doux commerce*: Josiah Child again captured the temper of the times in writing, "All trade [is] a kind of warfare."[8]

Trade was not conceived as necessarily being mutually beneficial and the focus in contemporary writings was exclusively on national gain. Because of the narrow focus on national gain and the jealousy of other's gains, there does not appear to be any recognition in the mercantilist literature of a prisoner's dilemma element to government intervention, in which international cooperation to control export promotion could make all parties better off. The focus on export competition and rivalry makes mercantilist thought similar in outlook to that of strategic trade policy.

Mercantilist Economic Policy: The East India Trade as an Illustration

Having described the similarities of outlook in strategic trade policy and mercantilist economic policy, how might mercantilist trade rivalries may be amenable to interpretation by use of strategic trade models? To be specific, the Anglo-Dutch rivalry for the East India trade provides an example in of a mercantilist trade rivalry in which the economic conditions of that trade fit very well with the Brander and Spencer (1985) modeling framework.[9]

For many centuries before the foundation of the English East India Company, goods from India and Southeast Asia, particularly spices and silks, were in great demand in western Europe. Ancient and medieval trade between the two regions entailed the transportation of goods across the Asian continent in large caravans. Despite the exorbitant cost of transport, merchants still found it profitable to carry on a small trade with regularity. In 1498, the Portuguese explorer Vasco da Gama opened an entirely new route between Europe and Asia, traveling by sea around the Cape of Good Hope. Although this heralded a new age of trade between the two regions, a century elapsed before the sea route was fully exploited for commercial purposes.[10]

After individual English voyages to Asia in the 1590s yielded mixed results, a group of merchants founded the East India Company in 1600 as a joint-stock company designed to take advantage of the new trading opportunities with Asia. A royal charter from Queen Elizabeth I granted the company a fifteen-year exclusive monopoly to all trade beyond the Cape of Good Hope, as well as customs concessions and permission to export specie. These privileges were renewed and expanded by subsequent royal decrees. The purpose of the joint-stock arrangement was to allow investors to pool their capital, lease or purchase ships, hire crews and finance their provisions, and send the ships to India and Southeast Asia with bullion to make purchases and English goods to trade. Good fortune would have the ships return with a tremendous booty of Asian goods—such as pepper, cloves, nutmeg, indigo, silk, tea, and cotton goods—ready to fetch high prices in England and Europe and thereby compensate the joint stockholders several times over for their expense and risk. In the first half of the seventeenth century, the company was simply a shipping concern, arbitraging large price differentials between European and Asian markets, but not engaging in production.

During its first decade, the English East India Company dispatched one ship a year on average to Asia, but by the mid-1620s sent about four ships a year (Steensgaard 1974:170). Losses due to shipwreck diminished with time—about 7 percent of the roughly 135 voyages before 1630 never returned (Krishna 1924:334ff)—although the threat of looting and piracy was an additional concern. Yet the East India trade proved to be profitable: the first two voyages earned a 95 percent profit, and net returns on early individual voyages ran as high as 230 percent (Chaudhuri 1965:209). These profits arose from the tremendous arbitrage opportunity open to the company: in the twenty years ending July 1620, purchases of £356,288 worth of goods in Asia fetched £1,914,600 in Europe (Khan 1923:17). This excludes transportation costs but is indicative of the markup (by a factor of five) achieved by the company. Pepper from Indonesia dominated the company's trade in both value and volume for the first several decades of the East India trade. Profit margins shrank as the trade expanded, with pepper prices falling in Europe by roughly a quarter between 1609 and 1626 (Chaudhuri 1965:151; see also O'Rourke and Williamson 2002).

For a few years before the formation of the English company, independent Dutch merchant groups had been engaged in routine commerce with Southeast Asia. In 1602, the States General (the Dutch governing body) initiated and helped finance the formation of the Dutch United East India Company, or VOC (Vereenigde Oostindische Compagnie), which was granted exclusive monopoly rights to engage in trade with Asia. By this stroke, Dutch trade was consolidated under the management of a single company in a government-sponsored effort to compete more effectively with trade rivals. Like the English, the Dutch mainly imported and reexported spices, with pepper accounting for nearly 60 percent of company trade by value in 1619–21 (Glamann 1958:13). But the VOC clearly dominated shipping volume in the early East India trade, returning sixty-five ships to England's thirty-five during 1615–25 (Steensgaard 1974:170), with shipping losses comparable to those of the English (Bruijn, Gaastra, and Schoffer 1987, 1:91).

How closely do the economic and institutional details of the early-seventeenth-century East India trade (from 1600 to roughly 1630) bear resemblance to the Brander and Spencer (1985) analysis of duopolistic export competition? To assess whether the conditions of the East India trade conform to the assumptions of this framework, consider eight key elements of their model in light of the trade from the perspective of the English East India Company.

Partial Equilibrium

The partial equilibrium assumption is appropriate here because the early seventeenth-century East India trade was a very small and emerging trade, if a particularly intriguing and exotic one, in contrast with the more mundane intra-European trade that accounted for the overwhelming proportion of England's international commerce. Even by 1663, according to Davis (1962:17), only 8,000 of the total 126,000 tonnage of ships engaged in England's foreign trade was taken up servicing the East India trade route.

Single Homogeneous Good

Brander and Spencer abstract from product differentiation, an assumption in accord with the early East India trade in homogeneous commodities such as pepper and other spices.

Duopoly with No Entry

Brander and Spencer assume that only two firms of different nationality are engaged in export competition and that there is no free entry, despite the existence of monopoly profits. This assumption is quite accurate in describing the rivalry between the English and Dutch companies in this early period. Entry by other English and Dutch merchants was explicitly prohibited under the terms of the government charters granting the companies exclusive rights to the trade, rights legally enforceable against interlopers.[11]

Other European countries were not competitors at this time because their maritime capabilities were not sufficiently advanced in long-distance overseas trade. (France did not form an East India company until 1664; the Swedish East India Company dates from 1731.) Spain and Portugal ruled the seas in the sixteenth century, but different seas owing to a papal decree in 1493 that allocated trade with the Americas to Spain and trade with Asia to Portugal. In the early seventeenth century, however, Portugal distinguished itself only in the rapidity of its decline, a decline accelerated with forceful encouragement from the Dutch. The Portuguese quickly became a residual trader in Asia, and the English and Dutch accounted for about 80 percent of the East India pepper trade by the early 1620s (Chaudhuri 1965:144). Moreover, as Wake (1979) and Steensgaard (1974:171ff) document, overseas shipments of Asian goods to Europe after 1600 entirely displaced the more costly land transport of such goods via the Levant.

Monopoly Profits

Imperfect competition gives rise to monopoly profits that are shared by the duopoly. As previously discussed, there is little doubt that the early East India trade was lucrative, suggesting that such rents did exist for the trading companies engaged in the trade. An English East India Company investor received an annual average return of about 25 percent over the first decade of the trade (inclusive of shipping losses), about three times the market rate of interest in London, although profits fell off after 1615 owing in part to increased Dutch competition (Chaudhuri 1965:211–217). This was high enough to elicit numerous complaints against the monopoly from resentful merchants who were excluded from the trade. Figures in Krishna (1924:77) suggest comparable profitability for the VOC: a total dividend of 307.5 percent was returned to Dutch investors over 1605–20, amounting to roughly 20 percent annually.

Cournot-Nash Game

The assumptions of the Cournot duopoly framework, which entail two firms engaged in a static, noncooperative, one-period, simultaneous-move game, fit very few cases at any period in history but can be partially justified here. The competition was clearly noncooperative to judge by the tense relations between the firms and by the failure of collusive agreements to hold.[12] The two companies made decisions about how many ships to return to Europe in a given year more or less simultaneous because of the nature of the annual sailing season to the East Indies. Ships returning to European ports had to depart within a window of less than six months to avoid the monsoon season in Asia and to avoid passage around the Cape of Good Hope in winter (Davis 1962:258).[13] Neither firm had the ability to determine precisely how many rival ships were to be sent or returned in a given season.

Once the separate, simultaneous decisions had been made, the annual season would end with all goods auctioned off on wholesale markets on arriving in European ports. Consequently, the firm's choices are modeled as a repeated game, each of whose constituent subgames has a significant probability of being the terminal period (the monopoly charters could expire, be revoked, or be rendered moot by interlopers). The repeated one-shot game is motivated by the fact that, in the early years of the trade, the companies were busy arbitraging prices of goods between the two markets and were not incurring fixed costs of production, undertaking irreversible ship investments, or engaging in preemptive acquisition of territory. Under these conditions, the unique subgame perfect equilibrium may be described by the static Nash equilibrium in each period.

Cournot (Quantity) Competition

A key assumption of the Brander-Spencer model is that the firm's choice variable is output (Cournot competition) instead of price (Bertrand competition) and that the firm makes no conjecture (a Cournot reaction) regarding the impact of changes in its output on its rival's output. As Eaton and Grossman (1986) demonstrate, the optimal trade policy associated with the duopolistic rivalry depends critically on the nature of the competition and the conjectural variation entertained by each firm. In contrast to the Brander-Spencer finding that an export subsidy could increase national welfare under Cournot competition, Eaton and Grossman found that the optimal policy becomes an export tax with Bertrand competition. This is an important critique of the Brander-Spencer model because it is often difficult to assess whether firms are competing with quantities or prices.

No such ambiguity arises in considering the East India trade because the firms clearly competed with quantities. The choice variable for both companies was the number of ships to have return in a given sailing season, thus determining the quantity of goods that would arrive at European ports in the coming months. Once both companies' ships arrived from Asia loaded with a fixed quantity of goods, these goods would be auctioned on European wholesale markets. Because the cost of each voyage was paid up front and the private investors had an interest in receiving dividends immediately to retire current debts, in most instances all returning goods were placed onto the market on arrival.

Less appealing is the idea that the companies necessarily entertained Cournot conjectures about how one's competitor would respond to changes in one's output. The assumption underlying the "Cournot conjecture" is that the domestic firm maximizes its profits by taking the foreign firm's output as given, and that the foreign firm's output will not change even if the domestic firm does change its output. This assumption is simply false because a change in the domestic firm's output does change the profit-maximizing level of output by the foreign firm. Yet alternative assumptions about how a rival will respond to a change in one's output are equally difficult to defend. In the case of "consistent conjectures," in which a firm perfectly anticipates how its rival will react to a change in its output, there is no scope for strategic trade policies (Eaton and Grossman 1986). Indeed, the entire conjectural variation approach to these Cournot models is now out of favor with economists because of their arbitrary assumptions about the way in which firms interact with one another. Thus, in this critical aspect of these models, we must be agnostic for the moment.

Constant Costs

In contrast to many models of imperfect competition in international trade, Brander and Spencer assume that the single good can be produced under conditions of constant or increasing marginal cost and without recoverable fixed costs. The assumption of constant costs is taken to be a reasonable reflection of the two cost components of the East India trade, shipping and acquisition. First, the cost of ships was not fixed because there existed a well functioning capital market in ships. The East India Company could lease ships from the competitive intra-European shipping market in the event that it was short of available tonnage in a given year. Pricing in the rental market for ships was based not on a fixed charge per ship, but on a flat freight rate on the required tonnage.

Second, the English and Dutch East India companies made only marginal demands on many goods produced and available in Southeast Asia during the early years of the trade. There is little evidence that the companies had much scope to exercise monopsonist power at this time. Prices in Asia could still vary from port to port depending on local conditions and from year to year depending on production. Yet cost prices of pepper in Asia were roughly constant in the early 1620s despite variation in the volume of English East India Company shipments (Chaudhuri 1965:148). Consequently, acquisition costs are treated as constant in a given year, with the various sources of supply in the Asian market as a whole ensuring that the trading companies could purchase as much as they could fill ships with at a given price.

Exports to Third Markets

Brander and Spencer assume that all trade occurs in third markets so that calculations of national economic welfare do not require an accounting of consumer surplus and the profits of the exporting firm become equivalently identified with national welfare. This assumption is reasonably accurate here: About 80–90 percent of English East India Company pepper was re-exported to northern Europe and the Mediterranean because of the limited market for pepper in England.

Thus, the circumstances of the early East India trade seems to map well into the basic assumptions underlying the Brander-Spencer model. The next question is why the Dutch soon came to dominate the trade. Steensgaard (1965) finds that the Dutch had no advantage in shipping costs over the English in the East India trade. If the English and Dutch companies traded a homogeneous commodity for which they received the same price and paid the same acquisition and shipping costs, then what accounts for the larger trade volume and hence greater profits achieved by the Dutch? Linear demand and Cournot conjectures, for example, establish the presumption that the Nash equilibrium is perfectly symmetric in output and profits for identical firms. Neither firm had an entrenched advantage initially because there were no major sunk costs involved in the trade in the first quarter of the century, since forts and factories were to come later. While territorial control was an important long-run factor accounting for the Dutch success, at this stage all aspects of the East India trade were still open to each firm. So what was the difference between the firms?

By all accounts, the competition between the two firms was intense, but the Dutch are considered to have been more aggressive and more ruthless than the English. While the rivalry between the English and Dutch companies in Asia was not plagued by outright commercial wars like the frequent conflicts in the European theater, the Dutch were tenacious in their efforts to eliminate foreign competitors from the spice islands of Indonesia. The VOC sought monopoly contracts with the principal spice-supplying regions to foreclose competitors and, unlike its English counterpart, was empowered to make treaties, acquire land, and build forts, thereby laying the groundwork for future colonization. The VOC penchant for looting rival vessels on occasion and intimidating English merchants in the region led to constant tensions and even an outbreak of hostilities in 1617–19 when the Dutch seized four English ships. After the mid-1620s, the English gradually ceded further trade with the Spice Islands to the Dutch and withdrew to trade in the far western points of Southeast Asia and with the Indian subcontinent at initially reduced trade volume and profits.

While territorial control (either direct or indirect) ultimately provided the basis for the Dutch domination of the region's international trade, a particular type of strategic policy facilitated the Dutch success. Comparison of the structure and objectives of each firm reveals a mechanism that facilitated Dutch ascendancy in the trade. This policy did not have anything to do with government subsidies, but with managerial incentives.

The English East India Company was a private firm organized and run solely by merchants, with no government stake or involvement beyond granting the monopoly charter. It seems very clear from the institutional makeup of the company that its exclusive objective was to choose the quantity of pepper to ship each year to Europe in order to maximize the returns to investors. Thus the English East India Company is assumed to maximize profits, represented by the expression

$$\pi = p(x, x^*) \cdot x - c \cdot x$$

where π is profits, p is the inverse demand function for pepper in Europe, x is the quantity of pepper carried to Europe (and x^* by the Dutch), and c is the constant marginal (shipping and acquisition) cost. Choosing x to maximize profits yields the following first-order condition:

$$\partial \pi / \partial x = p - c + v \cdot x,$$

where $v = (dp/dx) \cdot [1 + (dx^*/dx)]$ and is the firm's perceived marginal revenue, consisting of the first effect of changes in its output on price and the indirect effect of changes in its rivals output on price in response to changes in its own output (that is, the conjectural variation, with $dp/dx = dp/dx^*$).

The institutional structure and economic objectives of the VOC, however, differed significantly from those of the English company. Before the formation of the VOC, Dutch trade with the East Indies was managed by the *bewindhebbers*, who made business decisions regarding the details of particular voyages and the sale of Asian goods in European markets. The *bewindhebbers* were directly accountable to shareholders (*participanten*), who were guided solely by the profit motive. But the granting of monopoly privileges and establishment of close government ties that accompanied the formation of the VOC in 1602 eroded the influence of the *participanten* on the *bewindhebbers*. In effect, stockholder control over the management of the company was supplanted by the government (Glamann 1958:6ff; Steensgaard 1974:126–141). In characterizing the objective function of the VOC, one must look to the particular incentives facing the *bewindhebbers* who determined the company's shipping schedule. Steensgaard (1982:243) describes these incentives:

Maximization of dividends was the obvious aim of the participant. The *bewindhebbers* were participants themselves, but for several reasons they would tend to have other aims. *Their remuneration by provision made it their interest to maximize the turnover of the company, even at terms that were not advantageous to the participants.* For the same reason they might prefer consolidation and maximum growth rather than dividends. The social and political distinction attached to their offices would work in the same direction. Finally, the close relations to the Dutch political leaders and the ultimate dependence on the political authorities for the continued existence of the company would tend to influence business decisions. So the charter of 1602, in spite of formal continuity, created a managerial group with interests deviating from those of the participants." (Emphasis added)

As a consequence, for the first decades of the company, "the trading partnership was replaced by a permanent, anonymous capital; the *bewindhebbers* became a managerial group with close affiliations to the political authorities; the participants became holders of negotiable shares with not much more influence on company business than a holder of government bonds has on government policy, and the strategic aims of the company were radically changed" (Steensgaard 1982:250).

By design, as mandated in the government's monopoly charter, the *bewindhebbers* derived income both from their position as stockholders, for which they earned dividends that arose from profits, and from their role as managers, for which they earned a percentage of gross revenue. According to the charter, the sixty directors of the VOC were obligated to hold shares in the company and were to receive 1 percent of the value of equipment and ships and 1 percent of the proceeds of sales from each returning voyage. This changed in 1647, when the directors received a fixed salary as compensation (see Bruijn, Gaastra, and Schoffer 1987, 1:11ff).

In essence, the *bewindhebbers* can be thought to have chosen x^* to maximize a linear combination of profits and revenue,

$$\mathcal{L} = \lambda\{p(x, x^*) \cdot x - c \cdot x\} + (1 - \lambda)\{p(x, x^*)\}$$

where λ (which is between zero and one) is the weight put on profits in the objective function. This yields a first-order condition in which modifies the standard profit-maximizing condition in attaching to marginal cost the weight the firm places on profits in its objective function:

$$\partial\mathcal{L}/\partial x^* = p - \lambda \cdot c^* + v \cdot x^*.$$

The key difference between this first-order condition and the one for the profit-maximizing English company is that here marginal costs are discounted by λ (<1). If the firm only cares about profit maximization (i.e., $\lambda = 1$), then the conditions are the same; otherwise, the more weight the firm puts on revenue maximization, the more it discounts costs and the greater output it will produce. Thus, the *bewindhebbers* would be willing to sacrifice profits for revenue the more they earned from their managerial role, leading the firm to understate marginal cost relative to its true value and thereby produce more output than a profit-maximizing firm.

At first glance such an objective portends conflict between managers and investors. However, there is no trade-off between "power" and "plenty" in the context of a Cournot duopoly: Credible Dutch commitment to a strategy of maximizing a mix of profits and revenues dominated the English strategy of maximizing profits because it prompted the Dutch to market a larger quantity, and hence earn greater profits, at the expense of the English. When the Dutch States General helped form the VOC in 1602, created managerial incentives in the charter to increase shipping volume, and insulated its managers from the demands of investors, it institutionalized a contractual incentive mechanism enabling the company to commit to a higher level of trade and to achieve something that approached a Stackelberg leadership position against the English.

This example provides an is excellent illustration of the Fershtman and Judd (1987) and Sklivas (1987) discussion of how hiring an output-maximizing manager can serve as a commitment that nets the principal a larger profit in a Cournot duopoly setting.[14] By contrast, the English could not convincingly sustain such a strategy because private investors remained in charge of, and did not wish to relinquish control of, the company and the government had no role in its operation or activities beyond the enforcement of the monopoly charter.

After the formation of the VOC in 1602, the peaceful commerce of the earlier Dutch traders was abandoned in favor of more aggressive behavior to oust rivals from the East India trade. Shipping volume increased sharply and exclusionary tactics were initiated, including harassment of foreign merchants and pursuit of monopoly contracts. Indeed, Dutch stockholders quickly became distressed about the use of company resources for ends not directly related to profits. Their concern over the principal-agent problem proved to be well founded, as the company refused to open its books to investors, declared dividends with reluctance, and repudiated provisions of early agreements with investors by insisting that *participanten* sell their shares instead of receiving their original investment plus dividends if they wanted to reduce their stake in the company. Their concerns may even have been well based: Even though the Dutch as the Stackelberg leader earned greater profits than otherwise, investors might still be worse off if revenue payments to the *bewindhebbers* left the overall pool of disbursable profits smaller than in the profit-maximizing equilibrium.

Conclusions

Heckscher and Viner engaged in a spirited debate over the relative importance of power versus plenty in mercantilist policy. This essay has suggested, consistent with the contentions of Viner, that there need not be a tradeoff between the two objectives. Power, or a commitment to high levels of output and an aggressive form of competition, has a deterrent effect on potential rivals. This deterrence induces rivals either to limit their participation in the market or to stay out of the market completely. The complementarity of power and plenty may be an important feature of early long-distance international trade between Europe and Asia.

Of course, even if mercantilist policies can be seen with new light through the lens of strategic trade policy, this does not mean that government policies were optimally chosen or even welfare improving. Not only must the optimal level of intervention be determined, but government policy was also subject to the rent-seeking influence of private merchants. As Adam Smith appreciated, and as Grossman and Maggi (1998) show in the context of a strategic trade policy model, private influence on government policy can distort that policy to serve the interests of the merchants rather than the interests of the nation.

Notes

1. "For both periods power and wealth were both ultimate ends, i.e., valued for their own sakes. In neither period were they ordinarily regarded as conflicting ends, and on the contrary it was the general view in both periods that the attainment of the one was a means to the attainment of the other; power bred wealth, and wealth power. If there was occasional recognition that the maintenance of power was economically costly, this should not be interpreted without clear evidence as a denial that the loss or surrender of power would be even more costly economically." Viner (1935:100).

2. Quoted in Viner (1991:27–28).

3. This thesis will not appear to be particularly novel to those familiar with Frederic Lane's (1979) collection entitled *Profits from Power*, but the link to models of strategic trade policy provides a systematic framework in which to think about these issues.

4. For example, Robert Ekelund and Robert Tollison (1981, 1997) stress that mercantilist policies arose mainly as a result of rent-seeking merchants is enlightening and surely captures a very important aspect of the economic policies pursued during this period.

5. Brander (1995) provides an excellent survey of the literature on strategic trade policy.

6. This section draws on Irwin (1992) and Irwin (1996), chapters 2 and 14.

7. In cautiously advocating a shift in the burden of taxation from exports to imports, Henry Robinson (1641:8) warned that "here it is worth remembrance that a great part of foreign commodities brought for England are taken in barter of ours, and we should not have vented ours in so great quantity without taking them."

8. Quoted in Letwin (1963:44).

9. This section draws on Irwin (1991).

10. On the East India trade in general, see Khan (1923), Steensgaard (1974), and Furber (1976). The best references on the early English East India Co. are Krishna (1924) and Chaudhuri (1965); on the Dutch East India Co., see Glamann (1958) and Bruijn, Gaastra, and Schoffer (1979–87). On long-distance trade in general, see Tracy (1990, 1991). For recent work on the East India trade, see O'Rourke and Williamson (2005).

11. Consequently, the East India trade experienced almost no entry or smuggling from other English or Dutch merchants for much of the century, although the English East India Co. was eventually challenged by interlopers in the 1680s.

12. Government representatives met in London in February 1619 and agreed to split the spice trade (one-third for the English and two-thirds for the Dutch, with an equal division of the pepper trade), but company actions ensured that the agreement was moot not long after the ink was dry (see Glamann 1958:76).

13. Dutch shipping records indicate that from 1602 to 1624, over 64 percent of ship departures from the East Indies were concentrated from November to January, and over half of all departures from the Netherlands took place between December and February (with about 85 percent by May) (see Bruijn et al. 1987, 1: 63, 78).

14. See also Das (1997) for a discussion of managerial incentives and strategic trade policies.

References

Brander, J. A. 1995. "Strategic Trade Policy." In G. Grossman and K. Rogoff, eds., *Handbook of International Economics* 3:1395–1455. Amsterdam: Elsevier.

Brander, J. A., and B. J. Spencer. 1985. "Export Subsidies and International Market Share Rivalry." *Journal of International Economics* 18:83–100.

Bruijn, J. R., F. S. Gaastra, and I. Schoffer, eds. 1979–87. *Dutch-Asiatic Shipping in the 17th and 18th Centuries*. 3 vols. The Hague: Nijhoff.

Chaudhuri, K. N. 1965. *The English East India Company: The Study of an Early Joint Stock Company, 1600–1640*. London: Cass.

———. 1978. *The Trading World of Asia and the English East India Company*. Cambridge: Cambridge University Press.

Child, J. 1693. *A New Discourse of Trade*. London: Everingham.

Das, S. P. 1997. "Strategic Managerial Delegation and Trade Policy." *Journal of International Economics* 43:173–188.

Davis, R. 1962. *The Rise of the English Shipping Industry in the Seventeenth and Eighteenth Centuries*. London: Macmillan.

Eaton, J., and G. M. Grossman. 1986. "Optimal Trade and Industrial Policies Under Oligopoly." *Quarterly Journal of Economics* 101:383–406.

Ekelund, R. B. Jr., and R. D. Tollison. 1981. *Mercantilism as a Rent Seeking Society: Economic Regulation in Historical Perspective*. College Station: Texas A&M University Press.

———. 1997. *Politicized Economies: Monarchy, Monopoly, and Mercantilism*. College Station: Texas A&M University Press.

Fershtman, C., and K. L. Judd. 1987. "Equilibrium Incentives in Oligopoly." *American Economic Review* 77:927–940.

Furber, H. 1976. *Rival Empires of Trade in the Orient, 1600–1800*. Minneapolis: University of Minnesota Press.

Glamann, K. 1958. *Dutch-Asiatic Trade, 1620–1740*. The Hague: Nijhoff.

Grossman, G. M., and G. Maggi. 1998. "Free Trade vs. Strategic Trade: A Peak into Pandora's Box." In R. Sato, R. V. Ramachandran, and K. Mino, eds., *Global Competition and Integration*, 9–32. Boston: Kluwer Academic.

Grossman, G. M., and J. D. Richardson. 1985. *Strategic Trade Policy: A Survey of Issues and Early Analysis*. International Finance Section, Dept. of Economics, Princeton University.

Heckscher, E. F. 1935. *Mercantilism*. 2 vols. London: Allen & Unwin.

———. 1936. "Revisions in Economic History, V, Mercantilism." *Economic History Review* 7:44–54.

Irwin, D. A. 1991. "Mercantilism as Strategic Trade Policy: The Anglo-Dutch Rivalry for the East India Trade." *Journal of Political Economy* 99:1296–1314.

———. 1992. "Strategic Trade Policy and Mercantilist Trade Rivalries." *American Economic Review* 82:138–143.

———. 1996. *Against the Tide: An Intellectual History of Free Trade*. Princeton, NJ: Princeton University Press.

Khan, S. A. 1923. *The East India Trade in the XVIIth Century*. Oxford: Oxford University Press.

Krishna, B. 1924. *Commercial Relations Between India and England, 1601–1757*. London: Routledge.

Lane, F. C. 1979. *Profits from Power: Readings in Protection Rent and Violence-Controlling Enterprises*. Albany: State University of New York Press.

O'Rourke, K. H., and J. G. Williamson. 2002a. "After Columbus: Explaining the Global Trade Boom 1500–1800." *Journal of Economic History* 62:417–456.

———. 2002b. "When Did Globalization Begin?" *European Review of Economic History* 6:23–50.

O'Rourke, Kevin H., and J. G. Williamson. 2005. "Did Vasco da Gama Matter for European Markets? Testing Fredrick Lane's Hypothesis Fifty Years Later." NBER Working Paper No. 11884. December 2005.

Petty, W. 1680. *Britannia Languens, or a Discourse of Trade*. London: Dring.

———. 1690. *Political Arithmetick*. London: Clavel.

Reynell, C. 1685. *A Necessary Companion or, the English Interest Discovered and Promoted*. London: Brown.

Robinson, H. 1641. *England's Safety, in Trades Increase*. London: Bourne.

Sklivas, S. D. 1987. "The Strategic Choice of Managerial Incentives." *Rand Journal of Economics* 18:452–458.

Steensgaard, N. 1965. "Freight Costs in the English East India Trade 1601–1657." *Scandinavian Economic History Review* 13:143–162.

———. 1974. *The Asian Trade Revolution of the Seventeenth Century: The East India Companies and the Decline of the Caravan Trade*. Chicago: University of Chicago Press.

———. 1982. "The Dutch East India Company as an Institutional Innovation." In M. Aymard, ed., *Dutch Capitalism and World Capitalism*, 232–257. New York: Cambridge University Press.

Tracy, J. D. 1990. *The Rise of Merchant Empires: Long-Distance Trade in the Early Modern World, 1350–1750*. New York: Cambridge University Press.

———. 1991. *The Political Economy of Merchant Empires: State Power and World Trade, 1350–1750*. New York: Cambridge University Press.

Viner, J. 1935. "Mercantilism." *Economic History Review* 6:99–101.

———. 1948. "Power versus Plenty as Objectives of Foreign Policy in the Seventeenth and Eighteenth Centuries." *World Politics* 1:1–29.

———. 1991. *Essays on the Intellectual History of Economics*. Ed. D. A. Irwin. Princeton, NJ: Princeton University Press.

Wake, C. H. 1979. "The Changing Pattern of Europe's Pepper and Spice Imports, ca. 1400–1700." *Journal of European Economic History* 8:361–403.

11

Mercantilism, the Enlightenment, and the Industrial Revolution

Joel Mokyr

Economic historians will insist on claiming Eli Heckscher as one of their own. His magisterial *Mercantilism* bears every sign of the true economic historian: a reliance on the sources, a clear and analytic framework, a good "nose" for asking the right questions, and an excellent "feel" for the period. Yet the book seems to have been strangely neglected by economic historians in recent decades.[1] Mercantilism as a major topic in the institutional development of Europe has not yet been taken up by the New Institutional Economics. One can only speculate as to the reasons, but it is clear that once the relations between the state and the economy start to attract the interest of this school, they will find a treasure of insight and information in those two volumes. Where Heckscher's work has been better appreciated has been among the scholars working on the political economy of the eighteenth century, especially in the work by Ekelund and Tollison (1981, 1997) and Root (1994), whose interest in rent-seeking led them inevitably to the mercantilist state. While these scholars have not always agreed with Heckscher's view of mercantilism, they have clearly shown due respect for his work.

My perspective here will be somewhat different, if overlapping with their work. The central question with which I am concerned is not economic policy or regulation as such, but long-term economic growth, which began in earnest in Europe just about at the time that classic mercantilism went on the defensive and eventually declined. Heckscher, of course, noted this in passing (1955, 1:275) as well as that the growing aversion to compulsory limitations on economic activity, while going back to the middle ages, was felt most strongly in England and was thus a cause of the Industrial Revolution. But it is fair to say that explaining the Industrial Revolution was not the main focus of his work.

In pointing this out, however, Heckscher identified something that subsequent economic historians have been ignoring at their peril, namely that the causes of the Industrial Revolution include intellectual changes, that is, autonomous changes in what people knew and believed to be true. It is not enough to postulate economic change in terms of changes in technology, prices, demand, population, and physical constraints: what people *believed* about their world and one another was central.[2] Such belief systems can be self-reinforcing and constitute a system that can produce a multiple of equilibria, some of which are more conducive to economic progress than others. In that sense, the Industrial Revolution may have been more "contingent" than economic historians often tend to believe (Mokyr 1998:31–32).

To understand what is known as the "Great Divergence" or the "European Miracle," it seems natural to examine the intellectual roots of economic progress beside the economic and social ones. In Mokyr (2002, 2005), I explore one set of reasons explaining why intellectual factors mattered next to the standard tales of factor endowments and sociopolitical environment. In eighteenth-century Europe, this key development involved a movement I have labeled "the Industrial Enlightenment." Although the Enlightenment was composed of many diverse and often contradictory streams, one common denominator was that economic progress could be achieved by studying natural phenomena and regularities, reducing them to general principles wherever possible, summarizing them in systematic and accessible forms, and applying what was learned to "the useful arts" (that is, production). The Industrial Enlightenment was firmly committed to the Baconian ideal that the purpose of useful knowledge was to bring about material progress to mankind, and asserted that this could be achieved by rational means.

In this essay, I propose to explore a different and more elusive way in which the Enlightenment affected the Industrial Revolution, namely through its impact on institutions. Without changes in the institutional environment of Europe, the technological progress underlying the Industrial Revolution might have been slower in coming and, more important, might have been arrested, as it had before, by what might best be called negative institutional feedback. This involves political and social changes resulting from economic growth that tended to slow down and even reverse growth. Throughout much of history, the wealth resulting from economic growth has tended to attract predators and parasites the way jam attracts houseflies. Successful commercial and industrial regions (for example, Northern Italy and the Low Countries) and groups (for example, Jews and Rhineland Mennonites) raised the envy and greed of less fortunate or resourceful neighbors. Enterprise, industry, and ingenuity created opportunities for internal rent seekers who found politics or violence more remunerative than hard work. Regional commercial and financial success "invited" tax collectors, pirates, invaders, and default-prone borrowers. Either way, it generated in almost dialectical fashion the means to its own demise. The most visible form of negative institutional feedback before 1815 was, of course, war.[3] Economic growth often indirectly helped instigate these conflicts.

It hence stands to reason that, had nothing changed in the eighteenth century but the means and will to improve technology, the process of economic change would have run into serious barriers. Moreover, as I have noted before (Mokyr 1999, 2002), technological progress itself is always in danger of running into resistance by groups that were opposed to innovation for a variety of reasons. With some important exceptions, most Enlightenment figures were favorably disposed to innovation and opposed to attempts to arrest it through political or mob action. Resistance to new technology never disappeared, but because the essence of such institutional resistance was to use *non-market* means to prevent new techniques from being adopted, the growing belief in the beneficence of markets over controls in the nineteenth-century West favored innovators.

In what follows, I submit that institutional changes formed a synergistic whole with the technological advances. Both were triggered, in different ways, by the Enlightenment in the eighteenth century and had a significant intellectual component. Of course, one could, debate the extent to which intellectual developments take priority over "real" changes determined by supply and demand and political facts on the ground. Ekelund and Tollison (1997:14) dismiss ideological causation as a position that "may possess some merit as an auxiliary, supporting" explanation. They feel that intellectuals have been flattering themselves to think that their thought affects public policy, but they fail to realize the impact of the Enlightenment on institutional changes (in fact, the term does not appear in their book). Instead, they claim that because a positive theory of idea formation or the role of ideology is absent, they prefer to focus on economic activity as the basis of institutional change. Ideology, they claim, is "a grin without a cat." This seems a peculiar position to take in view of the events in the West in the last quarter of the eighteenth century, during which two political revolutions were a source of profound institutional change, subsequently spilling over to the entire Western world. Are we to conclude that the Enlightenment's impact on the thought and consequent actions of Mirabeau, Sieyès, Jefferson, Paine, Hardenberg, and the likes, and the institutional changes they wrought was really a "grin without a cat?" Even if we cannot understand the "causes" of the Enlightenment at all—a point I do not accept—it could still be a bona fide explanation of the phenomena that followed it.[4]

Institutional Progress and the Enlightenment

Economic historians speak of "technological progress" without—as yet—the misgivings of many well-meaning but misguided historians and social scientists who feel that the normative tinge of the word "progress" reeks of Whiggish positivism or worse. While technological progress is itself not a neutral term, at least technology has tended to move in one direction. Institutional change is much trickier. Few have been audacious enough to use the term "institutional progress." Effective markets can disintegrate as fast as they can emerge. The trust in contracts and rule of law, to say nothing of peace and the respect for life and property on which efficient allocations depend, have been abruptly reversed more than once. Some Enlightenment thinkers made the leap that individuals and social institutions were subject to similar regularities as natural phenomena and that once these regularities were understood, society could be manipulated and harnessed in the same way.

All the same, the impact of the Enlightenment on the economies of the West transcended its impact on useful knowledge.[5] Had nothing else changed, the institutional negative feedback mechanisms characteristic of pre-1750 societies I have delineated might well have sharply reduced any social gains from technological creativity. Vested interests and rent-seeking could have—and in many places did—threaten continuing technological progress. Without question, "institutional progress" (defined, for instance, as a reduction in the rate of return on rent-seeking activities relative to those in productive activities, or as the reduction in the sum of the deadweight losses from foregone gains from trade or factor mobility) was less monotonic and far more subject to reversals and setbacks than was technological progress. Yet nonmonotonicity does not mean there was no trend. Lacking the full impact of the Enlightenment, economic growth in the non-Western world remained more vulnerable. Many areas were certainly capable of growth, but unable to overcome the negative institutional feedback and thus to sustain it. It has turned out to be easier to transfer Western technology than Western institutions to other areas, and the delicate coevolution of the two was often absent altogether in non-Western economies, leading to a great deal of political tension and social upheaval.

"Institutions" here might be seen to include the formal rules and conventions by which society organizes its economic affairs as well as the accepted collective *beliefs* about the behavior of others that generate regularities in social interactions (Greif 2006). During and after the technological advances of the late eighteenth century, struggles ensued about their implementation. The outcomes of these struggles were by no means inevitable. Economic interests were of course important, but so was persuasion. Logic, coherence, facts, appeals to authority—in short, rhetoric—played an importance role in the emergence and shaping of the institutions that shaped and supported material progress. Without arguing that some institutions are uniformly "good" or "bad," reasonable conjectures about their impact on growth can be made.

Enlightenment economic thought was dominated by the growing realization that the economic game was not zero-sum: exchange was a positive-sum game, and redistribution a negative-sum one.[6] In pointing out the fallacy of the mercantilist zero-sum assumption, David Hume and Adam Smith in Scotland were the most eloquent and influential spokesmen for this tradition.[7] Smith's celebrated statement was that the doctrine, invented by the spirit of monopoly, taught nations that "commerce, which ought naturally to be, among nations as among individuals, a bond of union and friendship, has become the most fertile source of discord and animosity" (1776, 1:519). These opinions were common Enlightenment views, especially among physiocrats such as Turgot, enlightened antimonopoly thinkers such as Diderot, and early critics of mercantilism such as Davenant, Barbon, and Vanderlint.[8] Mercantilist thinking was based primarily on the idea that in order to win the competitive game overseas, domestic producers required subsidies and their competitors should be slapped with tariffs. But by 1773 Matthew Boulton told Lord Warwick that Birmingham manufacturers would defeat their Continental competitors by mechanization and the "separation of process" (that is, the division of labor and specialization) (Uglow 2002:212). In other words, the competitive game should be played in competitive and free markets with productivity as the main control variable.

The importance of institutional change on subsequent growth thus falls into three broad categories: bad institutions that impeded the efficient allocation of resources and the emergence of welfare-enhancing exchange and imposed deadweight burdens, those that channeled human creativity, energy, and talent into nonproductive and possibly destructive uses, and those that failed to encourage technological progress and created obstacles to it. Some forms of economic change were more dependent on institutional progress than others. The emergence of spot markets, local fairs, short-term labor contracts, and land rentals could be arranged without a great deal of institutional support as long as a minimum of law and order could be provided. But technological progress and the supply of long-term venture capital that carried it required more complex arrangements and were often encumbered by incomplete contracts, poorly defined property rights, coordination failures, asymmetric information, and the threat of default. Patent licensing, firm-specific human capital, the agency problems generated by expensive overhead capital and durable equipment, and the division of knowledge, all required institutional change for their support.

Rent-seeking and Institutional Progress

Adam Smith's eloquent case against rent-seeking is well known.[9] In many ways, however, *The Wealth of Nations* is the crashing coda of many decades of enlightenment thought, both in the British Isles and on the Continent.[10] Among those, one of the most interesting is the Frenchman Pierre de Boisguilbert and his compatriot Vincent de Gournay, both of whom used the term *laissez-faire* before it was taken over by the physiocrats (Hutchinson 1988:107–115, 224–225). More ambiguous is the exact position of the Dutch emigrant Bernard de Mandeville, yet his statement that "unhappy is the people, and their constitution will be precarious, whose welfare must depend upon the virtues and consciences of ministers and politicians" boiled down, in Hutchison's (1988:124) words to one of the "earliest and most brilliantly penetrating cases for the market economy." There is also some evidence that Smith was indebted to the Italian Pietro Verri (Groenewegen 2002:278–279). The Scottish enlightenment, long before Adam Smith, increasingly realized the positive-game nature of commerce: David Hume said as much when he noted in his famous essay on "The Jealousy of Trade" that "it is impossible but the domestic industry of every one must receive an increase from the improvements of the others." Yet Hume himself was deeply indebted to the work of his teacher Lord Henry Kames, who was the first to work out the full theoretical significance of property rights. Almost as influential as the *Wealth of Nations* was Adam Ferguson, Smith's contemporary who invented the term "Civil Society" (Ferguson 1767).[11]

The central idea of an enlightened economy was that market forces should be allowed to prevail, rent-seeking and regulation kept at a minimum, and the state limited to its essential functions. These ideas were transnational, propounded by a "Republic of Letters" that was the essence of the European Enlightenment. Where the big differences between European societies came into play was in the implementation stage. The entrenched interests and mercantilist ideas fought back, and the outcome of the battle differed from country to country, often the result of personalities, the timing of events, and historical contingency.

The idea that rent-seeking, privileges, and unearned transfers were not only unjust but harmful as well turned out to be extraordinarily powerful.[12] Any economic system—including the European economy during the Industrial Revolution—is at the mercy of its incentive structure, specifically the opportunities for rent-seeking as they led not only to inefficiencies but also to the possibility that opportunistic behavior would extinguish technological creativity itself. Modern economists have returned to the issue (Baumol 1993, 2002; Murphy, Shleifer, and Vishny 1991; Shleifer and Vishny 1998; Ekelund and Tollison 1997). It has been increasingly realized that rent-seeking and corruption were more than just a minor irritant or a redistributive mechanism with only second-order effects on overall economic performance. Not all corruption is created equal, of course, and many cases of bribery and graft may be interpreted as an attempt to save the free market from those who would regulate it out of existence (Root 1994). More importantly, rent-seeking is far more pervasive than venality: it is the manipulation of the formal (non-market) institutions and informal customs of a society to redistribute income. It is perfectly consistent with "a rule of law"—when the law meant to redistribute income rather than stimulate growth. In the Britain of 1700, government-enforced monopolies, privileges and prohibitions, tariffs, rules and regulations, and rent-seeking in other forms still imposed a heavy toll. Britain was not unique, nor the worst case.[13] But efficiency and economic performance were seriously impeded by the continuous attempt of well-connected, able, and resourceful "entrepreneurs" to harness the state and its apparatus as well any other organization to divert resources their way. Enlightenment thought realized that these actions reduced the size of the national pie, but on the Continent the abolition of the institutions that supported them had to be imposed by force by French revolutionaries or Prussian civil servants, whereas in Britain it grew organically within the existing political structure, so to speak. Enlightenment-inspired reforms reduced the opportunities for rent-seeking, though they never eliminated them. In the Middle East, India, East Asia, or Africa, however, it is hard to find any trace of such reforms until the Europeans showed the way. There is no evidence that on the eve of the Industrial Revolution rent-seeking in Europe was in any way less serious than in China.[14] China may not have had an Enlightenment; it did not have mercantilism either. But, unlike China, in the areas of Europe most affected by the Enlightenment, rent-seeking increasingly clashed with the free market ideology that many Enlightenment thinkers espoused. For at least a critical time period, it was on the defensive. Here, then, is the second taproot of Western exceptionalism.

Rent-seeking, Shleifer and Vishny argue, is subject to economies of scale. In part this is the case because there are fixed costs in setting up the institutions and arrangements that produce rents, and in part it is because by reducing the rate of return to productive entrepreneurship, rent-seeking makes the return on itself relatively more attractive. It may therefore seem plausible that the existence of rent-seeking was consistent with multiple equilibria—a high-income (with little or no rent-seeking), and a low-income equilibrium in which the returns to all activities are low but the returns to rent-seeking remain above those to productive entrepreneurship. The simple setup proposed by Murphy, Shleifer, and Vishny (1993) implies that the "bad" equilibrium is stable, and it requires a fairly substantial change in the rate of return to rent-seeking relative to its opportunity cost in order to shift the economy from one in which there is a lot of rent-seeking and concomitant underdevelopment to one in which rent-seeking is dominated for most people by making money the honest and socially beneficial way.[15] Enlightenment-spawned reforms—whether revolutionary as in France or America, reactive as in Prussia and Austria, or more gradual as in Britain—had led to a decline in the returns to rent-seeking as an economic activity by the middle of the nineteenth century. Governments reduced their own sponsorship of rent-seeking, and worked to weaken private rent-seeking institutions from journeymen's associations to pirates and pickpockets.

In France and elsewhere on the continent, the post-1789 Revolution implied a valiant attempt to put an end to corrupt, inefficient rent-seeking regimes and the introduction of economic institutions that purported to be more "rational" that is, maximize the public welfare.[16] The reforms enacted during the post-1789 years were permeated with the ideas that we associate with the Enlightenment.

Institutional progress inspired by the Enlightenment in the Western world took place on a number of frontiers. The regulation of the grain trade and grain prices was another area in which liberalization, freedom of entry and action, and the erosion of exclusionary arrangements were replaced by increasing reliance on free markets. This process is described in detail by Persson (2000). Enlightenment thought, whether physiocratic or otherwise, nourished and stimulated these reforms and contributed to their eventual triumph despite strong resistance. The issue was complicated because, as was often the case, the "case" for restriction was justified by some social good, in this case price stability of a necessary means of subsistence and concerns about political instability and food riots.

Another area of liberalization was the elimination of a variety of costly barriers to entry, whose effect was to secure exclusionary rents for insiders. Guilds were among the first targets of the revolutionary reformers, monopolies were another. In Britain the golden age of the great trading monopolies was largely over by 1720 (Harris 2000), but the notion that free entry into an industry or an occupation was a natural right gained acceptance very slowly. Root (1994:157) notes that the philosophical argument in favor of a free market took a long time to penetrate the public policies of Parliament. Harris points out (2000:135) that the main barrier to entry into the state of joint-stock enterprise was not so much to convince Parliament to vote a private incorporation bill, but the money required to overcome resistance from existing firms or other vested interests.[17] By the late seventeenth century the seeds of change had already been planted: in international trade, monopolistic practices became increasingly difficult to maintain, and Lockean ideas of natural law and personal liberty—a harbinger of Enlightenment views—were already in the air after 1688, though the battle for free trade would continue through much of the eighteenth century (Ormrod 2003:126–127). Locke himself was still clearly in the mercantilist camp, but in the eighteenth century antimercantilist views gradually grew in influence. After Smith, the long-term trend in British economic policy was to create a more open and competitive society, although the triumph of enlightenment thought was dealt a setback in the 1780s and 1790s when the *philosophes* allied themselves with American revolutionaries and French Jacobins. The great monopoly of the East India company was ended by two parliamentary acts in 1813 and 1833, the restriction on the emigration of skilled artisans was removed in 1824, the export prohibition on machinery in 1843, and the Navigation Acts were repealed in 1849 after having declined for many decades.[18]

Rent-seeking in ancien régime Europe relied on the concept of *privilèges* or sanctioned liberties: the legal and customary rights that certain groups had obtained to keep out others from their status regardless of the merit of a claim.[19] Such rules created exclusion rents.[20] Rent-seeking institutions benefitted the *noblesse d'epée* of France, the great trading monopolies of Britain, the oligarchs of the United Provinces, the guilds of Germany, and the powerful Catholic Church of southern Europe. The main *privilège* in prerevolutionary France was of course a tax exemption, but the country could count many petty municipal offices such as "wardens of the oysters sellers' guild, gaugers of cheese and curds, and inspectors of tripe who gloried in their small dignities and enjoyed their exemptions" (Schama 1989:68).

It is possible to exaggerate the negative impact of guilds. In Britain they had already been weakened considerably by the beginning of the eighteenth century, whereas in France they showed a remarkable ability to adapt to the capitalist market, while at the same time "guilds and regulations...created zones of solidarity, credit, and trust in which family and matrimonial strategies played an important role" (Roche 1998:149). Guild regulations could be evaded by moving the process to the countryside or employing women workers. Some recent literature has tried to cast the craft guilds in a more favorable light, arguing that under some circumstances they may even have favored more technological progress than traditionally believed. Yet Ogilvie (2004) has disputed this revisionist interpretation, and Deyon and Guignet (1980) point out the inherent tensions in the ancien régime between local vested interests, which were invariably conservative, and more progressive forces inspired by the Enlightenment.[21] Progressive thinkers, whether physiocrat, late-mercantilist, or liberal, all felt an aversion to those who took advantage of political or social power to appropriate a larger portion of the surplus. Turgot, in many ways, personifies the institutional elements of the Enlightenment. His idea was that free competition should be implemented if necessary by using state compulsion as a weapon of persuasion to abolish all exclusive organizations such as associations, fraternities, and unions.[22] The abolition of guilds was at the center of his plan to reform the French economy, as he realized the extent to which guilds constrained the mobility of labor (Heckscher 1955, 1:216–217). Yet the plan failed, in large part because the guilds were indispensable in the complex system of royal finances in the ancien régime.[23]

The State and the Industrial Revolution

The era before the Industrial Revolution witnessed in some areas the rise of a powerful state with a precommitment to a minimum protection of property rights and the ability to solve the contestabilities and coordination failures of premodern societies (Epstein 2000). In other areas the rise of a modern state was more slow and wobbly.[24] A prevalent notion among the New Institutionalists is that the main source of uncertainty of property rights was the state itself, and that "better" property rights and less rent-seeking occurred when the state could commit itself to abstain from unilaterally grabbing assets from its citizens. The standard institutional interpretation proposed by what O'Brien (2002:245) has called the "North American Whigs" is that following the Glorious Revolution of 1688, Britain adopted a set of institutions that assured better property rights, restricted the government from arbitrarily taxing Britons, defended free enterprise and innovation, made contracting and transacting less uncertain and in general created the kind of economy that inexorably led to economic growth.[25] Yet it is not wholly clear how lower transactions costs and more certain property rights led to technological innovations. There also is a problem of timing: as O'Brien has pointed out, the institutional achievements made during the British civil war (the valiant attempts of the Stuart restoration notwithstanding), turned out to be largely irreversible. Yet the technological momentum of the Industrial Revolution did not start in full swing until the second half of the eighteenth century.[26]

The government, of course, was not the only predator: any pirate, con artist, pickpocket, forger, or highwayman was a rent seeker and increased transaction cost, lowering the net marginal product of capital and weakening incentives to engage in "productive" activity. When the state gradually assumed a monopoly on violence, the potential dangers it imposed to Smithian growth came to overshadow the others. The fear that those who were assigned to protect property would themselves become the main threat to it never quite abated, but in eighteenth century Europe such "predatory absolutism" in its purer forms existed nowhere. In England there was not even a professional police force to protect private property, and much of the enforcement against local violence depended on private mechanisms.

Protectionism was the best-known set of policies through which mercantilism promoted rent-seeking (the two are often considered interchangeable). The redistribution was meant to be primarily from foreigners to the citizens of the country in question, but protection of course also redistributed resources from some citizens to others. Mercantilist policies were at the heart of the negative institutional feedback that shrank the commercial profits of the United Provinces, and this helps explain why the Netherlands did not become the originating region of the Industrial Revolution. In the decades after 1660, the defensive efforts and the discriminatory policies of other European economies slowly eroded Dutch leadership (Ormrod 2003; De Vries and Woude 1997).

Arguably, then, the main risk to Smithian growth imposed by the state was not the threat it imposed to property rights as such, but the dangers that political and military actions imposed on the gains from international trade, through the actions of armies, blockades, and privateers. By the 1760s, the main Enlightenment thinkers and their clientele belonged to a global village, a "Republic of Letters," and nationality meant little to them (Darnton 2003). Coupled with their growing cosmopolitanism was a growing pacifist approach.[27] The costly wars fought between the European powers between 1793 and 1815 are thus in a sense ironic, because they were the very result of an Enlightenment-inspired revolution, as was the antiliberal reaction in Britain after 1795. After 1815, however, the Pax Britannica meant that at least within most of Europe predatory wars of the kinds waged by Louis XIV or Frederick the Great were no longer a likely threat.

The problem in ancien régime Europe was not just the insecurity and uncertainty of property rights, but the nature of these rights themselves. A government monopoly, a tax farm, or a law prohibiting the manufacturing or import of a rival product or the export of a complement might be regarded as a property right and was in many cases nearly perfectly secure, yet it *reduced* efficiency.[28] The correlation of the power of distributional coalitions and vested interests with the increasingly powerful and centralized state is rather unclear. Epstein (2000:36) argues that the rise of the modern state increased efficiency: in his view, the main institutional bottleneck to economic growth in premodern states arose from coordination failures caused by the absence of undivided sovereignty over the political and economic spheres. Because these states did not have a monopoly of power within their borders, various bodies derived income from "jurisdictional rights that constrained Smithian growth." This conclusion is contestable: rent-seeking could and did occur under autocratic unified governments as it did under the parcelized authorities that Epstein feels jeopardized Smithian growth. Indeed, some scholars have argued exactly the reverse: the strong absolutist state was ideally located for low-cost rent-seeking, while a government such as Britain's in which authority was fragmented between two authorities (royal vs. parliamentary) that competed in the supply of restrictive legislation eventually experienced the rise of "a free economy" as a by-product of this competition.[29] Parliament and local authorities could be just as profligate in handing out and enforcing exclusions and exemptions, but after 1750 increasingly elected not to do so. That is not to say that rent-seeking and what Hilton Root calls "the corruption of the spoils system" were absent in Britain, only that it was becoming more costly to bribe Parliament into redistributing income and controlling access. Such rent-seeking took place throughout the eighteenth century and was at times successful. Adam Smith was guilty of only a little exaggeration when he exclaimed that Britain's woolen manufacturers have been more successful than any other class of workmen in persuading the legislature that the prosperity of the nation depended upon the success and extension of their particular business (Smith 1776, 2:165).

Indeed, the ancien régime in Europe redistributed income and wealth in many ways and through many channels. A minimalist approach to rent-seeking might blur the many distortions of this system. One issue that has engaged historians is the redistribution due to grain price control. Many European governments felt that grain was somehow different from other commodities and implicitly recognized that the population at large were entitled to stable grain prices and reliably cheap bread, a sentiment surely reinforced by bread riots that were rife in Europe. Root (1994:85) notes that the regulations of the "moral economy" served some interests at the expense of others, and in the process imposed a deadweight interest on the economy. Food rioters were primarily urban dwellers, and could organize more easily than those who paid the price for these transfers. The logical conflict that this created for Enlightenment thinkers could not be easily resolved. Poverty was clearly unacceptable to the *philosophes*, but direct interventions in the market mechanisms were increasingly recognized as harmful. Adam Smith and the physiocrats could agree on freeing the grain trade, and their influence was central to the economic Enlightenment on both sides of the channel (Persson 2000). In Britain, despite food riots, grain market regulation became unpopular in the second half of the seventeenth century (Outhwaite 1981), and redistribution increasingly took place through outdoor relief. In France, too, this institution was coming under pressure in the second half of the eighteenth century (Kaplan 1976; Persson 2000:2–5). Growing market integration was seen as a better mechanism to stabilize prices than government regulation (Persson 2000:131–155). But there was more than that: by recognizing that poverty was primarily an economic and political problem and not a moral one, and by realizing that by increasing the prosperity of the nation through free international and internal trade poverty would eventually be diminished as well, eighteenth-century thought helped pave the road the classic liberalism that secured the gains of the Industrial Revolution (Norberg 2003).

Enlightenment ideas had an unmistakable impact on politics, perhaps beyond the wildest dreams of the *philosophes*. Again, the ideas outlined by Adam Smith in book V, chapter 1 about the responsibilities of the state reflect French and Scottish Enlightenment thought. The astonishing fact is that these ideas had a real impact. The influence of Enlightenment thinkers on eighteenth-century public policy could be found in the institutional reforms associated with the so-called enlightened despots.[30] The locus classicus of the impact of Enlightenment thinking on institutional change was in France. Although Turgot's Enlightenment-inspired reforms failed, Quesnay's disciples in positions of power (known as the *économistes*) were quite influential in reforming the French grain trade in the 1760s.[31] After 1789, of course, reform became the norm. The revolutionary assembly in France abolished feudal privileges, guilds, tax exemptions, and every other "liberty" it could think of. Such a radical reform would still have been unthinkable at the time of the death of Louis XIV in 1715, and in fact was still viewed as absurd at the time of the dismissal of Turgot in 1776.[32]

Some of the most widely observed "rational" reforms in eighteenth-century Britain, such as the Parliamentary enclosures and the establishment of turnpike trusts were explicitly aimed at enhancing economic performance. A pet project of Enlightenment rationalizers such as Condorcet was standardization, especially that of weights and measures, leading to the introduction of a standardized system in the Anglo-Saxon world and the metric system everywhere else. A unified and rational code of commercial law embodying laissez-faire ideas is another example in point. In Britain, many of the old rules were weakened or simply repealed by Parliament in the early nineteenth century, including the Statute of Apprentices and Artificers in 1814 and the Bubble Act in 1825. Britain's political institutions were nimbler and more flexible, so that they could be changed at low social cost by a body assigned to changing the rules and laws by which the economic game was played. Following North (1990:80) we might call this adaptive efficiency, meaning not only the adaptation of the allocation of resources but of the institutions themselves. To bring this about, what was needed was a meta-institution such as Parliament that was authorized to change the rules in a consensual manner, another paradigmatic Enlightenment idea.

Enlightenment and Free Trade

Another margin at which the Enlightenment was successful was the liberalization of trade and the elimination of both internal and external toll and tariff barriers. Foreign trade had always been the pivot of mercantilist thought, and in part the result of a misguided obsession with the Balance of Trade, in part because of rent-seeking. The Corn Laws, first passed in 1670 and reinstated in 1815, were the crowning achievement of rent-seeking landowners. In the eighteenth century and deep into the nineteenth, Anglo-Saxon liberalism simultaneously advocated free internal trade with continued protection for external trade. The later stages of the Enlightenment, inspired and informed by post-Smithian political economy, extended liberalism to foreign trade, but its triumph was late in the making, and after 1815 much of the Continent had a greater commitment to free international trade than the English-speaking areas (Nye 1991).

It is debatable whether free trade theory and ideology were wholly a consequence of the Enlightenment, and even more so if Enlightenment ideas necessarily led to support of free trade.[33] We should not rashly equate Smith with the Scottish Enlightenment, much less with the entire movement.[34] The Enlightenment did advocate a "civilized

consortium of nations" (Howe 2002:195), and in all its forms disapproved of any kind of commercial policy motivated by what Hume
called "the Jealousy of Trade." To be sure, Enlightenment writers were
never unanimous on commercial policy (Irwin 1996).[35] Yet the post-
Waterloo movement toward free trade would be unthinkable without
the political economy that the Scottish Enlightenment produced.

The origins of this movement, of course, predated the nineteenth
century. William Grenville, William Pitt the younger's cousin and foreign secretary of state, was strongly influenced by Smith's teaching
and opposed price regulation of flour, pointing out that it would lead
to scarcity.[36] He repeatedly lectured the prime minister on the virtues
of free trade, and had a strong impact on younger Whig MPs such as
Francis Horner, Henry Brooke Parnell, and David Ricardo, whose influence on the reform movement of the 1830s was decisive.[37]

The dominant figure in the "liberal Tory" governments in the mid-
1820s was William Huskisson—most famous among economists for
being, apparently, the first person ever killed by a moving train on the
opening day of the Manchester and Liverpool Railway—who passed a
series of tariff reductions and was instrumental in reforming the Navigation Acts (though they were not formally abolished until 1851).[38] In
Prussia, figures deeply influenced by Smith were Peter Beuth, a local
administrator in Westphalia, subsequently head of the Department of
Trade and Industry and considered the "father" of Prussian industry.
A convinced Smithian, Beuth was one of the chief figures in the transformation of Prussia from a rent-seeking to a competition-oriented
society, and served, among other things, as director of a variety of
academies and colleges to support industry. Other Prussians in his
mold were Theodor von Schön, an East Prussian advisor to Stein
(taught by Smith's main disciple in Königsberg, Christian Jacob Kraus)
and Ludwig von Vincke, the governor of Westphalia, who religiously
read a chapter a day in *The Wealth of Nations* and referred to Adam
Smith as "the Divine Smith" (Behrens 1985:187; Kindleberger 1978:190;
Schumpeter 1954:501). Stein himself, of course, was in every aspect a
child of the Enlightenment, and his successor, Hardenberg, considered
the free market system for goods and labor the way to maximize
economic efficiency and forge a new public spirit.[39] To be sure, the influence of the Enlightenment might have been less of a stimulus for reform than concern about French military power after the defeat of 1806
and the need to reform the Prussian state if the country was to maintain its position as a great power. The Prussian Enlightenment, more

so than the British one, carried the germs of the Enlightenment's deadliest offspring—nationalism—and its statism clearly was in some way an "illiberal" interpretation of Smith and led to the ideas of *Nationalökonomie* that would eventually extinguish free trade.

What tends to be overlooked, however, is that the Enlightenment, even when it was ambiguous about free trade, was always in strong support of free *internal* trade: the U.S. constitution's commerce clause, as well as the French reforms of 1791 (abolishing internal tariffs) and the post-1815 movement toward a German *Zollverein* reflected this sentiment.[40] Internal trade in Sweden was liberalized in the late 1770s (Persson 2000:139). The system of tolls and duties on Germany's magnificent river system that hampered trade in the eighteenth century was dismantled. Arguably, the lion's share of gains from trade were secured through internal rather than external trade.

The success of the Enlightenment thinkers in affecting legislation and policy should not surprise us: they were telling the most dynamic and resourceful segment of society what it wanted to hear. The triumph of the *philosophes* must be explained by their ability to act against the status quo from within the establishment. Many of the leading lights of the eighteenth century *philosophes* and political economists were well born and politically well connected. Even when they ran afoul of the regime, the relations rarely degenerated into hostility. This "cosy fraternizing with the enemy" as Gay (1966:24) calls it, did not come without a price, but it allowed the *philosophes* to be politically effective without necessarily threatening the status quo. In France, this relationship in the end imploded (though it was soon restored), but elsewhere it made it possible for their ideas to be adopted by the men who voted on policy decisions. Moreover, as I have argued elsewhere (Mokyr 2005), the success of the Enlightenment in Europe was in part due to the fragmentation of political power, which allowed rebels and deviants to play one power against another.

To be sure, intellectual factors were not exogenous to the system. Kindleberger (1975:35) cites Mill's statement that a good cause seldom triumphs unless someone's interest is bound up with it, but adds that in the British case it was more a view of the world at peace with cosmopolitan interests served as well as national. Such liberal views, inspired by the Enlightenment, soon ran afoul with national interests. The intellectual triumph of the political economists, which "overwhelmed the Tories when it did not convert them," are to Kindleberger the most consistent and persuasive explanation of the rise of free trade in the first half of the nineteenth century. The real point is not to realize that "someone's interests" were enhanced by economic rationalization but to ask how and why these interests defeated the resistance of those whose interests were not. Ideological change involved above all *persuasion*, and here the importance of the *philosophes* and their influence on policy makers must be an integral part of the story.[41]

Technology and Institutions in the Industrial Revolution

The distinction I have drawn between the impact of the Enlightenment on technology and its impact on institutions is of course arbitrary and we must consider their overlap. As noted, rent-seeking can thwart innovation through the siphoning-off of talent.[42] It is up to society and its institutions to set up the incentives for innovators correctly. In this area, too, the Enlightenment wrote a new page and helped draw the distinction between "the West" and much of the world that missed out on the movement.

One mechanism at work here was the degree to which society wanted to and could reward inventors. Intellectual property rights in useful knowledge was a major issue with which eighteenth-century society struggled (Hilaire-Pérez 2000). On one hand, Enlightenment thinking increasingly abhorred state-enforced monopolies, realizing full well that they were more often than not rent-seeking devices. On the other hand, patents were realized by some Enlightenment writers to be one of the more effective ways of encouraging invention and channeling talent into where it could be of most use to society, and where markets, rather than officials, would determine the value of an invention.[43] The growing use of patents to reward and encourage invention was thus a typical Enlightenment-inspired phenomenon, even if the origins of the institution precede the Enlightenment. Yet the *philosophes* remained deeply divided about the matter.[44] A typical Enlightenment idea is that useful knowledge be made accessible: the patent system, while protecting the intellectual property rights to the use of a novel technique, reduced the incentive to keep technological knowledge secret and placed the technical details in the public domain. In Britain this was laid out in a decision by chief justice Lord Mansfield, who decreed in 1778 that the specifications should be sufficiently precise and detailed so as to fully explain it to a technically educated person.[45]

The other main area in which technological innovation and institutional change overlapped was in the resistance of vested interests to new technology (Mokyr 1994, 2002). Historians of technology, with some important exceptions, have paid scant attention to the political economy of technological change. For most of recorded history, vested interests have banded together to try to stop progress, because it clearly threatened the value of their human and physical capital.[46] The resistance derived from two separate sources: one was the rational selfish behavior of powerful lobbies protecting their assets, standing in society, and political power base. The other came from those who were sincerely concerned about the unknown effects of new technology and unwilling to face the inevitable risks that radically new technologies imply. As noted already, economic historians have long pointed to the urban guild system as it emerged in the centuries before 1800 as a serious brake on innovation.[47] Enlightenment thinkers took a dim view of the rent-seeking lobbies such as craft guilds representing vested interests, perpetuating the technological status quo, and imposing limitations on economic freedom.

At one level, then, most Enlightenment thinking viewed technological change as "progress" and implicitly felt that social resistance to it was undesirable. Yet there was a strand of thought, associated with Rousseau and with later elements in romanticism such as Cobbett and Carlyle, that viewed industrialization as dangerous at best and as evil and destructive at worst.[48] Ideological resistance to technological change is deeply ingrained in the human psyche. Most of the *philosophes* did not support this line, yet they also realized that technological change was often disruptive and could lead to social tensions. The struggle between innovators and those who resisted novelty came to a crashing crescendo during the Industrial Revolution when the old regulations in the wool industry were repealed in 1809, followed by the abolition of the 250-year-old Statute of Artificers in 1814. The Luddite rebellion—a complex set of events that involved a variety of grievances, not all of which were related to innovation—was mercilessly suppressed. The debate between old regulations and privileges and the Enlightenment forces of laissez faire coincided with the debate between the force opposed to innovation and those that favored it.[49] Whether British entrepreneurs managed to take advantage of a historical opportunity, or whether the fear of popular uprising was only a pretext for passing a program favoring powerful industrial interests, it appears that rent-seeking-inspired resistance against new technology had been driven into a corner by that time. As Paul Mantoux put it many years ago, "Whether [the] resistance was instinctive or considered, peaceful or violent, it obviously had no chance of success" (Mantoux 1928:408). Had that not been the case, sustained progress would have been severely hampered and possibly brought to an end.[50] The growth of international trade and the gradual opening-up of the British economy to foreign competition in the eighteenth century strengthened the forces favoring innovation, and in this way the two movements reinforced each other.[51]

Conclusion

The transformations in Europe that weakened the negative institutional feedback in the age of Enlightenment were invariably slow, muddled, and contested. Had there been no institutional progress in the critical years after 1750, whatever gains were made through greater efficiency, improved trade, or better technology might have been grabbed by tax collectors, monopolists, lawyers, or foreign invaders, threatening to terminate economic growth. In this counterfactual scenario, it seems likely that the first wave of inventions we often identify with Ashton's famous "wave of gadgets" would have fizzled out as had happened in the past. Institutional changes required, however, intellectual foundations and beliefs to catch on, perhaps as a necessary rather than a sufficient condition. What made the Industrial Revolution different from the previous "spurts" of technology or commerce, then, was that it came after the Enlightenment.

It is easy to overstate the novelty of the institutions that emerged in the eighteenth century. Greif (2006, 25–26, 393) sees a continuity between the late Middle Ages and the emergence of modern institutions in the late eighteenth century. Late medieval Europe, he maintains, experienced forms of individualism, formal law, corporatism, self-governance, and rules that were determined through an institutionalized process in which those are subject to them could be heard and have an input. Yet these elements did not trigger modern growth. In between the Middle Ages and modern growth, notes Greif, came an interlude of absolutism and mercantilism.

Ideological changes are not the entire story. A desire for improvement and even the "right" kind of institutions alone do not produce *sustained* growth unless society steadily produces new useful knowledge. Knowledge growth occurs because in each society there are people who are creative and original, motivated by some combination of greed, ambition, curiosity, and altruism. All four of those motives can be seen to be operating among the people who helped make the Industrial Revolution, often combined in the same person. Yet in order to be translated from personal predilections to facts on the ground and from there to economic growth, the correct incentives and social interactions had to be there. The greatness of the European Enlightenment was that it created that kind of environment.

There was nothing inexorable or self-evident in those changes. Nothing like them took place in China, despite its being a sophisticated commercial economy and the rather remarkable process of growth in the eighteenth century Chinese economy. Likewise, nothing of the kind took place in the Ottoman world, Japan, or South America. Some of the European nations, such as Spain and Russia, were for one reason or another so lightly touched by it that their institutions—despite some sincere attempts at reform—seriously slowed down the pace of economic modernization.[52] Whatever subsequent economic growth occurred in these economies was subsequently spurred by prior economic success in the West. At the time, surely, it looked anything but preordained even in the West. In 1784 Kant reflected that the "age of Enlightenment" in which he lived was not yet "an enlightened age." Peter Gay assesses that this distinction was penetrating and important, because even late in the eighteenth century the *philosophes* had ample reason for uncertainty and occasional gloom (1966:20). Certainly, at that time, the prospects for an age of relatively free market economies and a curtailment of rent-seeking activities on the Continent still looked anything but inevitable.

Is it possible to speculate as to the "causes" of the Industrial Enlightenment? Explaining why the Enlightenment itself took place when and where it did is a daunting task that clearly lies outside the comparative advantage of the economic historian. The Enlightenment, much like the Renaissance and the Reformation that preceded it, were based on a foundation of skepticism and rejection. It amounted to a reexamination and eventual rejection of deeply entrenched traditional concepts and beliefs. In the study of the natural world, this was tantamount to a new approach summarized by the Royal Society's motto *nullius in verba* (take no one's word): a rejection of authority and an insistence on empirical verifiability. In the economic organization of society this led to challenges to such venerable institutions as the sanctity of privilege and "liberties." Challenges were posed to vested interests and exclusions that had ruled for centuries, to old customs and local monopolies, to the prevalence of chaotic weights and measures, to rights to levy tolls and taxes on goods and people that moved, to customary rights to veto the rearrangement of land use, to tax exemptions, and to the divine rights of kings. The question is not so much why such ideas occurred—they did in every society that suffered from built-in inefficiencies—but why they *succeeded*. Success was more likely to occur in a world in which political fragmentation placed limits on the resistance to and suppression of new ideas that reactionary coalitions in defense of the status quo could generate.

It also stands to reason that the emergence of free market capitalism, the growth of long-distance commerce, and the intellectual changes we associate with the Enlightenment reinforced one another in subtle ways. Indeed it is often thought that commercial capitalism brought about the Industrial Revolution as its inevitable culmination. This approach fails to take into account the vulnerability of prosperity based on Smithian growth and its susceptibility to mercantilist and other rent-seeking policies that eventually might have throttled the economic progress triggered by commercial expansion (Goldstone 2002).[53]

Not everything in the Enlightenment mattered equally to subsequent economic development. Needless to say, the movement affected only a small portion of the populations of the West. But perhaps that is all that mattered. Much of the economic growth was brought about by a relatively small group of inventors, entrepreneurs, engineers, and their counterparts in politics, administration, justice, and social thought. To paraphrase Keynes's oft-cited observation, practical men, who believe themselves exempt from intellectual influences, were usually the slaves of some defunct Enlightenment *philosophe*. Keynes was "sure that the power of vested interests is vastly exaggerated compared with the gradual encroachment of ideas. . . . Soon or late, it is ideas, not vested interests, which are dangerous for good or evil" (1936:383–384). As has often been pointed out, Keynes's own impact on economic policy after 1945 illustrates this statement. The same is true for the emergence of modern economic growth.

Acknowledgments

The comments of Peter Meyer, Maristella Botticini, Avner Greif, Sheilagh Ogilvie, Örjan Sjöberg, and the participants at the Heckscher Conference are acknowledged with gratitude. The research assistance of Hillary King and Michael Silver is also acknowledged.

Notes

1. Of the forty-five references to Heckscher's work on mercantilism in the two leading economic history journals, thirty-five were made before 1971, and only four since 1980. Of the thirteen citations in the entire economics and history sections of J-STOR to Heckscher's work on mercantilism, only five papers qualify as economic history proper. A recent well-reviewed book (Epstein 2000), clearly concerned with similar issues, does not even refer to it.

2. It is interesting to note that the one economist who can claim to have continued in Heckscher's tradition of combining international economics and economic history, Charles Kindleberger, identified intellectual and doctrinal forces as a powerful agent of economic change and liberalization (see Kindleberger 1975).

3. O'Brien (2003) notes that between the Nine Years War (starting in 1688) and the Congress of Vienna in 1815, Britain and France were at or on the brink of war for more than half the period, justifying the term "Second Hundred Years War."

4. Ekelund and Tollison's observation that ideas need to be "sold" does not really weaken the thrust of the point I am making here. The "selling" of ideas can take place through persuasion and rhetoric, the use of improved logic and facts, without a necessary concomitant change in the economic environment. The impact of Malthus's theory of population, a cornerstone of classical Political Economy and subsequent public policy—for example, the Poor Law Reform of 1834—is a case in point.

5. For a more detailed argument about the impact of the Enlightenment on technology, see Mokyr (2002, 2003).

6. The mercantilists, as Sir Josiah Child (1630–99) put it, held that "all trade is a kind of warfare" (Gay 1969:346). The idea that the production and exchange are not a zero-sum game is actually quite counterintuitive, and has taken a great deal of persuasion and struggle to catch on. See Rubin (2002:22) and Wright (2000:327).

7. Smith's understanding of this point was well expressed by Nathan Rosenberg (1960:560ff), who notes that Smith recognizes that "the pursuit of one's economic interest is not necessarily confined to the economic arena. When it spills over to the political arena, it leads to actions which detract from, rather than add to, the economic welfare of society . . . the competitive order which Smith advocated was an institutional arrangement which was characterized by the absence of all special privilege and sources of market influence." It is in this light that we have to understand Smith's well-known objections to the apprenticeship system, joint-stock corporations, and other forms of potential rent-seeking.

8. Turgot noted in 1773 that "there is no merchant who would not like to be the sole seller of his commodity. . . . These fools do not see that this same monopoly which they practice . . . against their own fellow citizens who are sellers in their turn . . . in this balance of annoyance and injustice . . . there is no advantage to any party; but there is a real loss to the whole of national commerce" (Groenewegen 1977:183–184).

9. The people living off the "public revenue," wrote Smith, "themselves produce nothing [and] are all maintained by the produce of other men's labour. When multiplied to

an unnecessary number, they may in a particular year consume so great a share of this produce as not to leave a sufficiency for maintaining the productive labourers...next year's produce will therefore be less than that of the foregoing" (Smith 1776, 1:363–364). This famous paragraph summed up much of Enlightenment thinking of the time, and its influence on the changes that were introduced in the way the economic game was played in the West were far-reaching.

10. For evidence of Smith's debts to French economic thought, see Groenewegen (2002:125–143, 363–378).

11. In it, Ferguson gets fairly close to a denunciation of rent-seeking in almost modern terms: "we think that a people cannot be impoverished by a waste of money which is spent among themselves. The fact is that men are impoverished...by having their gains suspended or by having their substance consumed...while money circulates at home, the necessaries of life, which are the real constituents of wealth, may be idly consumed; the industry which might be employed to increase the stock of a people may be suspended or turned to abuse.... We should place on the side of the loss every name that is supernumerary on the civil or the military list, all those orders of men who, by the possession of fortune subsist on the gains of others...all those who are engaged in the professions of law, physic, or divinity, together with all the learned, who do not, by their studies promote or improve some lucrative trade." He admitted, however, that a society of perfect virtue was impossible, and so some resources would have to be allocated to such unproductive occupations. Yet in a society dominated by avarice and vanity "the individual considers his community so far as it can be rendered subservient to his personal advancement and profit" (Ferguson 1767:350, 357). The sharp distinction between rent-seeking and a productive form of competition is not yet fully ripe, but clearly the idea is "in the air." As Herman (2001:189) notes, Ferguson's work was enormously influential on the Continent and was admired by Herder, Schiller, and Hegel.

12. Emma Rothschild (2001) has challenged the view that many of the more extreme liberal views came from Smith himself and argues that they emanated in Britain after Smith's death.

13. Not all monopolies were necessarily inefficient, poorly managed, and economically harmful, as Carlos and Nicholas (1990) have shown, though others have contested their approach. And yet the danger that they would eventually be tempted into rent-seeking was quite real. The same is true for craft guilds which, as Epstein (1998) has argued, may at some time have met a real economic need of organizing and transmitting useful knowledge and yet increasingly became a technologically reactionary entrenched distributional coalition. In the absence of competition such organizations will slide into rent-seeking even if that was not their original intent.

14. Indeed, Wong (1997:133) notes that "trade was never as exhaustively exploited by Chinese rulers as it was by European ones."

15. Shleifer and Vishny (1998:55), much in Adam Smith's spirit, define all government service, military work, and organized religion as rent-seeking. Such a definition seems inappropriate as it contains too much and too little. Rent-seeking is an activity that aims purely at redistribution and produces little or nothing of value itself. Some bureaucrats, lawyers, soldiers, and priests catered to a real social need such as national defense or the enforcement of property rights. Some talented "entrepreneurs" worked hard within the government bureaucracy to produce something of value that the private market turned out to be incapable of. Classic examples are the careers of Marriner Eccles and Mary Swit-

zer, documented in the last two chapters of Hughes (1986). Organized religion, too, seems to be responding to market signals, and defining it as rent-seeking altogether must be seen as inconsistent with the consumer sovereignty of those who demand this service.

16. The *opus classicus* on the institutional impact of the French Revolution in wiping out local *priviléges* remains Rosenthal (1992). In his recent book, Gillispie (2004:8) has pointed out that Enlightenment thought, with its deeply-rooted belief that human institutions should be arranged "naturally," formed the basis for the expectations for reform in the early years of the French Revolution.

17. The best-known example is the Calico Act of 1700 (reinforced in 1721) which prohibited the printing of calicoes and later even the wearing of printed cotton goods (passed at the urging of the light wool and silk industry lobbies). It seems a stretch to argue with O'Brien, Griffiths and Hunt (1991) that this blatant act of rent-seeking was an example of British pragmatism. Perhaps a better example of British pragmatism was the rather matter of fact manner in which the Act was repealed in 1774 at the urging of Richard Arkwright, the inventor of the spinning throstle.

18. By all accounts, the enforcement of these prohibitions had left a lot to be desired. Witnesses to an 1841 Select Committee admitted that exportation of prohibited machinery took place through the major ports rather than through remote moonlit beaches; insurance premiums against customs detection were quoted at 30 to 45 percent in 1825, providing some indication as to the social costs of this exclusionary policy (Jeremy 1981:42–43).

19. The idea that rent-seeking lay at the bottom of the institutional failures of the ancient régime in Europe was proposed in the early 1980s in a series of papers and books by Ekelund and Tollison (1981, 1984, 1997) but virtually ignored by economic historians.

20. Epstein (2000:15) points out that "freedoms" or "liberties" were concepts that defined inequalities in social and economic status and the entitlement to an income stream that such privileges conferred. It is not always easy to tell whether the monopolies of the time were invariably rent-seeking institutions or whether they were in part the result of scale economies and other sources of "natural" monopolies. Ville and Jones (1996) have pointed out that much of the evidence adduced by recent writers to support the notion that the large monopolies were efficient organizations is also consistent with a rent-seeking interpretation, but the evidence on this is still in dispute (Carlos and Nicholas 1996).

21. The French inventor Jacques Vaucanson, in his capacity of inspector-general of silk for the kingdom, tried in 1744 to overhaul the rather restrictive regulations of the Lyons municipal codes; the workers rose against the Paris intruders who barely escaped with their lives (Gillispie 1980:416). Even in the supposedly liberal United Provinces, guild regulations in the cities could protect long-established rights and vested interests "at the expense of the general interest" (Ormrod 2002:111).

22. In his famous *Eloge de Gournay*, Turgot made an eloquent plea against monopolies or exclusionary restrictions of any kind, practices we would identify today with rent-seeking behavior (Groenewegen 1977:26–29).

23. In Spain, the once powerful guilds or *gremios* were weakened under the reformist King Carlos III, who ordered in 1777 that all local guilds were to admit craftsmen from other parts of Spain in an attempt to weaken their local monopolies (Herr 1958:124–126).

Despite the vigorous campaign against them led by Carlos's government, the rent-seeking economy in Spain was not really dislodged.

24. Ekelund and Tollison (1981) rightly point out that there was a difference between the political forces supporting the liberalization of labor markets and those supporting the liberalization of commodity markets. In their view (52–53), common law courts tried to enforce monopolies in output markets, while weakening them in labor markets.

25. The *opus classicus* of this literature is North and Weingast (1989).

26. For a criticism of the North-Weingast view of institutional change triggered by the Glorious Revolution, see Epstein (2000); O'Brien (2002); and Sussman and Yafeh (2002).

27. The best example is Voltaire's famous quote from his *Philosophical Dictionary* (1766) in which he sounded uncharacteristically emotional in describing people on the battle field dying in indescribable torment seeing in their last moments the city of their birth destroyed amidst the cries of women and children perishing among the ruins. Two years later the Académie Francaise ran a competition on the best essay that "explained the advantages of peace and invited nations to unite in order to secure general tranquillity" (Guicciardi 2001:1412–1413). The complaints about war were primarily about its moral consequence, with the economic costs relegated to a secondary position, but David Hume in his *Of Commerce* (1754) presented a typically brilliant analysis of the social consequences not just of war but of being a "very martial people" and the general equilibrium effects of war on incentives and occupational choice.

28. Adam Smith (1978:11) observes that "not only property but all exclusive rights are real rights" yet it was clear that many of these real rights were regarded by him with horror. Simon Schama (1989:69) points out that before the Revolution the venal offices that collected one form of rent or another were treated as simply another kind of private property, and no one could imagine their expropriation without adequate compensation.

29. See, for instance, Ogilvie (1999). Ekelund and Tollison (1981:51–52, 66) argue that the struggle between Parliament and King in the seventeenth century was not a confrontation between those who favored free markets and those who favored monopolies and privileges but about who would get the right to issue the monopolies that generated the rents.

30. One example is the Austrian Joseph von Sonnenfels (1732–1817), the first professor of political economy at the University of Vienna, who influenced public policy under Maria Theresa (curtailing the power of the guilds and reforming the judiciary). "As a publicist, Sonnenfels had learned how to mobilize public opinion to act as a lever applying pressure to government" (Wangermann 1981:135; see also Wangermann 2003). Another eighteenth-century Austrian reformer was Karl von Zinzendorf who had come under the influence of radicals in Milán and physiocrats in Paris (Persson 2000:144). In Milan, the Supreme Economic Council set up in 1765 to reform economic and social policy counted such Enlightenment heavyweights as Cesare Beccaria and the brothers Alessandro and Pietro Verri. Although the success of these prerevolutionary Enlightenment reformers was spotty, since they depended on the cooperation of powerful governments, they can be viewed as precursors to the more fundamental reforms introduced by the revolutionary authorities after 1790.

31. Pierre du Pont de Nemours, a loyal physiocrat and a staunch believer in a limited role of government, was active in French public policy until the waning days of the ancien régime and worked tirelessly to bring about free trade. He helped establish the free port of Bayonne and was instrumental in bringing about the 1786 Eden treaty between

France and Britain. In addition, he served as an adviser to the Margrave of Baden as well as education administrator of Poland. He was quite active in the early stages of the Revolution (he proposed the famous "tennis court oath"). In his *De l'Origine et des Progrès d'une Science nouvelle* he firmly committed to laissez faire as meaning freedom of work, freedom of cultivation, and freedom of exchange and commerce (Groenewegen 2002:265).

32. Even at the time itself, the victory of free markets over privilege and restriction was far from a foregone conclusion. As many of the famous *cahiers de doléances* (complaints written on the eve of the French Revolution) contained concerns about encroachments on rent-seeking limitations as did those complaining about the arrangements themselves.

33. Kindleberger (1975:23) notes that the first case of practice following theory goes to Grand Duke Francis of Tuscany who permitted the free export of Siennese grain after reading Sallustio Bandini's *Economical Discourse* in 1737.

34. David Hume, while certainly no mercantilist, was of two minds about it and noted that a "tax on German linens encourages home manufactures and thereby multiplies our people and our industry" (Hume 1985:98).

35. Thus, for instance, Alexandre Vandermonde, a noted mathematician and scientist, who turned to economics late in life and taught it at the newly founded École Normale, and who knew his *Wealth of Nations* inside out, never converted to free trade and preferred the protectionist doctrines of Smith's contemporary, James Steuart (Gillispie 2004:513).

36. William Pitt himself was known to have a deep admiration for Smith. Ross (1998:xxv) notes that the doctrines of *Wealth of Nations* "exerted a a seminal influence on this outstanding British statesman of the era." There is a possibly apocryphal story of Pitt telling Smith during a London visit "Sir, we will stand till you are first seated, for we are all your scholars" (Ross 1995:375–376).

37. Smith's student Dugald Stewart was a prime producer of nineteenth-century "whiggery," and an enormously effective and eloquent teacher at Edinburgh. It was Stewart's lectures that turned *Wealth of Nations* into the fountainhead of all economic theory. Stewart "made the book virtually Holy Scripture to generations of Edinburgh-educated thinkers, economists, and politicians who in turn spread its influence to Oxford, Cambridge, London, and the rest of the English-speaking world" (Herman 2001:229–230; see also Rothschild 2001). Among Stewart's pupils were two future prime ministers, Palmerston and John Russell, as well as other senior officials.

38. Huskisson's interest in and debt to political economy—in particular Smith and Ricardo—had been part of his entire political career. His program was to remove all state support and protection for manufacturing and agriculture to weaken and remove the private interests that hampered free trade (Howe 2002:199). Huskisson "zealously and consistently subscribed to the theories of Adam Smith. Smith's teaching is reflected in practically every reform in the twenties" (Brady 1967:133).

39. Hardenberg, even more than Stein, believed "competition to be the greatest incentive and regulator of our industry" (cited by Koch 1978:178). His 1810 General Taxation Laws sought to reduce rent seeking in the form of tax exemptions and guilds, created an income tax which would be assessed equally on all Prussian residents as a proportion of income, and introduced freedom of occupational choice which meant anyone who paid a trade tax could carry on any trade.

40. The Zollverein was preceded by the Prussian Maassen Tariff Law of 1818 which abolished all internal tariffs in Prussia and was influenced by a memorandum by G. J. C. Kunth, Beuth's mentor.

41. Persson (2000:139), who supports a functionalist explanation of the liberalization of the grain trade in Enlightenment Europe, still notes that in the liberalization of the Swedish grain trade the French (physiocrat) intellectual inspiration is obvious.

42. The choice of Lavoisier as an example of a rent-seeker by Shleifer and Vishny (1998:55) is somewhat ironic. Lavoisier was a tax farmer rather than a tax collector, and as such he was undeniably a rent-seeker since tax farming was hugely profitable. And yet Lavoisier was a distinguished public servant apart from his scientific career. He did not actually "choose" to become a tax collector, as they suggest, but rather married into the occupation as was the custom then. There is little evidence to suggest that his political activities reduced his scientific accomplishments—unlike his star student Armand Seguin, who ended up abandoning his career as a scientist to enrich himself by selling shoes to the French army.

43. In a celebrated statement, Adam Smith (1978:83) noted that "the inventor of a new machine or any other invention has the exclusive privilege of making and vending that invention for the space of 14 years...as a reward for his ingenuity....For if the legislative should appoint pecuniary rewards for the inventors of new machines etc., they would hardly ever be so precisely proportional to the merit of the invention as this is."

44. The British Society of Arts, founded in 1754, was a classic example of an organization that embodied many of the ideals of the Industrial Enlightenment. Its purpose was "to embolden enterprise, to enlarge science, to refine art, to improve manufacture and to extend our commerce." Its activities included an active program of awards and prizes for successful inventors: over 6,200 prizes were granted between 1754 and 1784 (Wood 1913; Hudson and Luckhurst 1954). The society took the view that patents were a monopoly, and that no one should be excluded from useful knowledge. It therefore ruled out (until 1845) all persons who had taken out a patent from being considered for a prize and even toyed with the idea of requiring every prizewinner to commit to never take out a patent (Hilaire-Pérez 2000:197).

45. In the Netherlands, where patenting had existed since the 1580s, the practice of specification was abandoned in the mid-1630s but revived in the 1770s (Davids 2000:267). In the United States, Thomson (2002) has listed the various ways in which knowledge about and contained in patents was disseminated (including lists and descriptions of new patents in Scientific American and the Franklin Institute). "Through their mediation, private knowledge became public" writes Thomson (2002:11), although he notes that only a select few could make effective use of this public knowledge. Perhaps, however, that is all that mattered. The creation of new techniques—as opposed to widespread application— is confined to a very small minority of society, and to understand why it occurred we have to look at the opportunities and capabilities of those few rather than at society-wide averages.

46. One student of the history of technology (Cyril S. Smith, cited by K. D. White 1984:27) sighs that "every invention is born into an uncongenial society, has few friends and many enemies, and only the hardiest and luckiest survive."

47. Heckscher noted that conflicts emerged everywhere between those who "would attempt something new" and mistrustful fellow professionals, often relying on lawsuits and administrative interventions. While the outcome of these struggles was not inevita-

bly in favor of the entrenched vested interests, "every opportunity was taken to render it impossible to introduce a novelty without expensive and tedious conflicts.... The system normally penalized innovation" (1955, 1:171).

48. Peter Gay (1966:25) points out that Rousseau was treated by the other *philosophes* as a madman long before his clinical symptoms became apparent.

49. Thus Horn (2002) suggests that the Combination Acts and other legislation restricting personal liberty in the 1790s was not only intended to save the regime from French-inspired revolutionary turmoil, but also to protect the Industrial Revolution from resistance "from below."

50. As Randall has shown, in the west of England the new machines were met by violent crowds, protesting against jennies, flying shuttles, gig mills, and scribbling machines (Randall 1986, 1989). Moreover, in these areas magistrates were persuaded by fear or propaganda that the machine breakers were in the right. The tradition of violence in the west of England, writes Randall, deterred all but the most determined innovators. Worker resistance was responsible for the slow growth and depression of the industry rather than the reverse (Randall 1989). The west of England, as a result, lost its supremacy in the wool industry to Yorkshire. Horn (2003) has indeed argued that the waves of machine-breaking that swept over France in the early years of the French Revolution delayed mechanization and consolidated the lead that British manufacturing held over the French by discouraging the introduction of British machines. In 1830 the French inventor Barthélemy Thimonnier devised a working sewing machine using a chain-stitch system that made it a combination sewing and embroidery machine. Thimonnier ran into violent opposition from tailors. His army uniform factory in Paris, in which he had the new devices installed, was raided twice in the 1840s, and the machines were destroyed. Like many other French inventors, he died a poor and bitter man.

51. A resolution passed by the Justices of the Peace in Preston in 1779 fully summarizes the position of the British authorities: "Resolved that the sole cause of great riots was the new machines employed in the cotton manufacture; that the country notwithstanding has greatly benefited by their erection; that destroying them in this country would only be the means of transferring them to another country, and that, if a total stop were put by the legislature to their erection in Britain, it would only tend to their establishment in foreign countries, to the detriment of the trade of Britain" (cited in Mantoux 1961:403).

52. The case of Spain is especially instructive. There can be no doubt that there was a Spanish Enlightenment, culminating in the *Discurso sobre el fomento de la industria popular* published in 1774 and attributed to Pedro Rodrèguez de Campomanes, and which has been compared to *The Wealth of Nations* by no less an authority than Schumpeter (1954:173). In his younger days, Campomanes had tried to implement a long list of enlightened economic reforms under the reform-minded king Carlos III. Yet the impact of the Enlightenment on Spain remained superficial. Many of the key books of the Enlightenment, including the *Encyclopédie* remained banned, and while clandestine circulation was rampant, the Spanish Enlightenment collided with deeply entrenched interests which eventually defeated it (Storrs 2003). Herr (1958:198–200) estimates that less than 1 percent of the Spanish population welcomed the Enlightenment, a tenth as many as in France.

53. As Peter Gay (1969:347) notes in his monumental work on the Enlightenment, the philosophes' passion for decency and shrewdness in political economy had its part in overthrowing mercantilism, but the Enlightenment could not have done its work in isolation: expanding trade and increasing productivity invited the conception of a dynamic

world economy. Yet he fails to explicate fully how much of the "expanding trade and increasing productivity" were themselves a consequence of the Baconian ideology of knowledge and the emergence of the Industrial Enlightenment. In that sense the technological elements of the Industrial Enlightenment fed back into the political economy, just as the political elements encouraged and buttressed innovation. It is of such positive feedback that the stuff of sustainable economic growth is made.

References

Acemoglu, D., S. Johnson, and J. Robinson. 2001. "The Colonial Origins of Comparative Development: An Empirical Investigation." *American Economic Review* 91, no. 5: 1369–1401.

Baker, K. M. 1981. "Enlightenment and Revolution in France: Old Problems, Renewed Approaches." *Journal of Modern History* 53, no. 2: 281–230.

Baumol, W. J. 1993. *Entrepreneurship, Management, and the Structure of Payoffs*. Cambridge, MA: MIT Press.

———. 2002. *The Free-Market Innovation Machine: Analyzing the Growth Miracle of Capitalism*. Princeton, NJ: Princeton University Press.

Behrens, C. B. A. 1985. *Society, Government, and the Enlightenment: The Experiences of Eighteenth-Century France and Prussia*. London: Thames and Hudson.

Brady, A. 1967. *William Huskisson and Liberal Reform: An Essay on the Changes in Economic Policy in the Twenties of the Nineteenth Century*. London: Oxford University Press.

Carlos, A., and S. Nicholas. 1990. "Agency Problems in Early Chartered Companies: The Case of the Hudson's Bay Company." *Journal of Economic History* 50, no. 4: 853–875.

———. 1996. "Theory and History: Seventeenth-Century Joint-Stock Chartered Trading Companies." *Journal of Economic History* 56, no. 4: 916–924.

Cipolla, C. 1968. "The Economic Decline of Italy." In B. Pullan, ed., *Crisis and Change in the Venetian Economy in the Sixteenth and Seventeenth Centuries*, 127–145. London: Methuen.

Darnton, R. 2003. "The Unity of Europe." In *George Washington's False Teeth*. New York: Norton.

Davids, K. 2000. "Patents and Patentees in the Dutch Republic between c. 1580 and 1720." *History and Technology* 16:263–283.

De Vries, J., and A. M. van der Woude. 1997. *The First Modern Economy: Success, Failure, and Perseverance of the Dutch Economy, 1500–1815*. Cambridge: Cambridge University Press.

Deyon, P., and P. Guignet. 1980. "The Royal Manufactures and Economic and Technological Progress in France Before the Industrial Revolution." *Journal of European Economic History* 9, no. 3 (Winter): 611–632.

Ekelund, R. B. Jr., and R. D. Tollison. 1981. *Mercantilism as a Rent-Seeking Society*. College Station: Texas A&M University Press.

———. 1984. "A Rent-Seeking Theory of French Mercantilism." In J. Buchanan and R. D. Tollison, eds., *The Theory of Public Choice*, 206–223. Ann Arbor: University of Michigan Press.

———. 1997. *Politicized Economies: Monarchy, Monopoly, and Mercantilism.* College Station: Texas A&M University Press.

Epstein, S. R. 1998. "Craft Guilds, Apprenticeships, and Technological Change in Preindustrial Europe." *Journal of Economic History* 58, no. 3: 684–713.

———. 2000. *Freedom and Growth: The Rise of States and Markets in Europe, 1300–1750.* London: Routledge.

Ferguson, A. 1767. *An Essay on the History of Civil Society.* Dublin: Boulter Grierra.

Gay, P. 1966. *The Enlightenment: An Interpretation—The Rise of Modern Paganism.* New York: Norton.

———. 1969. *The Enlightenment: An Interpretation—The Science of Freedom.* New York: Norton.

Gillispie, C. C. 1980. *Science and Polity in France at the End of the Old Regime.* Princeton, NJ: Princeton University Press.

———. 2004. *Science and Polity in France: The Revolutionary and Napoleonic Years.* Princeton, NJ: Princeton University Press.

Goldstone, J. A. 2002. "Efflorescences and Economic Growth in World History: Rethinking the 'Rise of the West' and the Industrial Revolution." *Journal of World History* 13, no. 2: 323–389.

Greif, A. 1994. "Cultural Beliefs and the Organization of Society: A Historical and Theoretical Reflection on Collectivist and Individualist Societies." *Journal of Political Economy* 102, no. 5: 912–950.

———. 2006. *Institutions and the Path to the Modern Economy.* Cambridge: Cambridge University Press.

Groenewegen, P., ed. 1977. *The Economics of A.R.J. Turgot.* The Hague: Martinus Nijhoff.

———. 2002. *Eighteenth-century Economics: Turgot, Beccaria and Smith and Their Contemporaries.* London: Routledge.

Guicciardi, J.-P. 2001. "War and Peace." In M. Delon, ed., *Encyclopedia of the Enlightenment* 2:1411–1414. Chicago: Fitzroy Dearborn.

Harris, R. 2000. *Industrializing English Law: Entrepreneurship and Business Organization, 1720–1844.* Cambridge: Cambridge University Press.

Heckscher, E. F. 1955. *Mercantilism.* 2 vols. Trans. M. Shapiro. London: George Allen and Unwin.

Herman, A. 2001. *How the Scots Invented the Modern World.* New York: Crown.

Herr, R. 1958. *The Eighteenth-century Revolution in Spain.* Princeton, NJ: Princeton University Press.

Hilaire-Pérez, L. 2000. *L'invention technique au siècle des lumières.* Paris: Albin Michel.

Horn, J. 2003. "Machine Breaking in England and France During the Age of Revolution." Unpublished ms., Manhattan College.

Howe, A. 2002. "Restoring Free Trade: The British Experience 1776–1873." In D. Winch and P. O'Brien, eds., *The Political Economy of British Historical Experience, 1688–1914,* 193–213. Oxford: Oxford University Press.

Hudson, D., and K. W. Luckhurst. 1954. *The Royal Society of Arts, 1754–1954.* London: John Murray.

Hughes, J. 1986. *The Vital Few: American Economic Progress and Its Protagonists.* 2nd ed. New York: Oxford University Press.

Hume, D. [1742] 1985. "Of the Rise and Progress of the Arts and Sciences (1742)." In *Essays: Moral, Political and Literary.* Ed. E. F. Miller. Indianapolis: Liberty Fund.

Hutchinson, T. 1988. *Before Adam Smith: The Emergence of Political Economy, 1662–1776.* Oxford: Basil Blackwell.

Irwin, D. A. 1996. *Against the Tide: An Intellectual History of Free Trade.* Princeton, NJ: Princeton University Press.

Jeremy, D. 1981. *Transatlantic Industrial Revolution: The Diffusion of Textile Technologies Between Britain and America, 1790–1830s.* Cambridge, MA: MIT Press.

Kaplan, S. L. 1976. *Bread, Politics and Political Economy in the Reign of Louis XV.* The Hague: Martinus Nijhoff.

Kellenbenz, H. 1974. "Technology in the Age of the Scientific Revolution, 1500–1700." In C. Cipolla, ed., *The Fontana Economic History of Europe* 2:177–272. London: Fontana.

Keynes, J. M. 1936. *The General Theory of Employment, Interest, and Money.* New York: Harcourt, Brace.

Kindleberger, C. P. 1975. "The Rise of Free Trade in Western Europe, 1820–1875." *Journal of Economic History* 35, no. 1: 20–55.

———. *Economic Response: Comparative Studies in Trade, Finance, and Growth.* Cambridge, MA: Harvard University Press.

Koch, H. W. 1978. *A History of Prussia.* London: Longman.

Mantoux, P. 1961. *The Industrial Revolution in the Eighteenth Century.* New York: Harper Torchbooks.

Mokyr, J. 1994. "Progress and Inertia in Technological Change." In J. James and M. Thomas, eds., *Capitalism in Context: Essays in Honor of R. M. Hartwell,* 230–254. Chicago: University of Chicago Press.

———. 1998. "Editor's Introduction: The New Economic History and the Industrial Revolution." In J. Mokyr, ed., *The British Industrial Revolution: An Economic Perspective,* 1–127. Boulder: Westview Press.

———. 1999. "The Second Industrial Revolution, 1870–1914." In V. Castronovo, ed., *Storia dell'economia Mondiale,* 219–245. Rome: Laterza.

———. 2002. *The Gifts of Athena: Historical Origins of the Knowledge Economy.* Princeton, NJ: Princeton University Press.

———. 2005a. "The Intellectual Origins of Modern Economic growth." *Journal of Economic History* 65:285–351 (presidential address).

———. 2005b. "Long-term Economic Growth and the History of Technology" Prepared for the *Handbook of Economic Growth.* Ed. P. Aghion and S. Durlauf. Amsterdam: North-Holland, forthcoming.

Murphy, K. M., A. Shleifer, and R. W. Vishny. 1991. "The Allocation of Talent: Implications for Growth." *Quarterly Journal of Economics* 106, no. 2: 503–530.

———. 1993. "Why Is Rent Seeking So Costly to Growth." *American Economic Review* 83, no. 2: 409–414.

Norberg, K. 2003. "Poverty." In A. C. Kors, ed., *Encyclopedia of the Enlightenment* 3:347–353. New York: Oxford University Press.

North, D. C. 1990. *Institutions, Institutional Change, and Economic Performance.* Cambridge: Cambridge University Press.

North, D. C., and B. Weingast. 1989. "Constitutions and Commitment: The Evolution of Institutions Governing Public Choice in Seventeenth Century England." *Journal of Economic History* 49, no. 4: 803–832.

Nye, J. V. 1991. "The Myth of Free-trade Britain and Fortress France: Tariffs and Trade in the Nineteenth Century." *Journal of Economic History* 51, no. 1: 23–47.

O'Brien, P. K. 2002. "Fiscal Exceptionalism: Great Britain and Its European Rivals from Civil War to Triumph at Trafalgar and Waterloo." In D. Winch and P. O'Brien, eds., *The Political Economy of British Historical Experience, 1688–1914*, 245–265. Oxford: Oxford University Press.

O'Brien, P., T. Griffiths, and P. Hunt. 1991. "Political Components of the Industrial Revolution: Parliament and the English Cotton Textile Industry, 1660–1774." *Economic History Review* 44, no. 3: 395–423.

Ogilvie, S. 1999. "The German State: A non-Prussian View." In J. Brewer and E. Hellmuth, eds., *Rethinking Leviathan: The Eighteenth-century State in Britain and Germany*, 167–202. Oxford: Oxford University Press.

———. 2004. "Guilds, Efficiency, and Social Capital: Evidence from German Protoindustry." *Economic History Review* 57, no. 2: 286–333.

Olson, M. 1982. *The Rise and Decline of Nations.* New Haven, CT: Yale University Press.

Ormrod, D. 2003. *The Rise of Commercial Empires: England and the Netherlands in the Age of Mercantilism, 1650–1770.* Cambridge: Cambridge University Press.

Outhwaite, R. B. 1981. "Dearth and Government Intervention in English Grain Markets, 1590–1700." *Economic History Review* 34, no. 3: 389–406.

Persson, G. 2000. *Grain Markets in Europe, 1500–1900: Integration and Deregulation.* Cambridge: Cambridge University Press.

Petty, W. 1679. *A Treatise of Taxes and Contributions.* London: Obadiah Blagrave.

Pirenne, H. 1936. *Economic and Social History of Medieval Europe.* New York: Harcourt Brace & World.

Randall, A. J. 1986. "The Philosophy of Luddism: The Case of the West of England Workers, ca. 1790–1809." *Technology and Culture* 27, no. 1: 1–17.

———. 1989. "Work, Culture and Resistance to Machinery in the West of England Woollen Industry." In P. Hudson, ed., *Regions and Industries: A Perspective on the Industrial Revolution in Britain*, 175–198. Cambridge: Cambridge University Press.

Roche, D. 1998. *France in the Enlightenment.* Cambridge, MA: Harvard University Press.

Root, H. 1994. *The Fountain of Privilege: Political Foundations of Markets in Old Regime France and England.* Berkeley: University of California Press.

Rosenberg, N. 1960. "Some Institutional Aspects of the *Wealth of Nations.*" *Journal of Political Economy* 68, no. 6: 557–570.

Rosenthal, J.-L. 1992. *The Fruits of Revolution: Property Rights, Litigation, and French Agriculture, 1700–1860.* Cambridge: Cambridge University Press.

Ross, I. S. 1995. *The Life of Adam Smith.* Oxford: Clarendon Press.

———. *On the Wealth of Nations: Contemporary Responses to Adam Smith.* Bristol: Thoemmes Press.

Rothschild, E. 2001. *Economic Sentiments: Adam Smith, Condorcet, and the Enlightenment.* Cambridge, MA: Harvard University Press.

Rubin, P. H. 2002. *Darwinian Politics: The Evolutionary Origin of Freedom.* New Brunswick, NJ: Rutgers University Press.

Schama, S. 1989. *Citizens: A Chronicle of the French Revolution.* New York: Knopf.

Schumpeter, J. 1954. *History of Economic Analysis.* New York: Oxford University Press.

Shleifer, A., and R. Vishny. 1998. *The Grabbing Hand: Government Pathologies and Their Cures.* Cambridge, MA: Harvard University Press.

Smith, A. 1776 [1976]. *The Wealth of Nations.* Ed. E. Cannan. Chicago: University of Chicago Press.

———. 1762–63 [1978]. *Lectures on Jurisprudence.* Ed. R. Meek, D. D. Raphael, and P. G. Stein. Oxford: Clarendon Press.

Storrs, C. 2003. "Spain." In A. C. Kors, ed., *Encyclopedia of the Enlightenment* 4:109–112. New York: Oxford University Press.

Sussman, N., and Y. Yafeh. 2002. "Constitutions, Commitment, and the Historical Evidence on the Relation between Institutions, Property Rights and Financial Development." Working paper, Hebrew University of Jerusalem.

Thomson, R. 2002. "Mediating the Public and the Private: The Patent System, Technological Learning, and Invention in the Antebellum U.S." Presented at the 2002 Economic History Association Meetings, St. Louis.

Ville, S., and S. R. H. Jones. 1996. "Efficient Transactors or Rent-Seeking Monopolists? The Rationale for Early Chartered Trading Companies." *Journal of Economic History* 56, no. 4: 898–915.

Voltaire. 1766 [1962]. *Philosophical Dictionary.* Ed. Peter Gay. New York: Basic Books.

Uglow, J. 2002. *Lunar Men: Five Friends Whose Curiosity Changed the World.* New York: Farrar Straus and Giroux.

Wangermann, E. 1981. "Reform Catholicism and Political Radicalism in the Austrian Enlightenment." In R. Porter and M. Teich, eds., *The Enlightenment in National Context*, 127–140. Cambridge: Cambridge University Press.

———. 2003. "Austria." In A. C. Kors, ed., *Encyclopedia of the Enlightenment* 1:100–103. New York: Oxford University Press.

White, K. D. 1984. *Greek and Roman Technology*. Ithaca, NY: Cornell University Press.

Wong, R. B. 1997. *China Transformed: Historical Change and the Limits of European Experience*. Ithaca, NY: Cornell University Press.

Wood, H. T. 1913. *A History of the Royal Society of Arts*. London: John Murray.

Wright, R. 2000. *Nonzero: The Logic of Human Destiny*. New York: Vintage Books.

12

The Contemporary Relevance of Heckscher's *Mercantilism*

Deepak Lal

Like many great books, Eli Heckscher's *Mercantilism* is more often cited than read. I had known of it for a long time, but only came to read it in the late 1980s when I was preparing the synthesis volume of a multi-country comparative study of "the political economy of poverty, equity and growth" in twenty-five developing countries for the World Bank (Lal and Myint 1996). It was a revelation and suddenly allowed me to make sense of the cycle of economic repression and reform that I had observed in many developing countries over my thirty-year professional career working on them. Hence, perhaps the best way to show the contemporary relevance of Heckscher's great work on *Mercantilism* is by providing a personal account of why I came to see its relevance in explaining the ongoing worldwide Age of Reform.

Through the Looking Glass

In the 1960s and 1970s my work took me to many developing countries. The similarity of the means of economic repression through trade, foreign exchange and price controls, industrial licensing, and inefficient state monopolies soon became apparent. My natural instinct as an economist was to look upon these as the result of the bad economics perpetrated by what went under the banner of "development economics." I wrote a critique of these in the early 1980s from the viewpoint of what has been called the neoclassical resurgence in the economics of developing countries (Lal 1983, 2002), and blamed it all on the purveyors of the dirigiste dogma.

But this still left a worrying void in the explanation of why so many countries had chosen these patently dysfunctional policies. I ascribed this cognitive dissonance in a paper in 1985 to what I saw as the resonance of three ideas in the Third World: nationalism, socialism, and planning. These ideas I argued were Janus-faced and allowed the modernizing elites in these countries to reconcile tradition with modernity. The professed aim of the postindependence leaders of most of these countries was nation-building, and they found that these ideas allowed them to reconcile various atavistic attitudes concerning trade and commerce and communalism versus individualism with the modernity promised by the Enlightenment.

Then, in the mid- to late 1980s while working at the World Bank, I walked through the looking glass and first encountered the Alice in Wonderland economies of Latin America. Here the ongoing debt crisis starkly exposed the dysfunctional nature of the dirigiste dogma. But, most surprisingly many of these repressed economies began to reform. Similarly, China, which I visited for the first time in 1984, also very surprisingly seemed to have turned its back on Maoist economics with Deng Tsao Ping's initiation of the policy of the Open Door. In my adopted home in Britain, Margaret Thatcher did what had seemed impossible: she took on and defeated the trade unions. Why was the world moving toward the classical liberal economic policies that so many neoclassical resurgents had been preaching for about two decades? It could not have been the power of the ideas. For India, from which many of the neoclassical resurgents came and on which many others worked, had known of these ideas for nearly two decades, but nevertheless seemed impervious to them and set in its ways. These reflections led to my formulating the "crisis" theory of economic liberalization—namely, that it is only when the state seems to be withering away under the twin and related burdens of a fiscal and balance of payments crisis that it seeks economic liberalization (Lal 1987). This theory has since been substantiated in numerous studies (including Lal-Myint 1996 and Little et al. 1994), and in practice by the economic crisis in India in 1991, which led to its program of economic liberalization, and most momentously the sequence of crisis and reform that led to the implosion of the Communist system in the Soviet Union and its satellites.

In the late 1980s, the large multicountry comparative study that Hla Myint and I were codirecting came to an end. We had enough incontrovertible evidence of the role of nation-building in leading to economic repression and the eventual crisis that engendered reform. Then, before drafting the synthesis volume, I at last read Heckscher's *Mercantilism*, as I had often promised myself I would. It was a revelation. What I had thought was an original theory explaining economic repression and reform was all in Heckscher!

Mercantilism

Heckscher had argued that the mercantilist system arose as the Renaissance princes sought to consolidate the weak states they had inherited or acquired from the ruins of the Roman Empire. These were states encompassing numerous feuding and disorderly groups which the new Renaissance princes sought to curb to create a nation. The purpose was to achieve "unification and power," making the "State's purposes decisive in a uniform economic sphere and to make all economic activity subservient to considerations corresponding to the requirements of the State." The mercantilist policies—with their industrial regulations, state-created monopolies, import and export restrictions, price controls—were partly motivated by the objective of granting royal favors in exchange for revenue to meet the chronic fiscal crisis of the state—a problem shared by many countries of the contemporary Third World. Another objective was to extend the span of government control over the economy to facilitate its integration.

These were also the stated aims of many of the postindependence rulers of the Third World. They too, very often inherited artificial states created by their colonial predecessors which were riven by pervasive cleavages of race, religion or tribe. Like the Renaissance princes of sixteenth- and seventeenth-century Europe, they also saw neomercantilism as a means of forging a nation out of the subnational groups within their inherited states. Most of the practices described in the first volume of Heckscher's masterpiece concerning the regulation of both internal trade and industry and external trade and commerce will be resonant with anyone familiar with the economic policies of the postwar Third World, as until very recently they were ubiquitous.

But, as Heckscher showed, these attempts to extend the span of government control, to create order, only bred disorder. As economic controls became onerous, economic agents attempted to escape them through various forms of avoidance and evasion. By the eighteenth century this dirigisme bred corruption, rent-seeking, tax evasion, and illegal activities in underground (or "black") economies. The most serious consequence for the state was that this "tax" avoidance and evasion eroded its fiscal base, and led to the prospect of an un-Marxian withering away of the state. It was this dire prospect which prompted economic liberalization to restore the fiscal base and thence government control over what had become ungovernable economies. In France this changeover could only come about through a Revolution. For it must be noted that the events leading to it occurred because the king had to call the "Etats General" in order to deal with a severe fiscal crisis.

The nineteenth-century Age of Reform was motivated less by the writings of Adam Smith than the desire of governments to regain their fiscal bases, which had been destroyed by the unintended consequences of mercantilism. The results were spectacular. As Heckscher noted, the new found economic liberalism achieved the goal sought by mercantilism: "Great power for the state, the perpetual and fruitless goal of mercantilist endeavour, was translated into fact in the nineteenth century. In many respects this was the work of laissez-faire, even though the conscious efforts of the latter tended in an entirely different direction."

The result was attained primarily by limiting the functions of the State, which task laissez-faire carried through radically. The maladjustment between ends and means was one of the typical features of mercantilism, but it disappeared once the aims were considerably limited. In laissez-faire they consisted, indeed, only in certain elementary and unavoidable functions of foreign policy, defense, legislation, and the administration of justice, nicknamed by Carlyle "Anarchy plus the Constable." Disobedience and arbitrariness, unpunished infringements of the law, smuggling and embezzlement flourished particularly under a very extensive state administration and in periods of continually changing ordinances and interference with the course of economic life. It was because the *regime de l'ordre* bore this impress that disorder was one of its characteristic features" (Heckscher 1955:325).

From Control to Liberalization

An uncannily similar process accounts for the contemporary move from mercantilist controls to economic liberalization in the Third World. In Lal-Myint (1996) we document how many of the twenty-five countries that had set up dirigiste neomercantilist regimes switched policy in the 1970s and 1980s in the face of fiscal cum balance of payment crises.[1] A major consequence of dirigisme is that it creates politically determined current and future income streams for various favored groups in the economy (such as infant, declining or sick industries, industrial labor, regional interests, the deserving poor, old age pensioners, to name just a few). As these entitlements are implicit or explicit subsidies to particular groups, they have to be paid for by implicit or explicit taxation of other groups in the economy. In fact, all government interventions including regulation are equivalent to a set of implicit or explicit taxes or subsidies. However justifiable on grounds of social welfare, the gradual expansion of the transfer state entailed by burgeoning neomercantilism leads to some surprising dynamic consequences, like those adumbrated by Heckscher for the seventeenth and eighteenth centuries.

The gradual expansion of politically determined entitlements creates specific property rights. The accompanying tax burden to finance them leads at some stage to generalized tax resistance, leading to avoidance and evasion, and to the gradual but inevitable growth of the parallel or underground economy. This was the case with both developed and developing countries in the 1960s and 1970s. Faced with inelastic or declining revenues but burgeoning expenditure commitments, incipient or actual fiscal deficits become chronic. These can only be financed by three means: domestic borrowing, external borrowing, or the levying of the inflation tax.

Many countries, particularly in Latin America, tried all three with dire consequences. Domestic borrowing to close the fiscal gap crowds out private investment, damaging future growth and thereby future tax revenues. The fiscal deficit maybe financed by foreign borrowing for a time. But this form of financing is inherently unstable. The debt-service ratio can become unviable if, as in the late 1970s, world interest rates rise and the ability of the economies to generate the requisite surpluses to service the higher interest costs of public guaranteed debt is limited. This is often due to the policy-induced distortions inhibiting exports—such as overvalued exchange rates and high and differentiated effective protective rates of protection which are an indirect tax on exports—along with the difficulty in generating fiscal surpluses to match the interest on the debt. Thereupon, foreign lending can abruptly cease, leading to the kind of debt crises that plagued Latin America in the 1980s. The third way of financing the deficit, through the use of the inflation tax is also unviable over the medium run, for it promotes a further growth of the parallel economy and a substitution of some indirect or direct form of foreign-currency-based assets for domestic money as a store of value. The tax base for levying the inflation tax thus shrinks rapidly as the economy veers into hyperinflation.

With taxes being evaded, domestic and foreign credit virtually at an end, and private agents having adjusted to inflation to avoid the inflation tax, the government finds its fiscal control of the economy vanishing. It may not even be able to garner enough resources to pay the

functionaries required to perform the classical state functions of providing law and order, defense, and essential infrastructure. This dynamic process, whereby the expansion of the transfer state leads to
the unexpected and very un-Marxian withering away of the state, has
rarely reached its full denouement, although in some countries—Peru,
Ghana, Tanzania—it came close.

But well before things come to such a dire pass, attempts are usually
made to gain government control. Two responses are possible—an illiberal and a liberal one. The former, which is rare, consists of a further
tightening and more stringent enforcement of direct controls. Nyrere's
Tanzania provides an example. If this tightening is effective, however,
and the private utility of after-tax income received from legal productive activity declines to the level at which untaxed subsistence activities
are preferable, producers may seek to escape the controls by ceasing to
produce the taxed commodities altogether. The tightening and enforcement of controls could lead to an implosion of the economy. The government then finds that as producers return to untaxable subsistence
activities, its very tax base has fled into the bush. This is what happened in both Ghana and Tanzania.

The more usual response is to regain a degree of fiscal control
through some liberalization of controls on the economy. Typically,
however, these liberalization attempts are half-hearted and include
some tax reform, monetary contraction, and some measure of export
promotion. Their aim is to raise the economy's growth rate as well
as the yield from whatever taxes are being paid, and to improve
the debt-service ratio, in the hope that this will lead to a resumption
of voluntary lending. But unless the underlying fiscal problem (which
is largely that of unsustainable public expenditure commitments)
has been tackled, these liberalization attempts have usually been
aborted.

It is only when the complete breakdown of the society and economy
poses the danger of an even greater loss of future income streams than
that resulting from the rescinding of the existing political entitlements
created by past dirigisme—and are the source of the problem—that
the bitter pill of a complete change in policy regime is swallowed.
Many countries in Latin America, Africa, and Asia in the 1980s did finally swallow the pill, ushering in another Age of Reform. But as in
the nineteenth century, it is once again threatened by a new dirigisme.
It maybe worth seeing why, as it also provides a clue to a question on
which *Mercantilism* is silent, namely why was the nineteenth-century

Age of Reform followed by first a creeping and then a galloping dirigisme in much of the twentieth century.

Individual and Anti-individual

The missing answer is provided in part by the British political philosopher Michael Oakeshott. He makes a crucial distinction betwen two major strands of Western thought on the state: the state viewed as a *civil* association, or alternatively as an *enterprise* association. The former view goes back to ancient Greece, the latter has its roots in the Judeo-Christian tradition. The view of the state as a civil association sees it as a custodian of laws that do not seek to impose any preferred pattern of ends (including abstractions such as "social welfare" or fundamental "rights"), but that merely facilitate individuals to pursue their own ends. The enterprise view by contrast sees the state as the manager of an enterprise seeking to use the law for its own substantive purposes, and in particular for the legislation of morality. The classical liberalism of Smith and Hume entails the former, whereas the major secular embodiment of society viewed as an enterprise association is socialism, with its moral aim of using the state's power to equalize people.

He distinguishes three versions of the collectivist morality that the state viewed as an enterprise asociation has sought to enforce. The first was a religious version epitomized by Calvinist Geneva and in our own day by Khomeni's Iran. The second is a productivist vision seeking to promote nation-building, which was the enterprise undertaken by the Renaissance princes and the leaders of most ex-colonial states. The third is the distributionist version with its aim of promoting some form of egalitarianism. Both the secular enterprise visions involve dirigisme.

Oakeshott notes that as in many other preindustrial societies, modern Europe inherited a "morality of communal ties" from the Middle Ages. This was gradually superseded from the sixteenth century by a morality of individuality. This individualist morality was fostered by the gradual breakdown of the medieval order which allowed a growing number of people to escape from the "corporate and communal organization" of medieval life.

But this dissolution of communal ties also bred what Oakeshott terms the "anti-individual," who was unwilling or unable to make his own choices. Some were resigned to their fate, but in others it provoked "envy, jealousy and resentment. And in these emotions a new disposition was generated: the impulse to escape from the predicament by imposing it upon all mankind" (24). This, the anti-individual sought to do through two means. The first was to look to the government to "protect him from the necessity of being an individual" (25). A large number of government activities epitomized by the Elizabethan Poor Law were devoted from the 16th century onwards "to the protection of those who, by circumstance or temperament, were unable to look after themselves in this world of crumbling communal ties" (25).

The anti-individual, second, sought to escape his "feeling of guilt and inadequacy which his inability to embrace the morality of individuality provoked" (25) by calling forth a "morality of collectivism," where "'security' is preferred to 'liberty,' 'solidarity' to 'enterprise' and 'equality' to 'self-determination'" (27). Both the individualist and collectivist moralities were different modifications of the earlier communal morality, but with the collectivist morality in addition being a reaction against the morality of individualism.

This collectivist morality inevitably supported the view of the State as an enterprise association. While this view dates back to antiquity, few if any premodern states were able to be "enterprising," as their resources were barely sufficient to undertake the basic tasks of government—law and order and external defense. This changed with the creation of centralized nation-states by the Renaissance princes and the subsequent Administrative Revolution, as Hicks (1969:99) has labeled the gradual expansion of the tax base and thus the span of control of the government over its subjects' lives. Governments now had the power to look upon their activities as an enterprise.

In the Third World, as with the European anti-individualists, jealousy, envy, and resentment were based on the dissolution of the previous communal ties that industrialization and modern economic growth entails, but these emotions were supplemented by the feeling among the native elites of a shared exclusion from positions of power during the period of foreign domination. Not surprisingly, the dominant ideology of the Third World came to be a form of nationalism associated with some combination of the productivist and distributivist versions of the state viewed as an enterprise association. The dysfunctional nature of the dirigisme this led to has made them retreat from but not abandon their past dirigisme, with planning being replaced by regulation. So, there is no guarantee that the pendulum will not swing back once again towards full scale economic repression, as it did in Europe after the brief Age of Reform.

This period of economic liberalism was short-lived, in part due to the rise of another substantive purpose that most European states came to adopt—the egalitarian ideal promulgated by the Enlightenment. Governments in many developing countries also came to espouse this ideal of socialism. The apotheosis of this version of the state viewed as an enterprise association were the Communist countries seeking to legislate the socialist ideal of equalizing people. The collapse of their economies under similar but even more severe strains than those that beset less collectivist neomercantilist Third World economies is now history, though I cannot help remarking on the irony that it took two hundred years for 1989 to undo what 1789 had wrought!

The Future

What of the future? Is this new worldwide "Age of Reform" likely to be more permanent than its nineteenth-century predecessor? There are auguries, both favorable and unfavorable.

Let us take the latter first. The desire to view the state as an enterprise association still lingers on, as part of social democratic political agendas in many countries. It has ancient roots and is unlikely to die. It has now adopted a new voice, which Ken Minogue (1995) has labeled "constitutional mania." This emphasizes substantive social and economic rights in addition to the well-known rights to liberty— freedom of speech, contract, and association—emphasized by classical liberals. It seeks to use the law to enforce these "rights" based partly on "needs" and partly on the "equality of respect" desired by a heterogeneity of self-selected minorities differentiated by ethnicity, gender, and/or sexual orientation. But no less than in the collectivist societies that have failed, this attempt to define and legislate a newly discovered and dense structure of rights (including for some activists those of nonhuman plants and animals) requires a vast expansion of the government's power over people's lives. Their implementation, moreover, requires—at the least—some doctoring of the market mechanism. Then there is the global environmental scare and the population scare. Finally, the UN has taken up the cause of the world's poor and is seeking to establish a worldwide welfare state through a UN economic security council. Classical liberals can clearly not yet lay down their arms!

Equally worrying is the "Delors" vision of Europe, which seems to be a form of mercantilist nation-building, in the manner of the Renaissance princes documented by Heckscher.[2] Many voices are also resurrecting the threat from pauper labor imports to U.S. and European living standards (particularly of the low-skilled), and thence their social harmony. This is particularly worrying as it echoes various fears in the late nineteenth century of the social disruptions and discontent caused by the Industrial Revolution. Though recent historical work has questioned the bleak picture painted by novelists such as Dickens,[3] their fears were nevertheless influential in propagating the dirigiste cause, which led to the gradual unraveling of the nineteenth-century liberal international economic order (LIEO) as the distributive consequences of trade integration led to the rise of protectionist political coalitions in the US, Germany and France after 1870.[4]

Another great structural change is taking place in Western economies, whose short-term consequences could be equally painful and trigger another dirigiste reversal of the emerging LIEO. It maybe worth spelling this out. Hicks saw the substitution of fixed for circulating capital as the distinguishing feature of the Industrial Revolution.[5] But, as Ricardo, in his chapter on "Machinery," noted, during the period of adjustment there could be a reduction in employment and output; though at the end of the process the productive power and hence the level and growth rate of output and employment would be higher. This explains why it took a long time in Britain for the Industrial Revolution to raise overall living standards, and why during the period of adjustment, the older handicraft workers (using circulating capital in various forms of the "putting out" system) initially suffered, until they were eventually transformed into much richer industrial workers.

Today a similar process is underway in the West, with the increasing substitution of human for fixed capital in its newly emerging "information age" service economies. This process has been accelerated by the emerging liberal international economic order (LIEO) as the countries of Asia with abundant unskilled labor—particularly China and India—go through their own industrial revolutions, and increasingly specialize in the production for export of those manufactures on which workers—particularly the low-skilled—had depended in the past in the West. The ongoing substitution of human for fixed capital is an unavoidable means for maintaining and raising living standards in the West. But during the process of adjustment it may cause severe social strains.

In this adjustment process it is inevitable that initially the premium on human capital should rise, as this provides the signal for workers to upgrade their skills. This rising skill premium accompanied by stagnation in the wages of the unskilled is evident in all Western countries. Those countries, mainly in Europe, which have prevented this signal from working, have found that, instead of low and stagnant wages for the unskilled they have the much worse problem of high and rising unemployment. Despite the siren voices calling for protection from Third World imports to ease these problems, for the West to follow their advice would be a snare and a delusion. But, as the rise of protectionism based on the equally deluded infant industry arguments of Hamilton and List in the late 19th century demonstrates, such snares are not always avoided. At a time when the third and second worlds have enthusiastically embraced the LIEO, it is the temptation for harried Western governments to turn their backs on the world they have created that constitutes the greatest threat to the future of the new global LIEO.[6]

Then, there is the creeping and continuing dirigisme to promote various "social policies" in many Western states (including the United States). These include demands for the inclusion of environmental and labor standards in the WTO (which has replaced GATT), as well as recent attempts to thrust Western moral values (democracy and human rights) down foreign throats—using the threats of unilateral trade restrictions. All these inevitably poison international relations. The nagging bad temper that is generated could lead to a gradual erosion of the liberal international economic order, as in the late nineteenth century.

Meanwhile there are more immediate worries that the recent financial crises in Asia might lead to a backlash against the globalization of capital flows in developing countries.[7] There is a pervasive fear in the Third World that continuing capital market liberalisation will lead to a greater volatility in their national incomes, damaging growth performance. The recent Asian crisis which has taken the stripes off so many of the region's tigers has merely accentuated these fears. Mahathir's reimposition of stringent capital controls in Malaysia maybe the harbinger of a trend towards the resucitation of economic nationalism.

This fear of volatility is an ancient worry of the Third World, earlier expressed as the purported adverse effects on growth of the export instability engendered by the integration of primary product exporting countries in the world economy.[8] In the twenty-five-country study covering the period since World War II, Myint and I could find no statistical evidence that the volatility of annual growth rates effected overall growth performance—a conclusion in consonance with the numerous studies of the effects of export instability on growth. Thus Hong Kong has had one of the most volatile growth rates among developing countries, while India one of the most stable—but the long-run growth performance of Hong Kong puts the Indian one to shame. Thus though there may undeniably be greater volatility in national incomes of countries integrating with the world economy, this need not damage their long-run growth rates.

Against these dangers there are many hopeful signs. As in premodern times, today's states are finding it more and more difficult to find the resources to continue (or increase) their enterprise. This is partly because of the worldwide growth in tax resistance,[9] and most important the virtually complete integration of international financial markets. The latter has strengthened the former. Nor is a reimposition of exchange controls to stop this process likely, if for no other reason than that it would now have to be adopted and enforced worldwide.

The instincts of the state through most of human history have been predatory. The integration of world financial markets provides a bulwark against these base instincts—like tying Ulysses to the mast. Every government is now concerned about the rating of its country and its enterprises by world capital markets. Bad policies—or at least those disapproved of by world capital markets—can lead to an instantaneous reduction in a country's wealth, and the terms on which it can acquire the means to increase it, a painful lesson many southeast Asian countries have recently learned. The worldwide movement toward fiscal rectitude and the creation of an economic environment that is transparent and rewards efficiency is no longer a matter of choice but of necessity. With massive global flows of capital triggered at the press of a button, governments are now faced with an instantaneous international referendum on their economic policies. The Central Bank or Treasury proposes, but the money market disposes!

The same actual or incipient fiscal crisis which has ultimately prevented the State from giving in to the "enterprise" voice, or led to forced reversals in its past dirigisme, also threatens the major form of its continuing enterprise in the West—the welfare state. The partial dismantling of the New Zealand welfare state and its continuing erosion in that social democratic beacon of hope, Sweden, are surely more than straws in the wind.[10]

Finally, there is the recent spectacular movement from the plan to the market in China and India. The future progress of these ancient civilizations raises unresolved questions about the relationship between culture, democracy and development.[11] Can the market survive in polities which are undemocratic? Will globalization necessarily lead to the worldwide spread of a homogenized Western culture? On the latter I have my doubts, partly because the very mainspring of Western culture—its individualism—is paradoxically leading to social decay and decadence in the West.[12] There is a triumphalist tendency in the West, most noticeable in the United States, to identify its own cultural and political forms as necessary conditions for its economic success. This raises complex issues that I cannot go into on this occasion.[13] There is, however, one point that needs to be stressed, and that concerns the first of the questions posed in this paragraph. Many, including the major contemporary advocate of the classical liberal order—Hayek[14]—have posited a necessary connection between economic and political liberty (nowadays translated into the market cum democracy). I disagree.[15] Oakeshott's distinction between a civil and enterprise association is more useful in judging the sustainability of a market order. For after all, until 1997, the only "country" that was clearly a civil rather than enterprise association—in Oakeshott's terms—was Hong Kong, and it was a colony, now extinguished!

I argued in my Ohlin lectures (Lal 1998b) that their cosmological beliefs have a tenacious hold on the minds of different civilizations. The West, as I argued, is still haunted by St. Augustine's *City of God* and its narrative of a Garden of Eden, the Fall, the Day of Judgment that leads to paradise for the saved. I showed how much of secular Western thought from Marxism to Freudianism to environmentalism regurgitates the same narrative. It clearly has a tenacious hold on Western minds. But promoting these secular Augustinian visions again requires dirigisme, and it would not be surprising if the West were to once again chase another enterprise vision which would end the current Age of Reform. We would then have the third Heckscherian cycle (as it maybe called) between economic repression followed by reform since the emergence of the modern world from the Middle Ages.

Notes

1. The following section is based on Lal-Myint (1996:292–293).

2. See Wolf (1994).

3. See Hayek (1954).

4. See Rogowski (1989).

5. See Hicks (1969), esp. the appendix, and Lal (1978), appendix A.

6. This fear is also echoed by Williamson (1996).

7. The remainder of this section is based on Lal (1998a, 1999).

8. See Lal (1983).

9. In a rearguard action, the OECD has just announced a task force that will study how to prevent tax competition between states, which is rightly feared to be eroding the ability of states to extract the maximum revenue from their citizens. Whether one should applaud this attempt to create a cartel of predatory states to maximize the exploitation of their prey depends upon whether one sides with the predator or the prey. But even if such a cartel could be formed, it would be subject to the form of cheating that undermined the OPEC cartel, for instance: some country or other would find it in its interests to attract mobile factors of production with the inducement of lower taxation. By so openly avowing the cause of the predatory states that control its purse strings, the OECD would seem to have signed its death warrant in the eyes of economic liberals.

10. I may claim some foresight in seeing trends earlier than most others. See chapters 8 and 15 in Lal (1993).

11. I deal with some of these in my 1995 Ohlin lectures (Lal 1998b).

12. See Lal (1998b) for details and substantiation.

13. But see Lal (1998a, 1998b).

14. See Hayek (1979).

15. See Lal (1996).

References

Aftalion, F. 1990. *The French Revolution: An Economic Interpretation*. New York: Cambridge University Press.

Hayek, F. A. 1954. *Capitalism and the Historians*. London: Routledge.

———. 1973–79. *Law, Legislation and Liberty*. 3 vols. London: Routledge.

Heckscher, E. F. 1955. *Mercantilism*. 2 vols. London: Allen and Unwin.

Hicks, J. R. 1969. *A Theory of Economic History*. New York: Oxford University Press.

Lal, D. 1978. *Men or Machines*. Geneva: International Labor Organization.

———. 1983–2002. *The Poverty of "Development Economics."* London: Institute of Economic Affairs; Cambridge, MA: Harvard University Press. 2nd ed., London: Institute of Economic Affairs; Cambridge, MA: MIT Press.

———. 1993. *The Repressed Economy*. London: Edward Elgar.

———. 1996. "Participation, Markets and Democracy." In M. Lundahl and B. J. Ndulu, eds., *New Directions in Development Economics*, 299–322. London: Routledge.

———. 1998a. "Renewing the Miracle: Economic Development and Asia." Inaugural Harold Clough lecture, Institute of Public Affairs, Perth, July 1998.

————. 1998b. *Unintended Consequences: Factor Endowments, Culture and Politics.* Cambridge, MA: MIT Press.

————. 1999. "Taxation and Regulation as Barriers to International Investment Flows." *Journal des Economistes et des Etudes Humaines* 9, no. 1: 3–29.

Little, I. M. D., et al. 1994. *Boom, Crisis and Reform.* New York: Oxford University Press.

Minogue, K. 1995. *Politics.* Oxford: Oxford University Press.

Rogowski, R. 1989. *Commerce and Coalitions.* Princeton, NJ: Princeton University Press.

Williamson, J. G. 1996. "Globalization, Convergence and History." *Journal of Economic History* 56:277–306.

Wolf, M. 1994. *The Resistible Rise of Fortress Europe.* Rochester Paper No. 1, Trade Policy Unit, Center for Policy Studies, London.

Part V   The Continental Blockade

13

The Continental System After Eighty Years

François Crouzet

The Continental System: An Economic Interpretation was published in Oxford, by the Clarendon Press, in 1922. Eighty years later, it remains the only global survey of the Continental System, a synthesis basic to any study of the problem. It can, of course, be criticized on various points, but this applies to any book; and I want to start this essay by paying tribute to the great scholar who wrote it. However, this classical work was *un livre de circonstance*, the product of developments at the time it was written. Unfortunately, those circumstances are not perfectly clear.

The Continental System is part of a collection of over 150 volumes on the economic and social history of World War I, which was sponsored by the Carnegie Endowment for International Peace, a foundation established by the steel magnate Andrew Carnegie in 1910. In 1911 it organized an international conference in Rome, which decided to launch a large number of studies on the causes of war; the inspiration was pacifist, and the idea was to expose the illogic of war and its nefarious consequences. Actually, war broke out not long afterward, and the Carnegie Endowment had to change its plans; eventually they decided to refocus the project toward a large-scale historical and interdisciplinary study of the world war's effects upon the economies and societies of both belligerent and neutral countries. James T. Shotwell of Columbia University was appointed director of the project. In 1919, he organized national editorial committees. The committee for Scandinavia had as chairman Harald Westergaard, professor of political science at the University of Copenhagen (who had attended the Rome conference of 1911); the other members were Heckscher for Sweden and N. Rygg for Norway.[1]

In the preface of the book, Heckscher wrote that Westergaard "proposed that I should treat the subject" (of the Continental System) for the Carnegie series. But he did not have to start from scratch: in the preface again, he stated that the book "represents a sort of synthesis of earlier studies of the mercantile system, on the one side, and the result of extensive theoretical and practical work—private, academic, and government—in the field of present-day war economics, on the other" (indeed, Heckscher had published in 1915 a book on the economics of the world war).[2] "In its original form," the study of the Continental System was "written very rapidly during the winter of 1917–18, under strong pressure of other work, and was presented to my history teacher, Professor Harald Hjärne, of Uppsala," on his seventieth anniversary in May 1918.[3] After accepting Westergaard's proposal, Heckscher writes, "I overhauled my earlier text, changing its outward arrangement in several respects and making a number of additions" (vii). This work was done rather quickly, as the author's preface is dated July 4, 1919 (viii). But the text had to be translated into English and revised by Westergaard and, most likely, because it was the rule for the collection, by Shotwell (though his name does not appear).

This is only one of the mysteries that surround the book. Unlike all other volumes in the Carnegie collection, this one includes neither the list of the other works published or to be published in it, nor the membership of the national editorial committees, nor a preface by Shotwell. However, the most important fact is that *The Continental System* is the only volume in the large Carnegie collection to be a historical study *stricto sensu* and to deal with developments much earlier than World War I. Admittedly, Westergaard wrote in his preface (v) that the Continental System "in many ways throws light on the economic blockade among the belligerent powers involved in the World War." On the other hand, it is rather surprising that no study of the World War I blockades was published by Carnegie, though several volumes on the subject had been planned; we only know that one volume on French blockade policy was written but that Shotwell decided not to publish it, because it gave a "method of carrying on a blockade" in a future war!

I shall add that Heckscher did some more work for the Carnegie project; he wrote the chapters on Sweden in one collective volume on the economic effects of World War I in the Scandinavian countries.[4]

So the origins of the book on the Continental System are not perfectly clear. The Shotwell papers, which are deposited at Columbia University's Library, ought to contain some useful materials.

The Continental System was written within a rather short span of time. Moreover, because the war prevented him from working abroad,

Heckscher could only use materials available in Sweden; actually, he found Swedish libraries rather well equipped (1922:vii, 374), with Napoleon's correspondence, British Parliamentary debates[5] and some good monographs which had come out in the prewar years. Still, he was unable to get hold of some recent American and British books.[6] He wrote in the preface (viii) that his chapter on "Policy of the United States" ought to have been "either enlarged or omitted altogether"; actually, that chapter is satisfactory and stresses quite well the important role the United States played in the history of the Continental System.[7] However, one must point out that, for lack of better sources, Heckscher some times had to rely upon materials of dubious value, such as memoirs and pamphlets.[8] On the other hand, he distrusted too much British trade statistics, and did not realise that those of exports from Britain included goods that were to be smuggled into enemy countries (172 n. 1, 244).

It is therefore striking that Heckscher, despite this shortage of materials, succeeded in building a solid and durable edifice.

First his book has very few factual errors or *à peu près*, like calling Louis XVI an "autocratic king" (18), or stating that American trade with enemy colonies "created a market in America for the industrial products of the Continent which competed with those of Great Britain herself" (102, 104, 105).[9]

Second, Heckscher is fair and impartial. In his introduction he had condemned recent attempts "to transform scientific work into a species of propaganda,"[10] and clearly stated, "I have pursued to the best of my humble ability a purely scientific aim ... I have not sought to take sides in the struggles that are barely finished" (3). He kept to his word. Occasionally (but rarely), one word might suggest a pro-German bias,[11] but then comes a sentence that reveals him as strongly Anglophile and somewhat anti-German.[12] One may, however, wonder about Heckscher's silence about German submarine warfare, which was more cruel toward neutral ships and crews than the arbitrary and brutal treatment they had suffered from both the British and the French during the Twenty-three Years War, and which he condemned (1922:46, 48–49, 371).

As for Heckscher's view of Napoleon, it is rather critical: "Throughout his career [he] renounced all moral traditions and made self-assertion his loftiest lodestar" (9); he had a "cynical sense of reality for everything that had to do with means," (198) "ruthless consistency" (93), "obstinacy" (99), "calm effrontery" (140); still, one feels some admiration for "such an almost super-humanly equipped ruler as Napoleon" (161).[13]

Though it was explicitly stated at the start, by both Westergaard and Heckscher (1922:v, 3), that comparisons between the Napoleonic Wars and World War I would be illuminating, such comparisons are neither systematic nor extensive; references to the recent war are not infrequent, but generally rather short, even in the conclusion, despite its subtitle: "Comparison with the Present Day." Heckscher had written in his preface (1922:vii): "Probably the atmosphere of a rather strict blockade in a neutral country will be found to pervade it [the book] as a more or less natural consequence of the time of its production." Indeed, Sweden suffered, from 1917 onward, from serious shortages (particularly of food) and from inflation. This is probably one of the reasons why Heckscher considered, as we shall see later, that the most efficient form of blockading a country was to prevent it to import. Altogether it seems that to have lived through a blockade did not have— except in some instances—any negative effects on Heckscher's view of the Continental System, and on the contrary helped him to better understand the latter.[14]

On the other hand, Heckscher sometimes displayed the arrogance which is not unusual among economists (especially those of the liberal persuasion). Napoleon's "line of thought was as inconsistent as that which is constantly found outside the circle of professional economists" (198); his "amateurishness in dealing with matters of credit" (63), the fact that "he was still in the pre-mercantilist or bullionist stage" (71) are also stigmatized. Occasionally, this haughtiness leads Heckscher close to anachronism.[15]

However, this is a minor shortcoming, while Heckscher, who always stressed how important theory was for understanding economic history, successfully used, in some parts of his book, the economist's deductive approach. For instance, he starts his chapter on British reactions to Napoleon's blockade by examining "Possible lines of British policy," and his part IV, on the effects of the Continental System, by analyzing the "different types of effect" that could be expected according to the countries concerned. Not infrequently, also, Heckscher starts an analysis with some categorical (and controversial) statement and then adds some significant qualifications.[16]

The Continental System is divided into four parts; the first on its antecedents, the second on its "origin and external course," the third on its "internal history and working," and the fourth on its effects. The drawback of this arrangement is some arbitrariness in distributing some problems between parts II and III; the reader of part II wonders if some matter has been left out, but finds later that it is examined in part III.

I shall also mention a question of terminology. Nowadays, we call "Continental Blockade" Napoleon's economic war machine against Britain, and "Continental System" the political organization that was intended to enforce the blockade on the Continent. Heckscher does not make this distinction. This is a minor matter,[17] and after these preliminary remarks, I shall now try to analyze the interpretation of the Continental Blockade and the Continental System, which Heckscher elaborated, and his views of the system's working and failure.

Origins of the Continental System

As I just mentioned, the first part of Heckscher's book is devoted to "the antecedents of the Continental System." Typically, he had ruled that, to understand the nature of the System, "we must first consider the body of ideas whence it proceeded" (9, also 4), as "the economic policy of a country is not determined by actual conditions but by the popular ideas concerning those conditions" (23).[18] To him, the antecedents of the Continental System were in mercantilist ideas and in the long commercial war between Britain and France to which they had led. Five chapters deal with this economic struggle, and the study becomes more detailed from the beginning of the Revolutionary wars in 1793. But Heckscher stresses that "the connection with the past" was very strong (23); the leaders of the French Revolution "stood unconsciously, but almost entirely under the all-pervading influences of the old economic conceptions" (24). Like their ancient regime forerunners, they were convinced that the economic system of Britain was artificial, unnatural and fragile, that it showed signs of economic decay, especially the fast increase and heavy burden of the National Debt, and the existence of an unredeemable paper currency. A vigorous commercial war against British exports, by France and her satellites, could ruin the whole credit system, which depended upon foreign trade, and deprive Britain of the means to wage war abroad and to subsidize Continental allies (59–70). All the measures against British trade, which were taken during the Revolution, had antecedents before 1789 (28).[19] According to Heckscher, those traditional views of British economic power were "afterwards taken over by

Napoleon," who even was dominated by "simpler economic notions" (58, 71, 73).

Heckscher's analysis of the "intellectual origins" of the Continental System is well founded. Undoubtedly, the views, which prevailed in France, on the fragility of Britain's economy, played a key role in its preparation. In addition, he did not overlook the circumstances of the System's inception and of its later changes. He states that, during the French Revolution, the general political situation was chiefly responsible for the return to the policy of commercial warfare (24), and that the resumption of war in 1803 gave "rise to the most unlimited developments of the ideas which we have previously traced" (80). Moreover, he has emphasized the "epoch making character" (92) of the Berlin decree (November 21, 1806), after the "mere skirmishes" of the years 1803–1806 (83), and its connection with the defeat of Prussia at Jena: "Napoleon's victory on the Continent was as complete as his defeat at sea" (an allusion to Trafalgar) (88), as he now controlled the coasts of Germany and particularly Hamburg, which had become the major channel for introducing British goods on the Continent. For the first time the combination of most European countries for excluding British goods had been achieved (actually, it had to wait for the alliance with Russia at Tilsit, some months later) (51, 92).[20]

However, one may regret that Heckscher did not stress that economic warfare was the only weapon that was left, after Trafalgar, to Napoleon to fight (and, hopefully, to defeat) his implacable enemy (in other occasions, also, he seems to forget that "there was a war on"!), but he well pointed out that, because of British naval mastery, Napoleon's blockade only could be a "self-blockade" (93).

Heckscher has also well analyzed the "British counter-measures" in answer to Napoleon's decrees, particularly the Orders in Council of 1807, though they are "marvels of obscurity and rambling" (114). He clearly perceived that those orders were mainly directed against the very large carrying trade in colonial produce from enemy colonies to the Continent, by American ships and via American ports, which was harmful to the British West Indies (101–103, 105, 117, 120). He did see that the West India interest had demanded action against this trade, but he did not insist on this point, for lack of documents (113).

The meaning and impact of those Orders, which remained up to 1814 the foundation of British policy (114), were also well understood by Heckscher: to compel Napoleonic Europe to "have no trade but with England" (120), and thus to encourage—and even force—

Continental merchants and peoples to violate the prohibitions edicted by their own governments. He gave a good account of the British licensing system, which, despite some dysfunctioning, combined a formal blockade of the Continent with the encouragement of exports (and also of imports of necessities) on neutral ships (205–210); through this system, the British government effectively controlled the sea trade of Europe.[21] It might have been stressed that British sea power made possible a strict enforcement of the maritime blockade. And Heckscher does not mention that considerations of prestige influenced British policy: Britain had to answer by drastic retaliations the insolence of the Corsican usurper, who proclaimed the blockade of England, while his own navy was rotting in port.

From the preceding remarks, it is clear that Heckscher considered the Continental System as the apex of mercantilist policies—of which, a decade before his great book, he was already critical.[22]

In his view, the Continental System "originated . . . on one side in a blockade that followed the general lines of mercantilist trade policy, especially on the part of France, and, on the other side, in a maritime blockade dominated by the same ideas which proceeded from Great Britain but was imitated in a still more intensified form by France,[23] where, owing to the British mastery of the seas, it acquired the character of a self-blockade" (51). Indeed, such an "attack on enemy exports not imports" was in a "strictly mercantilist spirit"; the idea was not "to inflict military damage on the enemy," "not to kill [a] trade altogether, as is the case nowadays, but to seize it" to one's benefit (35–37). The mercantilist tinge (and the suggestion of an internal contradiction, about which more later) is obvious in the definition of the Continental System at the beginning of the book: it aimed both at "crushing a political enemy by economic means and at the same time building up [the] commercial and industrial prosperity" of France (9).[24]

The Blockade

Heckscher must be praised for his narrative of the fluctuations in the blockade's enforcement, which has been confirmed, with some adjustments, by later research. There were three periods during which the self-blockade was practically ineffective: from the Berlin decree to the summer of 1807, from mid-1808 to mid-1810, and finally after the Russian disaster. Heckscher has rightly stressed—to explain the second phase—the impact of the Spanish rising[25] and then of "diminished vigilance during the Austrian campaign" of 1809, especially on Germany's northern coasts (149, 178–180). On the other hand, in late 1807, early 1808, and from the summer of 1810 to the end of 1812, the blockade was seriously enforced.

However, in his detailed study of the latter period, Heckscher—who calls it "the Second Continental System"—has concentrated on the changes in Napoleon's policy, which led eventually, in his words, to "the self-destruction" of the Continental System. Napoleon transformed his system for two reasons: the prevalence of large-scale smuggling, which had to be repressed, and the fall in customs revenue. Therefore, he adopted the Trianon tariff (August 5, 1810): colonial produce would be admitted but imposed with heavy duties. According to Heckscher, Napoleon did not realize "the great extent" to which this new policy jeopardized his struggle against Britain. "This meant that fiscalism had definitely gotten the upper hand.... The object was no longer to exclude goods, but to make an income by receiving them instead," two aims that were incompatible (197–199).

I suggest that Heckscher has overestimated this policy change,[26] which only applied to colonial produce, while the prohibition of British manufactured goods was not only maintained, but aggravated by the Fontainebleau decree (October 18, 1810), which, inter alia, prescribed the public burning of confiscated goods. Actually Heckscher describes the "most violent methods," which the French used late in 1810 to enforce the new measures, as the "culmination of the oppression involved in the Continental System" (202–203, 222). But he goes rather far in writing that the latter "was perverted into a gigantic system of exaction" (205).[27]

Heckscher has also overestimated the importance of the licensing system which Napoleon developed from 1810 onward. It was indeed "a breach of the self-blockade," but not "one more nail into the coffin of the Continental system" (214). Actually, many licences were granted to American ships, for trading with their country, and they were blockade-runners, in violation of the British blockade. Though some direct trade with Britain took place under licenses in 1812 (with France importing colonial produce), it was not very large and, from the French point of view, cannot be called an "almost complete fiasco" (214). It is an overstatement that the licensing system removed Napoleon "still further from his great aim" (Britain's defeat)[28] (214). Heckscher has likewise made too much of a project, which Napoleon delineated in January 1812, of importing under licenses large quantities of colonial produce, which would bring in much money and revive the economy; as this project was not "formally accepted," still less implemented, one cannot assert, "this means that the principle of the Continental System had been abandoned." Nonetheless Heckscher wrote: "One may call this the 'self-destruction' of the system"; and he gave this title to one of his chapters, which he thus concluded: owing to that self-destruction, "we have good reasons to doubt the possibility of its [the System's] continuance... even if the Russian campaign and the wars of liberation had not intervened" (248–251, 254).[29]

I disagree with this point, and indeed I have an opposite position. I doubt whether Britain could have withstood several years of efficient blockade, if Napoleon had come back victorious from Moscow;[30] at least I maintain that she would have been in a dangerous position.

Economic Effects

This brings us to the problem of the Continental System's effects upon the British economy, which is crucial, as the system's aim was to ruin it.[31] Heckscher was fully conscious that it was a difficult problem, as the Blockade's effects had to be disentangled from those of several contemporaneous factors (327–328). He candidly admitted that opinions on the feasibility and consequences of the Continental System "must remain divided" (254)—a view I fully share.[32] Nonetheless his judgements were rather categorical, as he was convinced that Napoleon's attack against British exports was bound to fail. His analysis actually mixes up two demonstrations: that the System could not succeed, and that it did not succeed.[33] Early in his book, he had mentioned a pamphleteer of 1797, who "turned out to be a true prophet in his exposition of the futility of all attempts to shut out the British" (54). And at the very end, he concluded that the Continental System had "very small prospects of attaining its object" (373).

One argument was that, before the Berlin decree, Continental Europe only received 40 percent of Britain's total exports, and this was a "serious weakness" for Napoleon's plans (324–325). However, Heckscher shrewdly added that the blockade's chances of success would markedly improve if the United States (he had rightly seen their crucial role) also established a self-blockade. And he observes that the British government actually gave help to Napoleon by its harsh policy toward America (325). Indeed, the worst periods for Britain occurred when both most of the Continent and the United States were closed—or almost closed—to British exports. I shall add that Napoleon was also brutal toward America and waited until 1810 to start a clever cat-and-mouse game, which contributed to the United States starting war against Britain in 1812 (too late to be really useful to France). Heckscher stresses that, anyhow, the Continental System could not disturb trade with the rest of the world; however, that "rest" was made up of "colonial" countries, and their purchasing power for British manufactures depended partly from reexports by Britain to the Continent of their primary products. Heckscher asserted that Britain, if the Continent's self-blockade had been complete, would have turned toward overseas countries; but, in the short term, such a reorientation would have been painful (325–326).

Another point Heckscher stressed is that "the particular kind of dislocation in Great Britain due to the Continental System...was necessarily of a comparatively superficial nature, just because it was a dislocation caused by obstacles in the way of exports," because "the economic function of exports is absolutely limited to providing payment for imports" (332, 335). He was overlooking that Britain had become an "export economy," which would suffer if many export markets were closed for years. He added that "a failure of exports can always be alleviated by production with a view of accumulating stocks" (332)—an expedient that cannot actually last long.

Still, Heckscher accepted that Britain suffered a crisis in 1811–12, but he states several times that it was not very serious. He is brief on the depression that struck British industry in 1811 and for most of 1812, on the unemployment and hardships which ensued. He does not even mention the campaign by thousands of businessmen for the repeal of the Orders in Council, which showed how critical the economic situation was early in 1812.[34]

On the other hand, he took pains to prove that the crisis which broke out in Britain in the summer of 1810 and the depression which followed "cannot be regarded wholly, or even mainly (though certainly in part), as a fruit of the blows of the Continental System against Great Britain" (330).[35] This is typical of Heckscher's effort to minimize the effects of the System by asserting that difficulties Britain encountered "had no direct connection with Napoleon's proceedings" (173). One could answer that an indirect connection is nonetheless a connection and can be a strong one, especially when the link is some development which was unlikely to have taken place, but for the Continental System. Anyhow, according to Heckscher, the "principal cause" of the crisis was "the all but inevitable rebound from the large speculations" of 1808–9, specially in Latin America, and thus "a phenomenon having no direct connection with the Continental System" (240). Actually, the connection is indirect but strong: British businessmen made massive, speculative, and largely unpaid exports to Brazil and some Spanish colonies because, at the beginning of 1808, European markets were closed and because the Portuguese court had fled to Brazil and opened its ports after Portugal's invasion by a French army, charged with enforcing the Blockade; later the rising of Spain resulted in the opening of some of its colonies. Likewise, Heckscher writes that the depression of British industry in 1811 resulted from the "strangling" of exports to the United States by the Non-Importation Act, "factor, which likewise lacked any direct connection with the Continental System" (240). Again the connection, though indirect, was strong, as the Non-Importation Act was a retaliation against British blockade policy, which was itself a retort to the Continental blockade.[36]

However, in another passage, Heckscher wrote that it would be a serious mistake "to regard the crisis [of 1810] as entirely uninfluenced by the policy of Napoleon" (241): the stricter application of the Blockade in 1810 brought about the collapse of speculations in colonial produce (of which enormous stocks had accumulated in Britain), which triggered off the crisis; and he comments: "The connection with the Continental System thus seems to be manifest" (243; also 241, 244, 246).

If Heckscher was sceptical about the effectiveness of a blockade against a country's exports, his view was different about "the failure of imports, for if irreplaceable commodities are irretrievably left outside no measures can be of any avail," and, unlike exports, "imports are ends in themselves, because they satisfy the wants of the people directly, which is the final function of all economic activity" (332, 335). The experience of World War I is obvious here.[37] He therefore wondered whether Napoleon's chances of success would have been better if he had attacked Britain's imports (especially of grain) rather than its exports. He calculated that imports were only a small share of Britain's wheat consumption: 5–6.5 percent for the whole period 1801–10, 12–16 percent for the year 1810, which had the worst shortage. Even if those imports had been completely stopped, the deficit would have been "a mere trifle in comparison with what we had to accustom ourselves" during World War I: in Sweden, in 1917–18, the total supply of grain was "probably less than half of the normal." "The shortage of one hundred years ago consequently dwindles into comparative insignificance" (337–338).

Heckscher therefore rejected the view of J. Holland Rose, who had "blamed" Napoleon for having missed an opportunity to starve out Britain (where the harvest had failed in 1809), by delivering hundreds of licenses for exporting grain from France and the Low Countries to England. And yet this was a typically mercantilist policy: Napoleon wanted to help French farmers after a superabundant crop and to oblige Britain to send gold in payment (340–341, 344–345).

Nonetheless, Heckscher accepted that, on several occasions—1795, 1800, and 1812—Britain had "a severely felt shortage" plus "serious food disturbances." But to him, the assumption that a stoppage of imports would have "forced the conclusion of peace, or overthrown the British government is one which is more or less refuted by experience," that is, the situation in 1812: wheat prices at their peak, low imports (the harvest has also failed on the Continent), much unemployment.[38] "Despite all this, difficulties could be overcome" (339–340). "The very fact that the working classes of Great Britain acquiesced with comparative patience in their tremendously heavy sufferings, shows how limited the possibilities in reality were of putting an end to British power of resistance by any social movements caused by economic dislocations" (334–335). Heckscher explains this stoicism by "the character of the people": Englishmen were "phlegmatic," little "trained to rely on the state," and thus ready "to leave the conduct of the state entirely undisturbed even in times of serious distress." On the contrary, "an impulsive race [obviously the French], which has also become accustomed to receive help from the state in all things great and small,[39] may be led by a mere trifle to overthrow a government." And he stresses that "the rage of the unemployed was directed in the 'Luddite riots' against the new machinery ... but not really against the government" (331). I would add the adverb "mainly," as the troubles of 1812 were not entirely apolitical:[40] there was an explosion of popular joy after the murder of Prime Minister Perceval!

The monetary effects of the Continental System were also discussed by Heckscher, as Napoleon was hoping that the stoppage of British exports would prevent Britain from intervening on the Continent. Heckscher accepts the view that Britain needed a positive balance on current account in order to pay subsidies to her allies, but such a balance was achieved,[41] because the Napoleonic self-blockade ceased to be effective whenever Britain had continental allies, to which she could export freely (349, 351–353). Yet, the British government had serious difficulties in making payments on the Continent and had to send precious metals. But, Heckscher considers that those difficulties "lay in the matter of technical organisation and were not due to profound economic obstacles"; when organization improved, thanks to the Rothschilds, difficulties vanished (354–356). As for the outflow of gold, its major cause was the depreciation of sterling and the Continental System only played a minor role (361).[42] Heckscher refers briefly to the bullion debate and, as one can expect, he asserts that Ricardo's thesis "goes to the heart of the matter" (359). One can find him too optimistic when he denies that a fall in the Bank of England's reserves would have been dangerous, and that the British credit system could have been thrown into disorder by dislocations resulting from the Continental System. The argument that "the experience of the recent war has largely suggested that our credit organisation has a much more robust physique than anyone had previously suspected" is somewhat anachronistic (362–363).

As the immediate effects of the Continental System on the British economy were small, in Heckscher's view, it is normal that he did not dwell on its possible long-term consequences, inasmuch as quantitative studies of British growth only started in the interwar period, and debates on "crowding out" and related problems belonged to a distant future. Still, he wrote that Britain displayed no "visible signs that the uniquely rapid industrial development which is characteristic of this period was retarded by the Continental System. ... There was certainly no pause in the industrial revolution" (328–330).[43]

The Failure of the System

Though Heckscher was convinced that "the whole of Napoleon's plan ... cannot be regarded as having had any great prospect of attaining its object, that is, the crippling of Great Britain's military power by undermining the foundations of her economic life" (331), he did not neglect the actual causes of its failure. Foremost were to him the internal contradictions of the Continental System (between its attack against England and its other aim—to promote the development of France), which led to the "self-destruction" that has been discussed earlier. However, he also stressed, and rightly, the role of smuggling, which was omnipresent and jeopardized the enforcement of the blockade. However, smuggling could not have developed as much as it did but for the corruption and "systematic dishonesty of Napoleon's tools" of all ranks—from customs officer to field marshal—who tolerated or even helped fraud (164–166). And Heckscher made some excellent remarks upon the "general weakness of authority in those days," and "the enormous difference in the effectiveness of government then and now" (160–161, 164–166, 195, 366–370).[44]

Moreover, the Continental Blockade was, except in France, the product of foreign rule and it was increasingly disliked, inasmuch as many people came to think that it was not "for the good of Europe," but only aimed "to line French pockets" (158–159, 188). As for Napoleon's allies, except Denmark, their governments applied reluctantly the blockade; Heckscher rightly observes that its adoption by Sweden in 1810 was "a merely verbal profession of no very great importance" (151).

Consequently, smuggling "flourished throughout Europe to an extent of which the world since, and perhaps before then, has rarely seen the like"; it was well organized and enjoyed the complicity of most people (187, 192, 194–195). It flourished "from Gothenburg... around all the coasts of Europe to Saloniki" (191), a statement that goes too far, because the amount of smuggling sharply fluctuated, because shifts of its dominant sectors frequently occurred, and because, during some periods, it was held in check.

Heckscher's views have received strong support from the most recent of important books on the Continental System, *The Boulevards of Fraud*, by Silvia Marzagalli, which studies the three ports of Hamburg, Bordeaux, and Livorno.[45] The author insists on corruption, on the weakness of the administrative machinery, on the hostility to the blockade of merchant groups,[46] which thwarted it by all means they had, on the structural impossibility of enforcing the bans against trading with Britain.

On the other hand, Heckscher overlooked two causes of the Continental System's failure, which seem to me crucial.

The first was the remarkable ability of the British economic system to stand up to Napoleon's attack, thanks to its flexibility, to its adaptability, and to the entrepreneurship of its businessmen. It enabled the export trade to adapt quickly to changing political and military circumstances, to shift from traditional markets, when they closed, to new commercial routes and outlets. Sometimes exporters were too adventurous, but their dynamism was a major factor of Britain's successful resistance, inasmuch as it was supported by sea power (thanks to which any opening could be exploited), by an elaborate credit system, and by high productivity. Britain was able at the same time to bear the heavy financial burden of war and to go on with its Industrial Revolution.

Another (and more controversial) factor was time; I mean that the Continental System was not seriously enforced during a period long enough (possibly four or five years) to bring Britain to her knees.[47] It lasted for six years, but during over two and half years (up to mid-1807, and from mid-1808 to mid-1810), the blockade was ineffective, British goods entered the Continent in large quantities; the British economy did not suffer and even enjoyed a boom in 1809. On the other hand, during the three years and a half from Tilsit to the Spanish rising, and from mid-1810 to the Russian disaster, the blockade was enforced; it never was, of course, hermetically sealed, but British exports to "Napoleonic" Europe fell to very low levels (especially for manufactured goods). As, in addition, the American market was closed in 1808, and in 1811–12, the British economy greatly suffered: exports and industrial production fell markedly (in 1811, Britain's total exports were at 64 percent of their 1809 level), unemployment and hardships were severe.[48] I do not share, therefore, the view that Britain only had minor dislocations and that the Continental Blockade was ineffective; I even venture to say that its failure was not inevitable.

As for the reason why the blockade was not enforced long enough, they are obvious and of a military nature—the rising of Spain in 1808, and the Russian disaster. In both cases, Napoleon's own decisions to dethrone the Bourbons and to invade Russia resulted in the fall of the "Great Wall" he had painfully built against British trade.[49] I incline to share the view of my old master, Georges Lefebvre, that Britain was saved not by the laws of economics, but by the winter of Russia.[50] Actually, however, despite the economic and social difficulties that she suffered—and that were more serious than Heckscher conceded, those difficulties never reached the point at which either capitulation or revolution could not have been avoided.[51]

Economic Effects on the Continent

A last problem is the economic effects of the Continental System on the Continent. In this respect, Heckscher rightly distinguishes France and "the rest."

In France, those effects "were all that a protectionist policy pursued with absolute ruthlessness can involve for a country that adopts it," particularly "a hot house development of industrial production" (259). Actually, Heckscher observed a significant impact of the Blockade for only three industries: cotton, chemicals, and sugar.[52] The cotton industry had a fast expansion, thanks to the Continental System, as it was threatened by English competition (269–270). However, there was "no point where the two opposing tendencies" of the System "were so much in conflict with one another," where its "irremediable self-contradiction" was so clear: from 1807, the supply of raw cotton was under threat from the Blockade and the industry suffered (258, 272–277). Heckscher also stresses the collapse of the French cotton industry after Napoleon's fall (actually it was far from complete)[53] (279), which shows that industry "had by no means become capable, during the time of the blockade, of holding its own against foreign competition. Nor is the great prosperity which...occurred under the Restoration any real evidence of its competitive efficiency, inasmuch as a prohibition of the importation of foreign textiles was almost immediately reintroduced" (281).

On the other hand, Heckscher has a good word for the French chemical industry (especially the making of soda from sea salt, according to the Leblanc process) and for the beet sugar industry, though it collapsed after Napoleon's fall. He sees them as a positive, progress-promoting side of the Continental System, which removed some of the obstacles which impeded the use of recent and important inventions (286–294).

Still, they were exceptions, and Heckscher considers that the technical progresses of French industry, under the Continental System, "were not, on the whole, very great, and they still fell far behind Great Britain in almost every respect" (281),[54] and he concludes: "France and the Continent in general were even at the time of Napoleon's fall far from being in a position to take up the new fundamental processes on which the industrial life of England had been based for quite a long time" (282). He blames the Continental System for isolating French industries from British influences, which were indispensable for "participating in the fruits of the great economic revolution" (286). Actually, the isolation had started with the beginning of the Twenty-three Year War, well before the Berlin decree, and British prohibitions against exports of machinery and emigration of skilled workmen must not be overlooked.

In other Continental countries, the Continental System had roughly, according to Heckscher, the same effects as in France: it "came to work as a gigantic protectionist policy pursued to the limit ... enforced with the greatest violence ... for a short period"; therefore, it stimulated the production of all kinds of goods, but the latter suffered, like in France, of the self-contradiction, which created a shortage of raw materials, especially cotton (257–258). Still effects varied between countries and regions, according to the degree of control by Napoleon, to the level of development, and to the dependence upon foreign trade.

However, Heckscher mainly stresses "the French policy of interests," the selfish policy of Napoleon, who kept to a narrow mercantilist tradition. Like many historians, he highlighted a sentence, in a letter from the emperor to his stepson, Prince Eugene, viceroy of Italy, in 1810: "My fundamental principle is France first and foremost" (297). The Continental System thus became "a means of promoting the interests of France" at the expense of her vassals and allies (230).[55] Heckscher has described the hardships of three victims: the Kingdom of Italy, "which he [Napoleon] was anxious to transform into an economic dependency of France" (297); Switzerland, of which some parts suffered "widespread and frightful distress" (306–310); the Great-duchy of Berg, an industrialized "miniature England," on the right bank of the Rhine, which "suffered nothing but injury from the Continental System," as Napoleon refused to its manufactured goods entry into the French market (311–315).[56]

Still, Heckscher concedes that "the whole of this egoistical system" was more irritating than injurious for the vassals of France, those in Germany included (299). Indeed, one German state, Saxony, was the main beneficiary of the Continental System outside France; its cotton industry, which, before the blockade, had suffered from English competition, grew markedly, though, like its French counterpart, it did not keep pace with technical development in Britain (302–306). And Heckscher generalized the remark he had made about France: "Although the Continental System had a very strong stimulating effect on industrial development in many directions ... yet it had not built up industry so firmly as to prevent a relapse for some years after the close of the blockade; and this was due to *the incapacity of protection* [emphasis added] to provide for the adoption of the technical advances that had not been introduced before the beginning of the blockade" (306).

As for the "General situation on the Continent," Heckscher eventually concluded that "the effects of the Continental System on the actual material foundations of the life of the people ... were far less than those which accompanied the recent blockade," when the standard of living continuously fell. Except for colonial produce, the wants of the people could be satisfied more or less as usual. The reason was the "far-reaching sufficiency" of European countries (far greater than in 1914–18), especially in food, plus the smuggling of goods from Britain into the Continent (320–322, 365–366).[57]

I shall briefly return to Napoleon's "selfish policy," for it raises interesting questions. Heckscher rightly noticed that the emperor did not listen to some of his counselors, who recommended combining the Continent of Europe into an economic unit and establishing a customs union between France and her vassals and allies (259–295). Indeed, when, at St. Helena, he spoke about uniting Europe under his scepter, he mentioned unifying weights and measures, currencies, laws, but not a customs union or a free trade area. During his reign, he refused proposals to create a customs union between the Confederation of the Rhine member states, and did not try to unify economically Italy. Moreover, he closed French borders to manufactured goods from allied countries, and one of his dreams was "the French continental market design," which has been stressed by G. Ellis (who also calls it "a one way common-market"). Exports from France would fill the vacuum left by the exclusion of British goods from the Continent and France would become "the workshop of Europe," its dominant industrial power. However, this "design" was only a grandiose and vague dream of Napoleon and some of its officials.[58] Heckscher rightly pointed out that French exports to the rest of the Continent did not progress after 1806 (299–302).[59]

Moreover, one can assert that Napoleon's "selfishness" was not unjustified. France was the center of his system, but also the country that suffered most from the British sea blockade and from the loss of her colonies; her economy had to be defended. As for blaming him for not having opened the French market to exports from Switzerland, Berg, and so forth, it is anachronistic: such a liberal policy was foreign to the ideas and practices of the time. Admittedly, France exported manufactures and imported primary produce, but this does not allow us to call "colonial" relations between her and "the rest." The exploitation of Europe by Napoleon was achieved through war indemnities, requisitions and other politico-military exactions, and not through trade. It is certainly far-fetched to see the Continental System as an antecedent of the European Union. Nonetheless, it was an attempt to organize the European economy, to impose upon European countries a common economic policy—even though it boiled down to exclude British goods, and even, with the Trianon decree, a common external tariff. Moreover, in Western Europe at least, the Continental System had some structural consequences, which were to be durable, while all continental economies—and not only France—suffered from the dominant position her final victory gave to Britain.

Conclusion

Heckscher would not have agreed. One quotation will give the gist of his conclusions: "The Continental System had little success in its mission of destroying the economic organisation of Great Britain, and most of the things it created on the Continent lasted a very short time. The visible traces that it left in the economic history of the past century are neither many nor strong. Indeed it is difficult to find any more obvious and lasting effect than that of prolonging the existence of the prohibitive system in France far beyond what was the case, not only in Great Britain, but also in Prussia. Thus there are good grounds for doubting that the material development of our civilisation would have been essentially different if this gigantic endeavour to upset the economic system of Europe had never been made" (364).

G. Ellis has called *The Continental System* a "not impartial account," which was "influenced by liberal economic ideas."[60] I would not go so far, but it is not unfair to Heckscher (and to a book that remains a masterpiece) to remark that his position of free-marketeer and free-trader, his hostility to state intervention in economic affairs, and his pacifist feelings introduced bias in some parts of his study.

"On the whole," he wrote, "it may be regarded as a general rule that purely coercive laws in the sphere of economics have far fewer possibilities of being made effective in a positive direction than in a negative one" (217). And later: "From a purely economic point of view every trade war is, strictly speaking, a paradox, for it is directed against intercourse which is profitable to both parties and therefore inevitably inflicts sufferings on its author no less than on its intended victims." Heckscher did see the Continental System as an attempt "to destroy the texture of economic society," while he was convinced that such attempts "can generally do little more than retard the process of development" (364). However, he did not forget this time that there was a war on and he added that the system "mainly had immediate ends in view. It was in the first place a link in a life-and-death struggle" (364). As in other instances, he thus qualified a statement that had been rather categorical.

Notes

1. I am heavily indebted on this question to unpublished papers by two young scholars: A. Chatriot, "Comprendre la guerre. L'histoire économique et sociale de la guerre mondiale. Les séries de la Dotation Carnegie pour la Paix Internationale" (2002), and J. L. Harvey, "Henri Hauser et les historiens américains pendant l'entre-deux-guerres" (2003). I thank them heartily.

2. Heckscher (1915). Heckscher writes that he had attempted, "to some little extent," "an analysis of the economics of the recent war" and some general comparison with the Napoleonic Wars (1922:374, 386).

3. Heckscher (1918).

4. Bergenland and Heckscher (1930).

5. But the *Parliamentary Papers*, some volumes of which are full of important evidence for the subject, were not available.

6. He mentions, particularly, F. E. Melvin, *Napoleon's Navigation System* (New York, 1919), which is indeed a good work (219, n. 2).

7. His own experience may have helped him to understand how delicate the position of a neutral country is in a major war. Yet, he did not realize that a strong body of British opinion wanted war with the United States.

8. For instance, he praised (106) James Stephen's *War in Disguise or the Frauds of the Neutral Flags* (London, 1805), the author of which was the spokesman of a lobby of lawyers working at Courts of Admiralty, who wanted more prizes, which would bring them more income, and so on.

9. Heckscher (1922) also believes that Vergennes made the 1786 trade treaty, because he was influenced by physiocrats (18); actually he wanted to consolidate peace with England. There are also mistakes on the origins of the expression *Perfide Albion* (51), and on the cause of the fall in British exports in 1803 (80), plus misunderstanding of an address to Napoleon by the Chamber of Commerce of Cologne in 1811, "where a plea was coolly put forward to move the population from the unfertile right bank of the Rhine to its fertile left bank"; actually, the Chamber only said that, if the Emperor stated that Berg (on the right bank) would never be annexed to the Empire, its textile manufacturers would "delocalize" to the left bank. This was not a Stalinist plan of mass deportation! (314).

10. He complained that German works on the Continental System were often anti-British (295, 376).

11. For instance, calling Mulhouse Mülhausen (270–271).

12. The bombing of Copenhagen in 1807 is only called "quite superfluous" (122); Marshal Davout, governor of Hamburg, was "a man of the same type as the German generals who during the recent war governed occupied territories" (197). See also page 315, on the benefits of French rule on the left bank of the Rhine.

13. And Heckscher points out that the burning of prohibited goods, which Napoleon ordered in 1810, "was following precedents...in English legislation of the 17th century," which was repeated as late as the 1760s (203). See, however, infra, on his scorn for Napoleon's economic views.

14. It is strange that Heckscher made no reference to other cases of blockades, for instance of the Confederacy by the North during the American Civil war.

15. Heckscher (267–268) condemns Napoleon's support for "luxury" industries (like silk), as "such a policy diverted productive forces from turning out what was necessary for the support of the people as well as for the prosecution of the war." To him, this is one more case of government's "lack of intelligence in the sphere of economics," but he shrewdly adds: "This shows how comparatively gentle after all, was the pressure of the Continental System in comparism with that of recent wars."

16. He also asserts that "the connection between cause and effect...must always to a great extent have to be solved by theoretical reasoning" (238).

17. I shall generally use Heckscher's expression, the Continental System.

18. This assumption (which underlies Heckscher's great work *Mercantilism*) has been criticized by Coleman (1969:9, 12, 102, 113), as it "ignores the extent to which the force of economic circumstances frequently dictated the shape of policy enactments."

19. Heckscher adds that some practices that are typical of the period, such as smuggling and the granting of licenses by belligerents to violate their own prohibitions, had existed in the eighteenth century (15–17). Likewise, the British blockade policy also followed tradition (44).

20. Still, one may note Heckscher's remark: "In every respect...the Berlin Decree stands out as a culmination of earlier thoughts and measures" (89).

21. It seems that trading with the enemy, through licenses, neutralization of ships and cargoes, false ships' papers, was morally repugnant to Heckscher (40, 210–213).

22. The Anglo-French commercial war had become inevitable "after mercantilism had become firmly established in both countries" (13).

23. The British had transformed maritime blockade, which at the start was contrary to mercantilist ideas, into "merely an outcome of the mercantilist commercial policy" (30–32).

24. See also page 28, on the "dualistic character" of the Continental System, which thus involved "an irremediable self-contradiction."

25. Heckscher stresses that developments in Iberia opened to Britain new "transmarine markets," but he overlooked that, in this respect, Brazil was more important than the Spanish colonies (173, 175–176).

26. Cf. Ellis (1991:97): "In essentials, the twin aims of the original blockade decrees survived all their later modifications, notably those of 1810."

27. Heckscher asserts that the "system of corruption, created by Napoleon's tools" became worse, briberies and embezzlements more frequent (203–204). I doubt his interpretation of the examples he quotes.

28. However, Marzagalli (1999:265) asserts that the French authorities were unable to control the trade under licenses; also Ellis (1991:100).

29. Actually, there is a contradiction with Heckscher's previous assertion (154) that "the disintegration of the system ... was conditioned by external causes"—Napoleon's defeat in Russia, the risings in annexed and occupied countries.

30. Crouzet (1987:859–860).

31. Heckscher considers this problem in chapter IV of part IV, but also in chapter V of part III ("The British Crisis of 1810–12"). We shall come back briefly later to the effects on France and "the Rest of the Continent."

32. Crouzet (1987:853).

33. Plus, in the case of Continental countries, the view that it did not have any durable positive effects.

34. Earlier on, he had minimized the losses suffered by the British in the Baltic in October 1810 (234–235), and overestimated the "new commercial routes" which were opened to British goods, particularly across the Balkans (230–233, 236).

35. Heckscher went further in another passage: the crisis of 1810 "has no direct connection with the Continental System, but only the indirect connection that follows from the influence of the Continental System in bringing about general unrest in the world" (238–239; also 248).

36. Heckscher had written earlier that the shortage and high price of cotton early in 1808, the recession of the cotton industry which followed were linked "at the most with the Orders in Council" (173–174).

37. "This result [rather conclusion], which was reached early in 1918, is in accordance with later German developments" (332n). See also page 373: the blockade of World War I, which was "primarily directed against the enemy's imports," "had a far more correct economic object than that of Napoleon."

38. Heckscher considered that the poor law system made things worse and was "extremely pauperising" (328).

39. A strange statement, which may be correct in 2003 but not in 1922, and still less two centuries ago. Heckscher also made a mistake in calling *coups d'état* the popular risings (*journées révolutionnaires*) during the French Revolution.

40. A hotly debated topic, especially since the book of E. P. Thompson (1963).

41. This is far from sure, as Heckscher used official values of imports and exports, which can serve many purposes, except calculating their balance!

42. Actually, late in 1808 and early in 1809, Britain's *actual* balance of payments became suddenly negative, and the exchange rate of sterling fell; Crouzet (1987:537–542).

43. The evidence for this statement is flimsy: Heckscher compared figures of coal exports from Newcastle and of cotton wool imports for the five-year periods 1801–5, 1807–12, and 1816–20; 1796–1800 ought to have been added.

44. Heckscher insisted on this comparison, both in part III and in his conclusion; he stressed "the increased honesty and efficiency of public administration," and also the technical factor of railways and telegraphs. Thus, during World War I, the belligerents were able to control trade quite strictly.

45. Marzagalli (1999); see particularly pages 263–267.

46. Which Napoleon did not dare to punish; repression fell only upon "small people."

47. Marzagalli (1999:278) disagrees.

48. See Crouzet (1987).

49. Some historians answer that Napoleon took those two decisions in order to improve the blockade's enforcement; actually, neither Spain in 1808 nor Russia in 1812 were large markets for Britain; I do not agree with Heckscher (152) that "the apostasy of Russia" in 1810 was "the strongest possible blow" against the Continental System. Dwyer (2001:132) writes: "The real reason why Napoleon invaded Russia has nothing to do with international politics or the Continental System."

50. Lefebvre (1935:368–369).

51. One more case of "the Revolution that never was"! Heckscher observed incidentally: if the exclusion of British goods from the Continent had lasted, Britain would have aimed at more self-sufficiency; this would have damaged her economic position "immensely" and reduced her national income (263).

52. In his view, the silk, wool and flax industries were not affected (266–268); likewise, the iron industry, which remained in an "incredible backwardness" (283–284), a view that is not confirmed by Woronoff (1984), who observed some progress.

53. Ellis (1981) concludes that the blockade period left in Alsace "solid assets which survived the final agonies of the Empire" and had enriched Alsatian merchants and manufacturers (273). Those developments were one of the reasons why Alsace was, after 1815, one of the most progressive industrial districts on the Continent.

54. One could remark that six years is a short period for "catching up."

55. Also Napoleon "directed his policy against the countries of his own continental vassals and allies" (259).

56. Actually, these criticisms of Napoleon's policy toward these countries are excessive, their difficulties exaggerated; and Heckscher admitted that machine-spinning of cotton in Switzerland was rescued from English competition and grew.

57. However, Heckscher observes that agricultural countries somewhat suffered—but not much—from obstacles to their exports of primary produce (261–262, 317–318). But he stressed the serious deterioration of economic conditions on the Continent in 1811–13 and suggested that "conditions would have come to develop in a direction more like our own experience if the fall of Napoleon had been delayed a few more years" (322).

58. See Ellis (1981:104ff; 1991:98); Woolf (1990:201–203).

59. Woolf (1990:206, 210) writes that the industries of vassal countries were strong enough to resist an invasion of French goods, and were indeed more competitive, because of cheaper labor and raw materials.

60. Ellis (1981:7; 1991:135).

References

Bergenland, A., and E. F. Heckscher, eds. 1930. *Norway, Denmark, Sweden, and Iceland in the World War.* New Haven, CT: Yale University Press.

Coleman, D. C. 1969. *Revisions in Mercantilism*. London: Methuen.

Crouzet, F. 1987. *L'économie britannique et le Blocus Continental, 1806–1813*. Paris: Economica.

Dwyer, P. G. 2001. *Napoleon and Europe*. London: Longman.

Ellis, G. 1981. *Napoleon's Continental Blockade: The Case of Alsace*. Oxford: Clarendon Press.

———. 1991. *The Napoleonic Empire*. London: Macmillan.

Heckscher, E. F. 1915. *Världjkrigets Ekonomii: En Studie af Nutidens Näringslif under Kriget Inverkan*. Stockholm: Bonniers.

———. 1918. *Kontinental Systemet*. Stockholm: Bonniers.

———. 1922. *The Continental System: An Economic Interpretation*. Oxford: Clarendon Press.

Lefebvre, G. 1935. *Napoléon*. Paris: Presses Universitaires de France.

Marzagalli, S. 1999. *Les boulevards de la fraude: Le négoce maritime et le Blocus Continental, 1806–1813*. Lille: Presses Universitaires du Septentrion.

Thompson, E. P. 1963. *The Making of the English Working Class*. London: Gollancz.

Woolf, S. 1990. *Napoléon et la conquête de l'Europe*. Paris: Flammarion.

Woronoff, D. 1984. *L'industrie sidérurgique en France pendant la Révolution et l'Empire*. Paris: Editions de l'EHESS.

14

Eli Heckscher, Economic
Warfare, Naval Blockades,
and *The Continental
System*

Lance E. Davis and Stanley L.
Engerman

Eli Heckscher is one of the major economic historians of the twentieth
century, as well as a scholar who has had a major impact on the study
of economics, particularly in the fields of international trade and economic policy. His works as an economic historian have been concerned
with method as well as substance, and he wrote three essential books
that have been translated into English. These works—*Mercantilism*
(1935), *The Continental System* (1922), and *An Economic History of Sweden* (1954)—have had great staying power and remain the starting
points for scholars studying and debating these topics.[1] Heckscher's
main concern in these writings was with the role of government policies in peace and war and the role played by policy choices in economic growth.

Mercantilism is the examination of government trade regulation in
Western Europe from the Middle Ages until the age of laissez-faire. As
with many such classic works, most of the subsequent criticisms have
been anticipated. Given the enormous literature on mercantilism, a literature that is basically a debate with what scholars argue to have been
Heckscher's major points, the central issues he raised about unification,
state power, power and plenty, and the relative smallness of the difference between mercantilism and laissez-faire, continue to be debated. In
The Continental System the central concern was with the wartime blockades of the Napoleonic Wars—blockades that were initially imposed
by the British, but had then been introduced by Napoleon to promote
French production and to reduce British economic and military power.
These wartime measures were concerned with the achievement of both
power and plenty to the extent that they were not in conflict with each
other. Heckscher places the Continental Blockade in broader perspective in the book's last chapter, comparing its means and ends with the
World War I blockades. In a 1926 Swedish publication, abridged and

translated by the Carnegie Endowment in its Economic and Social History of the World War series in 1930, Heckscher briefly discusses the impact of the World War I blockade on neutral Sweden, but that discussion is given limited attention relative to that accorded Swedish wartime economic and monetary policy.[2]

In this essay we wish to focus on one aspect of Heckscher's work in economic history, that concerned with economic warfare or blockades. As mentioned, in addition to his analysis of the Continental System, Heckscher's interest in the impact of blockades on national rivalries reflected several of his long-term interests. The remainder of this essay is divided into two sections: (1) a general discussion of the nature of blockades and their legal framework; and (2) a short survey of the Continental System, a rather unusual form of blockade, with some brief attention given to more recent data.

The Nature of Economic Warfare

In this section we wish to expand upon the discussions of economic warfare presented by Heckscher and by others, and to survey the pre–twentieth century history of blockades and embargoes. During a war there are a number of alternative military and naval strategies that a belligerent can pursue in that country's efforts to defeat its enemies. Obviously one such strategy is conquest by force of arms in direct combat. Such a strategy involves the siege or the invasion of an enemy's territory, the destruction, capture, or surrender of the enemy's armed forces and, perhaps, the permanent occupation of its territory. Economic warfare, by weakening the enemy's ability to pursue military action, can substitute or complement a strategy of direct combat. Such an economic strategy is designed to sever the trading links between the enemy and their allies and also with neutral powers, and, in so doing, to reduce the level of military and civilian goods that are available to support military ventures. Historically, the blockade, usually sea-based but occasionally land-based, has been the most common form of economic warfare; however, in the more recent past other forms of economic warfare have been utilized. They include the imposition of higher tariffs, nontariff exclusions, and policies aimed at encouraging the production of substitutes by the targeting and neutral nations—all tactics designed to reduce enemy exports. In addition, the scope of economic direct warfare has recently been expanded to include the aerial bombardment of economic objectives, sanctions designed to restrict trade to neutral countries, sabotage of economic targets, preemptive purchases of strategic material, and, more generally, psychological warfare (Medlicott 1952, 1:xi). Although naval blockades remained their major concern, this widening of the scope was mirrored in the British government's decision to change the name of the department charged with implementing that county's economic warfare efforts from the Ministry of Blockade during World War I to the Ministry of Economic Warfare during World War II (Medlicott 1952, 1:1–3).

Wartime and Pacific Blockades

For centuries, land and sea blockades have been initiated unilaterally by belligerent powers for military or commercial motives. It was, however, only in early modern Europe that the rules and laws of blockade, like the laws of war, were formalized and enshrined in a series of international agreements, the most important of which were the treaty that emerged from the Congress of Paris of 1856 and the never ratified end product of the Conference of London of 1909 (Colombos 1959:417–423). Both spelled out a set of rules that were accepted, formally or informally, by most developed nations. Nevertheless, as with most rules of law, their acceptability and applicability varied with the intensity of the conflict and with changes in the technology and organization of warfare.

In simple terms, a naval blockade can be viewed as an attempt by one belligerent through the "interception by sea of the approaches to the coasts or ports of an enemy" to cut "off all his overseas communications" (Colombos 1959:649). The general aim is to reduce the enemy's ability to effectively carry out military operations, by stripping imports of supplies and also to prevent exports. Blockades designed to starve or weaken the enemy's civilian and military population by reducing imports of food supplies have received the most attention; however, blockades have also been aimed at the importation of munitions, other war supplies, and critical raw materials—petroleum and minerals in particular. In addition to reducing imports, blockades have frequently also been directed at a country's exports. In this latter case, the goal is usually to reduce the enemy's ability to obtain the wherewithal to pay for imported resources. In a somewhat parallel fashion, the blockading power may attempt to use political pressure or military threat against neutrals to limit the enemy's ability to acquire loans and capital from neutral nations.

Strictly speaking, a legal blockade entails the right to stop all merchant vessels seeking to enter a previously designated area. The legal right to seize contraband, the definition of which will vary over time, on the other hand, applies only to a limited and specific list of war materials; but these materials can be seized anywhere in the world. A country's decision to deploy a blockade designed to limit enemy exports or imports has a counterpart in the use of embargoes to limit that country's own exports to foes and neutrals. The aim of such embargoes often appears to be less economic than political—by creating a shortage of specific goods, the nation or coalition adopting the embargo hopes to influence a third country's behavior toward the other belligerent. Although there have been some notable, if not particularly effective, embargoes—Jefferson's early-nineteenth-century embargo of all American exports, and the South's embargo of cotton exports during the Civil War, to cite two examples—the relative importance of blockades and embargoes in history can be effectively proxied by the coverage given to the two strategies in the standard works on international law.[3] In those publications, embargoes received less than ten percent of the coverage given to blockades.

Although most blockades are deployed by belligerents in wartime, there have been some that involved neither war nor belligerents. For example, blockades have been used to deter war by weakening a potential enemy before an official declaration of war. The legal status of such pacific blockades is rather uncertain; but, in recent years, under the newly coined rubric of "economic sanctions," they have been deployed both by individual countries and by international organizations (for example, the UN and NATO).

Not all blockades have been deployed for political or for purely economic reasons. For example, during the years following its political decision to halt its transatlantic slave trade in 1808, Britain mounted a blockade of the African coast. The British government drew on existing antipiracy laws to justify its decision, and at times their naval squadron engaged in military skirmishes with vessels from France and other powers.[4] Earlier, during the long series of eighteenth-century wars between Britain and France, the British maintained a mainly military blockade of French ports on the Atlantic. That blockade was designed to keep the French fleet bottled up in port and, thus, to prevent it from supporting an invasion of the British Isles.

The major legal and political problems engendered by blockades arise not only from the impact of the intervention on enemies, but also from their effect on neutral "third" countries. Neutrals often represent potential alternative sources of supply; and, given that goods from anywhere can be routed through those neutrals, a blockade that does not restrict neutral trade with the enemy may well prove ineffective. Neutrals are, however, not belligerents; and as nonbelligerents they often believe that their commercial activities should not be constrained. Attempts to limit their exports and imports can bring them into direct conflict with the blockading power. Attempts to resolve those disputes have generated an extensive body of international law. Moreover, the issues involving neutral rights go beyond those raised by a naval blockade—such concerns are relevant only to controversies arising from contacts at sea. For a blockade to be effective, it must be extended to cover neutrals contiguous to or connected by land with the enemy; and, therefore, international laws must be extended to cover the myriad of political policies designed to deal with neutral overland trade.[5]

The expected benefit of a successful blockade seems clear—a loss of enough of the enemy's military power to shift the probability of victory in a favorable direction. But these benefits are not pure profits; there are costs involved in any decision to deploy a blockade. These costs include the direct expenditures on vessels and manpower that are needed to mount the blockade or the opportunity costs of diverting resources from alternative employments, the potential costs (in men and vessels) from damage or destruction by enemy action, and the possible costs that might result should the blockade induce a neutral to enter the war on the side of the enemy. Any military planner who sets out to design an "optimum naval blockade" must take into account the geography (the length of the relevant shoreline), the available technology (ships, aircraft, equipment), the level of military organization, economic power, and the probable response of neutral countries.

International Laws and Treaties

Blockades—interdictions whose "primary purpose is to prevent the enemy from receiving goods which may be used in warfare and that are designated as contraband" and to limit the ability of a neutral to trade with the enemy by making it legal to capture and condemn all neutral vessels sailing for enemy ports—not only directly involve the belligerents, but obviously also those of neutral third countries (Parmelee 1937). Such blockades have long raised major issues of international legal concern.[6] Beginning at least as far back as the late sixteenth century, in a long series of proclamations and international treaties, the concept of a "legal" blockade has been defined and its rules formally specified.

These principles, however, were not universally recognized. In the case of Britain, before 1815, prize courts had recognized a similar but different set of rules—rules that were less focused on the rights of neutrals: (1) "a blockade to be binding must be effective"; (2) "only a belligerent can establish a blockade"; (3) "to be valid a blockade must be duly declared and notified; the declaration must state the exact geographical limits of the blockaded area and the days of grace allowed to neutral vessels to enable them to come out of the blockaded port"; (4) "the blockade must be limited to the ports and coasts of the enemy" (Medlicott 1952, 1:4). Thus, there was room for differences concerning the legal basis of a blockade and sufficient ambiguities to leave substantial room for both judicial and military conflict. For example, a disagreement over neutral rights arose between the United States and Great Britain; that disagreement, as well as other issues, relating to the control of the American West and Canada, ultimately led to the War of 1812.

Were Blockades Successful?

The history of blockades over many years has shown that the success of any economic blockade depends, to a large extent, upon three factors—factors that vary with the domestic resources and the geographic location of the nation that the blockade is directed against and the military resources at the disposal of the blockading power. First, "the economy of the blockaded power must be vulnerable"—thus, given the resource and industrial base of the United States, a blockade against it would be almost certain to fail. Second, the blockading nation must have sufficient military power to control the land and sea routes that connect the enemy with the "outside world." Third, "the blockading power must be able, [either through military force or diplomatic pressure,] to secure the acquiesance or co-operation of neutral powers that might be able to supply the blockaded country (Medlicott 1952, 1:2–3). In summary, then, economic warfare, to be successful, depends on being able to restrict the enemy's economic ability to expand its stock of basic resources.

Although blockades have been affected by technical and political changes, it has been the shifting efficiency of blockades relative to what has become the most efficient antiblockade weapons—the substitution of steam for sail, the convoy—that probably represents the single most important chapter in the history of the blockade (see Colombos 1959:694–700 on legal aspects of convoys). Naval convoys were hardly a new innovation. In fact, convoys antedated the first effective naval blockades. However, then as now, convoys were not costless, since there were time costs in assembling the entire convoy, the gathering of the vessels for the convoy tended to jam harbors, and the speed of the convoy was limited by the speed of the slowest vessel.

Even a cursory glance at history suggests that, to a large extent, the relative efficiency of naval blockades vis-à-vis countering strategies—in the recent past those strategies have almost all involved convoys—has, in large part, depended on the nature and responses to five major regime changes. The first was technological changes. In the fifteen century changes in vessel design led to changes in the capability of sailing ships, permitting the development of effective blockades, while centuries later, steam and steel replaced wind and wood in both the convoying and the blockading force. Later telegraph and radio replaced visual signals, radar greatly increased the range of effective search, and submarines, aircraft, mines, and aircraft carriers greatly changed the nature of the opposing forces. The second was related to the increasing size and scope of major conflicts—it remains a question whether the American Civil War can be viewed as the earliest example of "total war," but there is no question that the first and second world wars qualify for that dubious distinction. Total war, as its name implies, tends to infer a willingness on the part of the belligerents to do anything required to win. Third, as trade expanded and nations attempted to pursue their competitive advantage, they became more dependent on international trade. As a result, they faced greater costs, should a blockade prove effective. Fourth, at least in the West, as nations grew economically and their governmental structures became more solidly emplaced, those governments were better able to control the actions of their own military forces. Finally, the size and power of both the belligerents (individual states, grand coalitions, international organizations) and the neutral powers altered the political infrastructure that supported the blockading fleets and the naval forces deployed in attempts to break that economic stranglehold.

Blockades have a rather mixed success record, as have had sanctions (pacific blockades). The availability of alternative sources of supply from neutral nations, the inability to restrict overland shipments to replace sea transport, the use of convoys to improve shipping success, and the ability to increase domestic production, all limit what can be achieved by blockades as a wartime measure. And what is thought to be the success of some blockades was due less to the control of shipping lanes, but to the domestic difficulties of the blockaded economy, due to labor shortage or poor harvests, or else the blockaded nations incorporation of production reductions or export embargoes of particular crops or commodities. Even some positive benefits of a blockade cannot by itself end a war except in unusual circumstances, since while they do achieve a rise in the costs of pursing warfare, this higher price could still be one that the blockaded party might be willing to pay.

Britain, France, and Napoleon's Continental System, 1665–1815

From the late seventeenth century until the end of the Napoleonic Wars in 1815, France and Britain were at war more than half the time, in addition to frequent and quite visible manifestations of commercial rivalry (Wright 1965:643–645).[7] Other European nations were involved in some of these wars, for example, in the War of Spanish Succession (1702–1713) and the War of the Austrian Succession (1739–1748). In others, such as the Seven Years War (1756–1763), the French and British were the sole or primary antagonists in North America, but with other nations involved in Europe. In the American Revolution (1776–1783), despite their contribution to the final outcome, the French role was relatively small. But, for the years between 1793 and 1815, with a small pause from the Peace of Amiens (March 1802 to May 1803), the major fight for dominance in Europe was between France and England, with both nations seeking as many political and military allies as they could acquire, whether by military force (France) or by cash subsidy (Britain).[8]

The Wars to 1807

During periods of warfare, as well as during the intervals of peace, restrictions on trade, including tariffs and blockades were deployed by these two nations against each other, as well as against other, neutral, nations. These constraints were designed to influence the European power balance and also to encourage domestic economic development. Both Britain and France actively pursued mercantilistic policies; and, as a result, international economic and military rivalries characterized

Europe from at least the late seventeenth century. There was a brief pause in these rivalries after the Eden Treaty, between England and France, in 1786 (Heckscher 1922:18–25; Kaiser 1990:250–251). This treaty eliminated prohibitions of imports and lowered customs duties; however, these policies were widely believed to be beneficial to the British and were opposed by the French. The treaty was in force for only a limited time, since in February 1793 war again broke out between the French and the British. Both nations soon reverted to their earlier policies of trade control—policies that included prohibitions on specific manufactured imports, a policy particularly desired by French industrialists, and attempts to limit all of the carrying trade of their foe. In 1796 the French law was extended from prohibition on British goods to exclude all goods acquired by British trade. These provisions were extended in the Nivôce Law of 1798, which was, however, nullified in 1799. Moreover, both nations introduced measures designed to restrict the trade of neutral nations with their rival. In particular, laws were placed on trade in various foodstuffs, the French (1793) by capturing any neutral vessels that were carrying food that belonged to Britain or were carrying British goods, a policy basically the same as that of the British at the time (Heckscher 1922:25–27, 42–47; see also Rose 1893).

From 1793 until the end of the first part of the war with France, Britain had implemented a rather traditional type of naval blockade, a close blockade of the major French port of Brest as a means of observing and limiting the movement of the French fleet (Mahan 1898, 1:335–380; Morriss 2001:1–21, particularly 13–15). During the second part of the French-British war, from 1803 to 1815, both nations imposed blockades designed to limit trade and to control warships: and both met with some mixed success (Jack 1941:14–42). By 1800, the British had more than twice the number of warships than did the French, a dramatic change in the military environment since the beginning of the eighteenth century when the two navies were of roughly equivalent size (Modelski and Thompson 1988:68–71; Harding 1995:102, 118, 126, 131, 136; see also Glete 1993).[9]

The French navy suffered a severe setback with Nelson's victory at Trafalgar (1805). And although the French added warships in the first decade of the nineteenth century, the British navy grew by about the same amount. It is this difference in the size of the two fleets that was to influence both the nature of the two blockades and their relative successes. The difference also underscored the importance of France's need to induce the other continental nations to impose trade restrictions and blockades against the British. The attempt to control the continent and its external trade was the basis of Napoleon's Continental System, and it was central to his wartime efforts.

Within fourteen months of the failure of the Peace of Amiens, a number of military and commercial actions were undertaken by the British and by the French. The British seized all French and Dutch vessels in British ports (May 1803), regulated the neutral trade with the enemy colonies (June 1804), and proclaimed a blockade of the Elbe and Weser rivers (June–July 1803)—a blockade that limited the trade from German cities. In August 1804, the blockade was extended to all French ports on both the English Channel and the North Sea; however, the effects of these blockades gradually eroded in the years prior to 1806. France, for its part, employed policies that were designed to limit British trade with the continent. In part, those policies involved military occupation as well as political coalitions with continental nations; and, in part, they were directed at raising tariffs and imposing other types of prohibitions on the import of British goods. Napoleon was initially successful militarily on the continent, but the British dominated the war at sea (Heckscher 1922:81–83).

Although it is believed the Napoleon's decree was planned earlier, his dramatic political and military activities were triggered by a British Order in Council of May 1806—an order that included the placement of a blockade on the European coast, a strictly enforced blockade between the mouth of the Seine and the Ostend, with the remaining coast between the Elbe and Brest less strictly enforced (Heckscher 1922:81; Mahan 1898, 2:269–274). In November 1806, Napoleon responded by issuing the so-called Berlin Decree; it was followed, in November and December 1807, by the two Milan decrees. These three decrees provided the basic structure for the Continental System. The provisions of the Berlin Decree included: (1) prohibition of all trade with the British; (2) all British subjects in French-occupied areas were considered prisoners of war and their property was "fair prize," (3) all trade in British goods was prohibited and all goods from England and her colonies were "fair prize" (and one-half their value was to be used to indemnify French merchants for loses to the British), and (4) no ships coming from the ports of Britain or its colonies would be permitted to use any port on the Continent. The Second Milan Decree extended these regulations to cover all vessels from all nations, and it made any vessel that had called at or was on its way to any British port a fair prize. Given the weaknesses of the French navy and its inability to impose heavy costs on the British, the declaration of these blockades and the subsequent actions at sea were, as Heckscher points out, rather a "theatrical gesture." Heckscher describes the French action as the imposition of a "self-blockade"—that by cutting off imports by continental countries the blockade was aimed at restricting the sales of British and British colonial goods and, in this way, damaging Britain's economic power (Heckscher 1922:90–93, 96, 114–124, 389–407).

In 1807, in reaction to the Berlin and Milan decrees, the British responded with several related Orders in Council—proclaiming policies that were basically aimed at tightening the blockade of France, restricting the direct trade of Britain's enemies with their colonies, and limiting French maritime trade with neutrals (Heckscher 1922:16, 110–117; Smart 1910:154–161). The first order required that neutral vessels call at a British port before proceeding to the continent. Thus "all direct intercourse between the enemy countries and other ports is prohibited, except when the 'other ports' are either European British ports or ports in the vessel's own country" (Heckscher 1922:116). Taken together, the orders imposed economic and political costs on the trade both of enemies and of neutrals. The regulation of neutral trade by both the British and the French was to be the source of continuing international conflict with the United States, then the major neutral trader in Europe's overseas commerce. By the end of 1807, the basic contours of the Continental System, the British blockade, and the United States' policies that were to form that country's reaction to these measures were all set in place. Although their duration of these policies was to be only a few years, they did have a dramatic effect on the shape of the European and American economies.

The Aims of the Continental System

Although dictated by the relative military balance of power between the British and the French, Napoleon's aims in the deployment of the Continental System were somewhat unusual among the rationales for blockades (Rose 1936; Kaiser 1990:237–263). France was the strong military power on the European continent, at least until wars with Spain and Russia weakened its capabilities; but, relative to the British navy, it was weak at sea.[10] Thus France could not really impose a blockade aimed at halting British shipping or stopping imports from elsewhere going into the British Isles. Nor could it easily stop exports from Britain to the continental nations, unless the continental nations would refuse to purchase them. That, indeed, was Napoleon's continental strategy: to control, directly or indirectly, the imports of the continental nations from Britain and its colonies, and it was the strategy that underlay the concept of a "self-blockade"—a blockade designed to restrict British exports. This "self-blockade" resembled more closely a system of tariff and quota restrictions than the customary naval blockade; and the policy was aimed both at harming the British economy, and, as tariffs are also designed to do, to encourage production by the French and continental industries.

Because of its naval weakness, and because of Napolean's firm mercantilist beliefs, the Continental System sought ends unlike those of most other blockades. Whereas most blockades were intended to reduce the enemy's military and economic power by depriving them of certain critical commodities, particularly weapons and foodstuffs, Napoleon's aim was to weaken the British economy by adversely affecting its financial capabilities.[11] This strategy would not only limit Britain's exports—exports that would provide them with foreign earnings—but it would also encourage British imports of continental goods. Imports meant British expenditures for foreign goods; and, thus, if foreign transactions were sufficiently unbalanced, to specie outflows (see O'Brien 1989 and 2002 on British monetary policy and public finance in this period). Reducing British revenues and specie reserves would not only reduce Britain's wealth and power and, presumably, weaken that country's credit and ability to borrow; but it would also have a more direct impact. It would greatly lessen Britain's ability to subsidize continental nations—a subsidy that was a part of the British attempt to lure those nations away from France and to redirect their trade toward Britain. While both customary blockades and Napoleon's Continental System were aimed at reducing enemy exports, the specific reason for deploying such measures—measures designed to limit their revenues—were somewhat different. In one case, it was to reduce the ability to purchase imports; in the other, it was to increase the balance-of-payments deficits and cause specie outflows.

The peculiar nature of the French blockade is indicated by its rather paradoxical behavior during the British grain crises of 1810 (Heckscher 1922:336–347; Melvin 1919:88–90; Galpin 1925:168–188; Macksey 1989; Lewis 1959:205–207; Doughty and Raugh 1991:24–26). Rather than seeking to impose costs on Britain by forcing a reduction in British grain imports at a time of domestic shortage, Napoleon encouraged

exports to Britain from France and its allies on the continent, particularly Holland, as a means of generating an increased trade deficit at
this fortuitous time of high grain prices, as well as a means of supporting French farmers.[12] Grain exports from France stopped the following
year, not because of a desire to try to starve the British, but because
France was itself now suffering from poor harvests.

In evaluating the success (or not) of the Continental System, it
should be noted that Napoleon's aim was to reduce Britain's specie
supply (a goal he was successful in achieving in the years of the blockade, since bullion at the Bank of England fell from £6.9 million in 1808
to £2.2 million in 1814), rather than to limit the British acquisition of
resources that could be used for military purposes or for consumption
or production (Mitchell and Deane 1962:441–443). Further, the blockade was designed to contribute not only to a hoped-for military victory, but also to an increase in French industrialization—which would
further limit British exports of manufacturers, and thus its economic
power.

Since both Britain and France introduced restraints on trade with
neutral nations, neither nation was able to offset substantially the
effects of the blockades by obtaining needed goods through trade with
neutral powers. More importantly, by making neutral vessels fair
prize, the blockades engineered a significant response by the biggest of
the neutral powers, the United States. That response led, in 1807, to an
Embargo Act directed against trade with both belligerents, then to the
Non-Intercourse Act of 1809, and finally to a war between the United
States and Britain—a war that began in 1812 over neutral rights. Previously, in 1810, the United States had passed a law that stated that if
one of the belligerents revoked their trade regulations (and the other
did not follow suit within three months), the United States would use
the Non-Intercourse Act to reduce trade with the nonrevoking nation.
Napoleon adopted policies that appeared to meet these terms, and the
United States narrowed its concern with trade restrictions to only the
British. Soon, however, the restrictions regarding Britain proved ineffective, and the United States declared war. Although the British soon
rescinded the offending Orders in Council, the American declaration
of war was not withdrawn; and for three years Britain and the United
States remained at war. It is not clear which of the belligerents suffered
the most because of these extensive sets of rules restricting neutral trade.
It is, however, clear that the British triumphed militarily, against both
France and the United States. And, although disputes over neutral

rights frequently arose during the course of many blockades, such as those deployed during the American Civil War and both world wars, the Napoleonic Wars represents one of the unusual cases of disputes between a belligerent and a neutral leading to outright war.

Policy Changes

In the nine years between the Berlin Decree and the French surrender, there were numerous changes in policy and in behavior on the part of both France and Britain and of their allies. Some of these changes in policy reflected shifts in internal economic and social conditions, while others reflected changing military circumstances and shifting alliances among the continental nations. Although the Continental System existed for the entire period, it was not always effectively implemented; and, as a result it is difficult to evaluate its success or failure. It is argued that the Continental System was effectively used to control trade only from mid-1807 to mid-1808 and from mid-1810 to mid-1812, or a total of three years, one-third of the period in question.[13] Such a limited period in a world with economies marked by long lags in both shipping and production, as well as lags in trading responses, means that any attempt to pinpoint the effectiveness of the Continental System is difficult.

Both belligerents were not just seeking to implement successful blockades, they were also pursuing other goals. The French wished to maintain continental alliances, by military force or by commercial agreement, but they were also concerned with the expansion of French industry and commercial power. The British wished to maintain their commercial and military power. To that end, they attempted, both by paying subsidies and through other political policies, to draw continental nations away from the French.

In discussing the changes and reactions of the two nations during the blockade years, it is important to remember that there were many other events that influenced the economies and the societies of the belligerents.[14] The blockade was not the only component of the economic and political policies that changed, and any attempt to measure the ex-ante (or ex-post) profitability of the blockades needs to take these other factors into account. There were changes in military fortunes on land and at sea, fluctuations in the size of the harvest because of weather conditions, and the customary economic fluctuations that reflected the impact of economic conditions on business activity—conditions that influenced both domestic and foreign demands. Even more important, perhaps, were the variations in Napoleon's political and military relations with other nations. Some countries were added to his alliance, but, as with Spain and Russia, some managed to successfully withdraw, by military measures, from French domination to ally themselves with Britain.

In 1809, among the many several factors that influenced the extent of the British blockade was the attempt to attract nations away from France by providing them with more favorable trading conditions. An Order in Council of April of that year ended the blockade of all European countries except France, Holland (then ruled by France), and the northern provinces of Italy and Germany. By this time, Spain had succeeded in breaking away from French domination; and that country had shifted much of its trade to Britain. Not only Spain, but also the Spanish colonies of Central and South America, increased their trade with Britain; and that increase helped to offset the reduction in British trade with the continent.[15] In response, in 1810, France undertook several new measures to increase economic pressure on the British. The Trianon tariff of August, 1810 greatly increased the taxes on imports from foreign and colonial areas; this meant, however, increasing the prices of foreign goods in the home market. It did represent a marked shift in French goals, away from the exclusion of colonial goods to the more familiar regulation of foreign trade by use of tariffs (Melvin 1919:233). The Fontainebleau decree of October 1810 "prescribed the destruction of all British goods throughout the Continent," a measure that was clearly aimed at halting all imports from British manufacturers (Heckscher 1922:153). Even more important in influencing French policy and in effectively limiting the impact of the blockades, was the Licensing Decree of July 1810. Licensing was a practice that the British had originally introduced (Heckscher 1922:153, 205–220; Melvin 1919:235–310). The British government, at its discretion, had been granting licenses to shippers wishing to trade with foreign nations. The aim of the British policy was not to restrict, but to expand, British trade with the continent. The French adoption of the licensing system meant that traders could obtain licenses to trade with the British; however, since the British still prohibited imports from France, the French attempt to use these to increase their exports did not succeed. Nevertheless, this policy did lead to more trade between the belligerents, particularly during the British grain shortage of 1810, and it marked an apparent policy shift from trade limitation by naval blockade to the use of tariffs and direct regulation of trade to reduce imports. In administering licenses, there was a conflict between their role as a regulatory measure and their role of a means of raising revenue. Most of the continental nations did not, however, follow France in the magnitude of tariff increases; they raised tariffs slightly, if at all. They did, however, generally allow for licensing to regulate trade. Despite these important changes in foreign trade relations, there were, perhaps, more important matters in late 1810 that were to lead to France's ultimate loss to Britain. These were not, however, the direct impact of blockade-related matters. Rather, in reaction to various French pressures, Russia severed relations with France. This led to a shift in Russia's trade allegiance from France to Britain, giving rise to Napoleon's ill-fated invasion and subsequent military defeat by the Russians and various European nations in 1814 (Duffy 1989).

In late 1811, even during the war between the two countries, Britain did attempt to allow some trade reciprocity with France, but this new opening led to no effective changes in policy (Melvin 1919:256–283, 289–291). In June 1812, Britain did, however, repeal the Orders in Council that had influenced their trade with the United States and other neutral nations. This order had angered American merchants and politicians, but its repeal occurred a few days *after* the United States had declared war on Britain; and thus, it did not prevent the War of 1812. Not surprisingly, the war caused a massive decline in Anglo-American trade; but once the wars ended the decline was quickly reversed, although previous peaks were slow to be achieved (Mitchell and Deane 1962:311; Porter 1847:359–360, 380–381, 400). In 1812, Napoleon's policy again shifted. The new policy was to encourage French imports—preferably imports of raw materials—from other nations, including Britain, as long as they were balanced by an equivalent amount of French exports, preferably exports of manufactured goods. This change led to some increase in total French trade.

The period between 1810 and 1812 was one of economic difficulties in Britain, France, and Europe in general (Heckscher 1922:238, 247; Gayer, Rostow, and Schwartz 1953:83–109). Output declined; and, initially in Britain, there were grain shortages and limited food supplies. Britain benefited from grain surpluses in Spain; but, in addition, from grain imports from France, Holland, and Flanders, countries that also had grain surpluses in 1810 but that were still at war with Britain. The French aim, consistent with the overall goal of its blockade policy, was to both take advantage of the opportunity to sell at high prices in order to drain Britain of specie, and to provide expanded markets for those French farmers with surplus production. The next year, however, grain shortages led to the need of France to import grain (Galpin 1925:168–188). In response to the grain shortages, the French imposed embargos against grain exports but since sales under licenses were permitted, this policy was never fully enforced. The history of the years 1810 to 1812 indicates both the unusual nature of the Continental System and the somewhat strange French expectations of what the system could accomplish. The defeat of Napoleon in Russia in 1812 effectively ended any trade war with Britain; and, in 1814, with Napoleon's defeat at the hands of several continental nations and his subsequent abdication, the Continental System came to an end.

Effects on Trade

In discussing the success or failure of both the Continental System and of the British blockade, it is necessary to remember what goals the two sets of policies were intended to achieve. The British blockade was more traditional: an attempt to restrict French exports as well as the imports by France and its other continental allies from neutral nations (Heckscher 1922:98–100). For the French, one goal was that of achieving military victory by reducing the economic power of an adversary. The policies adopted were, however, not so much aimed at reducing British imports of foodstuffs and other goods, as they were at lowering British foreign earnings by reducing that country's exports and increasing its financial outflows by having them increase their imports of necessary items. The hope was to create a balance-of-payments deficit for Britain; a deficit that would lead to an outflow of specie, thus reducing British wealth and productive capacity (O'Brien 1989; Neal 1990:201–222). The second goal of the French policy was to use the Continental System to attack British economic power by, in effect, raising tariffs, and, it was hoped, increasing the costs and decreasing the availability of British manufacturers, in order to encourage the development of French industry (Rose 1906; Melvin 1919:xii–xiii). The Continental System seems a rather expensive means of deploying tariffs and trade exclusions. In regard to this second French aim, it is difficult to present a full evaluation of benefits and costs; there were clearly some positive effects—it spurred the growth of some industries, such as cotton textiles, chemicals, and beet sugar.[16] But there were also some negative effects. Trade limitations increased the price of imports, including those of raw materials needed for manufacturing; and, thus, it reduced production in some sectors. In addition, with the implementation of tariffs and the introduction of loans for industrial establishments, the industrial policy involved an increased role of government. The Continental System and the blockades also had an impact upon industry in the other continental nations similar to the impact on France, being rather mixed and relatively minor (Crouzet 1990; Heckscher 1922:295–323).

Both within the war period and in the longer term, there is a need to distinguish between military and economic benefits. The fact that France lost the war is suggestive of the failure of the Continental System, but it may be argued that the Continental System served to prolong and make closer a war in which the French were, initially, in a less than powerful position. Whatever may have been the relative power of the belligerents before 1789, the internal turmoil generated by the French Revolution greatly weakened the capability of the French military. By the time the Continental System was introduced, the French strength was on land; while the British clearly had superior power at sea. As a result, the French were not in a strong position to achieve success with a naval blockade of the standard type. There was little prospect that a French blockade designed to bring down England would be successful, but the introduction of the Continental System probably had a somewhat positive military effect from the French point of view.

Taken together, the Continental System and the British blockade did have an impact on the magnitude of international commerce, as well as on the geographic pattern and the commodity composition of trade (see Crouzet 1958, 1989, 1990; Mitchell and Deane 1962:281–282, 289–290, 295, 311; Chabert 1945–49:321–328; Imlah 1958). In the case of the British, during the early nineteenth century, the size of the official values of total imports and total exports fluctuated, with little trend and few large changes (Mitchell and Deane 1962:281–282). The largest deviation from the average was in the high level of imports in 1810, the year of grain shortage. Although there were no dramatic changes during the war period, there was a slowing down of the rates of growth of exports from the levels that had been reached over the preceding two decades. The rate of growth of British exports during the years 1802–1814 fell to 3.1 from the 6.4 percent per annum that had marked the years 1781–1802, while the growth rate of imports declined from 5.4 percent to 1.2 percent (Crouzet 1989:191). These declines are suggestive of the impact of the war, if not of the blockade itself. The Continental System also led to some shifts in British export markets, and the same is true for its conflict with the United States. There was a relatively small decline in the share of goods going to continental Europe from Britain, particularly after 1805, but there were some increases in trade with Spain and Portugal after those countries had freed themselves from Napoleon's rule. The major shift in the pattern of British trade was triggered by the growth in the South American market. In several years, exports to South and Central American markets were equal to the average level of exports to the United States in the years 1808 through 1814 (Mitchell and Deane 1962:311). Moreover, the enhanced Latin American market continued to draw high levels of British exports after the war ended. In the postwar period, there was increased trade with almost all markets—a set of markets that included the United States and Continental Europe. There was, however, only a small change in the level of trade with France. With the exception of the higher postwar level of imports (but not exports) coming from the British West Indies, the list of nations from which imports to Britain increased looked very much the same as the list of countries that had recovered or increased the levels of exports.

Despite the French policies designed to limit the expansion of British manufacturing industries, particularly the rapidly developing cotton textile sector, British exports of cotton textiles increased rapidly during the era of the Continental System (Mitchell and Deane 1962:295, 311; Edwards 1967:51–64, 243–247). Much of the increase in exports went to continental Europe, and that pattern persisted after the war. Raw cotton imports increased, but, otherwise, there was little change in the level of imports from the American colonies. And, as in the case of geographic patterns, there were no major long-term shifts in the commodity composition of British trade.

French foreign exports during the war period fluctuated, but within a range of about 15 percent above and below the mean level in the period (Chabert 1945–49). Exports to (and imports from) England declined very sharply between 1803 and 1809; but after 1810 they rose again to late eighteenth century levels. Thus there appears to have been a minimal long-term impact of the interruption of trade between the two nations. In part because of the British capture of several of the French West Indian colonies, in part due to the independence of Haiti, previously an extremely wealthy colony, and in part because of the impact of the blockade, French exports to their colonies fell to almost zero between 1798 and 1814. There were some variations in the level of trade with continental nations—nations that were dependent upon their alliance with France—as well as some differences in the level of trade with the United States—differences that were largely due to the then current interpretation of neutrality codes. France suffered a sharp decline in imports in 1813 and 1814, a decline that reflected its trade with many American and European nations, particularly the German states. The movements of French exports were similar to those for imports. French exports included both foodstuffs and industrial products, and, the value of manufactured goods exported increased, both relatively and absolutely. Imports of cotton textiles declined somewhat during the war period, as did imports of colonial products and foodstuffs; both the declines were influenced by the weakness of French shipping, as well as the blockade of the British. After the war, there were recoveries in the level of imports of most commodities; and there was a return to prewar sources of supply for these goods.

The Continental System was in effect, a variant of a protectionist tariff that, by precluding imports of British manufactures, was designed to spur French industry. There was some growth in certain French industries, cotton textiles for example, and the French began to produce beet sugar; but, given the short period of time that this tariff was effective, there was neither dramatic growth during the war, nor did growth continue in these industries in any major way once the war had ended and the blockade was lifted. Although both the French and the British saw more rapid growth and higher levels of trade with the return of peace, as a means of generating import substitution, the French policy was expensive and not effective (Melvin 1919:330–346; Heckscher 1922:364–374; Marzagalli 2002:189–194, especially 176; Cunningham 1917:676–695). These conclusions, it should be noted, are consistent with the much earlier analysis by Heckscher.

Although its loss in the Napoleonic Wars did not prevent France from growing rapidly in the remainder of the nineteenth century, it lessened its international political power and influence. France did not reappear as a major military rival of Britain, and during the period of European expansion to form colonial empires, France had only a secondary role to play vis-à-vis the British. But to attribute these changes to the outcome of the wars is not to claim that the blockades and the Continental System played a major role. The effects on world trade, and trade in specific commodities, were limited and insufficient to alone change the fortunes of the belligerents.

Thus, in most regards *The Continental System* remains firmly in place as the key source to study this episode. Little controversy has developed in regard to overall interpretation or specific events, and, unlike his *Mercantilism*, it is regarded as an essential work whose interpretations are still acceptable to scholars. As of yet, they have not triggered any major ongoing controversies.

Acknowledgments

We wish to thank participants at the conference, particularly François Crouzet and Patrick O'Brien, for useful comments.

Notes

1. These works appeared in Swedish in 1931, 1918, and 1935, respectively. The English translation of *The Continental System* was published by the Carnegie Endowment for International Peace, as part of their studies of World War I. The concluding chapter is a "Comparison with the Present Day" since, as the editor Harold Westergaard states in his preface, "the Continental blockade in many ways throws light on the economic blockade among the belligerent powers involved by the World War."

2. Heckscher (1935, 2:42–44, 98–100) notes early examples of the conflict between the aims of mercantilism, encouraging exports, and those of wartime blockades, discouraging imports by the enemy, including a 1303 British edict against trading with the enemy, and compares a similar 1304 French decree with the World War I blockades of Germany and Sweden, aimed at reducing exports in order to protect food supplies. See also Heckscher (1930:5–8 and 1954:270–272, in the supplement by his son, Gunnar).

3. Embargoes may, of course, be successful in limiting trade, even if they do not achieve their desired political end, since it seems easier to influence your own exports than those of other nations. See Irwin (2001) and Surdam (2001).

4. See Eltis (1987:102–240) for a discussion of the costs and effects of the British blockades, and Jennings (1988:144–167) on the disagreements between the British and the French in the 1830s and 1840s regarding the British proclaimed right-to-search in their attempt to end the transatlantic slave trade.

5. In World War I, the allied powers attempted to limit trade by European neutrals with Germany by rationing the allowed imports based upon their prewar levels. For the case of Sweden, see Bergendal (1930:82–124). See also Davis and Engerman (forthcoming).

6. Most blockades are based on control of the sea, although there have been some land blockades of interest, including Mohammad's successful seventh century blockade of Mecca. See Donner (1977).

7. Of the twelve conflicts involving Britain and France, in three they were on the same side, none after 1720. For a survey of the naval aspects of these conflicts, see Ranger (1989).

8. The most complete studies of the political and economic aspect of the Continental System of the Napoleonic era are Heckscher (1922), Melvin (1919), and Crouzet (1958).

Heckscher (1933) is a very brief summary of his argument (see also Rose 1906). On the role of British subsidies paid to continental nations, see Heckscher (1930:67, 253), Sherwig (1969:345–356, 362–369), and Emsley (1979:22, 80–81, 150–151, 169).

9. During the Napoleonic era, the total warships of France and Spain generally equaled that of the British.

10. For a discussion of the relative importance of the control of land versus sea, see Rose (1936:219, 239); Wilson (1906); and Lloyd (1965). On relative British and French naval losses, see Jack (1941:36–37) and Glover (1980:181–184, 197, 200).

11. See Lewis (1959:171–185, particularly 180) for the description of the Continental System as "the first full-scale experiment in economic warfare, a bold attempt to blockade Britain without warships." Mahan (1898, 2:197–200) describes the French system starting with 1793 as "commerce-destroying," and his chapters on 1793–1806 and 1806–1812 are entitled "The Warfare Against Commerce."

12. For discussions of whether it would have been possible for France to starve out England at this time, see Olson (1963:49–72); Galpin (1925:109–122, 168–201); and Rose (1936).

13. See Heckscher (1922:320–323, 348–352) on the limits to French success. See also Kaiser (1990:252–253); Rose (1906:368–370); Crouzet (1989:192–193, 2002); and Markham (1965:329).

14. See Bodart (1916:116–138) for details on the sequence of wars with the other continental nations that Napoleon fought, ultimately fighting with all European countries but Denmark. The importance of land battles in comparison with naval battles is seen in the comparison of 302 land battles and sieges with seven naval battles. For estimates of military deaths in the Napoleonic era see Bodart, and Dumas and Vedel-Petersen (1923:27–34).

15. See Heckscher (1922:245), Gayer, Rostow, and Schwartz (1953, 1:89) and Mitchell and Deane (1962:311). The official volume of exports to the Foreign West Indies and Spanish America rose from an average of £315,000 in 1804–1805 to an average of £6,176,000 in 1809–1810, and remained above £3,000,000 for the rest of the war and afterward. Exports of United Kingdom produce to Spain also rose, from (in "real" values) an average of £40,000 in 1805–1806 to an average of £1,890,000 in 1809–1810.

16. See Heckscher (1922:266), Crouzet (1989, 1990:262–340); Ellis (1981); Henderson (1972:24–34, 46–48), Bergeron (1981:159–190). In *Mercantilism*, Heckscher (1935, 1:203) notes that "mercantilist regulation in France had placed obstacles in the path of all innovations which had somehow succeeded in becoming established in England, and the Continental System, together with the general unrest that prevailed on the continent until 1815, again retarded fresh development in France."

References

Bergendal, K. 1930. "Sweden: Trade and Shipping Policy in the War." In A. Bergeland and E. F. Heckscher, eds., *Sweden, Norway, Denmark, and Iceland in the World War*, 41–124. New Haven, CT: Yale University Press.

Bergeron, L. 1981. *France Under Napoleon*. Princeton, NJ: Princeton University Press.

Bodart, G. 1916. *Losses of Life in Modern Times: Austria-Hungary; France*. Oxford: Clarendon Press.

Chabert, A. 1945–49. *Essai sur les Mouvements des Revenues et de l'activité Économique en France de 1798 a 1820.* 2 vols. Paris: Librairie de Médicis.

Colombos, C. J. 1959. *The International Law of the Sea.* 4th ed. London: Longmans.

Crouzet, F. 1958. *L'Économie Britannique et le Blocus Continental (1806–1813).* 2 vols. Paris: Presses Universitaries de France.

———. 1989. "The Impact of the French Wars on the British Economy." In H. T. Dickinson, ed., *Britain and the French Revolution, 1789–1815,* 198–209. New York: St. Martin's.

———. 1990. *Britain Ascendant: Comparative Studies in Franco-British Economic History.* Cambridge: Cambridge University Press.

———. 2002. "America and the Crisis of the British Imperial Economy, 1803–1807." In J. J. McCusker and K. Morgan, eds., *The Early Modern Atlantic Economy,* 278–315. Cambridge: Cambridge University Press.

Cunningham, W. 1917 (1882). *The Growth of English Industry and Commerce in Modern Times.* 2 vols. Cambridge: Cambridge University Press.

Davis, L. E., and S. L. Engerman. 2006. *Naval Blockades in Peace and War: An Economic History Since 1750.* Cambridge: Cambridge University Press.

Donner, F. M. 1977. "Mecca's Food Supplies and Muhammad's Boycott." *Journal of the Economic and Social History of the Orient* 20:249–266.

Doughty, R. A., and H. E. Raugh. 1991. "Embargoes in Historical Perspective." *Parameters* 21:21–30.

Duffy, M. 1989. "British Diplomacy and the French Wars, 1789–1815." In H. T. Dickinson, ed., *Britain and the French Revolution, 1789–1815,* 127–145. New York: St. Martin's.

Dumas, S., and K. O. Vedel-Petersen. 1923. *Losses of Life Caused by War.* Oxford: Clarendon Press.

Edwards, M. M. 1967. *The Growth of the British Cotton Trade, 1780–1815.* Manchester: Manchester University Press.

Ellis, G. 1981. *Napoleon's Continental Blockade: The Case of Alsace.* Oxford: Clarendon Press.

Eltis, D. 1987. *Economic Growth and the Ending of the Transatlantic Slave Trade.* New York: Oxford University Press.

Emsley, C. 1979. *British Society and the French Wars, 1793–1815.* London: Macmillan.

Galpin, W. F. 1925. *The Grain Supply of England During the Napoleonic Period.* New York: Macmillan.

Gayer, A. D., W. W. Rostow, and A. J. Schwartz. 1953. *The Growth and Fluctuation of the British Economy, 1790–1850.* 2 vols. Oxford: Clarendon Press.

Glete, J. 1993. *Navies and Nations: Warships, Navies, and State Building in Europe and America, 1500–1860.* 2 vols. Stockholm: Almqvist and Wiksell.

Glover, M. 1980. *Warfare in the Age of Napoleon.* London: Cassell.

Harding, R. 1995. *The Evolution of the Sailing Navy, 1509–1815.* New York: St. Martin's.

Heckscher, E. F. 1922. *The Continental System: An Economic Interpretation*. New Haven, CT: Yale University Press.

———. 1930. "Sweden." In A. Bergeland and E. F. Heckscher, eds., *Sweden, Norway, Denmark, and Iceland in the World War*, 3–39, 127–277. New Haven, CT: Yale University Press.

———. 1933. "Continental System." In E. R. A. Seligman, ed., *Encyclopedia of the Social Sciences* 11:310–311. New York: Macmillan.

———. 1935. *Mercantilism*. 2 vols. London: George Allen & Unwin.

———. 1954. *An Economic History of Sweden*. Cambridge, MA: Harvard University Press.

Henderson, W. O. 1972. *Britain and Industrial Europe, 1750–1870*. 3rd ed. Leicester: Leicester University Press.

Imlah, A. H. 1958. *Economic Elements in the Pax Britannica: Studies in British Foreign Trade in the Nineteenth Century*. Cambridge, MA: Harvard University Press.

Irwin, D. A. 2001. "The Welfare Cost of Autarky: Evidence from the Jeffersonian Trade Embargo, 1807–1809." National Bureau of Economic Research, Working Paper 8692.

Jack, D. T. 1941. *Studies in Economic Warfare*. New York: Chemical Publishing Co.

Jennings, L. C. 1988. *French Reaction to British Slave Emancipation*. Baton Rouge: Louisiana State University Press.

Kaiser, D. 1990. *Politics & War: European Conflict from Philip II to Hitler*. Cambridge, MA: Harvard University Press.

Lewis, M. 1959. *The History of the British Navy*. London: George Allen & Unwin.

Lloyd, C. C. 1965. "Armed Forces and the Art of War: B. Navies." In C. W. Crawley, ed., *The New Cambridge Modern History*, 9:76–90. Cambridge: Cambridge University Press.

Mackesy, P. 1989. "Strategic Problems of the British War Efforts." In H. T. Dickinson, ed., *Britain and the French Revolution, 1789–1815*, 147–164. New York: St. Martin's.

Mahan, A. T. 1898. *The Influence of Sea Power Upon the French Revolution and Empire, 1793–1812*. 2 vols. Boston: Little, Brown.

Markham, F. 1965. "The Napoleonic Adventure." In C. W. Crawley, ed., *The New Cambridge Modern History*, 9:307–336. Cambridge: Cambridge University Press.

Marzagalli, S. 2002. "Roundtable: Reviews of Silvia Marzagalli, Les boulevards de la Fraude: le negoce maritime et le Blocus continental, 1806–1813: Bordeaux, Hambourg, Livourne." *International Journal of Maritime History*, 14:151–194.

Medlicott, W. N. 1952. *History of the Second World War*. 2 vols. London: Longmans, Green.

Melvin, F. E. 1919. *Napoleon's Navigation System: A Study of Trade Control During the Continental Blockade*. New York: D. Appleton.

Mitchell, B. R., and P. Deane. 1962. *Abstract of British Historical Statistics*. Cambridge: Cambridge University Press.

Modelski, G., and W. R. Thompson. 1988. *Seapower in Global Politics, 1494–1993*. Seattle: University of Washington Press.

Morriss, R. A., ed. 2001. *The Channel Fleet and the Blockade of Brest, 1793–1801*. Burlington: Ashgate.

Neal, L. 1990. *The Rise of Financial Capitalism: International Capital Markets in the Age of Reason*. Cambridge: Cambridge University Press.

O'Brien, P. K. 1989. "Public Finance in the Wars with France, 1793–1815." In H. T. Dickinson, ed., *Britain and the French Revolution, 1789–1815*, 165–187. New York: St. Martin's.

———. 2002. "Merchants and Bankers as Patriots or Speculators?: Foreign Commerce and Monetary Policy in Wartime, 1793–1815." In J. J. McCusker and K. Morgan, eds., *The Early Modern Atlantic Economy*, 250–277. Cambridge: Cambridge University Press.

Olson, M. 1963. *The Economics of the Wartime Shortage: A History of British Food Supplies in the Napoleonic War and in World Wars I and II*. Durham, NC: Duke University Press.

Parmelee, M. 1937. "Blockade." E. R. A. Seligman, ed., In *Encyclopedia of the Social Sciences* 2:594–596. New York: Macmillan.

Porter, G. R. 1847 [1836–1843]. *Progress of the Nation: In Its Various Social and Economic Relations, from the Beginning of the Nineteenth Century*. London: John Murray.

Ranger, R. 1989. "The Anglo-French Wars, 1689–1815." In C. S. Gray and R. W. Barnett, eds., *Seapower and Strategy*, 159–185. Annapolis: Naval Institute Press.

Rose, J. H. 1893. "Napoleon and English Commerce." *English Historical Review* 8 (October): 704–725.

———. 1906. "The Continental System, 1809–1814." In A. W. Ward et al., eds., *The Cambridge Modern History*, 9:361–389. Cambridge: Cambridge University Press.

———. 1936. *Man and the Sea: Stages in Maritime and Human Progress*. Boston: Houghton Mifflin.

Sherwig, J. M. 1969. *Guineas and Gunpowder: British Foreign Aid in the Wars with France, 1793–1815*. Cambridge, MA: Harvard University Press.

Smart, W. 1910. *Economic Annals of the Nineteenth Century, 1801–1820*. London: Macmillan.

Surdam, D. G. 2001. *Northern Naval Superiority and the Economics of the American Civil War*. Columbia: University of South Carolina Press.

Wilson, H. W. 1906. "The Command of the Sea, 1803–1815." In A. W. Ward et al., eds., *The Cambridge Modern History*, 9:208–243. Cambridge: Cambridge University Press.

Wright, Q. 1965. *A Study of War*. 2nd ed. Chicago: University of Chicago Press.

15

The Hanoverian State and the Defeat of the Continental System: A Conversation with Eli Heckscher

Patrick O'Brien

Whosoever commands the sea commands the trade, whosoever commands the trade commands the riches of the world and consequently the world itself.
—Sir Walter Raleigh, *History of the World*, 1614

Eli Heckscher wrote the first draft for his book on Napoleon's Continental System while the "continent" (including neutral Sweden) experienced the rigors of a far more effective British naval blockade during the closing months of World War I. He examined three principal themes. First, he considered the mercantilist origins of economic warfare. Second, he explored the reasons for virtual failure that attended six to seven years of intensified attempts by the French, other European, and American governments to exclude British exports from markets nominally under their control. And third, and of greater interest to our generation of economic historians concerned with growth and structural change, he devoted Part IV (roughly a quarter of the book) to an examination of the "Effects of the Continental System on the Economic Life of Great Britain and the Mainland."

I intend to bypass that part of the book because the economic outcomes of wars, including the costs and benefits of major strategies designed for their prosecution, continue to pose intractable theoretical and empirical problems for economists, economic historians, and historians to analyze. Although Heckscher and all other scholars who have conducted research on the Continental System make interesting suggestions about "effects," they have found it altogether more feasible to trace its origins, to reconstruct the policy in operation, at every conceivable level of disaggregation, and to explain the failures of governments to close markets to British exports and thereby precipitate a fiscal and financial crisis that could conceivably have seriously undermined the capacity of the Hanoverian state to continue to wage war against the Napoleonic empire and its allies, as well as the United States.

Most of Heckscher's classical study falls within an established and ongoing tradition of economic history that preserves its status as a canonical survey of knowledge about the Continental System available in 1917–18. Several decades of subsequent historical scholarship (synthesized, elaborated, and virtually completed in the second edition of François Crouzet's magnum opus *l'Economie Britannique et le Blocus Continental*) confirms the status of most of parts I to III of Heckscher's text, which deals with the immediate historical antecedents and wartime operations of the blockade. More recent historical literature supplements Heckscher's analysis of why European customs and military administrations under direct French rule, or acting on instructions from governments in reluctant or enthusiastic diplomatic accord with the emperor's strategy, failed to enforce an evolving body of Napoleonic orders and decrees designed to obstruct and regulate trade between the United Kingdom and the mainland (including Russia).

As a historian, economist, and true scholar, Eli Heckscher would surely have anticipated the publication and interpretation of this new evidence from archival and other sources, as well as the development of sharper theoretical insights for purposes of analysis. Above all, and since he recognized all history as contemporary history, he would also have expected a "reconfiguration" of problems that now appear to have held deeper relevance for his generation of intellectuals who lived through the high tide of liberal imperialism, which carried forward the integration of international markets for commodities, capital and labour during that first long boom (1899–1914) and who worked tirelessly to reverse the relapse of the world economy into neomercantilism after World War I.

As an intellectual historian, Heckscher conceived of the Continental System as a paradigm example of an episode in European history that emanated from a body of mercantilist ideas about power and profit that had promoted more than a century of Anglo-French rivalry— which he traced in his opening chapter back to 1660. Today (and with all the advantages of hindsight that have cumulated during eight decades of research and interpretation since its publication), the book can now be "read": first, as Anglocentric and deficient in its appreciation of European geopolitical history from which the Continental System emerged, and second, as an underspecified analysis of how and why the British state first stimulated and then defeated Napoleon's desperate and (I will argue) doomed attempt to close continental markets to British trade.

To begin with geopolitics: since Charles II and James II were clients of Louis XIV and allies of France in seeking to undermine Dutch primacy in international commerce, historians of international relations would not begin their narratives of Anglo-French antagonism with the Restoration. They are more likely to trace the origins of a "Second Hundred Years War" to the formation of the League of Augsburg, which led to the opening of dynastic conflict with France—referred to by British historians as King William's War (1689–98), because the Dutch coup d'état of 1688 led to a dramatic reorientation in the new regimes' foreign policy that generated a pronounced and persistent uplift in the share of the kingdom's gross domestic product devoted to strategic, imperial, and commercial objectives.

Following from that "conjuncture" (the Glorious Revolution), Britain fought seven times against France and her allies. The two countries were formally in a state, or on the brink or recovery from war, for more than half the period from between 1688 and the Treaty of Vienna in 1815. All of these protracted conflicts (interspersed with interludes of cold war between France and Britain) witnessed the raising of tariffs to prohibitive levels, bans on direct trade, and the conduct of seaborne commerce under more or less comprehensive and persistent risk of armed attacks (by royal navies and privateers) on trades conducted by French, British, allied, and neutral shipping with their respective enemies. Finally, all mercantilist wars included strategies that involved the expropriation and destruction of British, French, Spanish, Dutch, and Portuguese property overseas in Asia, Africa, and the Americas.

It would be impossible to measure the costs incurred and the benefits that accrued to British, French and other European economies from sixty-one years of open warfare between 1689 and 1815, funded and organized by their states against each other's trade and settlements and bases overseas. The final phase of an era of mercantilism certainly included intervals of more peaceful competition (1715–31) and several attempts by "liberal" statesmen in both Britain and France to dismantle the apparatus of bans, quotas, tariffs, and navigation acts that seriously restrained the growth of trade and pursuit of comparative advantage everywhere in the world economy before 1846. Nevertheless, and within a European geopolitical order dominated by a pervasive mercantilist "episteme," Britain's massive and sustained investment in the

Royal Navy and an ever increasing fleet of merchant ships eventually paid off.

For war after war, including that failed military campaign to suppress the revolt of its thirteen colonies in the Americas (1776–83), the Hanoverian kingdom emerged: first, with improved fiscal and financial capacities; second, with enhanced organizational and technological means to inflict damage on the seaborne trade and overseas investments of its rivals; and third, with augmented and more efficient naval power required to defend the realm and growing stake of its citizens in assets located overseas for trade, shipping, and servicing the international economy.

From the time of Cromwell's First Anglo-Dutch War (1652–54), slowly but surely (and by way of investment in predation, violence, learning, and technological innovation) the state established conditions for a set of complementary comparative advantages in naval power and mercantile shipping and services. By the time Castlereagh signed the Treaty of Vienna, Great Britain had become the most successful of Europe's mercantilist powers, in possession of the largest occidental Empire since Rome and with an economy that would continue to reap cumulative benefits from the acquisition of extraordinary shares of the world's commerce in manufactured goods, shipping, and the supply of international services.

Heckscher's book is not located in European geopolitical history. As its subtitle indicates, he set out to write an "economic interpretation" of a single phase of Anglo-French economic warfare that would "represent a synthesis of earlier studies of the mercantile system and its outgrowths on the one side and the result of extensive theoretical and practical work in the field of present day war economics on the other." In short, the book was written for economists by an economist of strong liberal persuasions at a propitious moment in the history of the world economy. Heckscher's implicit agenda was to demonstrate the irrationality and futility of economic warfare, derived (in his conception) from a body of thought (mercantilism) that he represented unconvincingly (as Coleman demonstrated) as a "system" riddled with inconsistencies, irregularities, and malign outcomes that the "scientific" traditions of classical and neoclassical economic theory (derived from Adam Smith) had refuted and condemned to the dustbin of intellectual history.

If (as I suggest) the Continental System is moved away from Heckscher's implicit and preferred context as a case study in the history of the theory of international trade (where Napoleonic strategy could only appear as a prime example of irrational mercantilism) and is reconfigured in the geopolitical history of the long eighteenth century as another failed, but more aggressive and ambitious strategy, pursued by France, along with other continental powers and the United States, in order to contain Britain's naval and commercial hegemony at sea, then it become possible to point up misspecifications and omissions in Hecksher's narrative of this famous but by no means unique episode of conflict in Anglo-French relations from 1689 to 1815.

Strategic, maritime, and diplomatic histories that analyze the rise of Britain to the position of naval and commercial hegemony that it held from 1815 to 1939, usually begin with the first of four Anglo-Dutch wars and cover a chronology that runs to conclusive victory over the fleets of France and Spain at Trafalgar in 1805. That history need not be summarized here, but a long bibliography records the kingdom's armed conflicts and commercial rivalry at sea with almost all other European states with ambitions (or even pretensions) to naval power in the Channel, the North Sea, the Baltic, the Atlantic, the oceans and seas of Asia, and the Middle East; to colonies and bases anywhere; and finally, to shares of the profits derived from trade and servicing the international economy over the period from the First Navigation Act to victory at Trafalgar (1650–1805).

With France and Spain, animosity and conflict remained persistent and serious. By the time of the Treaty of Utrecht in 1713, other major maritime powers—Venice, Portugal, and Holland—had ceased to be serious rivals (although a Dutch navy made a brief and disastrous appearance as part of a French-inspired coalition against Britain during the American Revolution). With Russian, Sweden, Austria, Denmark, and Prussia, sporadic conflicts and diplomatic incidents erupted whenever and wherever their warships and programs for the expansion of navies appeared to threaten Britain's security and economic interests in the Baltic and North seas. Open hostility often occurred during times of Anglo-French warfare when the aristocratic governments, in tandem with merchants, utilized an increasingly powerful navy to regulate or interdict the seaborne trade of neutral ships with France and her allies and actively encouraged privateering (even piracy!) against their trade. This increasingly aggressive stance toward neutral commerce aroused antagonism even from European states resisting the ambitions of Bourbon, Revolutionary, and Napoleonic France on the mainland and led to defections from the coalitions sponsored by

Britain to preserve a balance of power, to retaliations against the kingdom's trade, and to the formation of naval alliances among states with small navies (armed neutralities) in order to resist attempts by the Royal Navy to interfere with their seaborne trade. British presumptions to "command the seas" led to a century of potential or actual conflict, not merely with the navies of France and Spain, but with those of Holland, Russia, Sweden, and Denmark as well. After granting independence to the United States, the Hanoverian state refused to allow the new republic to opt (as it did for a time during the world wars of the twentieth century) to remain neutral and to profit by trading during the endemic conflicts among Europe's great powers. For the first and last time, Anglo-Saxon navies were informally and formally at war from 1804 to 1814.

Born in 1879, Heckscher matured at a time when Pax Britannica and the Royal Navy guaranteed the freedom of national economies to trade even in wartime and when Victorian imperial and commercial policy actively promoted the removal of barriers to international movements of commodities, capital, labor, and technologies. As a classical Anglophile liberal, Heckscher was disposed to represent Napoleon and his admirers as misguided mercantilist architects of an ultimately futile continental system. But that system could be properly understood only as a chapter in a much broader and longer-run narrative in Europe's geopolitical history in which Britain occupied top position as the most consistent and enduringly successful mercantilist state of a warlike period from 1688 to 1815. His anglocentric account of the Continental System cannot be accommodated within perceptions held by European powers (and the United States) of the geopolitical and commercial power retained by Britain for decades before and throughout protracted conflicts with Revolutionary and Napoleonic France. Indeed, most "Britons" made no secret of their mercantilist ambitions. Advocates for a blue water strategy had long recommended that the security of the realm and the growth of the economy could be best maintained by high levels of investment in the navy. Apart from Adam Smith and his precursors, most mainstream British economists of the day linked profit to power and advised their ruling elites to allocate rising volumes of fiscal resources (appropriated by the state for the prosecution of warfare) in ways that redounded clearly to the benefit of the nation's commerce, industry, employment, and expansion overseas.

After the Cromwellian protectorate, British monarchs and their aristocratic advisers (who made foreign and strategic policy almost without reference to parliament and public opinion) accorded top priority to the stability of the Hanoverian regime and the security of the kingdom. But in addition kings and queens, statesmen and their satraps of mercantilist advisers, commentators, and intellectuals made no secret of their strategy (which sometimes coincided with their motives) for waging war against other European powers. For whatever reason, once at war, kings, aristocrats, parliamentarians, merchants, and all patriotic Britons expected the forces of the crown to secure territory, bases, assets, and access to markets out there in blue waters overseas and for the economy to emerge from persistent engagements in expensive geopolitical conflicts with enlarged shares of the returns obtainable from trade and from servicing an expanding international economy.

Apart from maintaining Hanover, British foreign policy excluded claims to territory on the mainland and eschewed alliances with commitments to and affirmative enmity toward any continental power, provided its rulers did not threaten the realm and its possessions overseas, either by building up large navies or occupying ports along the North Sea coastlines of Holland and the Netherlands from where military invasions might be effectively launched to land troops on the beaches of East Anglia.

With the largest fleet in Europe at its command, the Hanoverian state pursued objectives that simultaneously preserved the security of the realm and ensured that the massive allocations of resources to the Royal Navy became acceptable to taxpayers and looked profitable for the economy at large. First and foremost, heavily armed ships of the line, constituting the bulk of the British fleet, remained stationed at sea or docked in readiness at Plymouth, Portsmouth, Torbay, and other harbors to guard the Western Approaches to the English Channel, to escort convoys in and out of their home waters, and to blockade French naval bases at Brest, St Malo, La Rochelle, and smaller ports facing England, such as Boulogne, Dieppe, Le Havre, and Dunkirk. Another home fleet patrolled the North and Baltic seas to intimidate and, when necessary, to strike preemptively at the smaller naval forces constructed by Holland, Denmark, Sweden, Russia, and other powers, which might develop from a potential to a real threat to British interests. Over time the Royal Navy also utilized a string of bases and "friendly" stations around the Mediterranean (including Lisbon, Gibraltar, Minorca, Malta, Naples, Sardinia, and Sicily) to bottle up French and Spanish warships at anchor in Toulon and Cadiz, to protect convoys from Barbary pirates and Ottoman hostility and (from offshore) threaten the possessions of Venice, Austria, and France in the Italian peninsula. As the Royal Navy built up a permanent presence in waters, bases, and stations to the west, north, and south of the European mainland, the Hanoverian state found itself commanding maritime power that became overwhelming during the Napoleonic War. But long before Trafalgar, it could curtail the access of France, Spain, and Holland to their empires overseas and, with impunity, attack their colonies in Asia and the Americas and degrade their commerce on the Atlantic, Indian, and Pacific oceans with a measured, but rather minimal reallocation of cruisers, frigates, and sloops to distant theaters of war.

During and, particularly, at the close of every conflict, when settlements were negotiated (by way of treaties signed at Ryswick, Utrecht, Aix, Paris, and Vienna), mercantilist advocates of a more extensive, intensive, and profitable blue water strategy complained that British statesmen had neither pursued economic warfare to its cost effective limits nor cashed in on the spoils derived from the superiority of their powerful navy. Monarchs and aristocrats who formulated strategies for warfare and negotiated for peace and stability probably held a shrewder appreciation of the limitations of navies. They certainly paid closer attention to the political conditions required to hold fast to conquests overseas and to maintain a balance of power and allies on the mainland. They also sought to contain the widening and deepening anxiety among European states toward Britain's "maritime despotism."

Such labels and perceptions of "Perfidious Albion," which had arisen early in the eighteenth century, represented a widespread European antagonism to the strategies pursued by Britain to achieve "power and profit" within a mercantilist order of competing national economies. Europeans observed a consistent British antipathy to any commitment of troops to support allies on the mainland. If and when British (or, more often, foreign troops, paid for by the London exchequer) became engaged in such battles, they tended to be withdrawn without consultation or due notice. Dishonorable subsidies to mercenaries became, as Josiah Tucker suggested, cost-effective options for the British state and its taxpayers to pursue. At sea, several maritime rivals (including Venice, Holland, Portugal, Denmark, and Russia) chafed under the increasingly subordinate status of their navies and deeply resented the presumption to stop, search, and regulate neutral trade with Britain's enemies in times of war. Long before the extensive, sustained, and economically disastrous European conflict instigated by Revolutionary and Napoleonic France, the view from the mainland had hardened into a realization that time and again Britain emerged from the succession of geopolitical conflicts with its naval power, economy, empire, and commerce with Asia, Africa, and the Americas, enhanced at the expense not merely of Spain, France, and Holland, but of the rest of the continent as well. No wonder "all Europe gloated when George III lost his thirteen colonies in the Americas" and that the celebration on the mainland for Nelson's great victory at Trafalgar seemed "muted and confined." As well it might, because by 1808 Britain had captured all remaining French and Dutch colonies, destroyed the fleet and bombarded the capital of neutral Denmark, intimidated Sweden and Russia, and established protectorates over Iberia, Minorca, Sicily, Malta, and the Ionian Isles. Howicke, Britain's Foreign Secretary, boasted that "No other power shall have any intercourse with the Continent. The sea is ours.... There is but one navy in the World, the British Navy." When a Swedish historian visited the kingdom in 1803, be reported on Britain as "a nation whose thirst for gain and narrow egotism have stifled everything beautiful and noble."

Perfidious and greedy Albion are perceptions that crop up time and again in the discourses of statesmen, diplomats, travelers, and commentators of the day. Only the fears aroused by Louis XIV and more intensely and widely by Jacobinism and Napoleon led to favorable views of England as an ally against social revolution. However, at the time, few among the European elite bought into the rhetoric of English statesmen who represented the conflict as a struggle of "freedom against tyranny." They were more likely to be comforted by Pitt's "war for the defence of property" and inclined to form prudential alliances with a succession of Tory cabinets who believed that "rule by a favoured and privileged minority was part of the natural order of things, sanctioned by God, justified by prescription, enforced through the moral authority of the church."

Eli Heckscher's classic account inclines to a representation of the continental system as peculiarly malign and misguided outgrowth of Napoleonic mercantilism. Since he wrote, the historiography of

Europe's long and complex record of geopolitical warfare has reconfigured *le blocus* as a rather desperate response (by the French empire after another predictable defeat at Trafalgar) to reconstruct some alternative strategy that might conceivably undermine Britain's command of the seas and possibly generate the kind of fiscal and financial crises that had destroyed another ancien regime in 1789. Only modern Whigs (who have failed to comprehend the undemocratic structure of the Hanoverian state and its promotion of a repressive culture of loyalty to an aristocratic regime, and to deny its serious abnegations of constitutional rights and liberties during both the American and French Revolutions) now represent the struggle with France in xenophobic rhetorics of the day.

The Royal Navy and the Defeat of the Continental System

Thus, the Continental System can be reconfigured within geopolitical history in order to show that it can neither be persuasively represented as an episode in a struggle between liberalism and tyranny nor understood with reference to any system or general theory of mercantilism. Furthermore, the failure of the French blockade can no longer be comprehended without wider and deeper analysis of two British weapons primed and geared for persistent engagement in warfare. The first is the relative power of the Royal Navy, and the second includes the resources (especially credit) at the disposal of the most consistently effective fiscal state in Europe.

Of course, Heckscher recognized that to arrest the entry of exports to foreign markets and to control the procurement of imports from overseas could only have been simpler and cheaper to achieve for a maritime power, enjoying command of the seas, than for an embryonic European empire—with strictly limited methods and means for guarding its coastlines and monitoring the enforcement of French-inspired imperial decrees by satellite, client, and allied governments. Indeed he observed astutely that "coercive measures in the sphere of commercial policy have at all times found a palliative in smuggling. But that palliative was used to an infinitely larger extent now that coercion acquired a range previously undreamt of and outside the limits of France proper it represented a foreign dominion and lack moral support in all classes of the community." Most historical literature on the operation of the Continental System has been concerned to explain how, when, why, and with what degrees of difficulty and fluctuation British trade with

Europe (and the Americas) continued, despite attempts by customs, police, and military forces to control its flow between the Berlin decree of November 1806 and the Battle of Leipzig in 1813. What Heckscher and other historians have not covered in anything like the same detail or explained is the much greater degree of success that attended efforts by the Royal Navy to blockade the seaborne trade of France, Spain, Holland, the Netherlands, Denmark, and other enemies on the mainland, and especially with their colonies in Asia, Africa, and the Americas.

Throughout the wars from 1793 to 1815, all trade overseas between Europe and the rest of the world became even more tightly subjected to a framework of regulations promulgated and enforced by the Hanoverian state. Although the Royal Navy could forcibly arrest and degrade enemy trade, British statesmen experienced political and legal difficulties in dealing with "neutral" ships carrying "neutral" cargoes into and from the continent in wartime. With vacillating and varying degrees of flexibility and diplomatic concession, they refused to recognize that neutral ships carried neutral goods and ordered the Navy (and encouraged even more self-interested captains and crews of licensed privateers) to implement its orders in council and to operate under letters marque that authorized them to stop and search ships and to confiscate cargoes branded as contraband. This highly contentious area of economic warfare led, as it had in previous wars, to the formation of armed neutralities, the alienation of Denmark and Russia, and retaliation followed by open war with the United States between 1806 and 1814. Yet Heckscher's classic text displays a lack of appreciation for the role played by the Royal Navy in: (1) stimulating Napoleon and his advisers to embark on a futile allocation of resources designed to close European markets to British exports; (2) creating conditions at sea and in maritime ports whereby the competitive advantages of employing British ships and middlemen to transport merchandise by sea moved demand radically in their favor; and (3) lending the indispensable assistance of its firepower and intelligence to the British mercantile marine, endeavoring to circumvent Napoleon's Continental System.

The transparent success for maritime compared to military power in waging economic warfare has also long deserved more elaboration on the relative scale and efficiencies of navies in an age of mercantilism. For long stretches of the Second Hundred Years War, with its "natural and necessary enemy," Britain enjoyed superiority at sea over the

French fleet and over the combined fleets of several European powers. More than any other single factor that well established and carefully maintained comparative advantage enabled the kingdom to defeat Napoleon's Continental System. Yet any advantage that persisted for more than a century (between 1689 and the Treaty of Ghent in 1814), needs to be explained and not taken as given as national advantages often are by theorists of international and interregional trade.

Although they might originate in some ultimate sense in geopolitical endowments (such as an island location with abundant natural harbors), comparative advantages are never entirely natural. They are in some degree man-made, accumulate through time, and are usually path-dependent. Their significance can, moreover, only be properly comprehended by way of complex exercises in comparative history. Thus, British superiority at sea (which had matured to become overwhelming during the Napoleonic Wars) can only be understood with reference to the relative backwardness of rivals, particularly the French navy, but also the navies of Spain, Holland, Russia, Denmark, Sweden, and the United States (or any conceivable alliance of foreign naval forces) to countervail the Royal Navy's sustained command of the seas! Despite his extraordinary range of erudition, derived from his deep knowledge of the European literature on mercantilism (which is replete with information and analysis of power, including sea power), this metaquestion held virtually no interest for Eli Heckscher. Nor has it attracted much attention from scholars of the military revolution in European history. In the absence of an explicitly comparative historiography designed to specify and, where possible, measure salient differences, my list of suggestions are based on limited data, the perceptions of contemporaries, and the views of naval historians as to why Britain became and remained Europe's hegemonic naval power for more than two centuries after the Treaty of Utrecht in 1713.

First and foremost, in peace and war alike, the British governments consistently devoted higher proportions of their total income (taxes plus loans) to the Royal Navy. Since total revenues (taxes appropriated and money borrowed by that regime) placed the British state clearly at the head of the European league tables for fiscal and financial prowess, the priorities accorded to public expenditures upon maritime power could be translated into scalar magnitudes that would reveal the degree to which public investment by successive Governments on the warships, canon, manpower, harbors, docks, bases, inventories, victuals, organization, and technologies required for a larger and more effective navy exceeded comparable expenditures undertaken not merely by France, but, also for long periods, by the Bourbon alliance of France and Spain combined. From time to time France (and Spain) attempted to catch up with Britain, but previous centuries (1494–1659) of dynastic warfare had eroded the fiscal and financial bases the Bourbon's required to support sustained programs of naval rearmament. In any case, the geopolitical preoccupations of Bourbon, Napoleonic, Habsburg, and other continental regimes remained with the defense of frontiers and territorial aggrandizement, which seriously constrained shares of fiscal resources that could be reallocated from military to naval, commercial, and imperial objectives—a constraint that "perfidious" British diplomacy (backed by subsidies to European allies) maintained and strengthened.

Meanwhile, the history of the realm's navy from 1650 to 1815 can be represented as a record of growth accompanied by ever-increasing efficiency. That trend ended at a position from where the Royal Navy commanded the seas and oceans of the world throughout the Revolutionary and Napoleonic wars. The trend did not proceed monotically, was not achieved without difficulty, and suffered setbacks and reverses (particularly during the American rebellion, when the Royal Navy confronted the combined fleets of all its major European rivals). Nevertheless, and looking back over a period of 127 years from the vantage points of Trafalgar and Waterloo, the records show marked increases in the absolute (and relative) size of the fleet; clear changes in the scale, functional variety, and firepower of its battleships; and a progression in the numbers of experienced and skilled seamen mobilized for warfare and discernible improvements in the organization of the navy.

Progression rested upon the development and a highly effective maritime policy, designed and pursued to defend an island kingdom from invasion from the mainland and at the same time to degrade and obstruct both enemy and neutral trade by sea during decades of conflict. Heckscher and his cohort of economists, who tended to view any form of mercantilism through opaque lenses beautifully ground by Adam Smith, never perceived how mutually reinforcing and ultimately promotional for the development of the domestic economy the political priorities accorded by successive monarchical and aristocratic governments to ever high levels of public expenditure on the Royal Navy eventually became.

For example, although the Glorious Revolution of 1688 reaffirmed the traditional right of Parliament to modify, and even turn down, requests from the Crown for taxes and loans, it never refused supply. Members of the House of Commons certainly retained traditional English suspicions of standing armies as instruments of royal (and, within their living memories, republican) despotisms. Navies allayed that suspicion and avoided popular resistance to mass conscription and disorders associated with the demobilization of unemployable unskilled males. Warships and their crews could defend the realm effectively (on deferred pay) from offshore and most seamen could be reabsorbed in the mercantile marine of the end of wars. Such complimentaries and externalities became more numerous and flowed in both directions between every section of the domestic economy engaged with coastal, seaborne trade and fishing on one hand and the Royal Navy on the other. For example, the protection accorded by armed frigates and sloops to convoys of merchant vessels against enemy warships, privateers, pirates, and other predators on the high seas is familiar. Entry to markets abroad and the enforcement of contracts could be secured by the presence of ships of the line from offshore and if necessary by salutary bombardments of foreign ports and their fortifications. British naval bases along sealanes provided havens and reassurance for merchants and investors that their ships, cargoes, plantations, buildings, and connections overseas could secure some defense from "their" increasingly powerful national navy. In wartime, when fresh demands for protection and retaliation intensified, British merchants, shippers, and investors in markets, colonies, and sources of supply outside the realm welcomed the destruction of rival plantations and colonies as well as the interdiction of enemy and neutral competition for intercontinental trade. During conflicts when normal commerce became too dangerous or unprofitable to pursue, many firms (involved directly or indirectly through chains of feedbacks with overseas trade) could obtain compensatory profits by diversifying production into meeting intensified demands from the Royal Navy for the construction of cruisers, frigates, sloops, and other warships; for the hire of extra shipping capacity required for privateering and as transport for the army and navy; for dealing in timber, masts, hemp, pitch, tin, copper, and other stores needed for the construction, repair, and maintenance of warships at Plymouth, Portsmouth, Chatham, Deptford, Sheerness, and other royal dockyards; and supplying ordnance, small arms, and victuals. The reallocation of complementary resources (especially seamen) between the mercantile and armed marines stabilized the system and maintained the strategy of export-led growth upon which the long-term growth of the economy depended.

Thus the growing and increasingly effective presence of the Royal Navy operated to reduce risks associated with commerce and investment overseas and imparted a measure of stability to foreign trade, afflicted by the recurrence of irregular, but all too predictable bouts of economic warfare. In this sense, the Royal Navy and the Mercantile Marine, together with all the manifold commercial services and manufacturing linked to commerce overseas, could be represented and analyzed as a single interdependent sector of a national economy, connected horizontally and vertically to preserve the security of the realm and to maximize the gains from overseas trade and imperialism.

Political arithmeticians, mercantilist intellectuals, and other precursors and successors of Adam Smith wrote in unabashed ways about the connections between sea power and profit. At the end of every war many published balance sheets of ships and their cargoes lost and gained through the systematic use of violence at sea. They lauded peace treaties that retained the conquest of territories, particularly islands and maritime bases overseas, which strengthened the capacities of the Royal Navy to protect British commerce and to strike at the trade of enemies (and neutrals alike) in forthcoming wars. If, as they often did, aristocratic statesmen made concessions and returned bases, islands, colonies, and fishing rights as part of European settlements, their less than ruthless pursuit of potential long-term economic gains from trade and colonization usually provoked vociferous criticism from the Commons, the press, and an increasingly xenophobic nation of "Britons" entranced with the power of their navy to inflict humiliating defeats on the French and all other "foreigners." Almost nobody questioned the need to spend ever-increasing sums of money to construct, man, and maintain floating fortresses that would remain superior in scale and efficiency to the fleets of rival powers. Monarchs, ministers, parliament, the clergy, the press, poets, novelists, playwrights, and the public at large rarely displayed anything but pride in the officers and seamen who defended their liberties, religion, properties, and interests overseas. Tropes, images, medals, paintings, and fictional heroes celebrating Britannia's "rule of the waves," its "ship of state," gallant officers, and jolly jack tars proliferated across the classes and testify to a national consensus of approbation for a dominant, well-managed, and modern navy long before Nelson and Napoleon appeared on the scene. With occasional widely publicized lapses (which could be followed by salutary executions on the quarter deck) Britain's ancién regime, whose strategic imperatives were subjected to little more than parliamentary applause and public loyalty, provided Britons with the navy they demanded, enjoyed, and derived profits from. By the time war broke out with Revolutionary France, the political nation certainly recognized that the advantages derived from more than a century of sustained public investment in sea power conjoined with foreign trade and imperialism had cumulated to provide the Hanoverian state with security, combined with virtually unchallengeable hegemony at sea.

When that sustained quest for security culminated in total victory at Trafalgar, Napoleon really had little choice but to gamble on an unenforceable and unworkable Continental System. Reasons behind the failure of a strategy born of frustration and desperation—which the customs officials, police, and troops of the French Empire attempted to enforce with limited and oscillating degrees of success over a seven-year period (1806–13)—can now simply be mentioned. They are, after all, well surveyed by Heckscher and elaborated in greater depth and detail by Crouzet's definitive study of *le blocus*. First and foremost, the emperor and his advisers must have been actively aware of the enormous difficulties that all ancién regime governments, however powerful and determined, had experienced in their attempts to restrain smuggling. Bribery, corruption, duplicity, and the discovery of alternative ports, inlets, beaches, and offshore islands had long been the commonplace methods used by merchants, investors, and shippers to land and distribute commodities designated as contraband by mercantilist laws and decrees. For decades the British and other European states had found that the regulation of trade could only secure acceptable degrees of enforcement and compliance if: (1) the transportation of goods by sea could be cordoned into recognized ports; (2) large-scale companies of merchants monopolized regulated trades; (3) tariffs and duties were maintained at moderate ad valorem levels; (4) customs services were maintained with the manpower, integrity, and efficiency required to contain smuggling; and (5) these services possessed the cutters, seamen, armaments, and information required to apprehend contraband at sea.

Not a single one of these five preconditions favored the effective implementation of the Berlin, Fontainebleu, and Milan decrees. Even within France, the coastline of the Napoleonic Empire was not defendable, while central control and persuasion exercised from Paris over the administrations of satellite and client regimes hardly became more than tenuous. Above all, the more rigorous and efficient blockade by the Royal Navy and the active participation of its cruisers, sloops, and frigates along the sealanes and seaboards of every country in Western, Northern, and Southern Europe, protecting and guiding the smuggling of merchandise originating in Britain and its empire onto the continent doomed the strategy long before Napoleon took his Grand Army into Russia. Yes, the Continental System certainly increased the difficulties and losses from trade with the mainland, and as Crouzet documents, led to downturns in the British economy in 1807–8 and 1810–12. Yet the Royal Navy saw to it that the risks of interdiction at sea by the customs vessels, privateers, and warships of the enemy were minimized—which implied that the profits obtained from taking these risks by continuing to trade with Europe and the Americas became larger and more concentrated in the hands of British investors, merchants, and shippers.

Britain's Remarkable Fiscal and Financial Weapons

As Chaptal and his other advisers recognized (and Napoleon appreciated), the real (and perhaps the only) prospect for the Continental System resided in the economic impact that the more or less immediate oscillations and potentially significant reductions in British and colonial exports might exercise on three variables of direct and immediate concern to a state subsidizing and funding armies of British and foreign troops on the mainland, while maintaining command of the seas. To those key connections—the fiscal base for taxation, the capacity to borrow on London and European capital markets, and the supply of money and credit—this conversation finally turns.

Eighteenth-century wars became, as Henry Dundas observed, "contentions of the purse." Certainly the fiscal and financial resources at the disposal of the Hanoverian state aroused the anxiety and envy of sovereigns all over Europe. Napoleon sensed that a concentrated attack on these "sinews of British power" might not cripple but could seriously undermine the capacity of his enemy to continue to fund protracted warfare. For Pitt the Younger, Addington, Petty, and Vansittart (successively chancellors of the exchequer responsible for the government's fiscal, financial, and monetary policy during the long conflict with France), the funding required for the war in general and for the

incremental funding for the intensified risks that accompanied overseas trade in 1806–13 in particular, emanated from three intercon-
nected sources: taxation, irredeemable loans, and the short-term
credits provided by an evolving system of banks connected to the London money market presided over (but not controlled) by the Bank of
England.

Alas, it is not entirely clear from Heckscher's book (or subsequent
scholarship) on how Napoleon and his advisers on strategy conceived
of the operational mechanisms through which even a partially effective
blockade of the mainland might have constrained the fiscal and financial capacities of the British government to continue to wage war by
land and sea. French views that national economies dependent on
overseas commerce were inherently more vulnerable and unstable
than countries (like France) based more widely and securely upon agricultural and industrial production, for domestic markets remained
commonplace long after 1789. Napoleon's own correspondence and
pronouncements on the accumulation of sovereign debt and diffusion
of paper money ("the greatest foe of the social order") present little
more than the anxieties of a generation who had lived through the
debt crises of the ancién regime and the collapse of the assignats in the
early years of the Revolution. Those same anxieties afflicted most English statesmen, politicians, pamphleteers, and economists (including
Smith, Torrens, Lauderdale, Horner, Thornton, King, and, above all,
Ricardo) who all published gloomy prognostications about the relentless accumulation of the kingdom's national debt that doubled in
nominal value during the American rebellion and more than doubled
against between 1793 and 1803. Indeed, so deep was public anxiety
after the loss of the thirteen colonies that in 1786 Pitt had instituted
what the prime minister and Parliament regarded as "inalienable" or
"quasi-constitutional" provisions for the complete redemption of the
national debt by means of a sinking fund linked to the imposition of
permanent taxes, designed to operate during interludes of peace and
years of war alike. Clearly a persistent and substantial reduction, in
the volumes of domestic and colonial exports and re-exports of foreign
merchandise carried in British ships for sale to markets on the mainland could have had seriously adverse effects on the government's
ability to borrow money and to mobilize taxation from customs duties
levied on imports and from excises imposed on domestic products that
were exported directly (or embodied as inputs in the goods and services sold) to Europe and the United States. Nevertheless, the short-

run cyclical effects on total revenues from taxation hardly show up in the data and could not in any case have seriously disabled the British war effort, because the Hanoverian state's system of exemptions, drawbacks, and bounties operated to exclude almost all exports and re-exports (except coal) from any adverse effects flowing from indirect taxation. By way of multiplier and macroeconomic effects, only revenues from the income tax suffered directly and "somewhat" from downswings and slowdowns in exports. Although aggregate receipts from the tax (introduced by Pitt in 1799, and which provided something like 40 percent of the incremental revenue required to prosecute against Napoleonic France in 1803–15) continued to rise, the total amount collected under Schedule D from business profits remained virtually stable for some six years between 1806 and 1813.

Pitt's introduction of the first income tax not only marked an innovation in taxation, but also represented a clear change in the government's traditional strategy for the funding of protracted warfare. Between 1699 and 1799, five major conflicts had been funded overwhelmingly by borrowing on the London capital market. While approximately two-thirds of the incremental or wartime revenues allocated to forces of the Crown and their allies fighting Napoleonic France emanated from taxation. That new strategy had been introduced to contain the accumulation of the national debt; to allay the anxieties of investors about the decline and instabilities in the values of their portfolios of government stocks; and to rebuff hostile propaganda predicting (as Tom Paine did as early as 1796) the imminent collapse of Britain's uniquely efficient funding system.

Unlike his major enemy, Napoleon supported his armies and navies with entirely limited recourse to loans and certainly regarded the accumulation of debt as potentially dangerous to the safety of any state. Although he paid attention to matters of finance, it is not clear how much credibility the Emperor reposed in the predictions of European (including radical British) intellectuals, and his own advisers and ministers that the relentless accumulation of debt servicing obligations, even by the fiscally successful Hanoverian regime, could (and indeed would shortly) lead (as excessive borrowing had many time before in the political history of ancien-régime Europe) to some kind of fiscal and financial crisis of that state. French hopes and anticipations went up and down with fluctuations in the prices of bonds on the London capital market. Clearly, interludes of depressed confidence in the capacity of British governments to defend the realm against threats of invasion, to contain French military hegemony on the continent, and to appropriate enough taxes to service its mounting burden of debt, led to sharp falls in prices of government bonds publicly quoted in London. At the same time, a string of naval victories, Wellington's successes in the Peninsula and Napoleon's defeats at Moscow and Leipzig led to declines in rates of interest the Treasury paid to borrow the money required to cover the gap between tax revenues and total expenditures. Furthermore, for more than a century, the prices of bonds had risen high at the end of every war. Whatever Napoleon and his advisers anticipated, no correlation can be detected between monthly movements in the prices of government stocks and exports and re-export recorded as shipped to markets on the mainland. Between the Berlin decree of November 1806 and the Battle of the Nations in October 1813, the sinking fund operated as Pitt proposed to "assure" investors that some share of the taxes collected by the Hanoverian state would remain permanently on the statute book and committed to debt redemption. At the same time, chancellors of the day continued to raise rates of taxation in order to curtail demands for loans and to feed the sinking fund. Nevertheless, while the Continental System operated, the Treasury obtained some £172 million by floating irredeemable bonds on the London market at rates of interest that ranged between 4.3 percent and 5.8 percent— slightly lower than interest burdens incurred for heavier annual demands for loans during the wars against the thirteen colonies and Revolutionary France. Interestingly, rates peaked during years of invasion scares (1797–98 and 1805), when doubts about the Royal Navy's ability to defend the realm and its system of property rights loomed larger in the rational expectations of investors.

Napoleonic hopes of precipitating some kind of fiscal and financial crisis of the Hanoverian state by arresting or even curtailing its access to taxes and loans by way of an onshore and hardly enforceable blockade, certainly failed. Britain's taut and overstretched sinews of power held firm, while troops and embodied militias ruthlessly suppressed Luddism and all other social protests that occurred during the cyclical downturns in economic activity that accompanied the years of "difficulty" (1808 and 1810–12) when Napoleon's blockade, together with the actions of hostile governments in Washington, did indeed depress the flows of British and colonial exports and re-exports to the mainland and to North America.

Heckscher recognized that the normal way that otherwise efficient firms and mercantile houses dealt with temporary interruptions is to find ways through and round the obstacles placed by governments in the way of the smooth and continuous flows of exports and imports (and their counterpart payments)—moving from sources of supply (along chains of transport, distribution, and credit) to consumers. Of course, this was precisely how he analyzed how British merchants, shippers and producers responded to the Continental System. What he neglected to emphasize was the indispensable help they obtained from the Royal Navy. He did not elaborate on how their response involved the redesign of their day-to-day operations to deal with more circuitous chains of distribution and transportation; protracted and expensive delays between production and consumption; substantial increases in the uncertainties that attended commerce with Europe and the Americas and with an unavoidable need to stockpile (imports as well as exports) of commodities on an abnormal scale.

Above all, what Heckscher clearly failed to appreciate was that British political and "entrepreneurial responses" to the blockade were underpinned by an indispensable extension of medium-term loans, credit, and liquidity from a monetary system that had evolved in scale and scope within a wartime framework of regulations that freed the central bank (loosely connected to an interdependent system of London and country banks) from the traditional restraints of a fully convertible currency.

All previous wars from 1689 onward had been fought within the albeit flexibly interpreted rules of the gold standard. At a moment of threat, occasioned by the landing of French troops on Welsh soil, and following on from nearly two years of repeated warnings from the directors of the Bank of England that the level of their bullion reserves would no longer allow them to meet rising demands from both the state and the private sector for reserve currency (bank notes and deposit), in 1797 the prime minister persuaded a reluctant parliament, recalcitrant monarch, and exceedingly nervous body of public opinion to suspend the Bank of England's obligation to redeem its outstanding liabilities *in specie*.

Suspension passed off without disturbance, and for the rest of the war through to resumption in 1819, the army, the navy, the treasury, and other departments of state, as well as the entire private economy, conducted their transactions with government paper, commercial bills of exchange, bank notes and deposits, drafts, promissory notes, and other forms of "soft" money, with a surprising degree of confidence and absence of difficulty. The suspension of convertibility aroused antipathies from nervous economists and conservative politicians as well as opposition from radical opponents to anything that added to the potential authority of an aristocratic and monarchical state. Yet Britain's wartime monetary regime's successful evolution into another sinew of power amazed European diplomats and stimulated Napoleon's ministers to advertise its fragility and to predict its imminent downfall. For a state engaged in costly, protracted, and worldwide expenditures on warfare, access to elastic and acceptable supplies of paper credit quickly transformed suspension into a "measure of unquestionable convenience." Although Pitt and his successors as chancellor of the exchequer resolutely opposed any suggestion that they should legislate a framework of regulations, stipulating how an embryonic central bank might exercise some measure of control over the aggregate supply of money, their advice and examples in offering short-term government loans to hard pressed British and colonial businessmen in 1793, 1795, 1797, 1799, 1807, 1808, and 1811 led the bank's directors to suppose that their proclaimed policy of "meeting the needs of trade with prudence and discretion" while supporting the more pressing and unavoidable demands from a state at war enjoyed complete ministerial, parliamentary, and business approval. With the exception of some critical murmurings from Malthus and Henry Thornton in 1801 and from Lords, King, and Petty (who fancied their credentials as economists) three years later, almost no debate surrounded the conduct of monetary policy by the bank and the treasury until David Ricardo published his three famous letters to the *Morning Chronicle* in the fall of 1809—a year when Napoleon's military dominance over major powers, clients, and reluctant allies on the mainland looked almost total and a moment when prospects for the reinvigoration of a European-wide exclusion of Britain's domestic and colonial exports from continental markets seemed (and indeed subsequently became) more promising.

Ricardo's letters inaugurated widespread and sustained "clamour" among the "chattering classes" about the operation of Britain's wartime monetary regime, which subsequently became famous in the history of economic thought as the bullion controversy. Unsurprisingly, the appearance of Ricardo (Heckscher's "most acute of economic theorists"), Thornton, Malthus, Horner, and a plethora of minor figures in the history of economic thought deploying Hume's specie flow mechanism, citing Adam Smith, and using the rigorous rhetoric of classical liberal theory to expose the errors of their mercantilist opponents in a serious

debate about monetary policy, diverted Heckscher and made it difficult for him to think his way into the geopolitical context of warfare
and parameters surrounding a debate in macroeconomic policy.

In effect, his mediation and representation of the bullion controversy
crosses from economics to politics to support the theoretical and virtually ahistorical and apolitical positions adapted by Ricardo and his bullionist followers. In an otherwise erudite work of historical scholarship
concerned with origins, operations, and outcomes of the Continental
System, Heckscher (with some cautious asides and qualifications)
treated a major political controversy about monetary policy in wartime
as an opportunity to participate in a discourse about monetary theory.
He concentrates, as bullionists did at the time, in lending his authority to unverified and essentially unverifiable hypotheses as to why
(after some twelve years of a satisfactory experiment with an inconvertible currency) an "unregulated" and "excessive" increase in the
supply of paper money had led inexorably to price inflation, the substitution of bullion for other commodity exports, and a depreciated
rate of exchange.

It would be unfair and anachronistic to marshal modern macroeconomic theory (particularly the unsettled contentions in monetary
theory) against "primitive monetarist" explanations for observed and
(now more carefully calibrated) movements in prices, outflows of specie, and fluctuations in the external value of sterling, or to point out
that Heckscher shared Ricardo's pre-Keynesian ideology, opposed to
all discretionary monetary regimes.

Historians will agree that bullionist tests for what the latter represented as irrefutable indicators of "excessive," "dangerous," and even
"unnatural" increases in supplies of paper credit are worth discussing
and connecting to the operation of the Continental System. Most
would now, however, reject the post hoc support that Heckscher,
Viner, and a long line of economists have accorded to Ricardian and
monocausal monetarist explorations for currency depreciation from
1809 to 1813. They will observe that several other cyclical climatic and,
above all, geopolitical factors also operated on the macro economy at
that time. Any model or historical account that derogates or fails to
consider data, and to offer informed conjectures about the significance
of major and multiple influences operating on the British balance of
payments, levels of relative prices, the rate of exchange, the state of the
kingdom's gold reserves, and the world market price for bullion between 1809 and 1813 now seems parsimonious to the point of losing

touch with the complex realities of six years marked by extreme but temporary political and economic difficulties. Of course, the data required to isolate and test impact of monetary policy upon relevant, properly specified and measured dependent variables will never become available, but the elements for the construction of a rounded explanation or "model" were all brought forward during three years of protracted controversy at the time. They were, moreover, dealt with again in depth and historical perspective by Joseph Lowe, Thomas Tooke, and other political arithmeticians immediately after the war, when Ricardo's views on convertibility became hegemonic among the political elite and classical economists alike.

While the Continental System remained in operation, so many other influences and variables operated on prices, rates of exchange, and the world market price for gold that it is difficult to understand why Heckscher gave Ricardo's analysis on the primacy of "excessive" increases in the realm's supply of paper money such a privileged position in his text. Although Heckscher hardly mentioned the relentless elevation of tax rates and the intensified demands from the army and navy for manpower and resources, he did deal carefully with the seriously deficient grain harvests of 1808–10 and 1812–13 and noted Napoleon's insistence that British merchants must be compelled to pay *in specie* for corn and any other imports purchased from France and other European suppliers. His analysis also considered the heightened (but fluctuating) demand from the British government for gold coins, required to subsidize allied armies and Iberian guerrillas in combat with French troops on the mainland and to fund local payments by the largest British army committed since Marlborough to serve in a European theater of war. Nevertheless, and coming to what he conceived to be a simpleminded mercantilist obsession with the accumulation and conservation of bullion, as a great historian of early modern economic thought, Heckscher's inclination was to derogate the now extensively documented difficulties experienced by Wellington, Kotusov, and Blucher, not to mention Napoleon and his bevy of generals, and indeed by all military commanders in theaters of war right across Europe, who expropriated when possible and purchased when necessary the food, transportation, horses, equipment, and shelter for their troops from local suppliers and attempted to pay using bills of exchange and promissory notes drawn on distant governments. That ubiquitous payment problem plagued Wellington throughout his time in the Peninsula, even though his commissaries could draw bills on a relatively stable and reliable government in London. Not least because soldiers

(especially mercenaries and guerrillas) expected to be regularly remu-
nerated in coin, otherwise desertions and even mutinies could occur.

From the perspective of his own peaceable liberal age of more rapid
and unimpeded transportation by land and sea, of well-functioning
institutions to facilitate trade, and of multilateral payments across the
frontiers of European countries, Heckscher approached the predicament and difficulties of the British government in finding sufficient
specie to fund military payments overseas from the standpoint of
an outstanding theorist of international trade and payments inclined
to take as given the institutions built up over centuries for well-
functioning systems for multilateral commerce and payments. Yes, Pitt
and other chancellors could and did (as he suggested) reduce their
(obsession with!) dependence on bullion by employing merchants and
bankers (like the Rothschilds) to facilitate transfers of subsidies to foreign governments and payments by Wellington's army in the Peninsula through negotiable instruments, drafts, and bill of exchange.
Nevertheless, the serious constraints of global warfare and impediments to trade, interrupted and delayed flows of exports and imports,
tightened constraints, and thereby inflated both mercantile and military demands for specie. Fortunately, the inconvertible currency regime introduced by Pitt in 1797 allowed the state to allocate whatever
specie it could acquire in an endeavor to meet vigorous demands from
Wellington and his Spanish guerrillas in the Peninsula, as well as the
insistence by the realm's fickle partners (Austria, Prussia, Russia, Portugal, and Spain) who had joined fragile coalitions against France that
they preferred military aid in the form of hard currency rather than
goods or bills of exchange that their agents would inevitably be left to
negotiate (at no small discount) through the embryonic institutions of
a traditional international payments system. In the closing years of the
Napoleonic War (1809–14), that system came under severe pressure
from the extension and intensification of military campaigns all over
Europe, from fiscal demands for taxes and increased propensities to
hoard gold and silver as well as the impediments interposed in the
way of commerce by sea by the retaliatory embargoes and privateering
of the United States, by the British naval blockade of the mainland, and
(albeit far less effectively) by the onshore blockade of the Continental
System.

In such circumstances it is difficult to comprehend the equivocal, but
unconvincing support that Heckscher gave to the analysis and recommendations of Ricardo and the Bullion Report submitted to Parliament
in 1810. Could his position stem from an unqualified admiration for

Ricardo, from his own scholarly concerns to expose errors in mercantilist thought concerned with the balance of trade and bullion flows, or might the great Swedish economist have been fundamentally committed to demonstrating the heuristic and universal validity of theory regardless of time, place, and context? In this case, and because the controversy arose as a direct outcome of a challenge launched by Ricardo and the bullionists against the foundations and operations of a wartime monetary regime, Heckscher's contradictory support for his great classical predecessor now reads as the least convincing historical argument in the book.

Historians may not now repeat his view that the "dislocation" (and particularly the dislocations of 1808 and 1810–11) "was overcome by itself without any measure at all worth mentioning," that "British measures were limited to an issue of treasury bills for £6,000,000 for the support of embarrassed businessmen." That is a "large" sum, and why forget the Royal Navy? Furthermore, under sustained and rigorous criticism for maintaining a regime of inconvertible paper currency and confronted with the Select Committee of the House of Commons (dominated by economists) who recommended that the Bank of England should proceed to a resumption of specie payments within two years, Perceval, Vansittert, Castlereagh, and other statesmen reminded their critics time and again that the flexible monetary system was temporary, necessary for the continued prosecution of the war, and of real assistance to merchants and businessmen engaged in countervailing attacks on British and colonial trade by Napoleon and his allies, including the United States.

When Heckscher observed, moreover that "Napoleon was right to read the success of his war against the credit of England in the decline of the exchanges and in the difficulties of payment," he repeats points made by Francis D'Invernois to Herries (Wellington's commissary in the Peninsula) and to Spencer Perceval, the prime minister. D'Ivernois, a British agent, studied French newspapers, corresponded with contacts in France, and argued that the Bullion Report strengthened Napoleon's resolve to maintain the Continental System and prompted politicians in Washington to assume a "haughty and peremptory tone towards Great Britain." He quoted the *Paris Journal*: "the day on which the London Bank will be compelled to resume will be the day on which it will feel the full effects of the Berlin and Milan Decrees."

Given his anglocentric sympathies, Heckscher arguments in support of Ricardian positions in the bullion controversy are puzzling. He wielded Ockham's razor in order to agree with Ricardo that exports of gold did not arise from remittances on government account (which he asserted were probably self-equilibrating) or from "corn imports or all else" that the Continental System as such was not one of its principal causes; that Europeans did not need to make international payments in gold or silver. Heckscher reached for a bullionist and monocausal explanation that gold was exported to replace commodities because its purchasing power was higher in Europe than in the United Kingdom, and Ricardo's focus on the "super abundant circulation" provides an "account which goes to the root of the matter and can be regarded as conclusive in all essentials."

Years later, Heckscher's contemporary and another great historian of economic thought, Jacob Viner, took essentially the same line with Silberling's detailed objections to the bullionist arguments. Like Heckscher, Viner believed the British government could have prevented the depreciation of the exchange rate and the discernible rise in the market above the mint price for gold. As Viner represented the matter, "It was primarily because under the paper standard the English currency was not contracted as it would necessarily have been contracted under a metallic standard that foreign remittances resulted in such a market depreciation of the paper pound on the exchanges." With similar but less excusable academic detachment from their own times of crises, Ricardo and other monetarists maintained that it was precisely because under the paper standard, credit was not contracted as it would have been before the suspension of 1797 that such problems as the blockade of European and American markets, unusual grain imports, heavy purchases of Baltic stores, the widespread hoarding of precious metals, disorganized markets for international payments, military expenditures, subsidies to foreign armies, or any other reason advanced by supporters of official policy had resulted in an increased market price for gold and depreciation in the rate of exchange. Such criticism is unanswerable. All it means is that a sufficiently vigorous deflation of the money supply will, in any situation, preclude divergence between the market and the mint price for gold and restore an exchange rate to its established parity.

Yet by the end of his discussion on currency and credit (chapter IV), Heckscher equivocates and comes round to a recognition that "the very conception ... of metallic resources for the credit of a country with a paper currency lacks support both in theory and practice." He also backtracks to suggest complacently that "whether the remedy" (resumption of specie payments) "would have been less harmful than the disease" (a superabundant paper currency) "after the depreciation had gone so far is not easy to say."

Yet at the time, ministers of the Crown as well as Napoleon and his economic advisers had no doubt that implementing the proposals of the Bullion Committee would seriously compromise Britain's capacity to wage war on land and sea against France. Indeed, when the implications of following Ricardo became clear, several members of the Bullion Committee, including Henry Thornton (Hayek's favorite economist), Huskisson, and Canning, changed their positions. During the closing years of the Napoleonic Wars, when any loss of confidence in paper assets denominated in sterling could impair the realm's ability to finance military and naval expenditures and the capacities of merchants to run the gauntlets of Napoleonic blockades and American embargoes, critics also began to make invidious comparisons between the depreciated notes of the Bank of England, the assignats of Revolutionary France, the "forced paper" of the Habsburg monarchy, and the Congress of the United States. Ministers immediately recognized the dangers of a vocabulary that represented the directors of the Bank of England as irresponsible profiteers, the Bank's issues as "excessive" and "superabundant" and its bank notes as "depreciated." They mounted a concerted counterattack to assure British and foreign investors that Ricardian analysis was misleading and no risks attached to holding and transacting in sterling.

Just four years after the final defeat of Napoleon at Waterloo, tradition reverence for the sanctity of specie money reasserted its hold on the official mind. Ricardian analysis of how best to reconstruct and operate a monetary regime assumed a position of unquestioned hegemony in the parliamentary and ministerial discourse concerned with the economy's incompetently handled transition to fully convertible currency. The bank's directors moved rapidly to restore the value of sterling to its pre-1797 parity deflated the currency, redistributed incomes in favor of aristocrats and other rentiers on fixed incomes, and afflicted the kind of dislocation on the economy that would surely have promoted the cause of Napoleonic France during those difficult years before Leipzig and Waterloo.

Conclusion

I conclude my tribute to Heckscher's classic study of the Continental System by suggesting that his treatise combines many of the virtues of historical scholarship with the myopias of economic theory and the ideological biases of a classical liberal. It has been a privilege and a pleasure to converse with such a great and stimulating intellect.

Bibliographical Appendix

The editors of this volume agreed that it would not be necessary or indeed appropriate for me to footnote this essay because it has been constructed as a "conversation" with Eli Heckscher about the way he chose to write his scholarly study of the Continental System in 1917.

Except in the third part of my essay, which is directly concerned with British fiscal, financial, and monetary policy in the wars against Revolutionary and Napoleonic France, I did not confront, qualify, amend, or supplement Heckscher's scholarship on this famous and strategic episode in economic warfare from 1806 to 1813. The second edition of François Crouzet's magnum opus *L'Economie Britannique et le Blocus Continental* (Paris, 1987) and his chapter in this volume has performed that task so comprehensively that only details remain to be covered in any greater depth and sophistication.

I have opted instead to depart from Heckscher's preferred context in the histories of economic warfare and mercantilism and to "reconfigure" the Continental System as an episode in the Second Hundred Years War between Britain and France for domination of the Atlantic economy and global commerce. In short, my purpose has been to relocate Heckscher's classic text within a modern geopolitical historiography concerned with the rise of Britain's state and national economy in rivalry with other leading European powers—particularly France.

Since Heckscher wrote *The Continental System* and his famous history of mercantilist thought, historians have constructed a new metanarrative to explain why the United Kingdom became the most successful mercantilist state and economy over the period 1689–1815 and retained that hegemonic status in geopolitics down to World War I. This bibliography has been structured and selected to reference and reflect three themes of a modern metanarrative in which the Napoleonic Continental System has been reconfigured as part of broader and longer British and European geopolitical histories: namely, as chapters on mercantilism, on navies, and on fiscal military states. The bibliography will be brief and includes only up-to-date texts with bibliographies that refer to further reading and lines for research.

European Mercantilism and Geopolitics, 1689–1815

Aerts, E., and F. Crouzet, eds., *Economic Effects of the French Revolutionary and Napoleonic Wars* (Leuven, 1990)

Armitage, D., *The Ideological Origins of the British Empire* (Cambridge, 2002)

Baugh, D. A., "Great Britain's Blue Water Policy, 1689–1815," *International History Review* X (1988): 33–58

Black, J., *Convergence or Divergence? Britain and the Continent* (Basingstoke, 1994)

———, *A System of Ambition: British Foreign Policy 1660–1793* (London, 1991)

———, *European Warfare 1660–1815* (London, 1994)

———, *Britain as a Military Power 1688–1815* (London, 1998)

Coleman, D. C., ed., *Revisions in Mercantilism* (London, 1969)

Contamine, P., *War and Competition Between States* (Oxford, 2000)

Crouzet, François, "The Second Hundred Years War: Some Reflections," *French History* 10 (1996)

———, *Britain Ascendant: Studies in Comparative Franco-British History* (Cambridge, 1990)

Crowhurst, P., *The French War on Trade: Privateering 1793–1815* (Loughborough, 1985)

Davis, R., *The Rise of the English Shipping Industry in the 17th and 18th Centuries* (Newton Abbot, 1972)

Davis, R., *The Rise of Atlantic Economies* (London, 1973)

———, *The Industrial Revolution and British Overseas Trade* (Leicester, 1979)

Dickinson, H. T., ed., *Britain and the French Revolution* (Basingstoke, 1989)

Ellis, G. J., *Napoleon's Continental Blockade: The Case of Alsace* (Oxford, 1981)

———, *The Napoleonic Empire* (London, 1991)

Emsley, C., *British Society and the French Wars 1793–1815* (London, 1979)

French, D., *The British Way of Warfare 1688–2000* (London, 1990)

Glete, J., *Navies and Nations: Warships, Navies and State Building in Europe and America* (2 vols., Stockholm, 1993)

———, *War and the State in Early Modern Europe* (London, 2002)

Gomes, L., *Foreign Trade and the National Economy: Mercantilist and Classical Perspectives* (London, 1987)

Hampson, N., *The Perfidy of Albion* (London, 1998)

Harvey, A., *Collision of Empires: Britain in Three World Wars, 1793–1945* (London, 1992)

Holsti, K. J., *Peace and War: Armed Conflicts and the International Order 1648–1989* (Cambridge, 1991)

Horn, D., *Great Britain and Europe in the 18th Century* (Oxford, 1967)

Hutchinson, T. W., *Before Adam Smith: The Emergence of Political Economy* (Oxford, 1988)

Johnson, D., et al., *Britain and France: Ten Centuries* (Folkestone, 1980)

Jones, J. R., *Britain and the World 1649–1815* (Brighton, 1980)

———, *The Anglo-Dutch Wars of the Seventeenth Century* (London, 1999)

Kennedy, P., *The Rise and Fall of the Great Powers* (London, 1988)

Kindleberger, C., *World Economic Primacy 1500–1900* (Oxford, 1996)

Liss, P. K., *Atlantic Empires: The Networks of Trade and Revolution 1783–1826* (New York, 1983)

McKay, D., and H. M. Scott, *The Rise of the Great Powers 1648–1815* (London, 1983)

Marshall, P. J., ed., *The Oxford History of the British Empire: The Eighteenth Century* (Oxford, 1998)

O'Brien, P. K., *Power with Profit: The State and the British Economy 1688–1815* (London, 1991)

———, "Mercantilism and Imperialism in the Rise and Decline of the Dutch and English Ecnomies," *De Economist*, 148 (2000): 469–501

O'Gorman, F., ed., Britain and Europe: A special issue of *Diplomacy and Statecraft*, 8 (London, 1997)

Ormrod, D., *The Rise of Commercial Empires: England and the Netherlands in the Age of Mercantilism* (Cambridge, 2003)

Padfield, P., *Tide of Empires: Decisive Naval Campaigns in the Rise of the West* (2 vols., London, 1979 and 1982)

Parkinson, C. N., and A. Fayle, *The Trade Winds: A Study of British Overseas Trade During the French Wars 1793–1815* (London, 1948)

Tracy, J., ed., *The Rise of Merchant Empires* (Cambridge, 1990)

———, *The Political Economy of Merchant Empires* (Cambridge, 1991)

Semmel, B., *Liberalism and Naval Strategy* (London, 1986)

Smith, A., *Creating a World Economy: Merchant Capital Colonialism and World Trade 1400–1825* (Boulder, 1991)

Steele, I. K., *The English Atlantic 1675–1740* (London, 1986)

Stone, L., ed., *An Imperial State of War: Britain from 1689 to 1815* (London, 1994)

Teichova, A., and H. Matis, eds., *Nation, State and the Economy in History* (Cambridge, 2003)

Tilly, C., *Coercion, Capital and European States AD 990–1900* (Oxford, 1990)

Wallerstein, I., *Mercantilism and the Consolidation of the European World Economy 1600–1750* (New York, 1980)

Williams, J. B., *British Commercial Policy and Trade Expansion 1750–1850* (London, 1972)

Wilson, K., *The Sense of the People: Politics, Culture and Imperialism in England 1715–85* (Cambridge, 1995)

Winch, D., and P. K. O'Brien, eds., *The Political Economy of British Historical Experience 1658–1914* (Oxford, 2002)

The Royal and Rival European Navies, 1660–1815

Acerra, M., et al., eds., *Les Marines de Guerre Européennes XVII–XVIIIe siècles* (Paris, 1985)

Acerra, M., and A. Zysberg, *L'essor des marines de guerres européennes, vers 1680–vers 1790* (Paris, 1997)

Allen, D. W., "The British Navy Rules: Monitoring and Incompatible Incentives in the Age of Fighting Sail," *Explorations in Economic History* 39 (2002): 204–231

Baugh, D., "The Eighteenth-Century Navy as a National Institution," *Oxford Illustrated History of the Royal Navy* (Oxford, 1995)

Black, J., and P. Woodfine, eds., *The British Navy and Use of Naval Power in the Eighteenth Century* (Durham, 1988)

Buchet, C., *Marine, Économie et Société: Un exemple d'interaction: l'auitaillement de la Royal Navy Durant la Guerre de Sept ans* (Paris, 1999)

Coad, J., *The Royal Dockyards, 1690–1850* (Aldershot, 1989)

Cookson, J. E., *The British Armed Nation 1793–1815* (London, 1997)

Crowburst, P., *The Defence of British Trade 1688–1815* (Aldershot, 1977)

Dixit, A., "Incentives and Organizations in the Public Sector," *Journal of Human Resources* 37 (Fall 2002): 197–205

Duffy, M., ed., *Parameters of British Naval Power 1650–1850* (Exeter, 1992)

Gardiner, R., *Frigates of the Napoleonic Wars* (London, 2000)

Goodman, D., *Spanish Naval Power 1589–1665* (Cambridge, 1996)

Gray, C. S., and R. W. Barnett, eds., *Seapower and Strategy* (Annapolis, 1989)

Hall, C. D., *British Strategy in the Napoleonic Wars* (London, 1992)

Harding, R., *The Evolution of the Sailing Navy 1509–1815* (London, 1995)

Horstein, S., *The Restoration Navy and English Foreign Trade* (London, 1991)

Kennedy, P. M., *The Rise and Fall of British Naval Mastery* (London, 1976)

Lavery, B., *The Arming and Fitting of English Ships of War 1600–1815* (London, 1987)

————, *Nelson's Navy: the Ships, the Men and Organization 1793–1815* (London, 1989)

Lincoln, M., *Representing the Royal Navy: British Sea Power 1750–1815* (Aldershot, 2003)

Morriss, R. A., *The Channel Fleet and the Blockade of Brest* (Burlington, 2001)

————, *Naval Power and British Culture 1770–1840* (Aldershot, 2004)

Roberts, D. H., ed., *18th Century Shipbuilding: Remarks on the Navies of the English and the Dutch* (Rotherfield, 1992)

Rodger, N. A. M., *The Wooden World: An Anatomy of the Georgian Navy* (New York, 1986)

————, *The Safeguard of the Sea: A Naval History of Britain 660–1649* (New York, 1998)

————, "Form and Function in European Navies 1660–1815," in J. Akveld et al., eds., *Maritiem-historische Studies* (Amsterdam, 2003)

Starkey, D., *British Privateering Enterprise in the Eighteenth Century* (Exeter, 1990)

Syrett, D., *Shipping and the American War 1775–83* (Exeter, 1970)

Tunstall, B., and N. Tracy, eds., *Naval Warfare in the Age of Sail: The Evolution of Fighting Tactics* (Annapolis, 1990)

Wilson, J. Q., *Bureaucracy: What Government Agencies Do and Why They Do It* (New York, 1989)

The Fiscal and Financial Foundations of the British State, 1485–1815

Ashton, T. S., and R. S. Sayers, eds., *Papers in English Monetary History* (Oxford, 1953)

Bonney, R., ed., *Economic Systems and State Finance* (Oxford, 1995)

———, *The Rise of the Fiscal State in Europe 1200–1800* (Oxford, 1999)

Bowen, H. V., *War and British Society* (Cambridge, 1998)

Braddick, M. J., *The Nerves of State: Taxation and Financing the English State 1558–1714* (Manchester, 1996)

Brewer, J., *The Sinews of Power: War, Money and the English State, 1688–1783* (London, 1989)

Cameron, R., *Banking in the Early Stages of Industrialization: A Study in Comparative Economic History* (Oxford, 1967)

Cannan, E., *The Paper Pounds* (London, 1925)

Collins, M., *Money and Banking the United Kingdom: A History* (London, 1988)

Comin, P., et al., eds., *The Formation and Efficiency of Fiscal States in Europe and Asia* (Cambridge, 2006)

Crouzet, F., *L'Économie Britannique et le Blocus Continental* (Paris, 1987)

Daunton, M., *Trusting Leviathan* (Cambridge, 2003)

Dickson, P. M. G., *The Financial Revolution in England: A Study in the Development of Public Credit 1688–1756* (Aldershot, 1993)

Erhman, J., *The Younger Pitt: The Consuming Struggle* (London, 1996)

Feavearyear, A. E., *The Pound Sterling* (Oxford, 1931)

Fetter, F. W., "The Politics of the Bullion Report," *Economica* 26 (1959): 99–130

———, *The Development of British Monetary Orthodoxy* (Cambridge, Mass., 1965)

Gayer, A. D., et al., *The Growth and Fluctuations of the British Economy 1750–1820* (2 vols, Oxford, 1953)

Hoffman, P. T., and K. Norberg, eds., *Fiscal Crises, Liberty and Representative Government* (Stanford, 1994)

Kynaston, D., ed., *The Bank of England: Money, Power and Influence 1694–1994* (Oxford, 1995)

Lovell, M. C., "The Role of the Bank of England as a Lender of Resort in the Crises of the 18th Century," *Explorations in Entrepreneurial History* 10 (1957): 8–21

McCusker, J., and K. Morgan, *The Early Modern Atlantic Economy* (Cambridge, 2000)

Neal, L., *The Rise of Financial Capitalism: International Capital Markets in the Age of Reason* (Cambridge, 1990)

O'Brien, P. K., "The Impact of the Revolutionary and Napoleonic Wars, 1793–1815, on the Long Run Growth of the British Economy," *Review XII* (1989): 335–436

———, "Fiscal Exceptionalism: Great Britain and Its European Rivals from Civil War to Triumph at Trafalgar and Waterloo," D. Winch and P. K. O'Brien, eds., *The Political Economy of British Historical Experience 1658–1914* (Oxford, 2002)

Ormrod, M., ed., *Crises, Revolutions and Self-sustained Growth: Essays in European Fiscal History* (Stamford, 1999)

Pressnell, L. S., *Country Banking in the Industrial Revolution* (Oxford, 1956)

Price, J., *Capital and Credit in British Overseas Trade 1700–76* (Cambridge, Mass., 1980)

Roseveare, H., *The Financial Revolution* (London, 1991)

Silberling, J., "British Financial Experience, 1790–1830," *Review of Economics and Statistics* 1 (1919): 282–297

Sraffra, P., ed., *The Works and Correspondence of David Ricardo* (3 vols., Cambridge, 1951–73)

Tilly, C., ed., *The Formation of States in Western Europe* (Princeton, 1975)

Tooke, T., *Thoughts and Details on High and Low Prices 1793–1822* (London, 1824)

Tooke, T., and W. Newmarch, *History of Prices 1792–1837* (6 vols., London, 1838)

Tracy, J. D., ed., *The Political Economy of Merchant Empires* (Cambridge, 1991)

Viner, J., *Studies in the Theory of International Trade* (London, 1955)

Wood, E., *Theories of Central Bank Control* (Cambridge, Mass., 1939)

Part VI

Eli Heckscher and Swedish
Economic History

16 Swedish Industrialization 1870–1930 and the Heckscher-Ohlin Theory

Lennart Schön

Sweden represents one of the most successful examples of industrialization from the late nineteenth century onward. In this essay, Swedish development from 1870 to 1930 is discussed from two sets of forces inherent in the Heckscher-Ohlin theorem. Simplified, they can be denominated either as external, exogenous forces related to the evolving open economy or as internal, endogenous forces within the Swedish economy. On one hand, Swedish industrialization can be viewed mainly as a reaction to international factor-price equalization with relative price increase of abundant factors in Sweden, favoring the export sector, increasing competition on the domestic sector and reshaping income distribution. On the other hand, the industrialization can be viewed mainly as a creative response by indigenous, endogenous traditions and industrial knowledge to new circumstances—including, of course, the ability to integrate ideas and entrepreneurial talent from abroad. These perspectives are also related to contemporary macroeconomic theories of growth as well as to microeconomic and Schumpeterian theories of structural change. The relative importance of these forces over time in Swedish industrialization is addressed in this essay.

Two Perspectives on Industrialization from the Heckscher-Ohlin Theorem

To Eli Heckscher, market integration or internationalization in a broad sense was a primary factor behind successful Swedish industrialization. Internationalization had many dimensions—new institutions were established from the mid-nineteenth century when markets were integrated with expanding trade and a new mobility of capital and labor, new ideas flew from Western Europe into Sweden, and there was a technology transfer with the factory system in focus. Thus, integration brought the market economy and capitalist institutions more firmly into Sweden.

The Heckscher perspective on industrialization is particularly attached to the role of trade and more specifically expressed in the so-called Heckscher-Ohlin theorem or the theorem of factor price equalization in integrated markets.[1] When markets widen through integration of different national economies (in a process nowadays called globalization), relative prices will change in a systematic way. The flow of goods, labor, and capital will make prices and relative income levels converge within a globalized economy. In a given economy, prices of factors that prior to integration were relatively abundant will rise and consequently prices of scarce factors will fall. Thus, globalization will favor labor in labor-abundant economies and capital in capital-abundant economies. This mechanism of factor price equalization that Eli Heckscher and Bertil Ohlin presented is of course based upon the experience of market integration in the late nineteenth century and early twentieth century.

To Heckscher (and Ohlin) trade was the main force behind factor price equalization, since the mobility of the production factors was imperfect, especially the mobility of labor. Heckscher once noted that labor, next to land itself, was the least mobile of all resources— paradoxical that it may sound.[2] In particular, human capital as carriers of knowledge and traditions was regionally tied, a circumstance that created certain constancy in industrial specialization. Thus, trade was a substitute for labor mobility in the process of factor price equalization, while, with a modern concept, the social capability of a region had a lasting impact upon its economic behavior and development.

This remark opens, in a very broad sense, for two classical perspectives on the causes of the industrialization process, particularly in small countries such as Sweden. First, industrialization can be seen as caused mainly by the interaction with open-economy forces in the late nineteenth century globalization comprising the effects on the price structure that were spelled out as the Heckscher-Ohlin effects. In this interaction new opportunities were created to make use of abundant factors that met a rising and elastic foreign demand. Second, the industrialization process can be viewed as a development propelled primarily by the reactions of idiosyncratic, endogenous forces in the Swedish economy to new conditions, that is, internal traditions and country-specific knowledge came to interact with new market possibilities and with the flow of new technology from more developed economies.

Of course, every analysis that tries to explain the performance of a specific economy in this period should comprise both elements, but their relative magnitude may differ. In this essay, the open-economy forces and their impact upon Swedish factor prices will be discussed in relation to internal structures conditioning the comparatively rapid economic growth in the period 1870–1930.

Convergence or Divergence in Economic Growth

These two perspectives inherent in the Heckscher position and the Heckscher-Ohlin theorem are very much in focus in contemporary debate on industrialization or growth more generally, emphasizing either open-economy forces or endogenous forces of growth.

The Heckscher-Ohlin theorem is perhaps most strongly emphasized in analyses of globalization by Jeffrey Williamson and his collaborates. In these analyses of market integration or globalization in history, convergence of income levels and relative prices are at the forefront.[3] In computable general equilibrium models, based upon standard neoclassical economics with diminishing returns to the accumulation of factors of production, growth is not the direct object of study, but rather the contribution of factor mobility and trade to convergence and growth; convergence and growth run largely parallel. The reallocation of resources to more productive ends is the central mechanism in this analysis. According to Jeffrey Williamson, the interaction between labor, capital, and commodity markets should be in focus of studies in economic growth. Economic historians "should attack these issues first before elevating international technological transfer to the status of prime mover, a thesis so ably argued by Gerschenkron that it has dominated the convergence debate ever since."[4] Thus, one can draw the conclusion that in order to promote economic growth Williamson would prefer institutions of market integration rather than institutions that stimulate technological transfer.

The new growth theory that was launched within economics in the 1980s gives a very different perspective on the growth process and its outcome than traditional growth theory.[5] Through the accumulation of "broad capital" that includes knowledge, human capital, and innovations, technical change and growth were made endogenous to the process. Thus, knowledge was produced as any other investment good by the calculated use of labor and capital. In this perspective, institutions governing such investments come to the forefront. The inclusion of knowledge as a key factor and asset had further consequences. While other factors had diminishing returns and were consumed in the production process, knowledge grew when it was used. Furthermore, through externalities including spillovers and complementarities, the accumulation of knowledge was endowed with increasing returns. New complementarities arose through the advance of knowledge in different areas and new possibilities were created in the interaction between human capital and technology.

Convergence between economies at different income levels is not the logical outcome of a theory with increasing returns, externalities, and complementarities. Rather, it predicts divergence since initial differences are enlarged in an endogenously determined growth process with such characteristics.

There are of course modifications and qualifications of the two basic models that diminish the gulf between them. The concept of social capability emphasizes, for instance, that there are decisive socially determined differences in the ability to integrate productivity-increasing methods and to transform structures and thus differences in the ability to join convergence clubs at certain historical points of time.[6] This concept is very close to the arguments by Heckscher on the immobility of human capital and on the persistence of traditions behind regional differences in industrial development.

Innovations and Structural Change

The aspect of a creative response to new circumstances involves an analysis of the structural change in the industrialization process and of the creation of new innovating enterprises. Then the analysis is brought to a lower and more specific level than in the dominating macroeconomic models of growth referred to above. In a more microeconomic perspective, one may distinguish between two different types of firms (or industries) that are related to the two basic perspectives. On one hand, there are industries that mainly exploit the abundant factor in an economy taking advantage of the positive effect upon prices and income from market integration and international trade. These may be called Heckscher-Ohlin firms. On the other hand, there are firms (or industries) that exploit a specific innovation; such firms exploit knowledge that is specific to the firm and the entrepreneurs grasp these opportunities. These may be called Schumpeter firms.[7] In the present essay this typology will be used to further characterize Swedish industrial growth and industrial specialization.

At this point one should emphasize strongly that these juxtapositions of Heckscher-Ohlin and Schumpeter firms or of traditional and new growth theory with convergent/divergent behavior does not place Eli Heckscher firmly in any one of these boxes. In his analysis of Swedish economic development, Eli Heckscher was well aware of all of these aspects of growth. As noted earlier, Heckscher emphasized the paradox that knowledge, traditions, and human beings are the most stationary factors of production next to land, which formed a basis for the Heckscher-Ohlin theorem with trade as a substitute for factor mobility. From the same proposition, one could of course develop theories of, say, the role of firm specific knowledge in a regional context with spillovers and external effects of entrepreneurial behavior. Such insights are to be found richly in Heckscher's works. Furthermore, contrasting these two kinds of firms or industries does not mean that they develop independently of each other. Thus, over time relative price equalization may work to the detriment of original Heckscher-Ohlin industries and favor Schumpeter industries; that is, price changes by open-economy forces may favor structural change that is based upon internal factors.

The Schumpeterian analysis introduces a very different perspective that gives a contrast to both traditional and new growth theories. The behavior of the individual entrepreneur is in focus, and innovation is the prime mover behind economic growth. The motive is technological profits that may accrue to the entrepreneur for a passage of time due to imperfect monopolistic markets, but when innovations diffuse such profits melt away and markets become competitive. Thus, in the Schumpeterian perspective there is over time a dualism between the prime mover of growth and the workings of open economy forces. This perspective is fundamental to a Swedish tradition of analysis that focus both on relative price changes and the structural changes—that is, on the interaction between external and internal forces over time.

This Schumpeterian approach has been pursued and elaborated in Swedish economic history in mainly two successive ways. First, Erik Dahmén established the concept of development blocks. These were formed through complementarities around innovations that are at the center of the growth process.[8] Second, complementarity has further consequences that have been explored and elaborated in an analysis of growth performance and structural change with a model of structural change presented in works by Krantz and Schön and Schön.[9] Inventions may appear and knowledge accumulate at a rather constant pace, but their impact upon the economy vary very much over time due to properties such as complementarity and externality. Radical innovations that create important and far-reaching new complementarities as the steam engine, the railway, the electrical motor, the combustion engine, the motorcar, the microprocessor, and the Internet are rare, and their diffusion spread over long periods.[10]

The creation of new complementarities within a development block changes the relative price structure—as does market integration, but with another logic. In central areas of innovation, relative output prices will generally fall, intensifying competition against old combinations of production factors. The expansion of activities in the innovating areas will, however, increase demand for inputs of goods and services and for complementary production that are supplied less elastically and the prices of these goods will rise. Within the development block, remuneration to the factors of production will increase either as a consequence of increased productivity (supply push) or as a consequence of increased prices (demand push). Within old blocks remuneration will decrease.

Furthermore, complementarities around radical innovations appear suddenly and unexpectedly, despite the fact that the breakthrough has been preceded by a long period of innovative activity. The wider repercussions of the innovation that forms the development block make a new turn of events. Such was the case with the electronic revolution (the Third Industrial Revolution) following the advent of the microprocessor or with the Second Industrial Revolution following upon the accumulation of engineering and scientific knowledge at the end of the nineteenth century. In such periods of more rapid transformation, regions and nations react differently. There are clearly leading regions and nations, since innovations appear from the existence of geographically confined complementarities and externalities. Diffusion is more rapid to regions and nations that are favored by new demands, due to their resource endowments, their institutional characteristics, and their social capability. For the same reasons, the new turn of growth direction is unfavourable to other regions and nations. They may be firmly attached to old combinations and/or have endowments that are less advantageous under new circumstances. Under those conditions divergence will follow.

With more differentiated and sophisticated industrial production with stronger intra-industry ties and with closer contacts between producer and customer, the demand pushes at the early stage of innovation and diffusion will favor markets that are nearby geographically and socially, thus making the domestic market important.[11]

Over time, however, investments will make competencies, infrastructures, and institutions more generally adapted to the new complementarities. Hence the development blocks will be more widely diffused. Since further innovative activity (that is, economic use of potentially available new combinations from the accumulation of knowledge) is restricted by the structure of complementarities and interests created (that is, restricted by path-dependency), the accumulation of broad capital will be captured within the confinements of diminishing returns. Further growth will be more determined by diffusion of the new technology and by the working of the market mechanism. In that diffusion process, the favorable position of the leaders is undermined while laggards will improve their position. Thus, divergence in growth rates and income levels will turn into convergence (among countries involved in this process). In that same process, there will be factor price equalization and with greater transparency the price mechanism will be more important for the allocation of resources.

Thus, from this perspective the growth process may be periodized in two parts. The first period is characterized by radical transformation of structures when development in a geographical context is uneven with growth accelerating in small nuclei. The second period is characterized by rationalization when gaps are being leveled and the economy is made more homogenous with growth accelerating (to a certain point) in a wider context. Hence, divergence and convergence put their imprint on different phases and the new growth theory and the traditional evolve around properties that have characterized growth alternately. The Swedish position in an international pattern of convergence/divergence will be treated in this essay.

Factor Movements and the Convergence of Factor Prices

The second half of the nineteenth century witnessed a globalization with far-reaching consequences in terms of market integration and equalisation of factor prices. This development provided a rich soil for the Heckscher-Ohlin theorem that was based mainly upon experiences from the pre-1914 period of globalization.

Table 16.1

Annual growth in indexes of real wages and in GDP per capita in European countries and the United States, 1870–1910

Country	Real wage level 1870/1874 UK = 100	Annual growth of real wages 1870–1910	Annual growth of GDP per capita 1870–1910
Sweden	49	2.8	1.7
Denmark and Norway	49	2.6	1.3
France, Germany, and UK	84	1.1	1.2
USA	165	1.1	1.8
Italy, Portugal, and Spain	51	0.6	1.0

Sources: Real wages from Williamson (1995); GDP per capita from Maddison (1995).

The effects of integration upon relative factor prices were most clearly expressed in the relation between Europe and the United States. The relatively rich supply of both capital and labor in the old European economy met with new possibilities in the United States, while the price of the relatively scarce resource of land was depressed due to the competition from the land-rich United States. In the United States relative price movements of course moved in the opposite direction. Wages grew at a slower rate than GDP. Trade and factor mobility thus led to a convergence of prices.

These trends in Old and New World relations fit very well to the Scandinavian development and particularly to the Swedish one (table 16.1). From comparatively low levels at the beginning of the 1870s, Scandinavian real wages increase strongly up to 1910—much stronger than the GDP growth. In Scandinavia, globalization clearly favored the abundant factor of unskilled labor. Trade as well as mobility of capital and labor provides part of the explanation to this development.

In the Scandinavian countries, growth of investment and production accelerated from the 1850s. This growth was accompanied by growing deficits in the foreign affairs. Reconstruction of the trade balances indicates that there were large capital imports to Scandinavia, particularly to the economically leading countries of Denmark and Sweden.[12]

Sweden had a comprehensive and recurrent capital import from the 1850s until 1910. For Sweden a full estimate of the foreign debt—adding interest charges to the deficits in the trade balance—has been made. According to this estimate, the Swedish foreign debt was above

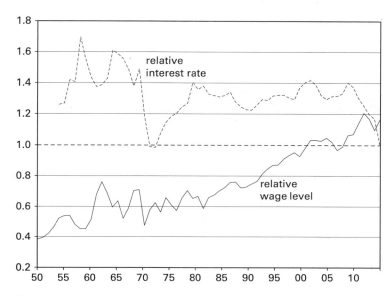

Figure 16.1
Interest rates and real wages in Sweden in relation to average interest rates (1855–1914) and wages (1850–1914) in Britain, France, and Germany
Source: Wages from Williamson (1995); interest rates from Homer (1977), Lindahl et al. (1937), and Schön (1994)

two-thirds of GDP around 1890, and it grew slightly faster than GDP until the war.[13]

Concomitant with the capital inflow, there was mass emigration from Scandinavia. In a global perspective the Scandinavian and particularly the Swedish position could be described as a mixture of the Old and the New World. In relation to the United States, Scandinavia had an abundant supply of labor, and mass emigration followed. In that perspective, Scandinavia was part of the Old World. The relation to the old industrial countries in Europe was different, however. In that respect, Scandinavia and particularly Sweden were rich of some natural resources while capital was scarce. Thus capital flowed to Scandinavia mainly through the emissions of bonds to develop her productive capacity.

These double flows of labor out of and capital into the country in combination with economic growth had profound consequences on Swedish relative prices (see figure 16.1). Relative capital/labor prices converged strongly between Sweden and the primary capital-supplying economies of Britain, France, and Germany. In the early stages of industrialization, Swedish interest rates were comparatively high with only a short interval of sharply rising Continental rates in conjunction with the war between France and Germany (1870–71). Swedish rates fell, however, somewhat in the long term and then dropped down close to the European level at the outbreak of World War I (and stayed low after the war). Swedish wages moved in the opposite direction. In the mid-nineteenth century the wage level has been estimated to be only half the average of the wage levels of Britain, France, and Germany in real terms. Relative wages in Sweden rose, however, particularly from the 1890s, when modern industrialization accelerated in Sweden. At the outbreak of World War I Sweden had become a country of comparatively high wages and low interest rates.

The strong rise in Swedish real wages was due not only to differences in relative nominal wage increases (the denominator of real wages) but also to a relative Swedish decrease in living costs thanks to trade (the nominator of real wages). Thus, trade had a particularly strong positive effect upon real wages in countries with rather barren soil such as Sweden. The impact from falling prices of grain upon income in agriculture was counteracted, however, partly by a transition to increased production of milk and meat and partly by tariffs that somewhat reduced the pressure toward structural changes in the economy.

Within Europe convergence was much weaker, which is clear from table 16.1. In Mediterranean Europe wages grew only very slowly and at a low level. It has actually been argued that convergence within Europe was insignificant for the world economy.[14] Convergence to the leading economies was to a great extent a Scandinavian phenomenon. As a matter of fact, there were parts of the European periphery that fell behind the leaders during the new surge of industrialization in the late nineteenth century. Thus economies in Europe diverged even in an era of reduced transactions costs internationally.

However, the classical gold standard era of 1870–1910 was not a very homogenous period from a growth perspective. As far as the trends of convergence/divergence are concerned, there was clearly a turning point around 1890. In the period 1870–1890, convergence was much more pervasive and growth rates much more even among countries—also in a Scandinavian/Latin European comparison (table 16.2). That was a period characterized by the decisive market integration that took place after the introduction of new institutions at mid-nineteenth century as well as the creation of a new infrastructure of

Table 16.2
Annual growth rates of GDP per capita in Europe and the United States, 1870–1910

Land	1870–1890	1890–1910
Scandinavia	0.9	2.0
United Kingdom	0.9	0.9
Spain, Portugal	0.9	0.7
Italy		2.1
Continental Europe	1.0	1.3
United States	1.6	2.0

Note: Continental Europe = Austria, Belgium, France, Germany, the Netherlands, and Switzerland.
Sources: see table 16.1.

railways, steamships, and telegraph cables. It was an expansion built upon innovations of the First Industrial Revolution (the steam engine with the factory system) and the ensuing infrastructure development and upon the complementarity between an industrial center and a largely raw material producing periphery. From 1890, development changed character, however. While growth of GDP and wages accelerated in Scandinavia (as in the United States), it decelerated in Latin Europe (and stagnated in the United Kingdom). Development diverged both in the European periphery and in the Atlantic core countries. There was divergence also within Latin Europe. The economies of Spain and Portugal stagnated almost completely, while there was a strong industrial spurt in Italy from around the turn of the century that within Italy served to increase the differences between the northern and southern regions even more.

The diverging growth rates from 1890 reflect different reactions to the new basis that was created for growth with the so-called Second Industrial Revolution. Manufacturing industry became more sophisticated with a more central role to engineering and science. Abramovitz and David stated that this decade meant a new basis for growth in the United States.[15] In the nineteenth century, and particularly 1850–1890, American growth could by and large be explained by the accumulation of the traditional factors of production—of land, labor, and capital. Capital accumulation was of particular importance in enabling a growing labor force to take into use the abundant resources of land. But from 1890 the importance of that accumulation diminished. From this point of time human capital became all the more important to the increase in growth rates and to a sustained increase in the productivity of the traditional factors (that is, in total factor productivity). Thus, the center of industrialization shifted from the building of railways, factories, and homes to the development of competent labor and management. The returns from investments in knowledge and education increased. A similar new turn was pointed out by Goldin and Katz that found a new complementarity between capital and skills arising in the United States in combination with the first wave of electrification.[16]

At the other extreme, United Kingdom failed to accelerate in the Second Industrial Revolution. According to Crafts, British capitalists behaved quite rationally when they accommodated to comparative advantages established from the First Industrial Revolution with comparatively high productivity within low-skilled manufacturing industries.[17] A failure to adopt new technologies has also been attributed to the high degree of British integration in the world markets, particularly in the financial market that gave weak linkages between risk capitalists and British industry.[18] One could also claim that Britain had already experienced some of the companions of the Second Industrial Revolution—such as accelerating urbanization and institutional changes—that were important in other parts of the world, which reduced the strength of the wider development block in the British case.

In continental Europe there was a western group consisting of France, Belgium, and the Netherlands with "close-to-UK" growth rates and only weak acceleration from the 1890s, and a central group of Germany, Austria, and Switzerland with "close-to-Scandinavian" growth from 1890. Thus, we find a sphere of Western Europe at the Atlantic from the United Kingdom down to Spain and Portugal with weak performance in the Second Industrial Revolution 1890–1910; in the core Atlantic economy, the initiative had gone west to the United States. In the other direction there was a strong central axis from Scandinavia (particularly Sweden with the new engineering industries) over Germany and Switzerland down to northern Italy, with Sweden and Italy matching U.S. growth rates.

The transformation of the late nineteenth century meant a shift in weight of factors. The First Industrial Revolution had, for instance, a strong reliance upon coal. The new technology and organization spread from England to Belgium, northern France, and western Germany, and the area of coal deposits made up the industrial core. With the technological shift in power generation from the 1890s, resources of coal became less strategic. Established structures may even have put up a resistance to change. On the other hand, in regions and countries endowed with hydropower and/or petroleum new expectations were raised and new profitable ends were opened. However, such a structural change required openness to new possibilities, flexibility in allocation of resources, an innovative bent, and supply of competence in new areas (this is no different from the First Industrial Revolution or from any major structural transformation, but each has its own configuration of forces). This essay will not go further into the background of the differing European reactions to this industrial revolution. It will only emphasize that the classical gold standard era holds two distinct periods that may not show up in aggregate growth rates. It also emphasizes that the reactions to the Second Industrial Revolution were strongly diverging among European countries, a divergence that seems to be due to idiosyncratic forces. This new divergence created scope for convergence at a higher level than the convergence of 1870–1890, a convergence that was to be delayed due to war and disintegration of markets until after World War II.

Thus, Scandinavian countries and Sweden in particular could benefit from the globalization and the European integration in the nineteenth century in order to achieve rapid economic growth. The industrialization of the Scandinavian countries with emigration, capital imports, and expanding foreign trade is largely a success story. Their success makes up a contrast to, for instance, the experiences on the Iberian and Balkan peninsulas, where capital imports are held to result not in development but rather in dependence upon the creditors and in restrictions upon further growth.[19]

Swedish Structural Change from the 1890s

From the 1890s, the Swedish economy became part of the transformation broadly called the Second Industrial Revolution. This structural change had two main components. First, industrial growth accelerated relative to the growth of the primary sectors of agriculture and forestry. Thus a new urban industrial economy expanded. Second, the industrial sector was upgraded. There was a shift from semimanufactured or traditional industrial commodities to more sophisticated goods.

At first sight, one might say that there was a clear continuity in Swedish specialization within this structural change. Traditional primary sources were refined. The exports of oats declined already in the 1880s and were replaced by increasing export of butter, made possible by the diffusion of the separator, invented by Gustaf de Laval, among other things. The export of timber and sawn wood stagnated while the production of chemical pulp and wood-based paper grew explosively. Similarly the traditional production of iron and steel grew only slowly, while new engineering industries emerged and grew successfully, many of them at the very frontier of the time, within the field of electrotechnology.

Undoubtedly this profound structural change was spurred by the new relative prices in the Swedish economy, in line with the Heckscher-Ohlin theorem. The initial specialization to the world market had been underpinned by relatively low prices of unskilled labor and of natural resources. That was no longer the case. The elastic demand for Swedish staple export goods had early on sustained growth and attracted foreign credit. It was no longer possible to sustain an industrial growth on that basis. Higher wages, more expensive timber, and new sources of hydropower propelled a profound technical and structural change within the characteristic commodity lines in Sweden.

One could say that this was merely an adaptation to new relative factor prices. However, logical as it may appear in face of the price change, one may turn the logic the other way around. One may also hold that it was the appearance of a new, more sophisticated industry with higher value added per worker that made it possible to keep up the relative increase in wages. That is logical, particularly since Swedish real wages continued to increase when the catching up process was completed after the turn of the century. Swedish growth became part of the new divergence that became even stronger after World War I (figure 16.2). Furthermore, in a microeconomic perspective one should emphasise that the new enterprises arose from new initiatives independently of old established interests. It was not old sawmills that turned to pulp and paper confronted with new set of prices. It was not old iron works that turned to engineering. Rather, the new industries emerged through independent entrepreneurial initiatives that took advantage of possibilities arising in the market by launching innovations, thus exploiting firm-specific knowledge. There was a shift from industries based on natural resources to knowledge-based industries, that is, from Heckscher-Ohlin industries to Schumpeter industries.

One can characterize Swedish industrial specialization in this Second Industrial Revolution as exploiting knowledge and innovations within

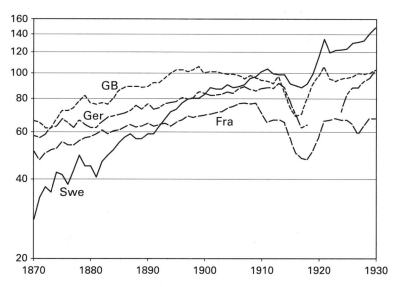

Figure 16.2
Real wages in France, Great Britain, Germany, and Sweden, 1870–1930
Great Britain wages 1905 = 100
Source: Williamson (1995)

the fields of power and communication, particularly related to energy-intensive processes and to electricity (both low and high voltages). This knowledge did not appear independently of old industries, though. Rather, it was knowledge that had been highly demanded by traditional Swedish industries and related to her natural conditions (vast country, energy-intensive processes, and rich supply of wood fuel and waterpower). It was also formally developed in technical universities in the second half of the nineteenth century.

There are indications that the relative price of labor did change, not only in an international perspective but also within Sweden (see figure 16.3). According to available wage series for unskilled and skilled municipal workers, the Swedish convergence to international wage levels was accompanied also with a convergence within Sweden between wages for unskilled and skilled labor up till the late 1910s. Available series indicate a similar development within iron industry with a stronger wage increase for the unskilled than the skilled labourer from 1870 to 1914. This may seem surprising, taking into account the more rapid growth of new skill-intensive industries that should have shifted labor demand within industry in this direction. There are, however, a

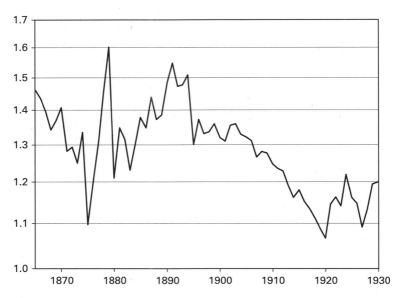

Figure 16.3
Skill premium of municipal workers, 1865–1930
Stockholm 1865–94; all towns 1894–1930
Source: Bagge et al. (1933)

couple of circumstances that can explain this seemingly paradoxical development. First, emigration that was on a high level up until World War I did probably lower the supply of unskilled labor relatively to skilled labor. The relative drain of unskilled labor is further indicated by the fact that agrarian wages closely followed the industrial wage level of the unskilled laborer up to the 1910s. Secondly, in conjunction with the new industrial development there was a strong urbanization with comprehensive construction works. Thereby the demand for unskilled labor increased particularly in the urban areas—many new entrants into the towns from rural areas had their first occupations in labor-intensive constructions. Thirdly, one can at least hypothesize, that the supply of skilled labor increased due to the increasing level of education as well as to learning processes in prior industrialization; the supply of skilled labor was relatively elastic.[20]

Furthermore, it took some time to carry through a structural change in accordance with new relative prices, particularly since the new structure emerged in a process of competition between old and new interests in Swedish industry. Although new industries such as engi-

Table 16.3
Composition of Swedish commodity exports 1872/74–1927/29 (Percentage shares in current prices)

Year	Primary and semi-manufactured goods*	Manufactured goods	Specific manufactured goods	
			Paper goods	Engineering products
1872–74	93.9	6.1	1.1	1.4
1888–90	83.5	16.5	6.4	2.9
1908–10	78.3	21.7	5.7	9.8
1927–29	45.8	54.2	25.0	19.6

*Primary and semimanufactured goods comprise agricultural goods and food, hides, timber and sawn wood, minerals, and semimanufactured metal goods.
Sources: BiSOS, SOS Utrikeshandel, Statistics of Sweden.

neering or pulp and paper showed very high growth rates from the 1890s, while sawmills and iron works were at a low level in that respect, the new industries were still not dominating the sector. This is very clear from the composition of Swedish exports. Even if there had been some expansion of paper exports up till 1890 and of engineering products until 1910, exports were still dominated by products of a traditional character, such as sawn wood, iron ore, steel, and food. The growth of new industries had at an early stage a strong domestic market component—for instance, paper to the strongly expanding printing industry and to retail trade and machinery to the industrial sector as a whole (see table 16.3). The shift in the export composition following the new export advances came after 1910 and particularly during the 1920s. At this stage, the industrial structure of the Second Industrial Revolution had come of age.

Thus, from the perspective applied here, one can say that in the 1920s Schumpeter industries, based on firm specific knowledge, got a stronghold in the Swedish manufacturing sector, to the detriment of natural resource–based Heckscher-Ohlin industries. The potential conflict between these industrial groupings was however reduced during the 1920s and 1930s when old and new interests within industry merged, creating strong blocks both in terms of financial and technological resources.

This shift in the basis from natural resources to specific knowledge also manifested itself in the other dimension of the analysis—that between convergence and divergence. Up to World War I there had been convergence and factor price equalization in many respects, both internationally, with Sweden (and Scandinavia) catching up on the leading countries, and nationally in Sweden with narrowing or stability of wage differentials between skilled/unskilled labor and between sectors. From World War I and in the 1920s this situation changed. In a European perspective, Swedish wages rather forged ahead (see figure 16.2), and in such a perspective Sweden became a European pioneer in introducing American scientific methods in industrial production, notably during the 1920s. Within Sweden, available wage series also indicate strong or even very strong divergence. Among municipal workers skill premium increased slightly (see figure 16.3), while the differences in wage growth between sectors became very large (see figure 16.4). Urban wages (industrial and municipal) rose strongly in relation to agricultural. This indicates that productivity within the new industrial structure increased rapidly in the 1920s, depicting both the expansion of new more sophisticated industries and the spread of rationalization based upon electricity and new machine technology. Wages in the urban service sector rose even more strongly in combination with an expansion of the local authorities in the 1920s. Agriculture,

Figure 16.4
Hourly earnings of unskilled municipal worker and manufacturing workers in relation to hourly earnings of agricultural workers in Sweden, 1870–1930
Source: Bagge et al. (1933)

on the other hand, lagged behind in this modernization process and was at the same time hit by falling prices internationally after the war.

Wage development in the 1920s had in many ways a dual character. The new industrial structure with knowledge-intensive industries and a thorough electrification of industrial mechanical energy had raised the technological level. On one hand, a new capital-skill complementarity arose in Swedish industry similar to the one that Goldin and Katz discovered in the United States.[21] Thus demand for skilled labor, which had become relatively cheaper in previous decades, increased. On the other hand, the relatively high wage level of unskilled labor increased efforts to rationalize and mechanize routines in industrial processes (further intensified through a reform of working hours in 1920). Rationalization and standardization of work procedures in combination with high wages increased demand for the lower paid female labor in industry. In the 1920s female employment and female wages increased substantially.[22] Thus, while demand for skilled engineers increased, female labor substituted for unskilled male labor. While male wages probably diverged during the 1920s, at least at a sector level, there was compression in the entire wage structure, taking female wages into account.

The diverging trends that appeared during and after World War I at international and sector levels can to some extent be analyzed within the framework of disintegration of markets compared to the situation before the war. On one hand, capital supply was substantially augmented due to the war in some of those countries that had been successful in the Second Industrial Revolution, such as the United States and Sweden. Financial markets, however, disintegrated and capital became less mobile. The capital-labor-ratio rose primarily in the urban modernized sector of these economies, where new technology was applied and demand for skilled labor increased. On the other hand, international labor migration was diminished or almost ceased. As a consequence, internal labor migration diminished, particularly the mobility of unskilled male laborers. Thus, the land-labor ratio in Sweden (or Europe) turned downward. At the same time, trade in primary products recovered, which depressed agricultural prices and reduced demand for unskilled labor in countries of import.[23] As a consequence, sectoral wages as well as international income levels diverged.

Divergence both in wages and in growth rates was, thus, to some extent the result of the war and the disintegration of markets, but it was more profoundly the result of the structural transformation of the industrial sector, denominated the Second Industrial Revolution. Divergence appeared already from the 1890s and was enlarged from the war. The Swedish transformation with a strong growth of Schumpeter industries played a part in this divergence. Within Sweden, within Europe, and in a wider international perspective, new structural tensions were created that were to increase in the 1930s and to be released only after World War II, in a new period of convergence and factor price equalization.

Conclusion

The weight of the two perspectives on industrialization—open-economy forces and the interaction with internal structures and traditions—involved in the Heckscher-Ohlin theorem shifted over time. Foreign trade was important in early industrialization to bring about an increased export sector based on Swedish natural resources and to lower subsistence costs with increased transformation pressure on agriculture. In combination with the flows of capital and labor, foreign trade fundamentally changed relative factor prices in Sweden, paving the way for further industrialization. In this process, it was of profound importance that factor mobility was high within Sweden so that the economy could adjust to a changing situation. In the long run, the foreign demand for timber, iron, and oats would stagnate, while at the same time new relative factor prices reduced Swedish advantage in such crude exports and raised the necessity to rely on more refined endowments. The Swedish economy had been complementary to the leading industrial countries at an early stage of industrialization, but from the turn of century it entered into a more competitive situation. Thus, the ability to undergo a profound structural transformation particularly from the 1890s onward was of utmost importance for long-run growth. While performing that transformation, the Swedish economy contributed to a new divergence in international economic development that was to succumb to convergence at a much later date.

Acknowledgments

I would like to thank Ylva Hasselberg and other participants of the Eli F. Heckscher Symposium at Stockholm School of Economics and the participants of the Economic History seminar at Universidad Carlos III, Madrid, for valuable comments on an earlier version of this paper.

I also gratefully acknowledge the financial support from the Bank of Sweden Tercentenary Foundation for the project "Economic Growth and Productivity in a European Perspective since 1870."

Notes

1. Heckscher (1919).

2. Heckscher (1968:272).

3. See O'Rourke and Williamson (1994, 1995a, 1995b) and Williamson (1995, 1996).

4. Williamson (1995:162).

5. Notably Romer (1986).

6. See Abramovitz (1986).

7. On these concepts, see Braunerhjelm and Oxelheim (1992).

8. Dahmén (1950, 1988).

9. Krantz and Schön (1983); Schön (1994, 1998, 2000a).

10. Cf. the concept of General Purpose Technologies, developed in the 1990s; see Bresnahan and Trajtenberg (1995).

11. Cf. Burenstam Linder (1961).

12. Generally, all Nordic countries had large deficits in the trade with goods but surplus in services due to the income of shipping. Overall, however, there were negative current accounts. Denmark and Sweden were leading Nordic capital importers both in time and in magnitude. Ljungberg and Schön (2001).

13. Schön (1989, 1990).

14. Hatton and Williamson (1994:23).

15. Abramovitz and David (1973).

16. Goldin and Katz (1996).

17. Crafts (1985).

18. Kennedy (1987).

19. Berend and Ranki (1982).

20. Cf. Sandberg (1979).

21. Schön (1991, 2000b) shows that new growth branches were characterized by a more intensive use of electricity relative to other energy carriers as well as a more intensive use of skilled labor.

22. Svensson (1995).

23. While the mobility of unskilled male labor diminished after the war, depressing wages in agriculture, the flow in Sweden of female labor from the rural to the urban sector increased, which may be seen as an reaction to a new demand in both the

manufacturing and the service sector. This was reflected in the female relative wages, emphasized earlier.

References

Abramovitz, M. 1986. "Catching Up, Forging Ahead and Falling Behind." *Journal of Economic History* 46:385–406.

Abramovitz, M., and P. David. 1973. "Reinterpreting Economic Growth: Parables and Realities." *American Economic Review* 63, no. 2: 415–426.

Berend, I., and G. Ranki. 1982. *The European Periphery and Industrialisation 1780–1914.* Budapest: Akademiai Kiado.

Braunerhjelm, P., and L. Oxelheim. 1992. "Heckscher-Ohlin and Schumpeter industries: The response by Swedish multinational firms to the EC 1992 Program." Working Paper of the Industrial Institute for Economic and Social Research, Stockholm. No 352.

Bresnahan, T. F., and M. Trajtenberg. 1995. "General Purpose Technologies: Engines of Growth?" *Journal of Econometrics* 65:83–108.

Burenstam Linder, S. 1961. *An Essay on Trade and Transformation.* Uppsala: Almqvist & Wiksell.

Crafts, N. F. R. 1985. *British Economic Growth During the Industrial Revolution.* Oxford: Clarendon Press.

Dahmén, E. 1950. *Svensk industriell företagarverksamhet. Kausalanalys av den industriella utvecklingen 1919–1939.* Stockholm: Industriens Utredningsinstitut.

———. 1988. "Development Blocks in Industrial Economics." *Scandinavian Economic History Review* 36:3–14.

Goldin, C., and L. Katz. 1996. "The Origins of Technology-Skill Complementarity." *NBER Working Paper 5657,* Cambridge, MA.

Hatton, T., and J. G. Williamson. 1994. *Migration and the International Labor Market, 1850–1939.* London: Routledge.

Heckscher, E. F. 1919. Utrikeshandelns verkan på inkomstfördelningen. Några teoretiska grundlinjer. *Ekonomisk tidskrift* 21:1–32.

———. 1968. *Svenskt arbete och liv. Från medeltiden till nutiden.* Stockholm: Aldus/Bonnier.

Homer, S. 1977. *A History of Interest Rates.* New Brunswick, NJ: Rutgers University Press.

Kennedy, W. P. 1987. *Industrial Structure, Capital Markets and the Origin of British Economic Decline.* Cambridge: Cambridge University Press.

Krantz, O., and L. Schön. 1983. Den svenska krisen i långsiktigt perspektiv. *Ekonomisk Debatt* 7.

Ljungberg, J., and L. Schön. 2001. Domestic markets and international integration. Paths to industrialization in the Nordic countries. Paper presented at the IV EHES conference, Oxford, September 20–23, 2001.

Maddison, A. 1995. *Monitoring the World Economy, 1820–1992.* Paris: OECD.

O'Rourke, K. H., and J. G. Williamson. 1994. "Late-Nineteenth Century Anglo-American Factor Price Convergence: Were Heckscher and Ohlin Right?" *Journal of Economic History* 4:892–916.

———. 1995a. "Open Economy Forces and Late Nineteenth Century Swedish Catch-Up: A Quantitative Accounting." *Scandinavian Economic History Review* 43, no. 2: 171–203.

———. 1995b. "Education, Globalization and Catch-Up: Scandinavia in the Swedish Mirror." *Scandinavian Economic History Review* 43, no. 3: 287–309.

Romer, P. M. 1986. "Increasing Returns and Long Run Growth." *Journal of Political Economy* 94:1002–1037.

Sandberg, L. G. 1979. "The Case of the Impoverished Sophisticate: Human Capital and Swedish Economic Growth before World War I." *Journal of Economic History* 1:225–241.

Schön, L. 1989. "Kapitalimport, kreditmarknad och industrialisering 1850–1910." In E. Dahmén, ed., *Upplåning och utveckling. Riksgäldskontoret 1789–1989*, 227–273. Stockholm: Allmänna förlaget.

———. 1990. "Capital imports, credit market and industrialisation in Sweden 1850–1910." Paper presented at The Tenth International Economic History Congress, Leuven, August 1990.

———. 1991. "Development Blocks and Transformation Pressure in a Macro-Economic Perspective—A Model of Long-Cyclical Change." *Skandinaviska Enskilda Banken Quarterly Review* 3–4:67–76.

———. 1994. *Omvandling och obalans, Mönster i svensk ekonomisk utveckling*. Bilaga 3 till Långtidsutredningen 94. Finansdepartementet. Stockholm: Fritzes.

———. 1997. "External and Internal Factors in Swedish Industrialization." *Scandinavian Economic History Review* 65:3.

———. 1998. "Industrial Crises in a Model of Long Cycles: Sweden in an International Perspective." In T. Myllyntaus, ed., *Economic Crises and Restructuring in History*. Frankfurt: 397–413.

———. 2000a. *En modern svensk ekonomisk historia. Tillväxt och omvandling under två sekel.* Stockholm: SNS.

———. 2000b. "Electricity, Technological Change and Productivity in Swedish Industry 1890–1990." *European Review of Economic History* 5, no. 2: 175–194.

Svensson, L. 1995. *Closing the Gender Gap: Determinants of the Change in the Female-to-Male Blue Collar Wage Ratio in Swedish Manufacturing 1913–1990*. Lund: Ekonomisk-historiska institutionen, Lunds Universitet.

Thomas, B. 1954. *Migration and Economic Growth: A Study of Great Britain and the Atlantic Economy*. Cambridge: Cambridge University Press.

Williamson, J. G. 1995. "The Evolution of Global Labor Markets Since 1850: Background Evidence and Hypotheses." *Explorations in Economic History* 2:141–196.

———. 1996. "Globalization, Convergence and History." *Journal of Economic History* 2:377–406.

17   Eli F. Heckscher's Vision of Economic Development

Johan Söderberg

An eyewitness, Axel Hirsch, has described Eli F. Heckscher's daily work habits in the following way. He went up at about five o'clock in the morning, made his morning tea or just drank a cup of hot water, and carefully read the newspaper. Then he started to work. This continued until 6 PM, interrupted only by a brief lunch, twenty minutes sleep, and half an hour's reading of some detective story of a reasonably high literary quality. After dinner he resumed work until he went to bed at about 9:30 PM. His life was calm and humdrum. He never traveled unless he had a particular mission. It would never have occurred to him to go out for a walk on a beautiful day to enjoy the sun or the flowers. Rarely did he visit the cinema, even more seldom the theater. Hardly ever did he go to a concert or to the Opera.[1]

Did this ascetic man have any vision of economic development? Did he have a view of the goals and probable outcome of economic growth? What were the main forces of change, economic and noneconomic, in economic development? How was economic growth related to the development of society as a whole?

I will argue that one of his contributions was to partially endogenize preferences in a long-term and gloomy view of economic development. He did not reflect much theoretically upon his own model, however, which also stands as empirically fairly tenuous.

Economics and the Aim of Economic Life

In some ways, Heckscher's conception of economics was conventional. Economics as a discipline, to him, was the study of scarcity in human society. Economic life rested on what he labeled the economic principle or the law of least efforts. This was the problem of making best possible use of available but limited resources with respect to covering the total needs of human beings. The price system played the important role of equilibrating supply and demand, enforcing a connection between the scarcity of resources and the strictness of economizing behavior.[2] Heckscher characterized the invisible hand (in Adam Smith's sense) as "wonderful machinery."[3]

Heckscher usually talked about "economic life" rather than about "the economy" or "the economic system." To him, economic life was the activities of human beings handling the problem of scarcity when making their living. Sometimes he used the term "the economy" to describe economic life as taken together. For instance, "the economy before 1750" was characterized by immobility, and agriculture formed the most inefficient part of this "economic system." The economy could have a greater or smaller impact upon other parts of society.[4] This usage appears to be in some conflict with Heckscher's statement that the economy is not a particular sphere of human activity, but one aspect of all human life.[5] However, this matters little when it comes to presenting his view of long-term economic development.

What, then, was the aim of economic life? Heckscher shared Adam Smith's opinion that consumption is the sole purpose of economic activity.[6] In what he must have thought was an equivalent statement, Heckscher also stated that economic life had only one task: consumers' welfare.[7] The goal of economic activity must be to gratify, in the best possible way, the needs of the population taken as a whole, among which the interests of all individuals should be equally valued. The greatest possible quantity of iron, electricity or any other sort of material product could not be the objective of human strivings. The aim should be a life as rich and valuable as possible.[8] All of this conformed to standard economics at his time.[9]

Exogenous or Endogenous Preferences?

Theoretically, Heckscher regarded preferences as exogenous. Human goals and needs are not part of the economy.[10] It was outside the domain of economics, for example, to make judgments as to whether or not certain needs should be encouraged while others should be discouraged. The price mechanism was useful only in its capacity to optimally allocate resources, given the needs of people. There might well be social or moral reasons for restricting, for example, demand for alcohol, or stimulating demand for higher education or museum visits through subsidies. This was not an economic issue, though. The explanatory value of economic theory ceased as soon as human beings were no longer considered as capable of acting in their own best interest.[11]

Similarly, economic theory could have no opinion as to priorities among ends. Despite scarce total resources, medieval people had spent far more on cathedrals and other religious purposes than later epochs with far greater material resources had done. This allocation of resources could only be explained by the fact that religious needs were more strongly felt in medieval than in modern society. The problem fell outside the field of economics.[12]

To Heckscher, this illustrated a basic limitation of economic theory. The economic principle, the adaptation of means to ends, had never been decisive in human life. The fundamental things could only be sought for in what human beings thought they needed, or—as Heckscher used what he labeled a loftier word—in their ideals.[13]

Heckscher did not use the term "preferences," which I think was not widely used in economics during his formative years. He must have been aware that Marshall did without the word (talking about "wants" instead).[14] But Heckscher's phrase "what human beings thought they needed" presumably comes close to the modern, and rather loose, meaning of "preferences."[15]

In an important 1930 article, Heckscher discussed "the character of demand," by which he meant a mental state, "the character of the wishes, inclinations, and wants of human beings." This was different from effective demand on the market, which was restricted by prices and budgets. But Heckscher thought that another issue should be confronted. Had people's eagerness for certain goods or services changed regardless of changes in prices or supply? Economic theory took demand as given, but another theory—the materialist conception of history—reversed the causation, letting the mode of production transform the aims of human beings. This should be tested, Heckscher thought.[16]

What is remarkable is that Heckscher conceded that the materialist conception of history had two good points here. First, the character of demand indeed was affected by modern advertising and marketing, that is, influenced by economic activity. Second, economic life constantly affected people's imagination and lust for various things. For instance, modern working life and urban life had altered the whole existence of workers, ranging from clothes and shoes to education and mental orientation. These effects were often unconscious.[17]

The view of perceived wants as exogenously determined thus was ambiguous in Heckscher's writings. On one hand, he admitted the possibility of endogenous wants and gave examples of this that were obviously not of marginal importance. On the other hand, he did not in any way attempt to revise standard economic theory, according to which this was not an option.

Heckscher discussed at some length the tendency of needs in modern societies to become more differentiated.[18] Rising living standards make it possible to satisfy more diverse needs, as well as weaker needs. Adam Smith had noticed this, and Heckscher quoted him: "The desire of food is limited in every man by the narrow capacity of the human stomach; but the desire of the conveniences and ornaments of building, dress, equipage, and household furniture, seems to have no limit or certain boundary."[19] Whereas Smith did not place this observation into a dynamic framework, Heckscher did. As elementary needs would demand an ever-smaller share of incomes, the agricultural sector would diminish in importance, precisely because its indispensable products became an ever-smaller part of the overall economy.

If Smith was right, total demand has no bounds. This is what Heckscher thought. When the most pressing demands have been met, people wish other, less indispensable but desirable things. The subjective needs had grown parallel to the possibilities to meet these needs, and could be expected to do so in the future as well. This tendency had played en enormous role in economic history, Heckscher argued.[20]

The view of unbounded and more various demands has a long history. Heckscher must have met it not only in Adam Smith but also in Jevons or Marshall.[21] In order to understand Heckscher's position, it is necessary to briefly relate a few of the nineteenth-century economists.

Nassau Senior argued in his *Outline of the Science of Political Economy* (1836) that the necessities of life are few and simple. A man's desires are soon extended, first to more varied food, then to variety in dress. Last comes the desire to build, to ornament, and to furnish. These tastes were seen by Senior as "absolutely insatiable," and they seemed to increase with every improvement in civilization. Our desires do not aim so much at quantity as at diversity. He called this the Law of Variety in human requirements. Besides the love of distinction, the love of variety was one of the most powerful principles of human nature.[22]

In his *Theory of Political Economy*, Stanley Jevons referred to the Law of Variety that Senior had formulated in his "admirable treatise." But

Jevons paid even more attention to T. E. Banfield, who had advanced his theory of consumption in a series of lectures in 1844. Banfield proposed that the satisfaction of every lower want creates a desire of a higher character. The satisfaction of a primary want (such as ordinary food) awakens the sense of more than one secondary privation (such as clothing and delicacy in food). Thus demand for objects of refined enjoyment (such as pleasure from the beauties of art) was depending upon the facility with which the primary wants was satisfied.[23]

There seems to be little to be found in Banfield over and above the remarks of Senior. Jevons did not elaborate the theory of wants held by these gentlemen. He used them to support two of his main tenets: that utility was not an intrinsic quality of things, and that the marginal utility of any article was diminishing.[24]

It was up to Marshall to transform the theory of wants into something new: a theory of wants and activities. Like several theorists before him, he noted that humankind, with the progress of society, rapidly developed more subtle and more various wants. Monotony was increasingly felt as irksome, and variety was demanded for its own sake. There was a growing desire for amusements such as athletic games and traveling, which developed activities rather than merely gratified the sensuous cravings. Marshall saw many commendable consequences of this, for instance the trend that those drinks that stimulated the mental activities (such as tea) largely were displacing those that merely gratified the senses (such as alcohol).[25]

This is clearly a case of endogenizing preferences. Marshall did the same thing once more when discussing the demand for housing. Demand for larger and better housing became more urgent, he thought, as people's higher activities developed (which they could do despite the fact that bad housing stunted the faculties and limited these higher activities). In modern society, the elementary need for shelter from the weather played little part in the effective demand for housing. When basic demands for housing had been met, a yet further and almost unlimited increase was desired as a requisite for the exercise of many social activities. Speaking broadly, Marshall stated, causation ran from new activities giving rise to new wants. The reverse applied only to humankind's earliest stages.[26] This idea is at the center of his conception. He regarded the development of new activities, rather than of new wants, as "the true key-note of economic progress."[27]

To Marshall, desires changed with economic development in another way than they did to Senior and Banfield. The "lower" desire for distinction still existed and could even expand. For instance, the efforts to obtain distinction by dress were extending themselves in the lower strata of English society. It could also decline, as the dress of men in the upper grades had become simple and inexpensive as compared with what it had been in Europe not long ago. But another and "higher" want, excellency for its own sake, was becoming more important. A large part of the demand for the highly skilled professional services, as well as the best work of the mechanical artisan, arose from the delight that people had in the training of their own faculties. Marshall characterized Nassau Senior's assertion that the desire for distinction is universally and constantly strong as a "great half-truth."[28]

Heckscher did not explicitly discuss the consumption theories of Senior and Banfield. He cannot have shared their view of a unilinear development from simple material needs to desires with more of a cultural content. What Heckscher observed was rather the reverse. Spiritual needs had been extremely important during medieval times, demanding enormous material resources, but subsequently material needs had been given priority. This trend obviously does not fit the Senior-Banfield theory. On the other hand, Heckscher approved of the idea that economic growth led to more varied demand.

Neither did Heckscher follow Marshall, probably for several reasons. Marshall had been inspired by McCulloch, who saw the gratification of a want or a desire merely as a step toward new pursuits that were undertaken with fresh energy.[29] Heckscher, on the other hand, characterized McCulloch as an unoriginal disciple of Ricardo's.[30]

More important, Heckscher was not attracted to the idea of evaluating human wants as lower or higher. The only needs that existed to him were those that people actually possessed, explicating that the word "actually" meant "according to their own subjective view."[31] This was sufficient to him, and distanced him from Marshall's (probably less useful) distinction between various kinds of wants. Some of these were seen as "artificial," related to a higher comfort, whereas other wants were worthy as they developed human faculties—intelligence, energy, and self-respect.[32] To Heckscher, economics must remain non-normative and devoid of any moral content, just as every other science should be.[33]

We also should keep in mind that Heckscher did not share the general optimism of the late nineteenth century. I will return to this important theme later. For the moment, let us just note that the one of the main conclusions that he drew from the shift toward expendable products in modern society was that demand tended to become unstable. This is in itself a far cry from the evolutionary optimism of the late nineteenth century.[34]

The newly developed needs were, Heckscher argued, far more changeable, more subject to changes in taste as well as in trade conditions, than the elementary needs of food for survival, clothes, and housing as protection against cold. Rising incomes and changing preferences among manual workers had led to many important changes in consumption. The new needs comprised objects such as radio, film, and gramophones, to which was added the enormously enlarged importance of already existing but uncared for needs such as sports, pleasure, and clothing. This growing capriciousness in demand in turn reinforced the general sense of insecurity that characterized the interwar period, for instance the notion that the economic system of the nineteenth century had served its time.[35]

Another effect, already mentioned, was the growth of advertising and marketing. These activities expanded with a certain degree of necessity, Heckscher argued, with the standard of living. The consumer could choose not only between various needs but also between alternative goods that could satisfy his needs. For this reason, stronger persuasion was needed from advertisers and sellers in order to make him choose one good before others. The more dispensable the goods were, the more marketing efforts were required. And modern advertising often seemed to reach its goal.[36]

The dwindling demand for luxuries provided yet another example of preferences being transformed by economic growth. The economic role of luxuries had strongly diminished in relative terms, and probably even in absolute numbers, in the long run, and particularly so during the nineteenth century. Heckscher related this phenomenon to two circumstances. First, a greater number of needs could be satisfied as a result of the transformations of the last century. Second, the interest in outwardly splendor had very much been reduced. Taken together, this contributed toward explaining the declining role of the goldsmiths during the nineteenth century.[37]

The other side of the coin was the growing propensity to save. Here, too, preferences appear to have been endogenous. On Heckscher's account, the rich and powerful during the Middle Ages were great spenders rather than savers, due to their demand for outwardly glamour and personal services. The situation changed with the subsequent commercial expansion, as the number of people grew whose incomes exceeded their cost of living. Later, the industrial expansion further reinforced this tendency, and the rich took the lead in savings.[38]

It is thus possible to find examples in Heckscher's work of preferences being transformed as an effect of economic activity. He sometimes endogenized preferences, and at least in a few cases he was conscious of doing so. Yet he held on to standard theory, which saw preferences as exogenous. He did not bring up Marshall's more systematic approach, linking preferences to the development of new activities in the process of economic growth, activities that in turn generate new preferences. Arguably, Marshall's argument was a more fruitful way of dealing with the problem. But that is another story.

Demand and the Forces of Change

Heckscher constantly discussed the forces of change in economic life. His approach seems to have been based on three notions:

1. Demand to an important degree was formed independently of the economic machinery itself.

2. Demand often worked as the active factor in relation to the productive forces.

3. Economic factors did not, in general, have any first-hand role in explaining changes in society. They did not acquire a primary role until the nineteenth century.

Let us have a closer look at these ideas.

The decline of servanthood provided one example of demand being transformed by noneconomic factors. With modern economic growth, human labor had become increasingly scarce. One consequence was a huge reduction in the extent of servanthood, Heckscher noted in the 1930s. This was, as he saw it, not an effect of relative price changes alone; neither could it be explained solely by changing demand or supply schedules. True, servants had become more expensive and more difficult to acquire, and modern household technology hade made it possible to refrain from demanding them as much as formerly. Yet, an American multimillionaire would not have any difficulty in paying for as many servants as he wished to have. There must be other explanations as to why he employed far less servants than an English aristocrat with a fraction of his income would have done up to World War I. The present-day millionaire had lost the lust for this kind of personal services, and this made him different from generations of lords before him, not only in the United States but in most European countries as well.[39] A mental change has taken place that affected economic life.[40]

This led to the question, Heckscher continued, if this mental change in itself was a consequence of changing relations of production. He believed, however, that other factors had played the major role. The taste for personal services in the form of servants was regarded by him as more unusual in the United States than in Europe, probably for many reasons among which religious and political ones appeared to be more prominent than the economic ones. Not only in the United States, but also in a European country like Sweden, the conception of the necessity and appropriateness of servanthood had shifted in connection with a changing view of our fellow beings and ourselves.

Heckscher saw changing human needs as a central impulse to the economy. Growing needs and new needs stimulated people to make harder efforts and to employ their mental capabilities further than before.[41] Conversely, static needs or an unchanging taste resulted in a lack of such impulses toward transformation.[42]

It may be added that not only demand but also supply to a large degree was formed outside the economic system, according to Heckscher. He made a distinction between economic history and the history of technology. As a human (or social) science, economic history did not deal with technology as such, only with the consequences of such conditions and changes for people's lives. Shipbuilding, for instance, remained a technological subject until the various types of ships were related to the ways of transporting people and goods in the service of humankind.[43] The cultivation of land or the transformation of raw materials into useful objects was as such a technical matter, not an economic one.[44]

Heckscher went so far as to state that changes in the fundamental conditions of economic life usually stemmed from phenomena outside the sphere of economic life, such as the state of technology or human needs.[45]

The servanthood example appeared to Heckscher as only one of many cases of the more general situation that demand often was a highly active factor.[46] People reacted strongly against downward pressures on acquired living standards. This was one of the most important forces in economic history, as Heckscher saw it. Such reactions were known not only in modern society but also, for example, from Imperial Rome. Yet, Heckscher reminded the reader that the desirable mechanism described by David Ricardo as "a taste for comforts and

enjoyments" among the laboring classes was far from being an historical constant. During long periods of history this tendency had been
very weak, as could be inferred from a more or less constant birth rate.
Things had changed, though, in modern society.[47] In the depression of
the 1930s, for instance, the strong demands for assistance from the
farmers had contributed towards a new and far-reaching policy of
state intervention.[48]

Heckscher argued that economic factors did not in general have any
firsthand role in explaining changes in society. Even when it came to
more limited task of explaining economic development, economic
phenomena could not in general be assigned a primary part. Nor could
any other factor—political, ideological, religious, and so forth—a priori
be considered as having any overarching role. This is what he called a
universalistic conception of history. Each phase, each change, had to be
studied in its own right.[49] More than perhaps any other leading economic historian, Heckscher tended to stress the role of noneconomic
factors, not only when explaining overall changes in society but also
when coming to grips with change within economic life.[50]

Heckscher advanced as a general statement that economic factors do
not play the decisive role in social and political change.[51] Rather, he
thought, most social changes had their origin in changes in attitudes.
These mental changes could in turn be traced back to a great number
of other phenomena such as religion, philosophy, literature, and art.[52]

However, there seemed to be a pattern over time in the relationship among explanatory factors. In Heckscher's view, economic forces
appeared rather late as the most important motive force in transform-
ing society. This did not happen until the nineteenth century. There
could be little doubt that the main difference between a person in 1800
and in 1900 was the economic condition. Previously, other sources of
change had been vital. In medieval times the Catholic Church had had
the decisive role in forming Western society. During the sixteenth century the formation of the nation-states had been central. In the eighteenth century, on the other hand, the most dynamic role was played
by the Enlightenment and the dissolution of the society of the ancien
régime.[53]

The early industrialization period provided another example of the
secondary role of economic factors. No milestone could be more important to economic history, Heckscher thought, than the changes that
came forward in the period 1750 to 1800, when the economy began to
depart from the traditional condition of immobility. But the impulse to

the most important economic transformation, the one that took place in England, did not primarily come from within economic life. It originated to a large extent in the political revolutions of the seventeenth century and the subsequent deregulation of the economy, combined with the new spirit of curiosity and discovery.[54]

During the nineteenth century, on the other hand, the impact of the economy upon other fields grew much stronger than previously. International relations, classes, lifestyles, science, religion, morals, the arts, and literature were all transformed under the greatest and most rapid economic transformation that had ever taken place.[55] The long-run relationship between economic and noneconomic factors thus had changed in favor of the former.

What Was the Outcome?

The goal of economic activity according to Heckscher, as stated earlier, was a life as rich and valuable as possible for humanity. To what extent had this goal been realized? Heckscher saw the 150 years preceding World War I as an outstanding, indeed as a "wonderful" epoch in history. This was a period in which human beings reached a new command over nature. Humankind had proven its ability to channel natural resources into a system that transformed life as a whole of the population, in a mental as well as in a material sense. The period was one of fermentation, but it appeared to him as far brighter than the one that started in 1914.[56]

In other texts, Heckscher was more explicit. A fairly long list of outstanding features of the liberal nineteenth century can be compiled from his various writings. This era succeeded in combining economic and social mobility with a far stronger sense of security than in present society.[57] In economic history, the role of the nineteenth century probably was as great as all the preceding epochs taken together. The rise in material standards of living during the nineteenth century had been unprecedented.[58]

Yet, this was not what was most remarkable. Heckscher thought that this period, despite all its deficiencies, would eventually appear as a "golden age, as one of the richest cultural epochs that mankind had ever lived through." A free intellectual and spiritual life had been established during the century. A new type of man was created, with new habits and a new view of his existence.[59] During the liberal era, human beings had possessed a great liberty of action and a great ability to influence the course of things.[60] Moreover, liberalism had created a state that was far more honest and efficient than any previous regime.[61]

The liberal era thus was conceived as having formed a golden age in the history of mankind. Yet, Heckscher's view was not unambiguous, as he added that much had been lost at the same time that much was gained. He concluded, indecisively, that all attempts to make a balance betweens gains and losses must remain subjective.[62] Obviously this was in some contrast to what he had just said, since his characterization of the period 1750–1914 would have little meaning if he had not valued humankind's increasing powers over nature, the liberation of the mental climate, and the formation of a new type of person as gains. The losses were more vaguely specified.[63]

What was wrong, then, with the post-1914 period? The major problem was the growing power of states over individuals. The state had gained new power in every respect. During the last decades of his life, this was a recurrent theme in Heckscher's writings.[64]

Whereas Heckscher usually emphasized noneconomic factors behind many other great changes in society, he did so to a lesser degree regarding the strengthening of the state. Modern states had far stronger power resources at their disposal, and this could only be explained by technical and economic factors. The "total" state, as Heckscher called it (within quotation marks) combined ideas from old absolutism with socialism. It could not only exercise power over each individual's thoughts, feelings, and acts. It also had developed an unprecedented military power and strongly intervened in economic life. This was based on new systems of command, leadership, and organization. They included the railway, the telephone and the telegraph, the electrical power systems, the press, and the radio, as well as large-scale production itself with the growing role of big industrial enterprises.[65]

Heckscher found it interesting to compare the present state of affairs with the stationary state as depicted by John Stuart Mill.[66] Mill described a society in which population and capital formation had ceased to grow. Technological progress continued, however, and working hours were shortened. Mill sympathized with this condition and painted it in bright colors. Heckscher thought that the stagnating population predicted by Mill had been realized in Western societies, and production had indeed come to place smaller demand on physical labor. Yet, he wrote in the 1930s, the feeling of security and the peacefulness in society now was lower than it had been for many generations.

Of course, political factors played a great part in creating the present uncertainty. But Heckscher also sought for more long-term explanations. He thought that the demands for safety and security, which tended to be perceived as self-evident claims, were an important source of insecurity. These claims were not matched by the basic economic conditions at present. As a result, new tensions were constantly produced.[67]

Democracy also had problematic consequences, at least in one vital respect. The broad layers of society were indifferent to the foreseeable deterioration of cultural and intellectual life. They made other priorities. In every society, new mental impulses must be a matter for a small number of persons only. This was thus unavoidable in a democratic system as well.[68] Presumably Heckscher meant that democracy would allow nonintellectual preferences to have a substantial impact, as the political system became more sensitive to voters' opinion.[69]

These trends in society after World War I were contrasted with the situation during the first part of the nineteenth century. Here, Heckscher stressed the role of political and psychological factors. The lack of intervention during the laissez-faire era allowed the technical and economic forces a free play, and society was indeed reshaped. The present ideals were precisely the opposite, not only in dictatorships but also in democratic states where the strivings for enlarged state power were usually denied. As regulation increased, the scope of economic forces had become reduced. Producers had become used to organize themselves as interest groups rather than to compete with each other.[70] Technology still was a dynamic factor, but it had not outweighed the tendency toward rigidity.[71]

Toward the end of his life, Heckscher admitted that he held a pessimistic view of development. In 1949, he declared his belief that the future would regard the transition from nineteenth-century society to the one that presently was being consolidated in about the same way as he and many others looked upon the transition from the Roman Empire to medieval times: the climax of a cultural development had relapsed into more primitive conditions. Culture stood considerably higher in the nineteenth century than now.[72]

The individual was disappearing. Aldous Huxley's *Brave New World* was correctly pointing at the trend that had characterized society since about 1900, Heckscher thought. He also held the opinion that Karin

Boye, a well-known Swedish author, was on the right track in her novel, *Kallocain*. This novel, published in 1940, depicts a future society in which the state gains total power over individuals by using a serum that forces them to speak the truth.[73]

Benny Carlson has noted the similarities between the ideas put forward by Heckscher and those of F. A. Hayek. To both, the argument involving the threat against individual freedom was essential, and to Heckscher this line of reasoning became prominent already in the 1930s.[74] The depression promoted state activism, as conceived by Heckscher, and it is quite possible that the early 1930s were decisive in turning him toward pessimism.[75] However, he certainly was affected by his reading of J. M. Keynes's *The Economic Consequences of the Peace* (1919). Reviewing this book (Heckscher 1920), Heckscher agreed with Keynes's devastating criticism of the Versailles Treaty. If applied, the treaty would destroy the whole future of the German people, Heckscher thought. He concluded that this would bring forth a catastrophe (*Ragnarök*), which it was highly unlikely that European civilization would be able to survive.[76]

The Collapse of the Nineteenth Century

To sum up, Heckscher regarded the nineteenth century as a rich cultural epoch, and obviously placed greater weight on this rather than on the material progress of the time. His argument was symmetrical when it came to the troubled interwar era. The main problems arising then were with individual freedom and the risk of a destructive and oppressive state; the fact that material living standards had advanced did not alter his overall evaluation of the period.[77] Both conclusions are well in line with his general view, referred to above, that the greatest possible material production should not be the aim of human efforts. The economic goal of providing as ample goods and services as possible according to the needs of the population was, after all, not more than a worldly matter.[78]

During his mature years, Heckscher's vision of economic growth was based on liberalism.[79] A free market society with a largely non-intervening state could achieve strong economic growth and rising living standards combined with individual freedom and cultural advance. What presented the major problem to him was that the successful development of the nineteenth century, which had relied on exactly those conditions, had been overturned in the post-1914 era.

True, the economy still grew in material terms, but it did not realize what was most priceless: a life as rich and valuable as possible. The market economy, however dynamic, had proved unable to resist the growing threat from the state.

Though worrying, this should not have presented any fundamental theoretical problem to Heckscher's grand view, since his universalistic interpretation of history usually had emphasized the strong impact of noneconomic forces upon the economy. Ideals and politics had changed, and so the economy must change. Economic organization was a social phenomenon, and the aim was to understand how humankind had changed throughout the centuries.[80] This change was not necessarily encouraging. Heckscher's evaluation stands in sharp contrast to Marshall's late-nineteenth-century optimism regarding what he called the "growing earnestness of the age" and "the growing intelligence of the mass of the people." Marshall saw the growing power of the telegraph, the press, and other means of communication as ever widening the scope of collective action for the public good.[81]

Given this universalism, however, it must have been disturbing to come to the conclusion that the forces making for instability and insecurity were to a considerable extent endogenous to the economic system.

Three key aspects of this have already been mentioned. The new systems of command and organization, placing more powerful instruments than ever in the hands of the state, clearly were a result of the combined economic and technological transformation of recent decades.

Second, the economy had developed a new volatility. The economic system became more subject to the fancies of demand, which could be reinforced by advertising and marketing. Demand changed in a more erratic way due to the improved standards of living that had been generated by the unprecedented growth during the last century.

Third, demand for safety and security was stronger in the interwar period than ever before. Since the economic system could not live up to these demands, tensions were increasing. Despite the new volatility just mentioned, Heckscher believed that the tendency toward a more rigid economy dominated.

Heckscher thus differed from many other liberals in his assessment of the outcome of the modern growth process.[82] Progress was certainly possible, but it never was a built-in part of his system. He made a clear distinction between the ideal type of the economy as a smoothly running system, given the free play of the factors of production, and the actual condition which could be reasonably close to that ideal (in the golden age of liberalism) or far from it (as in the interwar period). Even the state of affairs that was closest to the ideal had failed to produce results that were stable in the long run.

After all, the economic system was neither the foundation nor the prime mover of society, but just one vulnerable part of it.

A striking feature in Heckscher's writings is the marked borderline that he constructed between economic theory and economic history. Heckscher believed that economic theory could not explain the dynamics of the historical process. This task would require other tools, such as sociological theory. Economic theory as it existed was an indispensable aid, but only for the analysis of steady states.[83] Heckscher did not highly regard the attempts made at transcending static theory. Noteworthy results had been achieved in one field only: the study of business cycles. Economic theory had no room for the study of transitions from one set of underlying institutional conditions to another, nor could it explain changes in the basic conditions of economic activities. Heckscher even made the astonishing assertion that economic theory was unable to explain changes in the economic variables.[84]

This is a strange departure from Marshall's economics, with its emphasis on dynamics. It is also odd that Heckscher did not theoretically recognize that his own writings contained many examples of changes in the economic variables that were explained by the interaction of supply and demand.

Heckscher's restricted view of the role of economic theory is difficult to explain, even when taking into account his troubles in reconciling his role as an economist with his role as an historian. Be this as it may, it is obvious that the toolbox of economics was not much used in his proficient writings on economic history and the history of economic ideas. One of his major works, *Sveriges ekonomiska historia från Gustav Vasa*, for instance, contains little explicit economic theory.

These reservations concerning economic theory may explain why Heckscher made no serious attempt to bind together the various strands of his thinking on long-run economic development, and particularly the deplorable trends found in modern society, into a more consistent model. Or, possibly, he found this project to depressing to be carried out. Still, he presented the elements of such a model.

This model illustrates the well-known fact that Heckscher the ideologist was never far from Heckscher the scholar.[85] His model pinpoints his difficulties in keeping the roles apart. Its essential feature, the view of individuals becoming serfs of the state, was clearly biased. No systematic reviewing of the evidence was presented. Ordinarily, Heckscher was a very good, though not a first-rate, empirical researcher (many of his results have been questioned and revised by later researchers, but of course he did not often have the time to develop the most suitable methods or to dig deeply into the archives). In this case, he fell far below his usual standards. It would not be expecting too much, I think, that the thesis that the Western world reached an historical high tide in terms of culture and economy around 1900, only to decline after 1914, should be supported by some information regarding political rights and freedom, cultural development, education, or other indicators regarded as useful. Nothing of this was done or even attempted.

Much as I appreciate Heckscher the economist and, even more, Heckscher the economic historian, I find it difficult to escape the conclusion that his gloomy model was largely an ideological construction that had grown into an obsession. What we see is not only a dark model, which is perfectly legitimate, but also a dark side of Heckscher the scholar.

Acknowledgments

Thanks to Rolf Henriksson, Benny Carlson, Arne Jarrick, and Janken Myrdal for useful comments.

Notes

1. Hirsch (1953:229–231).

2. For example, Heckscher (1918:19–20). The price system did not, however, exist in all times and societies. Where it did not exist, the allocation problem had to be solved by other means. Heckscher (1922:17).

3. Heckscher (1918:228). See also Heckscher (1921:6–8).

4. Heckscher (1953:12, 16). Sometimes, Heckscher used the expression "the sphere of economic life," apparently in the same sense as "economic life." Heckscher (1922:54).

5. Heckscher (1922:11); Heckscher (1963:3).

6. Heckscher (1918:227). Heckscher repeatedly stressed this point; for other references see Carlson (1994:46).

7. Heckscher (1915:243).

8. Heckscher (1918:4). Heckscher saw a great difficulty with the principle of gratifying the needs of the population taken as a whole as far as possible: there was no way of balancing one person's needs against the needs of any other person. He did not offer any way of circumventing this problem, though he agreed with Wicksell that a skewed income distribution meant that a given sum of money did not represent the same need to different persons. Heckscher (1918:255–256); Heckscher (1926:23).

9. According to Jevons, "We labour to produce with the sole object of consuming." Jevons (1871:47). Marshall, whom Heckscher admired, also endorsed the view of consumption as the end of production. Marshall (1961:67). Heckscher expressed his admiration of Marshall (e.g., Heckscher 1926:52).

10. Heckscher (1921:78); Heckscher (1922:13, 54).

11. Heckscher (1921:77–78).

12. Heckscher (1922:13, 48).

13. Heckscher (1922:49).

14. Aspers (1999:655).

15. I assume that preferences conventionally refer to "whatever people take to be reasons for choosing one action rather than another" (Sugden 2000:198).

16. Heckscher (1930:64–67).

17. Ibid. Of course, Heckscher was far from accepting the materialist conception of history. His alternative, the universalistic conception of history, is discussed later in this essay.

18. Heckscher (1936:92, 100). See also Heckscher (1933:719).

19. Heckscher (1936:92).

20. Heckscher (1951:21).

21. Jevons (1871:48–51); Marshall (1961:86–90, 222, 227).

22. Senior (1938:11).

23. Jevons (1871:48–51). See also Bowley (1937:110–111).

24. Regenia Gagnier argues that the introduction of marginalism around 1871 implied a revaluation of human needs: from now on they were regarded as insatiable. She does not mention Marshall's reference to McCulloch or Jevons's account of Senior; neither is the reader informed that Banfield advanced his consumption theory more than a quarter of a century before Jevons published his *Theory of Political Economy*. Gagnier (2000:3–4, 44–45).

Disregarding the fact that the notion of unbounded and more various demands had been clearly formulated well before the pioneering publications of Jevons and Menger, she overstates the reorientation of marginalism. I think it can be doubted that marginalism meant anything at all with respect to the view of human needs as insatiable. If there was a continuity, this would undermine Gagnier's thesis that the marginal revolution caused economics to abandon its, in her evaluation, useful focus on productive relations in order to become subjective and psychological.

25. Marshall (1961:89 n. 1). However, Marshall's attitude was not unreservedly positive. He observed that the temptations of the modern money economy hindered savings. The

growth of new wants led to extravagances and to a subordination of the interests of the future to those of the present. This is yet another case of preferences being endogenized in Marshall's work. Ibid., 227.

26. Marshall (1961:88–89). Blaug summarizes, fairly I think, Marshall's view that activities "in some sense dominate and mold those very 'wants' that are taken as data in static equilibrium analysis" (Blaug 1985:397).

27. Marshall (1961:689). Aspers rightly highlights the wants-activities theory as pivotal in Marshall's work. Aspers (1999:655–658). He also makes the important observation that the positive side of this approach can be separated from the normative aspect that Parsons called attention to.

28. Marshall (1961:87–89, 115). Senior indeed considered distinction to be the most powerful of human passions. However, Marshall did not mention that Senior had in fact made the same observation as he did regarding the simplification of the male dress. To Senior, the taste for variety in dress quickly reached its highest point and subsequently, "in one sex at least, diminishes until even the highest ranks assume an almost quaker-like simplicity" (Senior 1938:11–12). Senior did not explain how this observation could be reconciled with his view of distinction and desire for variety as the most powerful principles of human nature.

29. Marshall (1961:90).

30. Heckscher (1904:168).

31. Heckscher (1918a:232).

32. Marshall (1961:689–690). See also Parsons (1982:189, 198).

33. Heckscher (1926:23–24).

34. On Marshall's evolutionary views, see Groenewegen (1995:166–168, 479–486, 510–513).

35. Heckscher (1953:353–354). Heckscher referred to Loveday (1931), who had noted the growing changeability of demand. See also Heckscher (1936:107); Heckscher (1939:47).

36. Heckscher (1953:346); Heckscher (1930:80); Heckscher (1939:47–48).

37. Heckscher (1949:531).

38. Heckscher (1946:170–171).

39. Heckscher (1930:82–83).

40. Another example of a demand change being determined outside the economy is the long-term decline in the consumption of fish in Sweden. Fish had played a great part in consumption during the Catholic era, partly due to its role during Lent. During the subsequent centuries the role of fish in popular diet declined, despite the fact that there was a great increase in the supply of herring during the last decades of the eighteenth century. Heckscher thought that the reason for the long-term decline was that the population gradually drifted away from Catholic habits. Heckscher (1949:283–285, 292).

41. Heckscher (1927:10).

42. One case of rigid tastes is the problem that landowners encountered when trying to introduce the potato as part of the diet of their servants at large landed estates in Sweden

during the latter part of the eighteenth century. Servants resisted this change in diet, as they did not like the taste and smell of the potato. As a result, potato cultivation did not grow much for several decades. Heckscher (1949:204–205).

43. Heckscher (1951:3–11).

44. Heckscher (1922:12).

45. Heckscher (1922:54).

46. Heckscher (1930:79, 83–84).

47. Ibid., 39. The Ricardo quotation is from *Principles of Political Economy and Taxation*, chap. 5.

48. Heckscher (1936:111).

49. Sometimes this universalism can be exasperating, as in the following statement: "How man has come to demand this and given up that can only be explained through the whole history of the human mind" (Heckscher 1933:719). When it comes to explanations, Heckscher often is remarkably unwilling to make clear propositions. His universalism, though a protection against economism and narrow-mindedness, made it easier for him to bypass conclusive statements as to causation.

50. Jarrick (1985:1–7). The historian Harald Hjärne, Heckscher's academic teacher in Uppsala, probably influenced him greatly in this respect.

51. Heckscher (1963:210).

52. Heckscher (1963:8).

53. Heckscher (1951:40). See also Heckscher (1944:28).

54. Heckscher (1953:11–16). See also Heckscher (1955:468–471).

55. Heckscher (1953:16).

56. Heckscher (1953:280).

57. Heckscher (1939:30, 35). Heckscher explained elsewhere that he, when talking about the nineteenth century, actually meant the period 1815–1914; Heckscher (1935:24).

58. Heckscher (1968:246); Heckscher (1950b:82–83).

59. Heckscher (1968:253, 344). These passages are not included in the American edition published as Heckscher (1963).

60. Heckscher (1950a:20).

61. Heckscher (1934:146). See also Heckscher (1918b:260).

62. Heckscher (1953:280).

63. Heckscher thought that the dynamic development of the nineteenth century had adversely affected great numbers of people. Heckscher (1934:149). Yet, he criticized the pessimistic interpretation of the consequences of the Industrial Revolution in terms of living standards, subscribing to the view of J. H. Clapham and T. S. Ashton. Heckscher (1953:105–106).

64. This is dealt with at length in Carlson (1994).

65. Heckscher (1939:42); Heckscher (1934:150–152). He presented an early formulation of the thesis of unprecedented power resources having been placed in the hands of the states in Heckscher (1918b:260–261). See also Carlson (1994:43–46).

66. Heckscher referred to John Stuart Mill, *Principles*, 1848, book 4, chap. 6. See also Heckscher (1948a:300, 305–306).

67. Heckscher (1939:48–49).

68. Heckscher (1934:166).

69. Heckscher took it for granted that no democratic polity could be indifferent to a strong public opinion (1934:163). If, for example, a majority the Swedish people would (unwisely) vote for a transition to socialism, those who did not wish so must to accept this according to the rules of democracy (1948b:10).

70. Heckscher (1939:39, 51).

71. Carlson (1994:45).

72. Carlson (1994:20); Heckscher (1950b:83, 86).

73. Heckscher (1950a:20–21). An English translation of *Kallocain* appeared in 1966.

74. Carlson (1994:109, 260). See also Lewin (1967:125–126, 131–132, 271).

75. In the early 1920s, Heckscher held an optimistic view of the potential of technological change in counteracting monopolies and limiting the powers of the state. Carlson (1992:66–71, 79). I am not aware of any evidence that Heckscher's pessimism was induced by his reading of the gloomy prospects outlined by Schumpeter (1918).

76. Heckscher (1920:144, 146).

77. Heckscher remarked in 1934 that few people suffered from distress in Sweden, and that a decline in the material standard of living might be less of a catastrophe than many other things. Heckscher (1934:163).

78. Heckscher (1934:163).

79. I do not here go into Heckscher's ideological transformation from conservatism to liberalism at about the time of World War I. On this issue see Carlson (1994:16–19).

80. Heckscher (1963:8); Heckscher (1944:26). There is a certain similarity between Heckscher and Marshall here. Historical study to Heckscher aimed at grasping how mankind has changed, while Marshall saw economics as a "science of human motives." His purpose with economics was to understand the influence of economic conditions on human character. Parsons (1982:183); Aspers (1999:652–653). Heckscher's restricted view of economics as a science made it impossible for him to share Marshall's view of the purpose of economic science. Rather, he placed similar hopes in the historical disciplines.

81. Marshall (1961:25).

82. See also Jarrick (1985:194 n. 11).

83. Henriksson (1991:165).

84. Heckscher (1963:5–6).

85. For example, Henriksson (1991:160–161, 166); Myrdal (1958:245).

References

Aspers, P. 1999. "The Economic Sociology of Alfred Marshall: An Overview." *American Journal of Economics and Sociology* 58, no. 4: 651–668.

Blaug, M. 1985. *Economic Theory in Retrospect*. 4th ed. Cambridge: Cambridge University Press.

Bowley, M. 1937. *Nassau Senior and Classical Economics*. London: Allen & Unwin.

Carlson, B. 1992. "Eli Heckscher and Natural Monopoly: The Nightmare That Never Came True." *Scandinavian Economic History Review* 40, no. 3: 53–79.

————. 1994. *The State as a Monster: Gustav Cassel and Eli Heckscher on the Role and Growth of the State*. Lanham, MD: University Press of America.

Gagnier, R. 2000. *The Insatiability of Human Wants: Economics and Aesthetics in Market Society*. Chicago: University of Chicago Press.

Groenewegen, P. 1995. *A Soaring Eagle: Alfred Marshall 1842–1924*. Aldershot: Edward Elgar.

Heckscher, Eli F. 1904. "Ekonomisk historia. Några antydningar." *Historisk Tidskrift* 24:167–198.

————. 1915. *Världskrigets ekonomi. En studie af nutidens näringsliv under krigets inverkan*. Stockholm: Handelshögskolan.

————. 1918a. *Svenska produktionsproblem*. Stockholm: Albert Bonniers.

————. 1918b. *Kontinentalsystemet*. Stockholm: Norstedts.

————. 1920. "För illa att vara sannt." *Svensk Tidskrift*, 138–146.

————. 1921. *Gammal och ny ekonomisk liberalism*. 2nd ed. Stockholm: Norstedts.

————. 1922. *Ekonomi och historia*. Stockholm: Albert Bonniers.

————. 1926. *Om ekonomiska studier. En handledning*. Stockholm: Norstedts.

————. 1927. *Nationalekonomien*. Stockholm: Albert Bonniers.

————. 1930. "Den ekonomiska historiens aspekter." *Historisk tidskrift*, 7–69.

————. 1933. "The Aspects of Economic History." *Economic Essays in Honour of Gustav Cassel*, 705–720. London: Allen & Unwin.

————. 1934. "Planhushållning." *Nationalekonomiska Föreningens förhandlingar, 1934*, 145–166, 190–192, 200. Stockholm: Nationalekonomiska Föreningen.

————. 1935. *Sveriges ekonomiska historia från Gustav Vasa* I. Stockholm: Albert Bonniers.

————. 1936. "Efterkrigstidens ekonomiska och sociala förskjutningar." *Ekonomisk-historiska studier*, 87–114. Stockholm: Albert Bonniers.

————. 1939. "Nutidssamhällets utvecklingstendenser." *Ekonomisk tidskrift*, 30–52.

————. 1944. *Historieuppfattning*. Stockholm: Albert Bonniers.

————. 1946. "Något om Keynes' 'General Theory' ur ekonomisk-historisk synpunkt." *Ekonomisk tidskrift*, 161–183.

————. 1948a. *Ödeläggelsen av 1800-talets hushållning*. Stockholm: Albert Bonniers Förlag. Reprinted in Kurt Wickman, ed., *Eli F. Heckscher om staten, liberalismen och den ekonomiska politiken*, 295–308. Stockholm: Timbro.

————. 1948b. "De nya skatteförslagen." *Nationalekonomiska Föreningens förhandlingar 1947*, 1–12, 25–27. Stockholm: Nationalekonomiska Föreningen.

————. 1949. *Sveriges ekonomiska historia från Gustav Vasa* II:1. Stockholm: Albert Bonniers.

————. 1950a. *Individ och samhälle*. Stockholm: Natur & Kultur.

————. 1950b. Intervention. *Nationalekonomiska Föreningens förhandlingar 1949*. Stockholm: Nationalekonomiska Föreningen.

————. 1951. *Studium och undervisning i ekonomisk historia*. Lund: Gleerups.

————. 1953. *Industrialismen*. 5th ed. Stockholm: Kooperativa förbundets bokförlag.

————. 1955. *Mercantilism*. London: Allen & Unwin.

————. 1963. *An Economic History of Sweden*. Cambridge, MA: Harvard University Press.

————. 1968. *Svenskt arbete och liv*. 5th ed. Stockholm: Aldus/Bonniers.

Henriksson, R. 1991. "Eli F. Heckscher: The Economic Historian as Economist." Bo Sandelin, ed., *The History of Swedish Economic Thought*. London: Routledge.

Hirsch, A. 1953. *Minnen som dröjt kvar*. Stockholm: Hökerberg.

Jarrick, A. 1985. *Psykologisk socialhistoria*. Stockholm: Almqvist & Wiksell International.

Jevons, W. S. 1871. *The Theory of Political Economy*. London: Macmillan.

Keynes, J. M. 1919. *The Economic Consequences of the Peace*. London: Macmillan.

Lewin, L. 1967. *Planhushållningsdebatten*. Stockholm: Almqvist & Wiksell.

Loveday, A. 1931. *Britain & World Trade: Quo Vadimus and Other Economic Essays*. London: Longmans, Green & Co.

Marshall, A. 1961. *Principles of Economics*. 9th ed. London: Macmillan.

Myrdal, G. 1958. *Value in Social Theory*. New York: Harper & Brothers.

Parsons, T. 1982. "Wants and Activities in Marshall." J. C. Wood, ed., *Alfred Marshall: Critical Assessments*, 1:181–199. London: Croom Helm.

Schumpeter, J. A. 1953 (1918). "Die Krise der Steuerstaates." In *Aufsätze zur Soziologie*. Tübingen: Mohr.

Senior, N. 1938. *An Outline of the Science of Political Economy*. London: Allen & Unwin.

Sugden, R. 2000. "Team Preferences." *Economics and Philosophy* 16:175–204.

18

From Wartime Provisioning to Barbarous Prosperity: Eli F. Heckscher's Investigations of Food Consumption in Early Modern Sweden

Mats Morell

When the first volume of *Sveriges ekonomiska historia från Gustav Vasa* (*The Economic History of Sweden Since Gustavus Vasa*) was published in 1935, it contained a chapter on the standard of living in the sixteenth century, which soon roused considerable debate among Swedish economic historians, ethnologists, and cultural geographers. In subsequent volumes published in 1936 and 1949, Heckscher carried the investigations further to cover the period up to 1815. The results were included in his abbreviated version of Swedish economic history, which stretched backward to the Middle Ages and forward to 1914 (*Svenskt arbete och liv* [1941], published posthumously in English as *An Economic History of Sweden* in 1954).[1]

The matter of discussion largely centered on Heckscher's choice of method and sources.[2] Heckscher's most important precursor was Hans Forssell, whose promising carrier as historian was aborted in 1875 when he was appointed minister of finance.[3] Forssell estimated mid-sixteenth century grain production and cattle stock by a massive working up of tithe records and cattle tax records for the Älvsborg ransom. He concluded that per capita grain harvest of the Vasa age (mid-sixteenth century) was almost similar to early-nineteenth-century harvests. Vasa age harvests actually reached two-thirds of the per capita harvest around 1870, by which time a century of massive reclamation had turned grain (oats) into a major Swedish export item. The per capita number of cattle according to Forssell had diminished sharply over the three hundred years between 1571 and his time of writing, indicating a lowered consumption of animal foodstuffs. It has been shown that Forssell underestimated sixteenth-century population, and thus his per capita production figures became suspiciously high, although his tithes records (according to Heckscher) underestimated grain harvests. To support his view of declining standards, however, Forssell—without much of a critical eye—had compared "food budgets" for the workers of royal estates with similar material from the seventeenth and eighteenth century and concluded that normal food provisioning was diminishing in these latter centuries. In particular consumption of meat and fish seemed to shrink.[4]

Heckscher distrusted the production figures that could be deducted from grain tithes rolls. He believed that the fact that they originated from a taxation process meant that they underestimated actual production.[5] Therefore, instead of trying to calculate production and deduct per capita consumption by dividing production estimates with population figures he preferred to use direct consumption data. For the sixteenth century he primarily used accounts of food provisioning of workers and other categories on farms and castles owned by the crown, found in the ledger of the realm (rikshuvudboken) of 1573. He also used—just as did Forssell—local food budgets from the crown's "stock farms," mining establishments, and smithies in the 1550s. These food budgets were to regulate what the concerned populations, mostly different categories of manual workers, were to be served to eat, as part of their wages. The material from the seventeenth century was much scantier since the state by the reign of Gustavus II Adolphus had disposed of its stock farms and sold or leased out its mining establishments and smithies. Heckscher used budgets from a couple of remaining castles and norms in a household advisory book for young nobles. For the period 1720–1815, finally, Heckscher based his study upon around thirty budgets mostly from private manors, referring mainly to male and female farm workers.[6]

A "Physiological Comparison" of Living Standard

Heckscher did not really aim at describing food consumption per se, but at finding quantitative measures of the level of the living standard amongst the broad masses of the population and its development since the middle of the sixteenth century. For that reason, he argued, we

ought to know how the entire needs of the Swedish people were met in that age ... in everything relating to human life.... Indubitably it is possible to catch glimpses of this as far as court and aristocracy are concerned.... But that route does not lead us far in the direction of a total picture of the subsistence of the people, and in particular it is impossible to arrive in that way at numerical results.

Therefore his exposition had to be confined to food supply only. Thus, the level of food consumption became an indicator of living standard in general.[7] This was perhaps somewhat annoying, as Heckscher was able to conclude from price relations that people of the sixteenth century were relatively well endowed with foodstuffs compared to other material necessities and that changes in food availability and agricultural production had been less dramatic than changes concerning industrial production.[8] For this reason concentration of food consumption would tend to understate the changes in living standards over the ages.

Furthermore, he had to resort not to an "economic" but to a "physiological comparison," by weighing different food stuffs by their energy content measured in (kilo)calories, rather than by their prices as would be natural for an economist. For one thing, it was not altogether easy to collect a body of plausible price data, but Heckscher described it more as a matter of the index problem:

Cash amounts of course tell us nothing in terms of comparisons with later times, and any conversion by reference to some supposed so-called price level is meaningless since in order to make any sense it has to be based upon largely unchanged consumption habits, while the characteristic feature of progress is precisely the reverse.[9]

This statement seems to imply that the index problem was impossible to solve when very long periods of time were involved. Paradoxically, Heckscher thereby indirectly proclaimed as impractical, attempts to use the "monetary approach," or the real income method in order to study the long term trend of the standard of living, which he, along with many other—indeed, perhaps most—economists in other circumstances, advocated.[10]

The problem with the physiological comparisons, according to Heckscher, granted that one kept to foodstuffs, was that "changes in taste . . . almost never found expression. . . . Such aspects have to be tacked on to the conclusions arrived at without even a thought of their being able to be expressed quantitatively."[11]

By now it may be suggested that Heckscher was unnecessarily pessimistic about the index problem concerning his long periods. In fact, his results showed convincingly that the type of (food) consumption was altered rather marginally between the mid-sixteenth and late eighteenth century. Consumption of beer, fish, and meat dwindled, rye gradually replaced barley, but still, a storage economy based on preserved (salted or dried) animal foodstuffs together with dried bread and beer dominated the menus of the working populations Heckscher studied. Had he really resorted to performing only a comparison of consumption levels or standard of living in the sixteenth, the seventeenth, and the eighteenth centuries, then it would have been possible to weigh the consumed amounts with their prices, using a fixed food basket. The disturbing changes in consumption patterns occurred later.[12]

But the fact is that Heckscher at least initially rather seem to have been inclined to compare food consumption levels in the sixteenth century with consumption levels of his own lifetime. In such a comparison for sure, the index problem might have been insoluble.

While there are problems with his having to resort to food consumption alone and to quantitative and qualitative statements of what was eaten, rather than the monetary value of it, this method also had its merits. It turned Heckscher into a historian rather than an economist, and it made him provide vivid (albeit on some points doubtful) illustrations of material life of sixteenth-century Sweden. It also provided him with elements needed to measure grain production (for human consumption) in preindustrial Sweden.[13]

As for the reason for this choice of method, for the resort to food consumption alone, the purely physiological comparisons, there is one very simple explanation: he had used it before.

The Food Provisioning Problem in World War I

Largely, Heckscher tried to qualify Forssell's statements, which I referred to above. But he received inspiration from elsewhere also. During the early years of World War I, Heckscher devoted considerable energy to the question of food provisioning in blockaded Sweden. This theme occurred in his *Världskrigets ekonomi* (*Economy in the World War*, 1915) and he wrote about it also in the periodicals *Svensk Tidskrift* (Swedish Review), which he founded and published together with Gösta Bagge, and *Ekonomisk Tidskrift* (Economic Review).[14] In short, Heckscher proposed a deliberate storage program. He asserted that by proper storage and distribution policy Sweden could manage self-sufficiency during blockades even without changing the direction of agricultural production, that is, without affecting the far-reaching specialization on production of butter and pork, which at that time necessitated voluminous peacetime grain imports.[15] To come to terms with the problem he proposed, already in 1915, a special commission on war preparedness (Statens krigsberedskapskommission, hereafter SKK), which was indeed inaugurated later the same year. The task of the commission was not to regulate food production during the ongoing war, to govern distribution of food, food storage or food rationing etc. Other authorities governed these matters. SKK rather "investigated the possibilities of self-sufficiency of the country and by discussions tried to indicate suitable ways for the arrangement of food provisioning during possible future blockades with or without domestic crop failures."[16]

Naturally, Heckscher was appointed to the commission, and he wrote large parts of the report, which came in five separate volumes, the most important one in this respect being the fourth, entitled *Folknäringen vid krig* (Popular Wartime nutrition) and prepared by a subcommittee led by Heckscher. It made use of Sweden's foremost experts of agricultural sciences and nutrition. It went into great detail: one appendix concerned the absorption of wheat and rye flour in the human intestinal canal, with special respect to grinding and sifting.[17]

The first chapter of *Folknäringen vid krig* dealt with the nutritive needs of the population, and, more specifically, the need for energy, proteins, fats, salt, and spices. Embarking from Hultgren and Landergren's classical study of consumption among Swedish farm hands in 1891 and a calculation based on German material by the nutritionist pioneer Carl Voit, it was concluded that the average male worker in Sweden needed 3,300 kilocalories (including 10 percent wastage) a day. With help of a scale of the relative requirements for men and women of different ages and age differentiated population figures, it was determined that the annual energy requirement of the total Swedish population in 1912–13 reached 5,247 billion kilocalories. Similarly the average male Swede worker needed, according to SKK, 80 grams of palatable protein a day, implying that the total population needed 133,498 tons. Furthermore, the male average worker needed 56 grams of fats, and totally 35,000 tons of salt was needed annually (16.5 g per person per day), whereas the need for spices most easily could be estimated from peacetime import volumes.[18]

The second chapter, written by Heckscher with support from Gustaf Leufwén, the director of the Swedish agricultural society, provided a statistical overview of peacetime food consumption in Sweden. Heckscher embarked from production figures, deducted vegetable products (and milk) used for animal feeding and processing to beer and spirits, calculated the net import of foodstuffs, and arrived at figures for domestic consumption in tons. With help of figures for energy contents of different foodstuffs it was concluded that the population consumed 6,956 billion kilocalories annually; 60 percent came from vegetable sources, 40 percent from animal sources; 14 percent of the kilocalories consumed accrued to net import. All in all, this meant 4,376 kilocalories per consumption unit (= average working adult man) and day. But the estimate excluded energy from alcoholic beverages, including beer—"which cannot really be seen as nutrients but still supply the human body with a considerable amount of kilocalories." Including alcoholic beverages, total consumption reached 7,142 billion kilocalories. Per consumption unit, this almost equaled 4,500 kilocalories a day, that is, 1,200 kilocalories more than the minimum requirement.[19] The rest of the chapter was devoted to the provisioning balance of fodder for animals, fertilizers, and so forth needed for sustaining domestic food production.

The third chapter, also written by Heckscher, consisted of calculations on food resources during blockades, and the fourth and last chapter dealt with the general grounds for food economy in wartime.

The calorie arithmetic of SKK 1918, *Folknäringen vid krig*, was Heckscher's main reference point in his sixteenth-century investigations. With some minor revisions, he returned to the figures for the energy content of SKK 1918, when he made his calculations concerning the energy content of sixteenth-century diets. Likewise, he used the average-working-man norm of caloric requirements from SKK 1918, and the note on beer not being viewed as a nutrient or at all a food element was withheld in his study.

Results: A "Barbarous Prosperity"

Even excluding beer, the quantitative results for the sixteenth century were comparable to those SKK had calculated for 1912–13. Only a few budget norms accruing to forested districts fell below the 3,300 kilocalorie limit stated by SKK. With beer included, most of the Vasa age data took on proportions that clearly surprised Heckscher. The most niggardly sixteenth-century food budget provided 3,752 kilocalories a day per worker, but the average worker of the ledger of realm of 1573 received 5,061 kilocalories a day. Corn, including corn for brewing and distilling, was the most important food item. No budget gave as little corn as the average adult man consumed in 1926–30 (175 kg). The average worker of the ledger of the realm in 1573 received close to 700 kg annually. All figures below 500 kg originated from forested or mining districts. Even so, consumption of animal-based food—foremost butter, beef, and fish—was far from insignificant. Excluding beer from the total, 30–40 percent of the energy intake originated from animal foodstuffs; including beer, the figure was 23–29 percent. Beef and butter consumption was on par with that of the early twentieth century, whereas fish consumption was much higher.

"And then finally," Heckscher noted, "there is the beer." According to Heckscher, regular statements in the sixteenth century talked of one jug, corresponding to 2.62 liters, as a minimum daily requirement for adults, men and women alike. Heckscher also refers to a letter where Duke Johan complained to his father the king that his guards needed 1.5 jugs on weekdays and 2 jugs on Sundays. This approached 1,500 liters per person a year, while total consumption of beer and small ale per consumption unit (grown men) was only 61.2 liters in 1911–15. Whereas beer consumption according to SKK gave on average 26 kilocalories per person and day, the average in the ledger of 1573 was close to 1,000 kilocalories for ordinary farm hands and around 2,000 kilocalories for members of the royal court.[20]

The seventeenth-century budgets testified to a decrease of the average energy intake by close to 30 percent. In particular there was a decrease in consumption of animal foodstuffs like meat and butter, and the animal-based proportion of diet sank by around 50 percent. After some discussion on the size of the grain barrel, Heckscher concluded that the energy intake of the eighteenth century was equivalent to about 90 percent of that of the sixteenth. It was thus 10 percent higher than during the seventeenth century. The gross consumption of corn was on par with that of the sixteenth century, which implies a rise of about one sixth compared with the seventeenth century figures. Beer consumption during the eighteenth century was only one-third of that of the sixteenth century and about half of that of the seventeenth. Distilled spirits constituted an uncertain factor; Heckscher assumed an increase in drinking during the eighteenth century, but he did not venture to estimate the extent to which this affected the net consumption of corn. The consumption of animal-based food continued to drop. Consumption of meat in the eighteenth century was 25 percent of that of the sixteenth century or 75 percent of that of the seventeenth. Fish consumption was likewise just a quarter of that of the sixteenth century and 69 percent of that of the seventeenth. Consumption of milk had increased, but Heckscher concluded that, all in all, a shift took place from animal to vegetable foodstuffs (meaning cereals, since he rightly considered potatoes of little importance before 1800). Furthermore, Heckscher found that corn consumption tended to increase in the course of the eighteenth century. Daily energy intake, exclusive of beer, was around 3,000–3,500 kilocalories per capita, according to the eighteenth-century budgets. The animal based proportion of consumed energy revolved around merely 10 percent.[21]

Albeit generous, sixteenth-century food provisioning was monotonous according to Heckscher. He did not consider total energy intakes for ordinary people exceedingly high, as they "rather were somewhat lower than figures for 1912–13," but figures for consumption of specific food elements was much higher than just before the world war. The explanation of this riddle was that much of what was considered normal in Heckscher's present day diet was totally missing in the food budgets: potatoes, other vegetables, milk, cheese, eggs, and sugar.[22] The diet was based on what he considered a "storage economy": "The commodities were accumulated in the storehouses while in season, and people thus lived on the stocks at least until the next season, and often longer. It seems as though on principle they actually disliked consuming fresh food on an everyday basis, perhaps out of fear of being tempted into reducing the stocks."[23]

Food production and food supply was discontinuous, Heckscher explained. Cereals along with meat came only in the autumn, when the cattle were fattened after summer grazing and had to be slaughtered, as winter feeding was usually deficient. Deficient winter feeding in turn meant that milk was produced mainly during summer, when the cows were grazing, often far away from the villages. Fish was—because of spawning seasons—caught mainly in certain brief periods. Thus foodstuffs had to be preserved. Milk was mainly stored as butter or cheese, but in general Heckscher assumed that what could not be dried effectively was salted. He based his belief on royal admonitions, primarily letters of Gustavus Vasa. The bulk of the requirements of the broad masses and the upper classes alike were met with coarse stored bread, beer, and, as far as animal-based foods were concerned, by "green-salted butter and by meat and fish both dried and salted, usually a year old and often much older than that."[24] Everything was "washed down with one single drink, namely beer."[25] Heckscher concluded that "for those parts of the broad layers of the people, which has been possible to study, one has again to assert an admittedly still very profound, but yet rather barbarous prosperity."[26]

Heckscher did not believe the type of diet underwent any profound changes as the broad masses of population was concerned, in the seventeenth or eighteenth centuries—even though *brännvin* (vodka), rye bread, and finally potatoes became more and more important. The storage economy was largely unaltered. As for the upper classes and in particular the court, they had already in the sixteenth century permitted themselves more fresh meat, game, along with wine, sugar, and other luxuries. During the seventeenth century the upper classes were able to develop "a more multi-faceted luxury, crude and barbarous admittedly...but with a European emphasis among magnates with cultural pretensions."[27]

In explaining the "barbarous prosperity" of the sixteenth century and development thereafter, Heckscher largely resorted to Malthus. He did account for the inner calm of the realm during Gustavus Vasa and for the general lack of wars. But of more principal importance was that the population seemed not to grow faster than food production capacity did in the sixteenth century. He was unclear why, but somewhat vaguely seem to have thought of the influence of restrictive inheritance and marriage patterns. Thus, sixteenth century Sweden was an "exception" to Malthus's otherwise "well documented theory" that "population has a tendency to surpass food resources."[28] The worsened situation of the seventeenth century followed largely from the burdens of the great power policies and the war coupled with a tendency for an out-of-proportion population growth: a Malthusian situation.[29] The fact, finally, that the improvement of the largely peaceful eighteenth century was not more profound was attributed to a Malthusian tendency of the population to increase too fast compared to the means of provisioning.[30]

Increased cultivation of rye at the expense of barley helped to explain the increased consumption of rye bread and the decreased importance of beer. The fact that diets became more and more based on cereals could be linked to reclamation, largely occurring at the expense of fodder producing meadows and pastures and thus at the expense of animal husbandry. Reclamation in turn was explained by relative price changes: grain prices were rising both compared to animal food prices and in relation to prices of manufactured goods for large parts of the eighteenth century. Relative price increases on grain promoted reclamation and grain production and explained the (relative) downturn of animal production.[31]

Heckscher had problems, however, in explaining this relative price change and its persistence. Taken for granted that increased consumption of animal foodstuffs follows from increasing prosperity, why did demand in animal products not raise their prices and thereby stimulate animal production? Heckscher makes two attempts at solving this riddle. At first, he proposes that "the downturn in animal production was not felt as any drawback among the broad layers and therefore did not raise the prices of animal foodstuffs, simply because the simple people could not have afforded them under any circumstances." Furthermore, Heckscher performs a comparison of wages and cost of living of craftsmen, indicating a profound downturn in their living standards. Therefore, "the source for the surplus accruing to large parts of the farmers" might be sought in "income redistribution between the agrarian population and the non-agrarian groups of the broad layers." But he was doubtful about this and found it hard to accept the thought "of a reduced standard of living for any large population groups what so ever since the seventeenth century when the wars pressed everybody except the nobility." Instead he ended up with a theory of changed preferences: he found it "far from excluded that a transformation of taste-habits had occurred and brought with it reduced demand for animal foodstuffs, so that the reduction in their production did not lead to price increases, bur rather the opposite."[32]

More recent discussions have been closer to Heckscher's first propositions. Relative price increases on grain have been attributed to population pressure driving up the prices of cheaper vegetable foodstuffs such as grain (and later potatoes). Increased grain production could (before the agricultural revolution), it has been argued, come about only by farmers taking marginal land in to use. Therefore average yields might have been pressed down implying that more grain could be produced only at rising unit costs. Moreover, by the income effect of rising grain prices, the spending power of poor working people's households shrank, and because demand for grain had lower elasticity of price and income than demand for meat, butter, and other animal foodstuffs—perhaps even to the extent that more grain was consumed per household when relative grain prices rose—this contributed to the relative rise of grain prices.[33] In the light of these discussions, Heckscher's theory of changing preferences seems to be an unnecessary hypothesis.[34]

Food Quality and Sensationalism

In part one of *Sveriges Ekonomiska historia*, dealing with the sixteenth century and comparing consumption levels with the (then) present days, Heckscher is lured into a degree of sensationalism. He seems trying to make the reader astonished at the result that farmhands of the Vasa age ate as much as workers of 1912–13. He describes with unhidden fascination the profound qualitative differences between sixteenth- and twentieth-century diets, the extreme monotony of diets revealed by the sixteenth-century food budgets, the heavy salting of food, the supposed poor quality of longley stored food items. When speaking of "green-salted butter," Heckscher clearly interpreted "green" as green with age and heavy salting. But in particular he marvels at the enormous quantities of beer that sixteenth-century people drank. The heavy beer drinking was explained by the "enormous thirst," provoked by the heavy salting of food, but the "oceans of beer" also "made it easier for people of the ages to wash down food, which not only a modern palate, but also those then living, must have found most unappetizing." Likewise, Heckscher explains the role of spices by the need to "deaden the taste of spoiled food and sour beer." Almost joyfully, he reports an anecdote concerning how King Gustavus himself ordered that a party of butter that had happened to be forgotten in the storehouse for three years "should be purveyed to dalkarlar (men from Dalecarlia) working on the castle, with their since long well known digestive capacity."[35] The statements concerning the quality of the food of the sixteenth century gave rise to criticisms. They seemed to imply that food staples in sixteenth century generally were of defective quality, which could not be asserted. According to Sam Hedar, "green salted butter" more likely meant butter salted lightly in fresh condition. The prefix "green" was, even misleading in connection with butter, according to Hedar. "Salt green" meat, as Phebe Fjellström has demonstrated, connoted "fresh meat immersed in a strong brine without first having been smoked or dried."[36] Beer was not only a drink among others. To prepare parts of the barley harvest into malt and subsequently beer was one particular way of preparing a nutritive food. Beer was used to soak dried bread and beer soup with dried bread or blood bread was a standard item in the seventeenth and eighteenth century hospital and orphanage menus. Still, in the early nineteenth century it was eaten instead of milk or butter with porridge.[37] And the role of spices could be interpreted in wholly other ways than

those Heckscher proposed: as culturally grounded luxurious stimu-
lants, precursors to the tea, coffee, and chocolate of the eighteenth
century.[38]

In the subsequent volumes this sensationalist trace withered away
and the author concentrates on emphasizing and discussing the
changes in consumption levels from the sixteenth to the eighteenth
century. Heckscher appears as much more of an analytic economic historian, when dealing with the same problem in the eighteenth-century
volume of his work in 1949.

Further Critique and Revisions

Some critics denied the possibility and meaningfulness of trying to calculate nutritive figures of diets of past time.[39] Most reviewers, however, accepted the principles but concentrated on the use of sources,
either their capacity to mirror consumption of the actual groups concerned, or their capacity to show representative figures for the population at large.

Heckscher firmly trusted the accurateness of his food budgets. He
argued that they furnished "conclusions reliable in all essentials," they
were "unlikely to contain any material source errors for the personnel
whose consumption they govern, since in a number of instances
the quantities of foodstuffs in question are issued and accounted
for."[40] The material "consisted ... for the most part ... of actual food
budgets extracted from the accounts of estates."[41] With this, however,
Heckscher did not really mean that the food budgets constituted
accounts of delivered foodstuffs, but merely that they were not simply
feeding suggestions of the type to be found in the ever-increasing flood
of eighteenth-century agricultural and housekeeping advisory literature. In the chapter on food consumption in the eighteenth century he
made this clear: it was a question of norms. Nevertheless they were
"part and parcel of an accounting for ongoing activities .... Even if it
must be admitted that their conformity with the figures in the accounts
themselves has not been verified."[42]

In fact, it has been shown that a few of Heckscher's budgets were
actual accounts, mostly however, they constituted norms to be applied
for future feeding. Thus in principle we meet with two types of sources
with differing source-critical problems. A priori it may be assumed that
the returns of accounts furnish more reliable information than the
norms, and obviously Heckscher agreed on that. With regard to the

norms, discussions focused on whether they were followed at all. Cultural geographer David Hannerberg doubted this and called for comparisons with other data. Historian Birgitta Odén, fellow economic historian Gustaf Utterström, and later Morell showed by examples that the norms generally functioned as guidelines. In many instances they were foregone, for sure it was no question of they stating "quantities actually available."[43]

Arthur Montgomery and Sven Ljung took up another issue. They argued that the food provisioning of the sixteenth-century royal stock farms represented wages in kind, and therefore the seemingly enormous portions included amounts that could either be sold to provide the recipient with other necessities or be distributed among his family. As the natural economy was more or less being replaced by a monetary one in the seventeenth century and wages payments most likely more took the form of cash allowances by then, it was more likely that food provisioning budget actually represented individual consumption in the seventeenth century. Odén shows convincingly that this critique largely overshot the mark, the food budgets most likely represented individual portions even in the sixteenth century. She also shows, however, that there seems to have been some mistaken use by Heckscher of the accounts in the ledger of 1573. Heckscher divided two different summary titles of provisioned food volumes entered in the ledger by census numbers referring only to people receiving provisioning according to one of the two entries. Therefore, per capita figures from that particular source—which in fact constituted actual accounts and which Heckscher considered most important since it involved over five thousand crown estate workers—became too high.[44]

Naturally, Heckscher was aware that the peasant population's food consumption could diverge from that indicated by the budgets from crown estates of the sixteenth century. He argued "that peasants in general existed at a lower level," but that the differences hardly were significant:

The only opinion one can express with complete certainty concerns the people of the crown estates and the more or less industrial establishments; and it is incontestable that physiologically the standard at which they lived was distinctly a high one according to modern conceptions. Furthermore it does not appear reasonable to assume any very great difference between them and the peasants, for one would then have to reckon upon a mass influx to places where better food was supplied; and nothing is known, to me at least, of any such phenomenon.[45]

Heckscher argued similarly concerning eighteenth-century food budgets from private estates. He also compared farmhand budgets, with budgets for hospital inmates and paupers, and as they received only little less, the comparison spoke for the accurateness of the estate food budgets and for the possibility to generalize from them. Calculations on per capita supply of corn in Stockholm in 1790, based on customs material, pointed in the same direction.[46] Why would the proprietors of estates "generally have paid their male (and female) workers more than what was normal for the sector of the populace to which they belonged or which simply enjoyed a social position substantially higher than that of the servant class."[47]

The presumptions are that there existed a rudimentary free labor market, that (potential) laborers were mobile, that they were informed about "wage conditions" and that their reaction to "wage" differentials were stronger than other social or cultural ties. In particular, Per Nyström opposed this and referred to indications that such freedom of movement did not exist in the sixteenth century. Peasants, on one hand, were economically weak and yet they crowded (as Gustavus Vasa complained) together on their homesteads despite royal exhortations to migrate and clear new land. Royal stock farms, on the other hand, obtained compulsory laborers who were guarded like prisoners.[48]

K.-G. Hildebrand attacked Heckscher's conclusions from a more empirical point of view. He showed that if the annual per capita salt consumption implied in Heckscher's sixteenth-century royal food budgets had applied to the entire Swedish population, then total salt consumption would have been three times larger than the entire annual import of salt. Thus, Heckscher's figures for salt consumption in the sixteenth century could not be generalized. Moreover, Hildebrand found no reason why the food budgets of crown establishments at all should be representative of the diet of the broad layers of the population who lived away from the crown establishments. The crown's accounts related to large-scale, necessarily systematically organized supply of foodstuffs. Rules were simple and uniform, quantities were ample, and measures, methods, proportions, and practices were stereotyped. He considered the possibility that total per capita consumption was much more modest among ordinary peasants than according to the food budgets used by Heckscher. He also argued that the special organization of the crown economy caused food purveyed by the crown to be more one-sided and more based on heavily salted items than was the diet of the peasantry.[49]

Similarly, Bertil Boëthius and Gustaf Utterström questioned the possibilities to generalize the diet from of eighteenth-century manorial food budgets. Boëthius argued that more of a lacto-animalic type of diet survived in peasant households than in the market-oriented large estates and that estates and iron works for practical reasons stuck to food that was easily stored and easily transported—corn. Utterström agreed and showed that inter alia contracts regulating the quantities of foodstuffs which peasants were obliged to supply to soldiers established on crofts on their land revealed an appreciably lower level of corn consumption than suggested by the food budgets.[50]

Finally, Boëthius and later Morell went on to show that there were important deficiencies in Heckscher's transformation of old measures. In brief, weight measures of the sixteenth and to a lesser extent the early seventeenth century was overrated, as was the volume of the grain barrel. On the other hand, the volume of the grain barrel of the eighteenth century was underestimated, as was the weight measures. The discrepancies were largest for the weight measures with which the animal foodstuffs were reckoned. Therefore, it has been concluded that Heckscher overstated consumption levels in the sixteenth century, and foremost the provisioning of animal foodstuffs. Likewise, he underestimated the provisioning of the eighteenth century, and foremost the provisioning of animal foodstuffs. Although the wavelike movement of provisioning levels remains, the magnitudes of change are largely evened out. Consumption levels of the sixteenth century appear less surprising, the fall in consumption to the seventeenth century and in particular the fall in the animal proportion of the diet appears less dramatic. In the eighteenth century this tendency was even broken, restoration of kilocalorie consumption since the sixteenth century was more or less complete by then and animal content of diets seemingly did hardly change at all from the seventeenth to the eighteenth century.[51]

Heckscher's Food Consumption Studies in Retrospect

In modified form, the result from Heckscher's food consumption studies has survived and been referred to in international standard writings. In spite of some obvious shortcomings, his investigations could indeed have constituted inspiring endeavors. But while international research into the topic was vigorous in the postwar period, it seems as if the massive critique that Heckscher's studies provoked put a lid on Swedish historical research into food consumption for several decades. Certainly his methods and sources were somewhat discredited by the criticisms, and mostly researchers who directly or in passing have addressed the food provisioning problem of preindustrial Sweden has embarked—like Forssell—from the production side.[52] But while most historians have remained skeptical of Heckscher's actual sixteenth-century consumption figures, new research has largely given support to his "vegetabilization" thesis of the eighteenth century and his notion of the heavy dominance for vegetable foodstuffs in general, and grain in particular, in preindustrial diets.[53] The ultimate irony is then, that Heckscher, despite distorted use of sources, despite deficient transformation of old measures and despite unfounded optimism concerning the possibilities to generalize results, seems to have arrived at conclusions that subsequently have been accepted by later research. Undoubtedly he had a deep understanding of the ages he studied, and a considerable amount of *fingerspitzgefühle*, but is it not somewhat discomforting for our profession that everything seems to have been wrong—except for the conclusions.

Notes

1. Heckscher published previews of his consumption studies concerning the sixteenth century in articles in *Dagens Nyheter* in 1931 and 1935 (Heckscher 1931, 1935a, and 1935b). Taken together, these brief articles already stated the main conclusions and methodical considerations. There was a reply by Sven Palme in 1931 criticizing Heckscher's alleged overstatement of the one-sidedness of sixteenth-century diet. Palme also wrote slightly ironically about Heckscher's conclusion that energy intake was as high in the 1570s as in the 1910s—in essence, of course, people had very similar nutritive needs at both points of time.

2. For a comprehensive and much more detailed overview of the debate, see Morell (1987).

3. Cf. Heckscher (1936:145).

4. Forssell (1884:54–60, 119–120).

5. The original effort in trying to estimate production by use of tithe records in Sweden was Forssell (1884). The argument about the usability of tithe records lingers on. Recent optimistic statements are found in Myrdal and Söderberg (1991), reworked in English in Myrdal and Söderberg (2002). See also Leijonhufvud (2001). A very skeptical view is presented in Palm (1993).

6. See Morell (1987:76–90) for references and a critical discussion.

7. Heckscher (1935–36, 1:88). The citation is translated in Morell (1987:71–72).

8. Heckscher (1935–36, 1:126).

9. Heckscher (1935–36, 1:91). Citation translated in Morell (1987:72). In the *Dagens Nyheter* articles this position is very clearly expressed also.

10. See, for example, Hicks (1939:697–700) and Hartwell (1980:95–104). The heart of that method is to let the real income be a proxy for standard of living. Rather than trying to think out and read off a number of objectively measurable indicators for nutritive standard, housing standard, health standard, and the like, the analyst permits a historical individual to choose for himself or herself what they want to utilize numerically defined resources for. For a vigorous statement of the critique of this subjective method, see Gustafsson (1965); cf. Lundh (1983). Heckscher principally, albeit perhaps implicitly, approved of the real income method by referring to *Wages in Sweden*, published in 1933 by Bagge, Lindahl, and Svennilsson (1933), as the outstanding source for knowledge about living standard in Sweden from the 1860s onward. See Heckscher (1976 [1941]:302; 1963 [1954]:259–260).

11. Heckscher (1935–36, 1:91); quotation translated in Morell (1987:77).

12. Indeed it has been argued, that it would have been easier, with the help of prices, to estimate the distribution of consumption on different items "than to bring about trustworthy calorie-calculus" (Söderberg 1987:346).

13. In doing so, he embarked from the food budget statements of grain provisioning to male and female farm workers, taking four barrels per adult worker annually as the norm. Concerning forested and fishery districts, he wrote down the norm to three barrels as indications that people in these regions ate less grain and proportionally more animal foodstuffs. Further, he took account of the age structure—possible only from 1750 onward—reducing estimated consumption by children and elderly people according to a physiological scale. He arrived at estimated figures for total human grain consumption and deducted the net import. The result pointed at an increase in grain consumption (and production) of 40.7 percent from 1750 to 1810. Naturally, this mainly reflected population increase. Therefore, since population increase of the entire period 1720–1815 reached some 70 percent, while food budgets indicated some increase of per capita consumption over the eighteenth century, he dared to estimate the increase of grain production at roughly 75 percent for the entire period 1720 to 1815. Cf. Heckscher (1949, 2:152–162).

14. For example, in Heckscher (1914) and Heckscher (1915b).

15. His argument was that a reorientation of agriculture would lead to a "bad use of the country's scarce productive forces." There were cheaper ways of securing wartime provisioning. See Heckscher (1915b:92). Naturally the problem reoccurred in the standard economic history of Sweden in the First World War, which he edited in 1926.

16. Mannerfelt (1926:87).

17. SKK (1918).

18. SKK (1918:8–15).

19. SKK (1918:17–49). The quote is from p. 48.

20. Heckscher (1935–36, 1:96–97, and appendix III). Mistakenly, Heckscher reckoned the sixteenth-century jug as corresponding to 2.62 liters, whereas it likely held no more than 2.45 liters. Cf. Morell (1987:98–99), and Morell (1988:33). Revisions of the measures of the

grain barrel, and the weight measures used for hops, led to revisions of the calorie intake from beer in Heckscher (1963 [1954]:69–70). Normally, budgets stated the amount of grain allowed without specifying its use. In most cases, Heckscher calculated, the amount used for brewing by help of a sixteenth-century recipe and the recorded figures concerning provisioning of hops.

21. Heckscher (1935–36, 2:420–422), Heckscher (1949, 1:176–180), and Heckscher (1949, 2:7–21). The drop from the sixteenth to the seventeenth century was most evident for Gripsholm Castle, as Heckscher had data from both centuries for this place. The summary of results herein is largely culled from Morell (1987:69–70). Cf. Morell (1989:17).

22. Heckscher (1935–36, 1:98, 99).

23. Heckscher (1935–36, 1:85). Citation translated in Morell (1987:70). Heckscher thought that the medieval economy was of the same type. Cf. Heckscher (1954:20–22).

24. Heckscher (1935–36, 1:84–87; translation in Morell (1987:71).

25. Ibid., 98.

26. Ibid., 99.

27. Heckscher (1936, 2:420). Citation translated in Morell (1987:71).

28. Heckscher (1935, 1:127). Cf. discussion in Myrdal and Söderberg (2002:24–25, 133–135).

29. Heckscher (1936, 2:422).

30. Heckscher (1949, 1:180; cf. 42, 57). This statement, according to which large parts of the population lived on narrow existential margins, formed the basis of his famous analysis of the mortality cycles of the eighteenth century as being based on, correlated by, and indeed determined by harvest fluctuations. Ibid., 37–41 and diagram I and V.

31. Ibid., 238–240.

32. Ibid., 240 (all quotations) and diagram XXIII. Concerning income redistribution between rural and urban groups, cf. Söderberg (1983:9, 11).

33. Morell (1989:48–49). Cf., for example, Postan (1976); Abel (1980:11, 116ff), Le Roy Ladurie (1980:74–75, 113); Söderberg (1987:341). A more general discussion is found in Myrdal and Söderberg (2002:10ff).

34. The theory of changed preferences as determinant of the shift in eighteenth-century consumption pattern seems all the more implausible, as Heckscher himself noted that the development of food consumption in the eighteenth century in fact took a turn that was "so far from paving the way for what we now name modern circumstances that it rather pointed in the opposite direction" (1949, 2:181). The theory therefore seem to imply that the eighteenth century was a parenthesis during which people preferred a more cereal-based diet, whereas fifty years later they started to prefer animal-based diets again. The hypothesis of changed preferences also tallies badly with Heckscher's Malthusian theory of the relation between harvest fluctuations and mortality, which presupposed that large layers of population constantly lived within very narrow margins—which was hardly a matter of choice as the changed preference theory seem to imply.

35. For the quotes of the paragraph, see Heckscher (1935–36, 1:86–88, 97). Cf. Heckscher (1954:21–22). In the articles of 1931 and 1935 as well as in other popular writings (e.g., Heckscher 1941), this scent of sensationalism is even stronger.

36. Hedar (1949:223ff); Fjellström (1970:63). Citation translated in Morell (1987:91), where a more detailed discussion is to be found.

37. Utterström (1978:158–161); Morell (1989:182–189).

38. See, for example, Schivelbusch (1980:11–21).

39. E.g. Barkman (1939:698). For a discussion largely supportive of Heckscher's efforts, see Morell (1987:92–93). Cf. Morell (1989:60–62).

40. Heckscher (1935–36, 1:90); citations translated in Morell (1987:76).

41. Heckscher (1949, 2:175); citations translated in Morell (1987:76).

42. Ibid., 152–153; citations translated in Morell (1987:77).

43. Cf. Morell (1987:78–80). Quote from Heckscher (1935–36, 1:92); translated in Morell (1987:80). On the degree of conformity between norms and accounts in pauper provisioning, see Morell (1989:120–123, 182–222).

44. See discussion and references in Morell (1987:80–85).

45. Heckscher (1935–36, 1:97–98); both citations translated in Morell (1987:85). Heckscher confines the agreement to years of normal harvests.

46. Heckscher (1949, 2:153–158).

47. Ibid., 180.

48. Nyström (1974:100–101).

49. Hildebrand (1954). There is a more detailed discussion, with more references, in Morell (1987:87–88).

50. See for references and details Morell (1987:88–90). For a discussion of the possibilities to generalize data from food budgets and in particular data on provisioning of paupers, see Morell (1989:289–294).

51. See Morell (1987:91–105) for details, references, and magnitudes of revisions.

52. See, for example, Hannerberg (1941, 1971), Isacson (1979), Lindegren (1980), Gadd (1983), Palm (1993), and Palm (1998). Utterström (1957) and Utterström (1978), however, like Morell (1989), used sources of the food budget type.

53. Foremost, perhaps, by Morell (1989) summoned up in Morell (1990) and Palm (1998), who, like Montelius (1975), emphasize the dominance of grain even in forested districts where production (but because of interregional trade not necessarily consumption) was more centered on animal husbandry. Perhaps one might state that modern researchers tend to let the heavy dominance of cereals be valid for the sixteenth century as well. See Myrdal and Söderberg (2002). Research into Swedish preindustrial food consumption published prior to 1987 is discussed at some length in Morell (1989:16ff). For a brief synthesis, see Morell (1997).

References

Abel, W. 1980. *Agricultural Fluctuations in Europe: From the Thirteenth to the Twentieth Centuries*. London: Methuen and Company.

Bagge, G., E. Lindahl, and I. Svennilson. 1933. *Wages in Sweden, 1860–1930.* London and Stockholm: P. S. King/Norstedt.

Barkman, B. C. 1939. *Kungliga Svea Livgardes historia.* Stockholm: Stiftelsen för Svea Livgardes historia.

Fjellström, P. 1970. "Nord- och mellansvenskt kosthåll i kulturekologisk belysning." In N.-A. Bringeus, *Mat och miljö. En bok om svenska kostvanor,* 41–64. Lund: Gleerup.

Forssell, H. 1884. *Anteckningar om Sveriges jordbruksnäring i sextonde seklet.* Stockholm: Samson & Wallin.

Gadd, C.-J. 1983. *Järn och potatis. Jordbruk, teknik och social omvandling i Skaraborgs län 1750–1860.* Göteborg: Meddelanden från Ekonomisk-historiska instituionen.

Gustafsson, B. 1965. *Den norrländska sågverksindustrins arbetare 1890–1913. Arbets- och levnadsförhållanden.* Stockholm: Almquist & Wiksell.

Hannerberg, D. 1941. *Närkes landsbygd 1600–1820. Folkmängd och befolkningsrörelse. Åkerbruk och spannmålsproduktion.* Göteborg: Meddelanden från Göteborgs högskolas geografiska institution.

———. 1971. *Svenskt agrarsamhälle under 1200 år. Gård och åker. Skörd och boskap.* Stockholm: Läromedelsförlaget.

Hartwell, R. M. 1980. "The Rising Standard of Living in England 1800–50." In A. J. Taylor, *The Standard of Living in Britain in the Industrial Revolution,* 93–123. London: Methuen.

Heckscher, E. F. 1914. "Krigsberedskap och handelspolitik." *Ekonomisk tidskrift,* 383–396.

———. 1915a. *Världkrigets Ekonomi.* Stockholm: Nordstedt.

———. 1915b. "Vår lifsmedelstillgång i krigstider." *Svensk Tidskrift,* 89–97.

———. 1926. *Bidrag till Sveriges ekonomiska och sociala historia under och efter världsskriget.* Stockholm: P. A. Nordstedts.

———. 1931. "Från Gustav Vasa till våra dagar. Den svenska levnadsstandardens utveckling." *Dagens Nyheter,* February 8, 1931.

———. 1935a. "Svenska folkets levnadssätt genom tiderna I." *Dagens Nyheter,* May 28, 1935.

———. 1935b. "Svenska folkets levnadssätt genom tiderna II." *Dagens Nyheter,* May 31, 1935.

———. (1935–36). *Sveriges ekonomiska historia från Gustav Vasa.* Stockholm: Albert Bonniers.

———. 1936. "Hans Forssell." In *Ekonomisk-historiska studier,* 137–160. Stockholm: Bonniers.

———. 1941. "Femtonhundratalets svenska samhälle." *Svenska Turistföreningens årsskrift 1941. 1500-talet,* 17–28. Stockholm: Svenska turistföreningens förlag.

———. 1949. *Sveriges ekonomiska historia från Gustav Vasa.* Stockholm: Albert Bonniers.

———. 1954. *An Economic History of Sweden.* Cambridge, MA: Harvard University Press.

———. 1976. *Svenskt arbete och liv från medeltiden till nutiden.* Stockholm: Aldus.

Hedar, S. 1949. "Gustav Vasa och det saltgröna smöret." *Historisk Tidskrift* 1949, 253–262.

Hicks, J. R. 1939. "The Foundations of Welfare Economics." *Economic Journal* 49:696–712.

Hildebrand, K.-G. 1954. "Salt and Cloth in Swedish Economic History." *Scandinavian Economic History Review* 2, no. 1: 74–102.

Isacson, M. 1979. *Ekonomisk tillväxt och social differentiering 1650–1860. Bondeklassen i By socken Kopparbergs län.* Uppsala: Almqvist and Wiksell International.

Le Roy Ladurie, E. 1980. *The Peasants of Languedoc.* Urbana: University of Illinois Press.

Leijonhufvud, L. 2001. *Grain Tithes and Manorial Yields in Early Modern Sweden: Trends and Patterns of Production and Productivity.* Uppsala: Almqvist and Wiksell International.

Lindegren, J. 1980. *Utskrivning och utsugning. Produktion och reproduction I Bygdeå 1620–1640.* Stockholm: Almqvist & Wiksell.

Lundh, C. 1983. "Levnadsstandarden—indikatorer och mått: engelsk och svensk debatt om lönearbetarnas villkor 1750–1850." *Meddelanden från Ekonomisk-historiska institutionen, Lunds universitet* 29.

Mannerfelt, C. 1926. "Livsmedelspolitik och livsmedelsförsörjning 1914–1922." In E. F. Heckscher, *Bidrag till Sveriges ekonomiska och sociala historia under och efter världskriget*, 1:43–143. Stockholm: P.A. Nordstedt.

Montelius, S. 1975. *Leksands fäbodar. Leksands sockenbeksrivning.* Leksand: Leksands Kommun.

Morell, M. 1987. "Eli F. Heckscher, The 'Food Budgets' and Swedish Food Consumption From the 16th to the 19th Century: The Summing Up and Conclusions of a Long Debate." *Scandinavian Economic History Review* 35:67–107.

———. 1988. "Om mått- och viktsystemens utveckling i Sverige sedan 1500-talet. Vikt- och rymdmått fram till metersystemets införande." *Uppsala Papers in Economic History* 16.

———. 1989. *Studier i den svenska livsmedelskonsumtionens historia. Hospitalhjonens livsmedelskonsumtion 1621–1872.* Stockholm: Almqvist & Wiksell.

———. 1990. "Studies in the History of Swedish Food Consumption: Food Consumption among Institutionally Supported Paupers, 1621–1872." In Aerts, E., and H. Van der Wee, eds., *Recent Doctoral Research in Economic History.* D-session Proceedings Tenth International Economic History Congress. Leuven: Leuven University Press.

———. 1997. "Kosthållets utveckling." In B. M. P. Larsson, M. Morell, and J. Myrdal, eds., *Agrarhistoria*, 211–228. Stockholm: Almqvist and Wiksell International.

Myrdal, J., and J. Söderberg. 1991. *Kontinuitetens dynamik. Agrar ekonomi i 1500-talets Sverige.* Stockholm: Almqvist & Wiksell.

———. 2002. *The Agrarian Economy of Sixteenth Century Sweden.* Stockholm: Almqvist & Wiksell.

Nyström, P. 1974. "Avelsgårdsprojektet 1555–56. Några anteckningar." In T. Forser, ed., *Historieskrivningens dilemma och andra studier av Per Nyström*, 84–105. Stockholm: PAN/ Nordstedts.

Palm, L. A. 1993. *Människor och skördar. Studier kring agrarhistoriska metodproblem 1540–1770.* Göteborg: Historiska Institutionen, Göteborgs Universitet.

———. 1998. "Efterblivenhet eller rationell tidsanvändning—frågor kring det västsvenska ensädet." In L. A. Palm, C.-J. Gadd, and L. Nyström, eds., *Ett föränderligt agrarsamhälle. Västsverige i jämförande belsyning*, 13–81. Göteborg: Göteborgs Universitet.

Palme, S. 1931. "Kosthållet i Sverige på 1500-talet. Komplettering till en utredning av professor Heckscher." *Aftonbladet*, February 17, 1931.

Postan, M. M. 1976. *The Medieval Economy and Society*. Harmondsworth: Penguin Books.

Schivelbush, W. 1980. *Paradiset, smaken och förnuftet. Njutningsmedlens historia*. Stockholm: Alba.

SKK. 1918. *Folknäringen vid krig*. Stockholm: Statens Krigsberedskaspkommission.

Söderberg, J. 1983. "Levnadsnivåer, reallönetrender och 1700-talets inflation: Stockholm i ett europeiskt perspektiv." Paper presented at Nordisk forskningssymposium Levevillkor i Norden fra ca. 1700–1945, Sandbjerg 1983.

———. 1987. "Hade Heckscher rätt? Priser och reallöner i 1500-talets Stockholm." *Historisk tidskrift* 3:341–356.

Utterström, G. 1957. *Jordbrukets arbetare. Levnadsvillkor och arbetsliv på den svenska landsbygden från frihetstiden till mitten av 1800-talet*. Stockholm: Tiden.

———. 1978. *Fattig och föräldralös i Stockholm på 1600- och 1700-talen*. Umeå: Umeå University.

Part VII   The Man

19

A Portrait of Our Grandfather

Eva, Einar, Sten, and Ivar
Heckscher

Eli Filip Heckscher was born in Stockholm on November 24, 1879. His parents, both of whom were Jewish, had moved there from Copenhagen just a few years earlier. Eli's father, Isidor Heckscher, had earned a doctorate in law from Copenhagen University and was employed as a bank attorney. In addition, he served as Danish consul general in Stockholm. Eli's mother, Rosa Meyer, made important contributions to social work. Our grandfather thus was raised in an economically comfortable and socially well established family.

In 1907 Eli Heckscher married Ebba Westberg, a gentile born in 1874. She had grown up in the small provincial town of Hedemora, located some two hundred kilometers northwest of Stockholm. There her father had been the postmaster, then considered a rather prestigious position. Before her marriage to Eli, Ebba had worked as a secondary school teacher in the fashionable Stockholm suburb of Djursholm, socializing in the same circles as Alice Tegnér, Elsa and Nathanael Beskow, and their friends. She also published a book on the history of female education in Sweden. The couple had two sons. Sadly, the youngest died of tuberculosis at an early age.

Their eldest son, Gunnar Heckscher, was born in 1909. At the time, the family lived in Danderyd, another wealthy Stockholm suburb. Not long thereafter, however, they bought a house in central Stockholm. Gunnar followed in his father's footsteps, earning a Ph.D. at Uppsala University in 1934 and then setting out on an academic career. He was appointed a professor of political science at the Stockholm School of Social Work and Public Administration in 1948, moving to a similar position at Stockholm University in 1958. During the years 1961–65, Gunnar was the leader of the Swedish Conservative Party, then, as now, part of the liberal opposition. He later served as Swedish ambassador, first in New Delhi (1965–70), then in Tokyo (1970–75) and finally as a delegate to the United Nations (1975–76). He died in 1987.

In 1934, Gunnar Heckscher married a law student, Anna Britta Vickhoff. Their union was blessed with four children. The eldest of these was Eva (1936–2004), who took a lively and active interest in the preparation of this book. She began a career as a journalist before switching to the Swedish Foreign Office. She rose to become Swedish ambassador in Bangkok (1992–1996) and head of the Security Department of the Swedish Foreign Office (1996–2001). The second child, Einar, was born in 1938. He is a radical intellectual, well known for his translations of complex poetry and other literature. Next, in 1942, came Sten. He studied law at Uppsala University and, inter alia, became an attorney, undersecretary of state in the Ministry of Justice, cabinet minister for industry and commerce, national police commissioner, and finally president of the Administrative Court of Appeal in Stockholm. The youngest of the four siblings is Ivar, born in 1943. He chose a career in teaching and is well known as a Swedish advocate of Rudolf Steiner's anthroposophy.

Eva Heckscher

My grandfather never wore an overcoat—not even in subzero weather. Why? Quite simply, he did not want to get caught up in idle chatter. That, however, did not indicate a lack of interest in other people and their views and ideas. Quite the contrary, he was very much interested in others, especially young people.

As the eldest of his grandchildren, I had the greatest opportunity to be with him one on one. On those occasions, I never felt that I was unwelcome or boring. We chatted about many things, but he seldom talked about himself. He talked about issues, about things. I remember two in particular.

We were spending a week together at Kolmården, a forested area south of Stockholm. He told me of his intense pleasure at having been given his own railway car by the Swedish Railways when he traversed the country researching his thesis. The second thing he told me concerned a dreadful railroad accident, the Getå disaster, that had occurred during the 1910s in the area where we were, and of the deep distress he had felt at the time.

Thus learning about him as a person requires a roundabout approach. One rather obvious such possibility is to look at his library.

Naturally it was filled with massive scholarly tomes. But there were also some more recreational titles, such as the works of Conan Doyle, Austin Freeman, Gilbert Keith Chesterton, Freeman Wills Crofts, and Dorothy Sayers. All these writers shared at least one characteristic with each other and with my grandfather, the analytical mind of a detective. Another is my grandfather's way of reasoning his way to a solution. He always had a sidekick, and the discussions in the books, between Father Brown and Flambeau or Sherlock Holmes and Watson, also are relevant to my grandfather's style. In addition, the impish sense of humor that characterized Chesterton was similar to that of my grandfather. Most of you readers are no doubt too young to remember "The Flying Inn," Chesterton's story concerning teetotalers, of which he was not very fond. While my grandfather also was teetotaler he was far from militant, and his sympathies would have been with the author.

My grandfather loved beauty and was very fond of the sea. He frequently went sailing but, being easily distracted by discussions on one topic or another, ran aground more often than not. His boat's name was inspired by Galileo Galilei. He picked Galilei's saying, "*E pur si muove*"—"and yet she moves." That, of course, is the essential characteristic of a sailboat.

I well remember our last summer together. I had begun to study philosophy at school and was interested in the question of free will. Naturally, that summer we had rather intense discussions on the subject. I don't remember what position each of us took, but of course my grandfather's was the opposite of mine, regardless of what he really believed. After all, he was a teacher. His desire to train minds certainly permeated his work in this very building, which was so very important to him. Two major events in his life occurred in 1909: his eldest son was born and the Stockholm School of Economics was founded.

To once again raise the question of free will, my grandfather certainly must have believed in freedom of choice. This belief is reflected in the motto he chose for his life, a quotation I believe is from Horace: "*Non propter vitam vivendi perdere causas*," do not lose the purpose for the sake of living.

Einar Heckscher

As if often the case with memories, it is quite possible that what I remember of my grandfather is a mixture of fact and fiction. I was only a child when I knew him, and we were never really close. Within our family, I saw him largely as an object of veneration. He remained something of an authority figure to my father, even when they disagreed. When speaking about him, my father referred to my grandfather as Eli, but face-to-face he rather formally called him "father." When I was a child during World War II, someone told me that if the Germans had conquered Sweden my grandfather Eli was third on Hitler's execution list and my father was seventh. My grandfather was not a religious man, but during those times one was acutely aware of being a Jew, even in my strictly secular family.

Early during the war, my grandfather asked my father, who at the time was working and living in Uppsala, to move with his family into the large, solid stone house in East Stockholm where my grandparents lived. I believe that Eli somehow intended to return fire if the Gestapo came, relishing not the idea of an invasion but the concept of giving tit for tat.

My grandfather lived on the first floor together with my grandmother, a school teacher from Djursholm, who was several years his senior and a gentile. I suspect that she had married him with a certain fixity of purpose, which had evolved into something akin to worship. They had lost a baby son to tuberculosis, and I believe that sorrow never left my grandmother. She truly loved my father, but, for no apparent reason, sometimes seemed a bit afraid of him. But then my father knew very little about women, having been thrown into the world of adults when he was still in the early stages of puberty.

My parents and we four children moved into the two middle floors of the Stockholm house, with a Hungarian refugee student as a house guest. A friend of my father's, together with his French wife, lived on the top floors. It is quite probable that the wife had wartime contacts with the French resistance, although it is also possible that this idea was just a childish fantasy of mine.

My grandfather's body was a continuous source of wonder for me; not an ounce of fat was to be seen, just sinews, skin, and bones. He began each day with a cup of silver tea and, sometimes, a hard-boiled egg. Then he worked, doing research and writing books on economics and economic history. His activities were treated with a reverence that to me as a child seemed at the same time both sacred and rather ridiculous. As far as I could tell, he nearly always worked. Now and then he would depart—sometimes without an overcoat, even in the depths of winter—for the Stockholm School of Economics, which was about a ten- to fifteen-minute walk, to attend a committee meeting or assembly. There he would greet the other more or less learned men and sit down. He seldom contributed to the discussion, however, at times even falling into peaceful slumber during the proceedings. At the meeting's end, he would punctually wake up, say a polite but brief farewell, and then hurry back home to his typewriter and books.

Each Thursday, our family dined with my grandparents on the first floor. The menu was always the same: peas, potatoes, and pork cutlets. The latter were something of a luxury during those times of rationing. After my grandmother had sliced the fat off her cutlet, she would meet grandfather's covetous glance and, with her fork, transfer the shreds of fat to his plate. After grandfather, with predatory joy, had consumed the fat together with a dab of mustard, my father would repeat the exercise. He parted with his fat with some regret, I believe, but also with a look of gleeful rebellion. To my sorrow, I was not allowed to participate in this fat-slinging ritual. This deprivation might well have contributed to my budding taste for rebellion. After dinner, grandmother would sit down at the piano, and I was supposed to perform romantic songs about nature, penned by members of the social upper crust, in my boy soprano voice. Being used to singing Bach chorals in church, I disdained these chirping sessions as boring and inferior. Since my grandmother was always nice to me, even if a bit ridiculous in my childish eyes, there was never any thought of not obliging her.

One Thursday, when I probably was four or five years old, I arrived in my grandparents' living quarters somewhat earlier than usual and went to see my grandfather in his study. He rather preferred my older sister, but he also treated me with benevolence, if in an absentminded sort of way. My grandfather used to keep a revolver lying on his desk. Being busy, he reached for something to distract me so that he could continue working. The first object his hand happened upon was the gun, which he handed to me. I was delighted, especially since overly frenzied shooting sessions had caused water pistols to be banned at home. Naturally, I touched the trigger. My grandfather had forgotten that the gun was loaded, a shot went off. Eli's temple received a burn and the bullet penetrated his writing desk. Grandfather looked at me with wonder and said: "Well, Einar, I think you had better go and play with grandma for a while." Whether or not this was a double entendre, I will never know. In any case, he left the bullet embedded in his desk with something akin to pride.

Grandfather had an unmarried sister, Aunt Ella, who was a noted genealogist in Uppsala. She was deeply, although of course with suitable chastity, in love with her brother. While she was rather testy with adults, she was firmly committed to our freedom as children. As a result, she was promptly obeyed by both groups. When she realized that her death was imminent, she summoned me for a visit. Although at the time I was a model of puberty induced confusion, she talked to me with an openness that I had not often experienced from adults. Indeed, much of the considerable advice she gave me I still deeply cherish. She spoke of my grandfather as if he were a child, which in many ways he probably still was.

My grandfather severed relations with me when I was between eleven and twelve years old. Family tradition required that his grandchildren present their school reports to him for inspection at the end of each term. He had become used to our presenting him with rather good grades. Recently, however, I had discovered soccer and had befriended working class kids with a more down-to-earth and irreverent attitude to life. Suddenly my school grades had sunk into mediocrity, my absences had become too frequent and my marks for behavior and demeanor, which then were included in school reports, were gravely disapproving. Grandfather read the report and, without looking at me, said, "Get out of here." Thenceforth, I only met my grandmother in his absence. I don't believe I saw him many times, if ever, after that. Indeed, I can't recall ever speaking to him again. I do remember sneaking a peak at him as he lay in state.

When grandfather died, I was fourteen or fifteen. It was Christmastime, and during the school vacation I was working at a paint store in order to finance my sinful behavior. Shortly before dinner he said to his wife, "I think I'll lie down on the sofa for a while." He never got up. I was told of his death at work, and, to my utter surprise, I felt nothing. I was shocked at myself. It was an entirely new experience for me. My life had been full of efforts to conceal my true feelings, sometimes with scant success. Now, perhaps for the first time, at least off the soccer field, I had dared to make an independent judgment and stick to it. I have never forgotten that moment.

My grandfather was profoundly devoted to scholarship. I am quite sure that he was not a mean person, even though he could utter rather harsh judgments about people. While he was a humanist, I also thought he was a bit of an intellectual snob. When he was a child, my father once came home with a school report full of the highest possible grades, except in drawing and physical education, which in our family did not count. Still, in one academic subject he had received only the second highest grade. Grandfather remarked grimly, or perhaps only teasingly, "If you go on like this, you'll end up deputy secretary in some chancellery." This unquestioned faith in the value of academic honors probably was passed on to my father, even though he also had a healthy and fruitful respect for actually getting things done, not just knowing best. Once, during a period when I dreamed of becoming a writer, my father commented to one of my siblings: "If he's not published at twenty-three, then he'll never become a writer, will he?"

Toward the end of her life, Kajsa Warg, an eighteenth-century Swedish working-class icon, said something to the effect that, "When at its best, life has been labor and toil." That pretty much sums up what made Eli tick. He was also fond of sailing, although mainly to enjoy the outdoors and to argue benevolently with his son or with acquaintances. With the latter, he sometimes displayed more irony than was to their liking. This according to my father, who also told me that Eli often utilized his charts to sail between a navigational marker and the shoal of which it warned. Not surprisingly, the results were sometimes drastic. What else went on in that relentlessly industrious mind of his must have been known to very few people.

I believe that the importance Grandfather placed on his chosen subject had its roots in a kind of stubborn humanism. He realized that outright socialism had little future, pure idealism having a short half-life in constructing and administering a society. He understood that any system will be corrupted by the sort of persons who will maneuver behind the scenes for powerful positions regardless of the official ideology. Democracy was just the least imperfect ideology. This was a private and sometimes rather cynical view of mankind, cynical not in the current pejorative sense but according to the original meaning of *kynos* itself. Politically, he was a liberal, although not being active in party politics.

I do not know the extent to which Grandfather foresaw the dramatic acceleration of modern life, although I believe he anticipated the neo-colonial rat race for primary products which is the underlying reason for so many of our planet's current ills. I also believe he would have seen through the many obscure and one-sided notions of economic growth that, in reality, mainly profit stock speculators, while allowing ordinary people to remain unemployed and far too many children to be deprived of an education. The powers that be, even in institutions

such as the WTO, the IMF, and the World Bank, often seem more interested in fictional stock market valuations and in helping to refine corrupt practices than in providing food for future generations. Such an
attitude would have been deeply offensive to Eli Heckscher.

Sten Heckscher

Let me first note that I was no more than ten years old when my
grandfather died. Thus I have few distinct memories of my own concerning him, and I may have difficulty distinguishing my actual experiences from what I have only been told. Of course, some of the stories
I have heard I know to be true from my own recollections.

One such story is the one my sister told you about my grandfather
not wearing an overcoat, even in the winter cold. Her explanation was
that he did not wish to be stopped in the street by people wanting to
discuss various issues with him. She also related that he was the first
in our family to have a sailboat. It was gone by the time I was born,
but there certainly are stories about it.

My version of these events differs somewhat from that of my sister.
For example, I believe that he hypothesized that navigation marks
were always placed with a margin for error, so that it should be possible to squeeze between the mark and the hazard. Not surprisingly, my
grandfather became famous for frequently running aground. Still, one
must agree that the acted like a true scientist, repeatedly trying out
and testing a hypothesis. Moreover, his navigation habits did not discourage later generations from sailing in the archipelago. We still have
sailboats in the family, so the tradition he started lives on.

When thinking about Eli in preparation for these few remarks, one
aspect has been particularly striking. My remembrance of him is a
strange combination of closeness verging on intimacy with a sense of
strict reserve. He could be, and usually was, very generous with his
time when he was on his own turf, in his own world. He seemed to be
always working. Only during the week before his death do I remember
him lying on a sofa in his study. Otherwise, I do not remember ever
seeing him away from his desk. Yet I must have since I know we sometimes celebrated Christmas Eve together.

Still, when as a child I visited my grandfather, he always had time to
tell me interesting things, for example about the important sixteenth-
century Swedish King Gustav Vasa. He described the living conditions
of the king, his court, and his army in considerable detail. Thus, when I

was six years old I knew all about the consumption of beer in the living quarters of the sixteenth-century army. Clearly he was a good story-teller. We small children sat at his feet and listened to fascinating stories based on his scholarly research. It was also the case that his wife Ebba was a great story teller. She invented fabulous sagas that were serialized day after day, much to the delight of her grandchildren.

From early childhood, I was aware that Eli wrote numerous, very lengthy books. In later years I have also encountered beautiful short publications addressing basic questions. A favorite of mine is a lecture he gave in 1909, I believe in the town of Gävle, located 170 kilometers north of Stockholm. In seven pages he explains why some people are rich while others are not. I like such succinct presentations.

Returning to the contrast I mentioned earlier, however, I remember almost nothing concerning personal matters, such as relationships or emotions. It is as if they did not exist. I do remember neither anger nor sadness or sorrow and barely any joy. My recollection is that he seemed uninterested or absent in regard to matters other than those that related to his work, as if he were immersed in his research to the exclusion of everything else.

I wonder what my father, who died fifteen years ago, would have said, had he been able to present his views at this symposium. Of course, there is no way for me to know for sure. I imagine, however, that he would have expressed great enthusiasm concerning the intellectual and scholarly conversations he had with my grandfather. Beyond those lively discussions on politics, economic problems and developments, and the state of the country, however, he probably would have said very little. I doubt that even he would have mentioned anything about the "soft" part of their relationship, which no doubt existed even if both of them pretended otherwise.

Here it is quite possible that I am being unfair. Perhaps they just believed that such personal and emotional matters should not be displayed before the children. In any case, I can only offer you my recollections and they were not objectively formed.

Perhaps this is the inevitable fate of my younger generation, especially since the age gap with our elders is so large: To learn of our grandfather through posterity and his large scholarly production, despite not having read much of it, to become acquainted with him mainly after his death and not as a living, breathing human being.

The question as to the influence my grandfather has had on me and on my life remains unanswered. Nevertheless, I would like to thank those responsible for organizing this symposium for making me pose and ponder over it.

Ivar Heckscher

As the youngest of Eli's grandchildren (I was only nine years old when he died), I have hardly any memories of him at all. Two images remain, however. The first is a dim memory of my grandfather lying in state. I remember that he felt cold when I touched him. My other mental picture is of him sitting at his desk. The visits I and my siblings made to him when we were small were very ritualistic. I was allowed into his study, picked up and put on his knee. As the result of an operation, he had a hole behind his left ear, and I was allowed to put my finger in it. He then displayed all the things on his desk. Most of them related to his calculations. To a small child, they seemed very strange and dangerous. He was very strict about us not touching any of them. One of the other objects on his desk was a clock in a glass case, which exposed its inner workings. Following this inspection of his possessions, it was candy time. He had a box of candy on his desk, and I was allowed to pick just one. There were perhaps seven or eight different kinds, some of which I liked better than the others. If a favorite was near the top, I could pick it, otherwise not.

This is just about all I remember of Eli, but I do have something else to share with you. At the time that I was invited to this symposium, I was in the middle of moving. In the process of packing my belongings, I unexpectedly found two large paper bags full of my grandfather's drawings and correspondence. Included was a school essay he had written when he was sixteen years old. It has been translated into English from the rather stilted and archaic version of Swedish then used in the schools. Inevitably some the original flavor had been lost in translation. Nonetheless, here are Eli Heckscher's reflections on a brief essay topic assigned by his gymnasium teacher in the year 1895:

What Career Do You Find Most Appealing?

The philosophy and the ideals each person sets for himself play an important role in all his actions, but perhaps especially so in his choice of occupation.

At least in their youth, everyone has a goal toward which they wish to devote all their efforts; this goal might be a noble struggle for good or the enjoyment of sensual pleasure or material advantages. This choice is a truly important matter when they must choose their career. Here, the desire for fame is also of major importance. If one wishes to be the strongest or the most powerful, it is ambition just as much as wanting to be the most learned, the noblest or the richest. In all cases, it is about being the foremost. Of course there are many humble persons, but that youth is usually ambitious can not be denied. (Besides, wishing to be most humble is itself a form of ambition.) For most people, this is a major driving force.

Another influence that sometimes plays an even greater role is the more or less consciously exerted force of one's surroundings, especially that of parents. Most fathers want their sons to continue on the path on which they themselves have wandered all their lives; or else to undertake with fresh resolve all the things that they themselves had wished, but had been able, to do. I am not here speaking of the case where the father compels his son to choose a particular occupation, since then his preference has no effect. No, I refer to a case where the father, while giving his son a free choice, still lets him know that choosing the parental occupation would be pleasing, or else lets the son know about all the good he could accomplish in that career.

This outcome is closely related to the influence of tradition. Even if his father is not so engaged, it can easily happen that a youth, again half against his will, turns to the occupation that his ancestors have practiced for centuries. Naturally, others in his surroundings, such as teachers at the school where he is educated, can exert an influence in one direction or another.

One factor that here, as in all aspects of life, enters in an unsubtle fashion is the question of money. Many a young man endowed with a good mind and far from being lazy, has been forced by poverty to work in an occupation for which he is not suited simply because it requires a less costly education.

Before turning to what the product—if I may express myself thus—of all these factors is, I wish to note that the career which might have been most appealing to us at one time, soon often losses its attraction. Perhaps because we get to see this occupation up close, making it seem less attractive, or because we enter into a new environment that exerts an opposing influence on us, or, finally, because we change our minds for no particular reason. Most people, almost since they first began to think, have conceived of some ideal occupation. Few of us, however, have clung to such a childish notion. I am here not talking about wishes such as becoming a cab horse or a locomotive, which could not possibly be realized, but about fairly reasonable and feasible ideas. Even these change more or less frequently, until the time finally comes for deciding on one or the other. This does not mean that one always makes the best choice. Often one has had far wiser plans earlier than at the time the final decision has to be made.

I shall now very briefly describe the product of the factors. This might seem to lie outside the scope of the topic, but in my view it belongs there since the occupation one chooses, in most cases, is most appealing at the very moment it is chosen. The final outcome depends on the strength of the various aforementioned factors relative to each other. If one could imagine being able to choose a career completely free of outside influences, it still seems highly unlikely that the result would be good. It would probably be much more advantageous if someone more experienced than oneself could offer advice, as long as one could be sure that they, as is surely the case with one's parents, wished one well. Parents, however, will be misled by their desire to see the child choose their own occupation. On the contrary, it would be beneficial for society if tradition ceased to compel anyone into a particular career and if the influence of money in that regard also ended. Sadly, at least the latter of these is totally unimaginable.

Since I have now described the various forces that contribute to a man's choice of career, I obviously did not interpret the topic as requiring not a presentation of my personal preferences, but instead a general survey of the forces that are of importance when a man chooses his place in society.

20

Eli Heckscher Today: A Bibliometric Picture

Bo Sandelin

Since the natural sciences provided a model for economics more than a century ago, measurement has been an important element in economists' thinking. These days the activities of economists themselves have also become an object of measurement. Since the establishment of the Institute for Scientific Information (ISI) in the United States in 1961, it has become easier to measure publications and citations in scholarly journals. Here we will concentrate on citations of Eli F. Heckscher in journals included in the ISI databases Social Sciences Citation Index (SSCI) and Arts and Humanities Citation Index (AHCI). The SSCI contains information on articles in about 1,700 social science journals, while the AHCI is based on about 1,130 arts and humanities journals.[1]

The citations of Heckscher in the SSCI and AHCI do not, of course, give a complete picture of his significance as a scholar and in public debate. For reasons linked to the selection process and discussed below, there is a tendency for his English-language scholarly works to be overrepresented in the databases at the expense of his Swedish writings and political contributions. Nevertheless, it is not uninteresting to get an idea of the quantity and pattern of citations of Heckscher in mainly English-language scholarly journals.

We will find that in the period 1986–2002 he was cited less than Myrdal and Wicksell but approximately as much as Ohlin, and more than Cassel and Lindahl. Though his list of publications includes more than 1,100 items, about 80 percent of the citations pertain to different versions of just four works: *Mercantilism*, the large but untranslated *Sveriges ekonomiska historia från Gustav Vasa*, the shorter *An Economic History of Sweden*, and his article "The Effect of Foreign Trade on the Distribution of Income."

Table 20.1
Number of citations in SSCI and AHCI journals, 1986–2002

	1986–1991	1992–1997	1998–2002	Total
Gunnar Myrdal	785	781	653	2219
Knut Wicksell	167	147	96	410
Eli Heckscher	89	91	69	249
Bertil Ohlin	104	74	61	239
Gustav Cassel	57	41	44	142
Erik Lindahl	49	33	29	111

Heckscher and His Contemporaries

Eli Heckscher (1879–1952) was partly contemporary with a number of Swedish economists who are still internationally cited. He was younger than Knut Wicksell (1851–1926) and Gustav Cassel (1866–1944), but older than Erik Lindahl (1891–1960), Gunnar Myrdal (1898–1987), and Bertil Ohlin (1899–1979).

In table 20.1 we see how Heckscher compares with his Swedish colleagues in terms of citations in SSCI and AHCI journals. Myrdal is clearly by far the most cited in every period, with about five times as many citations as Wicksell. As a broad social scientist, Myrdal differs from the others in receiving many citations in journals other than economics or economic history journals (Sarafoglou and Sandelin 1992). Heckscher and Ohlin come after Wicksell, though clearly ahead of Cassel and Lindahl. With one exception (the relative positions of Heckscher and Ohlin in 1986–1991), the order is the same for all periods. Recalculated as citations per year, there would also be an astonishing stability between the periods in the number of citations for each individual. This indicates that there is a certain constancy in the significance of these old economists, at any rate over such a limited time span as we embrace here.

It is a well-known fact that when a concept is sufficiently widespread and has become the common property of every economist, it often appears in an economic text without reference to the original book or article; the Pareto optimum, Keynesianism, IS-LM-analysis, and the Phillips curve are examples. The Heckscher-Ohlin theorem in international trade theory is another example. This means that the numbers for Heckscher and Ohlin in table 20.1 may underestimate their relative influence.

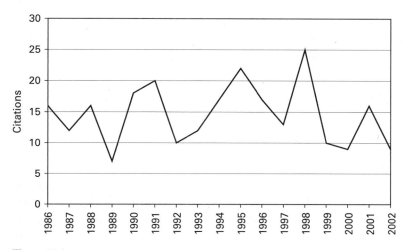

Figure 20.1
Number of citations of Heckscher, according to SSCI and AHCI

As mentioned, the numbers of citations calculated as an annual aver-age for each of the three periods are quite stable. For Heckscher we would get 15, 15, and 14 for 1986–1991, 1992–1997, and 1998–2002, re-spectively. However, when the averages are such low numbers, they may be composed of figures for individual years that differ relatively widely from each other. This is confirmed in figure 20.1, which shows the citations of Heckscher each individual year in 1986–2002. The number oscillates between a low of 7 citations in 1989 and a high of 25 in 1998.

Heckscher's Publications

Heckscher was an extremely prolific writer in more than one genre. Be-sides his great scholarly books, he contributed scholarly articles, espe-cially to the *Ekonomisk Tidskrift*, and he contributed books and articles to the general public debate; in the daily newspaper *Dagens Nyheter* he published about three hundred articles (Carlson 1994:3). Henriks-son (1991:141) asserts that of the more than thousand entries in Heckscher's bibliography, "his economic theoretical and historical writings, in number at least, constitute only a minor part. Most of these writings were comments on and analyses of current problems where he applied his historical knowledge and theoretical acumen with such distinction and brilliance that he became a leading personality in the political and cultural life of his day." Uhr (1987) provides some details: Heckscher's bibliography, published in 1950, "contains 1148 entries for his 36 books, 174 articles in professional journals, his chapters in government reports, and the more than 700 short articles he wrote for the weekend issues of Stockholm's leading newspapers. Only a few of his books and articles have been translated."

Selection Criteria

Of course, the distribution of citations in the SSCI and AHCI does not accurately represent the proportions of Heckscher's work as a scholar and a committed citizen. First, because these journals have the status of scholarly journals, there is in all likelihood a tendency for scholarly works to be overrepresented among the works cited in them, too. Secondly, not all scholarly journals are included. For possible inclusion in these databases, "ISI's editorial staff reviews nearly 2000 new journal titles annually, but only 10–12% of the journals evaluated is selected."[2] One of the criteria for including a journal is that basic information is provided in English. The following is printed in bold letters: "**English language article titles, abstracts, and keywords are essential.**" Besides, "English language cited references are also recommended" for those journals that wish to be included. In addition to highly international journals, "ISI seeks to cover the best regional journals as well." However, even then "English language bibliographic elements remain essential."

Against this background it seems reasonable to assume that there is a higher probability that an English-language journal will be included than a French-, or German-, or other-language journal of the same quality. In consequence, it also seems very likely that the references in the journals included will be biased toward publications available in English. Thus, of all citations of Heckscher's publications in different genres, citations of his scholarly works, especially those in English, are likely to be overrepresented in the SSCI and AHCI databases.[3]

With this in mind, we may look at table 20.2, where the proportion of citations of Heckscher's different publications is shown, and where we see that different versions of just four works account for about 80 percent of the citations.

Table 20.2
Citations of Heckscher in SSCI and AHCI journals broken down by publications (citations by Swedish authors in parentheses) Per cent

Publication	1986–91	1992–97	1998–02
Mercantilism (1935)	39 (0)	42 (1)	35 (1)
Der Merkantilismus (1932)	2 (0)	2 (0)	3 (0)
Merkantilismen (1931)	2 (1)	1 (1)	1 (1)
La Época Mercantilista (1943)	1 (0)		
Subtotal	44 (1)	45 (2)	39 (2)
Sveriges ekonomiska historia (1935)	12 (4)	11 (9)	3 (2)
Subtotal	12 (4)	11 (9)	3 (2)
An Economic History of Sweden (1954)	16 (3)	4 (0)	10 (3)
Svenskt arbete och liv (1941)	2 (2)	5 (4)	3 (3)
Subtotal	18 (5)	9 (4)	13 (6)
Utrikeshandelns verkan (1919)	9 (1)	8 (0)	7 (0)
The effect of foreign trade (1949)	2 (0)	7 (0)	1 (0)
Heckscher-Ohlin Trade Theory (1991)		7 (0)	13 (1)
Subtotal	11 (1)	22 (0)	21 (1)
Other	15	13	24
Total	100	100	100

Mercantilism

Heckscher's most cited work is *Mercantilism*, which together with the Swedish, German, and Spanish editions gets around 45 percent of the citations of Heckscher in 1986–1997, and slightly less after that. No citation is registered for the Italian edition *Il Mercantilismo* (1936). The work appeared in two volumes in Swedish in 1931, and in a revised second edition in 1953, but it is mainly citations of the English editions that are included in the database. As a classic in its field, several English editions have been published after the first one in 1935: a revised edition appeared in 1955, reissued with a new introduction by Lars Magnusson in 1994, and there have been reprints in between.

Its preeminent role is confirmed by many prominent authors. Henry Spiegel (1952:31) concludes that "Eli F. Heckscher (1879–) is an outstanding economic historian and the highest authority on the mercantilist period." Joseph Schumpeter (1954:149), discussing the literature on the period, says that he "shall mention but two well-known standard

works which in any case are, or ought to be, in every students hand:
E. F. Heckscher's *Mercantilism . . .* and P. Mantoux's *The Industrial Revolution of the Eighteenth Century."* D. C. Coleman (1957:25) concluded in
a review of the second English edition that as "a contribution to the
history of economic thought, there can be no doubt whatsoever that
Heckscher's work remains outstanding, still invaluable to the student
of the period" (but at the same time he found it "curiously unrealistic"
as Heckscher "shunned particular contexts and particular problems").
To Bob Coats (1957:187), *Mercantilism* "represented a pioneering effort
to delineate the major themes of economic ideas and policy in Western
Europe during some four or five centuries" (but "this undertaking was
necessarily bound to fail; indeed, few scholars have the learning or
breadth of imagination even to contemplate such an enterprise").
Mark Blaug (1986:31) states: "The outstanding historical study of mercantilism in all its phases is E. F. Heckscher, *Mercantilism."* Carl Uhr
(1987) declares that "one of [Heckscher's] major and most widely
known treatises was *Mercantilism."* Lars Magnusson (1994:33, 32) designates the book Heckscher's magnum opus, and states that "almost
instantaneously it made this liberal Swedish economist and economic
historian famous for a wide international audience."

Nobody can deny that the book has influenced writing on mercantilism immensely, and few deny that it is a great book. This does not
mean that criticism is lacking, but it is beyond the purpose of this essay
to go into the details.[4]

Sweden's Economic History

Heckscher's second major work is *Sveriges ekonomiska historia från Gustav Vasa* (Sweden's economic history from the reign of Gustav Vasa), of
which volumes 1 and 2 were published in 1935 and 1936, respectively,
and volumes 3 and 4 not until 1949. Both this work and *Mercantilism*
have their roots in Heckscher's licentiate thesis *Produktplakatet och dess
förutsättningar,*[5] presented in 1903 but not published until 1908 (Henriksson 1991).

Sveriges ekonomiska historia från Gustav Vasa accounts for 11–12 percent of Heckscher's citations during the first two periods in table 20.2,
and for only 3 percent in 1998–2002. This is considerably less than the
figures for *Mercantilism.* There are probably two reasons. First, none of
the four volumes has been translated, so only those who know Swedish can read them. As a result, a large share of the citations is made by

Swedes, while Swedes played a tiny role in the citations of the English version of *Mercantilism*.

Secondly, *Sveriges ekonomiska historia från Gustav Vasa* focuses on Sweden, and is consequently less international in contents, and less important for an international audience, than *Mercantilism*. But as a scholarly achievement *Sveriges ekonomiska historia från Gustav Vasa*, too, is outstanding, and it is not evident which of the two should be ranked first. In Söderlund's (1953:139) opinion, *Sveriges ekonomiska historia från Gustav Vasa* "is probably the best work Heckscher ever produced." Montgomery (1953), Uhr (1987), and Henriksson (1991) do not try to rank the two and seem to place them on an approximately equal footing.

An Economic History of Sweden

The next work, *Svenskt arbete och liv* (1941), was translated by Göran Ohlin under Heckscher's own supervision as *An Economic History of Sweden* (1954). The translation was provided with a supplement by Gunnar Heckscher and a preface by Alexander Gerschenkron. When the translation was published it was praised in a review by T. S. Ashton (1957) as "an antidote to many so-called introductions to economic history, clogged as these are with metaphysical rubbish and restrictionist doctrine. It offers a narrative disciplined by economic logic and informed by the wisdom that comes of contact with affairs" (82). The first half of the concluding sentence may come as a surprise: "The book has already had a salutary influence on the teaching of economic history in British universities, and as time goes on the circle of Heckscher's disciples in the English-speaking world will widen."

The book begins with an earlier epoch (the Middle Ages) than *Sveriges ekonomiska historia från Gustav Vasa* but can otherwise be regarded as a summary of the latter. We should not be astonished that the Swedish version is cited almost only by Swedes. Nor should we be surprised —taking into account the composition of the SSCI and AHCI databases—that the English version is cited more in total than the Swedish.

The Effect of Foreign Trade

So far, we have looked at works on economic history. Heckscher's work in pure economic theory is much less extensive. Nevertheless, among economists in general, Heckscher is probably known mainly for his contribution to the theory of international trade—the foundation of the so-called Heckscher-Ohlin Theorem—originally presented in his article "Utrikeshandelns verkan på inkomstfördelningen" in a special volume of the *Ekonomisk Tidskrift* dedicated to David Davidson in 1919. Flam and Flanders (1991:3) hold that this article (and one on intermittently free goods) "constitute [Heckscher's] whole output in economic theory." It was translated in slightly abridged form as "The Effect of Foreign Trade on the Distribution of Income" and published in *Readings in the Theory of International Trade* (1949). This translation was revised, corrected, and completed, adding parts that were omitted in the first translation, in a new book, *Heckscher-Ohlin Trade Theory* (1991), edited by Harry Flam and M. June Flanders.

We see in table 20.2 that citations of different versions of this article appear to constitute a fifth of the citations of Heckscher since the beginning of the 1990s. There is, however, a problem here. When it comes to the last version, included in the book *Heckscher-Ohlin Trade Theory*, it is impossible to determine from the database whether a citation originally refers only to Heckscher's article, or the translation of Ohlin's doctoral thesis in the same volume, or the introduction by Flam and Flanders, or even the foreword by Paul A. Samuelson. So the numbers for this book may include not only citations of Heckscher's article.

Scattered Citations

The aforementioned four works receive about 80 percent of Heckscher's citations in the SSCI and AHCI journals. The rest of his more than 30 books, 174 articles in scholarly journals, and nearly 1000 other items get zero or merely a few stray citations each. One exception is the short article "Växelkursens grundval vid pappersmyntfot" (The foundations of the exchange rate on the paper standard) in the *Ekonomisk Tidskrift* (1916). This article is not cited at all in the first two periods, but suddenly in 1998–2002 it is cited eight times. The names and affiliations of those who have cited it make it hard to believe that any of them understand Swedish; consequently, it seems likely that none of them has read the article. Thus, these citations may indicate something about the principles of the journals or the authors when compiling the list of references, but hardly anything about how much the article has been read.[6]

There is no citation of the Swedish book *Kontinentalsystemet* (1918), but four citations of the English version *The Continental System* (1922).

A few citations are also found for the collection *Bidrag till Sveriges eko-nomiska och sociala historia under och efter världskriget* (1926) (Contributions to Sweden's economic and social history during and after the world war), and one or two occur for Heckscher's doctoral thesis *Till belysning av järnvägarnas betydelse för Sveriges ekonomiska utveckling* (1907) (The role of the railways in Sweden's economic development), the essay collection *Svenska produktionsproblem* (1918) (Swedish production problems), the booklet *Gammal och ny ekonomisk liberalism* (1921) (Old and new economic liberalism), the collection *Ekonomi och historia* (1922) (Economics and history), the multi-edition book *Industrialismen* (1931), and a number of other titles. No citations are recorded for "Intermittent fria nyttigheter" (Intermittently free goods) in the *Ekonomisk Tidskrift* 1924, nor for many other pieces.

Conclusion

Heckscher was extremely studious, and his bibliography includes more than a thousand items, of which some are very comprehensive works. His citations according to SSCI and AHCI are concentrated to the latter, and to his theoretical article about the effect of foreign trade on the distribution of income. The distribution of the citations is partly a consequence of the selection criteria of SSCI and AHCI and does not necessarily give a true picture of his overall importance in public life. Had citations in books been included, his works as an economic historian would probably have been even more accentuated, inasmuch as economic historians seem to be more inclined to write books than economists. Had preference not been given to citations in English-language journals, his untranslated publications would probably receive more citations. His extensive writings on current political and economic questions attracted much attention in Sweden at the time, but are hardly cited in international scholarly journals.[7]

The citations reflect one aspect of Heckscher's significance: they simply indicate how much attention his works attract on the part of later authors of articles in selected, mainly English-language, scholarly journals. Even if incomplete, this information is not uninteresting.

Notes

1. In addition, the SSCI includes selected articles from about 3,300 science and technology journals, and the AHCI includes selected articles from about 7,000 science and social

science journals. We will not repeat this information later when talking about SSCI and AHCI journals. Information about the journals included and the selection process is given at http://www.isinet.com.

2. This and the next quotations are from http://www.isinet.com, December 13, 2002.

3. Another effect of the journal selection criteria in the ISI databases seems to be that when those databases are used to compare different countries with respect to scientific output, there is a bias not only in favor of English-language countries but also in favor of small-language countries (whose scholars write largely in English) in relation to non-English, large-language countries (whose scholars write largely in their domestic language). Cf. Sandelin, Sarafoglou, and Veiderpass (2000) and, in greater detail and for another period, Sandelin and Sarafoglou (2004).

4. Uhr (1979) and Magnusson (1994:32–33) give accounts of how *Mercantilism* was received by reviewers.

5. "Produktplakatet" of 1724 was a Swedish version of the Navigation Act.

6. It seems to me that editors have become more demanding in the last few decades and often require that any title mentioned or even intimated in the text should be included in the reference list, even if the author has never seen the work. Combined with the requirement that authors demonstrate familiarity with the literature in the area of research—and excessive willingness on the part of authors to try to do so—this results in huge lists of references.

7. It is interesting to note that in Carlson's (1994) detailed study *The State as a Monster: Gustav Cassel and Eli Heckscher on the Role and Growth of the State*, none of Heckscher's four most cited works according to SSCI and AHCI are included in the references.

References

Ashton, T. S. 1957. "An Economic History of Sweden." *Scandinavian Economic History Review* 5, no. 1: 82–85.

Blaug, M. 1986. *Great Economists Before Keynes: An Introduction to the Lives and Works of 100 Economists of the Past*. Brighton: Harvester Press.

Carlson, B. 1994. *The State as a Monster: Gustav Cassel and Eli Heckscher on the Role and Growth of the State*. Lanham, MD: University Press of America.

Coats, A. W. 1957. "In Defence of Heckscher and the Idea of Mercantilism." *Scandinavian Economic History Review* 5, no. 1: 173–187.

Coleman, D. C. 1957. "Eli Heckscher and the Idea of Mercantilism." *Scandinavian Economic History Review* 5, no. 1: 3–25.

Flam, H., and J. Flanders. 1991. "Introduction." In E. F. Heckscher and B. Ohlin, *Heckscher-Ohlin Trade Theory*, 1–37. Cambridge, MA: MIT Press.

Henriksson, R. 1991. "Eli F. Heckscher: The Economic Historian as Economist." In B. Sandelin, ed., *The History of Swedish Economic Thought*, 141–167. London: Routledge.

Magnusson, L. 1994. *Mercantilism: The Shaping of an Economic Language*. London: Routledge.

Montgomery, A. 1953. "Eli Heckscher som vetenskapsman." *Ekonomisk Tidskrift* 55:149–185.

Sandelin, B., and N. Sarafoglou. 2004. "Language and Scientific Publication Statistics." *Language Problems & Language Planning* 28:1–10.

Sandelin, B., N. Sarafoglou, and A. Veiderpass. 2000. "The Post-1945 Development of Economics and Economists in Sweden." In A. W. Coats, ed., *The Development of Economics in Western Europe Since 1945*, 42–66. London: Routledge.

Sarafoglou, N., and B. Sandelin. 1992. "Myrdal fortfarande mest citerad." *Ekonomisk Debatt* 20, no. 3: 229–232.

Schumpeter, J. A. 1954. *History of Economic Analysis*. Oxford: Oxford University Press.

Söderlund, E. 1953. "Eli F. Heckscher." *Scandinavian Economic History Review* 1, nos. 1 and 2: 137–140.

Spiegel, H. W., ed. 1952. *The Development of Economic Thought: Great Economists in Perspective*. New York: John Wiley & Sons.

Uhr, C. G. 1979. "Eli F. Heckscher, 1879–1952, and His Treatise on Mercantilism Revisited." *Economy and History* 23, no. 1: 3–39.

———. 1987. "Heckscher, Eli Filip." In J. Eatwell, M. Milgate, and P. Newman, eds., *The New Palgrave: A Dictionary of Economics*. London: Macmillan.

21 When Heckscher Changed Direction: From Social Conservatism to Economic Liberalism

Benny Carlson

For most of his life, Eli Heckscher was the most firmly principled economic liberal Sweden had. He fought against state-socialist tendencies, Keynesian crisis policy, and economic planning for many years, and he had only one real rival—Gustav Cassel—for the title of the most liberal Swede of the twentieth century. But whereas Cassel made one or another concession to protectionism at times, Heckscher never budged an inch from his free trade position.

However, there is another and less known Heckscher: the young conservative who, during the early twentieth century, adopted an almost state-socialist stance.[1] The social democrat Erik Palmstierna has told in his memoirs of "the crowd of intelligent young men who gathered themselves around Eli Heckscher ... these men of the historical school whose masters were Adolf Wagner and Ashley." Palmstierna speaks of a "junta" and recalls that during the general strike of 1909 a militia was formed with Heckscher at its head.[2]

The aim of this paper is to look closely at the young "junta leader" and try to date and explain his "change of direction," that is, his shift from a social-conservative or state-socialist position to a liberal one. This means that we must focus attention on the period from 1905 to 1918–19, the opening year being determined by when Heckscher began writing seriously on questions of economic policy and the closing year by the ending of World War I and Heckscher's emergence as a full-fledged economic liberal.

Authoritative Depictions of Heckscher

Let us begin by skimming through the depictions of Heckscher and his political stance and sources of inspiration which have been conjured up by sundry Heckscher authorities.

Arthur Montgomery emphasises how strongly Heckscher was marked by his teacher of history, Harald Hjärne, compared with his teachers (and eventually colleagues) in economics: David Davidson, Knut Wicksell, and Gustav Cassel. Heckscher's foremost master in the economic field was Alfred Marshall. Montgomery's account does not hint at any radical change of direction in the development of Heckscher's ideas other than the following: "There is no doubt that the move to the Stockholm School of Economics (1909) had very profound consequences for Heckscher's scholarly work during the next two decades. His interests were now led to a higher degree than formerly into the paths of economics." Montgomery also states that Heckscher, along with Cassel, was putting forward economic liberal ideas during the 1920s and that "Heckscher's liberalism was ... more uncompromising than Cassel's."[3]

One of the young Heckscher's partisans, Herman Brulin, with the help of some letters from Heckscher to his friend and colleague Gösta Bagge, has illustrated the "crisis of economic and political belief" Heckscher underwent during World War I. Heckscher explained in a letter of 1915 that he had "an abnormal need for unity of outlook, and therefore [I] continually endeavour to find an explanation of every separate point so that it comes into line with my total conceptual scheme. So in the end I arrive at a position which is clearly absurd; and then I start to pick the entire thing apart again in order to bring out another unbroken line, which goes the same way, and so on ad infinitum. Consequently I go from the one extreme to the other in the course of ten-fifteen years." In another letter of 1916, Heckscher spoke of "the road I am travelling at present, away from old gods and ideals and toward some goal of which I have no inkling myself." Brulin, for his part, argues that Heckscher's pilgrimage "led him a good way to the left of his former sympathisers." In Brulin's opinion, one reason for Heckscher's conversion is to be found in his "Anglomania," or better, his fear of the consequences of a German victory.[4]

Ernst Söderlund, too, had the idea that Heckscher's reorientation in a liberal direction resulted from the experiences of World War I. "It was mainly during this period, as far as can be judged, that Heckscher was working his way toward the thoroughly reasoned, almost Marshallian-liberal approach to economic questions which was to mark so deeply both his scholarly work and his participation in public debate."[5]

Heckscher's pupil above all others, Bertil Ohlin, summarized his mentor's political evolution: "He long considered himself a conservative in the spirit of Harald Hjärne. Little by little, however, his liberal approach to economic policy caused him to adopt a more independent outlook." Like Montgomery, Ohlin takes it for granted that Heckscher's appointment as professor of economics in 1909 caused him to turn his interest increasingly toward economic theory. Ohlin also mentions that "John Stuart Mill was one of the masters he admired."[6]

Björn Hettne has argued that it was natural for Heckscher, after being appointed to the chair in economics at the Stockholm School of Economics in 1909, "to become orientated more strongly toward neoclassical theory in the period that followed" and to adopt "a clearly negative attitude to the historical school."[7] Even though the question here is one mainly of attitude toward the use of economic theory, an ideological dimension is part of the picture: neoclassical theory leads thoughts in a liberal direction, the historical school in a social-conservative and state-interventionist direction.

One of our time's leading authorities on Heckscher, Rolf Henriksson, considers that Heckscher's change of stance happened during World War I: "The war had turned Heckscher's political views from moderate conservative to strongly liberal."[8]

Kurt Wickman, finally, denominates the young Heckscher not as a young but as an old-style conservative. Wickman explains Heckscher's switch to liberalism in terms partly of his study of Marshall and partly of the experiences of World War I.[9]

In other words, in the literature on Heckscher there is first of all an opinion (represented by Montgomery, Ohlin, Hettne, and Wickman) that he was influenced by his appointment as professor of economics. Thus he would have aligned himself more in the direction of modern neoclassical economics, which could explain his drift from conservatism toward liberalism. Second, there is an opinion (represented by Brulin, Söderlund, Henriksson, and Wickman) that he underwent an economic-political conversion during World War I with its multitudinous examples of state intervention and perhaps under the threat of a German victory; Germany represented state socialism at this time.

Heckscher's Own Picture

That Marshall greatly influenced the development of Heckscher's ideals is beyond doubt—he himself described Marshall's *Principles* as "the starting point of my theoretical studies."[10] Heckscher has also confessed that he was "indescribably green" when he started at the Stockholm School of Economics, which "for some years caused me literally to publish treatises to legitimise a professorship which I had already got."[11] However, Heckscher's own explanation of his drift toward an economic liberal standpoint bases itself on the negative experiences of state economic intervention during World War I. When asked during a newspaper interview of 1933 why he had changed from conservative to liberal he replied: "Yes, that is mostly a result of my changed economic stance. I was of a conservative way of thinking formerly, which chimed in with Hjärne's constitutional ideal. Then the Hammarskjöld government's national economic planning policy came along, which signified state intervention in every field. I really felt respect for the government's good intentions, but I got more and more of a depressing feeling that it had taken a wrong turning."[12]

In a summing-up of his "experiences of economics and economic policy over forty years" in 1944, Heckscher repeats his message to the effect that his scepticism about the state's ability to influence the economy successfully emanated from World War I: "It cannot be denied that my scepticism on this point had its root primarily in experiences of the working of government during the First World War; during my student years I had been almost as far from economic liberalism as anyone at that time." What Heckscher chiefly learned was that state interventions were marked by planlessness and deference to diverse special interests.[13]

Heckscher's Positions, 1905–18

We shall now follow the economic and political standpoints of the young Heckscher chronologically and use his attitude to the state as a clue in the search for Heckscher's ideological stance. In round figures the enquiry covers the period between 1905 and 1918.

The first item in Heckscher's bibliography turns up as early as 1897.[14] But Heckscher's first decade as a writer did not leave much to interest anyone concerned to know his standpoints on economic policy. Up to and including 1906 he wrote some seventy articles for sundry main entries in the *Nordisk Familjebok* (a Swedish encyclopedia), a major article on economic history, some miscellaneous articles on diverse topics, and some reviews. It was not until about 1905–6 that he began to bring forth products that lend themselves to ideological dissection.

Strikes were one of the young Heckscher's favorite topics, forming the subject of five articles between 1905 and 1909. In an article of 1905 he argued that employees in communications, guardians of law and order, and health and medical services ought to be designated as "public officials." A corps of conscripts should be formed under the local authorities as an extra insurance against strikes in these services.[15]

Early in 1906 Heckscher, along with Herman Brulin, went on to the offensive against "old liberalism" in *Svenska Dagbladet*. They spoke of "the general, well-deserved and international bankruptcy which has fallen upon the old historical liberalism." It was important to incorporate the workers into the nation, and there were possibilities here for a vigorous, thrusting right. Given a strong state power and sufficient energy it ought to be possible to hammer the masses out to the right as easily as to the left. "Socialism and true conservatism [can] meet here with an abundance of the prerequisites for cooperating with and understanding each other."[16]

When Heckscher, in a lecture that same year, discussed measures to combat problems of child and female labor, accidents at work, and long working hours, he believed that neither employers, trade unions, nor parents could solve these problems. The state was the only power that could push through the necessary protective measures. It was not a matter of individualism: "It is not a question of the interests of private individuals but of those of society.... It is *society's* interest which shall dictate the rules. That is the meaning of the expression *social* legislation, which is neither charity nor sympathy for the workers; it is not class legislation but social legislation; it is the means for a better organisation of society."[17]

In an article of 1906 on the development of the communications system—a forerunner of his doctoral thesis on railways the following year—Heckscher declared that the monopolistic nature of railways had created a strong argument for state railways and refuted the view held by the older political economists "concerning the universal validity and vitality of free competition, and of the unnaturalness of monopoly and the state's duty of passivity in the economic field."[18] The state could help to stabilize the economy, for example. In a debating contribution in the autumn of 1906 Heckscher presented, as Cassel had done some years earlier, a proposal for a countercyclical economic policy.[19]

Having administered this pasting to the old liberals, Heckscher turned on the old conservatives in 1907. In an article in *Det Nya Sverige*, a journal that had just been started up by Adrian Molin, the angriest representative of the Gothenburg young conservatives, Heckscher

accused the conservatives of having failed to understand what opportunities were opening themselves to the right—instead, they had
turned conservatism into a "moderate braking device." "They seem to
have no perception that developments in the social sphere over the
past century toward a strengthening of the state's position as the
proper guardian of the national interest constitute a great victory for
conservative ideas."[20]

In fact, however, 1907 is a lean year for anyone tracing the steps of
Heckscher the young economic policy activist. He went back to writing
articles for the *Nordisk Familjebok*, and he completed and defended his
doctoral thesis. In a debating article in *Social-Demokraten* in the autumn
of that year he presented himself as "a person who backs state intervention in principle without being a socialist." His opponents for their
part acknowledged that Heckscher "is state-socialist in outlook, not
a Manchester man." In the article, Heckscher challenged Stockholm
socialists to a public debate on the theory of socialism.[21]

The gauntlet thus thrown down was picked up, and early in 1908
Heckscher fought a memorable duel with leading social democrats at
the Stockholm community center. In the course of this, he declared
that it was a great mistake to believe that health and safety at work,
workers' social insurance and state railways were socialistic inventions. In all eras the state had intervened in every field, and liberalism
was merely a parenthetical phenomenon in this scheme of things.
"There is therefore not the least tendency for us to be slipping toward
a socialist state [just] because events are shifting us back into the
grooves in which they have moved for thousands of years with one
brief intermission."[22]

Heckscher made an appearance at the same time at the National
Economic Society with a state-interventionist message. He noted that
the task of the state had begun to be understood in a sense more wide-
ranging than fifty years earlier and he accepted this development: "For
the modern state has, as every state must do in the long run, resumed
its work of protecting and encouraging all aspects of the national life.
The state is no longer merely the supplier of the protection of the
law and the representative of the formal systematisation of the relation
between individuals but also intervenes itself as a positively active
power, supporting tendencies which seem to merit being developed
and assisted while counteracting others which cause harm within the
pale of the law." As an example of spheres that have been the object of
intervention, he specified public education, economic policy, and social

policy, and he added that everybody knew the extent to which Germany's economic expansion was the result of "direct intervention on the part of the state administration."[23]

Which enterprises ought to lie in the hands of state or local authorities? Well, replied Heckscher in a commentary on a local government strike: "It is chiefly—and ought to be—enterprises which firstly constitute more or less what one calls natural monopolies and secondly are indispensable to the health, welfare and legal protection of all members of society." Heckscher here made fun of the "timid old liberal theorists" who painted eloquent pictures of the dangers of economic enterprises in the hands of central and local authorities. However, one risk had been underestimated, and that was the risk that the workers of a democratic society would capture political power and in that way secure control over the enterprises in which they themselves were "subordinates." This risk was particularly serious precisely in natural monopolies and public utilities.[24]

In 1909 Heckscher was appointed professor of economics and statistics at the Stockholm School of Economics. That year left unusually few written traces. His reaction to the general lockout and general strike during the summer and autumn of 1909 is of interest of course. It was very resolute. In his very own person he went out with the dustcarts keeping Stockholm clean.

In the backwash of the general strike Heckscher complained of anarchy in the trade union movement, disobedience to the leaders, lack of centralization. His discourse climaxed in a tirade against democracy. "The chief casualty in all these phenomena is democracy—the word may be aptly translated as the sovereignty of the mob! If one wishes to appreciate properly the incredible silliness of pure democracy—the dominion of the stupid over the wise, the inexperienced over the experienced, the ignorant over the discerning—then one must go to the labour movement."[25] All in all, Heckscher seems to have viewed the result of the conflict as a useful lesson for the youthful and overweening labor movement.[26]

In 1910 Heckscher manifested his state-activistic stance anew in an article headed "Statssocialism och statsförvaltning" (State socialism and public administration). In it he repudiated the extremist alternatives of liberalism and socialism—"the state's absolute abstention from any involvement in economic questions on the one hand and the state's complete takeover of the nation's production on the other." State intervention was necessary and did not lead to a socialist state at all.

Heckscher declared "that economic activity inevitably needs effective
protection and supervision by state authorities, and as well as that
certain types of monopolistic activity are suitable for the state itself."
Socialist politicians, of course, wanted to expand the state's sphere of
activity but at the same time wished to limit the freedom of action of
state authorities. "The first prerequisite of every form of state socialism
is probably a strong executive power, equipped with far-reaching authority and unencumbered by involvement in matters of detail." Consequently Heckscher demanded "elbow-room for the government,"
transformation of the Riksdag into "a footstool of the executive
power," and an "efficient administration [which] is the A to Z of all
positive government action." The article ended with the following
complaint: "We find everywhere the same individualistic spirit, hostile
to vigorous government action."[27]

The first issue of *Svensk Tidskrift*, edited by Heckscher and his running mate Gösta Bagge, came out in December 1910. The two editors
declared that the journal aimed to defend "the Swedish state's internal
and external strength and the effectiveness of state action, in support of
the nation's common tasks, in nurturing the nation's international
standing, and in furtherance of the state's interest against encroachment or unjustified claims by all private parties and classes."[28]

When Heckscher delivered a lecture in the spring of 1911 on how
trade and industry could be "raised" the tone was palpably quieter.
"When one speaks of means for raising trade and industry, one's
thoughts probably turn in the majority of instances to the state," he began, but at once asked himself whether or not "the state's influence,
both positive and negative, over economic events is in a fair way to being overestimated." Taking labor legislation as an example, he expressed skepticism over the idea that the state "should seek to create a
condition of things desirable in itself"; the state should probably content itself with "giving the sanctity of law to a condition which has
already become the normal." Heckscher's lecture finished up with a
conclusion which was anything but state-activistic: "Without wishing
to deny the great importance of state action, therefore, I believe we
should hold to the basic principle that trade and industry should look
primarily to themselves for help."[29]

In an article toward the end of the year, Heckscher took up again the
question of "what our industry needs." Again the message was that
trade and industry must help themselves: "A flourishing industry
depends in the first instance on industrialists themselves. At the pres-

ent time, both in Sweden and in other countries, we have got so much into the way of being supported by the state—by 'trade policy,' 'industrial policy,' 'export policy,' 'shipping policy'—that sometimes the greatest danger seems to me to be that this simple truth may be forgotten." Heckscher's state-socialist stance of 1910 has more or less completely vanished here. A possible explanation of this changed attitude may be glimpsed: "Now, however, a fairly long liberal regime is approaching under which business and industry pretty obviously will have to expect less benevolent interest on the part of the state than hitherto." They must therefore stand on their own feet and "keep themselves afloat even in the face of very strong government measures for the benefit of other interests."[30]

Heckscher had now, as may be understood, become more doubtful about the state as entrepreneur. In an article of 1911, in a situation where he thought he detected "a strong aspiration to expand the sphere of the state's business activity," he weighed the advantages and disadvantages of government enterprise in the scales. Among the advantages were the economies of large scale and the scope for cheaper access to capital, while the disadvantages included rigidity, uniformity, lack of the pioneering spirit, and the risk of workers securing too much influence over the firm. Profit, as a measure of efficiency, must as a rule be the crucial factor in the choice between state and private enterprise.[31]

Heckscher's agitation against socialism was no longer introduced with any surprising announcement of unity in the matter of the important role to be played by the state. When the social-democratic movement emphasized more and more that the aim of socialism was to abolish poverty, Heckscher posed two questions: Can socialism increase economic growth? Can socialism prevent "pauperisation of the people"? By the latter question he meant that talk of society's guilt and the individual's innocence in the matter of individual poverty risked undermining "the spirit of personal responsibility" and creating a "poorhouse mentality."[32]

In an article of 1912 entitled "Sociala reformer" (Social reforms) Heckscher proposed the abolition of poverty as the highest goal of all economic and social work. He was prepared to allot a socially reformative role to taxation but underlined at the same time that poverty could not be abolished through distribution but only through growth. He could conceive of legislation dealing with maximum working hours and (with some hesitancy) minimum wages and social insurance.

"Security for the great mass of people can only be created, at least up to the present, by the most enduring of all social structures, viz the state itself, and for this reason social insurance is indispensable." However, care must be taken not to undermine "the sense of personal responsibility, that each and every one of us 'is the architect of his own fortune,' that poverty ... must never appear to the individual as not of his own making as long as he has had some opportunity of avoiding it." Therefore every responsible-minded person must strive to ensure that the forthcoming social reforms "do not lead to the pauperisation of the people, to the creation of a poorhouse mentality in the whole of society."[33]

The world war came, and with it the diverse state interventions in various directions on which Heckscher commented from time to time. "Maximum prices," he opined in 1915, "are a remarkably foolish stunt as a rule."[34] The less interference in the price-setting process the better. On the other hand there was nothing wrong with the state's appropriating unearned war profits, which otherwise risked "being squandered on champagne."[35]

Toward the end of the war, Heckscher delivered himself of some remarks that show that on its own merits he held to his earlier view of how the state ought to be but that he no longer believed it capable of living up to this ideal. First the ideal: "The correct solution can scarcely consist of anything other than a really strong and respected state power, independence and authority to the organs of state, a state administrative machine protected from party-political infection."[36] Then the overstrain: "Whether one wants to call wartime developments 'war socialism' or not, what is clear even to the most purblind observer is the extent to which during the war the state has extended its functions to more, bigger and increasingly difficult fields of action."[37]

The Full-fledged Liberal

Heckscher's magnificent entrance upon the scene as the prophet of economic liberalism in Sweden came with *Gammal och ny ekonomisk liberalism* (Economic liberalism old and new, 1921), a work that evoked the following exclamation from *Social-Demokraten*: "That a prominent man, Professor Heckscher, has been converted leftwards is one of the most sensational events of the age."[38] But even before this he had sharpened and launched his economic liberal message. In a lecture on the state and private initiative after the war, delivered in 1918, he preached

how the "invisible hand," or the "wonderful mechanism" of free pricing, was "the right engine for all true economic activity." Therefore
"the conclusion [can] be drawn at once that we ought to have the least
possible state management when the war is over."[39] In an article of the
same year on "State monopoly," he argued "that those who saw state
management at close quarters during the war generally incline to the
view that it is a contraction rather than an expansion of state enterprise, even such as it was prior to the war, that we are in need of."
Only by scrapping the wartime regime at once would it be possible to
achieve "self-limitation of the state." Heckscher spoke in the article of
a monster having been created during the war that was incapable of
being controlled.[40]

From this it was but a short step to "Frankenstein's monster," and
in 1918 Heckscher for the first time made use of this metaphor for
the menace of a state machine running riot: "Humanity in its adversity
seeks to bring in more and more and more, to include ever larger
areas within the compass of state organisation, and in so doing loses
all command of this mighty organisation as well as of the entire
situation produced by the maelstrom of war."[41] In the years that
followed Heckscher repeated this message in many variants and
declared that "the wartime planning fiasco made a great many people
wary of state intervention in matters great and small"; the state
had "overreached itself" and so forth.[42] In "Krigets oväntade avkomlingar" (The unexpected progeny of war), an article to which we
shall have cause to revert, Heckscher dissociated himself from "state
absolutism." The state exists for its citizens, not the other way round.
The state is a means to an end; to regard it as an end in itself was
idolatry.[43]

Conceivable Causes

With the help of testimony from Heckscher authorities, and from
Heckscher himself, we have arrived at a couple of possible explanations of Heckscher's conversion from social conservatism to economic
liberalism. Are there further explanations, of a social environmental character, of why, a decade or so into the twentieth century, a right-
ist should realign himself from social conservatism to economic
liberalism?

A dramatic event that caused many in the nonsocialist camp to
reevaluate their political stance was the general strike of 1909. Sven

Ulric Palme has described the general strike as "the strongly dominant experience which, more than any other, awakened the fear of socialism among middle-class Swedes."[44] Above all the strike may have destroyed all hope in the conservative camp of class cooperation under conservative leadership.

Another crucial sequence of events was the reform of the franchise in 1909 and the subsequent change of government in 1911. Nils Elvander describes the following scenario: The Conservative Party maintained a reformist course in a spirit of national solidarity from the dissolution of the union with Norway in 1905 until 1910, when it switched from social conservatism to economic liberalism. The main reason for the change of direction was that after the franchise reform, the Conservatives were faced with "the prospect that the reform policy would be carried further by a democratised government controlled by a radicalised liberalism with socialist support," fears which proved justified in 1911.[45] Elvander's conception of the timing of and explanation for the switch toward economic liberalism in the conservative camp has been confirmed by historian Åke Sundell.[46]

We can now present four hypotheses concerning when and why Heckscher's changeover from social conservatism to neoliberalism took place. According to these hypotheses it is conceivable that Heckscher's conversion may be related to:

1. The appointment to a professorship in 1909 and the subsequent stronger orientation toward neoclassical (liberal) economic theory;

2. The general strike of 1909 which awakened "fear of socialism" and cast doubt on the social-conservative project;

3. The franchise reform of 1909 and the subsequent power-shift from right to left in 1911, which meant that it was no longer a social-conservative government that directed reform policy;

4. The system of commissions, or "wartime socialism," during World War I, which had the effect of compromising state activism.

It is difficult on the basis of Heckscher's writings to free oneself from the impression that he changed course from social conservatism or state socialism to economic liberalism or state skepticism sometime between 1910 and 1911. His detailed studies of neoclassical economists at this time (hypothesis 1) may have had some influence, but the change of direction was so sudden as to provoke the suspicion that it may have been triggered by a more palpable change of ideological wind.

If the change of direction happened between 1910 and 1911 the general strike (hypothesis 2) can hardly have been of any significance. After all, one of his most state activist articles—the 1910 article on state socialism—was published *after* he had published reactions on the strike; he furthermore seems to have interpreted the strike primarily as a useful lesson for the workers.

The readiest explanation is probably to be found instead in the fact that in 1911 power passed from the right under Arvid Lindman to the left (liberals supported by the social democrats) under Karl Staaff (hypothesis 3). Heckscher, from his conservative horizon, must have interpreted the power-shift as a threat against the state which he wanted to see elevated above all special interests. Now the hour had struck, as he wrote in 1911, for "strong government measures for the benefit of other interests" (than those of trade and industry).

Heckscher's dawning economic liberalism was obviously fortified by the experiences of "wartime socialism" during World War I, and toward the end of the war he elaborated his well-reasoned and uncompromising liberal worldview. A number of other former young conservatives who, like Heckscher, moved in a liberal direction after 1910, fell back into right-wing radicalism and state socialism during World War I because they placed their hopes in a German victory. Heckscher was more inclined to favor the British side and therefore was not affected by any reversion.

But Heckscher's own testimony as to the all-overriding importance of his world war experiences—are we not to believe his own words? Yes, certainly. But at the same time it seems as though the war made him rest his full weight on the economic liberal foot rather than making him shift his center of gravity from one foot to the other. In fact it is not all that difficult to understand if Heckscher, when he afterward wanted to explain his switch from social conservatism to economic liberalism, preferred to emphasize (to himself as well as the outside world) the generally negatively loaded experiences of state intervention during the world war rather than the power shift, positively loaded in many quarters, which had been precipitated by a democratic reform.

Letters to Mother

In order to test this interpretation of Heckscher's conversion, which takes as its starting point two observed circumstances (hypotheses 1 and 4) and draws attention to one circumstance less noticed up to now (hypothesis 3), I have attempted to find some kind of "confession" in which Heckscher gives an account in confidence—that is, not to the public at large—of his change of stance. I have therefore inspected Heckscher's letters to his mother, Rosa Heckscher, during the period 1909 to 1922.[47] Heckscher explained his conversion in two of these letters, 1918 and 1919. The explanations were justified in terms of the article on "Krigets oväntade avkomlingar" in *Svensk Tidskrift* (which he had edited along with Bagge in the years 1911–18). He goes into the most detail in the second letter, which is worth citing at length:

Well, Mother, you are right that my essay in that issue is a sort of defection, but unfortunately not very substantial in positive respects. I have really thought this ever since 1915–16 but refrained from writing it down out of consideration for the others who were thought to have a right of censorship over my scripts as long as I was editor. Now Gösta consoles me by saying that no one should take any notice of it because it was nothing remarkable; on the former point he already seems to have been proved right, and the latter is also true. I cannot wait, I wish I could, for one's former belief always contain much that is not replaced by what is in the new, and if one had the power one would hardly give it up. But something like this is an inner compulsion and one can only go along with it. What caused the change is as usual lots of things. An inborn and inherited individualism probably plays a main part, it has emerged gradually during the silver-plating [?] which Hjärne and his school gave it at one time and which was of tip-top material. Then studying economics has had a lot to do with it; it weaned me away from my former protectionism, and much against my original thinking it took a lot more with it. A closer insight into what in reality lies behind the cliché of 'the state' then also became a main factor, especially the Hammarskjöld government's inability, even during its golden era and despite better intentions than we are likely to see again, really to act in accordance with what the general good required. The war came as the last big mouthful, especially the experiences during the study-tour of 1915.[48] None of this prevents me from feeling just as lost as most others do, whichever side they stand on, machine politicians excepted of course. For preference I would absolutely like to stop writing about political things in the usual sense, but there too one is driven to a certain extent by an inner force.[49]

In other words, Heckscher considers his studies of economics and the war to have been decisive in determining his conversion. Nothing new so far. What is new is that he turns the steak over, as it were—deep inside himself he was a liberal by birth and force of habit but for a time he became a conservative through his studies under Hjärne—and that he dates his conversion more exactly, at the years 1915–16. As far as his reference to Hjärne is concerned, one should perhaps keep in mind that Hjärne hardly ever displayed such a radical economic and social state-activist attitude as Heckscher did.

Conclusion

Eli Heckscher himself, outwardly (vis-à-vis the general public) and inwardly (in correspondence with his mother), has singled out his studies of economics and the experiences of wartime socialism during World War I as vital explanations of his conversion from social conservatism to economic liberalism. The authorities on Heckscher have similarly leaned toward one, the other or both of these explanations. The studies of economics began to exert their effect from 1909 onwards and the crucial experiences of wartime came from the years 1915–16. What is puzzling, however, is that a study of Heckscher's writings on the state suggests that in principle he "changed direction" sometime between 1910 and 1911. Thus there remains a suspicion, which cannot be confirmed by means of his statements or confessions (apart from a passage in an article of 1911), that the change—or perhaps even anticipated change—of government from right to left in 1911 played a part in his conversion. That Heckscher had lifted the liberal cup to his lips even before World War I is shown by the fact that he himself describes the war as "the last big mouthful."

Acknowledgments

This essay was translated from Swedish by Geoffrey French. I am grateful for comments on the paper at the Heckscher symposium, especially from Rolf G. H. Henriksson and Kurt Wickman.

Notes

1. When we speak of the young conservatives in Sweden, it should be clearly understood that in the early twentieth century there were two tendencies, a moderate wing in Uppsala consisting of the historian Harald Hjärne's pupils and with Heckscher at its head, and a radical movement in Gothenburg led by the philosopher Vitalis Norström, the political scientist Rudolf Kjellén and the versatile Adrian Molin.

2. Palmstierna (1951:34, 121).

3. Montgomery (1953:150–151, 154–157).

4. Brulin (1953:416–418). Heckscher's message was approximately the same in a letter to Bagge of August 1, 1923 (Kungliga biblioteket L67:65).

5. Söderlund (1953:63).

6. Ohlin (1971).

7. Hettne (1980:56–57).

8. Henriksson (1991:151).

9. Wickman (2000:14–15).

10. Heckscher in *Mercantilism* cited after Montgomery (1953:151).

11. *Tre tal* (1945).

12. Ingelson (1933).

13. Heckscher (1944:94).

14. *Eli F Heckschers bibliografi* (1950).

15. Heckscher (1905:222, 225).

16. Heckscher and Brulin (1906).

17. Heckscher (1906a:10).

18. Heckscher (1906b:314–315, 318–319).

19. *Berättelse* (1907:235–356).

20. Heckscher (1907a:178).

21. Heckscher (1907b).

22. *Socialismens grundvalar* (1908:20, 22).

23. Heckscher (1908a:3–4).

24. Heckscher (1908b:383–384).

25. Heckscher (1909a:8–9).

26. Heckscher (1909b).

27. Heckscher (1910:1–5, 7).

28. Bagge and Heckscher (1911:2).

29. Heckscher (1911a:3–4, 6).

30. Heckscher (1911b).

31. Heckscher (1911c:167–178).

32. Heckscher (1911d:231–233).

33. Heckscher (1912:411–417).

34. Heckscher (1915a:85).

35. Heckscher (1915b:248).

36. Heckscher (1917:444).

37. Heckscher (1918a:134).

38. "Gammalliberalismen" (1921).

39. Heckscher (1918b:5–6, 33).

40. Heckscher (1918d:520–522).

41. Heckscher (1918c:292). The article is not signed and not listed in Heckscher's bibliography. It is probably by Heckscher's hand, first because he was the editor of *Svensk Tidskrift* and second because he made use of the metaphor later on in the discussions about economic planning in the 1930s. Heckscher's use of the Frankenstein metaphor in fact led the present author to entitle his doctoral thesis *The State as a Monster* (1994, in the original Swedish 1988).

42. Heckscher (1919a) and (1921:314).

43. Heckscher (1919b:108–110).

44. Palme (1964:260).

45. Elvander (1961:298, 424, 467–468, 481–482).

46. Sundell (1989:109, 243, 251, 265). It is not quite obvious why a reform, carried out under a conservative regime in 1909, should cause a switch in the conservative camp around 1910. A conceivable explanation could sound like this: The conservatives had probably hoped that their social and franchise reforms should draw some gratitude and loyalty from "the masses." When this did not happen and when the conservatives could sense what would happen in the upcoming elections, feelings of disappointment took hold in the conservative camp.

47. Heckscher had a very confidential relationship with his mother (who was only seventeen years his senior), and wrote no fewer than 876 letters to her during the period 1894–1944 (Kungliga biblioteket L:67:85: 1–3).

48. Heckscher refers to the study tour he made in Holland, England, France, and Germany in the summer of 1915. See Heckscher (1915c).

49. Letter from Eli Heckscher to Rosa Heckscher 26 March 1919. In the earlier letter (29 December 1918) Heckscher speaks similarly of an underlying individualism, which was restrained by the Hjärne school, in combination with an inclination to go the whole hog theoretically, and of theoretical economics and the war causing him to change his opinion.

References

Bagge, G., and E. Heckscher. 1911. "Anmälan." *Svensk Tidskrift* 1:1–5.

Berättelse öfver förhandlingarna vid kongressen för fattigvård och folkförsäkring i Stockholm den 4, 5 och 6 oktober 1906. 1907. Stockholm: Svenska Boktryckeri-Aktiebolaget.

Brulin, H. 1953. "Eli Heckscher och Svensk Tidskrift." *Svensk Tidskrift* 43:407–425.

Carlson, B. 1994. *The State as a Monster: Gustav Cassel and Eli Heckscher on the Role and Growth of the State.* Lanham, MD: University Press of America.

Eli F Heckschers bibliografi 1897–1949. 1950. Stockholm: Ekonomisk-historiska institutet.

Elvander, N. 1961. *Harald Hjärne och konservatismen. Konservativ idédebatt i Sverige 1865–1922.* Stockholm: Almquist & Wiksell.

"Gammalliberalismen nyuppstånden." Professor Heckscher har blivit liberal." *Social-Demokraten,* November 29, 1921.

Heckscher, E. 1905. "Sträjkförslaget och renhållningssträjken i Stockholm." *Social Tidskrift* 5:220–225.

————. 1906a. *Industrialismen. Tre föreläsningar.* Stockholm: Centralförbundet för Socialt Arbete.

————. 1906b. "Kommunikationsväsendets betydelse i det nittonde århundradets ekonomiska utveckling." *Ekonomisk Tidskrift* 8:293–320.

————. 1907a. "Proportionalismen och det svenska statslifvet." *Det Nya Sverige* 1:173–182.

————. 1907b. "En avrättning av socialismen." *Social-Demokraten,* November 19.

————. 1908a. "Betydelsen af nationalekonomisk utbildning för statsförvaltningen och näringslifvets koprorationer." *Nationalekonomiska föreningens förhandlingar,* January 24. 1–18, 20–22.

————. 1908b. "Samhället och strejkerna. Några reflexioner med anledning af kommunalstrejken in Malmö." *Det Nya Sverige* 2:382–391.

————. 1909a. "Demokratien i den fackliga arbetarrörelsen." *Det Nya Sverige* 3:1–11.

————. 1909b. "Storstrejkens förutsättningar och följder." *Det Nya Sverige* 3:301–302.

————. 1910. "Statssocialism och statsförvaltning." *Det Nya Sverige* 4:1–9.

————. 1911a. *Något om medlen för det svenska näringslifvets höjande.* Gefle: Handelskammarens i Gefle.

————. 1911b. "Hvad vårt näringslif behöfver." *Stockholms Dagblad,* December 17.

————. 1911c. "Staten som företagare." *Svensk Tidskrift* 1:167–178.

————. 1911d. "Socialismen och fattigdomens afskaffande." *Svensk Tidskrift* 1:231–233.

————. 1912. "Sociala reformer." *Svensk Tidskrift* 2:409–420.

————. 1915a. "Maximipriser." *Svensk Tidskrift* 5:83–86.

————. 1915b. "Krigsvinster och statsbeskattning." *Svensk Tidskrift* 5:247–248.

————. 1915c. *Världskrigets ekonomi. En studie af nutidens näringslif under krigets inverkan.* Stockholm: P. A. Norstedt.

————. 1917. "Staten och storfinansen." *Svensk Tidskrift* 7:442–444.

————. 1918a. "Statsuppgifterna och deras bärare." *Svensk Tidskrift* 8:134–137.

————. 1918b. *Staten och det enskilda initiativet efter kriget.* Stockholm: Sveriges Industriförbund.

————. 1918c. "Frankensteins monstrum." *Svensk Tidskrift* 8:292–294.

————. 1918d. "Statsmonopol." *Svensk Tidskrift* 8:520–523.

———. 1919a. "Socialisering." *Sydsvenska Dagbladet*, February 2.

———. 1919b. "Krigets oväntade avkomlingar." *Svensk Tidskrift* 9:105–114.

———. 1921. "Den offentliga verksamhetens utväxter." *Svensk Tidskrift* 11:314–317.

———. 1944. "Erfarenheter av ekonomi och ekonomisk politik under fyrtio år." *Ekonomen*, 86–95.

Heckscher, E., and H. Brulin. 1906. "'Snar lösning.' Ur konservativ synpunkt." *Svenska Dagbladet*, March 13.

Henriksson, R. 1991. "Eli F. Heckscher: The Economic Historian as Economist." In B. Sandelin, ed., *The History of Swedish Economic Thought*, 141–167. London: Routledge.

Hettne, B. 1980. *Ekonomisk historia i Sverige*. Lund: Historiska institutionen.

Ingelson, A. 1933. "Eli F Heckscher." *Nya Dagligt Allehanda*, June 25.

Montgomery, A. 1953. "Eli Heckscher som vetenskapsman." *Ekonomisk Tidskrift* 55:149–185.

Ohlin, B. 1971. "Eli Heckscher." *Svenskt biografiskt lexikon* 18:377–381. Stockholm: P. A. Norstedt.

Palme, S. U. 1964. *På Karl Staaffs tid*. Stockholm: Aldus-Bonnier.

Palmstierna, E. 1951. *Ett brytningsskede*. Stockholm: Tidens.

Socialismens grundvalar. 1908. Stockholm: Wahlström & Widstrand.

Söderlund, E. 1953. "Eli Heckscher." *Historisk Tidskrift* 73:63–66.

Sundell, Å. 1989. *Den svenska högerns assimilering av ekonomisk liberalism. Studier kring en ideologisk förändringsproblematik*. Lund: University of Lund.

Tre tal hållna vid den middag som ett antal kolleger och lärjungar gav för Eli F Heckscher och hans anhöriga den 13 december 1944 på restaurangen Tre Kronor i Stockholm. 1945. Stockholm.

Wickman, K. 2000. "Eli Heckscher—pionjär utan efterföljare." In E. Heckscher, *Om staten, liberalismen och den ekonomiska politiken*, 11–49. Stockholm: Timbro.

22

Eli Heckscher on Jewish Assimilation and Zionism

Harry Flam

As the year 1942 was drawing to a close, Eli Heckscher wrote in his diary, "It is becoming increasingly clear that I see myself first and foremost as a citizen of Western society and a servant of the free search for truth, only second as a Swede, and third as a Jew. The mass murder of Jews now started by Hitler would otherwise be intolerable and haunt me day and night" (Koblik 1990:203).

Heckscher's ordering of identities was founded in a clear and strongly held view of the history and mission of Western civilization that not even Hitler and Nazism could shake. He saw himself foremost as a contributor to that civilization. In consequence, Heckscher argued that Jews should be completely assimilated into Swedish society, a common sentiment among his generation of Jews in Sweden. His priorities also led him to argue, both before and after World War II, against the creation of a Jewish state.

The purpose of my essay is to explain Heckscher's priorities of identity and views on assimilation and Zionism. I will do this by outlining Heckscher's Jewish background and the history of Jews in Sweden, stress the decisive influence by one of his university teachers, and then document and examine Heckscher's reasoning in more detail.

Heckscher's Background

The Swedish branch of the Heckscher family can be traced back to the merchant Ephraim Meyer Heckscher, who lived in Altona in the seventeenth century.[1] At that time, Altona, nowadays a central part of Hamburg, was a next-door competitor as port and trading center on the river Elbe and close to the North Sea. The Schleswig region where Altona was situated had been a duchy under the Danish crown since the twelfth century and remained so until a brief war with Prussia and

Austria in 1864. The Danish king invited people of all persuasions to Altona to stimulate trade and commerce, and many Jews settled there. A direct descendant of Ephraim Meyer moved to Copenhagen in the early eighteenth century, from which Eli's father emigrated to Sweden in 1875. Eli and Ephraim Meyer span eight generations.[2]

Isidor Heckscher, Eli's father, held a Ph.D. in law from Copenhagen University and frequently published articles in professional journals in economics and law. He was the Danish consul general, first in Gothenburg and then in Stockholm. His main occupation was in the bank, where his uncle, who had immigrated from Denmark before him, was general manager and chairman of the board. One may speculate that Eli's interest in economics was due to his father's influence.

Both of Eli's parents were Jewish. Eli himself married a non-Jew. Before 1952, Swedish citizens were required by law to belong to a church of some denomination or to some other religious community, and Eli was a member of the Jewish Community in Stockholm. He took no interest in Jewish religious life, but did publish articles and comments in Jewish journals.

The Jewish Community in Sweden in Heckscher's Time

Not until the late eighteenth century were Jews allowed to settle permanently in Sweden. The first wave of Jewish immigrants came from present-day northern Germany via Denmark throughout the nineteenth century. The immigrants were relatively wealthy merchants, bankers, and skilled craftsmen. At first, they were subject to numerous labor market and other restrictions, but these were gradually lifted and Jews received full rights as citizens in the 1860s. As had been the case elsewhere in Western Europe after emancipation, Jews became well integrated into Swedish society after one or two generations. In a short time, they attained far greater prominence as merchants, bankers, scholars, writers, painters, and patrons of the arts than warranted by their number. Intermarriage rates were high and assimilation rapid. Very few of the present-day descendants of the nineteenth-century immigrants identify themselves as Jewish.

A second wave of immigrants came from Russia at the end of the nineteenth and beginning of the twentieth century. The new immigrants were of a very different kind from the already established Jews in Sweden. They had little or no education, held low-skilled occupations, and were traditional or orthodox in their religious practice, whereas the Jewish establishment practiced what is called German Reform Judaism.[3] They were frequently looked down on by the established Jews. The immigrants from Russia were socially mobile, however, and within one or two generations, their descendants attained levels of education and income approaching those of the established Jews.

Heckscher belonged to the first group of established and assimilated Jewish immigrants. He had been raised in a prosperous family, had married a non-Jew (the daughter of a postmaster, a position with high status at the time), was a highly respected professor of economics and widely known to the general public through articles in the press and radio programs.

The Influence of Harald Hjärne

Heckscher entered Uppsala University in 1897 and received the degree of *filosofie licentiat* in 1904. His main subject was economic history, but he also studied political science and economics, the latter with David Davidsson, a fellow Jew and the founder of what later became the *Scandinavian Journal of Economics*. Although most of his studies took place in Uppsala, Heckscher also attended lectures in Stockholm and Gothenburg. He was attracted to Gothenburg by the most prominent Swedish historian at the time, Harald Hjärne. Hjärne was to have a strong influence on a generation of prominent Swedes, Heckscher among these.

European history in the nineteenth century was greatly shaped by the theory and practice of nationalism. We need only remind ourselves of the unification of Germany and Italy, and the breakup of the Ottoman Empire in Europe into new nation-states. Although Sweden had been independent since the sixteenth century, a nationalistic movement arose in the nineteenth century, recalling a glorious past, including Vikings and Swedish expansionism in the seventeenth and eighteenth centuries. Part of this movement was cultural and part was aggressively nationalistic, wanting to preserve the union with Norway and painting Russia as a new threat. There was also a strong movement among students for Scandinavian unity, stressing a common history, language, and culture.

Hjärne was critical of many aspects of the nationalistic movement. He pointed to its inwardness and that nationalists in all countries were engaged in a similar quest for national "peculiarities." Real national talent, according to Hjärne, was to achieve a higher cultural level on its own terms, which could only be achieved without the obsession for national traits. He deplored that nationalism threatened the political and cultural union of the Austro-Hungarian Empire and hindered the unification of Belgium and the Netherlands. He pointed out the tendency of nationalism to turn into racism and racial hatred, and denounced the idea of given racial characteristics as fatalistic and erroneous (Elvander 1961). In all of this, Hjärne went against the tide, displaying both independence of mind and some degree of courage.

To Hjärne, nationalism was a danger because it could hinder the progress and expansion of Western—European—civilization. He saw Western civilization as the primary achievement of humankind and its improvement as the highest good. Heckscher (1944a) described "this central part of Hjärne's preaching" in the following words:

Hjärne's studies were devoted to what he himself called 'the never fully eradicated unity of Europe,' the unbreakable inner togetherness of Western civilization, derived from a classical, mainly Greek heritage. During the Middle Ages this heritage was above all upheld by the church, but also by the empire, the two inheritors of the Roman Empire, with Latin as the language of unity keeping Western civilization together. At the same time, the Byzantine Empire kept the classical traditions more directly, with Greek as its language, and the Arabs appeared as the third keeper of the same heritage. This unity was endangered by the Reformation, but it was never completely eradicated by it. The Reformation upheld the unity of Western Christianity, the church remained universal in principle. The classical heritage was saved for our time through the Roman law and through *Volksrecht* as the Christian *Naturrecht*. In comparison with the overshadowing importance of all this, Hjärne looked at expressions of nationalism as admittedly important forms of the many-sided common heritage, determined by the political necessity and traditions of each people, but at the same time as a barbarian, divisive factor, always putting civilization in danger.

The cultural unity of Western or European civilization was central to Hjärne. Another element central to his thinking was that the fundamental task of the state—its raison d'être—was to create and uphold the rule of law. On this issue, Heckscher (1929) wrote: "Hjärne's thinking was that the protection of the elementary foundations for human co-existence, i.e. above all to uphold the rule of law internally and externally, was the real task of the state and that it amounted to superstition or something worse when one discriminated between people who wanted to cooperate achieving this." In other words, the rule of law was needed to prevent existing nationalistic, ethnic or other divisions from upsetting peaceful coexistence and hindering the progress of Western civilization.

Hjärne influenced a generation of Swedish historians and other academics. Heckscher was greatly influenced by Hjärne, as expressed by Arthur Montgomery (1953), a colleague at the Stockholm School of Economics, in his commemorative survey of Heckscher's contributions. Whenever Heckscher late in life discussed what his studies in Uppsala, Stockholm, and Gothenburg had meant to him, the dominating influence of Hjärne was always stressed. Hjärne frequently lectured to fellow historians in closed meetings, and these occasions gave him an opportunity to display his broad knowledge to a captivated audience. Montgomery writes of these meetings that "it was easy to understand that he made a particularly strong impression on those who, like Heckscher, were personally close."

From Hjärne, Heckscher received the world view of the universal character of Western or European history and civilization and a strong antinationalistic sentiment. This came to determine his views on anti-Semitism, Jewish assimilation, and Zionism.

Anti-Semitism

Anti-Semitic sentiment was widespread in Sweden until World War II, particularly in higher strata of society, but was mild compared to other countries in Western Europe, such as France and Germany, and insignificant compared to Russia and Eastern Europe. There were never concerted campaigns against Jews from the clergy or public officials as in other countries, but expressions of anti-Semitism were not uncommon in the press and in films, as documented by Andersson (2000).

As a consequence of his participation in public discussion, in particular on agricultural policy, Heckscher received anti-Semitic mail and became the target of public anti-Semitic attacks. In a commencement address to graduates at the Stockholm School of Economics in 1944, he writes that he has noted a shift toward intolerance in public discussion, in particular a tendency to look for scapegoats, "to put the blame for our eventual foolishness on others than ourselves":

The first time I came into contact with the new spirit was in connection with the heated battle about agriculture that erupted in 1929 and in which I was in the line of fire to a high degree. In my view, this is one of the very many instances where the spiritual victories which were so hard fought for in the 19th century are in the process of being lost; the supremacy of regimes of violence has of course exacerbated this tendency. It cannot be helped that one therefore becomes less willing to participate in public discussion on hot topics since one fears repercussions on bystanders and the innocent because of what one may say or write.[4]

It is true that Heckscher became a much less frequent participant in public discussion and policy making after 1930. Anti-Semitism was probably not the main reason, however. Heckscher simply wanted to spend more time and energy on research and a research professorship had been created for him at the Stockholm School of Economics in 1929[5] (Heckscher 1944b).

In its more principled form, anti-Semitism in Sweden and elsewhere in Europe in the latter part of the nineteenth century and until World War II took the form of "The Jewish Question," a euphemism for "The Jewish Problem."[6] After emancipation, Jews had moved out of the ghettos and become successful and influential in commerce, finance, politics, the arts, and universities out of proportion with their numbers. Jews were widely seen as foreign and having a detrimental impact, materially and spiritually, on the majority populations. For the majority populations, the Jewish problem was how to get rid of alleged Jewish economic power and exploitation, intellectual and political influence, and—ominously—racial contamination. For Jews, the problem was how to eliminate anti-Semitism.

The common Jewish response in Western Europe to anti-Semitism after emancipation was assimilation.[7] This was also the road followed by the Jews in Sweden. Heckscher, an assimilated Swedish Jew, therefore found it worrying that Jewish nationalism—Zionism—had taken a strong hold among the Jewish masses in Eastern Europe and found proselytes in Sweden. A Jewish state in Palestine would be proof that Jews were foreign to Europe and prompt anti-Semites to demand that Jews in Europe emigrate to their homeland.

Heckscher on Assimilation

For Heckscher, the solution to the problem of anti-Semitism was closely connected to the struggle between adherents of universalism and Western civilization on the one side and nationalists on the other: "The confrontation is between those who put the common Western cultural heritage first and fight all forms of nationalism, and on the opposing side nationalists of all color and nationalities. Whether the Jewish problem will be 'solved' or not is essentially tied to the outcome of *that* battle" (letter of 1939 from Heckscher to Hugo Valentin, reprinted in Koblik 1987.)

Heckscher had an essentially optimistic view on the possibilities for social and cultural progress; he believed that knowledge and reason could convince people of the value of universalism over nationalism. The rise of Nazism in Germany and the attendant anti-Semitism were of considerable concern to him and he was deeply disturbed by the atrocities committed against Jews, but he believed that reason and rationality would prevail.

One of Heckscher's main works as an economic historian, and the one that had the greatest influence on Swedish historians, is his monumental *Sveriges ekonomiska historia från Gustav Vasa* (The Economic History of Sweden from the Time of Gustav Vasa), consisting of four volumes covering the period from the early sixteenth century (the reign of King Gustav Vasa) to 1815, the end of the Napoleonic Wars.[8] Many of his other scientific writings deal with the Swedish economy. It may therefore seem surprising that Heckscher saw himself as a propagator of a universal Western civilization and as an antinationalist to the extent that nationalism was detrimental to Western civilization. However, a reading of *Sveriges ekonomiska historia* and other works makes it clear that Heckscher continually makes a point of the extent to which the development of the Swedish economy was dependent on foreign European influence, not least through immigration. In 1931, he published an article in the journal of the Association of Swedish Economists entitled "Swedish and Foreign in the Economic Life of Sweden," which attempts to show that much of economic progress was due to immigrants and imported technology, starting in the eleventh century when copper production was organized on a model practiced in Germany. It is only at the end of the nineteenth century that indigenous Swedes start to make significant innovations (Heckscher 1931).

Foreign influence was not only visible in the economic sphere. In an article in the Swedish daily *Dagens Nyheter* in 1929 with the heading "The Jews and Palestine," he devotes much space to the foreign influence on Swedish political and cultural elites, listing many who were considered originators of various aspects of Swedish culture but who were actually descendants of immigrants (Heckscher 1929). He adds with a touch of sarcasm: "What the Swedish culture would have been if it had developed in isolation on our peninsula I refrain from expounding; those who have an inkling of historical knowledge can easily imagine it themselves."[9]

It is clear that these examples were prompted by the rising anti-Semitism in Sweden and Germany. In the same article, he writes about racism in Germany: "it is difficult to imagine something more grotesque than the view that the Germans and the Prussians are at all pure 'Germans'....No one who can use his eyes and ears could be ignorant of how Slavic in origin a great part of the German people is."

Heckscher had the intention—never realized—to tackle the problem head-on, by writing about the contribution of Jews to European society. In a letter in 1933 to a leading Swedish publisher and fellow Jew, Karl-Otto Bonnier, he mentions his plan to write "a small pamphlet about the Jews in the cultured societies of Europe." However, he does not want to publish it with Bonnier because "everything that is written about the Jews is misinterpreted and vilified, and to reduce the possibility in the present case it has from the outset been clear to me that it should not be published by a publishing house which could be called Jewish." The letter is cited in Hansson (1988), which documents an interesting and revealing discussion among prominent Swedish Jews about assimilation as a defense against rising anti-Semitism in the early 1930s, in which Heckscher took an active part.

The solution to the problem of anti-Semitism in Western Europe was in Heckscher's view the eradication of nationalism, which would allow Jews and other groups to cooperate peacefully and fruitfully within the different European states. The Nazi terror against the Jews in Germany in the 1930s did not make him change his mind. If anything, it made him even more convinced that nationalism was the enemy, not only because it fueled anti-Semitism, but above all because it threatened Western civilization and everything that had been created over the past two millennia.

Nazism threatened to drive the Jews back into ghettos and cultural isolation and prevent them from contributing to the progress of Western civilization. In Heckscher's view, the Jews had contributed little during the centuries when they lived in isolation. The escape from the ghetto had allowed the Jews to use their creative powers for the common good.[10] To those who advocated Jewish nationalism and a Jewish state he made the analogy with the Scots: "No one can argue...that the Scots would have been more valuable for Britain and humanity by staying among their poor mountains instead of becoming

Photo 1
Eli Heckscher as a 12-year-old pupil at Nya Elementar (New Elementary) School in Stockholm during the fall term of 1891. Despite its name, the school was strictly a secondary school for boys. It was renowned among Stockholm secondary schools as a laboratory for pedagogical innovation.

Photo 2
Eli Heckscher as a young student at Uppsala University in 1902. At the University he concentrated on the study of history, with Professor Harald Hjärne as his academic mentor.

Photo 3
On the twentieth of June, 1907, Eli Heckscher married Ebba Westberg, who until then had been a secondary school teacher in the fashionable Stockholm suburb of Djursholm.

Photo 4
A class in economics at the Stockholm School of Economics (SSE) during the 1910s.
When the SSE was founded in 1909, Eli Heckscher, to his credit, was responsible for
making economics the lead subject. Indeed, "it generally constituted the foundation for
the business studies." He served as Professor of Economics and Statistics from 1909 to
1929, after which he received a research professorship in economic history. He continued in that position until his retirement in 1945.

Photo 5 and 6
Eli Heckscher was a workaholic who demanded as much as from himself as from his students. For him, a worthy life included working hard and being productive. He is pictured here in the study of his home at Baldersgatan 10 sometime during the early 1920s. It was in this room during World War II that his grandson Einar accidentally discharged the revolver that Eli had lying on his desk.

Photo 7
Eli F. Heckscher posing for the camera during the 1910s.

Photo 8
In August of 1911, Eli Heckscher, together with two old student friends from Uppsala University, Martin Fehr and Nils Edling, undertook a sailing tour of the Stockholm Archipelago in a so-called "Blekinge" skiff. Their log book reveals a certain reluctance by Heckscher's companions to let him take the helm since he had never before set foot in a sailboat. Source: Edling, Nils (1956), "Kring en gammal blekingseka," Svenska Kryssarklubbens Årsskrift, pp 96–105.

Photo 9
Eli Heckscher together with his son
Gunnar at the summer house on Utö in
the Stockholm Archipelago during 1921.

Photo 10
In addition to his scholarly endeavors,
Eli Heckscher found time to enjoy life
in the archipelago. He was enamored
of the sea and frequently went sailing.
His granddaughter Eva, however, has
recounted that while sailing Eli was
easily distracted by discussions on a
variety of topics and frequently ran
aground.

Photo 11
Eli Heckscher swimming with his two eldest grandchildren, Eva and
Einar, on a fine summer's day in the Archipelago. Snapshot probably
from 1941 or 1942.

Photo 12
Relaxing with a good book at the summer house in the Stockholm
Archipelago during the 1940s. Eli Heckscher was a voracious reader, and
not just of professional literature. His favorite authors included adventure
and mystery writers such as Conan Doyle, Freeman Wills Crofts, and
Dorothy Sayers.

Photo 13
The elderly Eli Heckscher. A photographic portrait from the mid 1940s.

Photo 14
Eva Heckscher, 1936–2004.

the ferment and backbone in a great culture, giving up all other special characteristics than what lies in character and intelligence."[11] Another analogy was drawn with the ancient Greeks: "No one can argue that the immeasurable importance of the Greeks for our world has the least to do with the present Greek state." The role that the Jews should play was clear to Heckscher: "My standpoint is that the Jews have the same task as all other peoples in Antiquity, namely to make the common Western culture as rich and valuable as possible" (from letters cited in Flakierski 1982).

According to Heckscher, the magnitude of the Jewish contribution to the progress of civilization depended on whether Jews were inherently different or just culturally different:

According to my philosophy of society, an inherent difference becomes a reason *for* assimilation—paradoxically as it may sound—whereas a difference created only by the environment strengthens the reasons for isolation. According to my philosophy of history, what we call culture has emerged and developed through a mixing of different contributions by individuals and peoples.... If now the Jews have a role as ferment among slower peoples... and if they keep their traits also in mixed marriages, then I see a reason *for* such, but the opposite if the valuable Jewish traits thereby disappear instead of being mixed.... My impression is that Jewish traits are persistent and survive also one or two generations of mixed marriages. (from letter cited by Hansson 1988)

The quote may give the impression that Heckscher believed in genetical differences. His commemorative lecture on David Davidson before the Royal Academy of Sciences in 1951 lends itself to the same conclusion:

It is of interest to find an answer to the question if Davidson's lineage to some significant degree can explain his kind of intellect. That there could not have been any significant influence from his parents seems rather obvious.... One may, however, imagine a more subtle influence from an ancestral tradition. As the following will show, Davidson's most characteristic intellectual trait was an unusual and subtle sharpness of mind, an ability to follow without fault a chain of thought through all its meandering to its end. This is a characteristic that not seldom has been considered a Jewish trait.... To the extent that one wants to speak of a Jewish disposition in this direction it becomes necessary also to think about the influence of the conditions of existence of Jewish communities. In their isolation from an unusually hostile surrounding, they sought support and protection in a theocratic constitution that dictated their daily lives down to the smallest detail; and subtle interpretations of the Talmud and ceremonial laws assumed an unusually strong and purely practical importance. (Heckscher 1951a)

When pressed on the issue of genetics vs. environment, Heckscher opted for the latter. His lecture on Davidson elicited a written response by a professor of "racial biology," who claimed that there existed no scientific findings of intellectual differences between races in general and of Jewish intellectual ability in particular. Heckscher (1951b) answered that he did not believe in the existence of a Jewish race (or, one can add, a Jewish nationality) and that what are considered racial characteristics are only historical products. The fact that there are indisputable differences between nations—he mentions France and Britain as an example—is due to environmental or cultural influences for generations, not genetic factors.

Heckscher on Zionism

Heckscher's view on Zionism, the struggle for a Jewish national home in Palestine as a solution to the Jewish problem, followed straightforwardly from his view on universal Western civilization *contra* nationalism. He saw nationalism as a threat to universal values and the progress of Western civilization and considered Jewish nationalism as no different than other forms of nationalism. In fact, he did not acknowledge the existence of a Jewish nationality. Jews had been dispersed among the various nations for so long that they had lost a nationality they once possessed and had adopted the culture of the nations of which they were citizens. They were as much Swedes as indigenous Swedes, as much French as indigenous French, and so on. In a letter about helping persecuted Jews from Germany, he writes: "You want that they be helped as flesh of our flesh. This I cannot feel. Friends from my youth, student friends, professional colleagues, yes even political adversaries are infinitely closer to my heart than a German, Russian, Polish or Romanian Jew" (from a letter quoted in Flakierski 1982).[12] More than being detrimental to Western civilization, Zionism would fuel anti-Semitism against the Jews who did not emigrate to Palestine and thus be a threat to the Jews themselves.

Heckscher wrote two major articles against Zionism in the leading Swedish daily *Dagens Nyheter* as far apart as 1929 and 1946. There also exists a private discussion spanning more than three decades in letters between Heckscher and Valentin, which has been documented and commented by Flakierski (1982).

Heckscher's arguments against Zionism are all clearly expressed already in the first article in *Dagens Nyheter*. After having acknowledged that migration to Palestine of the millions of "oppressed, mistreated and plundered" Jews of Eastern Europe and Russia would solve the Jewish problem for Jews and anti-Semites alike, he goes on to say (Heckscher 1929): "But Zionism has nevertheless not been able to avoid causing serious problems.... Both anti-Semites and Jewish nationalists have...been shown right. The former have said: now one can see that you do not belong here, since Palestine has been proclaimed your motherland and Hebrew your true language. The latter have said: now we must keep to our identity at all cost and to our language, avoid mixed marriages and other mixing with the strangers and return to religious practice in its most orthodox form." The repercussions for Jews that remained in the diaspora was a serious problem, since only a few percent of all Jews could be settled in Palestine due to its small size and lack of natural resources. An additional problem was the hostility of the Arabs and the political considerations that had to be taken by Britain, the main colonial power in the region:

Added to this is the present and utmost serious difficulty, the hostility of the previous inhabitants, the Arabs. (Parenthetically, this also shows how little this is a "question of race," since also the Arabs are Semites.) It is easy to realize the great dangers this holds, since the British empire, the original benefactor and supporter of Zionism, at the same time has the greatest number of Muslim subjects and can therefore hardly be led by exclusively humanitarian or pro-Jewish sentiments, and equally cannot sacrifice its prestige by capitulating before the Arab violence. One must fervently hope that it will be possible to save the Jewish colonies in Palestine; but the non-eradicable difference between them and the Arabs will place even more severe limits on future colonization than the economic conditions.

Here, Heckscher is in some ways prophetic. He concludes that Zionism is not the solution to the Jewish problem: "If there is an ounce of political wisdom in the world, it should lead to the inescapable conclusion that Jews should be treated like other citizens, that the conditions of peaceful co-existence must be allowed to dominate over nationalistic fanaticism and narrow-mindedness."

The second article in *Dagens Nyheter*, published in 1946, uses the same argument as the first, but puts much more emphasis on the economic difficulties of settling in Palestine and the rights and reactions of the Arabs. Heckscher claims that Zionism has contributed to anti-Semitism in Sweden and elsewhere and that a national home for Jews in Palestine is "a pure fantasy for the foreseeable future." The only practical solution to the problem of homeless Jews who survived the

Holocaust is to distribute them as evenly as possible among countries
with decent political conditions. Palestine is not even an acceptable
"surrogate" solution. Zionism is "a new Jewish tragedy added to the
many past" (Heckscher 1946).

A year later, in August 1947, Heckscher (1947a) published an article
in *Dagens Nyheter* about a meeting that had been held in the Jewish
community in support of the 4,300 Jewish refugees on the ship *Exodus*
on their way from Germany to Palestine, which the British had forced
to sail back to Hamburg. He argued that the British had had no choice
and that the Zionists were to blame, since they had declined an offer to
let the refugees disembark in France. He also deplored that the meeting
had not also called for free immigration to Palestine of Arabs, while
at the same time saying that if this were allowed, it would end in a
bloodbath.

The article gave rise to a discussion between Heckscher and Valentin
both in *Judisk Tidskrift* and in *Dagens Nyheter*. The former discussion
was animated while the latter was overly polite and respectful. In
Judisk Tidskrift, Valentin accused Heckscher of being fanatic, defeatist,
and hyperrationalistic and of making anti-Jewish statements. The exchange dealt both with Zionism as such and the British policy of trying
to limit or stop the inflow of displaced Jewish refugees from Europe
to Palestine. Above all, Valentin accused Heckscher of being incapable
of identifying with the physical and psychological plight of European
Jewry at the time. In closing the discussion, Valentin wrote that "the
human being is something totally different than the rationalistic atom
complexes that figure in the calculations of Heckscher" and that Heckscher had failed to understand the reality behind the Zionist ideology
because he was "ignorant of the existential conditions of the Jewish
people, their goals, yearnings and hope" (Valentin 1947). Heckscher
and Valentin had maintained a correspondence since 1919. It ended in
1951, when their disagreement had become too great.

In *Dagens Nyheter*, Heckscher (1947b) painted the Zionist project as
either unjust and politically impossible or as suicidal. It was unjust not
to allow Arabs to migrate freely into Palestine, since they had lived in
Palestine as a majority for 1,300 years, and it would be politically impossible to deny them this right. Alternatively, if free immigration of
Arabs were allowed, it would lead to a catastrophe for the Jews. Thus,
the conclusion was that the only possible solution was to settle the displaced Jews in Europe and elsewhere, not in Palestine. Valentin responded that he was a long-time supporter of a division of Palestine

between Arabs and Jews. Heckscher seized on the suggestion and declared that such a solution would "avoid some of the very greatest dangers that would otherwise follow if Zionism were realized" although he expressed skepticism about its practicability. He went on to argue that Valentin viewed the dangers presented by the Arab superiority in numbers and hostility against Jews too lightly. Finally, he reiterated his arguments that a Jewish state would give rise to anti-Semitism against the large majority of Jews that could and would not settle in the Jewish state (Heckscher 1947c).[13]

Conclusion

Heckscher's views that the Jewish problem should be solved by assimilation and that a Jewish state in Palestine would serve to exacerbate the problem by creating anti-Semitism in the diaspora and leading to a bloodbath in Palestine may seem surprising today, although such views were common among Jews at the time. How can they be explained?

I have already given one explanation. Heckscher held the view that safeguarding and promoting Western civilization was paramount. Jews had played an important role for the progress of civilization since their emancipation in the late eighteenth century and had contributed little when they were isolated in ghettos. Nationalism was threatening to reverse the process, with very negative consequences both for Western society and the Jews themselves.

Heckscher was a Jew by birth and reflected on the meaning of being a Jew, but he did not consciously identify with a Jewish culture or nationality. In his own words, he felt greater solidarity with friends, colleagues, and other Swedes than with Jews from other countries. In the words of Valentin (1951), he was "ignorant of the existential conditions of the Jewish people, their goals, yearnings and hope." This fact in combination with his rational intellect and—in the words of Bertil Ohlin (1971)—"somewhat doctrinarian disposition" can explain the attraction to a worldview resting on the grand scheme of things and disregarding more irrational or primitive aspects of human society.

Ohlin characterizes his teacher and colleague as "an ascetic and moralist." This may explain Heckscher's concern for the rights of the Arabs in Palestine. He also writes that "it is hard to understand Heckscher's personality without keeping in mind his love for and sense of belonging to Anglo-Saxon culture in its British form."

Heckscher had privately confided to Ohlin that he would very much like to see the Nordic countries become members of the British Empire, which is consistent with his view that it would be best for Palestine to remain a British mandate.

One must also consider that Heckscher came of age at a time when there was a relatively small distance in time between starvation, extreme poverty, epidemics, eternal wars, autocratic rule, superstition, and ignorance on the one hand, and rising living standards, improved health and longevity, enormous advances in science and technology, democracy, and a free press on the other. What had been won could easily be lost. A hundred years later, these advances are taken for granted. For Jews, the improvement in living conditions and their standing in society had been even more dramatic. Emancipation had freed them from a miserable existence as a badly tolerated minority, frequently the subject of oppression and abuse. Assimilation had been a successful strategy in Western Europe, where Jews had risen to relative affluence and many had become very prominent in their fields.

In conclusion, the antinationalistic and universal, multicultural worldview of his teacher was particularly attractive to Heckscher as a Jew. The paramount value he attached to Western civilization, his rational mind and his lack of identification with the Jewish people combined to make assimilation, and not Zionism, the solution to the Jewish problem.

Notes

1. Biographical data are from *Svenskt Biografiskt Lexikon* (1972).

2. One nineteenth-century member of the Heckscher family founded the largest bank in Hamburg at the time; another became ambassador and foreign minister of Prussia. Several Heckschers emigrated to the United States in the nineteenth century. They and some of their descendants became prominent merchants, industrialists, politicians, and patrons of the arts. The Heckscher Playground in Central Park and the Heckscher Museum of Art and the Heckscher State Park on Long Island testify to their prominence.

3. German Reform Judaism made radical changes in religious doctrine and changed the form of religious services, which became more like Christian Protestant services. Jews were no longer considered to be in exile, expecting a Messiah and the re-creation of a Jewish state. The anti-Zionist stand was changed after the Holocaust and the creation of the state of Israel.

4. In a fiercely anti-Semitic pamphlet listing Jews in prominent positions in Swedish society written by Oscar Landahl and published in 1936, Heckscher is virulently attacked for his views on Swedish agricultural policy.

5. The new chair was also connected to Heckscher's failed attempt to become rector of the Stockholm School. He gained no support from his colleagues, which disappointed him deeply and made him want to escape from the daily business at the school.

6. The label "The Jewish Question" was not invented by Karl Marx, but his well-known "Zur Judenfrage," published in 1844, certainly did much to popularize it.

7. Isaiah Berlin (1979) has written a highly interesting essay on the search for identity and assimilation of Jews after emancipation, focusing on the examples of Benjamin Disraeli and Karl Marx.

8. Heckscher (1935–49). A shorter version exists in English; see Heckscher (1954).

9. This is possibly an allusion to a familiar line by the early-nineteenth century Swedish poet Esaias Tegnér: "All that is educated is borrowed; only barbarism is our own."

10. This is precisely the argument made earlier by Thorstein Veblen (1919): "and when and in so far the Jewish people in this way turn inward on themselves, their prospective contribution to the world's collective output should, in the light of historical evidence, fairly be expected to take on the complexion of Talmudic lore, rather than that character of free-swung sceptical initiative which their renegades have habitually infused into the pursuit of the modern sciences abroad among the nations." I am grateful to Ronald Findlay, who directed me to Veblen's essay "The Intellectual Pre-Eminence of the Jews."

11. In another context, Heckscher characterizes the Jews as being a ferment *more* than a backbone of the societies in which they have lived (Heckscher 1929).

12. This should not be taken to mean that Heckscher was indifferent to the plight of fellow Jews. His mother had donated money for the purchase of a farm for the purpose of training refugee Jewish children from Germany in agricultural skills. Heckscher took an active part in the project, had an adolescent boy living with the family, and helped other Jews in distress. However, he did not acknowledge that he did this out of Jewish solidarity, but because no one else wanted to help.

13. Sartre (1946) also argued that Zionism leads to anti-Semitism and furthermore to a division between Zionist and assimilationist Jews: "The creation of a Jewish state constitutes in the eyes of the anti-Semite proof that the Jew does not belong the French people. Previously, he was criticized for his race, now he is considered to belong to another country. He has nothing to do with us—may he therefore go to Palestine. . . . The French Jew is irritated at the Zionist for further complicating a precarious situation, and the Zionist is irritated at the French Jew, whom he *a priori* accuses of non-authenticity."

References

Andersson, L. M. 2000. *A Jew Is a Jew Is a Jew: Representations of 'The Jew' in Swedish Comic Press 1900–1930s*. Lund: Lunds universitet.

Berlin, I. 1979. *Against the Current: Essays in the History of Ideas*. London: Hogarth.

Elvander, N. 1961. *Harald Hjärne och konservatismen. Konservativ idédebatt i Sverige 1865–1922*. Uppsala: Uppsala universitet.

Flakierski, G. 1982. "Rötter. Den judiska frågan i brevväxlingen mellan Hugo Valentin och Eli Heckscher." *Historisk Tidskrift*, 177–201.

Hansson, S. 1988. "Antisemitism, assimilation och judisk särart. Svenskjudisk elitdebatt vid Hitlers maktövertagande 1933." In G. Broberg et al., eds., *Judiskt liv i Norden*. Uppsala: Uppsala universitet.

Heckscher, E. F. 1929. "Judarna och Palestina." *Dagens Nyheter*, September 2.

―――. 1931. "Svenskt och utländskt i Sveriges ekonomisk liv." *Ekonomen*, no. 2.

―――. 1935–49. *Sveriges ekonomiska historia från Gustav Vasa*. Stockholm: Bonniers.

―――. 1944a. *Historieuppfattning. Materialistisk och annan*. Stockholm: Bonniers.

―――. 1944b. "Erfarenheter av ekonomi och ekonomisk politik under fyrtio år." *Ekonomen*, 86–95.

―――. 1946. "Sionismen." *Dagens Nyheter*, July 12.

―――. 1947a. "Svensk vädjan för judarna på Exodus." *Dagens Nyheter*, August 28.

―――. 1947b. "Öppna frågor." *Dagens Nyheter*, August 30.

―――. 1947c. "Slutreprik." *Dagens Nyheter*, September 1.

―――. 1951a. "David Davidson." *Ekonomisk Tidskrift*, 127–160.

―――. 1951b. "Finns det en speciell judisk begåvning." *Judisk Tidskrift*, 15–16.

―――. 1954. *An Economic history of Sweden*. Cambridge, MA: Harvard University Press.

Koblik, S. 1987. *Om vi teg skulle stenarna ropa: Sverige och judeproblemet 1933–1945*. Stockholm: Norstedts.

Landahl, O. 1936. "Judefrågan." http://www.abbc.com/historia/landahl.htm.

Montgomery, A. 1953. "Eli Heckscher som vetenskapsman." *Ekonomisk Tidskrift* 55:149–185.

Ohlin, B. 1971. "Heckscher, Eli Filip." In E. Gill, ed., *Svenskt Biografiskt Lexikon*, vol. 18. Stockholm: Norstedts.

Sartre, J.-P. 1946. *Réflexions sur la question juive*. Paris: P. Morihien.

Valentin, H. 1947. "Zionismen och verkligheten." *Judisk Tidskrift*, 370–371.

Veblen, T. 1919. "The Intellectual Pre-Eminence of the Jews." *Political Science Quarterly* 34:33–42.

23　　　　　　　　　Eva Heckscher, 1936–2004

Dag Klackenberg

Ambassador Eva Heckscher, who passed away in November of 2004, was raised in the renowned Heckscher family. She was the daughter of Gunnar Heckscher—professor, party leader and later ambassador—and his wife Anna Brita. Her grandfather, Eli Heckscher, was one of the greatest of all Swedish economists. Eva was profoundly influenced by her family and by growing up in such an intellectual atmosphere. As she used to say: "The dinner table discussions were my best university."

Eva graduated from secondary school in 1955 and began her academic studies at Uppsala University. There she was an active member of the anti-socialist student association Heimdal. She decided, however, to become a journalist, and from 1958 to 1965 she worked, first at the now-defunct *Högerpressens Nyhetsbyrå* ("The News Bureau of the Conservative Press"), and then for the venerable newspaper *Gotlands Allehanda*.

Having been appointed editor of the *American Swedish Monthly*, she moved to New York City in 1965. It was an important magazine published by the Swedish-American News Bureau. The latter was founded in 1921 by the Social Democratic leader Hjalmar Branting and the prominent banker and former foreign minister Knut Agathon Wallenberg in order to maintain contact with and preserve Swedish-American heritage in North America. Eva became part of a group of colleagues surrounding the head managers, Allan Kastrup and Anders H. Pers, all of whom were heavily engaged in the great American information project of the 1960s, "Meet Modern Sweden."

In 1966, when the news bureau was incorporated into the Ministry for Foreign Affairs as an autonomous division, "The Swedish Information Service," Eva transferred into the foreign service. She was "nationalized," as she herself liked to say. Her American experience was of great value when she and the director of information Kjell Öberg prepared a well-documented study of the history of the Swedish-American press. Of the original 1769 separate newspapers, barely ten remained at the end of the 1960s. Eva could take credit for successfully preserving this history.

Thus began her successful foreign office career. In accord with standard practice for transferring diplomats, various assignments in Stockholm (kanslisekreterare and byrådirektör) were followed by stationing in Nairobi, Bonn, and, once again, Stockholm. In 1985 Eva was named ambassador to Bangladesh. Her father Gunnar had served as ambassador to both India and Japan, and Eva had been deeply engaged in the preparation of his book *Asiatiskt maktspel* (*The Power Game in Asia*), including later editions. Asia became a constant presence in her life and when she returned home to the foreign office in 1989 she was made head of the Asian section of the political department (departementsråd). For several years during the 1990s she was ambassador to Thailand. Her simultaneous appointment in Cambodia gave her frightening insight into the Red Khmer reign of terror. Eva spent the last years before her retirement, 1996–2001, as Head of the Security Division of the Swedish Ministry for Foreign Affairs.

Eva Heckscher was a good example of those diplomats who successfully combine a sharp intellect, expert knowledge, and skillful report writing with sympathy and understanding for developments within the countries in which they serve.

Index